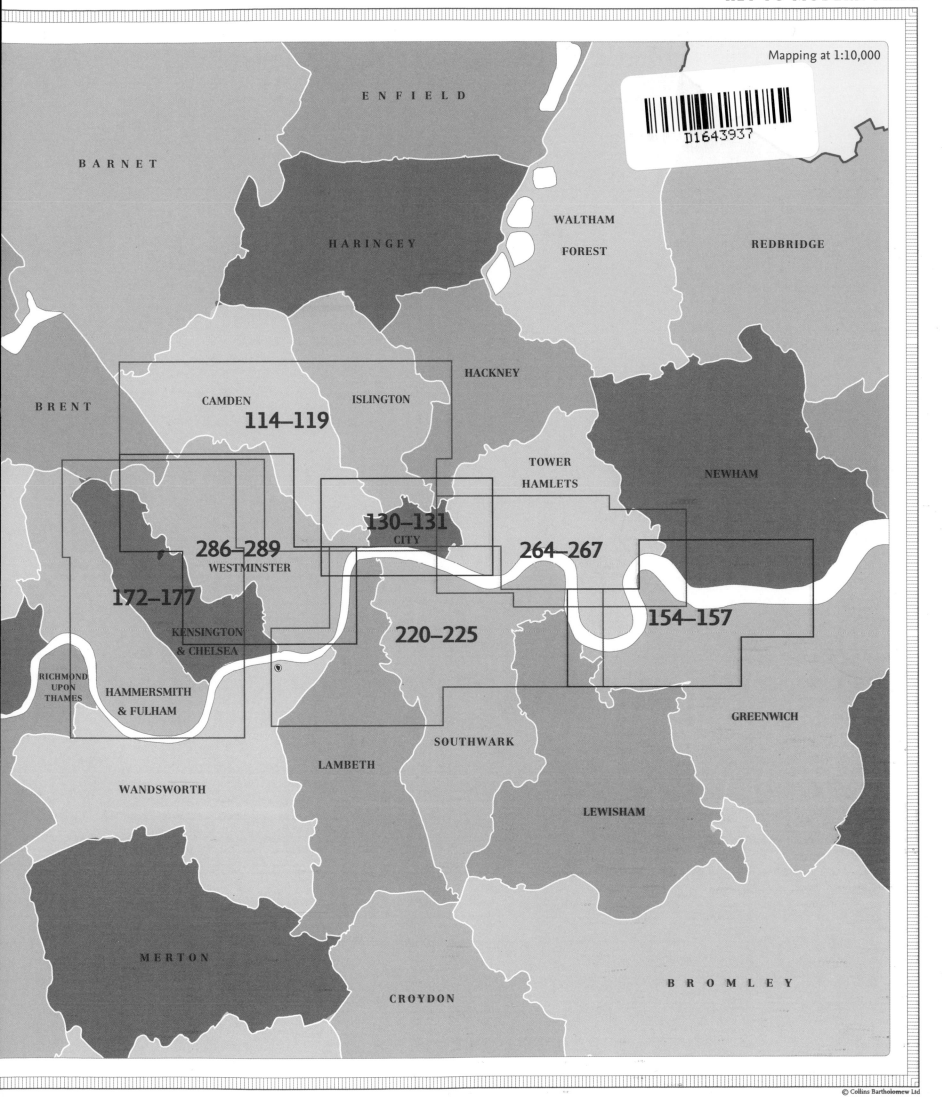

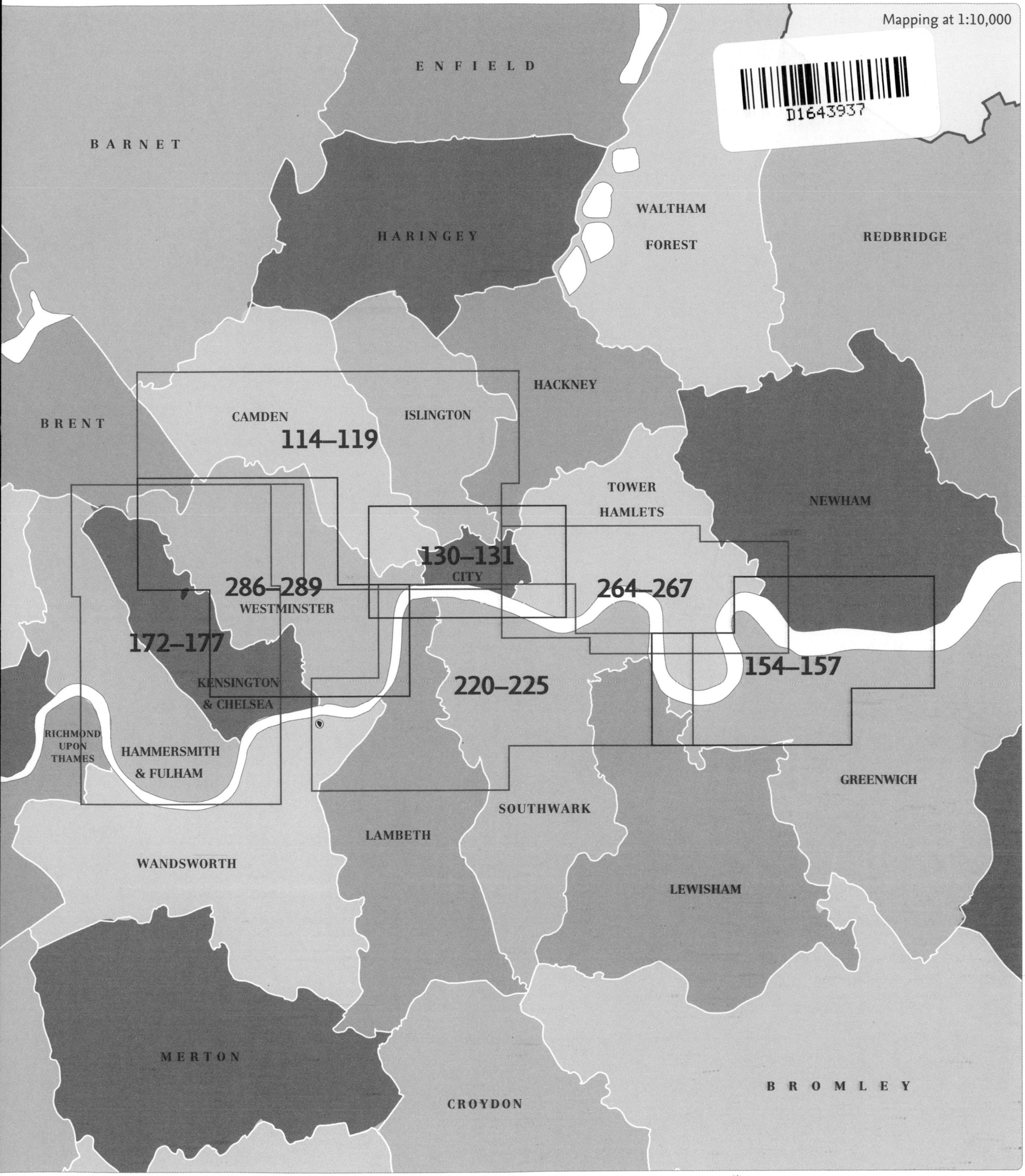
Mapping at 1:10,000
ENFIELD
BARNET
HARINGEY
WALTHAM
FOREST
REDBRIDGE
HACKNEY
BRENT
CAMDEN
ISLINGTON
114–119
TOWER
HAMLETS
NEWHAM
130–131
CITY
286–289
WESTMINSTER
264–267
172–177
KENSINGTON
& CHELSEA
220–225
154–157
RICHMOND
UPON
THAMES
HAMMERSMITH
& FULHAM
GREENWICH
SOUTHWARK
LAMBETH
WANDSWORTH
LEWISHAM
MERTON
CROYDON
BROMLEY

ATLAS OF LONDON

THE TIMES ATLAS OF LONDON

Times Books, 77-85 Fulham Palace Road, London W6 8JB

First Edition 2011

This edition produced for The Book People Ltd, Parc Menai, Bangor LL57 4FB

Author: Christopher Riches

Printed in China

British Library Cataloguing in Publication Data
A catalogue record for this book is available from the British Library

ISBN 978 0 00 790433 4/1
Imp 001

All mapping in this publication is generated from Collins Bartholomew digital databases.
Collins Bartholomew, the UK's leading independent geographical information supplier, can provide a digital, custom, and premium mapping service to a variety of markets.
For further information:
Tel: +44 (0) 141 306 3606
e-mail: **collinsbartholomew@harpercollins.co.uk**
or visit our website at: **www.collinsbartholomew.com**

If you would like to comment on any aspect of this publication, please write to:
Times Atlases, HarperCollins Publishers, Westerhill Road, Bishopbriggs, Glasgow G64 2QT
e-mail: **timesatlas@harpercollins.co.uk**
or visit our website at: **www.timesatlas.com**
Historical maps available to view and buy at: **www.mapseeker.co.uk**
twitter.com/timesatlas

Cover image (top): A general view of the City of London and the River Thames in 1794 © Getty Images
Cover image (bottom): The River Thames from the top of Tower Bridge, July 2011. See pages 302-303 for more information. © Mark Steward

THE TIMES
ATLAS OF LONDON

With special thanks to

MAPSEEKER ARCHIVE PUBLISHING
GATEWAY TO OUR HISTORIC PAST
www.mapseeker.co.uk

nls
National Library of Scotland

MODERN MAPS – KEY TO SYMBOLS

Symbols for mapping on pages 20–21

CITIES AND TOWNS

Population	National capital	Administrative centre / County town	District centre	Other town
5 million to 10 million	**LONDON** ▣	...	...	...
100,000 to 500,000		**Slough** ▣	Croydon ⊙	...
50,000 to 100,000		**Maidenhead** ▣	...	**Richmond** ◎
10,000 to 50,000			**Westminster** ⊙	**Wimbledon** ⊙
5000 to 10,000			City ○	Ewell ○
1000 to 5000			West Malling ○	Stoke Poges ○
under 1000				Mount Pleasant ○
Suburb				Mayfair ○

Built-up area

- Motorway
- Primary road
- Main road
- Secondary / other road
- Road tunnel (applies to all road classes)
- Long distance footpath
- Railway
- Railway tunnel
- Private railway
- Private railway tunnel
- International airport
- Regional airport
- Canal
- Minor canal
- Canal tunnel
- Administrative / County boundary
- London borough boundary
- 95 Spot height
- Lake
- River
- Dam
- Regional Park
- World Heritage site
- Site of specific interest

Symbols for 1:65,000 mapping on pages 36–53 and London borough maps

- M25 Motorway
- Toll Toll
- Level crossing
- Long distance footpath
- London City Airport Airport with scheduled services
- Railway line / Railway tunnel
- Railway station / Light rail station
- Underground / Overground station
- Heliport
- H Hospital
- Public building
- Built-up area
- Woodland / Park
- KENT County / Unitary Authority boundary & name
- CAMDEN Borough / District boundary & name
- Aquarium
- Battle site
- Castle
- Country park
- Ecclesiastical building
- Freight terminal
- Garden
- Golf course
- Historic house
- Historic site
- Major football club
- £ Major shopping centre
- Major sports venue
- Motor racing circuit
- Museum
- Nature reserve
- ★ Other interesting feature
- Racecourse
- Ski slope (artificial)
- Theme park
- University
- Wildlife park or zoo

Symbols for Central London 1:10,000 street mapping

- Street market
- Access restriction
- Long distance footpath
- CITY Borough boundary
- Main / Other National Rail station
- London Transport Overground station
- London Transport Underground station
- Docklands Light Railway station
- Pedestrian ferry landing stage
- Bus / Coach station
- Theatre
- \+ Church
- Mosque
- ✡ Synagogue
- ■ Other place of worship
- □ Glass houses
- Important building
- Shopping
- Market
- Major office
- Industry & commerce
- Other landmark building / Tower block
- Built-up area
- Golf course
- Woodland
- Public open space
- Park / Garden / Sports ground
- Cemetery

FOREWORD

The significant difficulty in recording the landscape of any city is that the physical, economic and demographic attributes that best describe it are in constant flux. For over 750 years, mapmakers have been attempting to portray the changing face of London. But a city that thrives on its vibrant trade, broad cultural heritage and pivotal role as the nation's capital might as well be built on shifting sands. The best that any one portrayal can hope to achieve is a snapshot, or, as this book reveals, a history of snapshots, so that previous incarnations of London might be brought together to tell the story of one of the world's great cities.

Wenceslaus Hollar's 1666 map of London after the Great Fire is one such snapshot. Shown on page 10 of this book, it dramatically illustrates the contrast between the empty areas, where buildings had been destroyed by the blaze, and the remaining densely packed houses beyond. It also draws attention to the opportunity for a grand rebuilding of the capital in a manner befitting of its growing world importance. Christopher Wren was on hand to deliver the plans to achieve such a transformation, and yet the street plan which re-emerged was little different from that before the fire. The citizens of London had proved resistant to such an organized scheme, preferring the urban fabric to evolve organically rather than by design. This typifies the way London has grown and spread, consuming the surrounding countryside and absorbing the many villages and towns that once lay beyond its walls. Evidence of this unplanned expansion can still be seen in the many small urban centres that are scattered throughout London, remnants of bygone satellites which add to the city's complicated and confusing anatomy.

The Atlas begins by looking at how the mapping of London has evolved since Matthew Paris first represented the city on his pilgrimage map in 1250. Historic mapping is used in many places in the book both to help tell the story of London and also to give the reader the opportunity to enjoy large reproductions of beautiful maps – what better way could there be to appreciate and observe the growth of London than by studying the changing face of London through a series of contemporary maps? Specially designed new mapping of London also plays an important role throughout this book. The street atlas section provides detailed, up-to-date maps for the whole of Greater London, and sections of larger scale street mapping are used to provide additional detail for particular areas of the centre of the city. There are also individual maps for each of the London boroughs.

The Atlas however contains much more besides maps. There are sections that place London in the context of its physical, economic and demographic position. The historic maps are reinforced by dramatic Victorian panoramas and a chronology of events. With statistics and photographs, there are also pages devoted to every borough in London, interwoven with London-wide thematic spreads covering everything from industry to art galleries, and fascinating 'before and after' studies that use either mapping or photographs to show how a particular area has been transformed.

Even during the relatively short period during which *The Times Atlas of London* was being prepared and compiled, the physical profile of the city changed significantly. The dagger-like silhouette of the Shard has forced its way into the London skyline and more skyscrapers will be following in the years ahead. The shape and character of London will continue to evolve but there is no doubt that the technology and imagination used to represent it will be equal to the task. The view from the top of the Shard on page 290 certainly rivals that of the imaginative Victorian balloonist shown on pages 70–1.

Edinburgh map makers John Bartholomew and Co. began producing maps of London in the 1880s, mostly publishing invaluable but unashamedly unromantic street maps and guides. With this book however, we offer a very different experience. Drawing on the approach adopted in *The Times Atlas of Britain* (published in 2010), this authoritative atlas is designed to encourage the general reader and the armchair tourist to explore and understand this great city and all that it has to offer.

CONTENTS

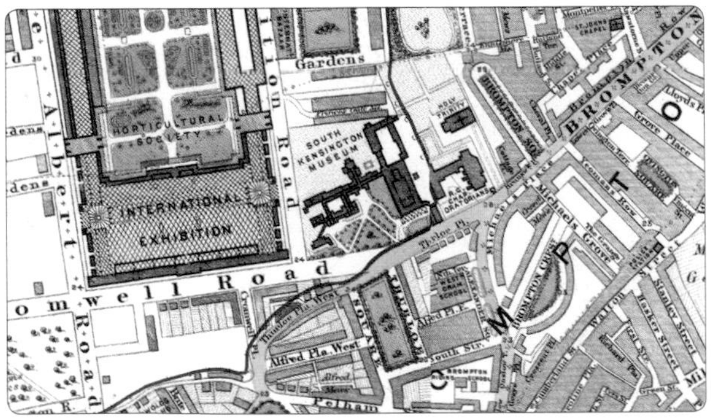
Gardens
INTERNATIONAL
EXHIBITION

MAPPING LONDON

Since its first representation in the map on this page, London has seen many innovations in how it has been presented in maps. In the pages that follow the changes in cartographic techniques move from Matthew Paris's idealized map through bird's-eye views to the ubiquitous street map and the latest advances in digital mapping. There are also examples showing the important part maps can play in epidemiological and sociological research, for example. In addition to the maps in this section, there are four large reproductions of London maps from the 1560s, 1769, 1851 and 1898 which are used to illustrate the growth of London on pages 54–61.

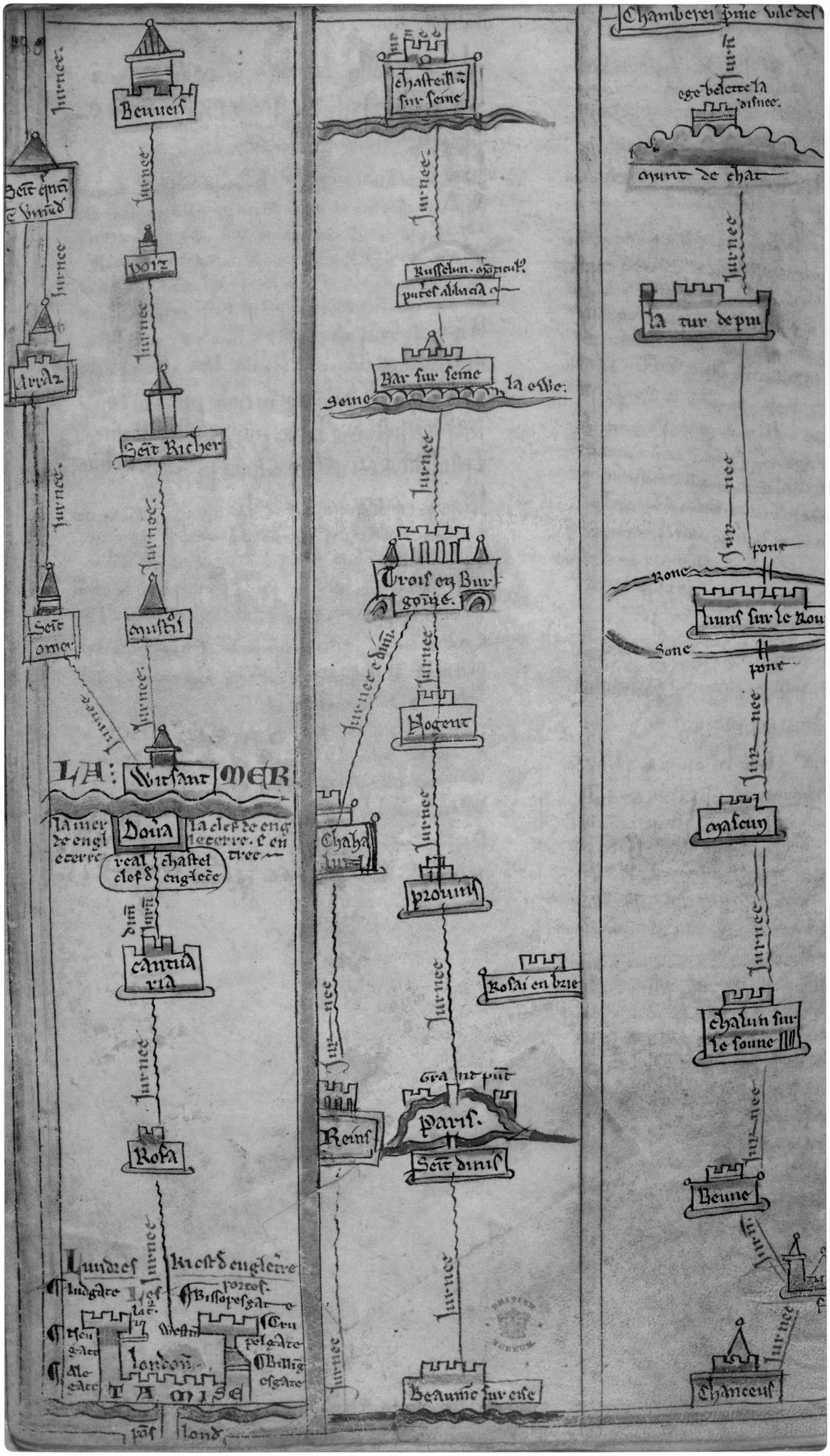

Matthew Paris's *Itinerary from London to Chambery*, 1250

Around 1250, Matthew Paris, Benedictine monk and prolific chronicler at the abbey of St Albans, produced what is the oldest surviving representation of London as part of his so-called *Book of Additions (Liber Additamentorum)*.

It features as the starting point on a pilgrimage map to the Holy Land by way of France and Italy. This was not a map in the conventional sense: rather, the route is presented schematically in the form of strips reading bottom-to-top and left-to-right on each page, showing major towns and stopping points linked by straight lines. Such linear strip maps were intended not as practical route maps but more as spiritual guides by which cloistered monks, forbidden from undertaking pilgrimage, could follow an inner journey to seek their Heavenly Jerusalem.

In many ways, Paris's schematic form, with its disregard of relative distance and surface detail, anticipates contemporary linear maps of motorways and diagrammatic maps of the London Underground (see page 15).

London itself is depicted rather simplistically, almost in the form of what would be recognized today as a map icon: the crenellated towers and wall presumably reference the major medieval landmarks of William the Conqueror's White Tower and the city's fortifications. In subsequent versions of the itinerary included in his *Chronica Majora* and *Historia Anglorum*, Paris adds greater detail to the thumbnail sketch of London and depicts the city walls and gates, London Bridge, St Paul's, Westminster and 'the great River Thames'.

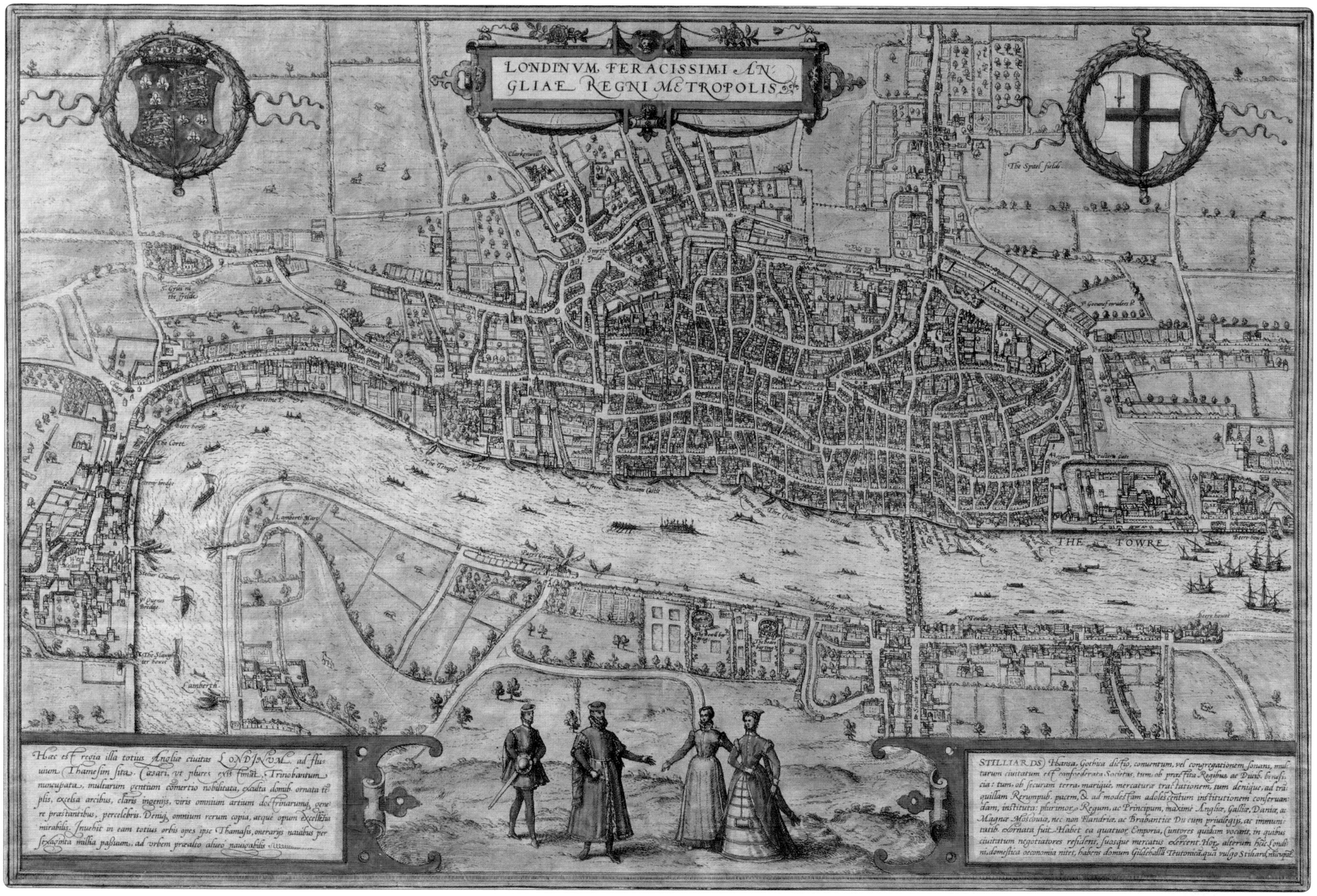

Braun & Hogenberg ***Londinium Feracissimi Angliae Regni Metropolis*****, 1572**

Georg Braun and Frans Hogenberg's map of London is the oldest surviving map of the capital, which it depicts around the time of Elizabeth I's accession to the throne in 1558. It first appeared in 1572 in their highly influential survey of European city mapping, *Civitates Orbis Terrarum*, but is assumed to be based on an earlier and now lost plan of the city, known as the Copperplate Map. London's inclusion in Braun and Hogenberg's publication is testimony to the city's political and commercial standing amongst contemporary European centres of power.

The map clearly illustrates the Tudor city that has expanded well beyond the still-extant walls of medieval London that run from the Tower in the east round to Blackfriars. Few streets are actually identified although sufficient locations are highlighted to allow orientation with the modern city: Westminster and Charing Cross at the bend of the river; Smithfield and Clerkenwell just beyond the western reach of the wall; Spitalfields and the various city gates in the north; and Southwark on the opposite side of the Thames.

While undoubtedly illustrating the city's plan, the map also has the strong pictorial quality that was common to the time. Buildings are drawn in perspective, animals stand in the fields, the surrounding hedges and trees cast shadows and individual oarsmen are clearly identifiable on the many watercraft on the Thames. The fashions of the day are also evident from the figures in the foreground while the adjacent bear- and bull-rings in Southwark hint at some of the main entertainments of the period.

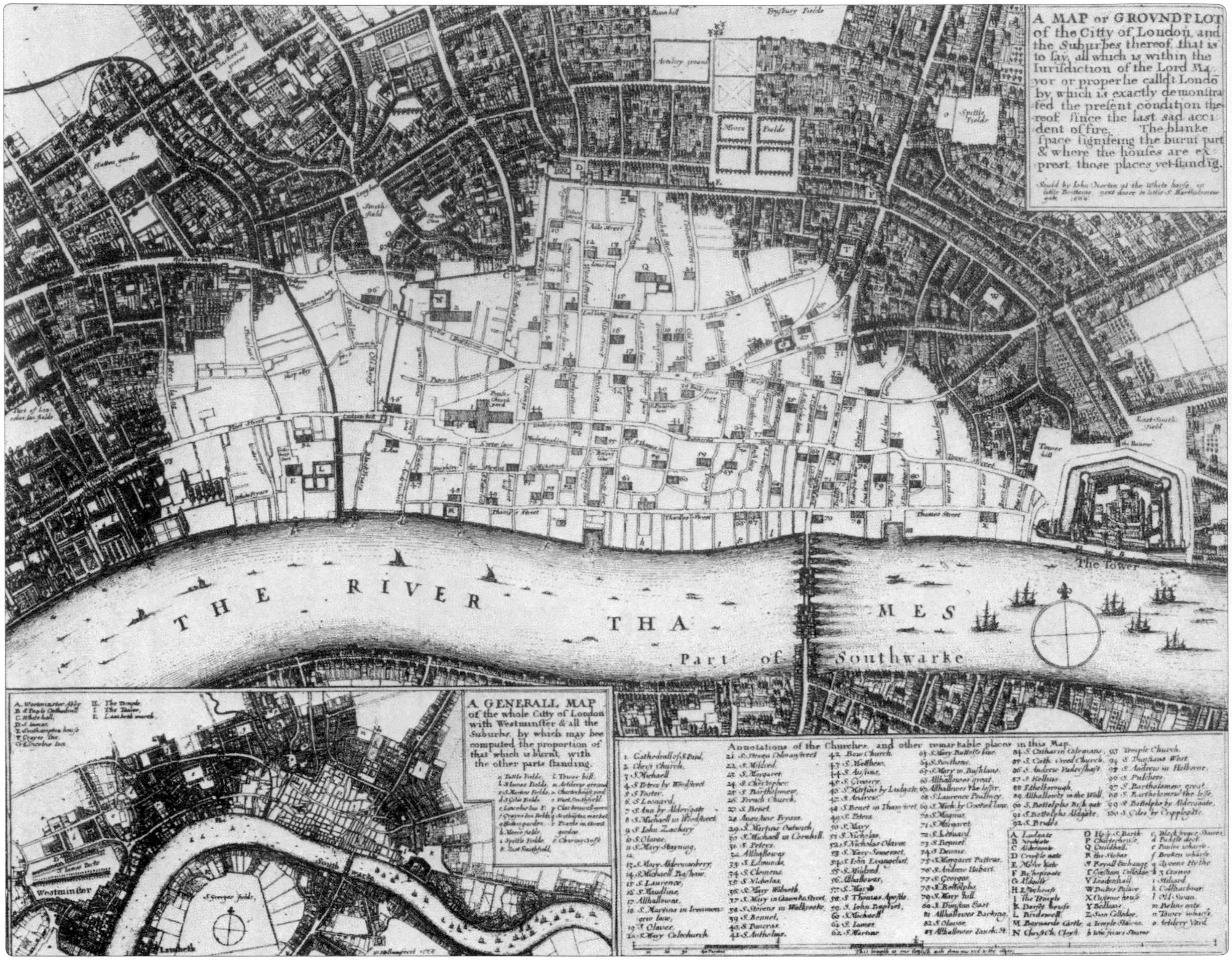

Wenceslaus Hollar *A Map or Groundplot of the City of London within the Suburbes thereof*, 1666

Over the course of three days in 1666, the Great Fire of London wiped out the original medieval city, destroying over 13,000 houses and 87 churches and laying waste to some 150 ha within the old walls. It also acted as catalyst for a cartographic revolution that ultimately saw the pictorial maps of the Braun and Hogenberg style (see page 9) replaced by functional scaled plans.

Wenceslaus Hollar, a Bohemian artist and engraver resident in London, had already surveyed and published highly accurate axonometric plan views, with horizontal and vertical axes to scale, of city districts before the fire struck. One element of this was that the destruction allowed previously impossible access to the tiny, complex streets and therefore an unprecedented opportunity to map the street pattern in detail. Within weeks he was able to produce this detailed and accurate ground plan of the razed areas, depicting the affected wards, streets and churches in simple plan format. This was a new departure in presentational terms although he still retains his signature three-dimensional depictions of surviving buildings on the perimeter.

Hollar's 'groundplot' map was clearly an important transitional step towards a new style of urban mapping. However, this new approach was not unique: Christopher Wren and others also submitted accurate plans as part of their ultimately unsuccessful redevelopment proposals for the city (see pages 134–135).

Hollar subsequently became part of the official team led by John Leake surveying the devastated areas to determine land ownership and insurance and he produced a further map in 1669 based on the results of this work. The age of the functional map had begun.

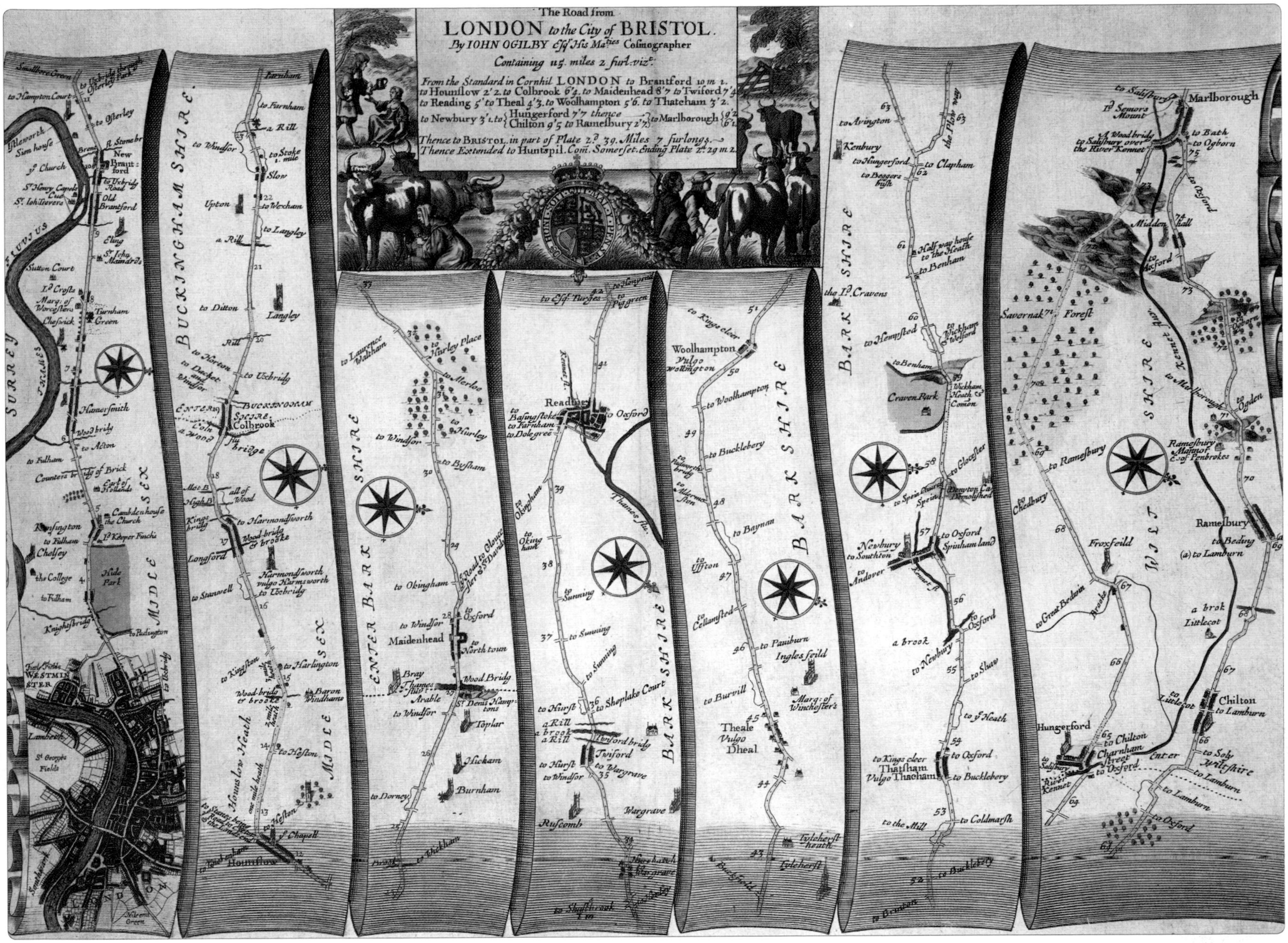

John Ogilby *Britannia ... an illustration of the kingdom of England and dominion of Wales: by a geographical and historical description of the principal roads thereof,* 1675

John Ogilby's *Britannia* was England's earliest road atlas and represented the first major advance in cartography since Tudor times.

With a team of assistants, Ogilby set about surveying and mapping the chief turnpike roads of England, measuring distances using a waywiser, an early form of odometer. He eventually mapped more than 2,500 miles of roads and in doing so standardized the length of the mile at 1,760 yards. In *Britannia*, Ogilby presented these as 100 end-to-end route maps between London and major cities and towns across England. Each route was depicted as a strip map, similar in style and format to that used by the medieval chronicler, Matthew Paris (see page 8).

In addition to representations of the road and the numerous towns and villages through which it passes, each strip records intervening distances and includes a compass rose to show changes in orientation. The routes illustrate few topographic details but are embellished with all manner of whimsical details including naturalistic vignettes of rural husbandry, hunting scenes and even the occasional mythological creature.

Thanks to Ogilby, travellers were now able to plan their journeys with more certainty and the popularity of his work was such that *Britannia* was republished in 1698, 1719 and 1720. Commissioned to produce three such volumes of road maps, Ogilby saw only the first published before his death the following year. Nevertheless, his achievements with *Britannia* secured his reputation as one of Britain's finest cartographers.

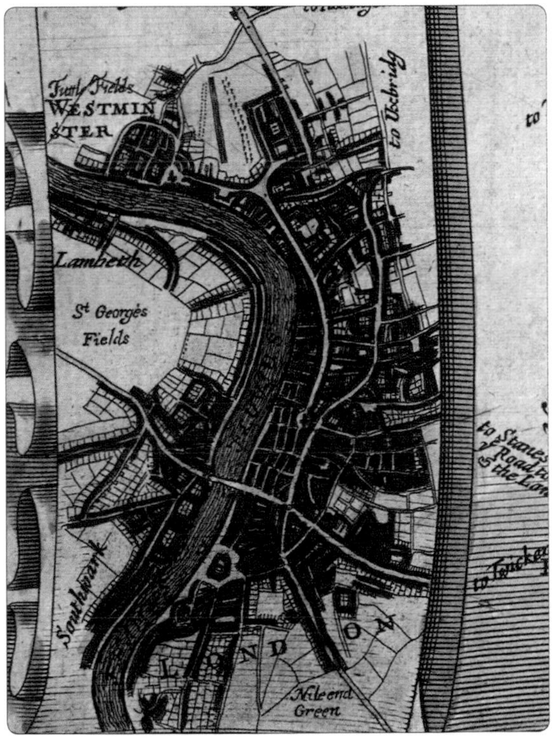

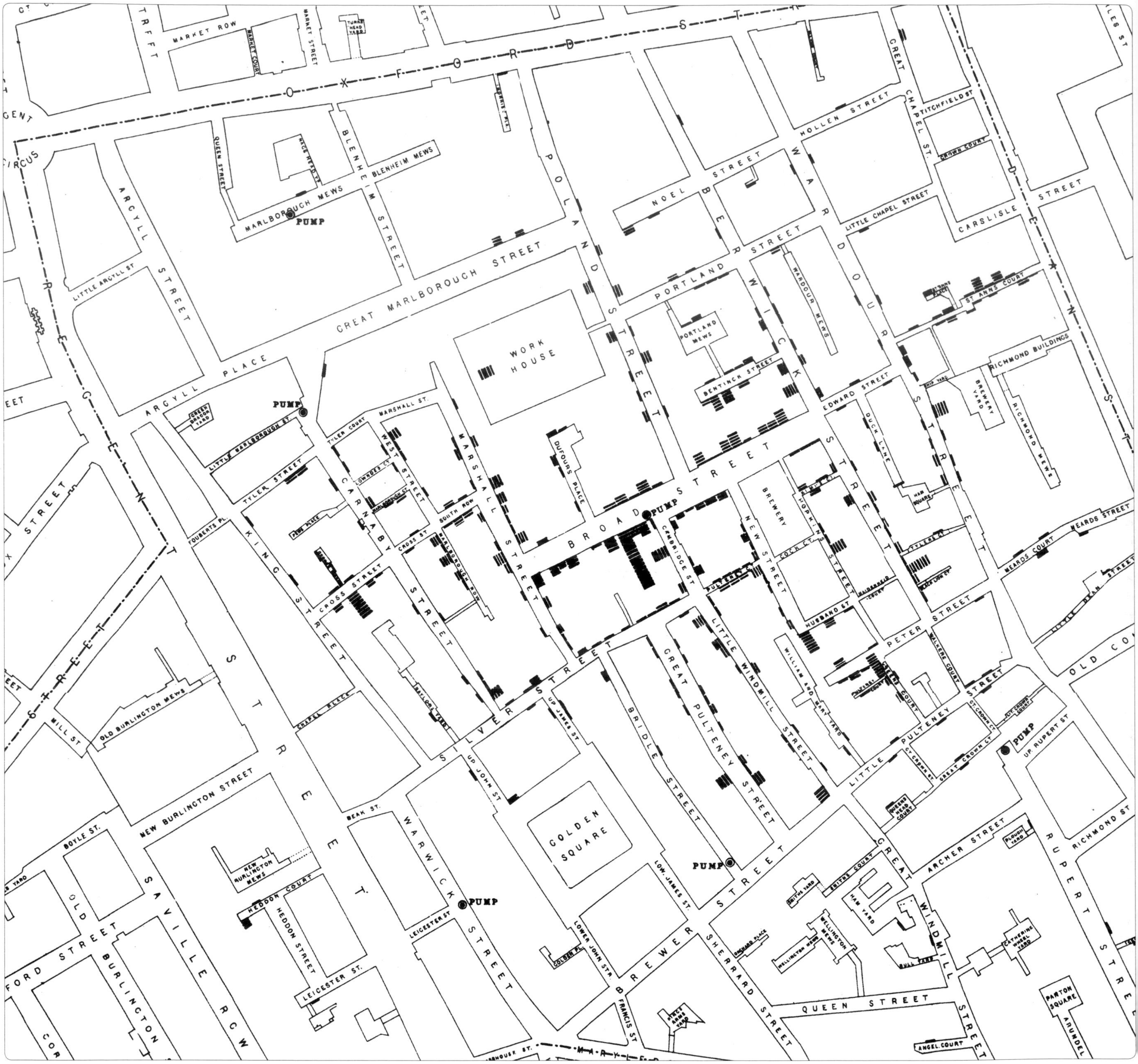

John Snow *On the Mode of Communication of Cholera*, 1855

This is one of two maps produced by the leading London physician, Dr John Snow, for his ground-breaking treatise on the causes and transmission mechanism of cholera.

While his use of maps to analyse disease was not original, Snow's 1855 maps were up to that point the most comprehensive study of a large-scale outbreak undertaken. The maps plot the spread of the disease on a commercial map of the Soho district during the 1853–4 outbreak, with bars used to represent deaths that occurred at specified households. The clustering of the bars in an area around a particular public water pump in Broad Street led Snow to conclude that this was the source of disease in that locality and, by extension, to conclude – correctly, as it emerged – that cholera was a water-borne, rather than an airborne disease. This view flew in the face of the prevailing scientific orthodoxy on the subject.

Snow was not a cartographer and he viewed his maps primarily as graphic summaries of the data he analysed in the texts of his report. However, they amply demonstrated to subsequent researchers how maps can be used to reveal patterns otherwise hidden in data. Yet in spite of the compelling evidence presented in Snow's maps as to cholera's true transmission vector, it was a further thirty years before the bacterium causing the disease was identified and the medical establishment accepted Snow's conclusions.

Charles Booth *Descriptive Map of London Poverty*, 1889

Between 1886 and 1903, industrialist and pioneering social researcher Charles Booth produced an astonishing series of maps of the capital that recorded the social class and wealth of Londoners on a street-by-street basis.

The scale and depth of data that Booth and his research team gathered for his *Inquiry Into the Life and Labour of the People in London* marked it out from other large-scale population surveys carried out during the 19th century. However, it was Booth's use of mapping as a key element in presenting his findings that was truly innovative.

The first *Descriptive Map of London Poverty* produced in 1889 used Stanford's *Library Map of London and Suburbs* (see page 14) as its base. Onto this were plotted the varying levels of poverty and wealth in every street in the capital using a seven-colour palette ranging from yellow (the wealthy upper classes) to black (the poorest and semi-criminal classes). The results were striking and allowed much of the minute detail of Booth's research to be communicated swiftly and with maximum effect. One immediate observation that the map provides is just how intermingled the social classes were in late-Victorian London: while there are clear pockets of obvious wealth, the colouration of many districts reveals a range of classes living in close proximity to one another, sometimes even within individual streets.

Booth's 'Wealth and Poverty map' as it became known, together with its subsequent revisions made a decade later, created the template for social mapping that became popular with demographic researchers, sociologists and city planners throughout the 20th century.

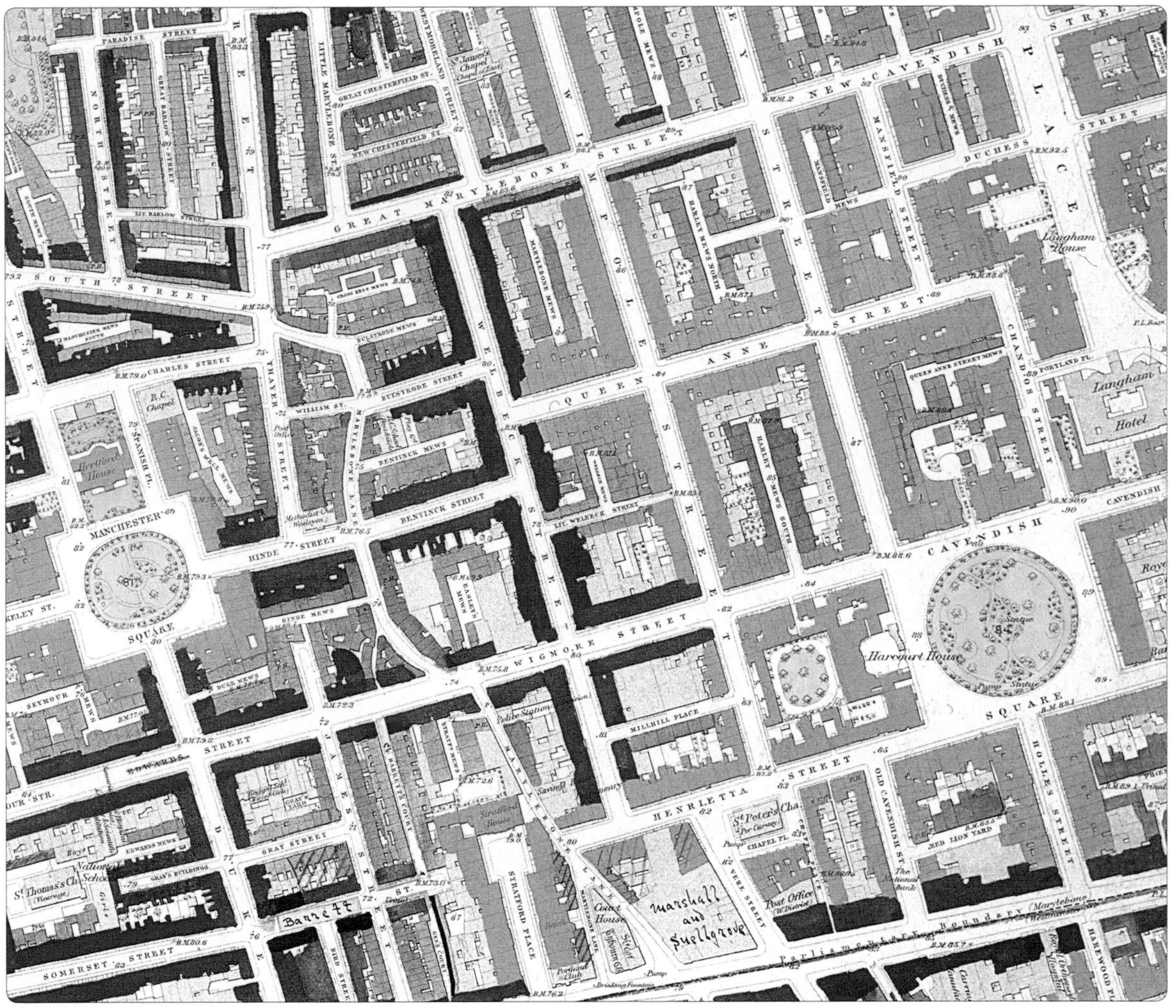

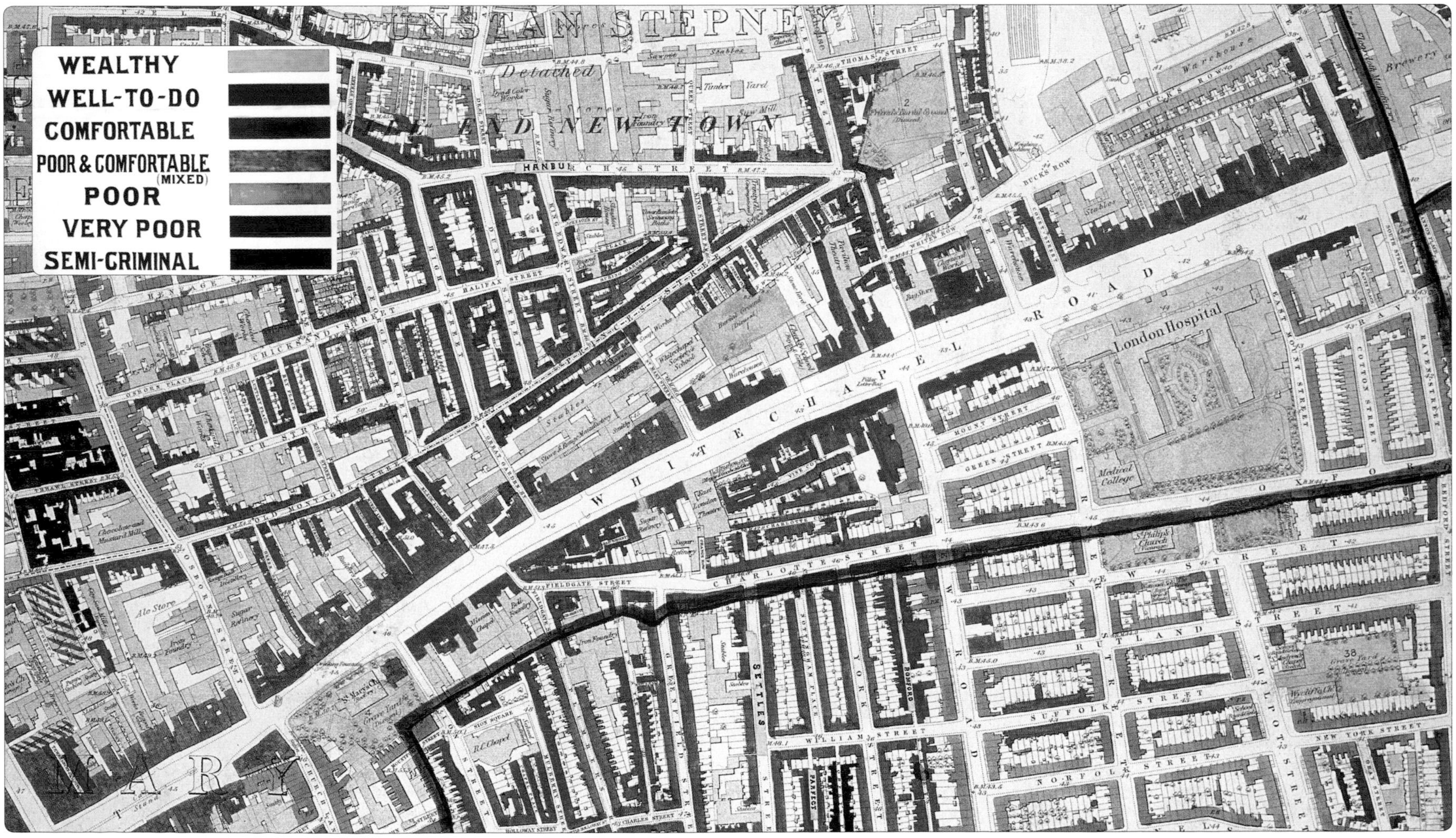

ap of Central London, 1897

…nticed as a printer, Edward Standford …tographic career at a London map seller's …ing quickly to own the business within four …nder his management, the company diversified …egan printing its own atlases and sheet maps. …n 1858, Stanford began to produce his *Library Maps*, …series of large copper-engraved wall maps of the continents, intended for libraries, schools and other public institutions. In 1862, a 24-sheet, 6 in. to the mile map of London was added to the series. With his eye ever on commercial opportunity, Stanford saw this primarily as a tool for the capital's administrators who were crying out for an up-to-date, large-scale map to help them keep pace with the rapid growth of London and its infrastructure. Several competing maps existed – including one by the Ordnance Survey – but none could match Stanford's for the sheer wealth of detail it provided.

Revised continually in the second half of the 19th century, this 1897 edition has been rescaled to 4 in. to the mile and defines central London as bordered by Kentish Town in the north, Clapham in the south, Bethnal Green in the east and Acton in the west. As with its predecessors, this edition displays an extraordinary accuracy and level of detail, pinpointing and identifying commercial and industrial properties, transport routes, schools, post offices, churches, police stations, workhouses, almshouses, hospitals and clubs.

The 'Library Maps' established the Stanford name as one of the foremost cartographers in Victorian England. Today, Stanford's map shop in Long Acre, London is widely regarded as the UK's leading specialist map and travel-book outlet.

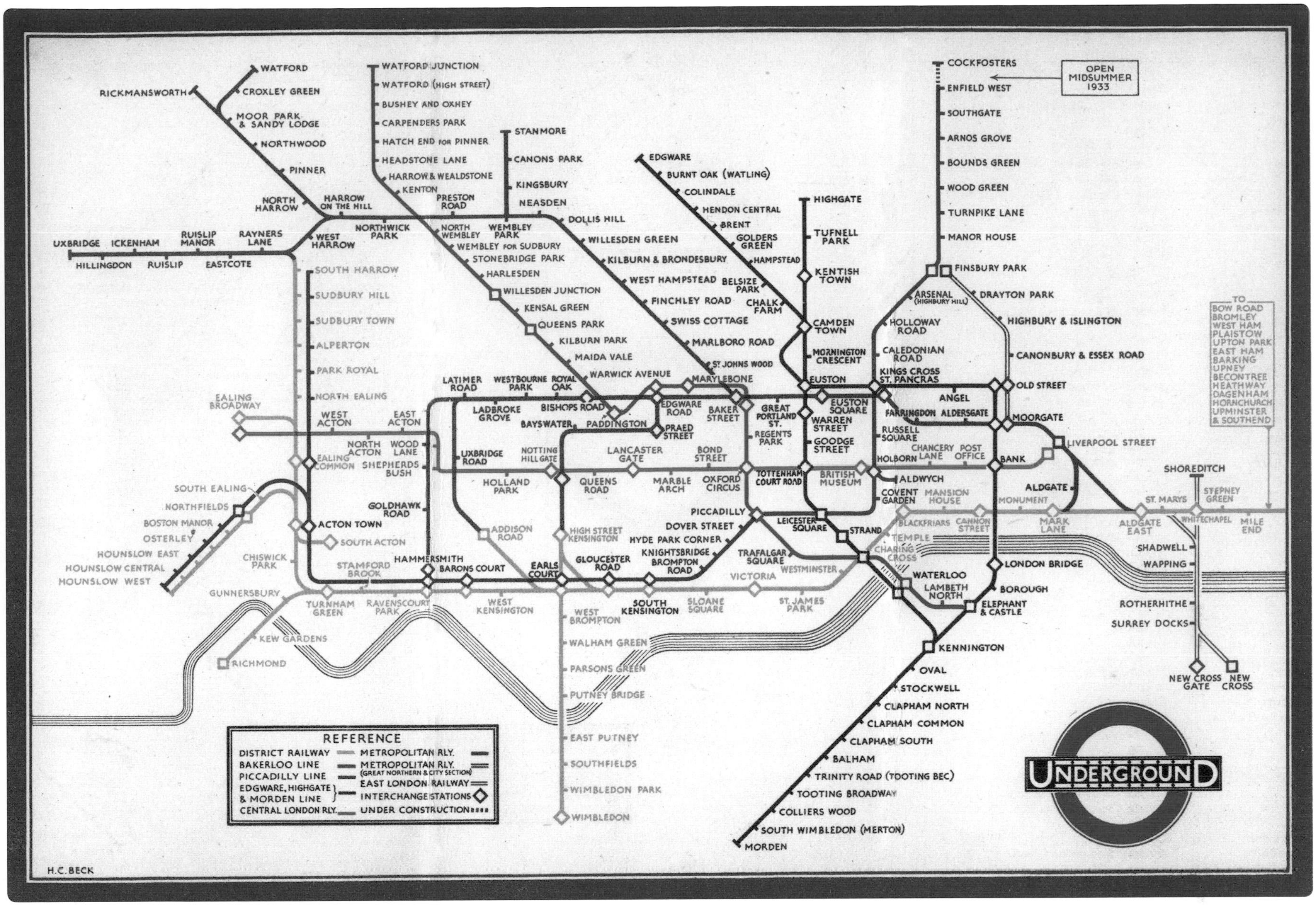

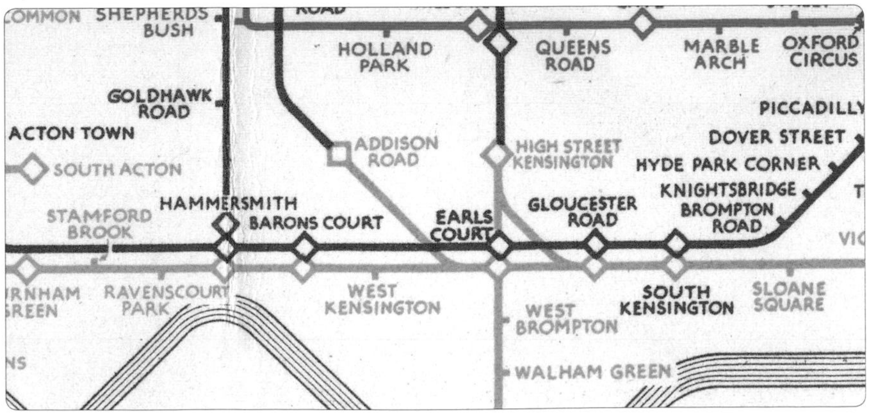

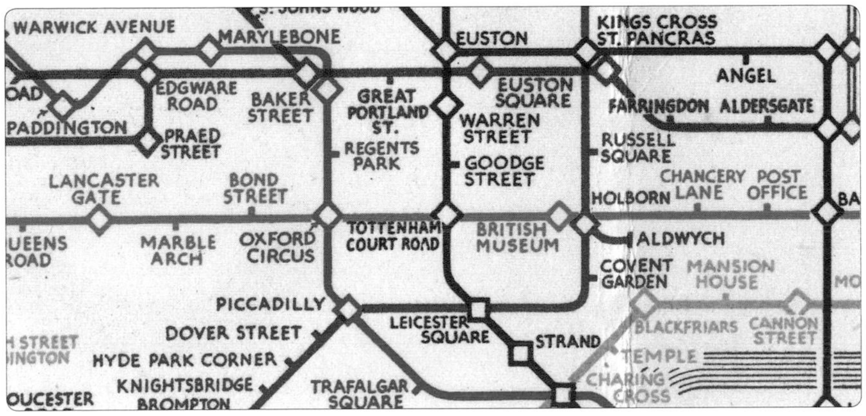

Harry Beck *London Underground Map 1st Edition*, 1933

Harry Beck, an engineering draftsman with London Underground, began to sketch out a new network map in his spare time in 1931. Prior to this, route maps were essentially geographic in arrangement, and were struggling with the increasing challenges of clearly depicting the tightly packed routes in central London while at the same time illustrating their suburban spread as the network expanded.

Beck's flash of genius came with the realization that, on a largely underground network, the stations' *relative* positions were more important to the traveller than the *actual physical distance* between them. Applying this principle, he devised a dramatically simplified schematic, where routes ran only vertically, horizontally or on 45° diagonals, stations were marked by neat ticks and interchanges differentiated by lozenges. Beck's designs were reputedly based on electric circuit diagrams although it is also claimed their inspiration came from maps of underground sewage systems. The influence of the prevailing Art Deco ethos, with its emphasis on elegance, functionality and modernity can also be seen in Beck's designs.

Beck was not a professional designer and his uncommissioned, radical new map met a cautious response from London Underground. Nevertheless, Tube travellers welcomed it enthusiastically from the outset and the innovative map has gone on to become not only a design classic but an icon of London itself.

Widely regarded as the epitome of information design, Beck's revolutionary map-cum-diagram now serves as the global blueprint for mapping many of today's complex transport systems.

Phyllis Pearsall *A–Z Atlas and Guide to London and Suburbs*, 1936

The A–Z street map as we know it today was the brainchild of Phyllis Pearsall in the early 1930s. Pearsall, an artist and writer, was the daughter of Alexander Gross, founder of the cartographic company Geographia. She conceived the idea for a simple, up-to-date map of the capital after having got lost using a 1919 Ordnance Survey map, the most recently published London street map then available.

To create her map, this remarkable woman set out daily to walk London's 23,000 streets, cataloguing street names, house numbers, bus and tram routes, stations, public buildings, museums and other attractions. She quickly decided that producing the map in the conventional sheet format would render it impractical for daily use; instead, she devised the now-commonplace format of dividing the map into small sections with street names keyed in to an accompanying alphabetical index. It was from this index that her publication took its name. Rejected by existing publishers, Pearsall set up her own business, the Geographers' Map Company (more commonly known now as the Geographers' A–Z Map Company Ltd), to produce and distribute her first A–Z in 1936.

The idea of street maps was not original to Pearsall nor indeed was her inclusion of street numbers, useful though this undoubtedly was. Where the A–Z triumphed was in its simplicity and ready availability through popular High Street outlets such as W.H. Smith. All of London was now accessible and Londoners took to it much as they did Harry Beck's map of the Underground (see page 15) produced a few years before.

Pearsall's creation has been hailed by the Design Museum as 'one of the most ingenious examples of early 20th century information design' and her A–Z concept is now ubiquitous amongst street-map publications.

Soviet topographic map of London, 1982

The Soviet political and military machine placed great value on accurate topographic mapping and devoted vast resources to its production. Through a combination of satellite imagery, high-altitude aerial reconnaissance, existing publicly available mapping and other data plus straightforward espionage, the USSR was able to map almost every country in the world with a level of detail and accuracy that is quite extraordinary.

The Soviets produced eighty or so British town plans at 1:25,000 and 1:10,000 between 1950 and 1990 including several of the capital. This map, dated 1982, shows a detail of east London. Built-up areas, rural structures, road networks, land and submarine contours, spot heights, river depths and widths are all visible amongst the wealth of detail provided. The Cyrillic script labelling even translates place names phonetically to overcome tricky local pronunciations.

An interesting feature of the maps – though not an unexpected one given their military origin – is their identification of buildings of strategic value. These are numbered, listed and colour-coded to signify different functions: military establishments (green), industrial plants (black), and administrative centres (purple).

The Soviets' highly secretive mapping efforts remained hidden until the collapse of the USSR in 1991 when the maps began to surface in the West. Interestingly, Ordnance Survey have attempted to ban them, claiming they were copied from OS maps and so contravened Crown Copyright. The British Cartographic Society and independent researchers have challenged this view but to date it remains untested in court.

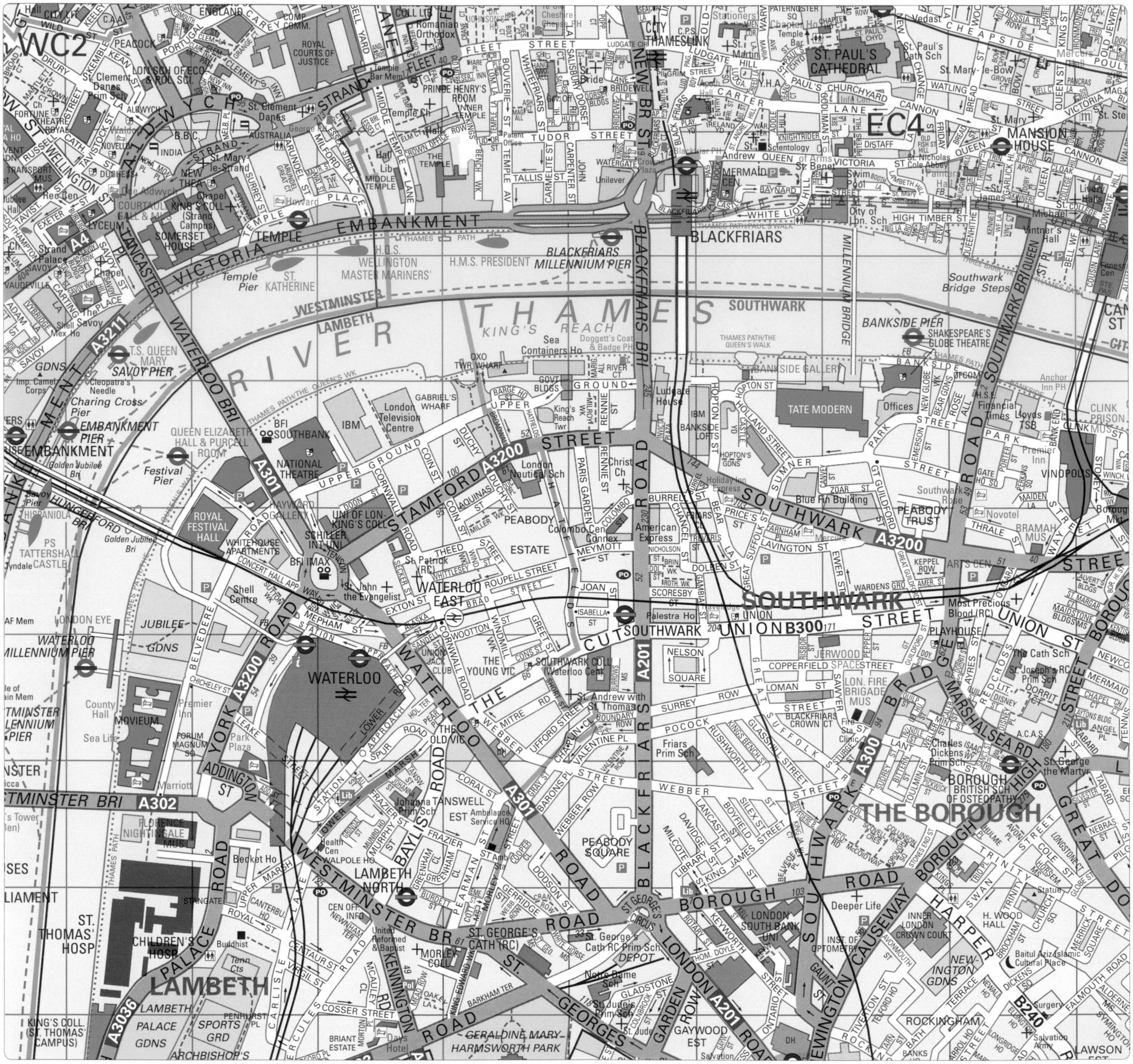

Modern Mapping

In the past, changing the design or 'specification' of a map invariably meant a re-draw from scratch. With digital technology it is now possible to change the design and content within a matter of minutes. The street mapping shown above is taken from the Collins Greater London Street Atlas. The same data, using a different specification, is used throughout this publication (see page 220).

The digital technologies available to today's cartographers also mean that London can now be mapped in extraordinary detail. OS MasterMap® is a cyclically updated map and aerial photography database produced by Ordnance Survey (OS), the UK's national mapping agency. It comprises millions of geographic features arranged in separate layers – buildings, landscape features, transport networks and addresses – and also incorporates an imagery layer consisting of high-resolution aerial photography. Such imagery is making an increasingly important contribution to the creation and revision of large-scale maps. A similar, if currently less extensive, product has been created by UKMap, the first direct commercial competitor to Ordnance Survey for such large-scale cartography.

While traditional printed maps tended to serve a single, specific purpose, the layered datasets of modern digital mapping can be combined and repurposed to allow a wide variety of uses. Depending on which data layers are used together, a single digital mapping resource can be used for demographic profiling, environmental analysis, civil contingency and transport planning. By overlaying these base layers with additional statistical data, it is possible to create maps which can be used to reveal patterns otherwise hidden in data.

LONDON IN CONTEXT

The pages that follow provide an outline of the key factors that influence all who live, work or visit the city. Its physical nature is examined first, by looking at its setting, its geology and its climate. The physical map of Greater London over the page provides a contrast to the map of Middlesex (below), which dates from 1877, for what was once a collection of settlements around London has now become part of the Greater London conurbation, absorbed by the economic might of the city and its ever-growing population, both themes studied in the pages that follow. As for the status of London, its importance to Britain has increased over the years as it has proved more adaptable to changing economic circumstances than the great industrial cities of the Midlands and the North, while its international standing has declined, though its 'economic clout' remains second to none in the world, according to PricewaterhouseCoopers in a recent survey.

One name that still regularly appears when talking about London is the lost county of Middlesex, which ceased to exist as a local government area when the Greater London Council was formed in 1965. Almost all of Middlesex was shared between a number of London boroughs, with a few areas in the north and southwest of the county being transferred to neighbouring counties.

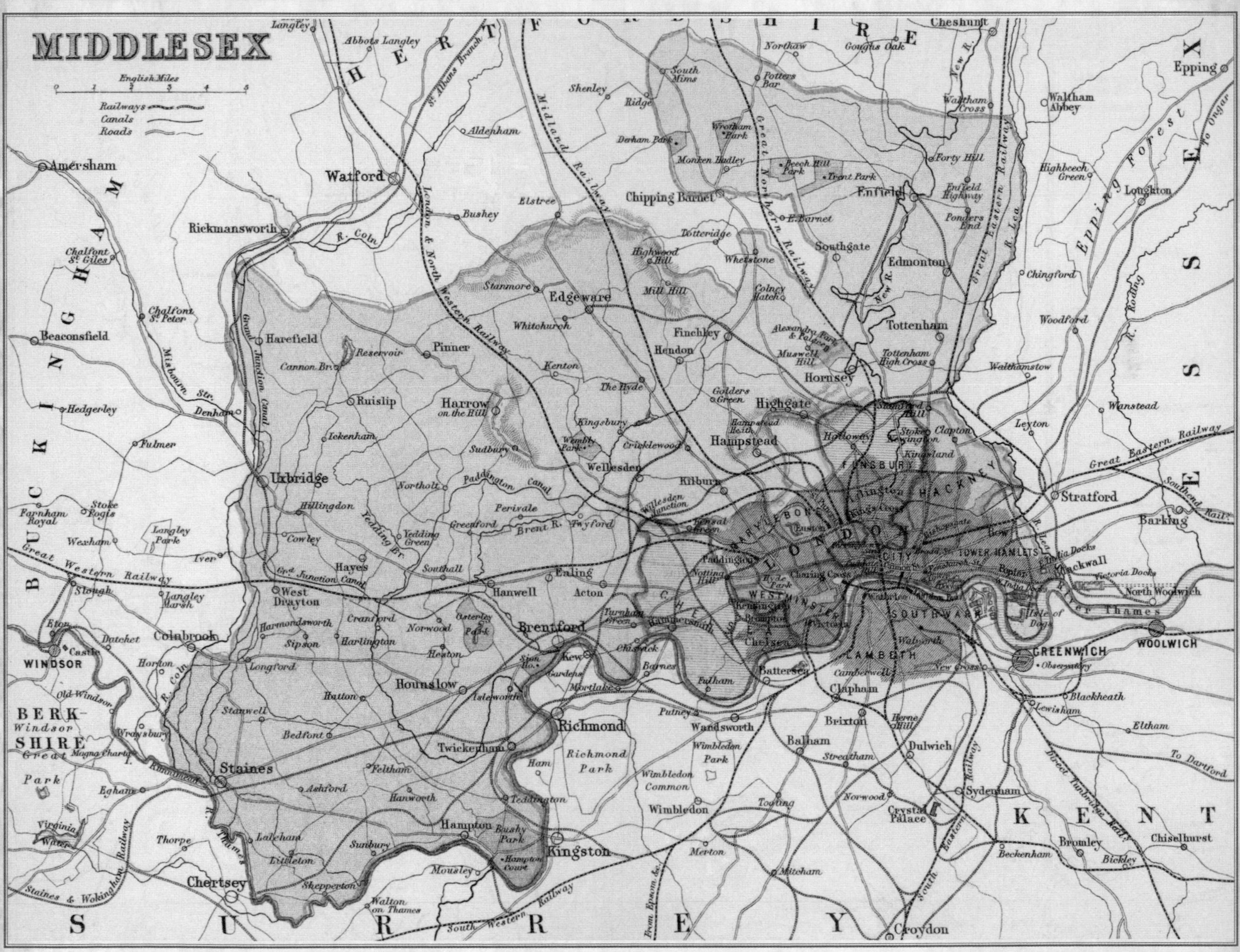

John Bartholomew, Gazetteer of the British Isles 1887
MIDDLESEX, *south-midland co. of England, bounded N. by Herts, E. by Essex, W. by Bucks, and S. by the river Thames, which separates the county from Surrey; greatest length, NE. to SW., 24 miles; greatest breadth, N. to S., 18 miles; area, 181,317 ac.; pop. 2,920,485. Excepting Rutland, this is the smallest of the English counties; but as it contains the greater part of London, its population is second only to Lancashire, which has the highest position in point of numbers. It is the metropolitan county of England. The appearance of the country is generally flat, with slight elevations on the Herts border and in the N. suburbs of London. The Thames, and its affluents the Colne, Lea, and Brent, are the only rivers, although there are several smaller streams in the co. Middlesex is likewise traversed by the Grand Junction, Paddington, and Regent Canals, also by the New River, an artificial watercourse constructed in the reign of James I. in connection with the water supply of the metropolis. The London clay forms the greater part of the soil, so that it is generally poor for farming operations except in some places on the banks of the Thames. Farming is carried on with much spirit, and with scientific attention. A large number of market-gardens, in connection with the metropolitan supplies are to be found in the co.*
The co. comprises 6 hundreds, 222 pars., the parl. bors. of London City, Bethnal Green, Chelsea, Finsbury, Fulham, Hackney, Hammersmith, Hampstead, Islington, Kensington, Marylebone, Paddington, St Pancras, Shoreditch, Tower Hamlets, and Westminster. It is mostly in the diocese of London.

1:171 000

Miles 0 1 2 3 4 5

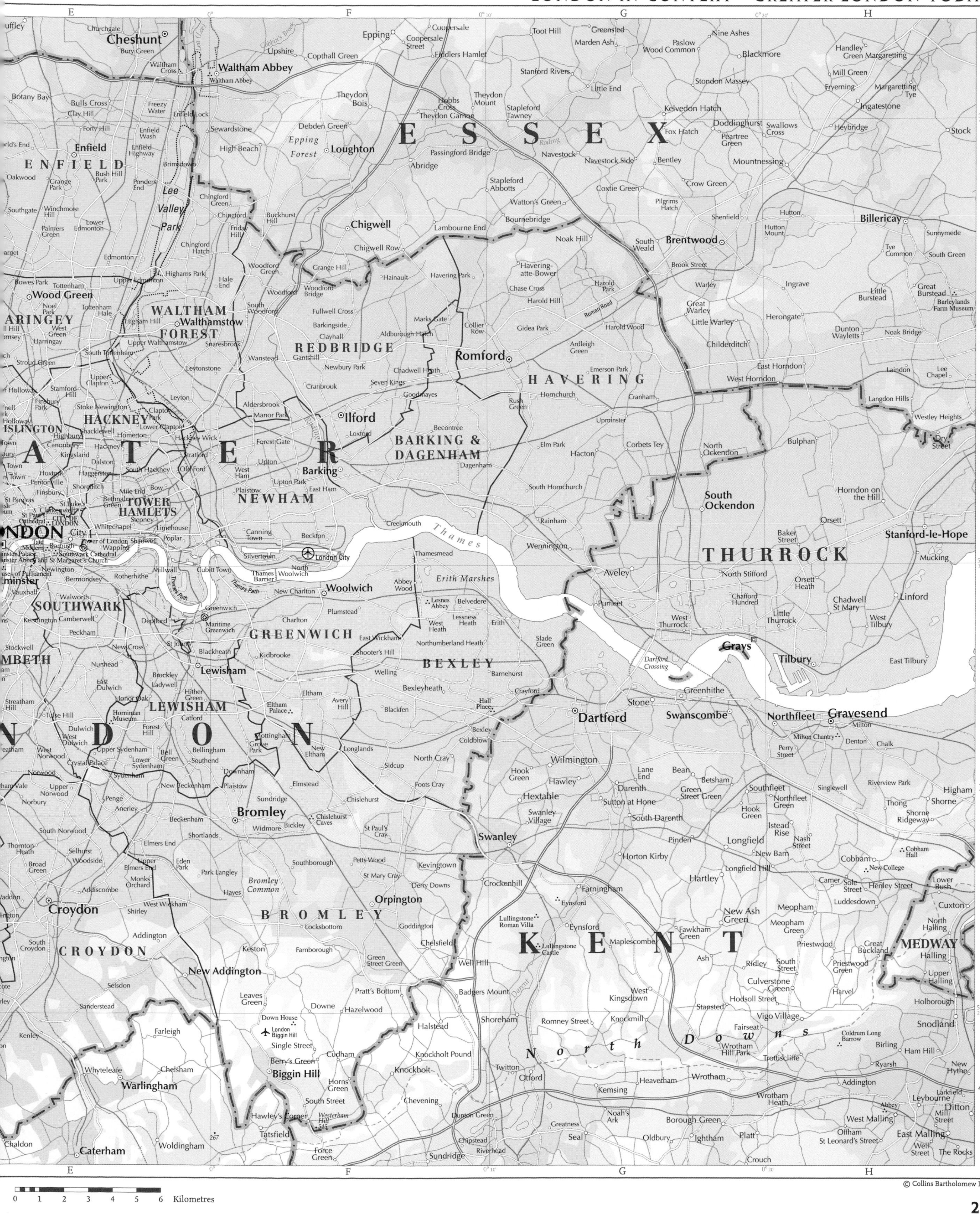
E
F
G
H
1
2
3
4
ESSEX
GREATER LONDON
THURROCK
KENT
MEDWAY
ENFIELD
HARINGEY
WALTHAM FOREST
REDBRIDGE
HAVERING
HACKNEY
ISLINGTON
BARKING & DAGENHAM
NEWHAM
TOWER HAMLETS
CITY OF LONDON
SOUTHWARK
LAMBETH
GREENWICH
BEXLEY
LEWISHAM
BROMLEY
CROYDON
Thames
Cheshunt
Waltham Abbey
Epping
Coopersale
Coopersale Street
Toot Hill
Greensted
Marden Ash
Nine Ashes
Paslow Wood Common
Blackmore
Handley Green
Margaretting
Mill Green
Fryerning
Margaretting Tye
Ingatestone
Upshire
Copthall Green
Fiddlers Hamlet
Stanford Rivers
Little End
Stondon Massey
Theydon Bois
Hobbs Cross
Theydon Garnon
Theydon Mount
Stapleford Tawney
Kelvedon Hatch
Doddinghurst
Swallows Cross
Heybridge
Stock
Fox Hatch
Peartree Green
Debden Green
Epping Forest
Loughton
Passingford Bridge
Navestock
Navestock Side
Bentley
Mountnessing
Abridge
Stapleford Abbotts
Coxtie Green
Crow Green
Watton's Green
Pilgrims Hatch
Bournebridge
Shenfield
Hutton
Hutton Mount
Billericay
Sunnymede
Chigwell
Lambourne End
Noak Hill
South Weald
Brentwood
Tye Common
South Green
Chigwell Row
Grange Hill
Hainault
Havering Park
Havering-atte-Bower
Brook Street
Warley
Ingrave
Great Burstead
Little Burstead
Barleylands Farm Museum
Chase Cross
Harold Park
Harold Hill
Great Warley
Little Warley
Herongate
Marks Gate
Collier Row
Gidea Park
Harold Wood
Roman Road
Dunton Wayletts
Noak Bridge
Childerditch
Ardleigh Green
Romford
Emerson Park
East Horndon
West Horndon
Laindon
Lee Chapel
Langdon Hills
Westley Heights
Hornchurch
Cranham
Upminster
Rush Green
Corbets Tey
North Ockendon
Bulpham
Dry Street
Elm Park
Hacton
South Hornchurch
South Ockendon
Horndon on the Hill
Orsett
Rainham
Baker Street
Stanford-le-Hope
Wennington
Mucking
Aveley
North Stifford
Orsett Heath
Chafford Hundred
Purfleet
Chadwell St Mary
Linford
West Thurrock
Little Thurrock
West Tilbury
Grays
Tilbury
East Tilbury
Dartford Crossing
Greenhithe
Stone
Swanscombe
Northfleet
Gravesend
Milton
Milton Chantry
Denton
Chalk
Dartford
Perry Street
Churchgate
Bury Green
Waltham Cross
Botany Bay
Bulls Cross
Clay Hill
Freezy Water
Enfield Lock
Forty Hill
Enfield
Enfield Wash
Enfield Highway
Sewardstone
High Beach
Brimsdown
Oakwood
Grange Park
Bush Hill Park
Ponders End
Lee Valley Park
Southgate
Winchmore Hill
Palmers Green
Lower Edmonton
Chingford Green
Chingford
Buckhurst Hill
Chingford Hatch
Friday Hill
Edmonton
Upper Edmonton
Highams Park
Woodford Green
Hale End
Woodford
Woodford Bridge
Bowes Park
Wood Green
Tottenham
Tottenham Hale
Noel Park
South Woodford
Fullwell Cross
Barkingside
Clayhall
Higham Hill
Walthamstow
West Green
Harringay
Upper Walthamstow
Snaresbrook
Aldborough Hatch
Stroud Green
South Tottenham
Wanstead
Gantshill
Newbury Park
Chadwell Heath
Seven Kings
Goodmayes
Leytonstone
Cranbrook
Upper Clapton
Stamford Hill
Finsbury Park
Leyton
Aldersbrook
Manor Park
Ilford
Stoke Newington
Clapton Park
Lower Clapton
Homerton
Hackney Wick
Forest Gate
Loxford
Becontree
Highbury
Canonbury
Kingsland
Dalston
Stratford
Upton
West Ham
Barking
Dagenham
Hoxton
Haggerston
South Hackney
Old Ford
Upton Park
Pentonville
Finsbury
Shoreditch
Mile End
Bow
Plaistow
East Ham
St Pancras
St Luke's
Bethnal Green
Clerkenwell
Stepney
St Paul's Cathedral
Whitechapel
Limehouse
Poplar
Canning Town
Beckton
Creekmouth
City
Borough
Tower of London
Shadwell
Wapping
Southwark Cathedral
Westminster Abbey and St Margaret's Church
Houses of Parliament
Newington
Silvertown
London City
Thamesmead
Bermondsey
Rotherhithe
Millwall
Cubitt Town
Thames Barrier
North Woolwich
Erith Marshes
Abbey Wood
Vauxhall
Walworth
New Charlton
Woolwich
Thames Path
Lesnes Abbey
Belvedere
Kennington
Camberwell
Greenwich
Maritime Greenwich
Charlton
Plumstead
Lessness Heath
Erith
Peckham
Deptford
West Heath
Stockwell
New Cross
St Johns
East Wickham
Northumberland Heath
Slade Green
Blackheath
Kidbrooke
Shooter's Hill
Nunhead
Lewisham
Welling
Barnehurst
Brockley
Ladywell
East Dulwich
Bexleyheath
Crayford
Eltham
Streatham Hill
Honor Oak
Horniman Museum
Hither Green
Catford
Eltham Palace
Avery Hill
Blackfen
Hall Place
Tulse Hill
Dulwich
West Dulwich
Forest Hill
Bexley
Coldblow
Wilmington
Mottingham
Grove Park
New Eltham
Longlands
Streatham
West Norwood
Upper Sydenham
Bell Green
Bellingham
Southend
Lower Sydenham
Crystal Palace
Sydenham
North Cray
Sidcup
Hook Green
Hawley
Lane End
Bean
Betsham
Norwood
Upper Norwood
Downham
New Beckenham
Plaistow
Elmstead
Foots Cray
Darenth
Hextable
Sutton at Hone
Green Street Green
Southfleet
Northfleet Green
Singlewell
Riverview Park
Higham
Shorne
Norbury
Penge
Anerley
Sundridge
Chislehurst
Swanley Village
South Darenth
Hook Green
Thong
Shorne Ridgeway
Beckenham
Bromley
Chislehurst Caves
Bickley
Widmore
South Norwood
Shortlands
St Paul's Cray
Swanley
Istead Rise
Nash Street
Pinden
Longfield
Thornton Heath
Selhurst
Elmers End
Horton Kirby
New Barn
Cobham Hall
Woodside
Eden Park
Southborough
Petts Wood
Kevingtown
Cobham
Broad Green
Upper Elmers End
Longfield Hill
New College
Hartley
Lower Bush
Monks Orchard
Park Langley
St Mary Cray
Derry Downs
Crockenhill
Camer
Sole Street
Henley Street
Addiscombe
Bromley Common
Farningham
Luddesdown
Croydon
Hayes
West Wickham
Orpington
Eynsford
Meopham
Cuxton
Shirley
Lullingstone Roman Villa
New Ash Green
Locksbottom
Goddington
North Halling
Addington
Meopham Green
South Croydon
Fawkham Green
Keston
Chelsfield
Lullingstone Castle
Maplescombe
Priestwood
Great Buckland
Halling
Farnborough
Ash
Ridley
South Street
Priestwood Green
Green Street Green
Well Hill
Upper Halling
Culverstone Green
New Addington
Selsdon
Pratt's Bottom
Badgers Mount
West Kingsdown
Hodsoll Street
Harvel
Holborough
Leaves Green
Downe
Hazelwood
Sanderstead
Down House
Stansted
Vigo Village
Snodland
Halstead
Shoreham
Romney Street
Knockmill
Kenley
Farleigh
London Biggin Hill
Fairseat
Coldrum Long Barrow
Single Street
North Downs
Wrotham Hill Park
Birling
Ham Hill
Trottiscliffe
Knockholt Pound
Berry's Green
Cudham
Whyteleafe
Chelsham
Biggin Hill
Horns Green
Knockholt
Twitton
Otford
Ryarsh
New Hythe
Warlingham
Heaverham
Wrotham
Addington
South Street
Chevening
Kemsing
Larkfield
Leybourne
Wrotham Heath
Ditton
Hawley's Corner
Westerham Hill
Dunton Green
Noah's Ark
Abbey
Mill Street
West Malling
Tatsfield
Greatness
Borough Green
Offham
Chaldon
Seal
Oldbury
Ightham
Platt
St Leonard's Street
East Malling
Caterham
Woldingham
Chipstead
Riverhead
Force Green
Sundridge
Crouch
Well Street
The Rocks
0 1 2 3 4 5 6 Kilometres

LANDSCAPE

The view from Parliament Hill, Hampstead Heath looking down towards Canary Wharf, with the North Downs rising in the background, showing London sitting in its topographic basin

Over the centuries, the debris of past generations – known as 'made ground' – and the bricks and mortar of present-day London, have masked the natural land surface. To understand the basic fabric of the city, we must start with its geology. London is located in the middle stretch of the Thames valley, near the heart of the London Basin. Moving north from Hyde Park, the suburbs present a switchback of hills before giving way to the slow haul into the Chilterns. These hills are fringed to the northwest by a prominent chalk scarp edge that overlooks an older plain of clay. Similar changes in topography occur to the west and south of central London. When these traverses are connected together, they constitute the bowl-like shape of the chalk, known as the London Basin. Clay and sands of younger geological ages – the marine London Clay and the sands of Bagshot Beds – are found inside the Basin. These materials make up the subsurface geology of the London area. Fifty million years ago, southern England lay beneath a warm tropical sea which, when it receded, left behind the London clay which can still be glimpsed in deep excavations. The layer of soft clay facilitated the excavation of the Underground railway, but it is notorious for causing subsidence of housing foundations.

Running water, and the sediments it carried, formed the main agent for shaping the natural landscape of southeast England. Early rivers, forerunners of the Thames, steadily removed much of the cover of sand and clay, reducing ancient ridges to the isolated hills of what are now suburban areas. Two or three million years before the present, the early Thames ran through what is now the Vale of Aylesbury, continuing east to the North Sea. This pattern persisted until 500,000 years ago, when the glaciers of the Ice Age blocked the drainage system, forcing the river to find a route further to the south. In this way the Thames evolved into its present course. What were originally floodplain deposits along the Thames were cut into by streams, and deposits of the sediments were formed into terraces which flanked the old river courses, the highest terraces being the oldest and the lowest the youngest. Archaeological remains, including the tools of early man who colonized the area during the past 500,000 years, provide the key to dating these terraces.

The Thames Basin

Around 120,000 years ago the sea level and the level of the Thames were much higher than they are now. For example, the pavement outside the National Gallery would have been lapped by tidal waters and the junction of Whitehall and Trafalgar Square would have been under water, even at low tide. Bones and fossils found in Trafalgar Square show that animals such as hippopotamus and elephant thrived in the warm climate. By 10,000 years ago the level of the Thames was considerably lower. At high tide it would only have reached the southern end of Northumberland Avenue, some 2 m above its present level at the Embankment. At this stage the River Fleet made a significant inlet where it joined the Thames close to Blackfriars. This inlet was an integral part of the port of Roman London.

London's lost rivers

The centre of London seems to be devoid of rivers apart from the Thames, but they are still there, hidden away in man-made tunnels. Indeed the Environment Agency has estimated that 70 per cent of London's river network of 600 km is covered over or altered in other ways by human intervention.

A romanticized view of the River Fleet joining the Thames, from the mid–18th century; in reality it was little more than an open sewer

The most significant of these hidden rivers is the Fleet. It rises in Highgate (Hampstead Ponds and Highgate Ponds were formed by dammed tributaries) and it was once used to supply drinking water to the city, to power watermills and to provide sheltered wharves for shipping. However, it was also widely used as a sewer so that, even in 1290, the monks of Whitefriars complained of its 'putrid exhalations' to the king. Over time parts of it were covered and channelled, but it only became completely subterranean as part of Sir Joseph Bazalgette's great sewage system, constructed after the mid-19th century cholera outbreaks. It now flows in tunnels for 6.5 km from Camden Town to the Thames, which it enters by Blackfriars Bridge. All that remains to the casual viewer are placenames along its course – Holborn (originally Holebourne, an old name for this part of the Fleet), Clerkenwell, Bridewell, Watergate and New Bridge Street, the latter dating from an early covering-over of the river.

Other rivers now flowing under central London include the Walbrook, which flows from Islington through the heart of Roman *Londinium* into the Thames south of Walbrook Street; it was on the banks of the Walbrook that a temple to Mithras was excavated in 1954. The Tyburn flows from Hampstead through St James's Park to Pimlico, giving its name to the area at the west end of present-day Oxford Street, where public executions took place. The Westbourne, part of which helped to form the Serpentine in Hyde Park, flows from Hampstead to Pimlico, at one point in a conduit above Sloane Square Underground station.

Further streams include Stamford Brook in West London, which flows directly into the Thames, and the Hackney Brook and the Moselle, both of which flow into the Lea, which is the major London tributary of the Thames, flowing down from Hertfordshire and through the Olympic Park. South of the Thames the Effa flows from Crystal Palace to Vauxhall and is now entirely underground as part of Bazalgette's scheme. Some other major rivers flow above the ground but in a modified state – the Wandle from Croydon to Wandsworth, the Brent from Hendon to Brentford and the Ravensbourne from Bromley to Greenwich. Interest in re-discovering these 'lost rivers' has increased and there are now schemes to start bringing small stretches of them back to life, such as the uncovering of a section of the River Quaggy in Sutcliffe Park, Lewisham.

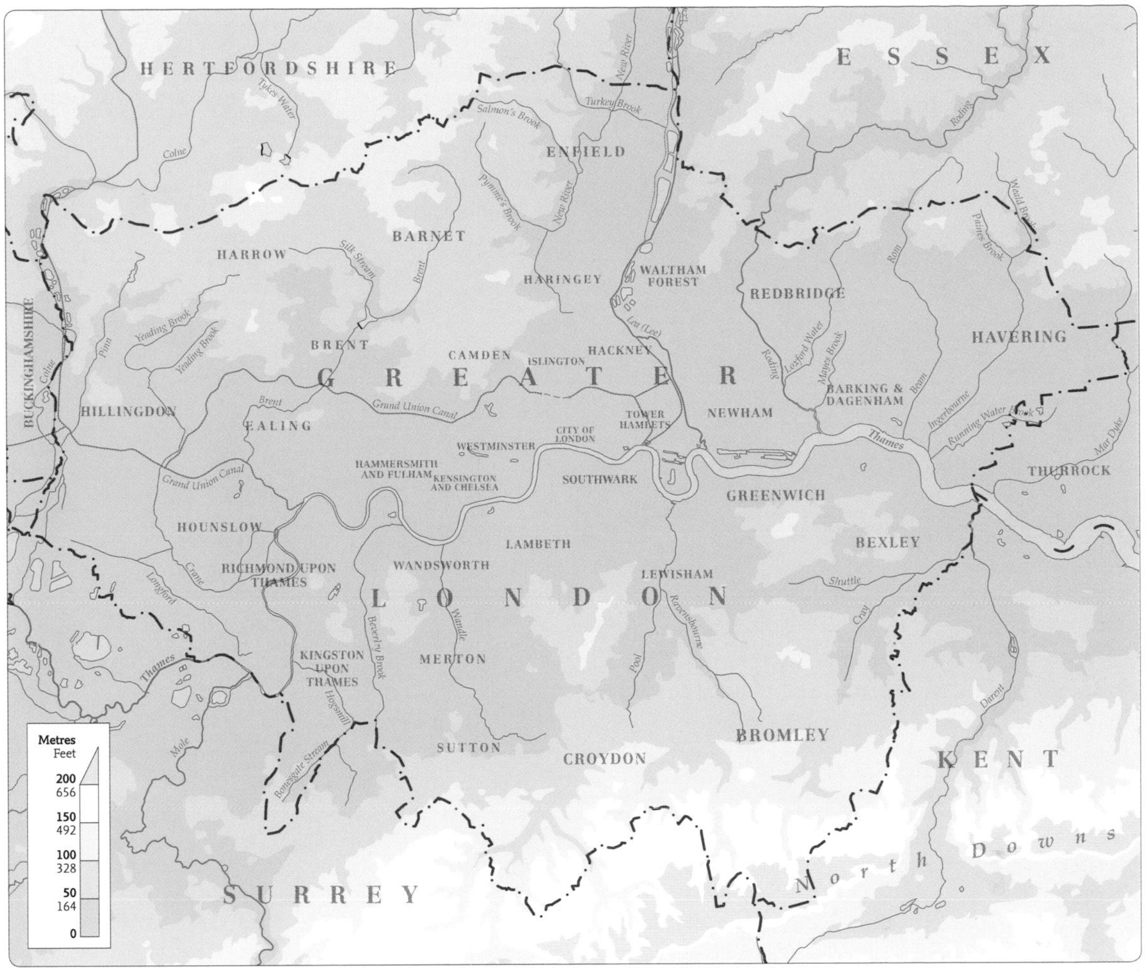

River map of London

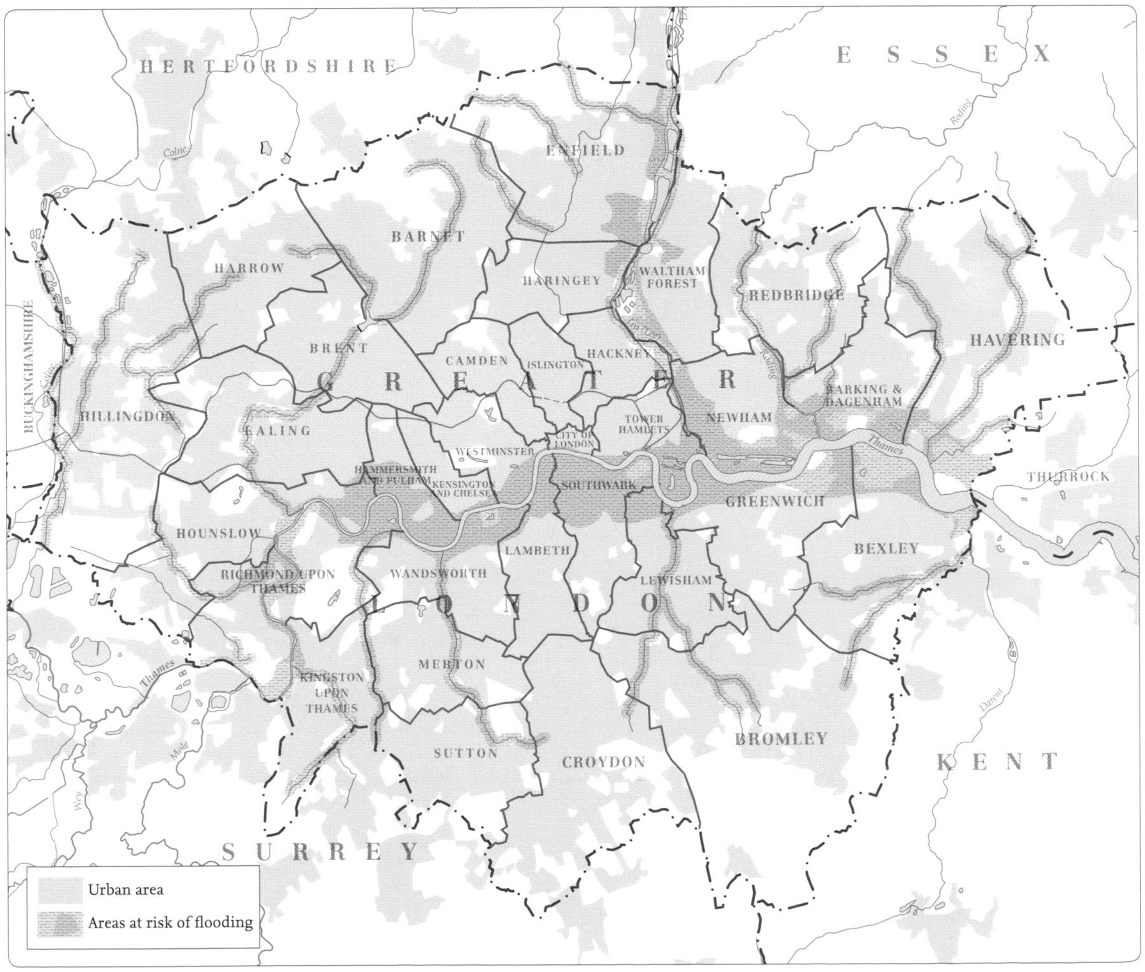

Areas at risk of flooding

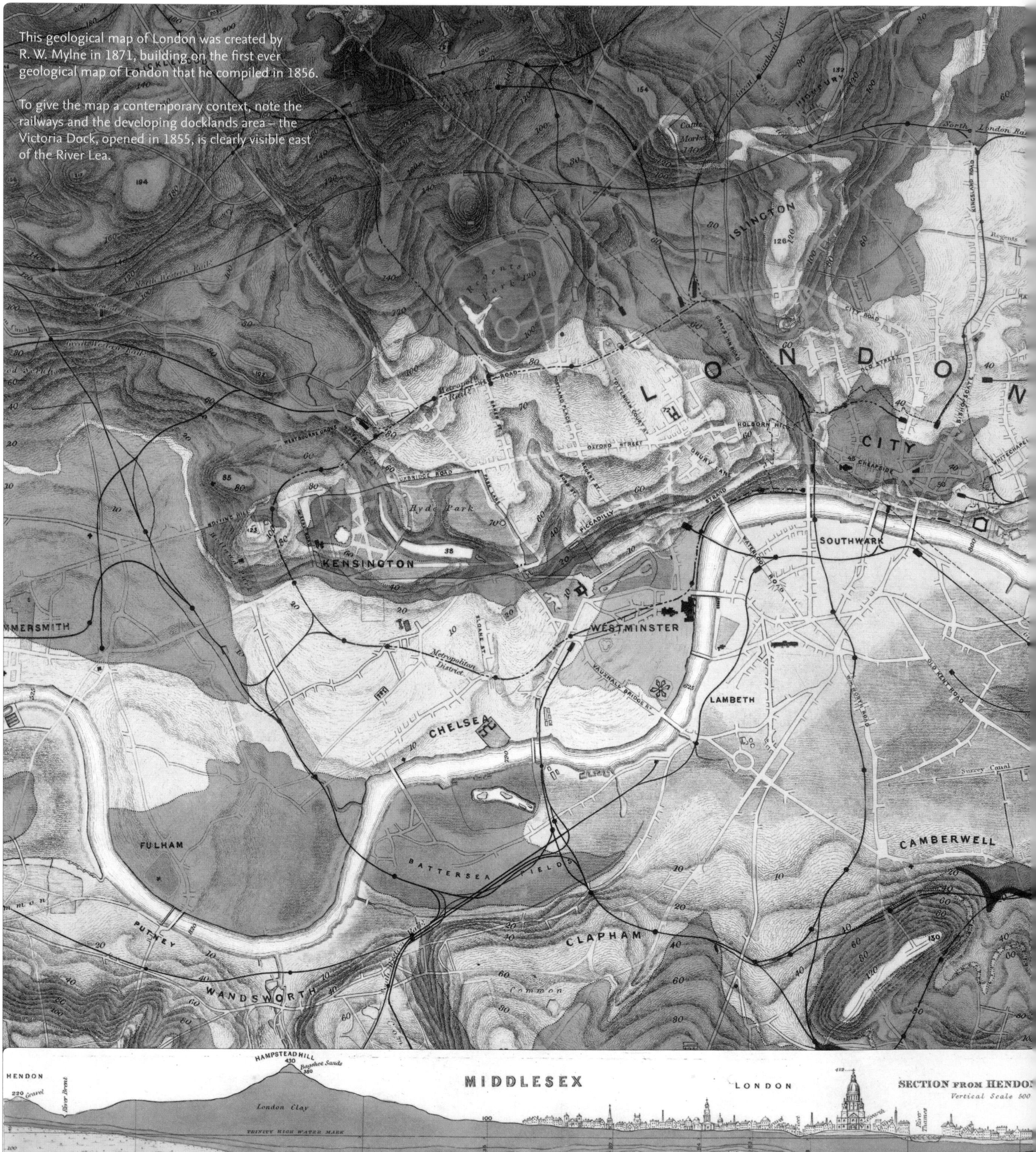

This geological map of London was created by R. W. Mylne in 1871, building on the first ever geological map of London that he compiled in 1856.

To give the map a contemporary context, note the railways and the developing docklands area – the Victoria Dock, opened in 1855, is clearly visible east of the River Lea.

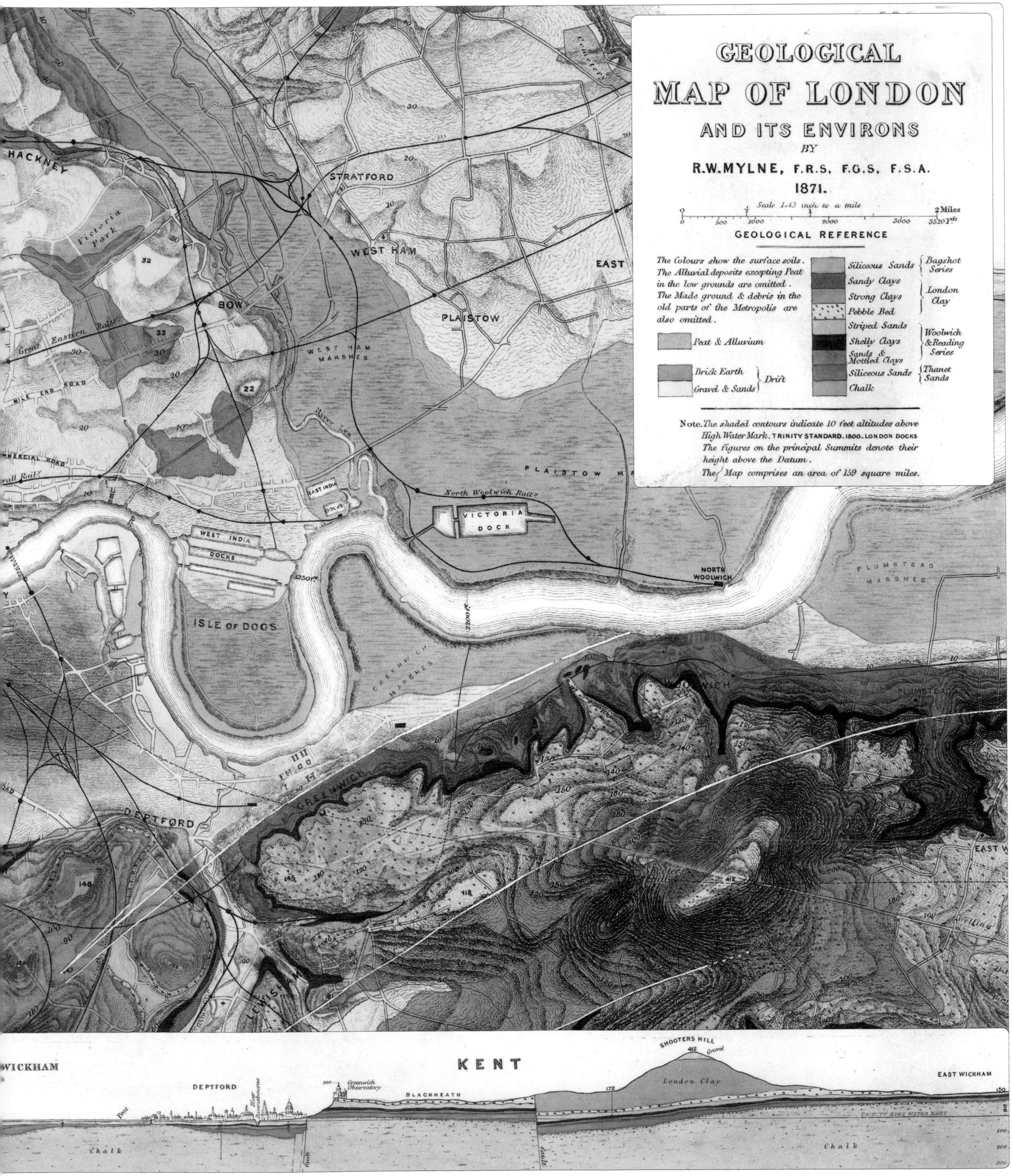
GEOLOGICAL
MAP OF LONDON
AND ITS ENVIRONS
BY
R.W. MYLNE, F.R.S, F.G.S, F.S.A.
1871.
Scale 1.43 inch to a mile
2 Miles
GEOLOGICAL REFERENCE
The Colours show the surface soils. The Alluvial deposits excepting Peat in the low grounds are omitted. The Made ground & debris in the old parts of the Metropolis are also omitted.
Peat & Alluvium
Brick Earth
Gravel & Sands
Drift
Siliceous Sands
Bagshot Series
Sandy Clays
Strong Clays
London Clay
Pebble Bed
Striped Sands
Shelly Clays
Sands & Mottled Clays
Woolwich & Reading Series
Siliceous Sands
Thanet Sands
Chalk
Note. The shaded contours indicate 10 feet altitudes above High Water Mark. TRINITY STANDARD. 1800. LONDON DOCKS
The figures on the principal Summits denote their height above the Datum.
The Map comprises an area of 159 square miles.
HACKNEY
Victoria Park
STRATFORD
WEST HAM
EAST
BOW
PLAISTOW
Great Eastern Rail
MILE END ROAD
WEST HAM MARSHES
River Lea
PLAISTOW M
North Woolwich Rail
VICTORIA DOCK
EAST INDIA
DOCKS
WEST INDIA
DOCKS
ISLE OF DOGS
NORTH WOOLWICH
PLUMSTEAD MARSHES
GREENWICH MARSHES
WOOLWICH
PLUMSTEAD
GREENWICH
DEPTFORD
EAST W
LEWISHAM
KENT
SHOOTERS HILL
WICKHAM
DEPTFORD
Greenwich Observatory
BLACKHEATH
London Clay
EAST WICKHAM
Chalk

CLIMATE

London has a maritime temperate climate, with neither great extremes of hot or cold weather. The winter months tend to be dull, with around 20 hours of sunshine a month, although in December 1890 no sunshine was recorded at all. Spring tends to be the driest season while July and August are the hottest months. In July the mean daily maximum is 22.5°C (the highest in Britain). The hottest temperature recorded was on 10 August 2003, when the temperature at Kew reached 38.1°C, just 0.4°C below the highest ever temperature recorded in Britain (38.5°C at Faversham, in Kent, on the same day). The city does not usually have particularly cold winters; the average is only around 30 days of frost. The coldest weather for which there are records was in the late 18th century. In more recent times, a low of –10°C has been recorded at Greenwich. The temperature in central London can be up to 5°C higher than the surrounding areas. This heat-island effect is caused by the buildings and hard ground surfaces absorbing radiation more effectively than open space, and then radiating this heat, so keeping air temperatures higher than less densely built-up areas.

Annual rainfall in central London is around 600 mm a year. It is wettest in the late summer and autumn, but overall rainfall is distributed throughout the year with a minimum of 37 mm in March and a maximum of 64 mm in November. The area is prone to heavy thunderstorms in July and August, the heaviest recorded being at Hampstead on 14 August 1975 when 169 mm fell in 2.5 hours, a quantity normally expected in three months. These storms can be very local – 6 km away from Hampstead hardly any rain was recorded. In 2009 and in both early and late 2010, London experienced some of its heaviest snowfalls for more than forty years, causing major disruption, most notably at Heathrow Airport. In the immediately preceding years snowfall in central London had been a rarity.

Office workers enjoy the sunshine in their lunch hour on Thursday 2 July 2009 when temperatures reached 32°C

Frost fairs

London winters were once much colder than they are today. In 1683–4, the Thames was frozen over for two months and a great fair was held on the river, complete with a street of shops and many fairground stalls – even bull baiting – while carriages went on the ice from Westminster to London Bridge. The last frost fair, which lasted just four days, was held in 1814. The Thames was able to freeze more easily then as the narrow arches of the old London Bridge (replaced in 1831) formed more of a barrier, slowing the flow of the river. 19th century river embankments also reduced the chances of freezing.

The Great Smog

London was once well-known for its dense winter fogs, exacerbated by smoke from coal fires. In December 1952 a dense, choking smog descended on the city, bringing public transport to a halt and

The great freeze of 1683–4 was the longest in London's recorded history

even causing the cancellation of an opera performance at Sadler's Wells when the smog filled the auditorium. It caused severe respiratory problems for a great many people and it was estimated that over 4,000 more people died during the smog than would have normally been expected at that time of year. This 'Great Smog' was the spur for legislation to restrict the burning of coal and led to a much better quality of air and the end of the London smogs.

The Great Storm

On the night of 15/16 October 1987, a great storm blew across southern England, and London was badly affected. Many trees were blown down, not just in the parks (Kew Gardens suffered badly) but also in the squares and streets of central London. Buildings were damaged and power supplies and public transport was disrupted. It could have been much worse if the centre of the storm had passed directly over London, as happened with a storm in 1703.

Dense smog was a hazard to transport and pedestrians in the winter of 1952

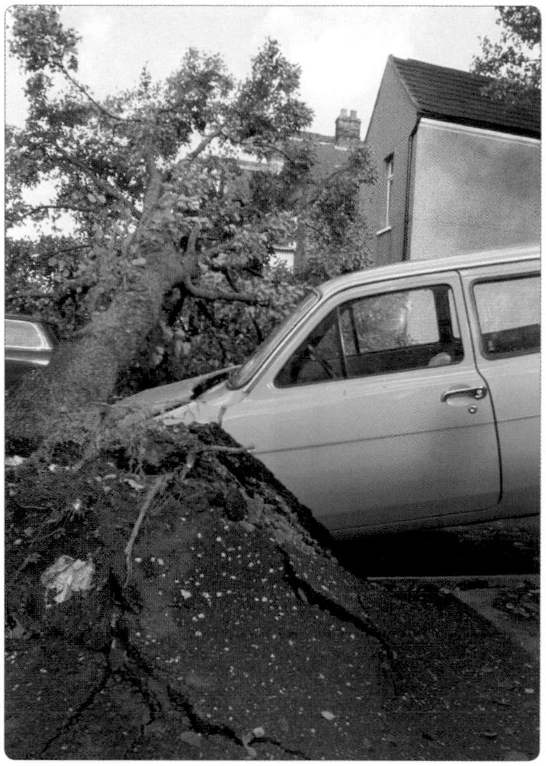

The storm of October 1987 left destruction in its wake

The climate by month

The figures below are based on the monthly averages recorded at Greenwich over a thirty year period between 1971 and 2000 and have been compiled by the Meteorological Office.

	Jan.	Feb.	Mar.	April	May	June	July	Aug.	Sept.	Oct.	Nov.	Dec.	Year
Max. average temp. (°C)	7.9	8.2	10.9	13.3	17.2	20.2	22.8	22.6	19.3	15.2	10.9	8.8	14.8
Min. average temp. (°C)	2.4	2.2	3.8	5.2	8.0	11.1	13.6	13.3	10.9	8.0	4.8	3.3	7.2
Days of air frost	7.4	7.4	2.9	1.1	0.1	0	0	0	0	0.3	3.0	6.9	29.1
Sunshine (hours)	45.9	66.1	103.2	147.0	185.4	180.6	190.3	194.4	139.2	109.7	60.6	37.8	1,461
Rainfall (mm)	51.9	34.0	42.0	45.2	47.2	53.0	38.3	47.3	56.9	61.5	52.3	54.0	583.6
Days with 1 mm or less rainfall	10.9	8.1	9.8	9.3	8.5	8.4	7.0	7.2	8.7	9.3	9.3	10.1	106.5

Climate comparisons

These charts show how London's climate compares with other major cities on a similar line of latitude. The blue bars at the bottom of the chart show monthly rainfall and the red bars show the average monthly temperature range. The maritime climate provides London with less extreme weather, either in terms of rainfall or temperature, when compared with these cities.

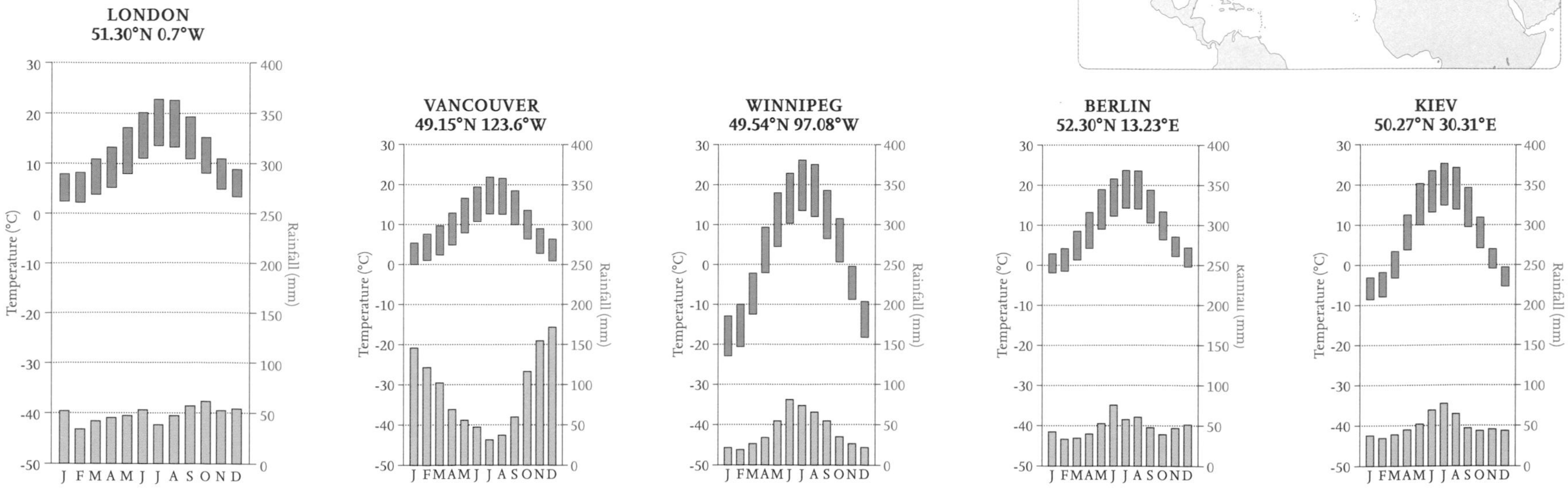

ECONOMIC ACTIVITY

London has been the commercial heart of Britain since Roman times. As it recovered from the Dark Ages, London (based around today's City area) developed as a commercial and trading centre. It had established its economic importance to the country long before Westminster began to be the major centre of government in the 12th century. The City has always been the financial centre of the country, the home of the major banks and trading companies. In the Industrial Revolution it was the financiers of London who helped fund the industrialization of Britain. The docks of London led to it becoming one of the world's main trading ports, handling a third of all Britain's trade. Around the docks grew many industries that needed to be close to a port – such as sugar refining and rubber processing in Silvertown. Manufacturing is now of limited importance to London while cargo shipping, with the arrival of containerization, has all moved to Tilbury, further down the Thames estuary and to Felixstowe in Suffolk. However, London's role as one of the world's major financial centres has increased its reliance on this sector even more, bringing great wealth to the city. Economic activity is now very unevenly distributed within Greater London, with a just a few Inner London boroughs dominating the economy of Greater London.

Overall, over a fifth of the UK's economic activity is provided by London, by far the greatest contribution of any region. When combined with the South East Region, the two areas contribute 36 per cent of the UK economy. Inner London alone contributed 14 per cent, equivalent to the total output of Scotland, Wales and Northern Ireland. The two leading sectors are business services (including property and renting) and financial services (45 per cent of all Gross Value Added from this sector in the UK).

Within London, economic activity is concentrated in certain areas, while some parts of the East End suffer from significantly low levels of economic activity, well below the UK average.

MAIN ECONOMIC SECTORS

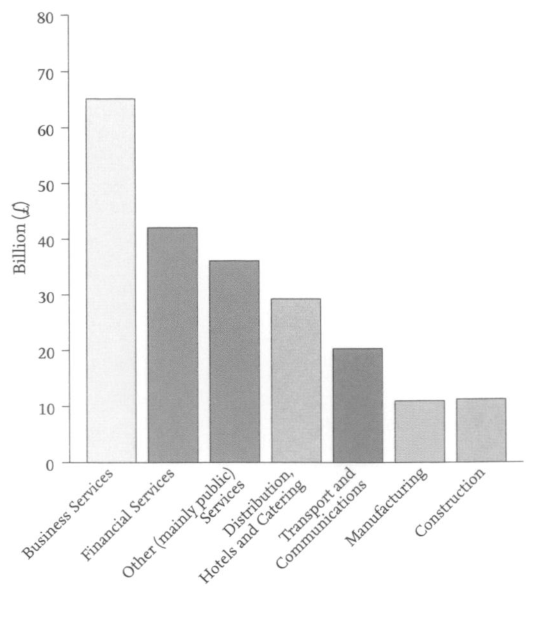

GROSS VALUE ADDED PER HEAD, 2008

United Kingdom	100
London	171
Inner London	295
West	525
East	163
Outer London	90
East and North East	68
South	87
West and North West	111

ONS Regional Trends data, 2011

Inside the Lloyd's Building in the heart of the City

GROSS VALUE ADDED BY REGION AS PERCENTAGE OF UK TOTAL, 2009

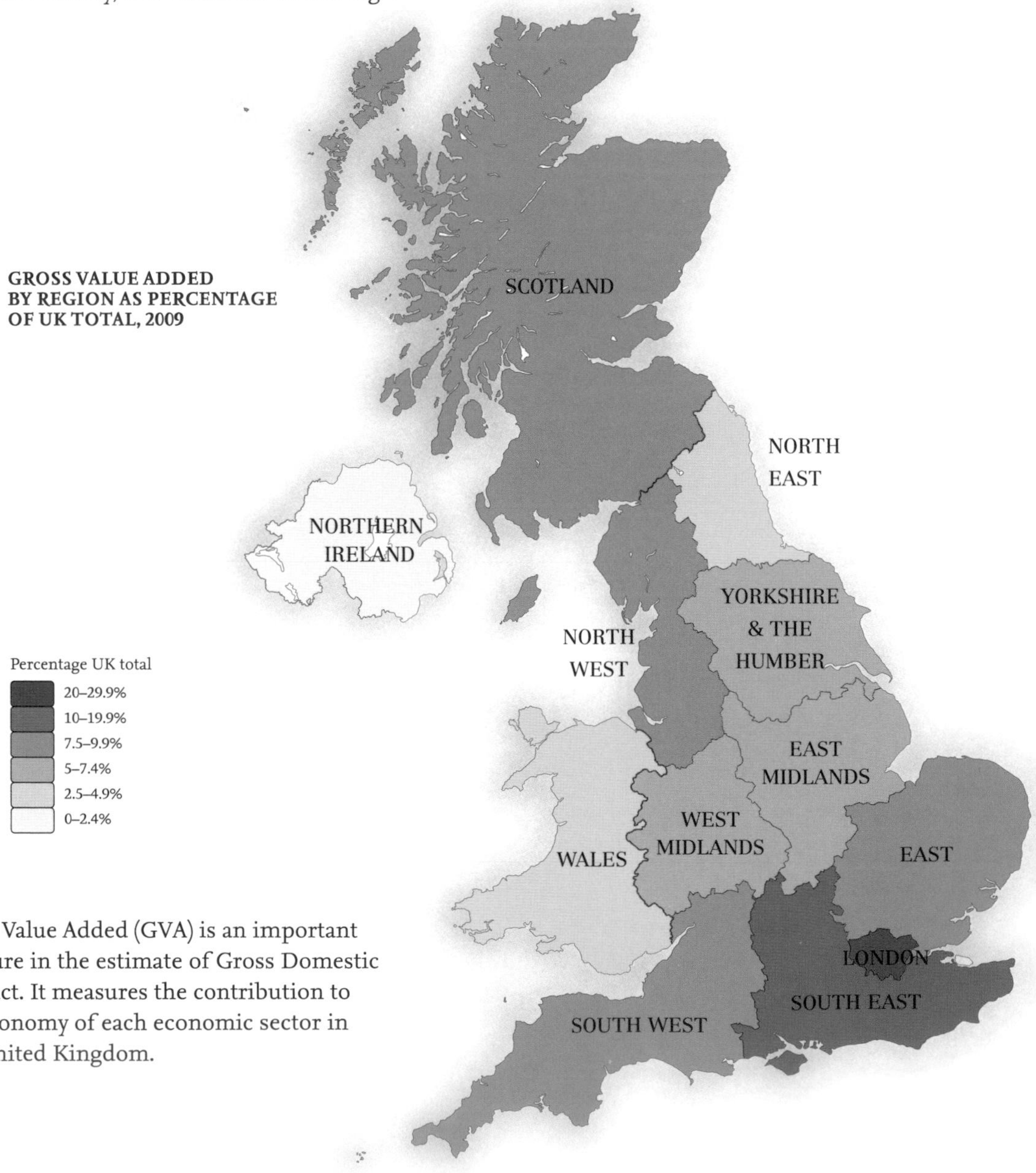

Gross Value Added (GVA) is an important measure in the estimate of Gross Domestic Product. It measures the contribution to the economy of each economic sector in the United Kingdom.

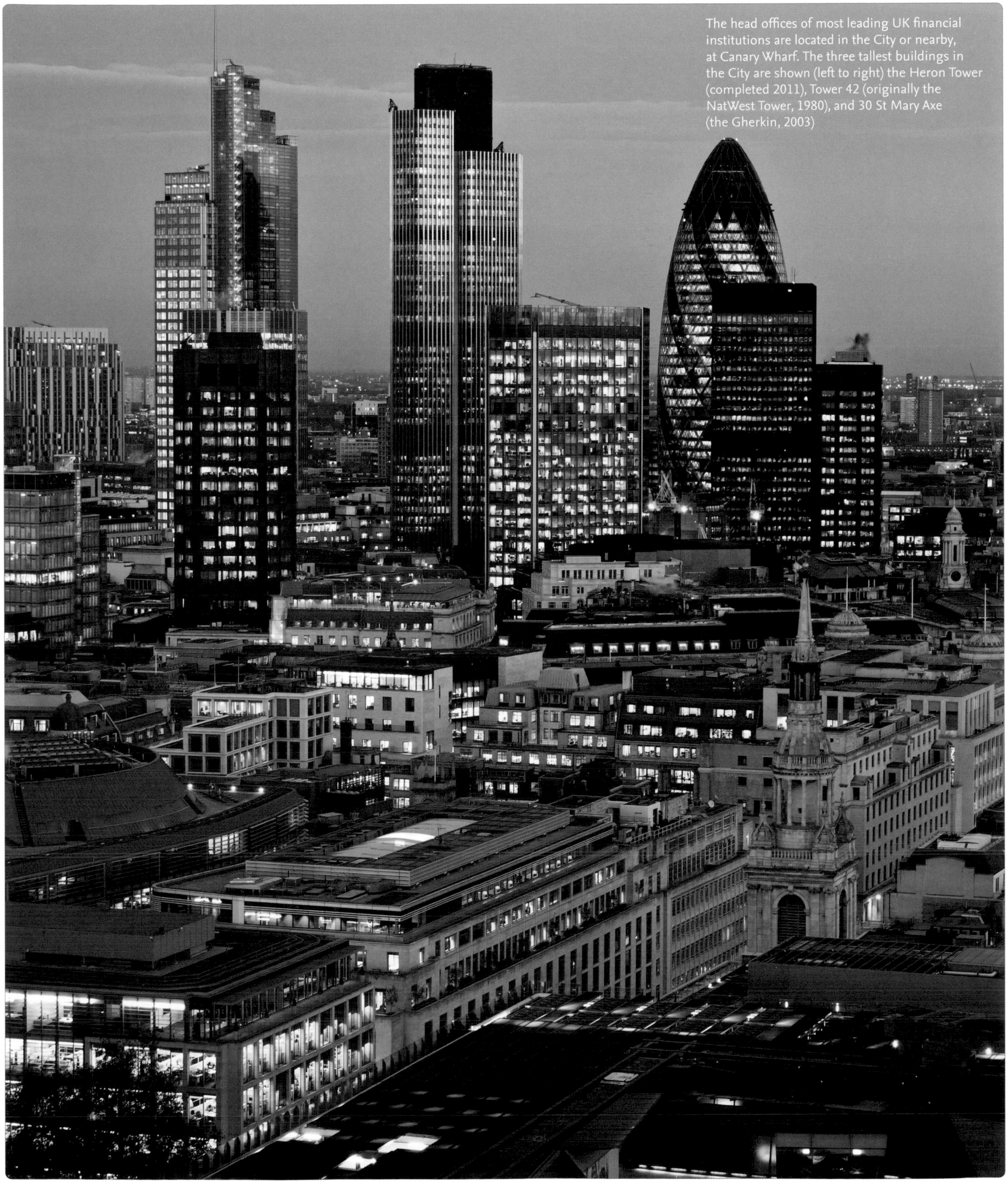

The head offices of most leading UK financial institutions are located in the City or nearby, at Canary Wharf. The three tallest buildings in the City are shown (left to right) the Heron Tower (completed 2011), Tower 42 (originally the NatWest Tower, 1980), and 30 St Mary Axe (the Gherkin, 2003)

EMPLOYMENT

The size of London's economy requires high levels of employment to support it. In London in 2009 there were over 4.7 million people either employed or self-employed (over 15 per cent of the UK total). In terms of employment sectors, there are some major differences with the UK as a whole – nearly 35 per cent of jobs are in finance, IT and other business activities compared with a UK average of 22 per cent while manufacturing accounts for only 4 per cent of jobs compared with 10 per cent in the UK. As the pie charts on the far right show, employment patterns in Inner London diverge significantly from the UK average. This pattern influences the skills required of workers – 54 per cent of London residents are in managerial or professional jobs compared with a UK average of 44 per cent, whilst productivity is 32 per cent above the English average (though not without personal cost to employees in terms or working hours, exacerbated by long commutes). London is an expensive city to live in, reflected in disposable household income being 28 per cent above the UK average. There are, however, unemployment blackspots within London and overall the jobless numbers were above the national average, between 9 and 9.5 per cent throughout 2010.

The shift in employment patterns has changed the nature of the workforce. Industrial unrest is mostly limited to the public sector. The militancy of the Bryant and May matchgirls (1888), the Great Dock Strike (1889) and others through to the dock closures of the 1970s and the Ford sewing machinists strike, seeking equality with male workers (1968) are in the past with the focus moving to public service and transport unions campaigning against job cuts and pension changes.

AVERAGE GROSS WEEKLY PAY

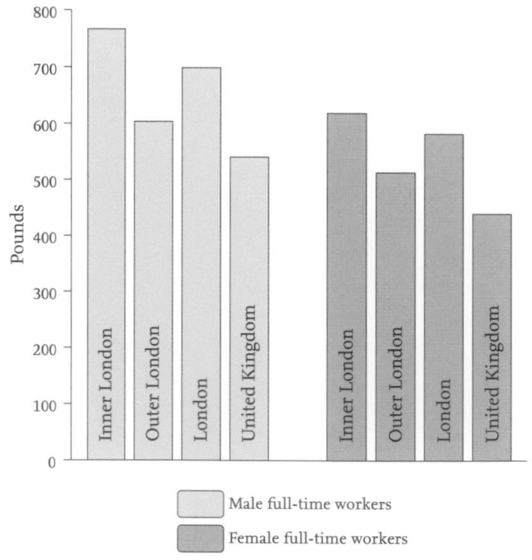

TOTAL EMPLOYEE JOBS

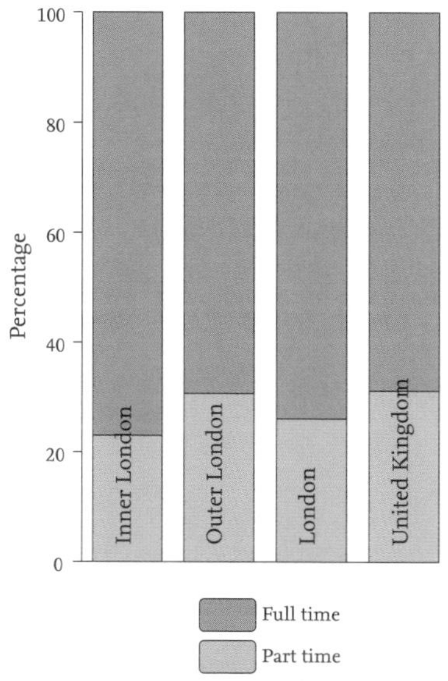

Wives of unemployed workers demonstrate in 1905

Marching against government spending cuts, 2011

Borough economies

Most of the individual boroughs are dependent on the central London boroughs of Westminster, Camden, Islington, the City and Tower Hamlets in meeting the employment needs of many of their residents. Of the Outer London boroughs only Croydon (an important business hub in its own right) and Hillingdon (effectively Heathrow) have major employment markets that pull workers in from other areas. Away from central London, public service plays a more important role in the economy. The four pie charts show the variety of employment patterns: the City has the highest number of workers in the finance sector, Barking and Dagenham in manufacturing, Greenwich in public administration and Hillingdon in transport (as a result of Heathrow).

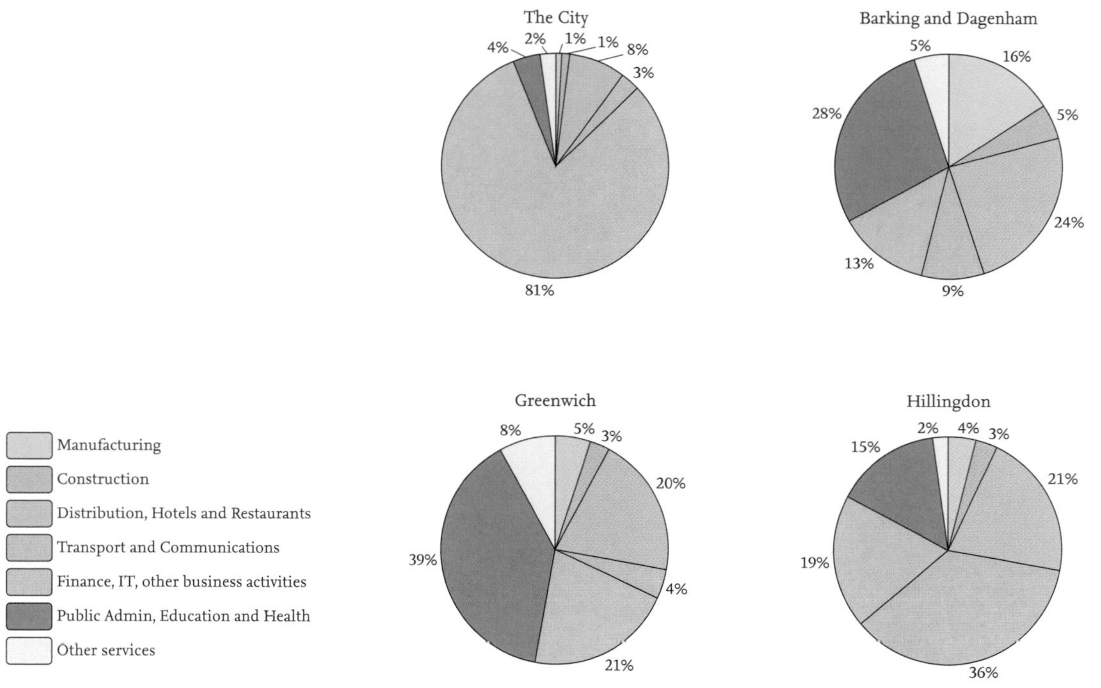

BUSINESS TURNOVER AND PRIVATE SECTOR EMPLOYMENT

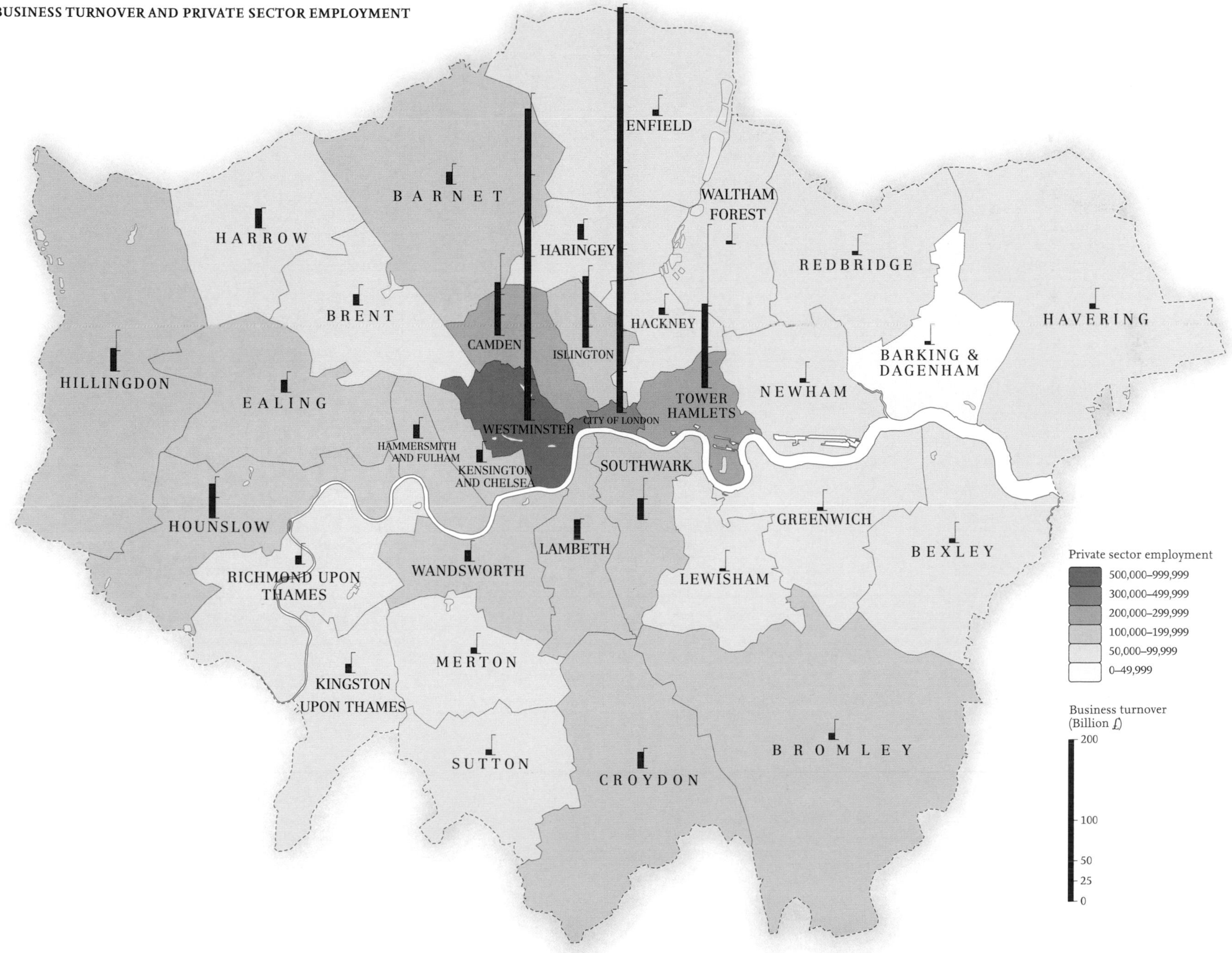

POPULATION

Once the new settlement of *Londinium* recovered from being sacked by Boudicca in AD 60, it quickly grew to become the largest town in Roman Britain, with a maximum estimated population of around 45,000 in the 2nd century. As with any fast-growing trading city, it drew people in from many places both from within Britain and from the wider Roman Empire. To thrive and prosper London has always relied on attracting people to live there and it has always had a much more diverse population than Britain as a whole.

After the 2nd century, its population declined and it was virtually abandoned in the 5th century. Renewed settlement, initially away from the old Roman city, began in the Dark Ages and by the 7th century it was thought to be the largest settlement in Britain again. By 1200 its population may have been 40,000 and perhaps up to 100,000 a century later. Famine and the Black Death reduced it to around 50,000 by 1500. The rule of the Tudors and Stuarts saw prodigious growth as London's position at the centre of a growing trading empire brought in people and wealth. It reached 200,000 in 1600 and over half a million in 1700.

The start of the 18th century saw the physical size of London expand as the built-up area spread west, and by 1760 the population was around three quarters of a million. Thereafter the growth of a colonial empire and of worldwide trading stimulated by the Industrial Revolution saw the population reach 1,111,000 in the first Census in 1801 and 6,227,000 by 1901. It reached its peak in 1951, at 8,164,000 after which it fell back to 6,608,000 by 1981. Since then it has grown again, the destination of choice for many migrants, making it a very cosmopolitan city of 7,754,000 in 2009, with a predicted population of 8,390,000 in 2021 and 8,841,000 in 2031. These last two figures, estimated by the Greater London Authority, suggest that the population will significantly surpass the previous population peak in the 1950s, although other estimates suggest a lower figure, almost matching the population of a century earlier.

POPULATION GROWTH FROM 1801 TO 2001

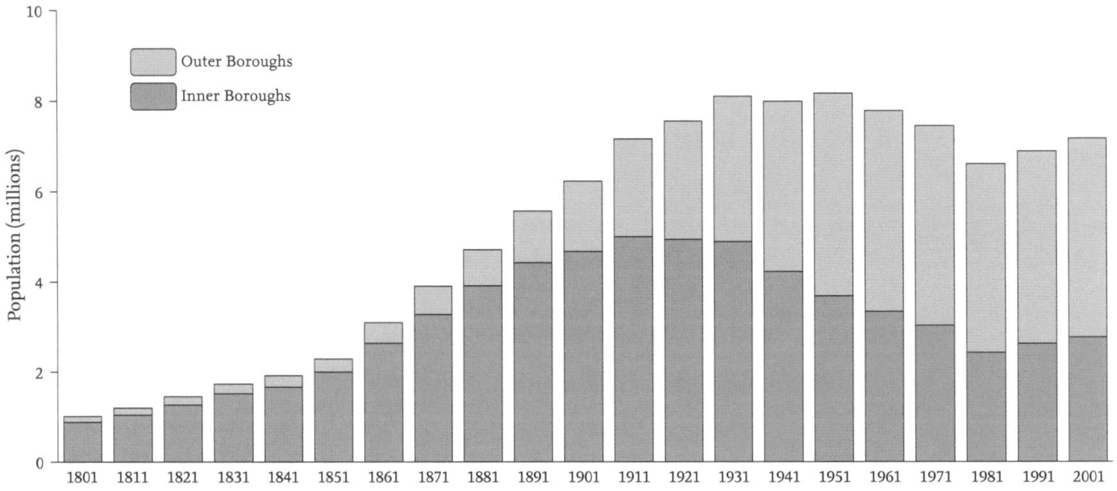

Source: *A Vision of Britain*

Population growth of London from 1801 to 2001
The figures used in this chart are based on Censuses from 1801 onwards and cover the whole of the area of Greater London, as we now know it. The different growth patterns for Inner London and Outer London show how the population has moved out of the centre of the city and into the suburbs, a trend only recently reversed. It was only in 1951 that the population of Outer London exceeded that of Inner London. In these figures Inner London consists of the boroughs of Camden, City of London, Hackney, Hammersmith and Fulham, Haringey, Islington, Kensington and Chelsea, Lambeth, Lewisham, Newham, Southwark, Tower Hamlets, Wandsworth and Westminster.

Multicultural London 2011
London is a city of great diversity. These charts provide a snapshot for 2011, as estimated by the Greater London Authority, showing Greater London and three contrasting boroughs: Havering, Newham, and Kensington and Chelsea.

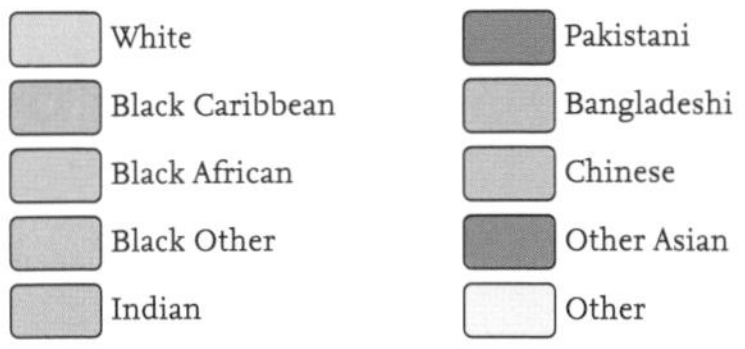

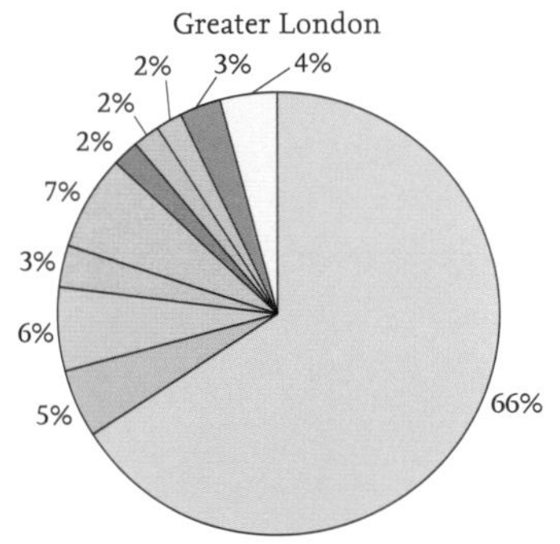

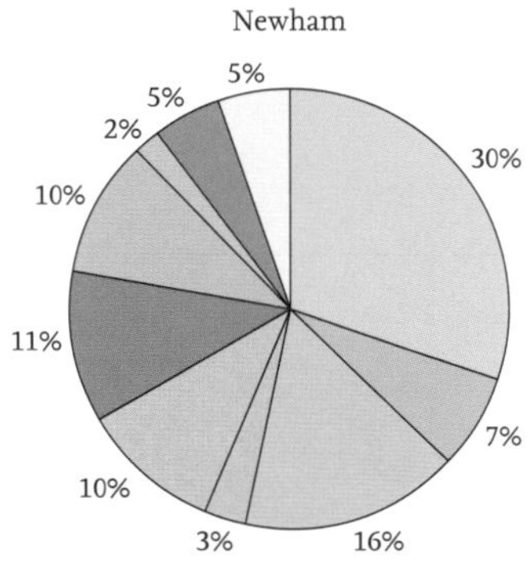

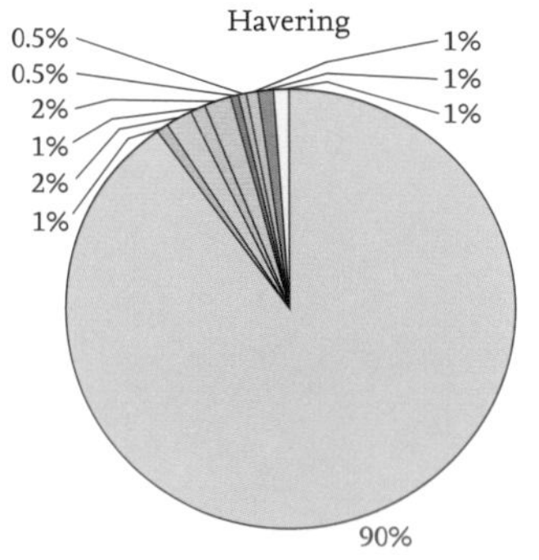

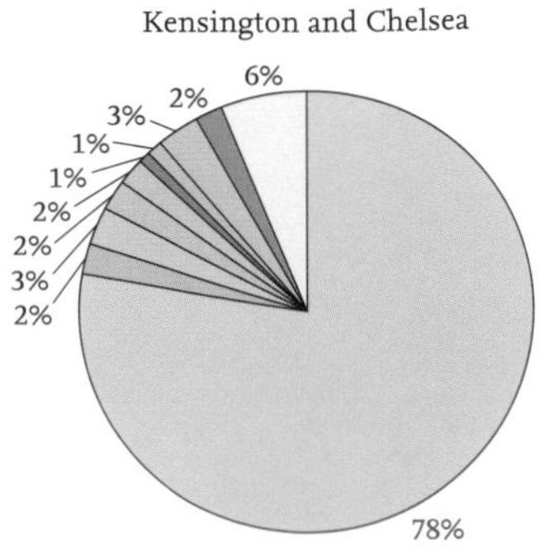

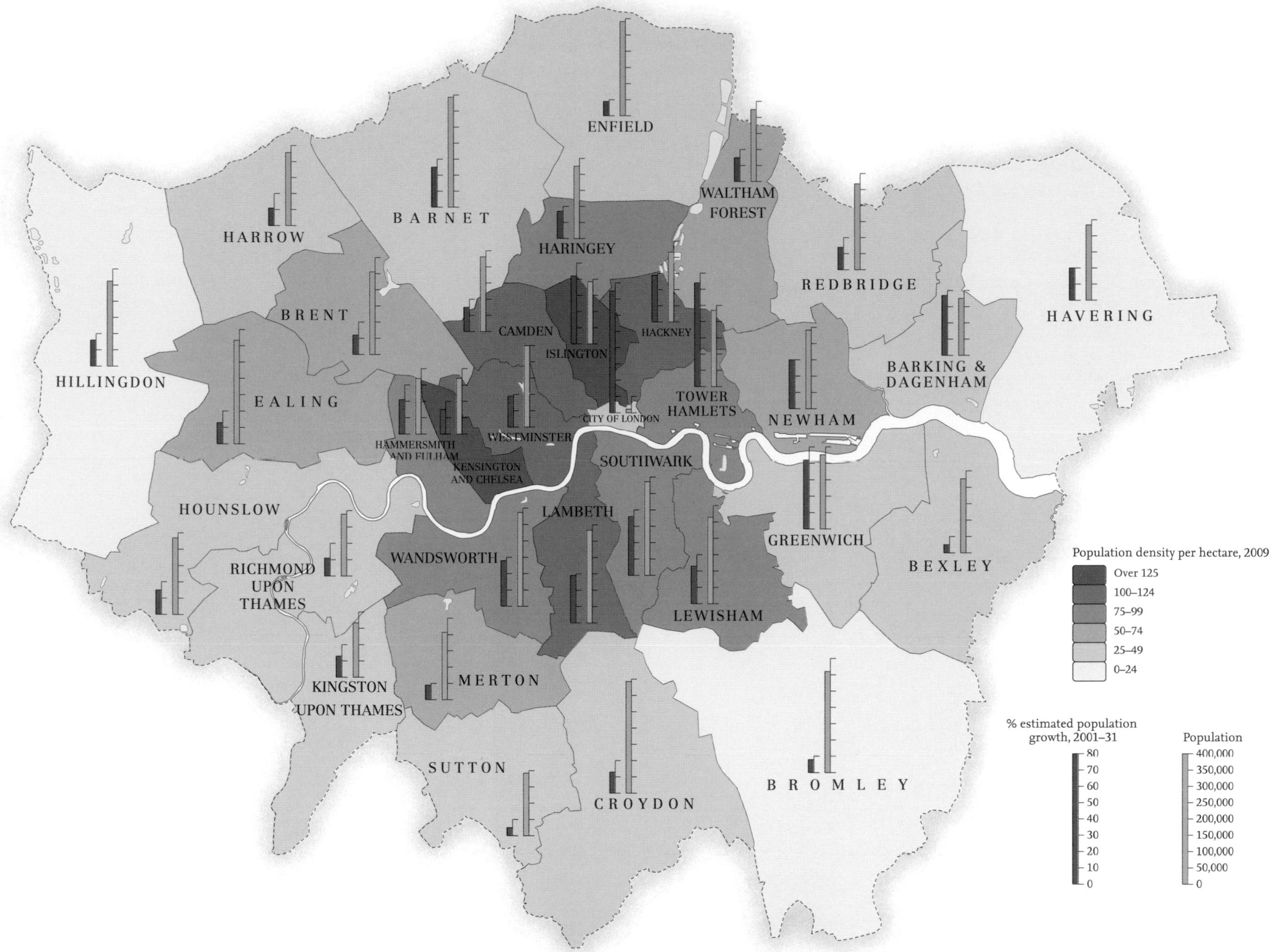

A multi-ethnic crowd at the Scoop amphitheatre next to City Hall

Population

The map above shows, by borough, the population density, resident population and estimated population growth.

Population density – people by hectare. As would be expected the Inner London boroughs have the highest density, led by Kensington and Chelsea.

Borough populations – the 2009 mid-year estimates produced by the Office for National Statistics. The City of London has the smallest population while Barnet has the largest.

Estimated population growth 2001–31. The Greater London Authority estimates that the population of Greater London will grow by 20 per cent between 2001 and 2031 (Inner London, 29 percent; Outer London, 15 per cent).

LONDON AND ITS PLACE IN BRITAIN

London is the capital of the United Kingdom of Great Britain and Northern Ireland, and it has always been the most important city in the country, both economically and politically. On this page we compare London with other parts of Britain by looking at a number of different areas.

Population

London is by far the largest conurbation in Britain. Around 12.5 per cent of the population of the UK live in London. A further 13.5 per cent live in the southeast of England, the area most dependent on London. The population of Scotland is only 10 per cent larger than the population of Outer London, while the population of Wales is 60,000 less than that of Inner London. The two charts below compare the population of Greater London with the other major conurbations in Britain and, secondly, the population of Inner London with other major British cities.

Looking east from the Shard, Britain's tallest building, located by London Bridge station in Southwark

MAJOR BRITISH CONURBATIONS COMPARED

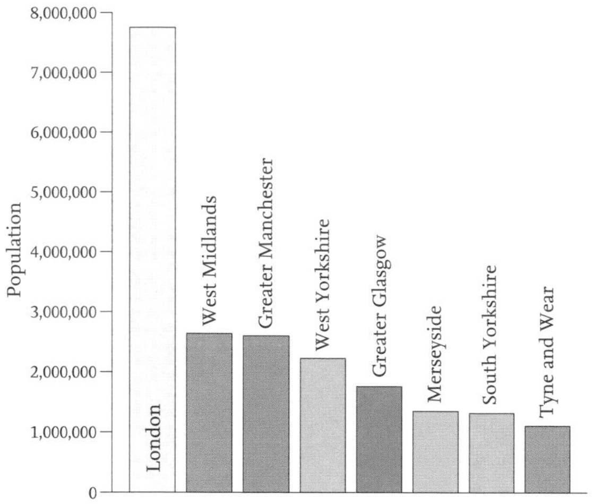

House prices

London is renowned for the high price of property, and these figures confirm how far ahead of the rest of Britain house prices are, and the gap is currently widening. Obviously within London there are significant variations, with the highest prices in Kensington and Chelsea and the lowest in Barking and Dagenham – but even then the price is just above the average cost for a house in the West Midlands.

Free school meals

Free school meals are used as an indicator of child poverty. The figures for London reflect the serious deprivation in parts of the city (and the higher than average number of children educated at private schools , so reducing the total number of pupils at state schools). It is also influenced by the many families that move out of London to bring up children, leaving London with a lower than average school population.

MAJOR BRITISH CITIES COMPARED WITH INNER LONDON

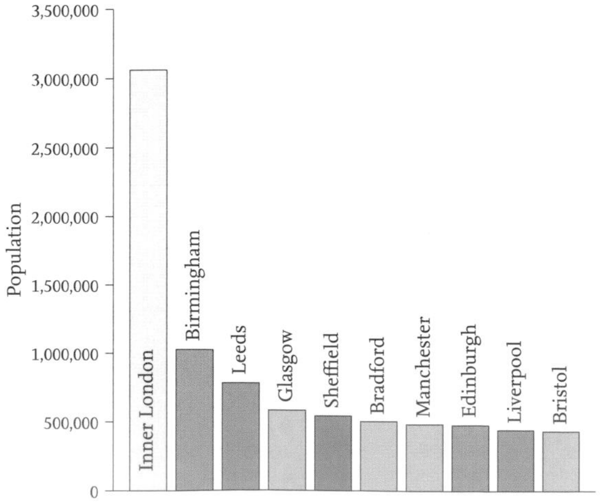

AVERAGE HOUSE PRICES OCTOBER–DECEMBER 2010

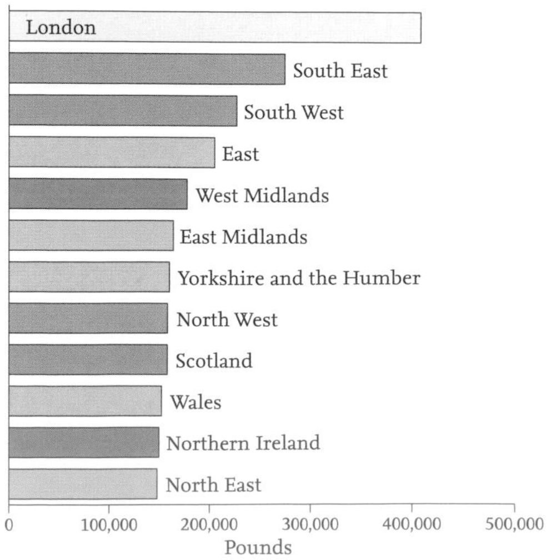

PRIMARY SCHOOL CHILDREN ELIGIBLE FOR FREE SCHOOL MEALS

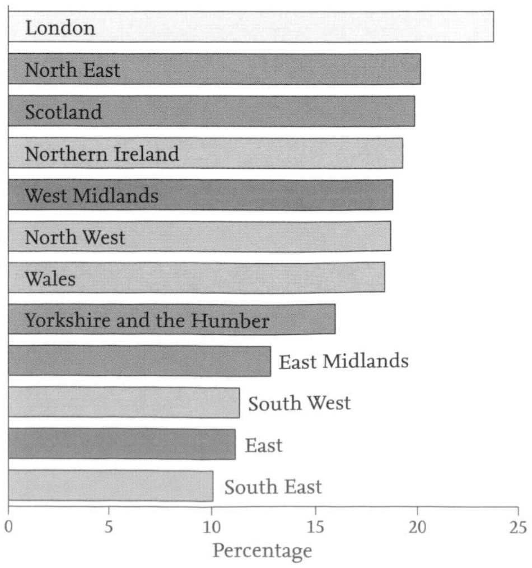

LONDON AND ITS PLACE IN THE WORLD

London once prided itself on being the capital of the world and its largest city – but that was in the 19th century. By 2011 the position is much altered. In a survey by the City Mayors Foundation, it had slipped down to 23rd position in terms of population.

Rank	City	City population	Metro population
1	**Karachi** *Pakistan*	**15,500,000**	18,000,000
2	**Shanghai** *China*	**14,900,000**	19,200,000
3	**Mumbai (Bombay)** *India*	**13,900,000**	21,200,000
4	**Beijing** *China*	**12,460,000**	17,550,000
5	**Delhi** *India*	**12,100,000**	16,713,000
6	**Buenos Aires** *Argentina*	**11,655,000**	12,924,000
7	**Manila** *Philippines*	**11,550,000**	13,503,000
8	**Seoul** *South Korea*	**11,153,000**	24,472,000
9	**São Paulo** *Brazil*	**11,038,000**	19,890,000
10	**Moscow** *Russia*	**10,524,000**	14,800,000
11	**Jakarta** *Indonesia*	**10,100,000**	24,100,000
12	**İstanbul** *Turkey*	**9,560,000**	12,600,000
13	**Bangkok** *Thailand*	**9,100,000**	11,970,000
14	**Mexico City** *Mexico*	**8,841,000**	21,163,000
15	**Tōkyō** *Japan*	**8,653,000**	31,036,000
16	**Tehrān** *Iran*	**8,430,000**	13,450,000
17	**New York** *USA*	**8,364,000**	20,090,000
18	**Kinshasa** *Congo D.R.*	**8,200,000**	10,100,000
19	**Dhaka (Dacca)** *Bangladesh*	**7,940,000**	12,797,000
20	**Lagos** *Nigeria*	**7,938,000**	9,123,000
21	**Cairo** *Egypt*	**7,764,000**	15,546,000
22	**Lima** *Peru*	**7,606,000**	8,473,000
23	**London** *UK*	**7,557,000**	12,200,000
24	**Tianjin** *China*	**7,500,000**	11,750,000
25	**Bogota** *Colombia*	**7,320,000**	8,361,000
26	**Ho Chi Minh City** *Vietnam*	**7,100,000**	no data
27	**Hong Kong** *China*	**7,055,000**	no data
28	**Guangzhou** *China*	**6,458,000**	10,182,000
29	**Dongguan** *China*	**6,446,000**	7,650,000
30	**Lahore** *Pakistan*	**6,100,000**	8,600,000

Living costs

Is London as expensive as it seems to everyone who lives there? A company called Mercer survey the cities of the world to find out which are the most expensive for companies to send expatriates to. London came out at 17th in their 2011 list, equal with Paris. While three cities above London, including Luanda at the top, appear because of the security costs of staying in potentially volatile places, London is seen as a cheaper place than Geneva, Hong Kong or Milan, for example. The ranking is calculated by comparing the costs of over 200 items, including housing (always a large component), food, travel and entertainment. With its expensive housing, London suffered in the overall ranking – however, for daily items, it fared much better, being among the cheapest places for a daily newspaper and a cup of coffee (see the chart below).

In further Mercer surveys, London came 39th for 'Quality of Living' (Vienna was first) and it did not make the top 50 in an 'Eco-Rating' survey, topped by Calgary, with Aberdeen, at 19th, the top British city.

Rank	City	Country	Rank	City	Country	Rank	City	Country	Rank	City	Country
1	**Luanda**	Angola	**6**	**Ōsaka**	Japan	**11**	**Singapore**	Singapore	**16**	**Beijing (Peking)**	China
2	**Tōkyō**	Japan	**7**	**Libreville**	Gabon	**11**	**Oslo**	Norway	**17**	**London**	UK
3	**Ndjamena**	Chad	**8**	**Zürich**	Switzerland	**13**	**Victoria**	Seychelles	**17**	**Paris**	France
4	**Moscow**	Russia	**8**	**Hong Kong**	China	**14**	**Seoul**	South Korea	**19**	**Tel Aviv-Yafo**	Israel
5	**Geneva**	Switzerland	**10**	**Copenhagen**	Denmark	**15**	**Milan**	Italy	**19**	**Nagoya**	Japan

EXPENDITURE AROUND THE WORLD

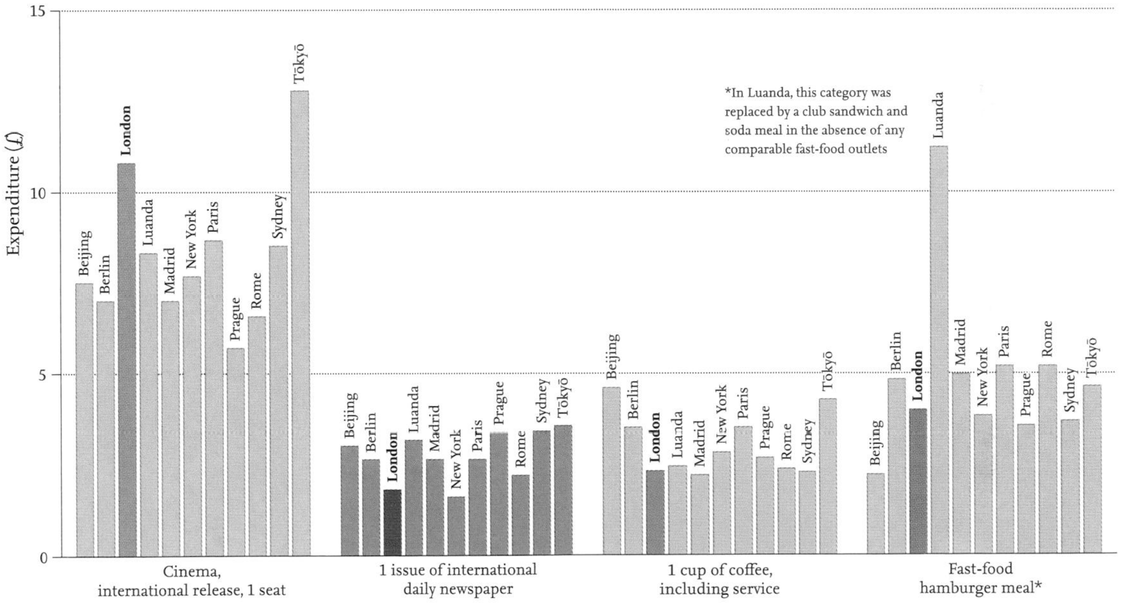

Which cities function best?

PricewaterhouseCoopers have analysed how twenty-six leading financial and commercial centres actually work, covering many aspects of living and working in a city including business factors, such as 'economic clout' and 'technological readiness' and personal factors such as 'health, safety and security'. In its 2011 Cities of Opportunity survey, London was ranked overall at sixth, behind New York, Toronto, San Francisco, Stockholm and Sydney.

LONDON'S RANKINGS IN 'CITIES OF OPPORTUNITY' SURVEY

	Rank		Rank
Economic clout	1	Health, safety and security	11
Lifestyle assets	3	Technological readiness	11
Ease of doing business	4	Sustainability	12
Transport and infrastructure	7	Cost	16
Intellectual capital & innovation	11	Demographics and liveability	17

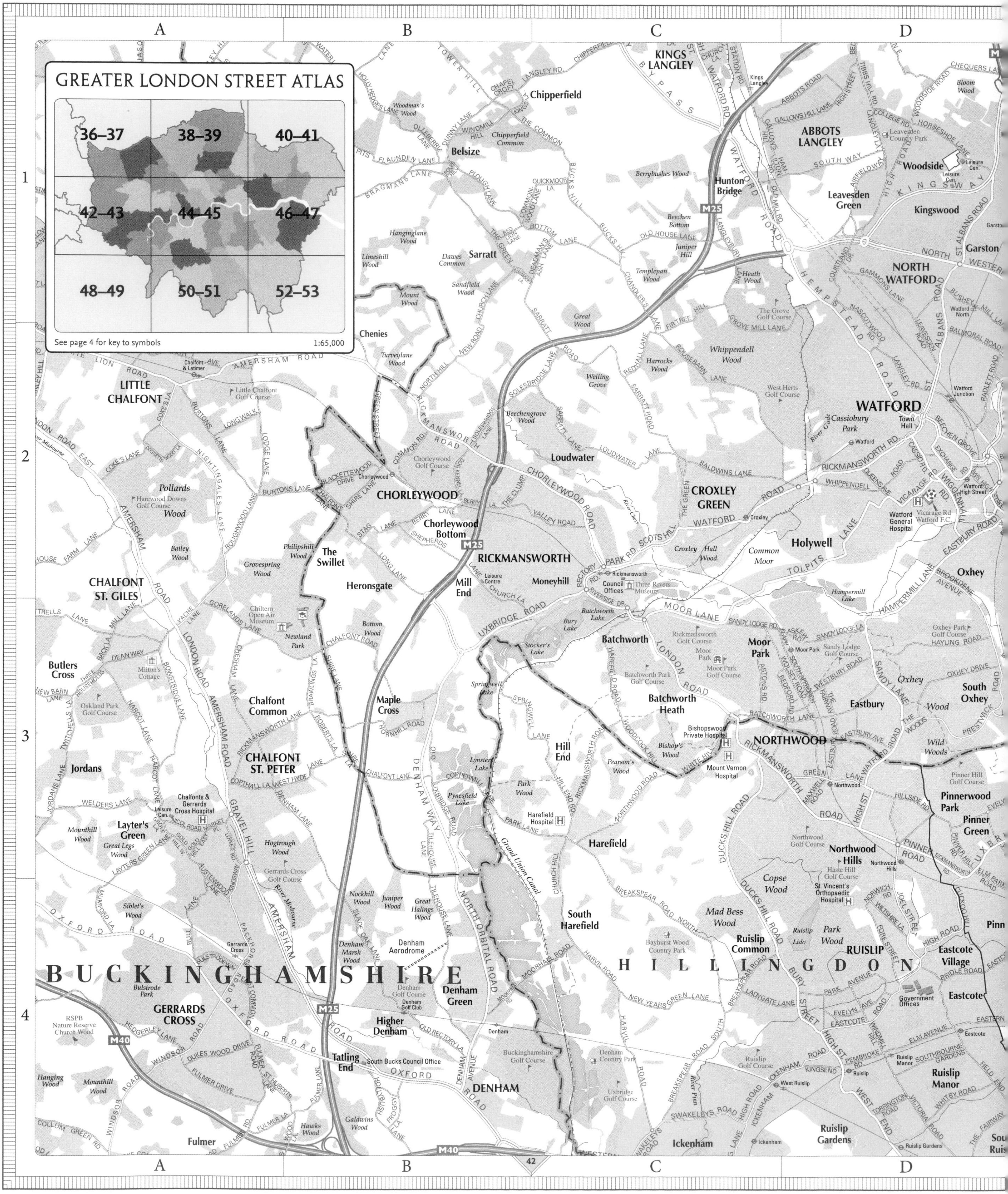
GREATER LONDON STREET ATLAS
36–37
38–39
40–41
42–43
44–45
46–47
48–49
50–51
52–53
See page 4 for key to symbols
1:65,000
A
B
C
D
1
2
3
4
KINGS LANGLEY
Chipperfield
Chipperfield Common
Belsize
ABBOTS LANGLEY
Leavesden Green
Woodside
Kingswood
Hunton Bridge
Sarratt
Garston
NORTH WATFORD
Chenies
LITTLE CHALFONT
WATFORD
Cassiobury Park
Loudwater
CHORLEYWOOD
Chorleywood Bottom
CROXLEY GREEN
Holywell
Pollards Wood
The Swillet
RICKMANSWORTH
Oxhey
CHALFONT ST. GILES
Heronsgate
Mill End
Moneyhill
Batchworth
Moor Park
Butlers Cross
Chalfont Common
Maple Cross
Batchworth Heath
Eastbury
South Oxhey
CHALFONT ST. PETER
Hill End
NORTHWOOD
Jordans
Layter's Green
Pinnerwood Park
Pinner Green
Harefield
Northwood Hills
South Harefield
Ruislip Common
RUISLIP
Eastcote Village
BUCKINGHAMSHIRE
HILLINGDON
GERRARDS CROSS
Denham Green
Higher Denham
Eastcote
Tatling End
DENHAM
Ruislip Manor
Fulmer
Ickenham
Ruislip Gardens
M25
M40
Grand Union Canal
42

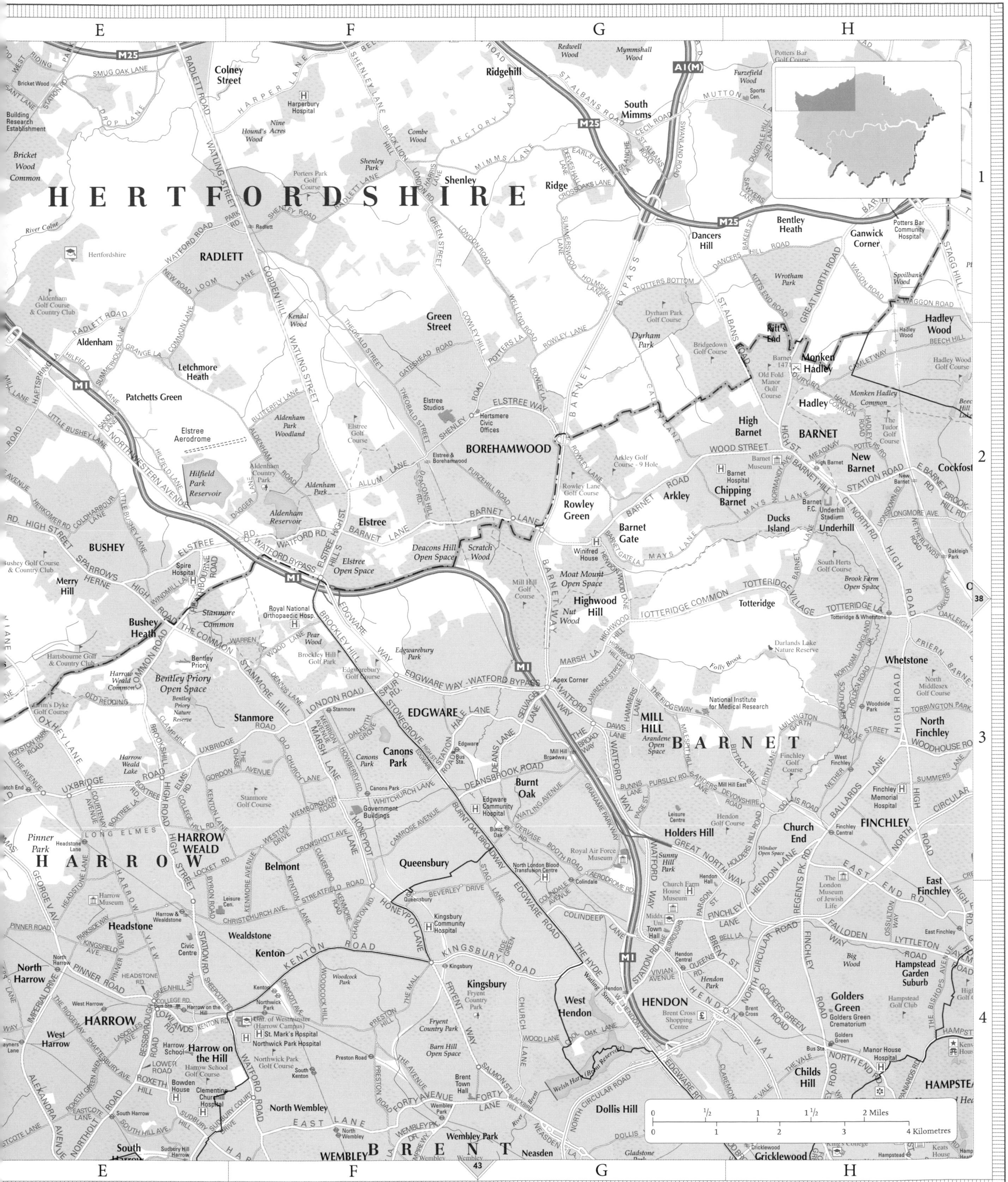
E
F
G
H
1
2
3
4
38
43
M25
A1(M)
M1
HERTFORDSHIRE
HARROW
BRENT
BARNET
Colney Street
Ridgehill
South Mimms
Redwell Wood
Mymmshall Wood
Furzefield Wood
Potters Bar Golf Course
Sports Cen.
Bricket Wood
Building Research Establishment
Bricket Wood Common
Harperbury Hospital
Hound's Wood
Nine Acres
Combe Wood
Shenley Park
Shenley
Ridge
Porters Park Golf Course
Radlett
River Colne
Hertfordshire
RADLETT
Dancers Hill
Bentley Heath
Ganwick Corner
Potters Bar Community Hospital
Wrotham Park
Spoilbank Wood
Aldenham Golf Course & Country Club
Kendal Wood
Green Street
Dyrham Park Golf Course
Dyrham Park
Bridgedown Golf Course
Kitt's End
Hadley Wood
Hadley Wood Golf Course
Aldenham
Letchmore Heath
Patchetts Green
Barnet 1471
Old Fold Manor Golf Course
Monken Hadley
Hadley
Monken Hadley Common
The Tudor Golf Course
Elstree Studios
Hertsmere Civic Offices
Elstree Aerodrome
Aldenham Park Woodland
Elstree Golf Course
Hilfield Park Reservoir
BOREHAMWOOD
Elstree & Borehamwood
High Barnet
BARNET
Arkley Golf Course - 9 Hole
Barnet Museum
Barnet Hospital
Chipping Barnet
New Barnet
High Barnet
Cockfosters
Aldenham Country Park
Aldenham Park
Rowley Lane Golf Course
Rowley Green
Arkley
Barnet F.C. Underhill Stadium
Underhill
Ducks Island
Aldenham Reservoir
Elstree
BUSHEY
Bushey Golf Course & Country Club
Spire Hospital
Elstree Open Space
Deacons Hill Open Space
Scratch Wood
Barnet Gate
Winifred House
Moat Mount Open Space
South Herts Golf Course
Brook Farm Open Space
Oakleigh Park
Merry Hill
Mill Hill Golf Course
Highwood Hill
Nut Wood
Totteridge
Totteridge & Whetstone
Stanmore Common
Royal National Orthopaedic Hosp.
Bushey Heath
Pear Wood
Brockley Hill Golf Park
Edgwarebury Park
Darlands Lake Nature Reserve
Folly Brook
Whetstone
Hartsbourne Golf & Country Club
Bentley Priory
Harrow Weald Common
Bentley Priory Open Space
Bentley Priory Nature Reserve
Edgwarebury Golf Course
Apex Corner
North Middlesex Golf Course
Grim's Dyke Golf Course
Stanmore
EDGWARE
National Institute for Medical Research
Woodside Park
MILL HILL
North Finchley
Arandene Open Space
Harrow Weald Lake
Canons Park
Edgware
Bus Sta.
Mill Hill Broadway
Finchley Golf Course
West Finchley
Burnt Oak
Mill Hill East
Stanmore Golf Course
Government Buildings
Edgware Community Hospital
Leisure Centre
Hendon Golf Course
Finchley Memorial Hospital
Pinner Park
Headstone Lane
HARROW WEALD
Belmont
Queensbury
Royal Air Force Museum
Holders Hill
Church End
Finchley Central
FINCHLEY
North London Blood Transfusion Centre
Colindale
Sunny Hill Park
Windsor Open Space
Harrow Museum
Leisure Cen.
Church Farm House Museum
Hendon Hall
The London Museum of Jewish Life
East Finchley
Headstone
Wealdstone
Kingsbury Community Hospital
Civic Centre
Middx. Uni. Town Hall
Kenton
Kingsbury
Hendon Central
Big Wood
Hampstead Garden Suburb
North Harrow
Woodcock Park
Fryent Country Park
Hendon Park
Hampstead Golf Club
West Harrow
HARROW
Northwick Park
Harrow on the Hill
West Hendon
HENDON
Brent Cross Shopping Centre
Brent Cross
Golders Green
Golders Green Crematorium
West Harrow
Uni. of Westminster (Harrow Campus)
St. Mark's Hospital
Northwick Park Hospital
Fryent Country Park
Harrow School
Harrow on the Hill
Harrow School Golf Course
Northwick Park Golf Course
South Kenton
Preston Road
Barn Hill Open Space
Welsh Harp (Brent Reservoir)
Childs Hill
Manor House Hospital
Bowden House
Clementine Churchill Hospital
Brent Town Hall
HAMPSTEAD
North Wembley
Wembley Park
Dollis Hill
South Harrow
Sudbury Hill Harrow
Wembley Park
Neasden
Gladstone Park
Cricklewood
WEMBLEY
M25
WATLING STREET
RADLETT ROAD
HARPER LANE
SHENLEY LANE
RECTORY LANE
MIMMS LANE
BARNET BYPASS
GREAT NORTH ROAD
ELSTREE WAY
EDGWARE WAY - WATFORD BYPASS
TOTTERIDGE COMMON
TOTTERIDGE LANE
HIGH ROAD
EDGWARE ROAD
KENTON ROAD
KINGSBURY ROAD
NORTH CIRCULAR ROAD
EAST LANE
0
1/2
1
1 1/2
2 Miles
0
1
2
3
4 Kilometres

A
B
C
D
1
2
3
4
HERTFORDSHIRE
HARROW
BARNET
BRENT
M25
A1(M)
M1
Colney Street
Ridgehill
South Mimms
POTTERS BAR
Harperbury Hospital
Nine Acres
Hound's Wood
Combe Wood
Shenley Park
Shenley
Ridge
Redwell Wood
Mymmshall Wood
Furzefield Wood
Potters Bar Golf Course
Potters Bar Mus
Porters Park Golf Course
Radlett
RADLETT
Hertfordshire
Aldenham Golf Course & Country Club
Aldenham
Letchmore Heath
Patchetts Green
Kendal Wood
Green Street
Dancers Hill
Bentley Heath
Ganwick Corner
Potters Bar Community Hospital
Wrotham Park
Dyrham Park Golf Course
Dyrham Park
Bridgedown Golf Course
Kitt's End
Monken Hadley
Hadley Wood
Hadley Wood Golf Course
Old Fold Manor Golf Course
Hadley
Monken Hadley Common
Elstree Aerodrome
Aldenham Park Woodland
Elstree Studios
Hertsmere Civic Offices
BOREHAMWOOD
Hilfield Park Reservoir
Aldenham Country Park
Aldenham Park
Aldenham Reservoir
Elstree Golf Course
Elstree & Borehamwood
Arkley Golf Course - 9 Hole
High Barnet
BARNET
Barnet Museum
Barnet Hospital
Chipping Barnet
Arkley
Rowley Lane Golf Course
Rowley Green
Barnet Gate
New Barnet
Cockfosters
Ducks Island
Underhill
Barnet F.C. Underhill Stadium
Elstree
BUSHEY
Spire Hospital
Merry Hill
Deacons Hill Open Space
Scratch Wood
Elstree Open Space
Winifred House
Mill Hill Golf Course
Moat Mount Open Space
Highwood Hill
Nut Wood
Totteridge
South Herts Golf Course
Brook Farm Open Space
Oakleigh Park
Bushey Heath
Stanmore Common
Royal National Orthopaedic Hosp.
Pear Wood
Brockley Hill Golf Park
Hartsbourne Golf & Country Club
Bentley Priory
Harrow Weald Common
Bentley Priory Open Space
Edgwarebury Park
Edgwarebury Golf Course
Darlands Lake Nature Reserve
Whetstone
North Middlesex Golf Course
Apex Corner
National Institute for Medical Research
Stanmore
EDGWARE
MILL HILL
Arandene Open Space
Harrow Weald Lake
Canons Park
Mill Hill Broadway
North Finchley
Woodside Park
Stanmore Golf Course
Burnt Oak
Edgware Community Hospital
Government Buildings
Finchley Golf Course
Mill Hill East
Finchley Memorial Hospital
Pinner Park
HARROW WEALD
Belmont
Queensbury
Royal Air Force Museum
Holders Hill
Hendon Golf Course
Church End
FINCHLEY
Harrow Museum
North London Blood Transfusion Centre
Sunny Hill Park
Church Farm House Museum
The London Museum of Jewish Life
East Finchley
Headstone
Wealdstone
Civic Centre
Kenton
Kingsbury Community Hospital
Colindale
Middx Uni
Town Hall
Hendon Central
Big Wood
Hampstead Garden Suburb
North Harrow
Woodcock Park
Kingsbury
Fryent Country Park
West Hendon
HENDON
Brent Cross Shopping Centre
Hendon Park
Golders Green
Golders Green Crematorium
Hampstead Golf Club
Highgate Golf Course
West Harrow
HARROW
Harrow on the Hill
Northwick Park
Uni. of Westminster (Harrow Campus)
St. Mark's Hospital
Northwick Park Hospital
Fryent Country Park
Barn Hill Open Space
Harrow School
Harrow School Golf Course
Bowden House
Clementine Churchill Hospital
Northwick Park Golf Course
South Kenton
Preston Road
Brent Town Hall
Welsh Harp (Brent Reservoir)
Dollis Hill
Childs Hill
Manor House Hospital
Kenwood House
HAMPSTEAD
Hampstead Heath
The Hill
North Wembley
Wembley Park
South Harrow
WEMBLEY
Neasden
Cricklewood
Uni. of Lon. King's College
Fenton Ho. (NT)
Burgh Ho.
Keats House
37
44

E
F
G
H
1
2
3
4
40
45
CHESHUNT
Bury Green
Cattlegate
Cattlins
Nursery Plantation
Cattlegate Wood
Lee Valley Park
River Lee Country Park
Waltham Cross
WALTHAM ABBEY
Holdbrook
Epping Forest District Museum
Crews Hill
Whitewebbs Park
Botany Bay
Freezy Water
Bullsmoor
Enfield Lock
Forty Hall
Forty Hall Museum
Kings Oak Hospital
Hilly Fields Park
Kingswood
Moat Wood
Ride Wood
Williams Wood
Chase Farm Hospital
ENFIELD
Enfield Wash
Albany Park
E S S E X
Sewardstone
High Beach
Honey Lane Quarters
Beech Hill Park
High Beech Golf Course
Deer-shelter Plain
Great Monk Wood
Little Monk Wood
King George's Reservoir
E N F I E L D
Trent Park Golf Course
World's End
Enfield Highway
Brimsdown
Gilwell Park
West Essex Golf Course
Round Thicket
Epping Forest
Sewardstonebury
Strawberry Hill
Buckhurst Hill
Grange Park
Bush Hill Park
Ponders End
Yardley Hill
Connaught Water
Bury Wood
The Hawk Wood
Chingford Golf Course
Queen Elizabeth's Hunting Lodge
Oakwood
Winchmore Hill
Jubilee Park
William Girling Reservoir
Chingford Green
Southgate
Grovelands Park
Grovelands Priory Hospital
Lower Edmonton
Holly House Hospital
Lord's Bushes
New Southgate
Palmers Green
EDMONTON
CHINGFORD
Friday Hill
Hatch Forest
Woodford Wells
Chingford Hatch
Larks Wood
Woodford Golf Course
Arnos Park
Pymmes Park
Lee Valley Park
South Chingford
Highams Park
Woodford Green
Bowes Park
Upper Edmonton
North Middlesex University Hospital
TOTTENHAM
Hale End
Banbury Reservoir
Walthamstow Stadium (closed)
Muswell Hill Golf Course
WOOD GREEN
Bruce Castle Museum
White Hart Lane Tottenham Hotspur F.C.
Northumberland Park
WOODFORD
Woodford Bridge
Uni. of London
Alexandra Palace
Alexandra Park
Noel Park
Tottenham Hale
Lockwood Reservoir
Higham Hill
W A L T H A M
WALTHAMSTOW
South Woodford
R E D B R I D G E
Clayhall
Muswell Hill
West Green
High Maynard Reservoir
Low Maynard Reservoir
William Morris Gallery
Upper Walthamstow
Thorpe Coombe Hospital
Roding Valley Park
Roding Hospital
F O R E S T
HORNSEY
H A R I N G E Y
Queen's Wood
Hornsey Central Hospital
HARRINGAY
St. Ann's Hospital
South Tottenham
Warwick Reservoirs
Reservoir
St. James's Park
Vestry House Museum
Hollow Pond
Snaresbrook
Snaresbrook Crown Court
Whipps Cross University Hospital
REDBRIDGE
Crouch End
Stroud Green
Leytonstone
Wanstead
Wanstead Golf Course
Wanstead Park
The Basin
St Mary's Church
The Temple
Highgate
Finsbury Park
STOKE NEWINGTON
Stamford Hill
Upper Clapton
Walthamstow Marshes
LEYTON
Aldersbrook
Ilford Golf Course
Cranbrook
Upper Holloway
Tufnell Park
Holloway
Emirates Stadium
Clissold Park
H A C K N E Y
Shacklewell
Lea Bridge
Lower Clapton
Lee Valley Park
Hackney Marsh
Leyton Orient FC
Manor Park
0
1/2
1
1 1/2
2 Miles
0
1
2
3
4 Kilometres
M25
M11

A
B
C
D
1
2
3
4
HERTFORDSHIRE
ENFIELD
HARINGEY
WALTHAM FOREST
REDBRIDGE
HACKNEY
M25
M11
CHESHUNT
Bury Green
Cattlegate
Cattlegate Wood
Nursery Plantation
Cattlins
Waltham Cross
Waltham Abbey
WALTHAM ABBEY
Holdbrook
Upshire
Copthall Green
Lee Valley Park
River Lee Country Park
Fernhall Wood
Rookery Wood
Crews Hill
Botany Bay
Whitewebbs Park
Capel Manor
Freezy Water
Bullsmoor
Enfield Lock
Enfield Wash
Forty Hill
Forty Hall Country Park
Forty Hall Museum
Hilly Fields Park
Kingswood
Chase Farm Hospital
Kings Oak Hospital
Ride Wood
Williams Wood
North London Nuffield Hospital
Trent Park Golf Course
World's End
Enfield Golf Course
Enfield Highway
Brimsdown
King George's Reservoir
Sewardstone
Sewardstonebury
High Beach
Epping Forest
West Essex Golf Course
Gilwell Park
Round Thicket
Strawberry Hill
Great Monk Wood
Little Monk Wood
Buckhurst Hill
Loughton
Grange Park
Bush Hill Park
Bush Hill Park Golf Course
Oakwood
Oakwood Park
Winchmore Hill
Ponders End
William Girling Reservoir
Jubilee Park
Lower Edmonton
The Hawk Wood
Chingford Golf Course
Queen Elizabeth's Hunting Lodge
Chingford Green
Southgate
Grovelands Park
Grovelands Priory Hospital
New Southgate
Palmers Green
Arnos Park
EDMONTON
Pymmes Park
Lee Valley Leisure Golf Course
CHINGFORD
Friday Hill
Hatch Forest
Woodford Wells
Holly House Hospital
Lord's Bushes
Chingford Hatch
Larks Wood
South Chingford
Higham Park
Highams Park
Woodford Green
Bowes Park
North Middlesex University Hospital
Upper Edmonton
TOTTENHAM
White Hart Lane
Tottenham Hotspur F.C.
Bruce Castle Museum
Banbury Reservoir
Lee Valley Park
Walthamstow Stadium (closed)
Hale End
Epping Forest
WOODFORD
Woodford Bridge
Hospital
WOOD GREEN
Noel Park
Alexandra Palace
Alexandra Park
Muswell Hill
Tottenham Hale
West Green
Lockwood Reservoir
High Maynard Reservoir
Low Maynard Reservoir
Higham Hill
WALTHAMSTOW
William Morris Gallery
Upper Walthamstow
Thorpe Coombe Hospital
South Woodford
Roding Valley Park
Roding Hospital
Clayhall
Snaresbrook
Snaresbrook Crown Court
Gants Hill
HORNSEY
Hornsey Central Hospital
HARRINGAY
St. Ann's Hospital
South Tottenham
Warwick Reservoirs
Reservoir
St. James's Park
Vestry House Museum
Hollow Pond
Whipps Cross University Hospital
REDBRIDGE
Crouch End
Stroud Green
Finsbury Park
STOKE NEWINGTON
Stamford Hill
Springfield Park
Upper Clapton
Walthamstow Marshes
Leytonstone
Wanstead
Wanstead Golf Course
Wanstead Park
The Temple
Aldersbrook
Cranbrook
Upper Holloway
Holloway
Tufnell Park
Emirates Stadium
Clissold Park
Shacklewell
Lea Bridge
Lower Clapton
Lee Valley Park
Hackney Marsh
LEYTON
Leyton Orient FC
Wanstead Flats
City of London Cemetery
Ilford Golf Course
Manor Park
39
46

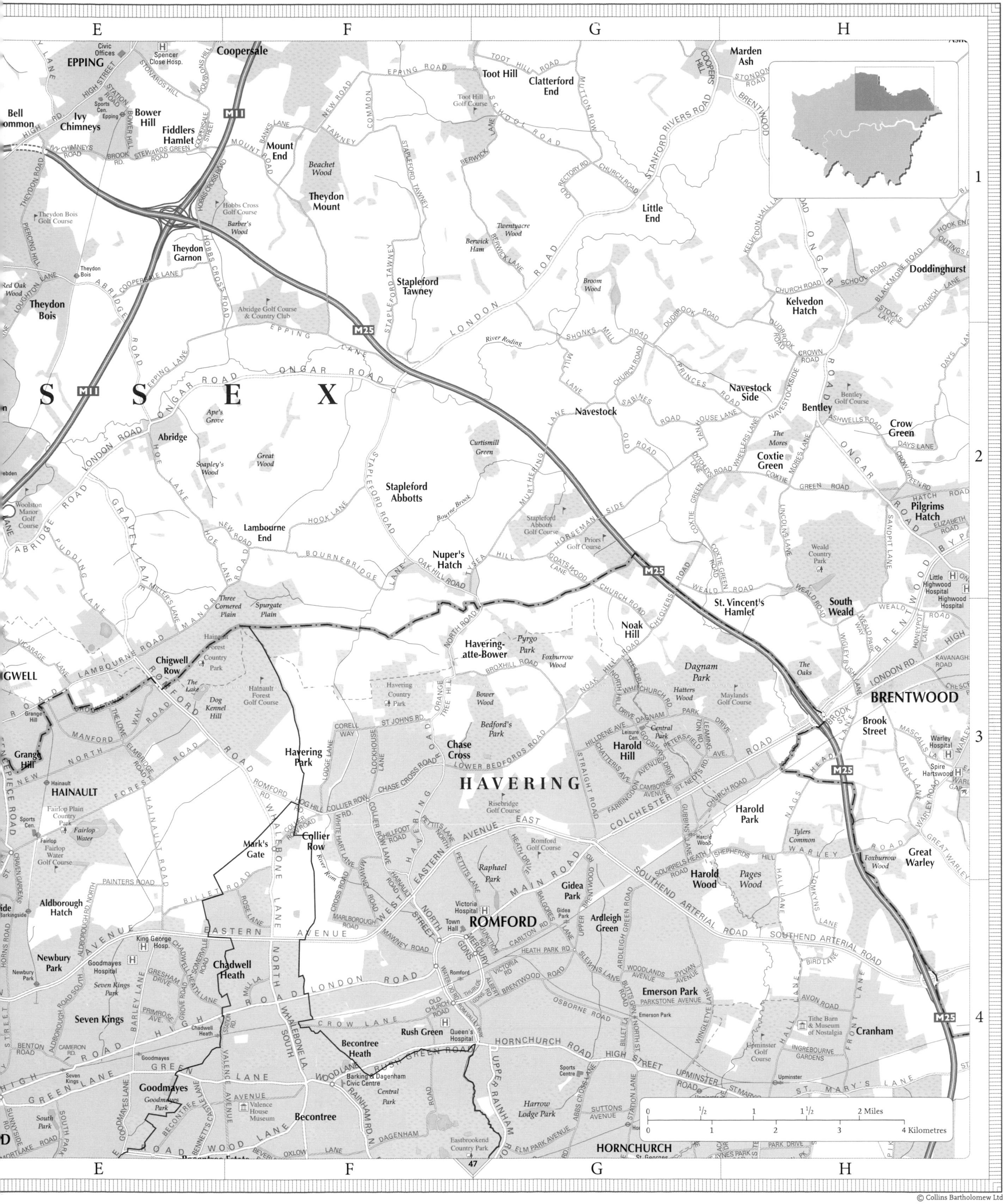
E
F
G
H
1
2
3
4
EPPING
Civic Offices
Spencer Close Hosp.
Coopersale
Toot Hill
Clatterford End
Marden Ash
Bell Common
Ivy Chimneys
Bower Hill
Fiddlers Hamlet
Mount End
Beachet Wood
Theydon Mount
Toot Hill Golf Course
Little End
Theydon Bois Golf Course
Hobbs Cross Golf Course
Barber's Wood
Theydon Garnon
Twentyacre Wood
Berwick Ham
Doddinghurst
Theydon Bois
Stapleford Tawney
Kelvedon Hatch
Broom Wood
Abridge Golf Course & Country Club
River Roding
Navestock Side
Bentley
Bentley Golf Course
S
S
E
X
Navestock
Crow Green
Abridge
Ape's Grove
Curtismill Green
The Mores
Coxtie Green
Great Wood
Soapley's Wood
Woolston Manor Golf Course
Stapleford Abbotts
Pilgrims Hatch
Lambourne End
Stapleford Abbotts Golf Course
Priors Golf Course
Weald Country Park
Nuper's Hatch
South Weald
Highwood Hospital
St. Vincent's Hamlet
Three Cornered Plain
Spurgate Plain
Noak Hill
Hainault Forest Country Park
Havering-atte-Bower
Pyrgo Park
Foxburrow Wood
Dagnam Park
The Oaks
Chigwell Row
The Lake
Hainault Forest Golf Course
Dog Kennel Hill
Havering Country Park
Bower Wood
Hatters Wood
Maylands Golf Course
BRENTWOOD
Bedford's Park
Brook Street
Grange Hill
Havering Park
Chase Cross
Harold Hill
Warley Hospital
Spire Hartswood
HAINAULT
HAVERING
Risebridge Golf Course
Harold Park
Fairlop Plain Country Park
Fairlop Water
Fairlop Water Golf Course
Collier Row
Mark's Gate
Romford Golf Course
Tylers Common
Great Warley
Foxburrow Wood
Raphael Park
Harold Wood
Pages Wood
Gidea Park
Aldborough Hatch
Victoria Hospital
Town Hall
ROMFORD
Ardleigh Green
King George Hosp.
Newbury Park
Goodmayes Hospital
Chadwell Heath
Seven Kings Park
Emerson Park
Seven Kings
Tithe Barn & Museum of Nostalgia
Cranham
Rush Green
Queen's Hospital
Becontree Heath
Upminster Golf Course
Upminster
Goodmayes
Barking & Dagenham Civic Centre
Central Park
Valence House Museum
South Park
Becontree
Harrow Lodge Park
Eastbrookend Country Park
HORNCHURCH
M11
M25
EPPING ROAD
ONGAR ROAD
LONDON ROAD
EASTERN AVENUE
COLCHESTER ROAD
SOUTHEND ARTERIAL ROAD
HORNCHURCH ROAD
HIGH STREET
GREEN LANE
NORTH STREET
MAIN ROAD
WHALEBONE LANE
ROMFORD ROAD
0
1/2
1
1 1/2
2 Miles
0
1
2
3
4 Kilometres
47

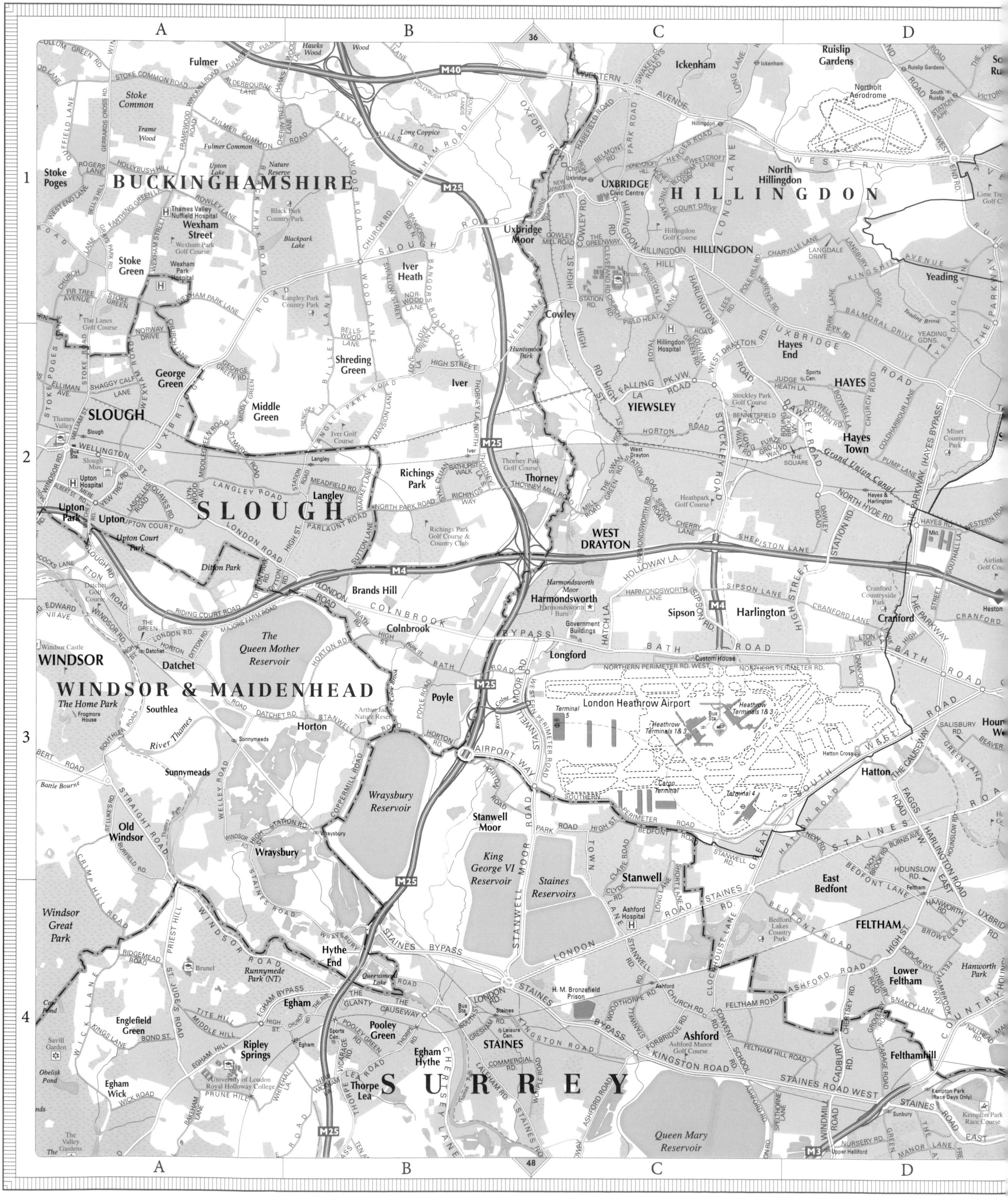
A
B
C
D
1
2
3
4
36
48
BUCKINGHAMSHIRE
HILLINGDON
SLOUGH
WINDSOR & MAIDENHEAD
SURREY
Fulmer
Stoke Common
Frame Wood
Fulmer Common
Upton Lake
Nature Reserve
Stoke Poges
Thames Valley Nuffield Hospital
Wexham Street
Wexham Park Golf Course
Black Park Country Park
Blackpark Lake
Stoke Green
Wexham Park Hospital
Iver Heath
Langley Park Country Park
The Lanes Golf Course
George Green
Shreding Green
Iver
Middle Green
Uxbridge Moor
Huntsmoor Park
Cowley
Ickenham
Ruislip Gardens
Northolt Aerodrome
North Hillingdon
UXBRIDGE
Civic Centre
HILLINGDON
Hillingdon Golf Course
Hillingdon Hospital
Brunel
Yeading
Hayes End
HAYES
Hayes Town
YIEWSLEY
Stockley Park Golf Course
West Drayton
Minet Country Park
Thorney Park Golf Course
Thorney
Richings Park
Richings Park Golf Course & Country Club
Langley
Iver Golf Course
Thames Valley
Slough Mus.
Upton Hospital
Upton Park
Upton
Upton Court Park
Ditton Park
Heathpark Golf Course
WEST DRAYTON
Brands Hill
Harmondsworth Moor
Harmondsworth
Harmondsworth Barn
Government Buildings
Sipson
Harlington
Cranford Countryside Park
Cranford
Heston
Datchet Golf Course
Windsor Castle
WINDSOR
Datchet
The Queen Mother Reservoir
Colnbrook
Longford
Custom House
The Home Park
Frogmore House
Southlea
Horton
Arthur Jacob Nature Reserve
Poyle
London Heathrow Airport
Terminal 5
Heathrow Terminals 1& 3
Cargo Terminal
Terminal 4
Hatton Cross
Hatton
River Thames
Sunnymeads
Battle Bourne
Old Windsor
Wraysbury Reservoir
Wraysbury
Stanwell Moor
King George VI Reservoir
Staines Reservoirs
Stanwell
Ashford Hospital
East Bedfont
Bedford Lakes Country Park
FELTHAM
Windsor Great Park
Brunel
Runnymede Park (NT)
Hythe End
Queensmead Lake
H. M. Bronzefield Prison
Lower Feltham
Hanworth Park
Cow Pond
Englefield Green
Egham
Pooley Green
STAINES
Ashford
Ashford Manor Golf Course
Felthamhill
Savill Garden
Obelisk Pond
Ripley Springs
Egham Hythe
Egham Wick
University of London Royal Holloway College
Thorpe Lea
Kempton Park (Race Days Only)
Kempton Park Race Course
Sunbury
Queen Mary Reservoir
Upper Halliford
The Valley Gardens
Grand Union Canal
Yeading Brook
M40
M25
M4
M3

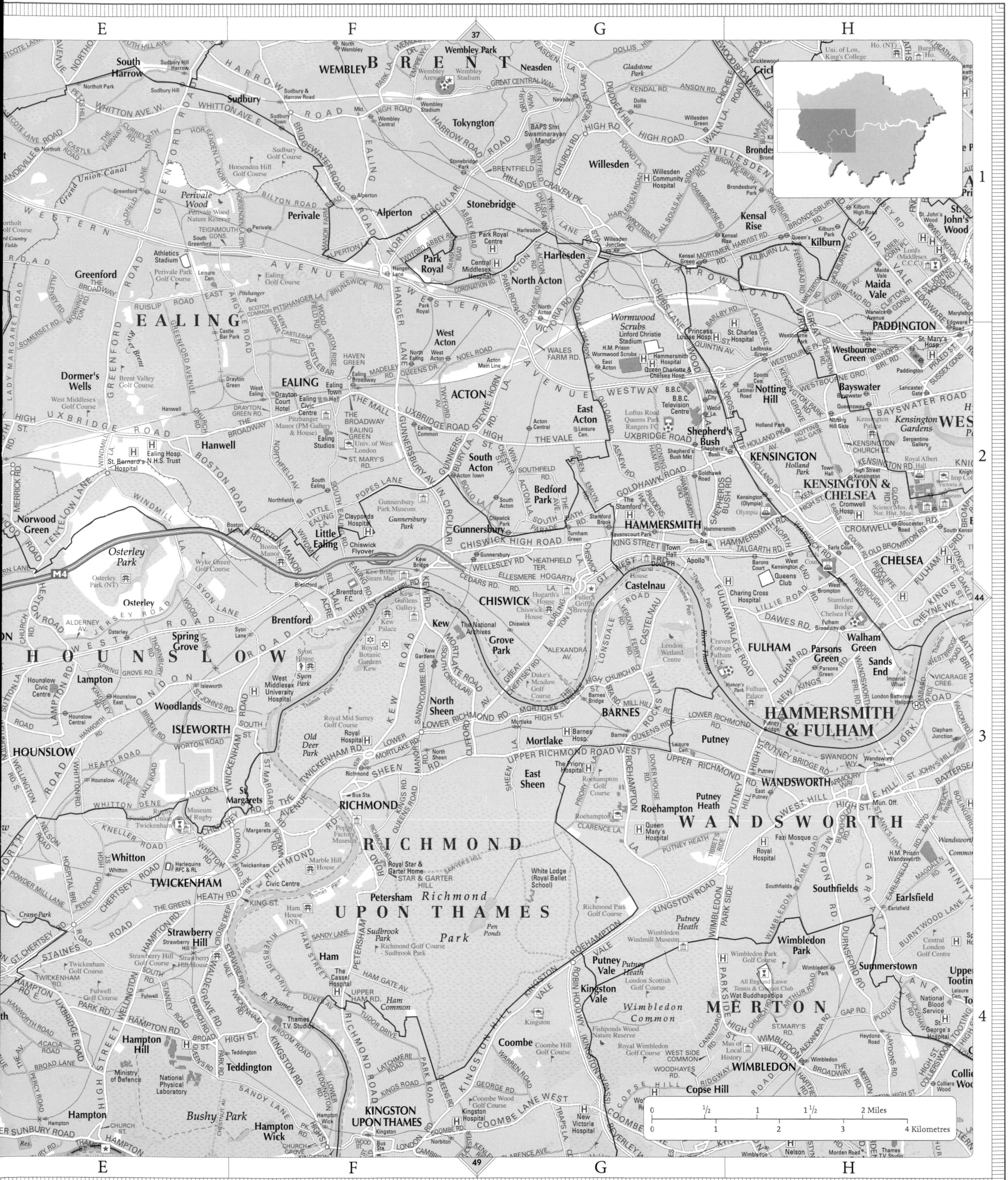
E
F
G
H
37
49
44
1
2
3
4
South Harrow
Sudbury
WEMBLEY
B R E N T
Wembley Park
Neasden
Wembley Arena
Wembley Stadium
Tokyngton
Willesden
Stonebridge
Alperton
Perivale
Perivale Wood
Greenford
Park Royal
Harlesden
North Acton
Kensal Rise
Kilburn
Maida Vale
PADDINGTON
St. John's Wood
E A L I N G
West Acton
Wormwood Scrubs
Notting Hill
Westbourne Green
Bayswater
Kensington Gardens
Dormer's Wells
EALING
ACTON
East Acton
Shepherd's Bush
KENSINGTON
Hanwell
South Acton
Bedford Park
KENSINGTON & CHELSEA
HAMMERSMITH
Norwood Green
Little Ealing
Gunnersbury
Osterley Park
Osterley
CHELSEA
CHISWICK
Castelnau
Brentford
Kew
Grove Park
FULHAM
Parsons Green
Walham Green
Sands End
Spring Grove
H O U N S L O W
Lampton
Woodlands
ISLEWORTH
North Sheen
BARNES
Mortlake
HAMMERSMITH & FULHAM
Putney
HOUNSLOW
Old Deer Park
East Sheen
WANDSWORTH
St Margarets
RICHMOND
Roehampton
Putney Heath
W A N D S W O R T H
R I C H M O N D
Whitton
TWICKENHAM
Southfields
Earlsfield
Petersham
Richmond
U P O N T H A M E S
Park
Strawberry Hill
Ham
Putney Vale
Wimbledon Park
Summerstown
Kingston Vale
Wimbledon Common
M E R T O N
Hampton Hill
Teddington
Coombe
WIMBLEDON
Copse Hill
Hampton
Bushy Park
Hampton Wick
KINGSTON UPON THAMES
M4
River Thames
Grand Union Canal
0
1/2
1
1 1/2
2 Miles
0
1
2
3
4 Kilometres

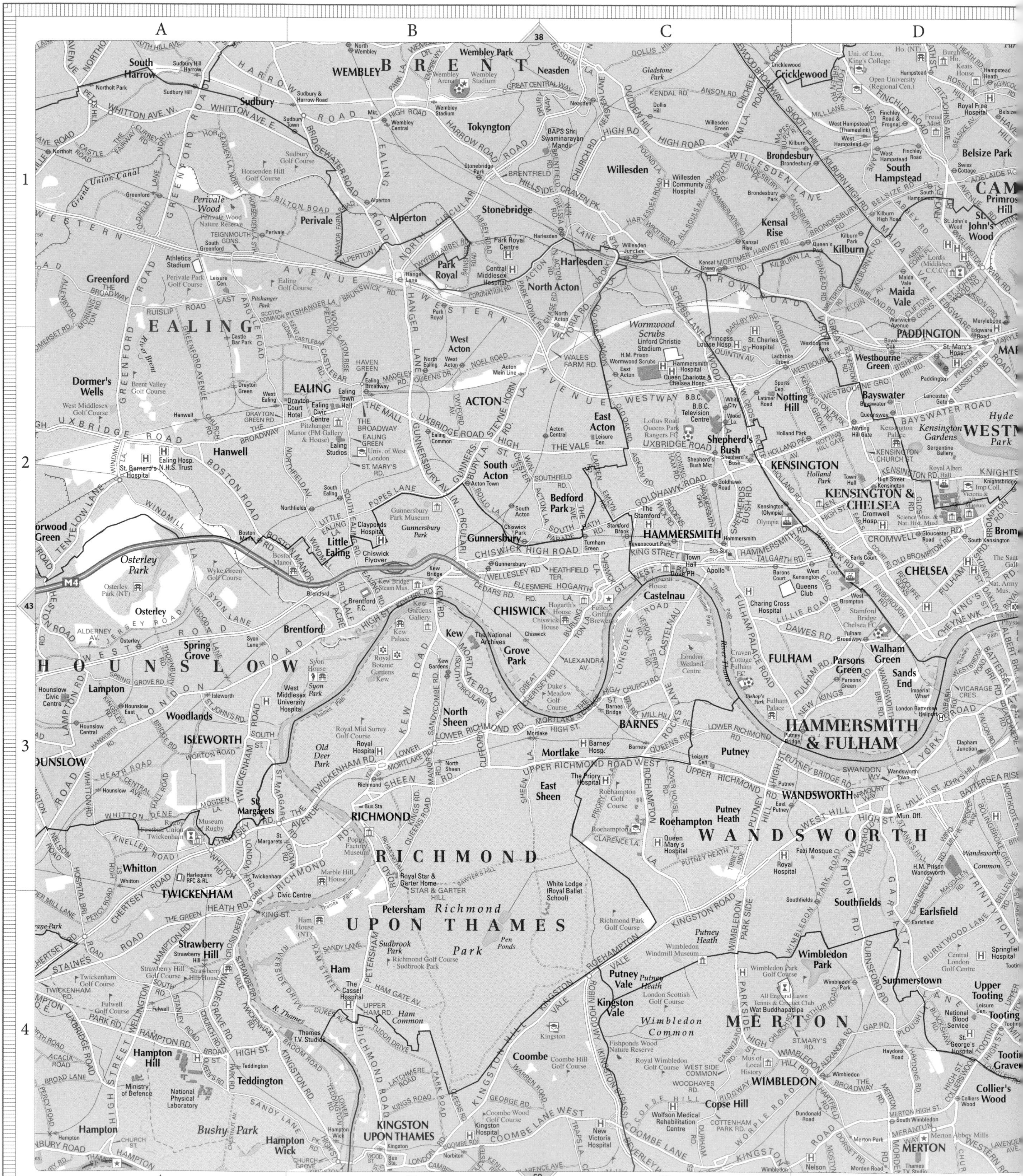
A
B
C
D
1
2
3
4
38
43
50
BRENT
WEMBLEY
Wembley Park
Neasden
South Harrow
Sudbury
Tokyngton
Willesden
Cricklewood
Brondesbury
South Hampstead
Belsize Park
Kensal Rise
Kilburn
Maida Vale
Alperton
Perivale
Stonebridge
Harlesden
Park Royal
North Acton
Greenford
EALING
Dormer's Wells
West Acton
ACTON
East Acton
Wormwood Scrubs
Notting Hill
PADDINGTON
Bayswater
Westbourne Green
Hanwell
South Acton
Bedford Park
Shepherd's Bush
KENSINGTON
KENSINGTON & CHELSEA
HAMMERSMITH
Gunnersbury
Little Ealing
Osterley Park
Osterley
Brentford
CHISWICK
Kew
Grove Park
Castelnau
CHELSEA
FULHAM
Parsons Green
Walham Green
Sands End
HOUNSLOW
Spring Grove
Lampton
Woodlands
ISLEWORTH
North Sheen
BARNES
Mortlake
East Sheen
HAMMERSMITH & FULHAM
Putney
WANDSWORTH
St. Margarets
RICHMOND
Roehampton
Putney Heath
Whitton
TWICKENHAM
RICHMOND UPON THAMES
Richmond Park
Petersham
Ham
Strawberry Hill
Southfields
Earlsfield
Wimbledon Park
Putney Vale
Kingston Vale
MERTON
Summerstown
Upper Tooting
Hampton Hill
Teddington
Coombe
WIMBLEDON
Copse Hill
Hampton
Bushy Park
Hampton Wick
KINGSTON UPON THAMES
Collier's Wood
MERTON
M4

E
F
G
H
1
2
3
4
39
46
51
HACKNEY
ISLINGTON
TOWER HAMLETS
NEWHAM
SOUTHWARK
LAMBETH
LEWISHAM
GREENWICH
BROMLEY
CITY
WESTMINSTER
HOLBORN
FINSBURY
SHOREDITCH
ST. PANCRAS
CAMBERWELL
BERMONDSEY
DULWICH
STREATHAM
SYDENHAM
BECKENHAM
WEST HAM
Holloway
Tufnell Park
Highbury
Kentish Town
Barnsbury
Camden Town
King's Cross
Hoxton
Haggerston
Dalston
Hackney
Shacklewell
Lower Clapton
Clapton Park
Homerton
Hackney Wick
Stratford
Victoria Park
Old Ford
Bethnal Green
Bow
Mile End
Bromley
Stepney
Whitechapel
Wapping
Shadwell
Limehouse
Poplar
Rotherhithe
Millwall
Cubitt Town
Deptford
Plaistow
Upton Park
Canning Town
Custom House
Silvertown
North Woolwich
New Charlton
Charlton
Bloomsbury
Soho
St. Luke's
Southwark
Walworth
Kennington
Vauxhall
Pimlico
Lambeth
Stockwell
Brixton
Clapham
Clapham Park
South Lambeth
Peckham
Nunhead
New Cross
New Cross Gate
St. John's
Blackheath
Kidbrooke
Blackheath Park
Eltham
Lewisham
Brockley
Ladywell
Honor Oak
Honor Oak Park
East Dulwich
Herne Hill
Tulse Hill
Streatham Hill
Streatham Park
Streatham Vale
Norbury
West Dulwich
West Norwood
Norwood New Town
Upper Norwood
Upper Sydenham
Lower Sydenham
Forest Hill
Catford
Hither Green
Lee
Grove Park
Mottingham
Bellingham
Bell Green
Southend
Downham
New Beckenham
Penge
Anerley
Norwood
Sundridge
Elmstead
Chislehurst West
River Thames
LONDON 2012 OLYMPIC PARK
Thames Barrier
The O2
London City Airport
Royal Victoria Dock
Royal Albert Dock
0
1/2
1
1 1/2
2 Miles
0
1
2
3
4 Kilometres

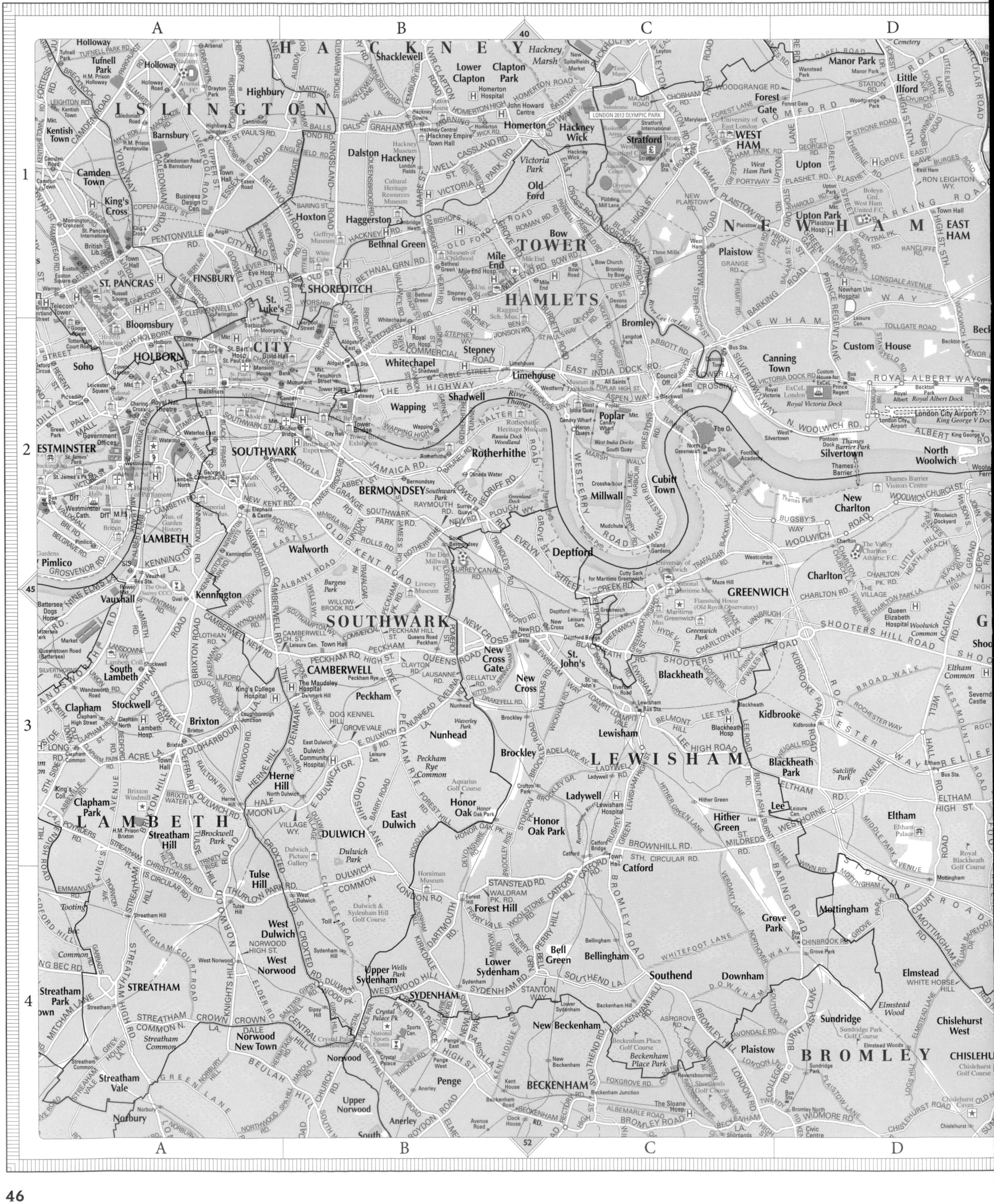
A
B
C
D
1
2
3
4
40
45
52
HACKNEY
ISLINGTON
TOWER HAMLETS
NEWHAM
SOUTHWARK
LAMBETH
LEWISHAM
BROMLEY
CITY
HOLBORN
FINSBURY
ST. PANCRAS
SHOREDITCH
BERMONDSEY
GREENWICH
CAMBERWELL
STREATHAM
BECKENHAM
Holloway
Tufnell Park
Kentish Town
Camden Town
King's Cross
Barnsbury
Highbury
Shacklewell
Lower Clapton
Clapton Park
Hackney Marsh
Homerton
Hackney Wick
Stratford
Dalston
Hackney
Victoria Park
Old Ford
Hoxton
Haggerston
Bethnal Green
Mile End
Bow
Bromley
Stepney
Whitechapel
Limehouse
Shadwell
Wapping
Poplar
Rotherhithe
Millwall
Cubitt Town
Deptford
Manor Park
Little Ilford
Forest Gate
WEST HAM
Upton
Upton Park
EAST HAM
Plaistow
Canning Town
Custom House
Silvertown
North Woolwich
New Charlton
Charlton
Blackheath
Kidbrooke
Blackheath Park
Lee
Hither Green
Eltham
Mottingham
Grove Park
Elmstead
Chislehurst West
Sundridge
Plaistow
Downham
Southend
Catford
Bellingham
Bell Green
Lower Sydenham
Forest Hill
Honor Oak Park
Ladywell
Brockley
Lewisham
St. John's
New Cross
New Cross Gate
Nunhead
Peckham
East Dulwich
Honor Oak
Dulwich
Herne Hill
Brixton
Stockwell
Clapham
Clapham Park
Streatham Hill
Tulse Hill
West Dulwich
West Norwood
Upper Sydenham
SYDENHAM
Norwood New Town
Norwood
Upper Norwood
Penge
Anerley
New Beckenham
Streatham Park
Streatham Vale
Norbury
Walworth
Kennington
Vauxhall
South Lambeth
Soho
Bloomsbury
St. Luke's
Pimlico
Thames
LONDON 2012 OLYMPIC PARK
London City Airport
Royal Victoria Dock
Royal Albert Dock
King George V Dock
The O2
Thames Barrier

E
F
G
H
41
53
1
2
3
4
Becontree Estate
HORNCHURCH
Upminster
Elm Park
Dagenham
South Hornchurch
HAVERING
Rainham
BARKING & DAGENHAM
Creekmouth
River Thames
Barking Flood Barrier
Ford Motor Company
Dagenham Breach
Thamesmead North
Thamesmead
Erith Marshes
Rainham Marshes
Wennington
Wennington Marshes
Aveley Marshes
Aveley
THURROCK
South Ockendon
Belhus Park
Purfleet
West Thurrock
Lakeside Shopping Centre
Abbey Wood
Abbey
Belvedere
Plumstead
Lesnes Abbey Wood
Lessness Heath
Erith
West Heath
Northumberland Heath
East Wickham
BEXLEY
Dartford Salt Marshes
Crayford Marshes
West Thurrock Marshes
Stoneness Lighthouse
Barnehurst
Welling
Falconwood
Bexley
Danson Park
Bexleyheath
Crayford
Barnes Cray
New Town
Dartford International Ferry Terminal
Stone
Greenhithe
Bluewater Shopping Centre
Blackfen
Old Bexley
DARTFORD
Lamorbey
Coldblow
Darenth Wood
North Cray
Joydens Wood
Wilmington
Hawley
Darenth
Ladies Wood
Lords Wood
Lane End
SIDCUP
KENT
Foots Cray
Green Street Green
Sutton at Hone
Hextable
Swanley Village
SWANLEY
St. Paul's Cray
M25
DARTFORD TUNNEL
QUEEN ELIZABETH II BRIDGE
0
1/2
1
1 1/2
2 Miles
0
1
2
3
4 Kilometres

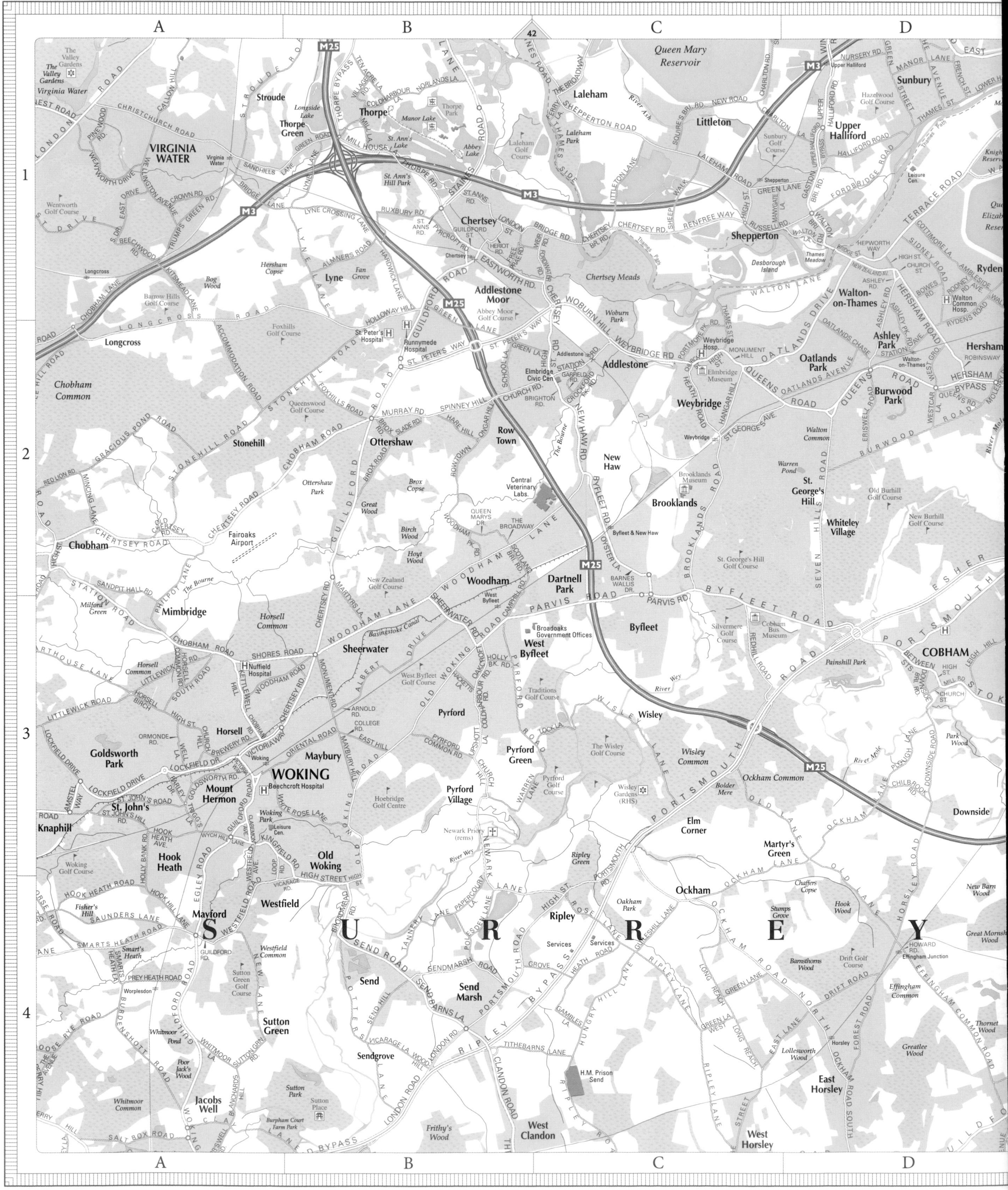
A
B
C
D
1
2
3
4
42
M25
M3
Queen Mary Reservoir
The Valley Gardens
Virginia Water
VIRGINIA WATER
Stroude
Thorpe
Thorpe Park
Thorpe Green
Manor Lake
St. Ann's Lake
St. Ann's Hill Park
Abbey Lake
Laleham
Laleham Park
Laleham Golf Course
Littleton
Sunbury
Upper Halliford
Hazelwood Golf Course
Sunbury Golf Course
Shepperton
Desborough Island
Chertsey
Chertsey Meads
Addlestone Moor
Abbey Moor Golf Course
Wentworth Golf Course
Longcross
Barrow Hills Golf Course
Bog Wood
Hersham Copse
Lyne
Fan Grove
Foxhills Golf Course
St. Peter's Hospital
Runnymede Hospital
Woburn Park
Addlestone
Elmbridge Civic Cen
Weybridge
Weybridge Hosp.
Elmbridge Museum
Walton-on-Thames
Walton Common Hosp.
Oatlands Park
Ashley Park
Burwood Park
Hersham
Ryden
Chobham Common
Queenswood Golf Course
Stonehill
Ottershaw
Ottershaw Park
Row Town
Brox Copse
Great Wood
Birch Wood
Hoyt Wood
Central Veterinary Labs.
New Haw
Brooklands
Brooklands Museum
Walton Common
Warren Pond
St. George's Hill
Old Burhill Golf Course
New Burhill Golf Course
Whiteley Village
St. George's Hill Golf Course
Chobham
Fairoaks Airport
Milford Green
Mimbridge
Horsell Common
New Zealand Golf Course
Woodham
Dartnell Park
Byfleet & New Haw
Byfleet
Silvermere Golf Course
Cobham Bus Museum
COBHAM
Painshill Park
Sheerwater
Basingstoke Canal
Broadoaks Government Offices
West Byfleet
Nuffield Hospital
West Byfleet Golf Course
Traditions Golf Course
River Wey
Wisley
Horsell
Goldsworth Park
Maybury
WOKING
Beechcroft Hospital
Pyrford
Pyrford Green
The Wisley Golf Course
Wisley Common
Ockham Common
Park Wood
Downside
Knaphill
St. John's
Mount Hermon
Hoebridge Golf Centre
Pyrford Village
Pyrford Golf Course
Wisley Gardens (RHS)
Bolder Mere
Elm Corner
Martyr's Green
Woking Park
Leisure Cen.
Newark Priory (rems)
Woking Golf Course
Hook Heath
Old Woking
Ripley Green
Ockham
Chaffers Copse
New Barn Wood
Westfield
Fisher's Hill
Mayford
Oakham Park
Stumps Grove
Hook Wood
SURREY
Ripley
Services
Great Mornshill Wood
Smart's Heath
Westfield Common
Send
Send Marsh
Barnsthorns Wood
Drift Golf Course
Effingham Junction
Effingham Common
Worplesdon
Sutton Green Golf Course
Sutton Green
Whitmoor Pond
Poor Jack's Wood
Sendgrove
H.M. Prison Send
Lollesworth Wood
Horsley
Thornet Wood
Greatlee Wood
Whitmoor Common
Jacobs Well
Sutton Park
Sutton Place
Burpham Court Farm Park
Frithy's Wood
West Clandon
East Horsley
West Horsley

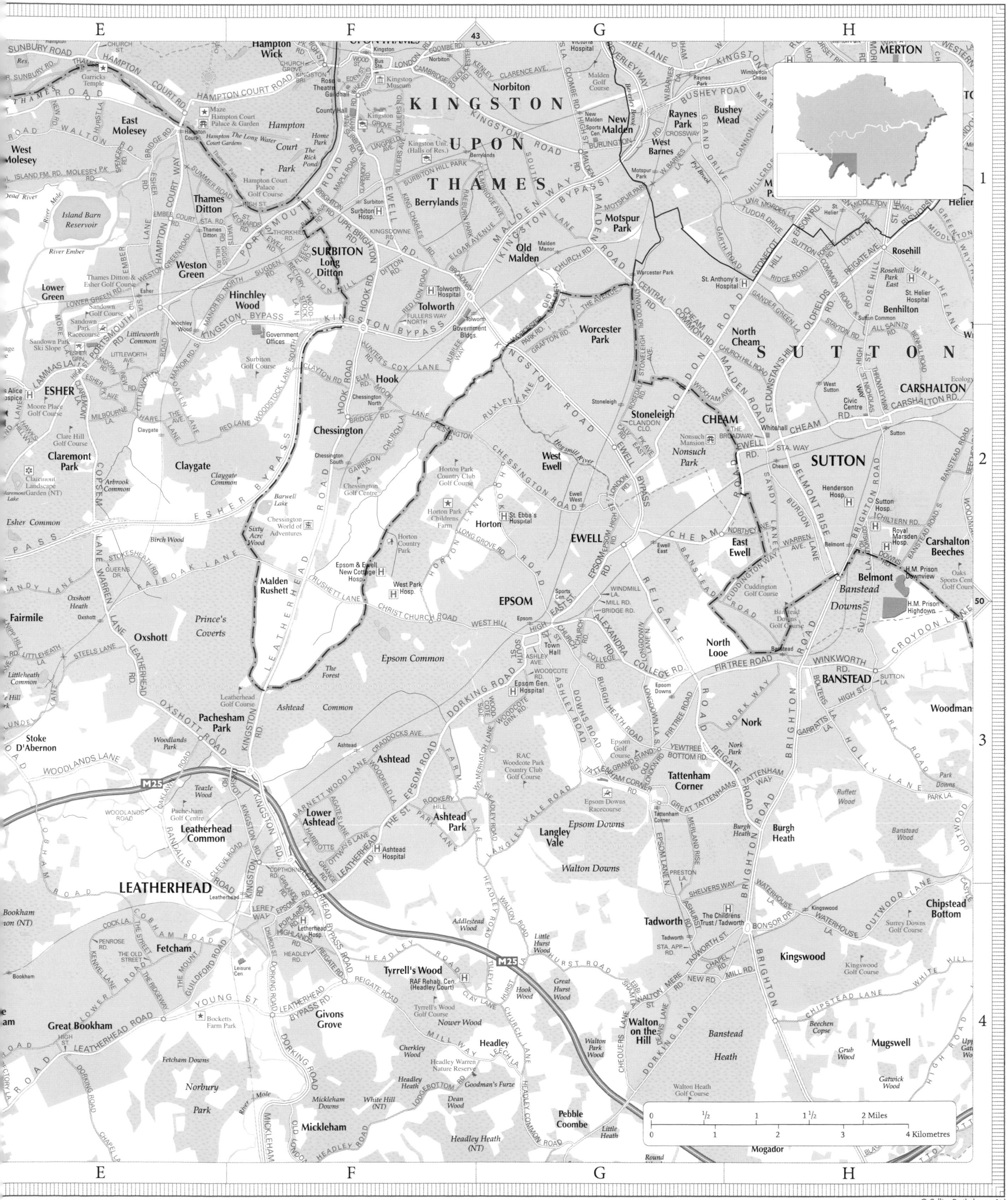
E
F
G
H
1
2
3
4
43
50
KINGSTON UPON THAMES
SUTTON
Hampton Wick
Norbiton
Merton
East Molesey
West Molesey
Hampton Court Palace & Garden
Thames Ditton
Surbiton
Long Ditton
Berrylands
New Malden
Raynes Park
West Barnes
Bushey Mead
Motspur Park
Old Malden
Tolworth
Hinchley Wood
Weston Green
Lower Green
Esher
Worcester Park
North Cheam
Rosehill
Benhilton
Carshalton
Hook
Chessington
Claygate
Claremont Park
Stoneleigh
Cheam
Nonsuch Park
West Ewell
Ewell
East Ewell
Horton
Epsom
Belmont
Banstead Downs
Carshalton Beeches
Malden Rushett
Fairmile
Oxshott
Prince's Coverts
Epsom Common
North Looe
Banstead
Nork
Woodmansterne
Stoke D'Abernon
Pachesham Park
Ashtead
Ashtead Common
Lower Ashtead
Ashtead Park
Leatherhead Common
Langley Vale
Epsom Downs
Tattenham Corner
Burgh Heath
Walton Downs
LEATHERHEAD
Fetcham
Tyrrell's Wood
Tadworth
Kingswood
Chipstead Bottom
Great Bookham
Givons Grove
Headley
Walton on the Hill
Banstead Heath
Mugswell
Norbury Park
Mickleham
Pebble Coombe
Mogador
M25
0 1/2 1 1 1/2 2 Miles
0 1 2 3 4 Kilometres

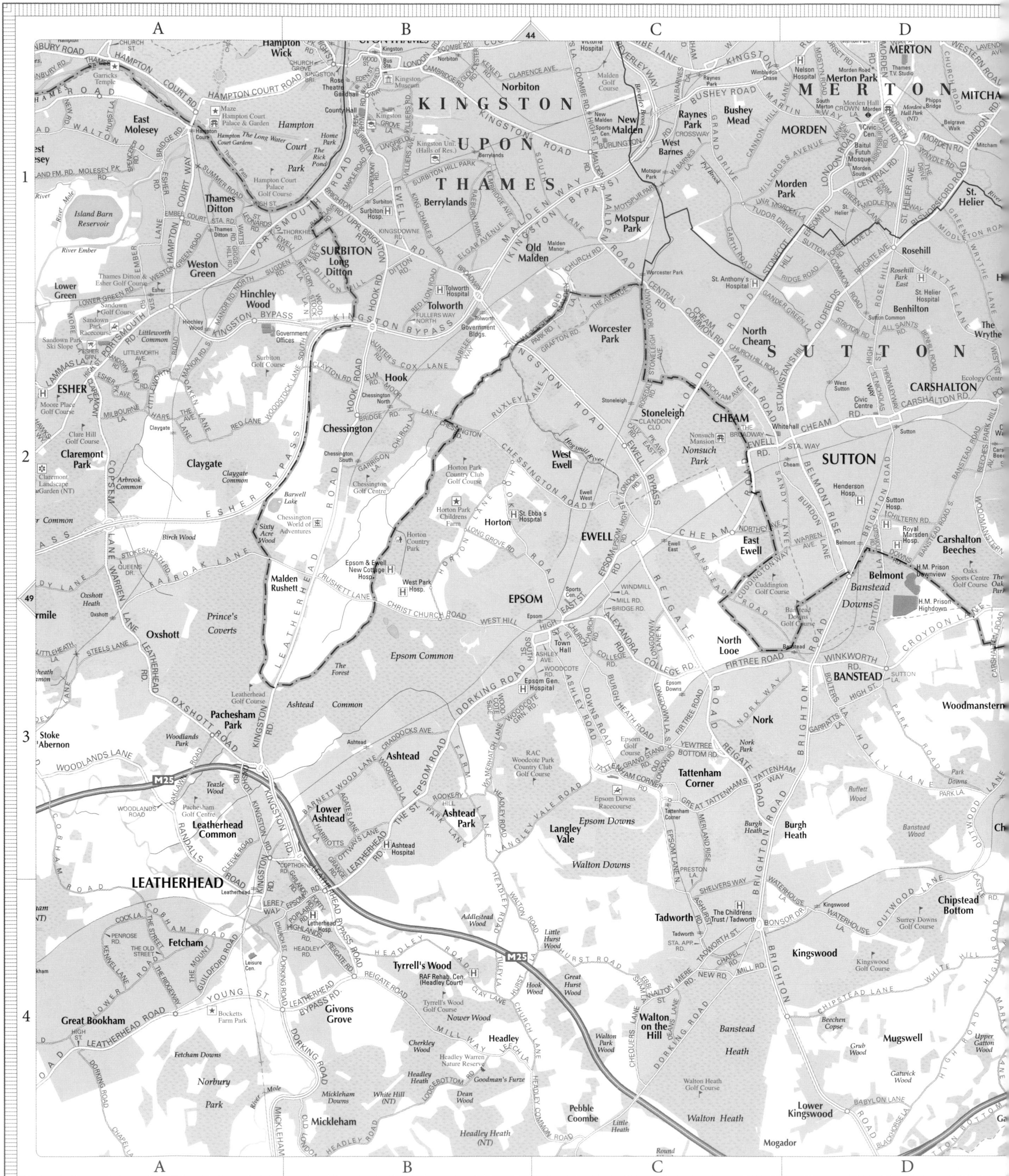
A
B
C
D
1
2
3
4
44
49
KINGSTON UPON THAMES
MERTON
SUTTON
Hampton Wick
Norbiton
Merton Park
MERTON
MORDEN
East Molesey
Hampton Court Park
Home Park
New Malden
Raynes Park
Bushey Mead
West Barnes
Thames Ditton
Berrylands
Motspur Park
Morden Park
St. Helier
Island Barn Reservoir
Weston Green
SURBITON
Long Ditton
Old Malden
Rosehill
Lower Green
Hinchley Wood
Tolworth
Worcester Park
North Cheam
Benhilton
The Wrythe
ESHER
Hook
Stoneleigh
CHEAM
CARSHALTON
Chessington
Claremont Park
Claygate
West Ewell
Nonsuch Park
SUTTON
Horton
EWELL
East Ewell
Carshalton Beeches
Malden Rushett
EPSOM
Belmont
Banstead Downs
Oxshott
Prince's Coverts
North Looe
Epsom Common
BANSTEAD
Pachesham Park
Ashtead Common
Nork
Woodmansterne
Stoke d'Abernon
Ashtead
Tattenham Corner
M25
Leatherhead Common
Lower Ashtead
Ashtead Park
Langley Vale
Epsom Downs
Burgh Heath
LEATHERHEAD
Walton Downs
Chipstead Bottom
Tadworth
Fetcham
Tyrrell's Wood
Kingswood
Great Bookham
Givons Grove
Headley
Walton on the Hill
Banstead Heath
Mugswell
Norbury Park
Mickleham
Pebble Coombe
Walton Heath
Lower Kingswood
Mogador

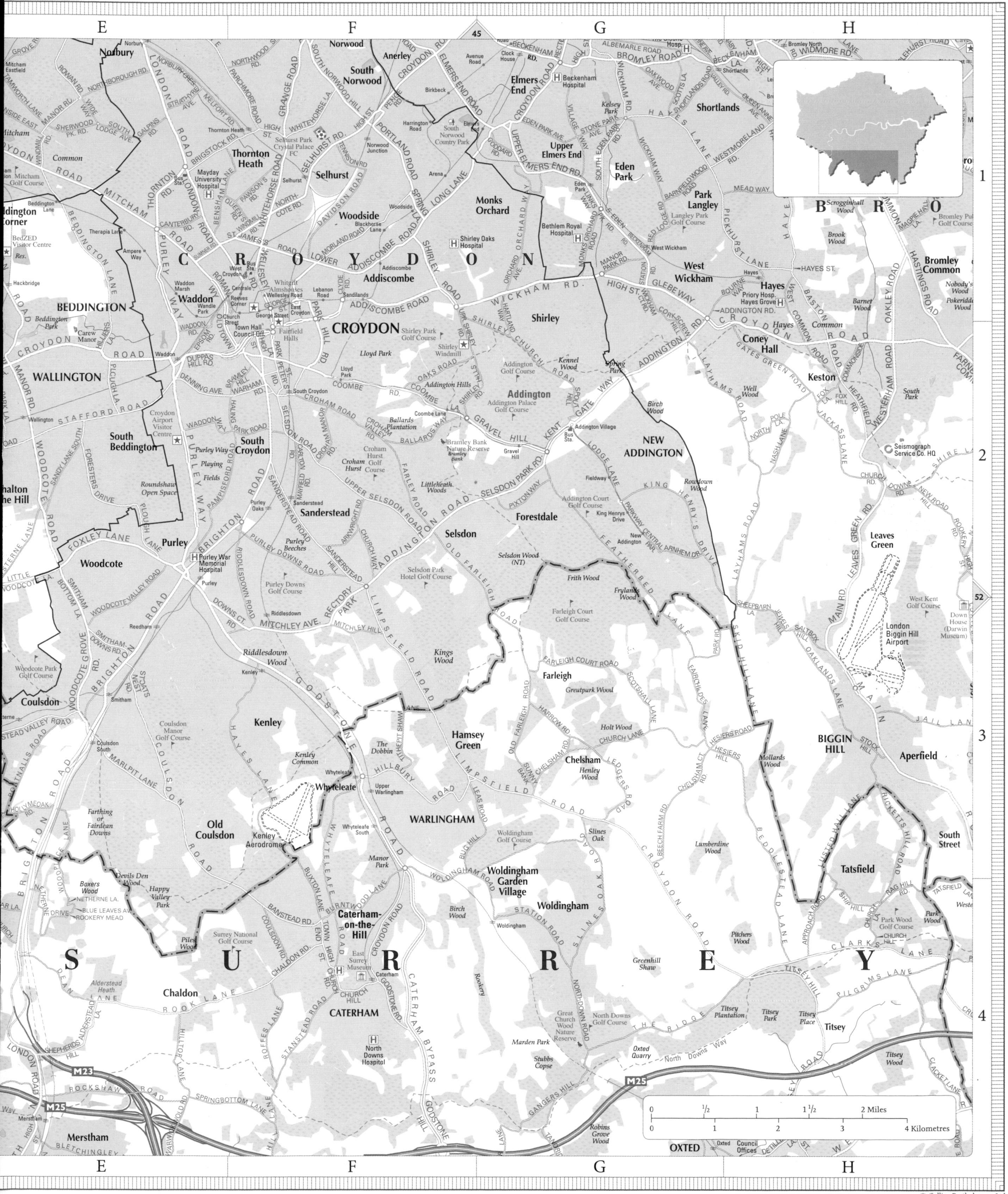
E
F
G
H
1
2
3
4
45
52
Norbury
Norwood
South Norwood
Anerley
Elmers End
Beckenham Hospital
Shortlands
Thornton Heath
Selhurst
Selhurst Park Crystal Palace FC
Mayday University Hospital
Woodside
Monks Orchard
Upper Elmers End
Eden Park
Park Langley
Bethlem Royal Hospital
Shirley Oaks Hospital
West Wickham
Hayes
Bromley Common
CROYDON
BEDDINGTON
Waddon
Addiscombe
Shirley
Coney Hall
Keston
WALLINGTON
Lloyd Park
Addington
Addington Hills
South Croydon
South Beddington
NEW ADDINGTON
Seismograph Service Co. HQ
Croydon Airport Visitor Centre
Roundshaw Open Space
Sanderstead
Selsdon
Forestdale
Purley
Woodcote
Purley War Memorial Hospital
Leaves Green
London Biggin Hill Airport
Down House (Darwin Museum)
Kings Wood
Farleigh
Riddlesdown Wood
Coulsdon
Kenley
Hamsey Green
Chelsham
BIGGIN HILL
Aperfield
Whyteleafe
WARLINGHAM
Old Coulsdon
Kenley Aerodrome
South Street
Tatsfield
Woldingham Garden Village
Woldingham
Caterham-on-the-Hill
East Surrey Museum
S U R R E Y
Chaldon
CATERHAM
North Downs Hospital
Titsey
Marden Park
Oxted Quarry
Merstham
OXTED
Oxted Council Offices
M23
M25
0 1/2 1 1 1/2 2 Miles
0 1 2 3 4 Kilometres

A
B
C
D
1
2
3
4
46
51
Norbury
Norwood
Anerley
South Norwood
Elmers End
Beckenham Hospital
BROMLEY
Widmore
Bickley
Shortlands
Civic Centre
Chislehurst
Thornton Heath
Selhurst
Selhurst Park Crystal Palace FC
Norwood Junction
South Norwood Country Park
Upper Elmers End
Eden Park
Park Langley
Southborough
Common
Mayday University Hospital
Woodside
Monks Orchard
Bethlem Royal Hospital
West Wickham
Scrogginhall Wood
Bromley Public Golf Course
Brook Wood
Bromley Common
B R O M
Shirley Oaks Hospital
C R O Y D O N
Addiscombe
Hayes
Priory Hosp. Hayes Grove
Nobody's Wood
Pokeridden Wood
Barnet Wood
BEDDINGTON
Beddington Park
Carew Manor
Waddon
Whitgift Almshouses
East Croydon
Town Hall Council Off.
Fairfield Halls
CROYDON
Shirley
Shirley Park Golf Course
Shirley Windmill
Hayes Common
Coney Hall
WALLINGTON
Lloyd Park
Addington Golf Course
Kennel Wood
Spring Park
Keston
Addington Hills
Addington
Addington Palace Golf Course
Well Wood
South Park
Croydon Airport Visitor Centre
Ballards Plantation
Birch Wood
South Beddington
South Croydon
Bramley Bank Nature Reserve
Addington Village
NEW ADDINGTON
Seismograph Service Co. HQ
Purley Way Playing Fields
Croham Hurst
Croham Hurst Golf Course
Littleheath Woods
Rowdown Wood
Roundshaw Open Space
Forestdale
Addington Court Golf Course
King Henrys Drive
Sanderstead
Selsdon
Leaves Green
Purley
Purley Beeches
Woodcote
Purley War Memorial Hospital
Selsdon Park Hotel Golf Course
Selsdon Wood (NT)
Frith Wood
Frylands Wood
Purley Downs Golf Course
Farleigh Court Golf Course
London Biggin Hill Airport
West Kent Golf Course
Down House (Darwin Museum)
Riddlesdown Wood
Kings Wood
Farleigh
Greatpark Wood
Coulsdon
Coulsdon Manor Golf Course
Kenley
Hamsey Green
Holt Wood
The Dobbin
Kenley Common
Chelsham
Henley Wood
Mollards Wood
BIGGIN HILL
Aperfield
Whyteleafe
Upper Warlingham
Farthing or Fairdean Downs
Old Coulsdon
Kenley Aerodrome
WARLINGHAM
Slines Oak
South Street
Whyteleafe South
Manor Park
Woldingham Golf Course
Lumberdine Wood
Devils Den Wood
Happy Valley Park
Boxers Wood
Woldingham Garden Village
Woldingham
Tatsfield
Westerham
Caterham-on-the-Hill
Birch Wood
Surrey National Golf Course
Piles Wood
Park Wood Golf Course
Pitchers Wood
East Surrey Museum
Greenhill Shaw
S U R R E Y
Alderstead Heath
Chaldon
Rookery
CATERHAM
Titsey Plantation
Titsey Park
Titsey Place
Titsey
Great Church Wood Nature Reserve
North Downs Golf Course
Marden Park
North Downs Hospital
Oxted Quarry
North Downs Way
Stubbs Copse
Titsey Wood
M23
M25
Limpsfield
Merstham
Robins Grove Wood
OXTED
Council Offices

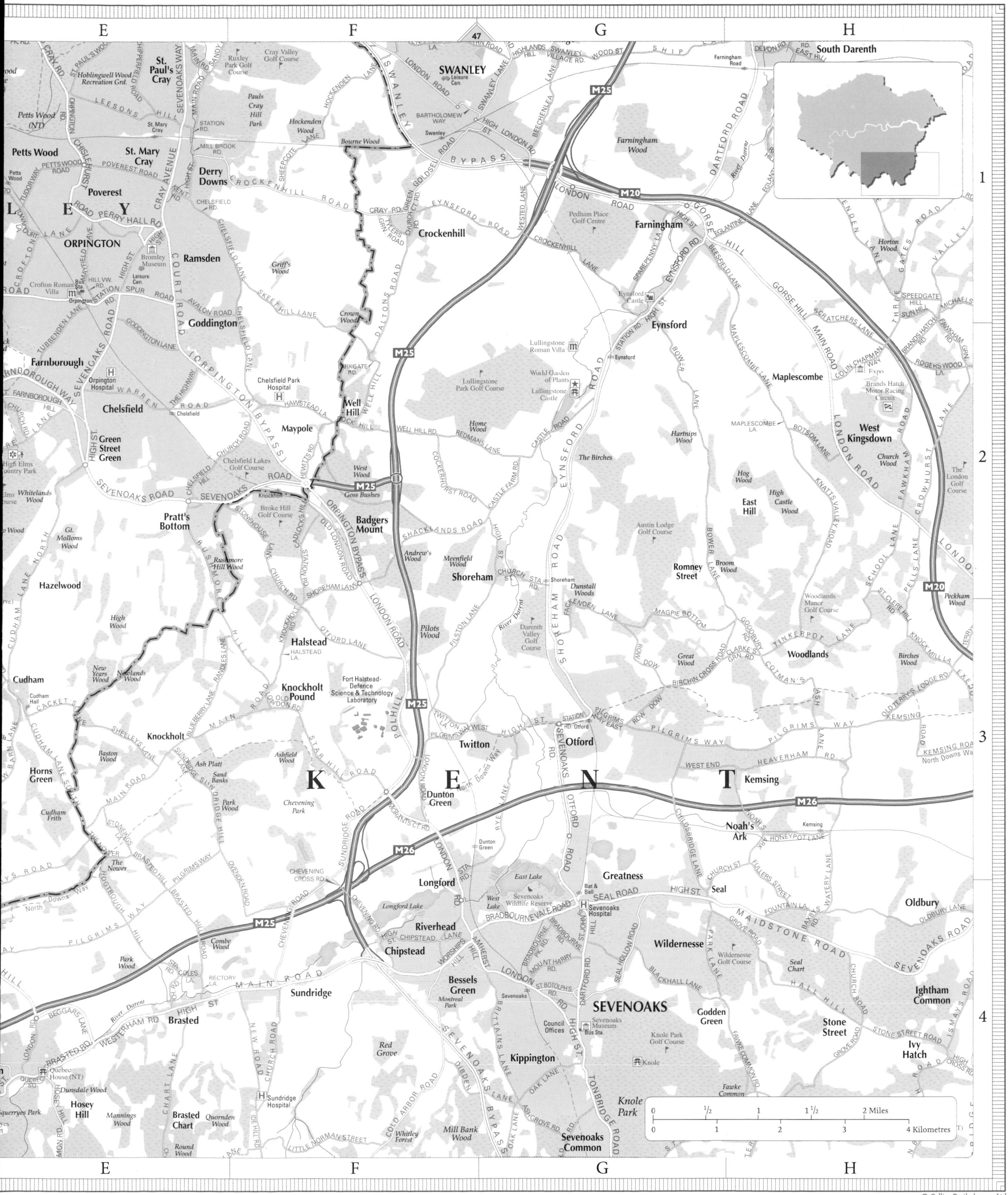
E
F
G
H
1
2
3
4
47
SWANLEY
St. Paul's Cray
St. Mary Cray
Petts Wood
Poverest
Derry Downs
ORPINGTON
Ramsden
Goddington
Farnborough
Chelsfield
Green Street Green
Pratt's Bottom
Hazelwood
Cudham
Horns Green
Knockholt
Knockholt Pound
Halstead
Badgers Mount
Maypole
Well Hill
Crockenhill
Farningham
Eynsford
Maplescombe
West Kingsdown
East Hill
Romney Street
Shoreham
Woodlands
Otford
Twitton
Kemsing
Noah's Ark
Dunton Green
Longford
Riverhead
Chipstead
Sundridge
Brasted
Bessels Green
SEVENOAKS
Greatness
Seal
Wildernesse
Godden Green
Stone Street
Ivy Hatch
Ightham Common
Oldbury
Kippington
Sevenoaks Common
Hosey Hill
Brasted Chart
South Darenth
K E N T
M25
M20
M26
Hoblingwell Wood Recreation Grd.
Ruxley Park Golf Course
Cray Valley Golf Course
Pauls Cray Hill Park
Hockenden Wood
Bourne Wood
Farningham Wood
Pedham Place Golf Centre
Bromley Museum
Crofton Roman Villa
Orpington Hospital
Chelsfield Park Hospital
Chelsfield Lakes Golf Course
Broke Hill Golf Course
Griff's Wood
Crown Wood
Lullingstone Roman Villa
World Garden of Plants
Lullingstone Castle
Lullingstone Park Golf Course
Home Wood
Hartnips Wood
The Birches
Eynsford Castle
Brands Hatch Motor Racing Circuit
Church Wood
The London Golf Course
Hog Wood
High Castle Wood
Austin Lodge Golf Course
Broom Wood
Woodlands Manor Golf Course
Peckham Wood
Dunstall Woods
Darenth Valley Golf Course
Great Wood
Birches Wood
Meenfield Wood
Andrew's Wood
Pilots Wood
West Wood
Goss Bushes
Fort Halstead-Defence Science & Technology Laboratory
High Wood
New Years Wood
Newlands Wood
Gt. Mollons Wood
Rushmore Hill Wood
Cudham Frith
Baston Wood
Ash Platt
Sand Banks
Ashfield Wood
Park Wood
Chevening Park
Combe Wood
The Nower
East Lake
Sevenoaks Wildlife Reserve
West Lake
Longford Lake
Sevenoaks Hospital
Wildernesse Golf Course
Seal Chart
Montreal Park
Council Offices
Sevenoaks Museum
Knole Park Golf Course
Knole
Knole Park
Fawke Common
Red Grove
Mill Bank Wood
Whitley Forest
Mannings Wood
Quornden Wood
Round Wood
Sundridge Hospital
Quebec House (NT)
Dunsdale Wood
Squerryes Park
Horton Wood
Ivy Hatch
Kemsing North Downs Way
North Downs Way
0 1/2 1 1 1/2 2 Miles
0 1 2 3 4 Kilometres

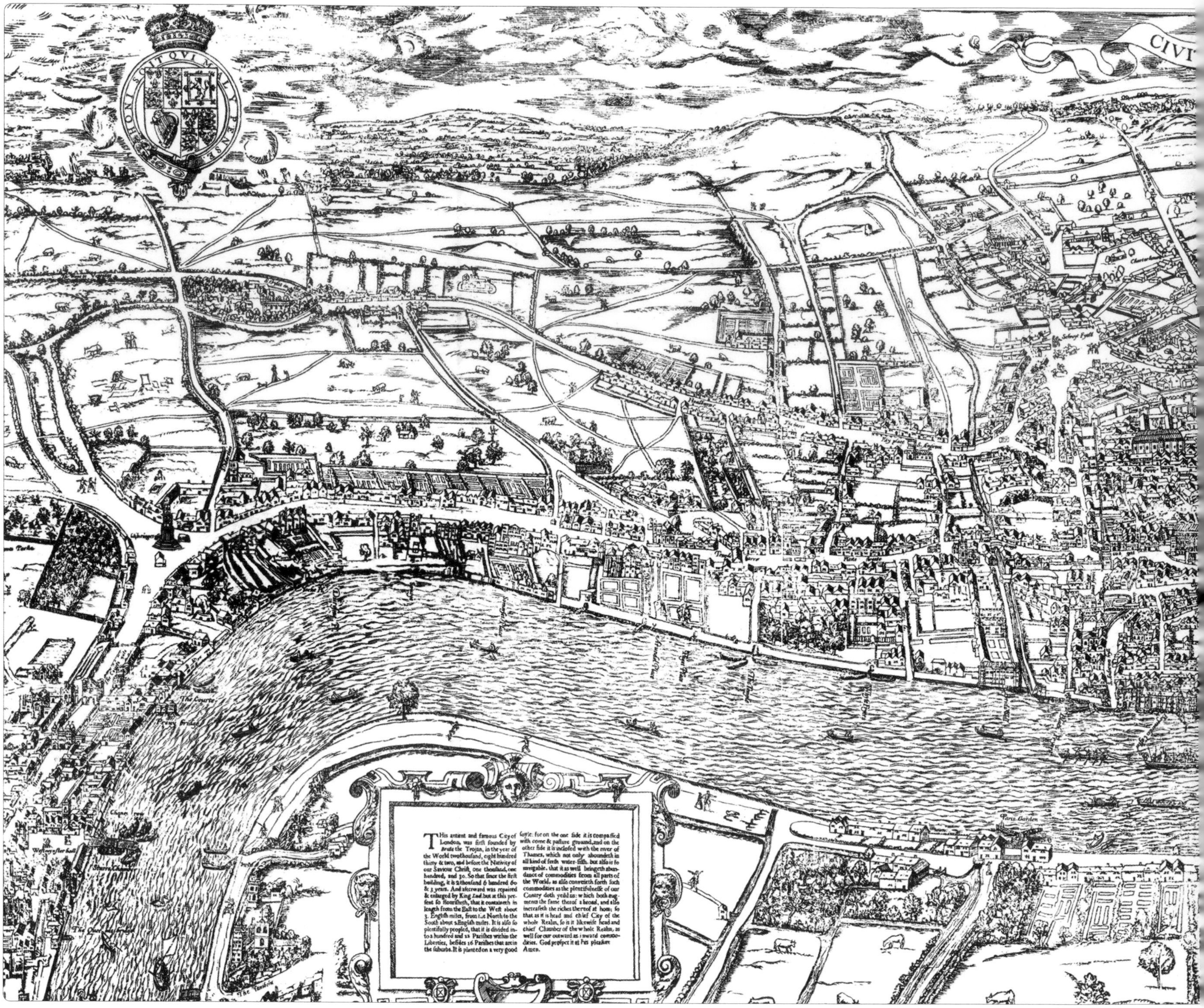

THE GROWTH OF LONDON

Whilst there is evidence of settlements in the London area in prehistoric times, London as we know it today was established by the Romans around AD 50 as a small civilian settlement at the northern end of their bridge across the Thames, close to today's London Bridge. After a turbulent start, *Londinium* emerged within 50 years as the largest settlement in Britannia and had prospered sufficiently to replace *Camulodunum* (Colchester) as capital. At its peak, Roman London had a population estimated to have been around 45,000 and boasted a sophisticated urban organization with major public buildings, a large fortress and a substantial defensive wall and ditch. This wall, which would last for over 1500 years, defined London's boundaries for several hundred years and its three access gates still survive in name in modern London: Aldgate, Aldersgate and Ludgate.

Under the Saxons, *Londinium* became part of the kingdoms of Mercia and subsequently Wessex, losing its status as capital to Winchester. In the process its fortunes declined as the centre of trade and its population deserted the old walled city and migrated westwards to an area known as *Lundenwic* ('London market'), corresponding to present-day Covent Garden and the Strand.

Sustained Viking raiding during much of the 9th century saw London repeatedly sacked until it eventually fell to the Danes in 871. Alfred the Great retook the city in 886 and began to restore it, resettling the old Roman walled area once more. The defensive walls were rebuilt, a new street plan was established and wharves were constructed along the banks of the Thames. A second defensive borough was established across the river at Southwark and in 994 a substantive bridge was built to link the two communities.

By the end of the 11th century, Westminster, with its abbey and royal palace, had emerged as a separate settlement and had effectively replaced the City of London as the centre of political power. William the Conqueror's White Tower – England's first stone castle – had been built just outside the east end of the city wall, a symbolic and practical expression of the dominance of

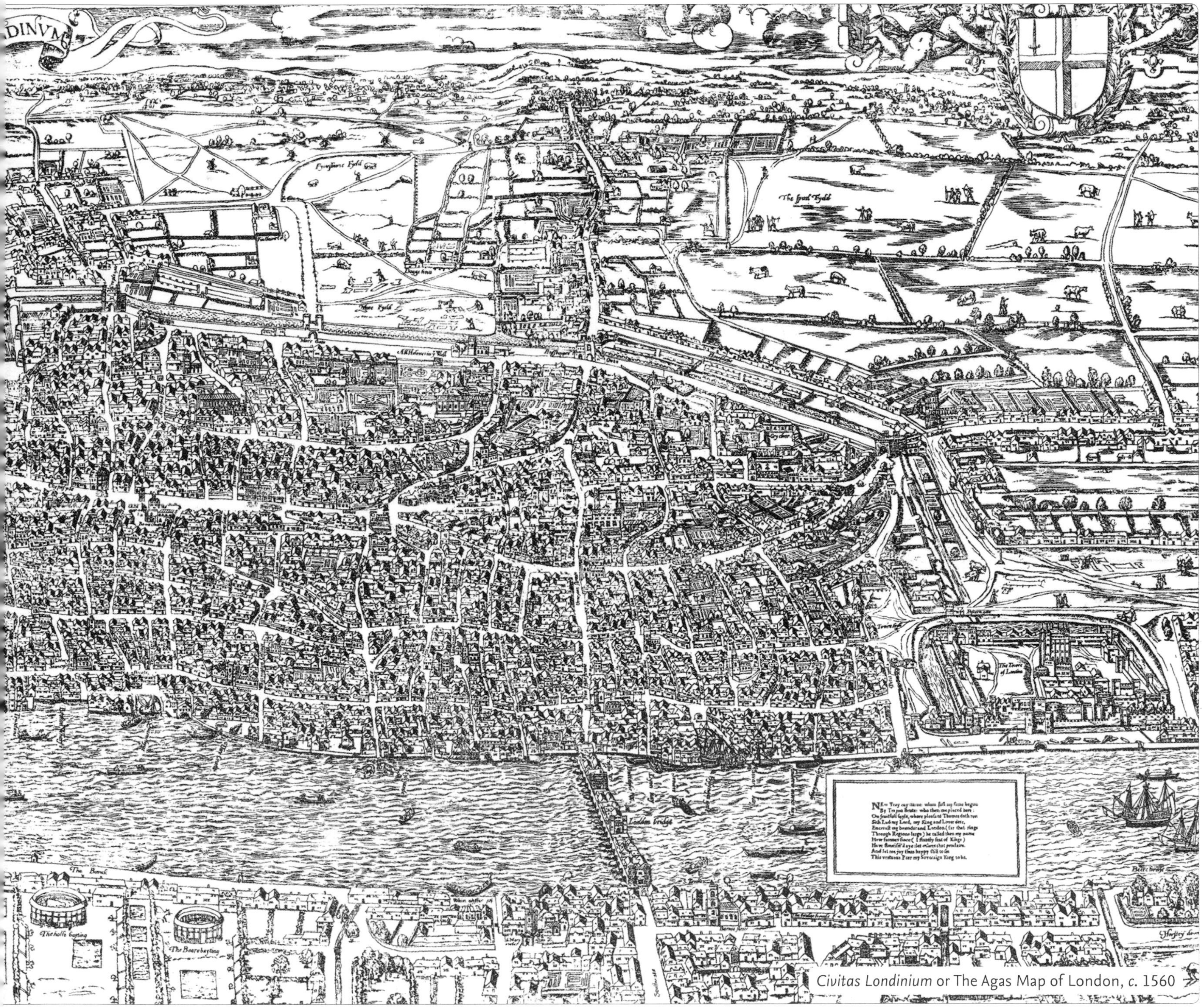

Civitas Londinium or The Agas Map of London, *c.* 1560

the new Norman ruling class. The city had ceded its political influence to Westminster, but its commercial and trading wealth continued to expand. Yet despite this burgeoning prosperity, London's physical development remained remarkably stable throughout the 300 years before the emergence of the first recognizable maps of the city in the mid 16th century.

What maps such as those by Braun and Hogenberg (see page 9) and Agas' *Civitas Londinum* (above) depict, therefore, is the essence of the medieval city, its 120,000 inhabitants still largely contained within the encircling walls with only tentative development beyond these to the north or east of the Tower. The satellite settlements at Westminster and Southwark are also still clearly distinct enclaves, albeit linked to the City by the great highway of the Strand and London Bridge respectively.

However, from around 1550 London embarked on a sustained period of growth and development that saw it emerge as one of the Western world's greatest metropolises. This transformation grew out of several inter-related developments in the late 16th and 17th centuries.

The main driver of these developments was the dramatic surge in London's population. The city was a magnet for all classes of people – nobility, traders, craftsmen and the poor – and by the outbreak of the Great Plague in 1665, some 370,000 people were crammed within its boundaries. However, the seizure of religious property during the reign of Henry VIII and its transfer to secular control fostered a more intensive use of the land and spurred on new development. This was particularly evident to the west between London and Westminster where, along the Strand and by the banks of Thames, many fine noble residences sprang up. To the east, areas such as Whitechapel and Spitalfields grew as incomers tended to settle outside the City and so avoid the strict regulation of the powerful trade guilds that controlled much of London's life and commerce. This eastward spread was a catalyst for the development of riverside hamlets such as Wapping, Stepney and Ratcliffe, which became the centres for the ships and services that powered the massive growth in English maritime trade during

the early 17th century. Consequently, although the Great Fire razed much of the medieval city in 1666 (see page 10), London survived because it had outgrown its historic core.

A comparison of contemporary maps such as those by Rocque from 1769 (above) and Tallis from 1851 (see page 58) graphically illustrates how the pace of growth continued and accelerated during the 18th and 19th centuries as London found itself at the hub of the emerging British Empire.

As its population grew from less than 700,000 in 1750 to well over two million a century later, London was forced to expand in all directions. Its westward development continued the trend of previous centuries and saw the rise of fashionable suburbs with elegant squares, terraces, parks and imposing houses. At the opposite point of the geographic and social compasses, settlement continued downstream on both sides of the river around a series of purpose-built docks. These new docks were replacing the old, crowded, city-centre wharves that were now unable to keep pace with London's growing importance as a trading port and shipbuilding centre. New bridges over the

London in 1769, updated from John Rocque's 1746 map; it includes Westminster and Blackfriars bridges and the New Road from Paddington to Islington (now Euston Road)

Thames in 1750 and 1769 also facilitated rapid growth along the south bank.

By the mid-19th century, not only were the once-satellite settlements of Westminster and Southwark now inextricably part of the city, many of the 'small and pleasant' villages that once surrounded the capital – such as Paddington, Shepherd's Bush, Camberwell, Richmond, Twickenham and Ealing – had been swallowed as London's footprint grew ever larger. This was due in large part to the development of the network of metropolitan railways and the Underground system that allowed people to commute from outlying suburbs to the city centre. In turn, this fuelled further the massive outward growth of the city that was recorded on the Royal Atlas map (see page 61) by the end of the century and which is evident on modern maps of Greater London (see page 20).

As the 20th century dawned, the *Bartholomew Gazetteer of the British Isles* proudly proclaimed London to be 'the greatest city of any age or country' whose 'immense size and population ... progress and pre-eminence form a very

CRICKLEWOOD
HAMPSTEAD
WEST END
WILLESDEN GREEN
SHOOT UP HILL
HIGHBURY
LOWER HOLLOWAY
REGENTS PARK
PADDINGTON
HYDE PARK
KENSINGTON GARDENS
EARLS COURT
LITTLE CHELSEA
CHELSEA REACH
LAMBETH REACH
PROPOSED BATTERSEA PARK
FULHAM COMMON FIELDS
WALHAM GREEN
PARSONS GREEN
SOUTH LAMBETH
BRIXTON
BATTERSEA RISE
COLOSSEUM
CHINESE EXHIBITION
MARBLE ARCH
CRYSTAL PALACE

remarkable feature in the history of civilisation'. Even allowing for the unshakeable self-confidence of the Victorian age, there was little doubt that London had indeed grown to become a political, financial and mercantile capital of global importance.

The creation of London County Council in 1888 brought some order to the ever-growing metropolis, and in the decades that followed, there were active slum clearance schemes and the building of new housing estates on the perimeters of the city. The extension of the Underground network stimulated more housing development in what are now the outer boroughs as people moved out of overcrowded central London. New industries were also established in the suburbs, from Ford in Dagenham to Beecham's in Brentford. World War II wreaked havoc on the city, accelerating its deindustrialization and the movement of people from the badly bombed areas of the East End to Outer London and beyond. The physical spread of London over the surrounding counties was restrained, however, by the imposition of a 'green belt' of countryside around the built-up area. From the 1950s, the population was transformed by mass immigration from the Caribbean and South Asia, making the city the most diverse in Britain. By now the metropolitan area far exceeded that of London County Council and in 1965 the Greater London Council was created, and, while the GLC no longer exists, its boundaries remain those of the Greater London area. The complete closure of the docks on the lower reaches of the Thames by 1981 has seen a reinvention of this part of London – the redevelopment of Canary Wharf makes a physical statement of London's importance now as a global financial centre. Through all these changes, many of which are covered in the pages that follow, London remains essential to the government and economy of Britain and, unquestionably, is one of the world's great cities.

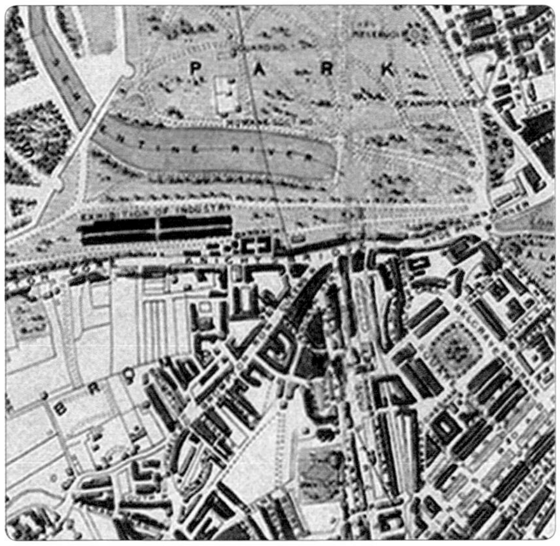

John Tallis's map of London, 1851 and extract; note the Crystal Palace shown on the southern side of Hyde Park

From Bartholomew Gazetteer of the British Isles, 1887

LONDON, *the capital of England and the principal town of the British Empire, on the river Thames, mostly in Middlesex, but also occupying parts of Surrey, Kent, and Essex, 60 miles (by the river's course) from the sea at the Nore; the centre of the dome of St Paul's is in lat. 50° 30' 48" W.*

The centre of the Government and commerce of the British Empire, London is the greatest city of any age or country. Politically, financially, and commercially, as well as on account of its immense size and population, its progress and pre-eminence form a very remarkable feature in the history of civilisation. Without entering upon the vague traditions which have survived from more obscure eras, we find that as early as A.D. 61 the 'Lundinium' of the Romans was a place of importance; 'Colonia Augusta' being another of its Roman designations. One of the principal evidences, however, of a much earlier existence of the town is found in the etymology of the name, which comes from the Celtic 'Llyn-Din'. Three important events have especial prominence in the pre-Norman history of London; namely, the foundation of the bishopric, supposed to have taken place in A.D. 179; the rebuilding and fortifying of the town by the Romans in 306; and the founding of St Paul's by Ethelbert in the year 597. Coming upon the firmer ground of authentic history, it is seen that in 1079 the Tower was built by William I., who, in the same year, granted the city its first charter, a document which is still extant. A charter granted by King John in 1189 authorised the annual election of a mayor and corporation.

Conspicuous landmarks in the subsequent course of the city's history are – Wat Tyler's Rebellion, 1381; Jack Cade's Rebellion, 1450; the foundation of Christ's Hospital, 1533; numerous pestilences, culminating in the Great Plague of 1665; and the Great Fire of 1666. The latter, although in itself a disaster of terrible magnitude, had one good effect, in so far that it swept away the old haunts of disease, and left room for the erection of the present city, the history of which, in a large measure, is the history of the progress of the British nation. Modern London has no clearly defined limits, and the determination of its unofficial boundaries is yearly becoming more difficult through its rapid and wide suburban extension. Roughly speaking, the whole metropolis may be estimated to cover, E. to W., 14 m., and N. to S. 10m.

As the seat of the government of the Empire, the commercial emporium of Britain, the home of British literature, art and science, and the place of residence, at special seasons, of the wealthier classes from all parts of the country, it is natural that London should abound with interesting, stately, and imposing buildings of all descriptions. Among the greatest of these are the Houses of Parliament, Westminster Abbey, Buckingham Palace, St James' Palace, St Paul's Cathedral, Lambeth Palace, the Tower of London, the Guildhall, the Mansion House, the Royal Exchange, the Bank of England, the General Post-Office, the British Museum, and the National Gallery. The Government departments, such as the Home and Foreign Offices, the Education Office, Somerset House (Inland Revenue), &c., are also important. There are over 1400 churches and chapels, 45 theatres, and 400 music halls concert rooms, &c. Thirteen bridges, besides 5 railway bridges, span the Thames; London Bridge being the most easterly, and Hammersmith Bridge that most westerly.

The metropolis is singularly fortunate in the possession of public parks, which for the extent and beauty are unsurpassed by any open spaces belonging to other large cities. The chief are:- In the W., St James' Park (80 ac.), the Green Park (70 ac.), Hyde park (390 ac.), and Kensington Gardens (360 ac.); in the N., the Regent's Park (470 ac.), containing the gardens of the Zoological Society and the Botanical Society; in the SW., Battersea Park (180 ac.); and in the E., Victoria Park (300 ac.).

London is the supreme seat of the judicature of the country. The principal courts are concentrated in the magnificent range of buildings known as the New Law Courts. The Inns of Court are to some extent colleges for law students, and include the Inner Temple, Middle Temple, Lincoln's Inn, and Gray's Inn. Altogether the different courts give employment to over 3000 barristers and 5000 solicitors. Exclusive of the Mansion House and Guildhall, in the City, there are 13 police courts in various parts of the metropolis, and the whole police force is about 14,000.

All the military affairs of the country are managed from the War Office and Horse Guards; the actual garrison of the metropolis mostly consisting of the Household cavalry, and Chelsea and Wellington barracks for infantry. The chief offices of the Admiralty, the Customs, and the mercantile marine service, are likewise situated in London.

Education is represented by many well-known institutions. London University is purely an examining body for conferring degrees, the tests being open to all comers, and certificates are obtainable by women. Of the colleges, University College and King's College are the principal, but there are also a number of others; notably the denominational institutions for the training of school teachers. Medical education, at the head of which stand the Royal College of Physicians and the Royal College of Surgeons, is actively carried on in the hospitals, especially at Bartholomew's, St Thomas', Guy's, St George's, and the Middlesex Hospital. In all there are about 35 general hospitals and infirmaries in the metropolis, besides a very large number of kindred institutions for the treatment of special diseases.

The chief public schools are Westminster, St Paul's, Christ Church (Bluecoat), Merchant Taylors' (Charterhouse), City of London Schools, and University College Schools. The School Board has in operation 368 schools, accommodating 334,309 children.

The water-supply of the town is drawn, and after filtration distributed, from the Thames and the New River. The gas-supply is in the hands of joint-stock companies.

Markets exist for almost every commodity that has a sufficient mercantile importance; those for food supplies being chiefly the London Central Market (meat and poultry), Billingsgate Market (fish), Covent Garden Market (fruit and vegetables), Borough Market (fruit and vegetables), Columbia Market (fish and general). A distinguished feature in metropolitan enterprise is the number and variety of means adopted for the conveyance of passengers and goods. It is impossible to describe the labyrinth of the rail system; but some conception of its intricacy and extent may be formed from the fact that the greater railway lines have 11 termini. The Metropolitan and the Metropolitan District Railways, popularly known as the "Underground," are the most convenient, and convey about 136 millions of passengers every year. The "Inner Circle," which completed the circuit, was opened in 1884. A gigantic traffic is also sustained by an immense number of omnibuses, tramway cars, and cabs. Of the latter it is estimated that there are about 10,000, while the cab-drivers number about 13,000. Hundreds of steamers ply upon the river, and a large goods traffic is carried on upon the Regent, Grand Junction, and the other canals. The trade of London comprises every department of active commercial enterprise that is usually associated with a great city. More particularly, however, it is known as the headquarters of finance, and the greatest emporium for merchandise in the world, rather than as a place of special manufacturing industry.

Financial interests have their chief centre in the Bank of England, which in November 1884 had notes to the value of £24,795,670 in circulation; at the same time, unemployed notes amounted to the sum of £9,741,690, and gold and silver in all the branches to £19,752,916. The number of private and joint-stock banks in London is 160. Their inter-official accounts are adjusted and settled through the medium of the Bankers' Clearing House, a splendidly organised establishment, dealing with enormous transactions, which average £1,000,000 a week, and which for the year ending April 1884 represented an aggregate sum of £5,838,158,000. The great centre of business is the Royal Exchange, which was founded by Sir Thomas Gresham in 1570. Other great exchanges, for special purposes, are the Corn Exchange, the Wool Exchange, the

LONDON, 1898

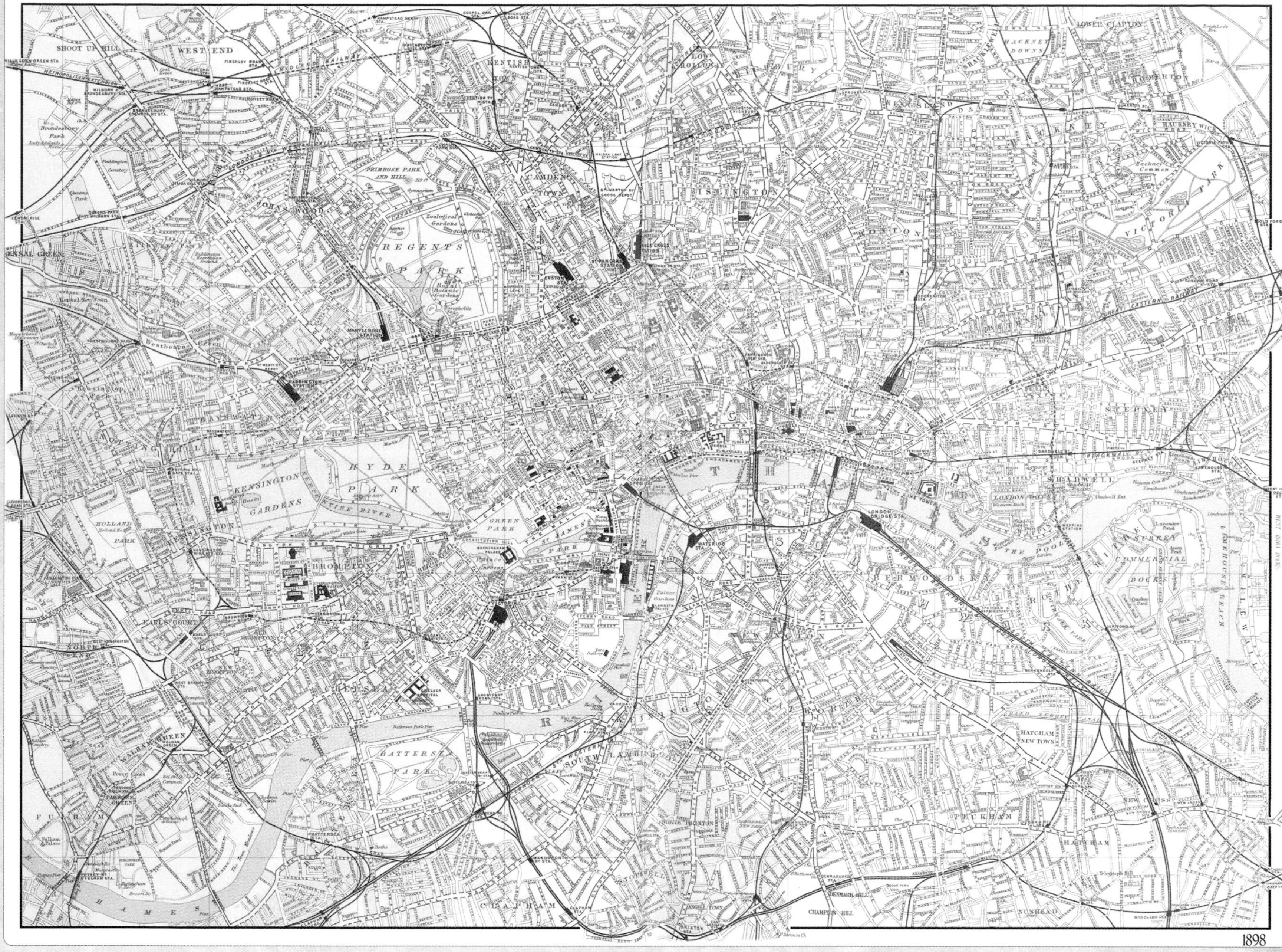

London, from the *Royal Atlas of England and Wales*, 1898

Coal Exchange, and an exchange for landed property.

In its purely mercantile aspects London shows an excess of imports over exports. This is due to the circumstance of its being a market for all descriptions of produce from every quarter of the globe; its especial trade with the East Indies and China almost amounting to a monopoly. To meet the exigencies of this multifarious traffic, a vast amount of dock accommodation has been provided. The chief docks are, the East and West India Docks, Blackwall; the London Docks, East Smithfield; Millwall Docks, Isle of Dogs; St Katherine's Docks, East Smithfield; Surrey and Commercial Docks, Rotherhithe; Regent Dock, Limehouse and the Royal Victoria and Albert Docks, North Woolwich. The new docks at Tilbury, constructed under the auspices of the East and West India Dock Company, have a water space of nearly 80 acres, with 12,000 ft. of quay room. With the completion of its railway system, this will be one of the most important undertakings connected with London shipping.

Brewing is, perhaps, the leading industry of London, which, however, may be said to carry on, more or less, nearly every mfr. known in the kingdom. Its potteries, glass works, tanneries, and chemical works are well known. Shipbuilding, which at one time showed a remarkable degree of industrial vitality, has seriously declined; the work now conducted on the Thames being almost confined to the construction of boats, barges, and yachts.

London has long been the great seat of the British publishing trade. Many of the book-publishing offices are situated in the neighbourhoods of Paternoster Row and Covent Garden, while newspaper offices are nearly all concentrated in Fleet Street and its vicinity. The number of newspapers published in London in 1884 was over 400, of which 24 were daily papers, morning and evening.

London from St Paul's Cathedral, 1846

...ING BY THOS ALLOM, ESQ: M.R.I.B.A.
...DON.
...of St. Paul's Cathedral

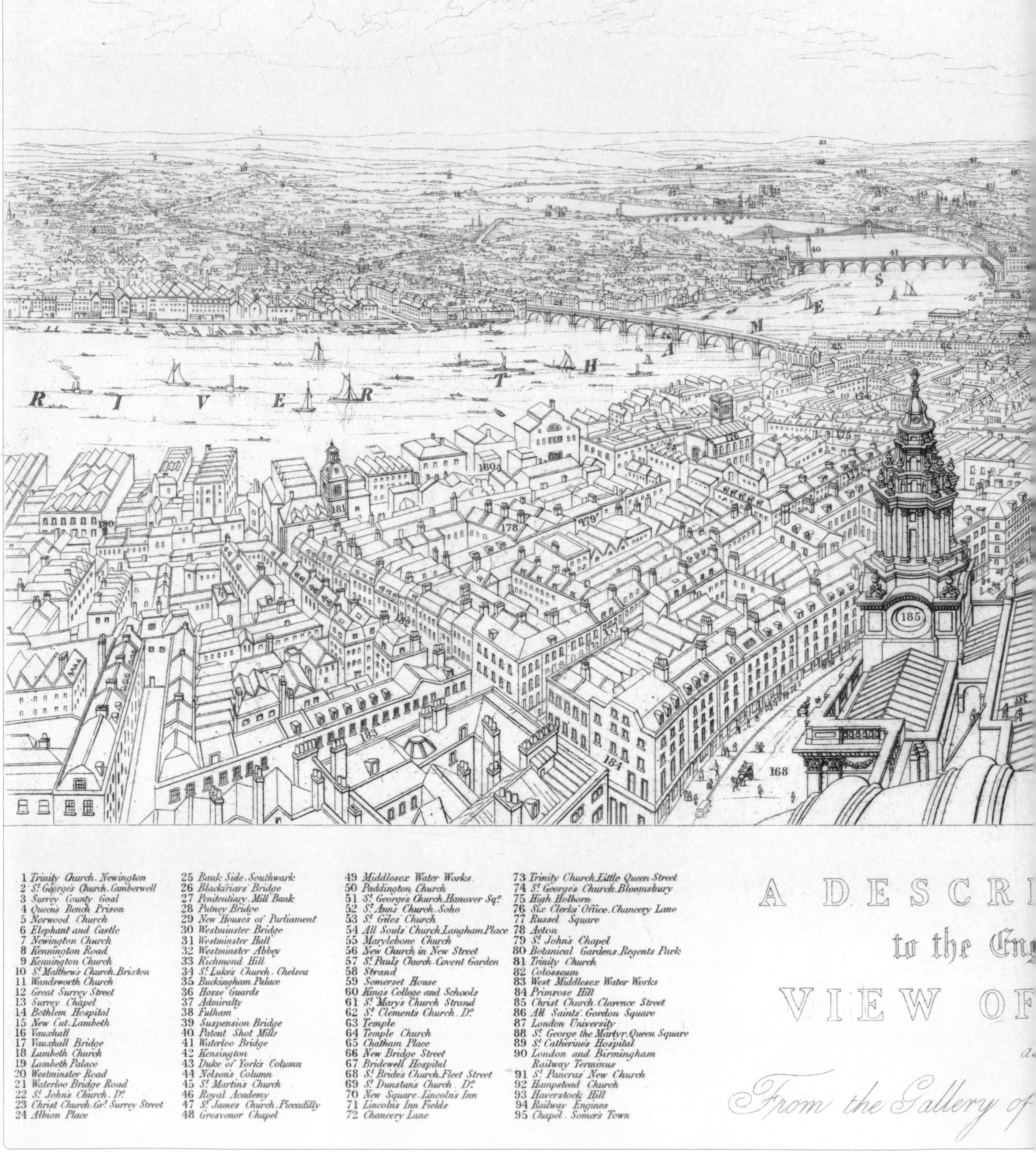

London from St Paul's Cathedral, 1846

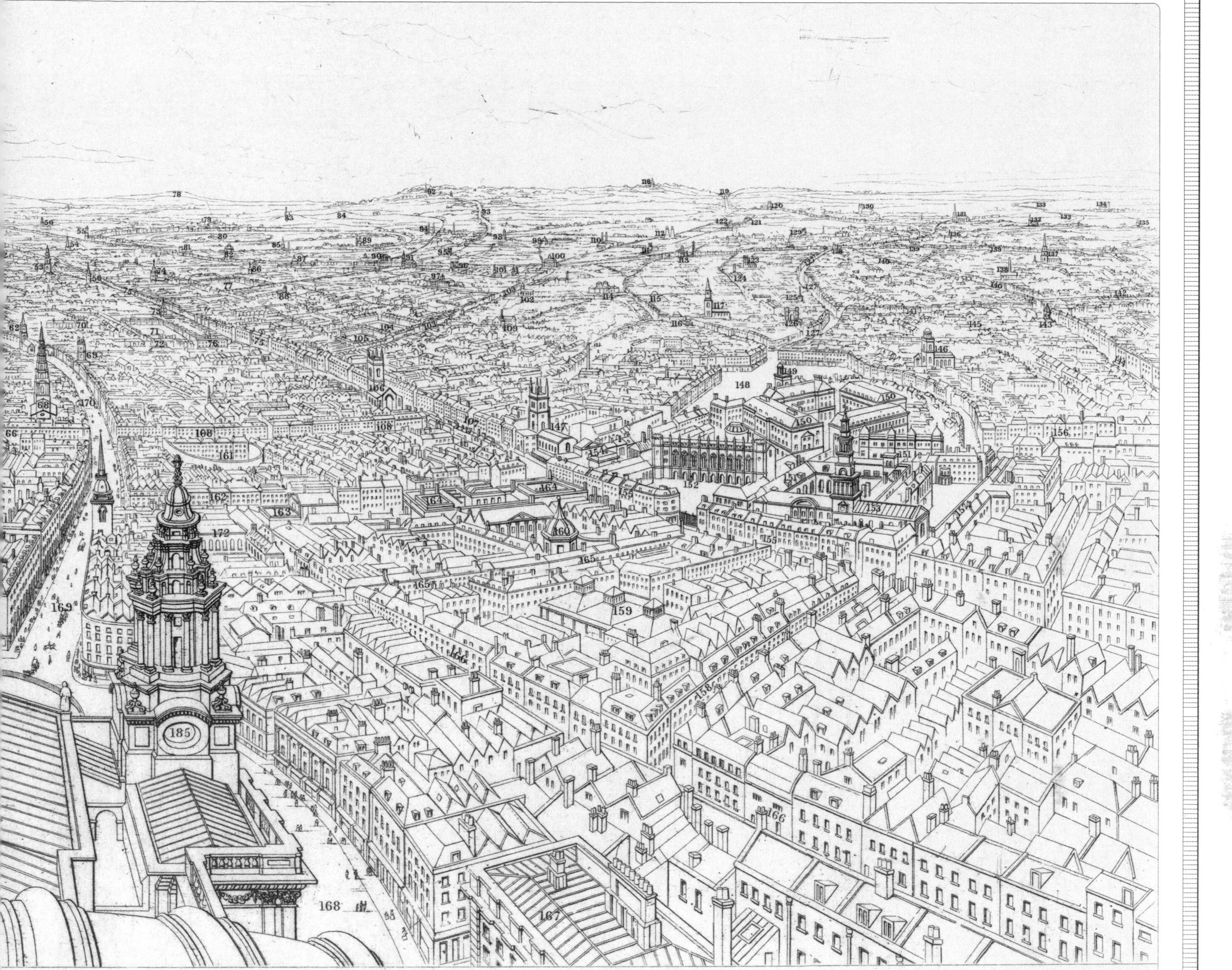

TIVE KEY

ing of the

ONDON,

n

int Paul's Cathedral.

96 Scots' Church. Regent Square
97 Foundling Hospital
98 Camden Town Chapel
99 St. Pancras' Old Church
100 Small Pox Hospital
101 Regent Square Chapel
102 Trinity Church, Gray's Inn Square
103 Gray's Inn Lane
104 Gray's Inn Gardens
105 Gray's Inn Square
106 St. Andrew's Church, Holborn Hill
107 Holborn Hill
108 Farringdon Street
109 Brewery. Liquorpond Street
110 Gas Works. Maiden Lane
111 All Saints' Church. Battle Bridge Road
112 Tile Kilns. Maiden Lane
113 St. James' Chapel. Pentonville
114 House of Correction
115 Spa Fields Chapel
116 Sessions' House. Clerkenwell Green
117 St. James' Church. Clerkenwell
118 Highgate Church
119 Highgate Archway
120 St. John's Church. Upper-Holloway
121 Caledonian Asylum
122 Model Prison
123 St. Mark's Church. Myddleton Squ.e
124 New River Head
125 St. John's Church. Clerkenwell
126 St. John's Gate
127 St. John's Street
128 Angel Inn. Islington
129 Trinity Church. Cloudesley Square
130 Chapel of Ease. Holloway
131 Islington Church
132 St. Stephen's Church. New North Road
133 New River
134 St. Paul's Church. Balls Pond
135 St. Peter's Church. Beauvoir Town
136 St. Peter's Church. River Lane
137 St. Barnabas' Church. King Square
138 Gas Works
139 City Road
140 Goswell Street Road
141 Wilderness Row
142 Old Street
143 St. Thomas' Church, Charterhouse
144 Goswell Street
145 Charterhouse
146 St. Bartholomew the Great
147 St. Sepulchre's Church Skinner Street
148 Smithfield
149 St. Bartholomew the less
150 St. Bartholomew's Hospital
151 Christ's Hospital, or Blue Coat School
152 New Hall of Do.
153 Christ's Church. Newgate Street
154 Giltspur Street Compter
155 Newgate Street
156 Little Britain
157 King Edward Street
158 Ivy Lane
159 Newgate Market
160 Old College of Surgeons
161 Fleet Prison
162 Ave Maria Lane
163 Sessions' House. Old Bailey
164 Newgate
165 Warwick Lane
166 Paternoster Row
167 London House
168 St. Paul's Church Yard
169 Ludgate Hill
170 Fleet Street
171 Creed Lane
172 Stationers' Hall
173 Little Bridge Street
174 The Times Printing Office
175 St. Andrew's Hill
176 St. Andrew's Church
177 Great Carter Lane
178 Prerogative Office
179 Knightrider Street
180 Upper Thames Street
181 St. Benett's Church. Paul's Wharf
182 Godliman Street
183 Little Carter Lane
184 Pauls Chain
185 Turrets of St. Paul's Cathedral.

ENGRAVED BY J. T. WILLMORE, A.R.A.
LON
From the Upper Gallery of the

London from St Bride's Church, 1846

DON.

teeple of St. Bride's Church

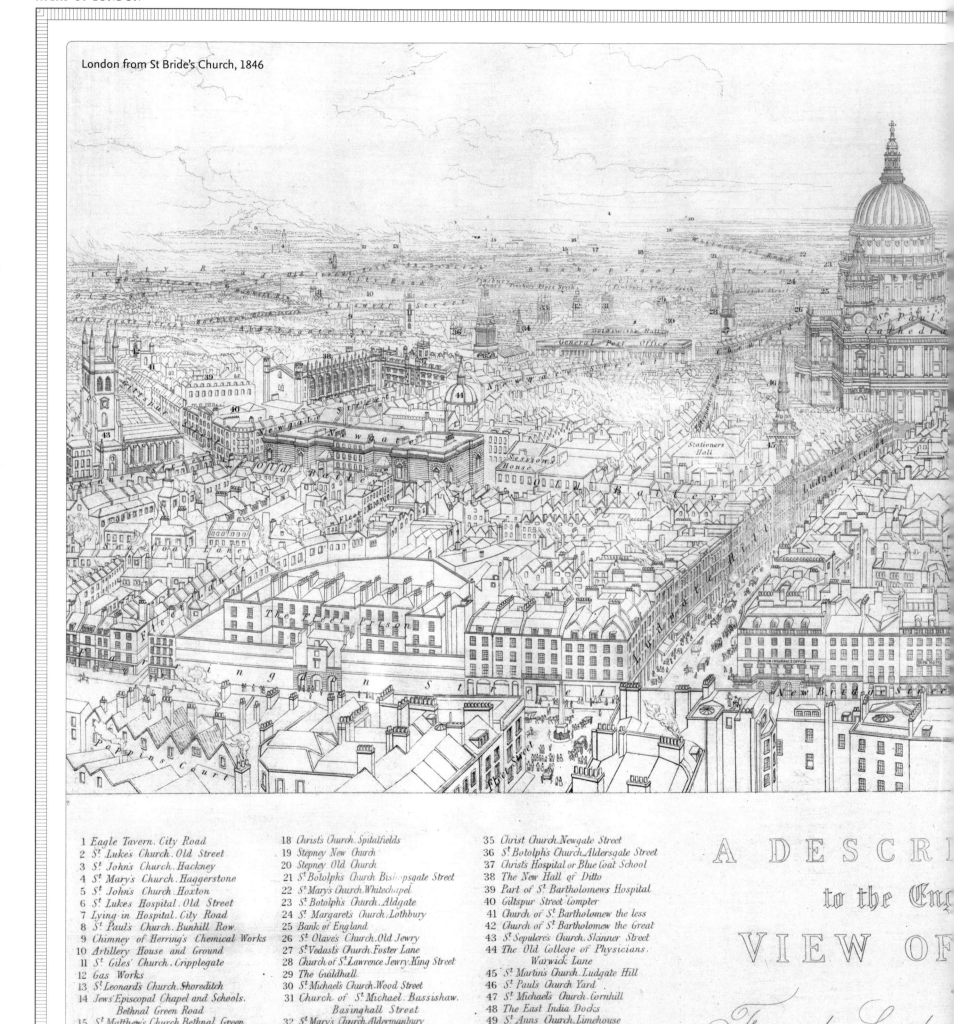

London from St Bride's Church, 1846

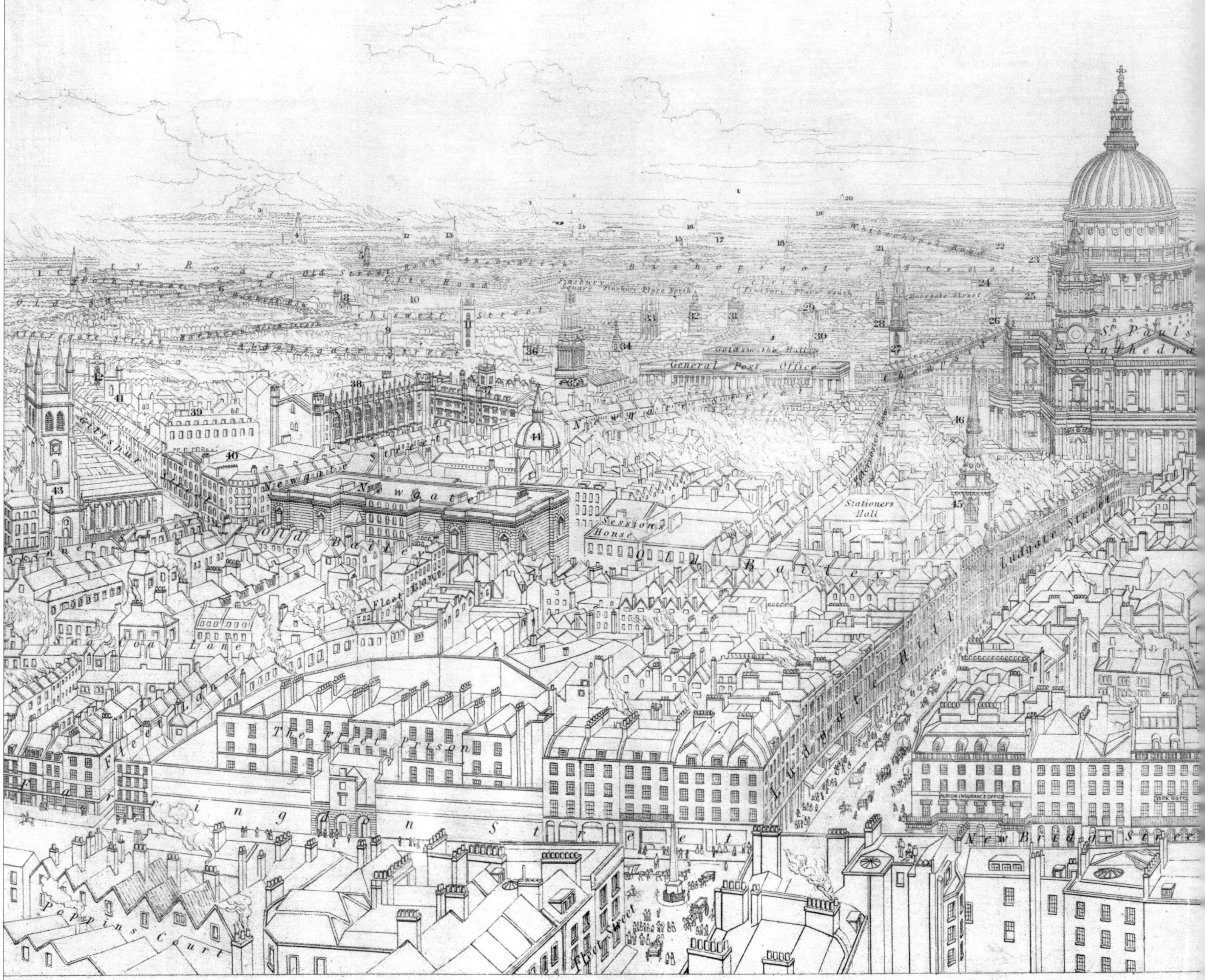

1 Eagle Tavern. City Road
2 S^t. Luke's Church. Old Street
3 S^t. John's Church. Hackney
4 S^t. Mary's Church. Haggerstone
5 S^t. John's Church. Hoxton
6 S^t. Lukes Hospital. Old Street
7 Lying-in Hospital. City Road
8 S^t. Paul's Church. Bunhill Row
9 Chimney of Herring's Chemical Works
10 Artillery House and Ground
11 S^t. Giles' Church. Cripplegate
12 Gas Works
13 S^t. Leonard's Church. Shoreditch
14 Jews' Episcopal Chapel and Schools. Bethnal Green Road
15 S^t. Matthew's Church. Bethnal Green
16 New Church. Bethnal Green
17 Lunatic Asylum. Bethnal Green
18 Christ's Church. Spitalfields
19 Stepney New Church
20 Stepney Old Church
21 S^t. Botolph's Church Bishopsgate Street
22 S^t. Mary's Church. Whitechapel
23 S^t. Botolph's Church. Aldgate
24 S^t. Margaret's Church. Lothbury
25 Bank of England
26 S^t. Olave's Church. Old Jewry
27 S^t. Vedast's Church. Foster Lane
28 Church of S^t. Lawrence Jewry. King Street
29 The Guildhall.
30 S^t. Michael's Church. Wood Street
31 Church of S^t. Michael. Bassishaw. Basinghall Street
32 S^t. Mary's Church. Aldermanbury
33 S^t. Alban's Church. Wood Street
34 Church of S^t. Ann and S^t. Agnes
35 Christ Church. Newgate Street
36 S^t. Botolph's Church. Aldersgate Street
37 Christ's Hospital or Blue Coat School
38 The New Hall of Ditto
39 Part of S^t. Bartholomews Hospital
40 Giltspur Street Compter
41 Church of S^t. Bartholomew the less
42 Church of S^t. Bartholomew the Great
43 S^t. Sepulcre's Church. Skinner Street
44 The Old College of Physicians. Warwick Lane
45 S^t. Martin's Church. Ludgate Hill
46 S^t. Pauls Church Yard
47 S^t. Michael's Church. Cornhill
48 The East India Docks
49 S^t. Anns Church. Limehouse
50 The West India Docks
51 Church of S^t. George in the East

A DESCR
to the Eng
VIEW OF
From the Steeple of

TIVE KEY

ing of the

ONDON,

en

aint Brides Church

52 The London Docks
53 St. Katherine's Docks
54 The Royal Mint. Tower Hill
55 Church of St. Hallows. Barking
56 Church of St. Dunstan's in the East
57 The Tower of London
58 The Custom House
59 The Monument. Fish Street Hill
60 St. Magnus' Church. Fish Street Hill
61 Church of St. Edmund the King. Lombard St.
62 St. Diones Back Church. Lime Street
63 St. Benet's Church. Gracechurch Street
64 St. Marks Church Goodman's Fields
65 Church of St. Mary Woolnorth. Lombard St.
66 St. Stephen's Church. Walbrook
67 St. Antholins Church. Watling Street
68 Church of St. Mary. Aldermary
69 Church of St. Swithin. London Stone
70 Church of Saint Mary Abchurch. Abchurch Lane
71 Church of All Hallows. Bread Street
72 St. Mildred's Church. Bread Street
73 Church of St. Mary Magdalene. Old Fish St.
74 Church of St. Nicholas. Cole Abbey. Ditto
75 Church of St. Michael. Paternoster. College Hill
76 St. James's Church. Garlick Hill
77 St. Michaels Church. Queen Street
78 Church of St. Mary Somerset. Thames St.
79 St. Benets Church. Pauls Wharf
80 Church of St. Andrew by the Wardrobe
81 Triangular Tower on Shooters Hill
82 Greenwich Hospital
83 St. Nicholas' Church. Deptford
84 St. Pauls Church. Ditto
85 Chapel in Greenwich Road
86 St. Mary's Church. Rotherhithe
87 St. James's Church. Bermondsey
88 St. Johns Church. Horsleydown
89 St. Olaves Church. Tooley Street
90 The Greenwich. Croydon. Brighton & Dover Railway Termini. Tooley Street
91 St. Saviour's Church. Southwark
92 St. Thomas's. Church and Hospital
93 Church of St. Mary Magdalen. Bermondsey
94 New Church. Peckham
95 St. Mary's Church. Kent Road
96 Trinity Church. Trinity Square. Newington
97 St. George's Church. Blackman Street
98 The District Church of Saint Peter. Sumner Street. Southwark
99 Gas Works
100 Bricklayers' Arms Termini of the Croydon & Dover Railway

This 'balloon view' of London from 1859 looking south was originally published by Banks in 1851

THE RIVER THAMES
CHELSEA BRIDGE
CHELSEA WATER WORKS
CHELSEA HOSPITAL
MILLBANK
Wilton Str
VINCENT SQUARE
REGENT STR
HORSE FERRY RD
MARSHAM ST
EARL ST
WESTMINSTER ABBEY
BROADWAY
BIRD CAGE WALK
ST JAMES'S PARK
THE QUEENS PALACE
CONSTITUTION HILL
Triumphal Arch
Wellington Statue
GREEN PARK
ARABELLA Row
EATON STR
GROSVENOR PLACE
BELGRAVE SQUARE
EATON SQUARE
WILTON PLACE
GEORGE STR
SLOANE SQUARE
SLOANE STREET
HANS PLACE
BROMPTON ROW
ALBERT GATE
BARRACK
Achilles
SERPENTINE
Reservoir
HYDE PARK
PARK LANE
MOUNT STR
BERKELEY SQUARE
SOUTH AUDLEY STR
GROSVENOR SQUARE
NORTH AUDLEY STR
REGENT STREET
QUADRANT
REGENT CIRCUS
OXFORD STREET
OXFORD STR
HYDE PARK CORNER
CONNAUGHT
ORCHARD STR
PORTMAN STR
PORTMAN SQUARE
BAKER STR
CAVENDISH SQUARE

History, Politics and Society

AD

43 Romans invade England.

50 Foundation of *Londinium*.

60 Sack of *Londinium* by Boudicca.

61 *Londinium* rebuilt and designated capital of province.

125 *Londinium* destroyed by fire.

200 *Londinium* designated as capital of Britannia Superior.

457 Britons defeated by mercenaries. *Londinium* disappears from historical record.

604 Mellitus appointed Bishop of London.

842 Viking attack on London: 'Great Slaughter'.

c.871 Danes occupy London. Recaptured by King Alfred (878).

911 Edward takes control of London after Alfred's death.

1016 Cnut captures London, becomes king.

1042 Edward the Confessor becomes king. London made capital of England.

1066 Harold killed at Hastings; William crowned at Westminster Abbey.

1085 Population c. 10-15,000.

1180 Population inside walls c.40,000.

1192 Permission granted for mayor and aldermen with own court.

1207 Archbishop of Canterbury takes up residence at Lambeth.

1215 Magna Carta: Mayor of London one of signatories.

1290 Expulsion of Jews from London ghetto in Old Jewry.

1327 First Common Council of City of London.

1348-9 Black Death epidemic: c.10,000 buried at West Smithfield.

1377 Population c.40,000.

1381 Peasants revolt led by Wat Tyler.

1397 First of Richard Whittington's four terms as Lord Mayor.

Commerce, Industry and Infrastructure

AD

50 Road network begun; Thames bridged; provision of port facilities.

125 New waterfront built.

c.290 London Mint established.

c.640 Gold coins minted in London; the first since Roman times.

899 First mention of Queenhithe.

949 First mention of Billingsgate.

1066 William grants London Charter.

c.1130 Charters establishing liberties.

c.1155 Vintner's Company granted Charter.

1170 Weekly horse fair at Smithfield.

1180 First mention of Goldsmith's Company.

c.1199 First building regulations introduced in the City.

1214 City Charter awarded by King John.

1272 First Craft Guild.

1274 First mention of 'Flete Street'.

c.1290 The Hop and Grapes in Aldgate High St: London's oldest Licensed House.

1358 138 shops on London Bridge.

1358 First Goldsmith's Hall.

1380 First Skinner's Hall.

1382 First Custom House.

1389 River wall built at Tower.

1394 Farringdon wards formed outside the wall.

Building and Architecture

BC

600 Middle Iron Age domestic sites at Rainham, Dewily, Bedfont, Heathrow.

AD

80-125 Building of basilica and forum, governor's palace, public baths, fort.

200 City wall built.

240 Mithraic temple built

c.600 Saxon London built mainly outside walls.

604 St Paul's Cathedral built.

606 St Mary Over Nunnery established on the site of present Southwark Cathedral.

898 Conference of King's Council re restoration of London.

c.1000 Earliest reference to London Bridge.

1067 Building of Tower of London and other castles began.

1089 Bermondsey Abbey founded.

1123 Building of St Bartholomew's Priory and Hospital begun.

1140 Priory of St John established at Clerkenwell.

1140 Nunnery of St Mary's established at Clerkenwell.

1176 Old London Bridge begun

1185 Temple Church consecrated.

1205 St Helen's Nunnery, Bishopsgate.

1212 Southwark Cathedral.

1220 Wakefield Tower at Tower of London begun.

1250 First Gothic arch (at St Bartholomew the Great).

1256 St Paul's Cathedral extended in Gothic style.

1290 Wall extended from Ludgate to Fleet River.

1375 First mention of Staple Inn.

Institutions and Popular Culture

c.1050 St James's Leper Hospital.

1148 St Katharine's Hospital founded by Queen Matilda.

1180 Leisure activities include cock fights, archery, wrestling, skating on Thames when frozen

1213 St Thomas's Hospital established at Southwark.

1247 Bethel Hospital for insane established.

1253 Elephant given to King and kept in Tower of London.

1272 Baynard's Castle handed over to Dominican Friars.

1297 Pig-styes banned from streets.

1371 Foundation of Charterhouse at Clerkenwell.

Science and the Arts

c.1173 Fitz Stephen, London historian, gave first description of the city.

1180 'Miracle Plays' performed at Clerkenwell.

1245 Westminster Abbey began to acquire art treasures.

1253 Sculptured bosses carved in Westminster Abbey.

1349-52 Stained glass windows made for St Stephen's Chapel, Westminster Palace.

1377 Effigy of Edward III by John Orchard placed in Westminster Abbey.

1396 Portrait of Richard ll painted for Westminster Abbey.

History, Politics and Society

415 Henry V leads victory parade after Agincourt (London Bridge to St Paul's).

422 First records of the Honourable Society of Lincoln's Inn.

440 First reference to the Honourable Society of the Inner Temple.

535 Sir Thomas More executed at the Tower of London.

550 Population c.80,000.

580 Proclamation forbidding housebuilding within three miles of any London gate.

583 Population c.120,000.

603 Outbreak of plague: 25,000 deaths.

605 Guy Fawkes' 'Gunpowder Plot'.

630 Population c.200,000.

642 Royalist Army defeated at Turnham Green.

649-60 Charles I executed in Whitehall; the Commonwealth declared.

662 Royal Society founded.

665 Bubonic Plague: c.70,000 deaths.

666 Great Fire of London.

700 Population over 500,000.

702-5 Buckingham House built.

Commerce, Industry and Infrastructure

1400 Billingsgate Market granted its charter.

1422 111 crafts recorded in London.

1425 First Draper's Company Hall.

1479 Billingsgate Market rebuilt by Hanseatic merchants.

1501 First printing press set up in Fleet Street.

1513 Foundation of Royal Dockyard at Woolwich and Deptford.

1554 First mention of The George Inn, Southwark.

1566 Royal Exchange instituted by Thomas Gresham.

1584 First mention of Ye Olde Cheshire Cheese Inn, Fleet St.

1593 Horse-driven water pump installed near Queenhithe.

1599 First dry dock built at Rotherhithe.

1613 Opening of 38-mile New River (from Herts to Clerkenwell) –London's main water supply.

1614 East India Docks built at Blackwall.

1651 Hay's Wharf opened.

1656 1,153 taverns in the city.

1663 First toll roads.

1667 Fleet Canal and Thames Quay project.

1669 Regular 'Flying Coaches' London – Oxford–Cambridge.

1680 'Penny Post' introduced.

1694 Foundation of the Bank of England.

Building and Architecture

1411 First Guildhall built.

1414 Shene Palace built by Henry V.

1490 Gatehouse, Lambeth Palace.

1512-19 Henry VII Chapel at Westminster Abbey.

1523 Bridewell Palace.

1547 Somerset Palace begun.

1571 Middle Temple Hall.

1616-35 Queen's House, Greenwich.

1619-25 Banqueting House, Whitehall.

1631 Kew Palace.

1635 Piazza, Covent Garden.

1665 Southampton Square, now Bloomsbury Square.

1670-7 College of Arms.

1670-1700 Rebuilding of City churches: 50 by Wren, one by Hawksmoor.

1671-77 The Monument.

1675-1711 St Paul's Cathedral rebuilt.

1698 Berkeley Square.

c.1700 Bedford Row.

1701 The Synagogue of Spanish and Portuguese Jews.

1711 Marlborough House.

1712 St Paul's Chapter House.

1714 St Alphage, Greenwich.

Institutions and Popular Culture

1509 St Paul's School founded by John Colette.

1539 St Bartholomew Hospital refounded after dissolution of monasteries.

c.1550 First use of private coaches.

1552 Christ's Hospital founded.

c.1560 First proper map of London by Ralph Agas.

1572 Harrow School founded.

1579 Gresham College founded.

1598 John Stow complains of 'terrible number of coaches, world run on wheels'.

1608 Great Frost Fair on Thames; taverns and football.

1611 Charterhouse School founded by Thomas Sutton.

1625 First Hackney carriages permitted to ply for hire.

1634 Sedan chairs for hire.

1637 Hyde Park opened for public use.

1637 50 licensed coaches (by 1652, 200).

1648-9 Frost Fair on Thames; printing press set up on ice.

1676 Foundation of Chelsea Physic Garden.

1682 Foundation of Royal Hospital, Chelsea (Wren)

c.1685 Sadler's Music House Theatre (now Sadler's Wells).

Science and the Arts

1476 First printing press set up in Westminster by William Caxton.

1510 Birth of Thomas Tallis, composer (died 1585).

1552 Birth of Edmund Spencer, poet and writer (died 1599).

1573 Birth of John Dunne, poet and Dean of St Paul's (died 1631).

1577 First London theatre built at Shoreditch by James Burbage.

1587 Rose Theatre built in Southwark.

1598 John Stow's *Survey of London* published.

1599 Globe Theatre built in Southwark.

1620 Birth of John Evelyn, diarist and writer (died 1706).

1633 Birth of Samuel Pepys, civil servant and diarist (died 1703).

1658 Birth of Henry Purcell, musician (died 1695).

1675-6 Foundation of the Royal Observatory, Greenwich.

1697 Birth of William Hogarth, artist (died 1764).

1705 Her Majesty's Theatre.

History, Politics and Society

1720 The 'South Sea Bubble'.

1732 Sir Robert Walpole offered 10 Downing St as official residence.

1751 Licensing Act.

1762 Westminster Paving and Lighting Act.

1767 Houses in city numbered for first time.

1780 Gordon Riots: c.850 killed.

1811 Population c.l,000,000.

1812 Prime Minister Spencer Perceval assassinated at House of Commons.

1825 Gallows and turnpike removed from Tyburn.

1829 Metropolitan Police Act.

Commerce, Industry and Infrastructure

1720 Charters granted to the Royal Exchange Assurance and London Assurance companies.

1729 2,484 private coaches, and 1,100 coaches for hire; 22,636 horses in London.

1734 Lloyd's List established as regular weekly publication.

1747 Coal Exchange opened.

1756 600 stage coaches licensed to towns within 19 miles of London; fixed routes from 123 stations in London.

1761 New Road from Paddington to Islington (first London bypass, now Euston Road).

1780 London bankers issued their own notes.

1785 First publication of *The Times*.

1794 Grand Junction Canal opened.

1798 7,000 watchmakers listed in Clerkenwell.

1802 West India Docks opened.

1802 Stock Exchange opened on new site.

1803 Surrey Iron Railway (Wandsworth–Croydon, horse drawn): first public railway.

1803 Dickens and Jones department store.

1803 Commercial Road opened: improved access to docks.

1807 Installation of gas lighting in Pall Mall.

1807–9 Royal Mint opened.

1815 First steamboat service on Thames.

1817 New Custom House.

1819 Burlington shopping arcade, Piccadilly.

1820 Regent's Canal opened.

1827 First publication of *Evening Standard*.

1828 Covent Garden Market.

1829 General Post Office opened.

1829 First omnibus service: Paddington–City.

Building and Architecture

1717 Cavendish Square.

1720 Hanover Square.

1729 Chiswick House.

1729 Marble Hill House, Twickenham.

1730 St George's, Bloomsbury.

1730 St Paul's, Deptford.

1735 The Treasury.

1739-53 The Mansion House.

1750-8 Horse Guards.

1750 Westminster Bridge.

1758 Kew Palace.

1758 Horse Guards, Whitehall.

1766 City Wall demolished and removal of gates begun.

1769 Kenwood House.

1772-4 Royal Society of Arts.

1775 Boodle's Club, St James's.

1776-86 Somerset House.

1778 Brook's Club, St James's

1786 Osterley Park House.

1788 White's Club, St. James's.

1789 The facade of Guildhall.

1802-3 Albany Chambers, Piccadilly.

1804 Russell Square.

1806 Sir John Soane's House, Lincoln's Inn Fields.

1824 Royal College of Physicians.

1824-31 London Bridge rebuilt.

1825 All Soul's, Langham Place.

1827-33 Carlton House Terrace.

1828 Marble Arch.

1829 Constitution Arch.

1829 Travellers' Club.

Institutions and Popular Culture

1715 Geffrye Museum (built as almshouses)

1718 Maypole removed from front of Somerset House.

1720 Westminster Hospital opened.

1722 Guy's Hospital founded.

1733 The Serpentine created in Hyde Park.

1739 Foundling Hospital, founded by Thomas Coram.

1741 London Hospital founded.

1759 The Royal Botanic Gardens, Kew founded.

1784 Balloon ascent from Artillery Ground, Finsbury.

1805 Moorfields Eye Hospital founded.

1818 Charing Cross Hospital founded.

1819 Brixton Prison opened.

1819 Bedford College for Women founded.

1828 University College, Gower Street founded.

Science and the Arts

1717 Birth of David Garrick, actor (died 1779).

1720 Theatre Royal, Haymarket.

1728 Birth of Oliver Goldsmith, writer (died 1774).

1732 Covent Garden Theatre (destroyed by fire 1808).

1746 Visit of Antonio Canaletto, Italian artist and painter of London views.

1755 Dr Samuel Johnson published his *Great Dictionary*

1757 Birth of William Blake, poet and mystic (died 1827).

1759 British Museum opened.

1763 James Boswell, biographer, meets Dr Johnson.

1768 Foundation of Royal Academy.

1776 Birth of John Constable, artist (buried Hampstead 1837).

1778 Birth of William Hazlitt, writer (died 1830).

1784 Birth of James Leigh Hunt, poet (died 1859).

1792 Birth of George Cruikshank engraver for Charles Dickens (died 1878).

1802 'On Westminster Bridge' sonnet by William Wordsworth.

1806 Birth of John Stuart Mill, philosopher (died 1873).

1809 Covent Garden Theatre rebuilt after fire (Smirke).

1816 Keats' house built, Hampstead.

1821 Haymarket Theatre opened.

1823 Royal Academy of Music opened.

1824 National Gallery founded.

1827-8 Zoological Gardens in Regent's Park opened.

1829 Cruickshank's 'March of Bricks' cartoon illustrates London's growth.

istory, Politics nd Society

832 Cholera epidemic.

835 Animal fighting made llegal.

837 Buckingham Palace ecomes permanent London esidence of the Court.

837 Typhus epidemic.

845 Mass meeting of Chartists n Kennington Common.

848-9 Major cholera epidemic.

850 Board of Health report on holera epidemic of 1848–9 and upply of water to metropolis.

853 Smoke Abatement Act.

853-4 Cholera epidemic.

857 Thames Conservancy Act.

858 'The Great Stink': pollution n the Thames.

859 Metropolitan Drinking ountain Association founded.

860 Metropolis Gas Act.

860 London Trades, Council ounded.

865 Foundation of the Salvation rmy in East End.

866 Last major outbreak of holera, 5,915 deaths in Poplar.

866 Sanitation Act.

868 Toll gates abolished.

868 Last public execution at ewgate Prison.

1870 School Board of London stablished.

1878 Epping Forest acquired by ity of London Corporation.

1885 Highgate Woods acquired y City of London Corporation.

1888 London County Council created.

1890 Housing Act enabling the LCC to clear slums.

1899 London Government Act: 28 new metropolitan boroughs created.

Commerce, Industry and Infrastructure

1834 Hansom Cabs introduced.

1836 First passenger railway in London: London–Greenwich.

1837 Euston station opened.

1838 Paddington station opened.

1840 Penny Post introduced.

1841 Fenchurch Street station opened.

1843 Thames Tunnel opened.

1848 Waterloo station opened.

1851-2 King's Cross Station opened.

1852 Poplar Docks opened.

1853 Harrod's store opened.

1855 Royal Victoria Docks opened.

1855 Metropolitan Board of Works created.

1863 Metropolitan Railway opened first Underground.

1863-9 Holborn Viaduct.

1864 First London bus with stairs.

1864 Charing Cross Station opened.

1864-70 Victoria Embankment.

1866 Cannon St Station opened.

1867-72 St Pancras Station.

1868 Millwall Docks opened.

1868 New Smithfield Market opened.

1868 Abbey Mills Pumping Station opened (Bazalgette).

1869 First Sainsbury's opened in Drury Lane.

1869 Last warship built at Royal Navy Dockyard, Woolwich.

1871 Lloyd's Incorporated by Act of Parliament.

1874 Liverpool Street Station opened.

1876 First arrival of refrigerated meat from abroad (America).

1879 First Telephone Exchange, Lombard St (ten subscribers).

1880 Royal Albert Docks opened.

1886 Tilbury Docks opened.

1886 Shaftesbury Avenue opened.

1888 First issue of the *Financial Times*.

1890 First 'Tube' railway: City and South London.

1897 Queen Victoria's Diamond Jubilee procession.

1899 Savoy Hotel and Theatre built.

Building and Architecture

1837-52 Houses of Parliament rebuilt after fire.

1841 St George's Roman Catholic Cathedral, Southwark.

1843 Trafalgar Square.

1848-51 Army and Navy Club.

1851-96 Public Record Office.

1853 Brompton Oratory.

1859 Floral Hall Covent Garden.

1862-4 First Peabody Trust buildings erected.

1866 Leighton House.

1868 Royal Albert Hall.

1871-82 Royal Courts of Justice, Strand.

1875-81 Bedford Park Garden Suburb.

1878 'Cleopatra's Needle' erected on Victoria Embankment.

1891 New Scotland Yard.

Institutions and Popular Culture

1831 King's College founded.

1833 London Fire Brigade established.

1834 University College hospital founded.

1835 Madam Tussaud's Waxworks opened.

1836 University of London founded.

1837 King's College Hospital founded.

1839 River Police formed.

1839 Highgate Cemetery opened.

1841 Last frost fair on Thames.

1842 Pentonville Prison opened.

1845 Victoria Park opened.

1845 Surrey County Cricket Club founded.

1849 Wandsworth Prison opened.

1852 Holloway Prison opened.

1853 Battersea Park opened.

1860 Battersea Dogs Home founded.

1863 Middlesex County Cricket Club formed.

1865 Metropolitan Fire Brigade formed.

1869 Southwark Park and Finsbury Park opened.

1873 Alexandra Palace opened.

1874 Wormwood Scrubs Prison opened.

1877 First Wimbledon Tennis tournament.

1880 First ever Cricket Test, England v. Australia, at the Oval.

1882 Central London Polytechnic, Regent St founded.

1895 First motor bus in London.

1897 Blackwall Tunnel opened.

Science and the Arts

1833 Soane Museum founded.

1834 Birth of William Morris, artist, writer, designer (died 1896).

1836 Birth of Walter Besant, London historian (died 1901).

1837 Royal College of Art founded.

1838 National Gallery completed (Wilkins).

1842 British Museum new building begun (opened 1847).

1851 Great Exhibition held in the 'Crystal Palace', Hyde Park.

1858 Alhambra Theatre opened.

1859 National Portrait Gallery opened.

1866 Birth of H. G. Wells, writer (died 1946).

1867 Birth of John Galsworthy, writer (died 1933).

1870 Royal Albert Hall opened.

1875 Bethnal Green Museum opened.

1876 Albert Memorial completed.

1881 Greenwich recognized as meridian.

1881 Natural History Museum opened (Waterhouse).

1883 Royal College of Music founded.

1888 Shaftesbury Theatre opened.

1893 Statue of Eros unveiled at Piccadilly Circus.

1895 First Promenade concert.

1897 Tate Gallery opened.

History, Politics and Society

1902 Metropolitan Water Board created.

1908-33 London County Hall built.

1908 Port of London Authority created.

1911 Population of Greater London c.7,252,000.

1915-18 German Zeppelins bomb London.

1919 'The Cenotaph' war memorial unveiled in Whitehall.

1920 'Unknown soldier' buried in Westminster Abbey.

1922 First Queen Charlotte Ball for debutantes.

1926 The General Strike.

1929 Local Government Act: LCC takes over hospitals and schools.

1931 Population of Greater London c.8,203,000.

1933 London Transport Act (Board formed).

1935 'Greenbelt' established by LCC.

1936 Jarrow unemployed march to London.

1939 Population of Greater London c.8.700,000.

1940 Air attacks on London docks.

1940 Second great fire of London: 30,000 incendiary bombs.

1941 National Fire Service formed.

1944 First flying bomb hits London.

1946 New Towns Act: eight new towns around London.

1948 First immigrants arrive from Jamaica.

1951 King George VI opens Festival of Britain.

1952 4,000 deaths attributed to 'smog' lasting several days.

1953 Coronation of Elizabeth II at Westminster.

1955 City of London declared 'smokeless zone'.

1957 Survey shows no fish in Thames from Richmond to Tilbury (40 miles).

Commerce, Industry and Infrastructure

1901 First electric trams in London.

1902 Spitalfields Market rebuilt.

1904 First double decker bus running in London.

1905 First telephone box in London.

1906 Bakerloo Line opened.

1906 Piccadilly Line opened.

1907 Northern Line opened.

1907 First Taxicabs in London.

1908 Kingsway Tram Tunnel opened.

1908 Rotherhithe Rd Tunnel opened.

1909 Selfridge's department store, Oxford St opened.

1911-22 Port of London Authority Headquarters erected (Cooper).

1912 Whiteley's department store, Bayswater, opened.

1921 King George V Docks opened.

1924 First Woolworth's store in London, Oxford St.

1924 British Empire Exhibition at Wembley.

1925 Great West Rd opened.

1926 London's first traffic roundabout at Parliament Square.

1927 Park Lane Hotel opened.

1930 Dorchester Hotel, Park Lane opened.

1930–55 Battersea Power Station.

1931 Liberty's department store, Regent St opened.

1931 Shell Mex Offices, Strand.

1932 Cockfosters, Arnos Grove, and Manor House Underground Stations (Holden).

1937 Earls Court Exhibition Hall.

1944 Port of London used as base for invasion of Europe.

1947 Last horse-drawn cab licence given up.

1947 King George VI Reservoir, Staines inaugurated.

1951 London Foreign Exchange Market reopened after 12 years.

1952 Last London tram journey for nearly 50 years.

1953 London Airport, Heathrow, opened.

1956 London Gold Market reopened after 15 years.

Building and Architecture

1899-1906 The War Office, Whitehall.

1903 Westminster Cathedral.

1905 Kingsway & Aldwych opened.

1905-8 The Quadrant, Regent St.

1907 Central Criminal Court (The Old Bailey).

1908 Rhodesia House, Strand.

c.1910 Duane Housing Estate, Hammersmith (LCC).

1910 Admiralty Arch.

1930 Y.W.C.A. Hostel, Great Russell St.

1931 Daily Express Offices, Fleet St.

1932 R.I.B.A., Portland Place.

1935 South Africa House, Trafalgar Square.

1936 Senate House, University of London.

1937 Bow Street Police Court.

1937 LCC Fire Brigade Headquarters.

1940 The Citadel, the Mall.

1955 Trade Union Congress HQ, Great Russell St (sculpture by Epstein)

1957-79 The Barbican Complex.

Institutions and Popular Culture

1904 London Fire Brigade formed.

1908 Twickenham Stadium opened.

1908 Olympic Games held at White City.

1910 London Palladium, Argyll St opened.

1911 'Pearly King' Association formed.

1914 Cinemas in LCC area total 266.

1921 Last horse-drawn fire engine in London.

1922 BBC begins broadcasting from Savoy Hill.

1923 First F.A. Cup Final at Wembley Stadium.

1927 First London greyhound track, White City Stadium.

1929 Dominion Theatre opened (became cinema in 1932).

1929 Tower Pier opened.

1930 Finsbury Park Astoria Cinema opened.

1930 First Chelsea Flower Show.

1930 Leicester Square Theatre opened (became cinema 1968).

1931 London public buildings floodlit for first time.

1932 Arsenal Stadium, Highbury, built.

1932 BBC moved to new offices in Portland Place.

1937 Empress Hall Ice Rink opened.

1940 Savoy Cinema, Holloway Road, opened.

1948 First jazz club opened by Ronnie Scott and John Dank worth.

1948 Olympic Games held at Wembley Stadium.

1951 National Film Theatre, South Bank.

1953 First 'coffee bar', 'the Mika'. opened on Frith St.

1955 'Bazaar': the first boutique, Kings Rd, Chelsea.

1958 The London Planetarium opened.

Science and the Arts

1900 Wallace Collection opened.

1901 Horniman Museum, Forest Hill opened.

1902 *Life and Labour of People of London published* by Charles Booth

1904 London Symphony Orchestra founded.

1904 London Coliseum Theatre opened.

1905 Strand Theatre opened.

1905 Aldwych Theatre opened.

1907 Queen's Theatre opened.

1909 Science Museum founded.

1911 Queen Victoria Memorial unveiled by George V in the Mall

1911 London Museum founded.

1914 Opening of King Edward VII Galleries at British Museum.

1926 J Logie Baird gave first demonstration of television in Frith Street, Soho.

1928 Discovery of penicillin by Alexander Fleming at St Mary's Hospital, Paddington.

1930 Whitehall Theatre opened.

1931 Windmill Theatre opened.

1932 London Philharmonic Orchestra founded by Sir Thomas Beecham.

1933 Open-air theatre, Regent's Park opened.

1934 National Maritime Museum Greenwich founded.

1935 Geological Museum, South Kensington founded.

1936 First regular television service from Alexandra Palace.

1948 'Eros' reinstated at Piccadilly Circus.

1951 Royal Festival Hall, South Bank opened.

1954 'Temple of Mithras' excavation at Bucklersbury.

1955 BBC TV Centre opened at White City.

1957 Imperial College of Science building, Kensington opened.

1959 Mermaid Theatre, Puddle Dock opened.

History, Politics and Society

1962 Commonwealth Institute, Kensington opened.

1965 Formation of Greater London Council to replace LCC.

1968 Large anti-Vietnam war demonstration in London.

1973 Statue of Sir Winston Churchill unveiled.

1974 First salmon caught in Thames for 100 years.

1976 Population of Greater London c.7,000,000.

1981 London Docklands Development Corporation formed.

1981 London Wildlife Trust formed.

1981 Greater London Enterprise Board formed.

1986 Greater London Council abolished.

1987 Fire at King's Cross underground station.

1989 Marchioness pleasure boat disaster on Thames.

1990 Population of Greater London c.6,500,000,

1992 IRA bombs Baltic Exchange.

1995 Aldwych bus bombed by IRA.

1996 Canary Wharf tower bombed by IRA.

2000 Establishment of the Greater London Authority.

2000 Election of Ken Livingstone as first Mayor of London.

2001 London's population 7,172,036.

2002 Mayors directly elected in boroughs of Hackney, Lewisham, Newham.

2003 UK's biggest street demonstration against Iraq War.

2005 Suicide bombers kill 52 on 7 July.

2008 Boris Johnson elected Mayor of London.

Commerce, Industry and Infrastructure

1960-64 Post Office Tower.

1961-3 Hilton Hotel, Park Lane, opened.

1966 Carnaby St Market.

1968 Closure of London and St Katharine Docks.

1968 Euston Station opened.

1968 Victoria Line opened.

1974 Covent Garden Market moved to Nine Elms.

1976 Brent Cross Shopping Centre opened.

1979 Jubilee Line opened.

1981 Royal Docks closed, last of London's docks to close.

1982 Enterprise Zone established in London docks.

1982 Billingsgate Market moved to Isle of Dogs.

1982 Thames Flood Barrier at Woolwich completed.

1986 Big Bang in City.

1986 Terminal Four completed at Heathrow Airport.

1987 Docklands Light Railway opened.

1987 London City Airport opened at Docklands.

1991 Spitalfields Market moved to Leyton.

1991 Queen Elizabeth II Bridge opened.

1994 Eurostar terminal completed at Waterloo station.

1999 Jubilee Line extension completed.

2000 Croydon Tramlink opens.

2003 Congestion Charge Zone established in central London.

2007 St Pancras International opened.

2007 Banking crisis begins.

2008 Terminal 5, Heathrow, opened

2009 Work on Crossrail began.

2010 Government rejects third runway at Heathrow.

2010 Bicycle sharing scheme started ('Boris bikes')

Building and Architecture

1961 United States Embassy, Grosvenor Square.

1962 Shell Centre, South Bank.

1963 Vickers Tower, Millbank.

1968 'Ronan Point' Tower Block collapses. Fatalities.

1978 London Central Mosque, Regent's Park.

1982 New British Library building founded.

1986 Lloyd's Building opened.

1987 Princess of Wales Conservatory, Kew Gardens.

1988 New Chapter House, Southwark Cathedral.

1989 Great storm causes much damage in London.

1990 Canary Wharf tower completed.

1991 Broadgate Centre completed at Liverpool Street station.

1995 Conversion of County Hall into flats.

1998 Construction of London Eye approved.

2000 Millennium Dome opened at Greenwich (now the O2)

2002 Millennium Bridge opened permanently.

2002 City Hall opened.

2003 Laban dance centre, Deptford wins Stirling Prize.

2004 Swiss Re building 'The Gherkin' opened.

2006 Broadcasting House extension opened.

2010 The Shard in Southwark became Britain's tallest building.

2011 Midland Hotel St Pancras reopened

Institutions and Popular Culture

1961 First Notting Hill Carnival.

1964 The Beatles recorded at EMI Studios, St John's Wood.

1968 Rolling Stones gave first open-air concert in Hyde Park

1968 London Weekend Television started.

1970 Radio London started.

1973 LBC began.

1973 Capital Radio began.

1985 'Band Aid' Concert, Wembley Stadium; 72,000 attend.

1987 First London Parade on new year's Day

1991 Open-air concert at Hyde Park.

1996 Proms in the Park started.

1997 First Thames Festival held.

2000 British Museum Great Court opened.

2005 2012 Olympics awarded.

2006 Emirates Stadium opened.

2007 New Wembley Stadium opened.

2008 Walthamstow greyhound stadium closed.

2011 Duke and Duchess of Cambridge married at Westminster Abbey

Science and the Arts

1961-2 Royal College of Art, Kensington Gore opened.

1967 Queen Elizabeth Hall, South Bank opened.

1968 Hayward Gallery, South Bank opened.

1969 Greenwich Theatre opened.

1970 The Young Vic Theatre opened.

1973 British Library formed.

1975 New Museum of London opened.

1976 National Theatre, South Bank opened.

1980 London Transport Museum opened at Covent Garden.

1982 Barbican Arts Centre opened.

1988 Museum of the Moving Image opened on South Bank.

1989 Design Museum opened on Butlers Wharf.

1990 Courtauld Gallery moved to Somerset House.

1991 Sainsbury Wing opened at National Gallery.

1993 Quaglino's opened.

1993 Buckingham Palace opened to general public.

1996 Millennium site confirmed at Greenwich.

1997 New Globe Theatre opened on Bankside.

1999 New British Library building at St Pancras completed.

2000 Tate Modern opened.

2004 University of the Arts, London established.

2008 Saatchi Gallery moved to the Duke of York's HQ, Chelsea.

2008 Rose Theatre, Kingston opened.

2011 Construction of the Francis Crick Institute (UK Centre for Medical Research) in Camden commenced.

THE BOROUGHS OF GREATER LONDON

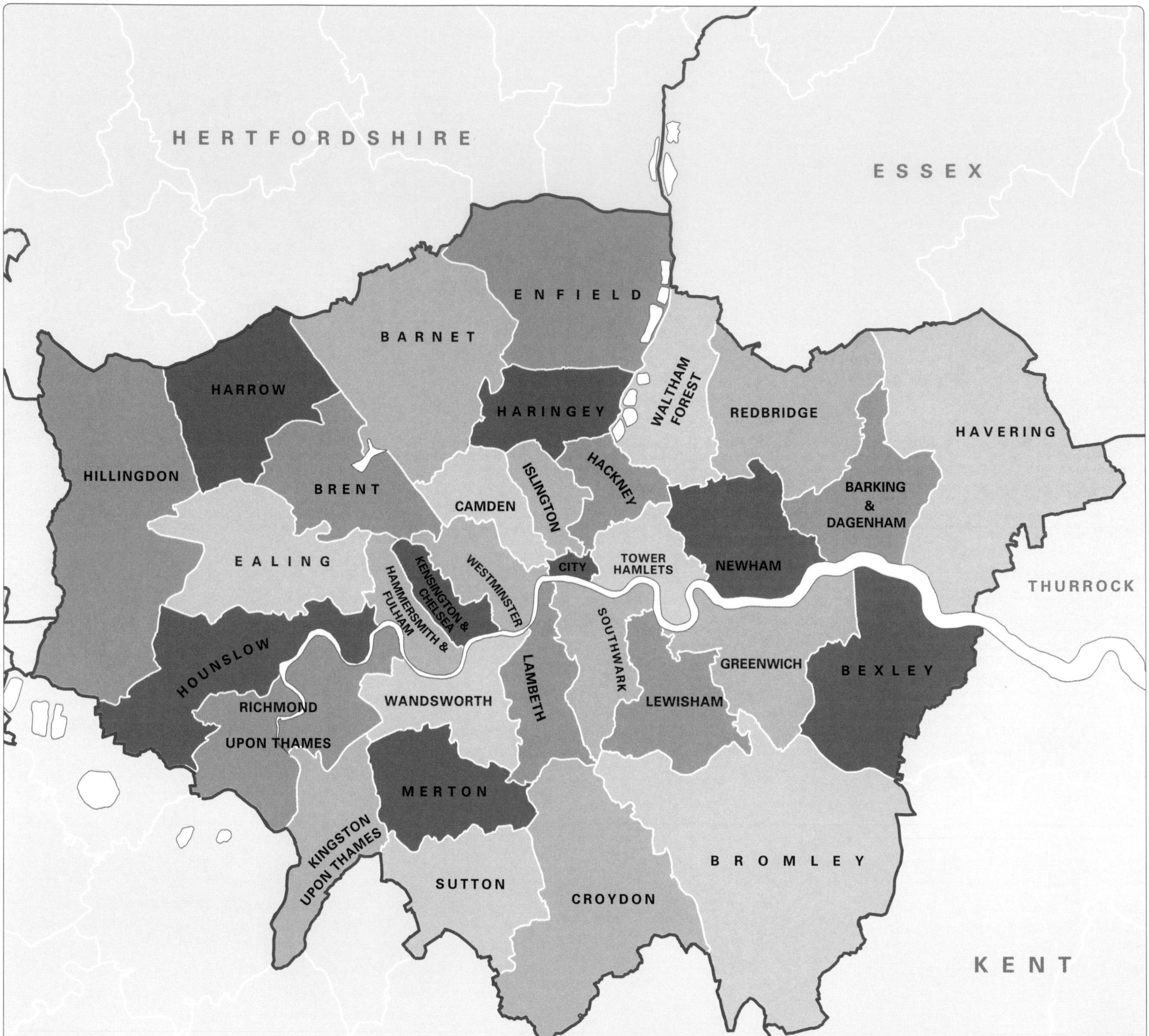
HERTFORDSHIRE
ESSEX
ENFIELD
BARNET
HARROW
HARINGEY
WALTHAM FOREST
REDBRIDGE
HAVERING
HILLINGDON
BRENT
CAMDEN
ISLINGTON
HACKNEY
BARKING & DAGENHAM
EALING
KENSINGTON & CHELSEA
HAMMERSMITH & FULHAM
WESTMINSTER
CITY
TOWER HAMLETS
NEWHAM
THURROCK
HOUNSLOW
SOUTHWARK
GREENWICH
BEXLEY
RICHMOND UPON THAMES
WANDSWORTH
LAMBETH
LEWISHAM
MERTON
KINGSTON UPON THAMES
SUTTON
CROYDON
BROMLEY
KENT
SURREY

THE GOVERNMENT OF LONDON

Various forms of local government existed for the City of London before the Norman Conquest. William I granted a charter to the city and administration was through a Court of Alderman, a Common Council and a Common Hall. The administration was headed by an elected mayor (from around 1283, a Lord Mayor), with many officials. In addition much influence was wielded by the various livery companies, initially protective craft guilds – such as Drapers or Fishmongers. With the rapid growth of London, however, increasing numbers of people lived outside the restricted boundaries of the City of London in parishes in the counties of Essex, Middlesex, Hertfordshire, Surrey, and Kent. While the City of London expanded into Southwark in 1327, various villages and related bodies administered the rest of London. These patchwork arrangements were thoroughly overhauled in 1888 when London County Council (LCC) was created, with, by 1900, twenty-eight metropolitan boroughs operating within the council area. County boroughs and municipal boroughs were created in the counties surrounding the LCC.

As the urban spread of London continued there was a need for further reform and in 1965 the Greater London Council (GLC) was created with thirty-three authorities underneath it, including the City of London. Primarily for political rather than administrative reasons the GLC was abolished in 1986 and all the boroughs effectively became unitary authorities solely responsible for the services within their borough, a process accelerated when the Inner London Education Authority was wound up in 1990. London thus became the only capital city not to have any central administration – the Conservative government even ensured that County Hall, the headquarters of the LCC and then the GLC, which sat across the Thames from the Houses of Parliament, was sold to the private sector so that it could never again become a political centre for London. In 2000 the Labour government established a Greater London Authority with the London Assembly and a directly elected Mayor of London; its strategic responsibilities included powers over policing, transport, economic planning and emergency services.

There are now four different levels of democratic government within London:

Boroughs
The Mayor of London and the London Assembly
Members of Parliament
Members of the European Parliament

The Boroughs

All London boroughs (except the City of London, which has a unique structure) hold elections every four years for councillors who represent a particular ward (a specified geographical area of the council). In the 2010 elections more than 6,000 candidates fought for 1,861 council seats. In those elections Labour ended up controlling 17 boroughs, the Conservatives 11 and the Liberal Democrats 2. In two councils there was no overall control. In addition, in the same elections mayors were directly elected for the boroughs of Hackney, Lewisham and Newham, the only boroughs that have agreed to have an elected mayor.

The Mayor of London and the London Assembly

The Mayor of London is directly elected by all London residents every four years. The 2012 election is the fourth for this particular position. The first mayor was Ken Livingstone, former leader of the GLC before it was abolished. He won the first election as an independent and his second representing Labour. He lost in 2008 to the Conservative Boris Johnson. The mayor and the administrative Greater London Authority are supervised by the 25-member London Assembly; 14 members are directly elected from very large constituencies (usually covering two boroughs) while 11 are elected London-wide by proportional representation. Organizations responsible to the mayor include Transport for London, the Metropolitan Police Authority, the London Development Agency and the London Fire and Emergency Planning Authority. Both the mayor and the Assembly are based in City Hall, on the south bank of the Thames, close to Tower Bridge.

Members of Parliament

Greater London is currently represented by 73 MPs. At the 2010 election, 38 Labour, 28 Conservative and 7 Liberal Democrats were returned. Under the current review of the size of constituencies, the Electoral Commission expects the number of MPs to be reduced to 68.

Members of the European Parliament

Greater London directly elects a group of eight members by proportional representation every five years. At the election in 2009 the elected members were Conservatives 3, Labour 2, UK Independence Party 1, Green Party 1 and Liberal Democrat 1.

City Hall, designed by Foster + Partners, on the south bank of the Thames in Southwark

BARKING AND DAGENHAM

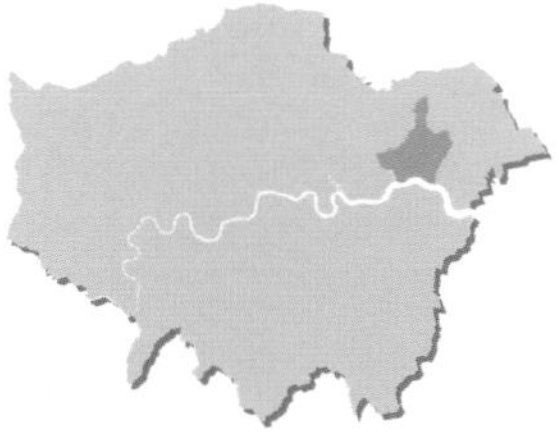

Population	175,600
Area	37 sq. km
Population density	4,745 per sq. km
Area of green space	12 sq. km
Jobs in borough	47,000
Average house price	£167,000

The borough of Barking and Dagenham takes its name from its two main settlements, both dating from Saxon times. Barking ('a settlement of the family of Berica') is located by Barking Creek, a major inlet on the Thames, and until the mid-19th century, home to a significant fishing fleet. It was also the site of Barking Abbey, a Benedictine nunnery founded in AD 666, and, prior to its dissolution in 1539 and subsequent destruction, one of the largest and wealthiest in Britain. All that remains is the 15th-century Curfew Tower, prominently depicted on the borough's coat of arms. Dagenham ('homestead of Daecca') remained a small village until the late 19th century development of docks.

The borough was formed in 1965 out of the Essex municipal boroughs of Barking and Dagenham (excluding a small area that went to the borough of Redbridge). Originally just called Barking, the borough's current name was adopted in 1980. The area changed dramatically after World War I. In 1919 the London County Council decided to build 24,000 houses in the Becontree Estate. Building was completed in 1934 but has since been extended, making it one of Europe's largest housing estates. Many of the residents were skilled workers from the East End, and found employment in the new industries that were established locally, most significantly in the Dagenham plant of the Ford Motor Company, the largest integrated car plant in the world when it opened in 1931. Car production ceased in 2002, but it is Ford's major centre for diesel engine manufacture, producing over a million engines a year and employing 4,000 people.

Reflecting the industrial heritage of the area, over 16 per cent of the jobs in the borough are in manufacturing, compared with a London average of 4 per cent. By contrast only 13 per cent of jobs are in finance, IT and other business activities compared with a London average of nearly 35 per cent. Traditionally an area of the skilled white working class, there has been a recent change in the population mix – in 1991 just under 7 per cent of the population were from ethnic minorities, but this is now estimated to be around 25 per cent.

The borough has also seen rapid population growth, with a population of 205,000 expected by 2020. The regeneration of the southern part of the borough through the London Riverside development scheme will help tackle social, health and economic problems – in 2007 it was the eleventh most deprived local authority in England.

FAMOUS FOR

Captain James Cook married Elizabeth Batts at St Margaret's Church in **Barking** in 1762.

Dick Turpin and his gang attacked **Longbridge Farm** in 1734, taking the family hostage and stealing their possessions. They allegedly threw money to bystanders as they escaped through Barking. The site of the farm became the Barking

Eastbury Manor House

campus of the University of East London until 2006 and is now used for housing.

Elizabeth Fry, the great campaigner for the improvement of conditions for women prisoners, was a Quaker minister attached to the **Barking** circuit, and was buried in 1845 in a Quaker burial ground at Barking next to the Meeting House (now the Gurdwara Singh Sabha London East Sikh Temple).

The Ford diesel engine plant at **Dagenham** is powered by three wind turbines.

The **Dagenham Breach** was an area of water and marshland originally formed when the Thames burst its banks in 1707. Much of the Breach has been reclaimed but the remaining ponds are now a nature reserve. In 1824, Elizabeth Fry's daughter described the scene: '… when night closed in over the wild marshy scenery, the cries of the waterbirds, the rustling of the reed beds, the strange sounds of the shipping on the river, gave the place an indescribable charm.'

Eastbury Manor House is a distinguished three-storey brick manor house built in 1557, where, according to Daniel Defoe, 'the Gunpowder Treason Plot was first contrived'.

The **1968 strike** of female sewing machinists at Ford's Dagenham plant over equal grading with their male counterparts directly led to the Equal Pay Act in 1970.

FAMOUS PEOPLE

Adam of Barking, Benedictine monk and poet, born Barking, *c.* 1176.

James Paroissien, military surgeon and diplomat, Brigadier-General, Peruvian Army, born Barking, 1784.

Sir Alfred (Alf) Ramsay, England football manager, born Dagenham, 1920.

Robert (Bobby) Moore, footballer, captain England 1966 World Cup winning team, born Barking, 1941.

Terence (Terry) Venables, football player and manager, born Dagenham, 1943.

Sandie Shaw (born Sandra Ann Goodrich), pop singer, first British winner of the Eurovision Song Contest, born Dagenham, 1947.

Stephen William (Billy) Bragg, musician and political activist, born Barking, 1957.

John Terry, footballer, England captain, born Barking, 1980.

John Bartholomew, Gazetteer of the British Isles (1887)
BARKING – *par. and market town, S. Essex, 2 miles N. of river Thames, 7 miles E. of London by rail – 12,307 ac., pop, 16,848; town, 3814 ac., pop. 9203. Market-day, Saturday. It has a large jute factory and other manufacturing works; there are also extensive market gardens.*

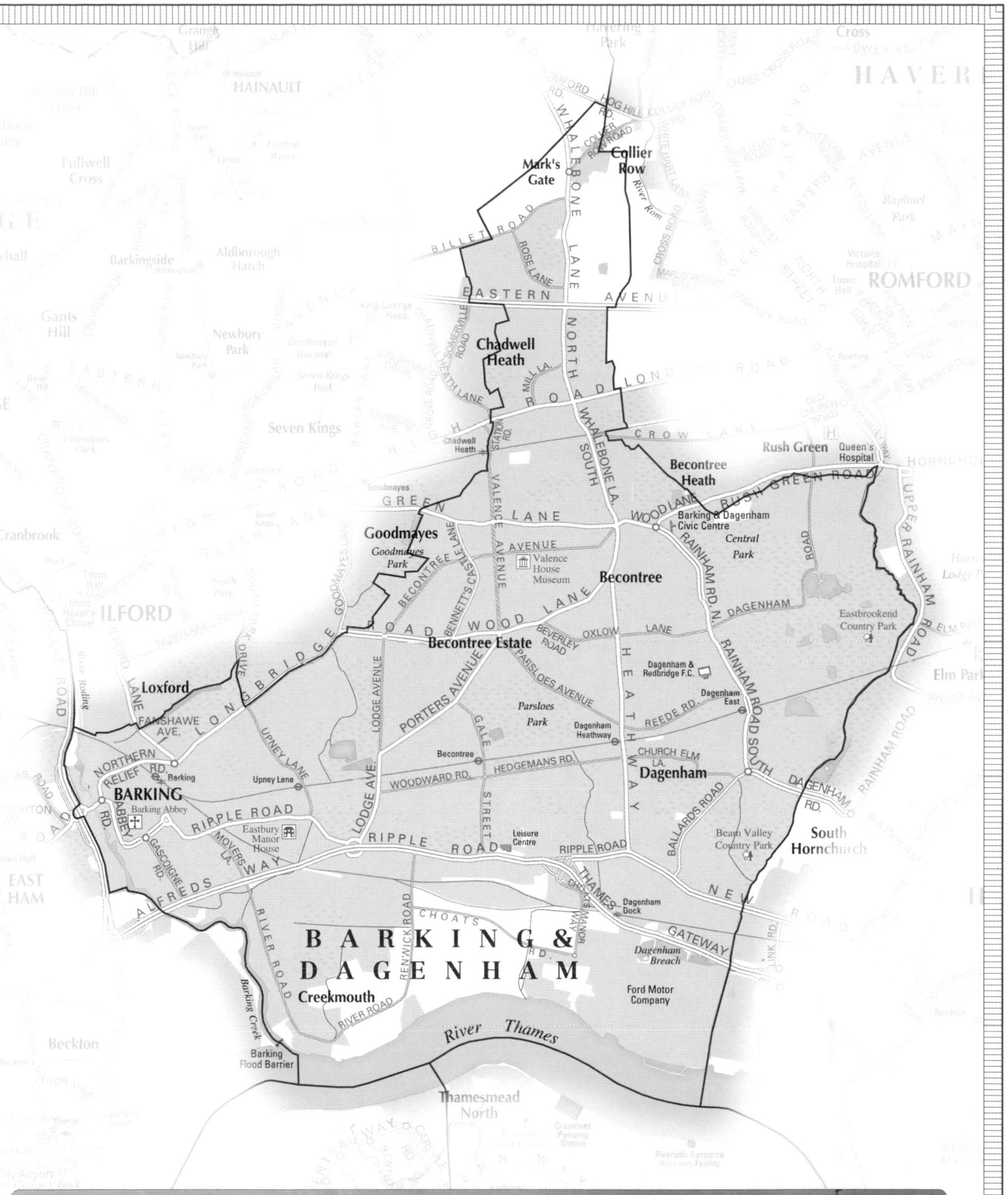

Barking Flood Barrier, managing flood defence at Barking Creek

INDUSTRIAL LONDON

Throughout its history London has been a trading centre and many crafts and small-scale manufacturing activities helped support this – from watchmakers to boat builders. In his *Journal of the Plague Year*, Daniel Defoe recalled workers whose trade stopped including 'riband-weavers, gold and silver lace makers, gold and silver wire drawers, seamstresses, milliners, shoemakers, hatmakers, glovemakers; also upholsterers, joiners, cabinet-makers, looking-glass makers, ... ship-carpenters, caulkers, ropemakers, dry coopers, sailmakers, anchorsmiths, blockmakers, carvers, gunsmiths, ship-chandlers, ... watermen, lightermen, boat-builders.' This listing is a reminder that in the 17th century all these goods had to be made in the city rather than brought to it.

Many of the early large-scale industries in London were concerned with food and drink. There were many flour mills around London, some water powered and some wind powered. Industrialization of the process came with the opening of the Albion Mill in Southwark in 1786, the first mill in Britain to be powered by James Watt's steam engine, which meant it could be located in the middle of the city rather than next to a power source. However, in 1791 it caught fire and was never rebuilt, although not before inspiring William Blake, who lived nearby, to write of 'dark, satanic mills' in 'Jerusalem'. The arrival of steam power had a major impact on London – any 19th-century picture of the south bank of the Thames will show numerous factory chimneys.

Brewing was also an important industry. Beer was frequently drunk as a safer alternative to water, and it was a major industrial activity to supply it – the Black Eagle Brewery in Spitalfields, founded in 1669, occupied 2.5 ha at its peak in the 19th century, while the Whitbread brewery in Chiswell Street was using another of Watt's steam engines in 1785, such a novelty that George III made a special inspection of it two years' later. The site continued as a brewery until 1976. As with much manufacturing, most brewing has moved away from London, Fuller's brewery at Chiswick being the largest active London brewery.

Printing was another industry that started in the heart of the city and then moved further out. The printing of *The Times* newspaper tells this story. The paper was started by John Walter in 1785 (for its first three years it was called the *Daily Universal Register*) at Printing House Square, once the site of Blackfriars Monastery. Printing remained there until 1974, when it moved to Gray's Inn Road and then in 1986 to Wapping, on the site of former docks, and then in 2008 it moved to the north of Enfield, at Broxbourne in Hertfordshire.

In the 19th century manufacturing moved east down the Thames along with the docks. Silvertown became a centre of sugar refining, rubber processing and many other industries that benefited from being close to the docks, while other newer industries, such as the manufacture of electric bulbs, established themselves in the Lea Valley. In the 20th century, greenfield sites became attractive for the new industries – Ford at Dagenham, the Park Royal industrial estate at Neasden, and the Great West Road at Brentford. In the 21st century, manufacturing plays a relatively minor part in the economy of London. In 2009 only 4.3 per cent of all jobs in London were in manufacturing compared with a national average of 10.2 per cent.

THE MAIN AREAS OF MANUFACTURING IN LONDON 2008

Business sector	No. of businesses	Percentage of UK businesses
Printing and reproduction of recorded media	3300	19
Clothing and textiles	1600	19
Metals and metal products	1600	6
Rubber, plastic and other non-metallic products	1200	6
Wood, wood products and furniture	1100	8
Food products and beverages	1000	9
Computer, electronic and optical products	700	10
Paper and paper products	300	10
Chemicals and chemical products	300	8
Electrical equipment	300	9
Motor vehicles and transport equipment	300	5
Pharmaceuticals	100	14

The Silvertown Explosion

Silvertown was the site of one of Britain's worst industrial accidents. During World War I the Brunner Mond chemical works were being used to manufacture the explosive trinitrotoluene (TNT). In the early evening of 19 January 1917, around 50 tonnes of TNT exploded. The blast was heard all over London and beyond, killing 73 people, injuring over 400 and destroying the factory, the fire station next door and around 900 houses close by.

TOP & BOTTOM BOROUGHS FOR MANUFACTURING JOBS AS PERCENTAGE OF TOTAL JOBS

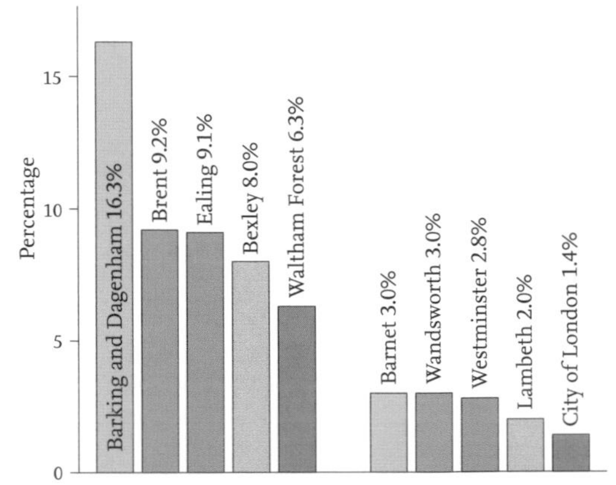

Beer has been brewed at Chiswick for over 350 years

Silvertown and the Royal Victoria Dock, 2007

Tate & Lyle sugar refinery, Silvertown, owned by American Sugar Refining since 2010

BARNET

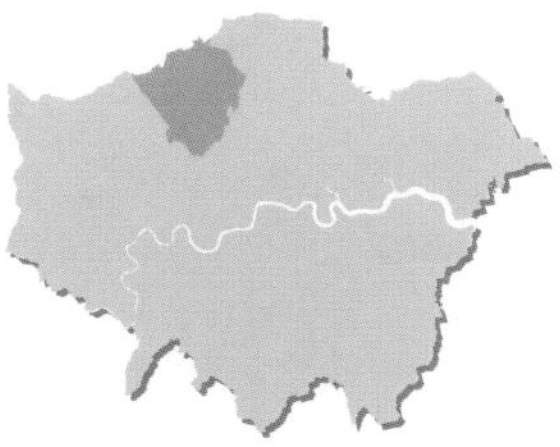

Population	343,100
Area	87 sq. km
Population density	3,940 per sq. km
Area of green space	36 sq. km
Jobs in borough	143,000
Average house price	£380,868

The borough of Barnet is named after the old market town of Barnet, formerly in Hertfordshire. The name comes from the Old English *baernet*, meaning 'land cleared by burning', a reminder of how wooded this area was in medieval times. In 1471 it was the scene of the Battle of Barnet during the War of the Roses, when Edward IV defeated his previous ally, the rebellious peer, Richard Neville (Warwick the Kingmaker), and so re-established his rule over England. The borough stretches down from rural Hertfordshire to the northern end of Hampstead Heath and contains Hampstead Garden Suburb, one of the world's first planned suburbs, dating from 1907, as well as the communities of Finchley, Hendon, Colindale and Golders Green. It was formed in 1965 from Barnet and East Barnet Urban Districts previously in Hertfordshire, the municipal boroughs of Finchley and Hendon, and Friern Barnet Urban District from Middlesex.

Barnet's population, like many London boroughs, has been growing swiftly over recent years, with a rise of over 18 per cent since 1988. Now around 32 per cent of the population come from ethnic minorities, the largest grouping being the Indian community of 31,000 people. Another distinguishing feature of the borough is that 19 per cent of the population profess the Jewish faith. This is by far the highest concentration in London and is based particularly around Golders Green.

As the railways spread out from central London, local communities grew rapidly – areas like Edgware and Finchley, served by the Northern line, became archetypal suburbs in the early 20th century. The Underground reached Hendon in 1926, and by 1931 its population was approaching three times that of a decade earlier. With good communications, by 2001, 59 per cent of the borough's residents travelled out of the borough to work, the majority to central London. Within the borough, the two most important job sectors are public administration, education and health (30 per cent of jobs) and retail, hotels and restaurants (at 28 per cent, a third higher than the average for London, boosted by such developments as the Brent Cross shopping centre).

Hendon RAF Museum

The Lawrence Campe Almshouses, Friern Barnet, built *c.* 1612

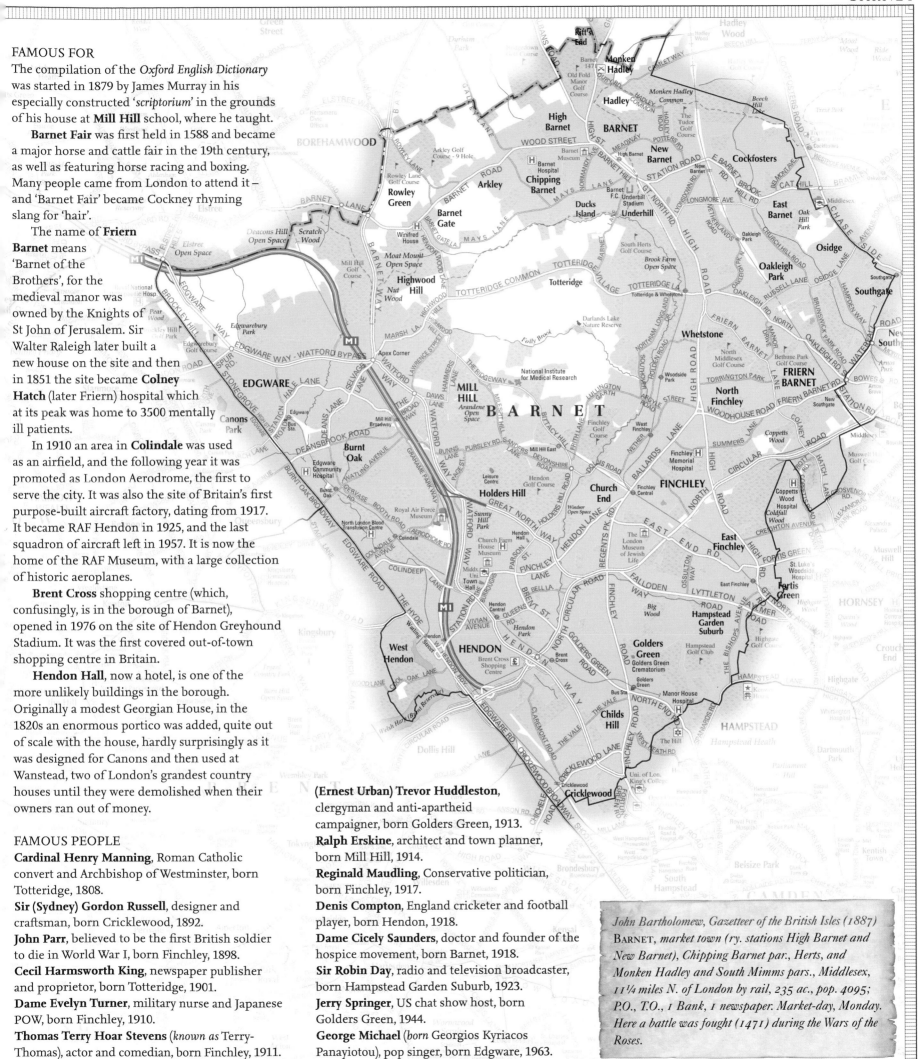

FAMOUS FOR

The compilation of the *Oxford English Dictionary* was started in 1879 by James Murray in his especially constructed '*scriptorium*' in the grounds of his house at **Mill Hill** school, where he taught.

Barnet Fair was first held in 1588 and became a major horse and cattle fair in the 19th century, as well as featuring horse racing and boxing. Many people came from London to attend it – and 'Barnet Fair' became Cockney rhyming slang for 'hair'.

The name of **Friern Barnet** means 'Barnet of the Brothers', for the medieval manor was owned by the Knights of St John of Jerusalem. Sir Walter Raleigh later built a new house on the site and then in 1851 the site became **Colney Hatch** (later Friern) hospital which at its peak was home to 3500 mentally ill patients.

In 1910 an area in **Colindale** was used as an airfield, and the following year it was promoted as London Aerodrome, the first to serve the city. It was also the site of Britain's first purpose-built aircraft factory, dating from 1917. It became RAF Hendon in 1925, and the last squadron of aircraft left in 1957. It is now the home of the RAF Museum, with a large collection of historic aeroplanes.

Brent Cross shopping centre (which, confusingly, is in the borough of Barnet), opened in 1976 on the site of Hendon Greyhound Stadium. It was the first covered out-of-town shopping centre in Britain.

Hendon Hall, now a hotel, is one of the more unlikely buildings in the borough. Originally a modest Georgian House, in the 1820s an enormous portico was added, quite out of scale with the house, hardly surprisingly as it was designed for Canons and then used at Wanstead, two of London's grandest country houses until they were demolished when their owners ran out of money.

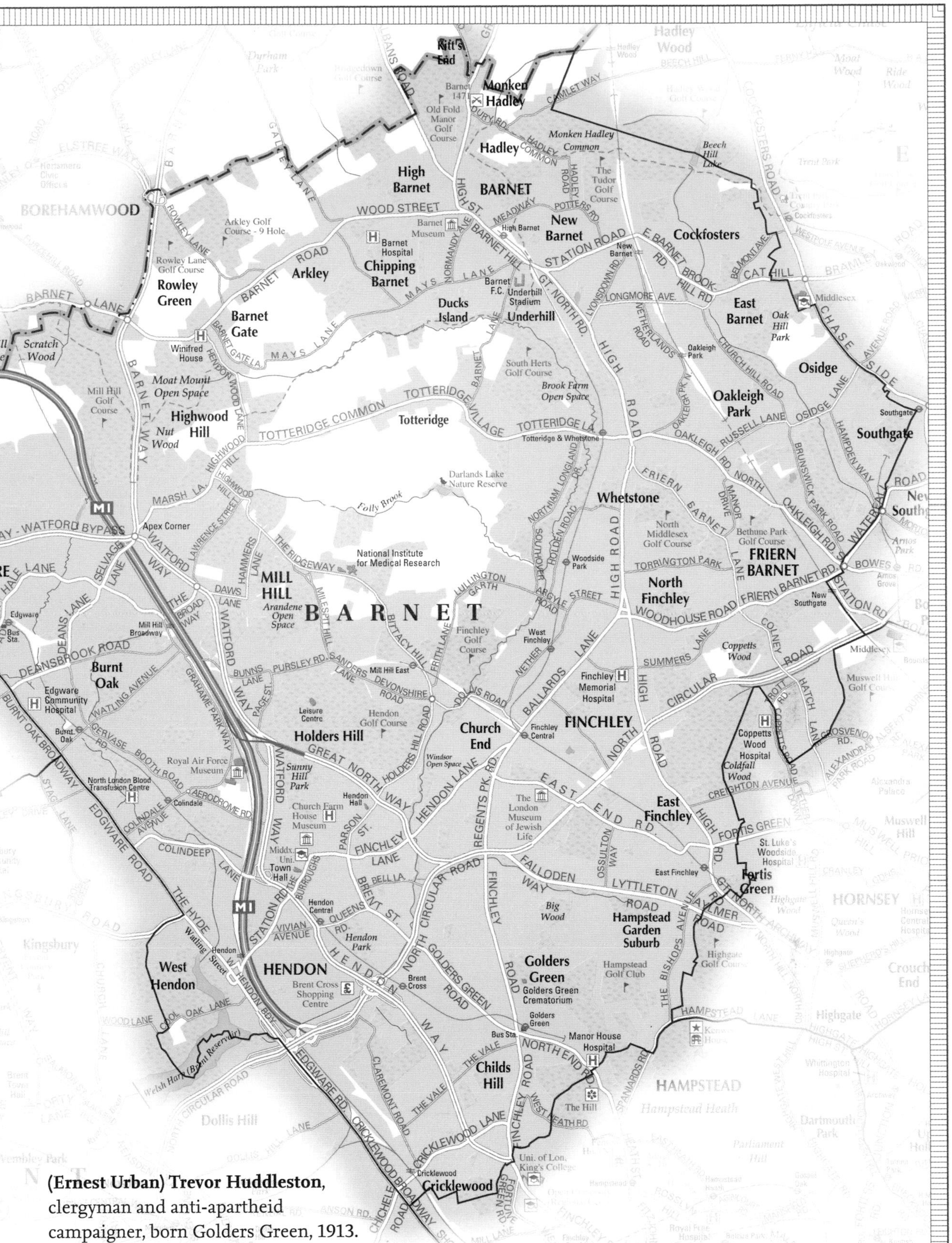

FAMOUS PEOPLE

Cardinal Henry Manning, Roman Catholic convert and Archbishop of Westminster, born Totteridge, 1808.

Sir (Sydney) Gordon Russell, designer and craftsman, born Cricklewood, 1892.

John Parr, believed to be the first British soldier to die in World War I, born Finchley, 1898.

Cecil Harmsworth King, newspaper publisher and proprietor, born Totteridge, 1901.

Dame Evelyn Turner, military nurse and Japanese POW, born Finchley, 1910.

Thomas Terry Hoar Stevens (*known as* Terry-Thomas), actor and comedian, born Finchley, 1911.

(Ernest Urban) Trevor Huddleston, clergyman and anti-apartheid campaigner, born Golders Green, 1913.

Ralph Erskine, architect and town planner, born Mill Hill, 1914.

Reginald Maudling, Conservative politician, born Finchley, 1917.

Denis Compton, England cricketer and football player, born Hendon, 1918.

Dame Cicely Saunders, doctor and founder of the hospice movement, born Barnet, 1918.

Sir Robin Day, radio and television broadcaster, born Hampstead Garden Suburb, 1923.

Jerry Springer, US chat show host, born Golders Green, 1944.

George Michael (*born* Georgios Kyriacos Panayiotou), pop singer, born Edgware, 1963.

John Bartholomew, Gazetteer of the British Isles (1887)
BARNET, *market town (ry. stations High Barnet and New Barnet), Chipping Barnet par., Herts, and Monken Hadley and South Mimms pars., Middlesex, 11¼ miles N. of London by rail, 235 ac., pop. 4095; P.O., T.O., 1 Bank, 1 newspaper. Market-day, Monday. Here a battle was fought (1471) during the Wars of the Roses.*

THE PEOPLES OF LONDON

There are a number of distinctive features about Londoners today that give their city a different character from the rest of Britain. It is a young place, with half the population aged 34 or under (compared with a UK average of 39), with the Inner London boroughs being younger than the Outer London boroughs. It is ethnically diverse; in 2011, the GLA estimated that nearly two-thirds of London is white (including those from Eastern Europe, North America and Australasia), while 14 per cent is Black Caribbean or African, 11.5 per cent of South Asian origin, and 5 per cent Chinese and other Asian in origin. Nearly a third of Londoners were born outside the UK compared with 7 per cent in the rest of the UK population (within London the figure ranges from 7 per cent in Havering to 52 per cent in Westminster). The birthplace of mothers of babies born in 2008 shows even more variation, with 42 per cent born in the UK, 16 per cent born in Africa and Asia, 12 per cent in the European Union, and 11 per cent elsewhere. Another snapshot is of the percentage of homes in which English is the first language. In London as a whole it is 78 per cent (compared with 95 per cent for the rest of the UK) and only around 45 per cent in Newham, the lowest figure in London.

A 1920s East End street entertainer imitates Charlie Chaplin, a Hollywood star with Cockney roots

Scottish pipes and drums parade in 1942

By the 1920s a large Jewish community was well-established in Spitalfields

While future population growth in London will be driven by an increasing birth rate, there is also a large flow of people both settling in and moving away from London, and in the process changing the mix of the population. Between 2001 and 2009, there was a net flow of around 40,000 people out of London, a figure that hides much larger numbers – 1.46 million came to London from the rest of the UK and 1.38 million came from overseas while 2.1 million left London for other parts of the UK and 0.8 million left to go overseas. In 2009, nearly 90,000 people came to live in London from areas in the UK beyond the East and South East of England, and it was only in the age range 20–29 that there was a net inflow of people.

Cockneys

The most traditional Londoner is the Cockney, once defined as being born within earshot of Bow Bells (the bells of the church of St Mary-le-Bow in the City, not Bow in the East End). The origin of the word (a puny or feeble town dweller, when compared with a hardy countryman) may come as a surprise, for the Cockney has a tough East End and working class image, as captured by Charles Dickens, with traditions exemplified by the Pearly Kings and Queens. The origins of the 'Pearlies' go back to an orphan, Henry Croft, who worked as a street sweeper with costermongers (street sellers) in the City markets. By tradition, costermongers sewed pearl buttons onto the seams of their clothes. In the 1880s Croft collected pearl buttons that fell to the ground and used them to cover a suit, which he used to raise money for costermongers. The costermongers then helped him with his charity work and a King and Queen, with elaborate pearly suits, were selected for each London borough, a tradition that endures.

Immigration to London

London has long attracted migrants from overseas. In the late 17th century, Huguenots (French Protestants) were expelled from France, and many came to London, bringing their textile skills with them to Spitalfields and the textile mills on the River Wandle. As the British Empire grew, more people from many parts of the world passed through London, from Indian aristocrats to Chinese sailors, but few permanent communities developed. In the late 19th century

The 19th century Cockney tradition of Pearly Kings and Queens continues in the 21st century

Chelsea Pensioners represent a London institution dating back over three centuries

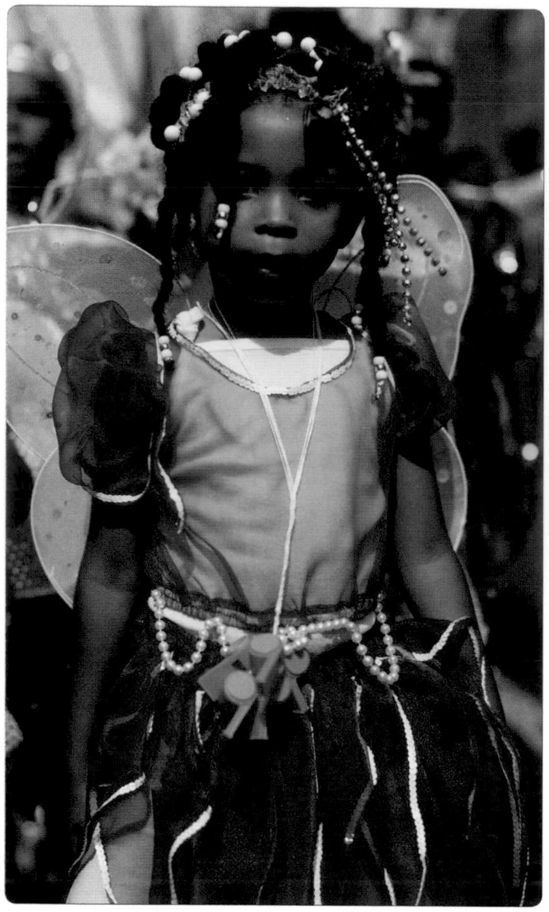

A young girl in costume at the Notting Hill Carnival

The Festival of Vaisakhi is one of the most important dates in the Sikh calendar

there was a significant influx of Jews escaping persecution in Eastern Europe, who also settled in Spitalfields, again working in the textile trade, and they displaced the Germans as the largest foreign community in London at that time.

The pattern of immigration only changed substantially after World War II, when Britain faced a great shortage of labour as it started to rebuild after the war. In 1948 the *Empire Windrush* docked at Kingston, Jamaica, to collect some Jamaicans who were returning to Britain to work in the Royal Air Force. There was extra space on board, and 492 Jamaicans paid £28 for the trip. The arrival of the *Empire Windrush* at Tilbury Docks on 22 June 1948 became the symbol of the start of immigration from the Caribbean. Many others followed, attracted by jobs within the National Health Service or with London Transport, and significant communities were established in Brixton and Notting Hill. More recently large African communities, for example from Nigeria, Ghana and Somalia, have formed.

Indians (mainly Sikhs and Hindus) started to arrive in the 1950s to work in factories in west London and later at Heathrow Airport, and settled in Southall and in the boroughs of Harrow and Brent. The arrival of Asians expelled from Uganda in 1972, saw small Asian businesses established across London. Pakistanis and Bangladeshis initially settled in the East End. Many worked in the textile trade and the area around Spitalfields was transformed by the presence of this large Asian Muslim population, and named by some as Banglatown.

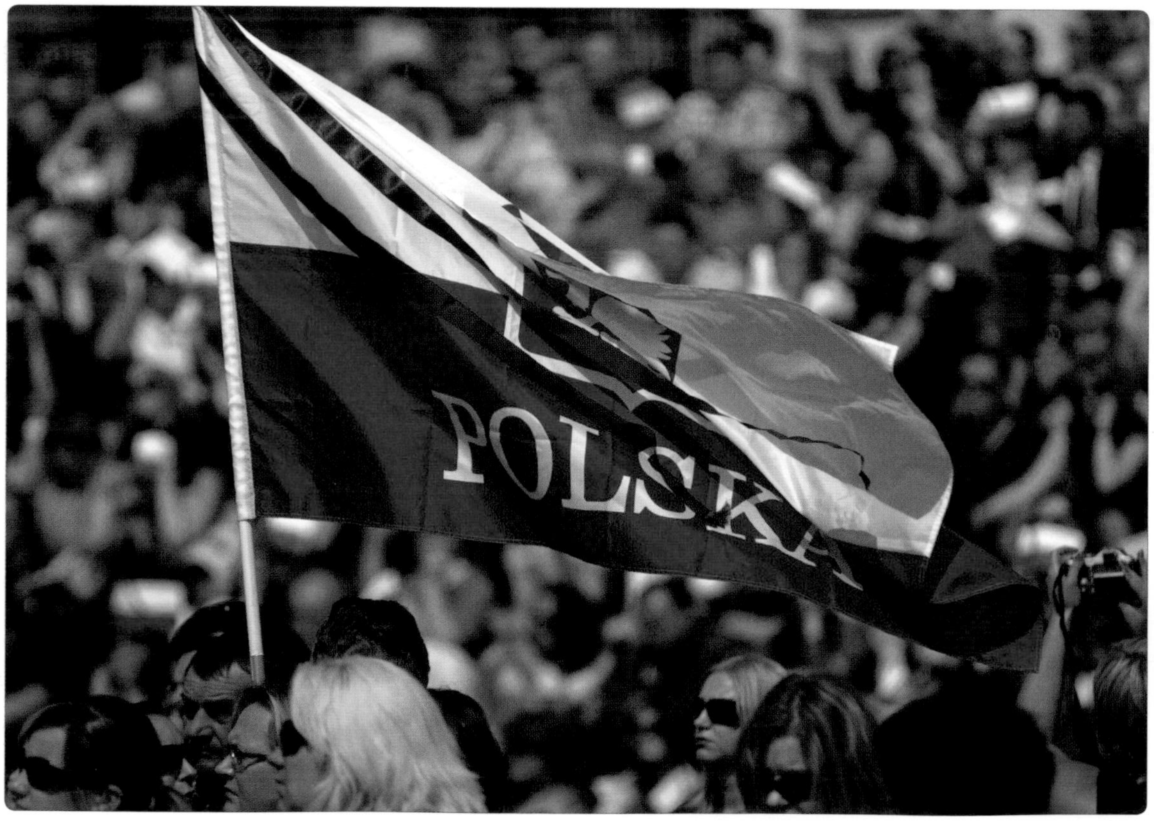

London's Polish community mourns the death of the Polish president, Lech Kaczyński, in 2010

In the 21st century, the immigrants have changed again, being a mixture of asylum seekers escaping from the many conflict zones in the world – from Somalia, Iran, Iraq and Zimbabwe, for example. People from European Union countries in Eastern Europe who have had free access to Britain since their membership in 2004 have also increased the cosmopolitan feel of the city, boosting the already well-established Polish community in West London and the Cypriot community of North London, for example.

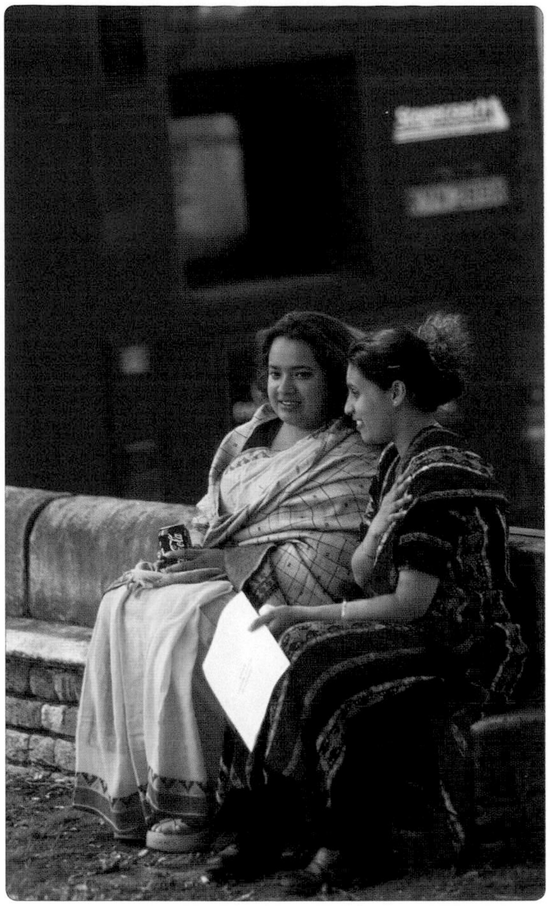

Many British Bangladeshis have settled in London

Celebrating Chinese New Year in London's Chinatown

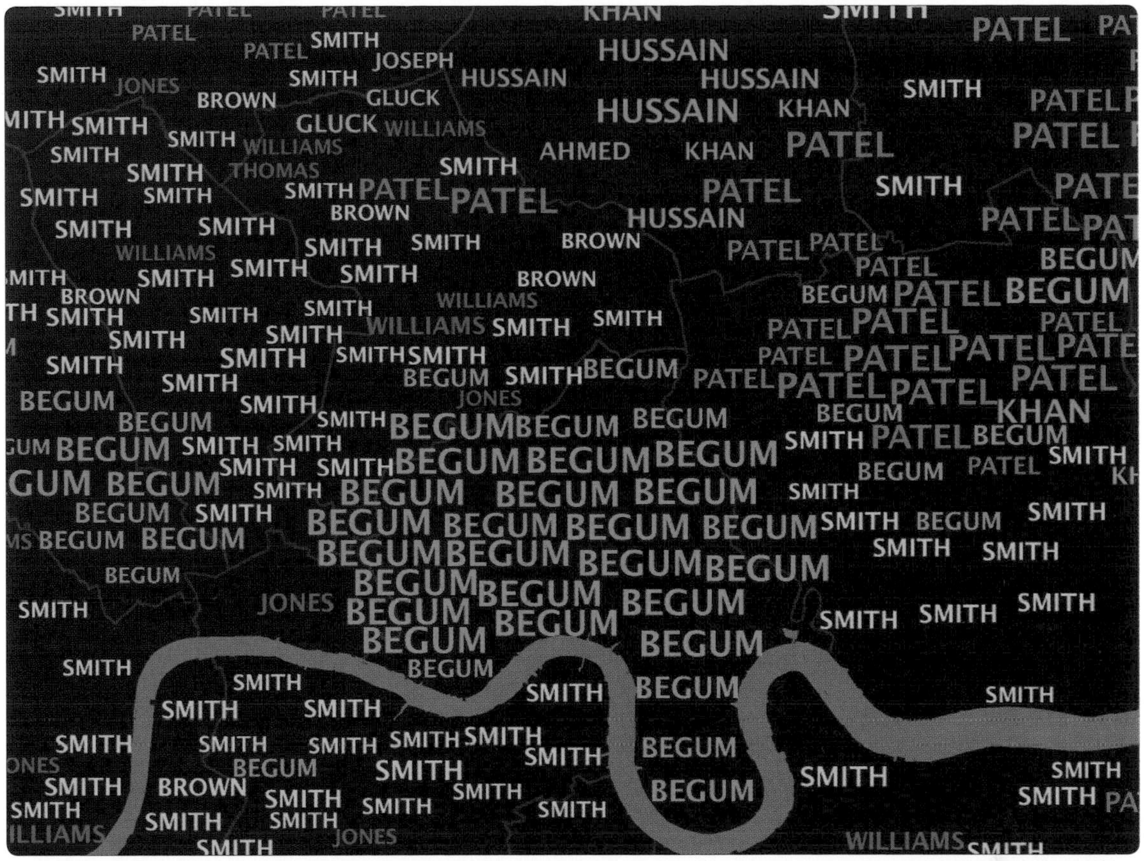

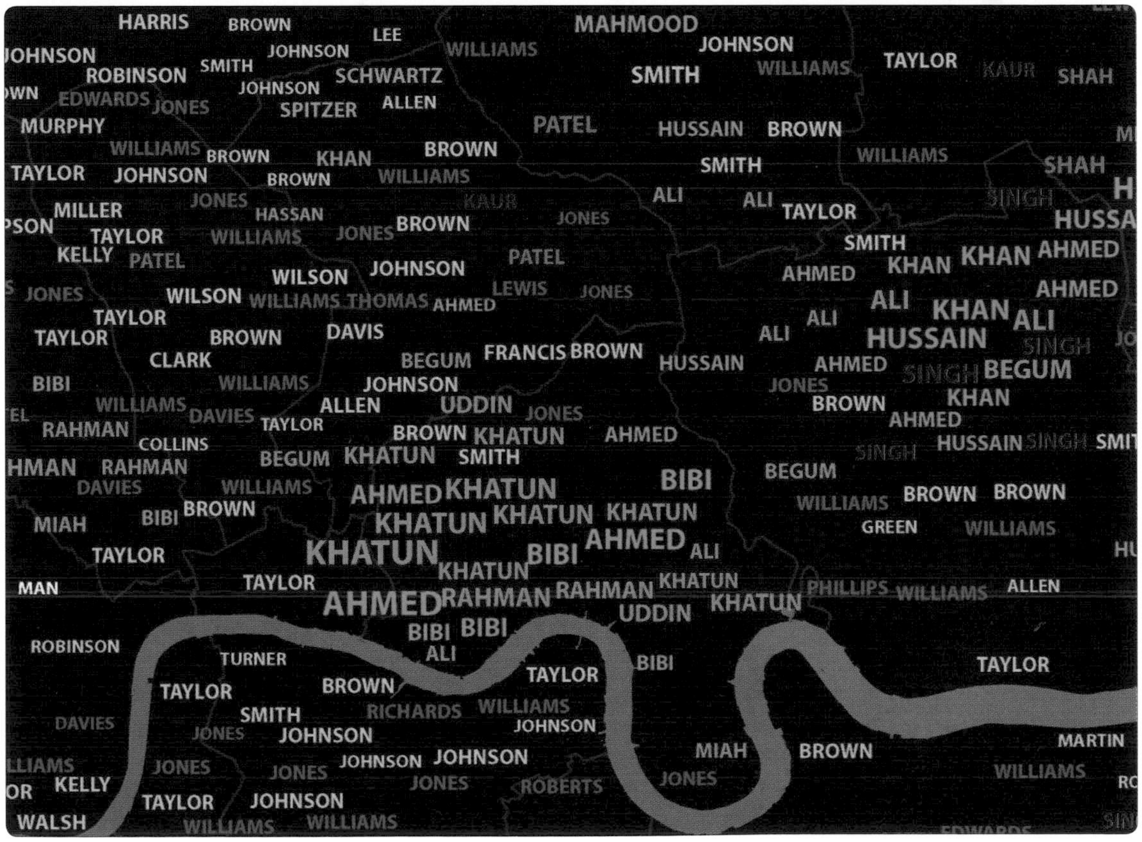

These two maps form part of a project to map the distribution of the most common surnames in London, based on the 2001 Electoral Roll. The first map shows the most popular surname in a given area and the second map shows the fifth most popular name. The size of the name is scaled to the number of people in the area and the colour indicates the origin of the name (but, importantly, not the origin of people bearing that name – the forebears of many Afro-Caribbeans, for example, were given British surnames by their slave owners). Note also that in the raw data 'Begum' (a female honorific title used by Bengalis) was classified as a surname and this is reflected on the maps. We are grateful to James Cheshire, University College London Department of Geography, for permission to reproduce these maps. A range of maps showing the first to fifteenth most common surnames can be seen at www.spatialanalysis.co.uk

BEXLEY

Population	225,900
Area	71 sq. km
Population density	3,182 per sq. km
Area of green space	23 sq. km
Jobs in borough	73,000
Average house price	£209,495

The borough of Bexley takes its name from the town of Bexley (in Old English 'a wood or clearing where box trees grow'). The borough was formed in 1965, from the municipal boroughs of Bexley and Erith, Crayford Urban District and part of Chislehurst and Sidcup Urban District, all traditionally in the county of Kent. The main settlements in the borough are Bexley, Bexleyheath, Crayford, Erith, Sidcup and Welling.

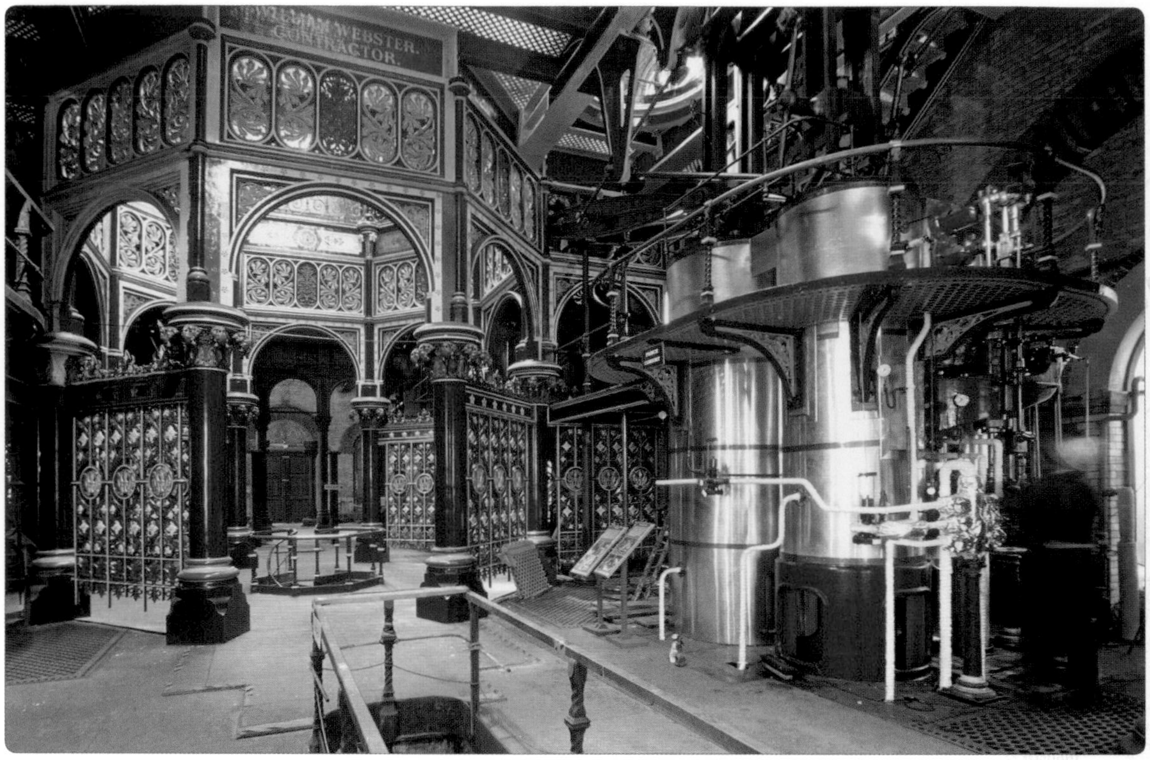

Restored Victorian interior of the Crossness Pumping Station

Whilst now primarily a suburban borough, with many of its residents working in central London, the main communities have a distinctive past. Crayford developed at the site where the Roman road from Dover to London crossed the River Cray. From the 16th century printing textiles became a major activity and in the late 19th century, the armaments industry developed, spurred on by Hiram Maxim's factory that made his machine gun. The harbour at Erith, meaning 'a muddy landing place', has been used since prehistoric times and became a naval dockyard under Henry VIII, but it was never a significant Thames port. The remainder of the borough was traditionally agricultural and heath land, and it was only from the late 19th century, with the coming of the railways, that the area developed, with many small villages becoming the focus of suburban developments for London workers.

The population of Bexley has grown slowly in recent years, and it is one of the least diverse London boroughs (in 2007, over 86 per cent of the population was of white ethnic origin). Around two-thirds of working residents commute outside the borough to their employment. Within the borough itself the largest share of jobs (nearly 27 per cent) are in public administration, education and health while only 20 per cent are in finance, IT and other business activities compared with a London average of nearly 35 per cent. Some manufacturing remains, including Caterham Cars, maker of sports cars, who are based at Crayford. More controversially, the Riverside Resource Recovery Facility, one of the UK's largest incinerators went on-stream in 2011. Located by the Thames at Belvedere, it is an energy from waste plant that can process over half a million tonnes of waste annually, brought from central and west London by barge, and can generate around 66 MW of electricity for the National Grid.

FAMOUS FOR

On 31 July 1894 at his home at **Baldwyn's Park, Bexley**, Hiram Maxim demonstrated his steam-engine powered biplane, which weighed over 3.6 tonnes. It flew an uncontrolled 281 metres at a height of 1.4 metres, ten years before the Wright brothers flew their aeroplane.

The borough of **Bexley** recycles 51 per cent of its domestic waste, the highest percentage of all London boroughs.

On the marshes by Erith stands the **Crossness Pumping Station**, designed by Sir Joseph Bazalgette and opened in 1865 as part of his extraordinary London sewerage system. Its four steam-powered rotative beam engines are the largest in the world, and a major restoration project in under way to restore this spectacular example of Victorian engineering.

The Red House, Bexleyheath, built for William Morris

Once London's most significant 'at risk' building, Bexleyheath's **Danson House**, a beautiful, compact Palladian villa designed by Sir Robert Taylor in 1766, has now been wonderfully restored and is open to the public.

The **Red House** in Bexleyheath was completed in 1860 for the great designer William Morris by Philip Webb. It led to a revolution in house design, both for its informal style and decoration and for how a house can be organized to work efficiently.

FAMOUS PEOPLE

Sir Francis Walsingham, Principal Secretary to Elizabeth I, born Foots Cray, *c.* 1532.

Francis Thynne, herald, antiquary and alchemist, born Erith, *c.* 1545.

Julius Jeffreys, surgeon and inventor of the respirator, born Bexley, 1800.

Dame Sidney Jane Browne, military nurse, first President of the Royal College of Nursing, born Bexley, 1850.

May Morris, designer and daughter of William Morris, born Bexleyheath, 1862.

Godfrey Martin Huggins, Viscount Malvern, prime minister of Southern Rhodesia, 1933–56, born Bexley, 1883.

Quentin Blake, children's book illustrator and cartoonist, born Sidcup, 1932.

Wendy Cope, poet, born Erith, 1945.

Alan Knott, Kent and England cricketer, born Belvedere, 1946.

Kate (Catherine) Bush, singer and songwriter, born Bexleyheath, 1958.

Steve Backley, athlete, Olympic javelin champion, born Sidcup, 1969.

Linda Smith, the greatly admired comedian who died in 2006, was born in ***Erith****, which she once described as 'not exactly a city that never sleeps, more a town that lies awake all night staring at the ceiling'.*

The 18th-century Five Arch Bridge, Foots Cray

John Bartholomew, Gazetteer of the British Isles (1887)
CRAYFORD, *par. and vil. with ry. sta., W. Kent, 8 miles SE. of Greenwich, 2457 ac. (29 water) and 144 tidal water and foreshore, pop. 4347; P.O., T.O.; has calico and felt carpet printing works, and silk and Brussels carpet manufactories*

THE THAMES

The Thames is one of the defining features of London. The river rises in the Cotswolds close to Cirencester and is the longest in England (the longer Severn rises in Wales), flowing around 340 km from its source to the sea. Before reaching London it flows through Oxford, Reading, Slough and past Windsor before entering Greater London by Hampton Court Palace.

The foundation of London was determined by the Thames. When the Romans first established their settlement of *Londinium*, the Thames was a much wider and less regulated river, but it was also shallower and had less of a tidal range. *Londinium* was located where it was because it was the lowest point on the Thames that could be forded at the time, and later, with Roman engineering skill, could also be bridged. As the city grew, so the gradual reclamation of land from the Thames began, as wharves were built and new land created behind the wharves. The process of extending the city into the area that was once occupied by the river continued through to the 19th century when the deeper and narrower Thames was finally established with the construction of the massive embankments that now define the river and its relation to central London. In some places the river has been shrunk by around 100 m. The islands and intertidal marshes that the Roman settlers would have been familiar with are now built over as part of Southwark and Lambeth.

As the width of the Thames has been constricted, so the dangers posed by flooding has increased, a danger exacerbated by the fact that southeastern England is slowly sinking. To help restrict the danger, the Thames Barrier was completed in 1982. The purpose of the Barrier was to protect central London from tidal surges coming up the Thames. When there is thought to be a danger of flooding, the gates in the barrier swing up 90 degrees from the river bed to form a solid wall across the river. The Barrier crosses the river between Silvertown and New Charlton and is designed to let shipping through. It has been raised 119 times for flood protection and rather more times (321) for testing between 1982 and February 2011. Barking Creek, further out towards the sea, is also protected by a major floodgate defence.

Travel on the Thames

Until the improvements in land transport in the 19th century, the river was a major transport route for people moving around London, from members of the Royal family in their elaborate state barges to simple ferries for workers. There are still two regular River Bus services (from Woolwich to Embankment and from Putney to Blackfriars) and many tourist boats and pleasure boats that use the Thames, along with commercial barge traffic, a few of which take some of London's rubbish to an incinerator at Belvedere.

Bridges over the Thames

London Bridge was so significant to the development of the city because the Thames was difficult to bridge. Until Putney Bridge was built in 1729, the next bridge upstream from London Bridge was at Kingston. Apart from Southwark, at the southern end of London Bridge, the south bank of the Thames was slow to be developed because of the lack of river crossings until the 18th century. The bridges across the Thames, starting with Tower Bridge, the nearest bridge to the sea within Greater London are given below (the nearest bridge to the sea is the Queen Elizabeth II bridge at Dartford, just to the east of Greater London).

Tower Bridge, between the Tower Hill and Bermondsey, is a massive drawbridge, completed in 1894, whose historic looks mask prodigious Victorian engineering skills. It is one of the iconic structures of London.

London Bridge, between the City and Southwark, was built 1967–72 as an unromantic three-spanned concrete structure. It was built on the site of John Rennie's stone bridge, opened in 1831 and now reconstructed at Lake Havasu City in Arizona. This bridge was built a little upstream from the old London

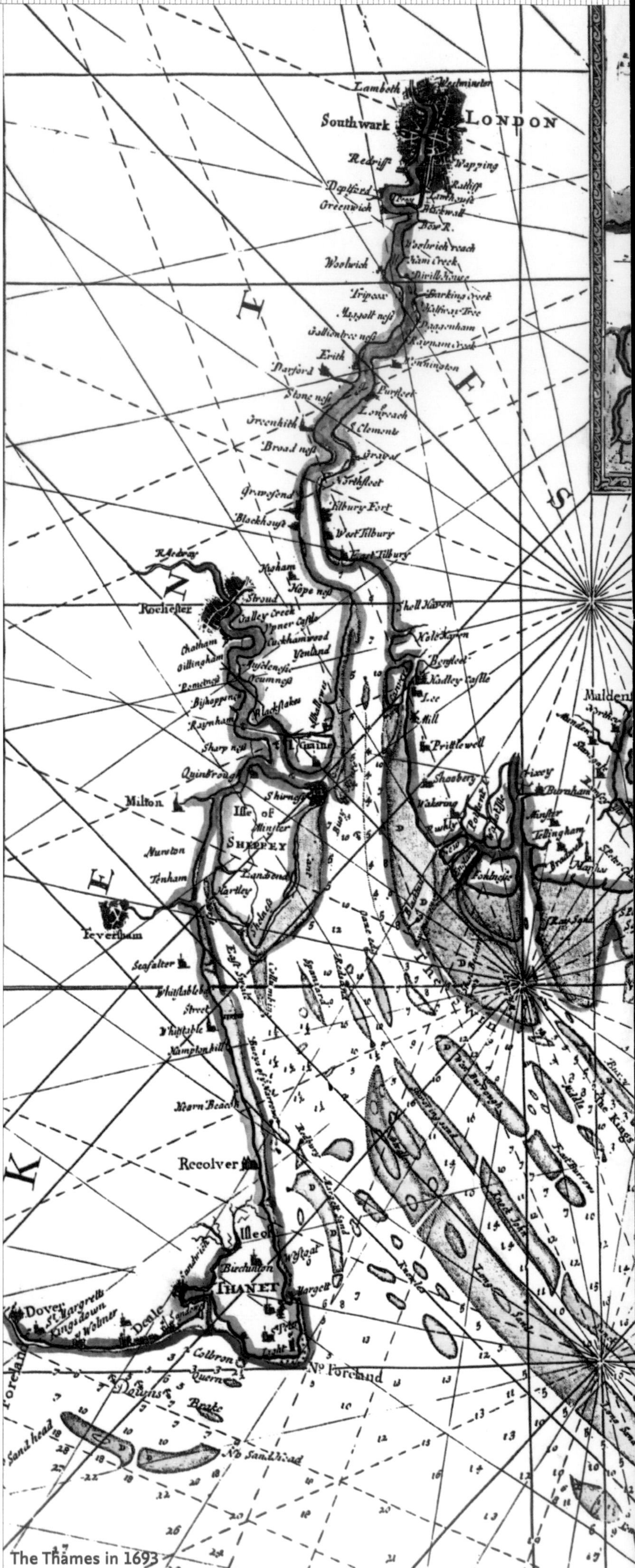

The Thames in 1693

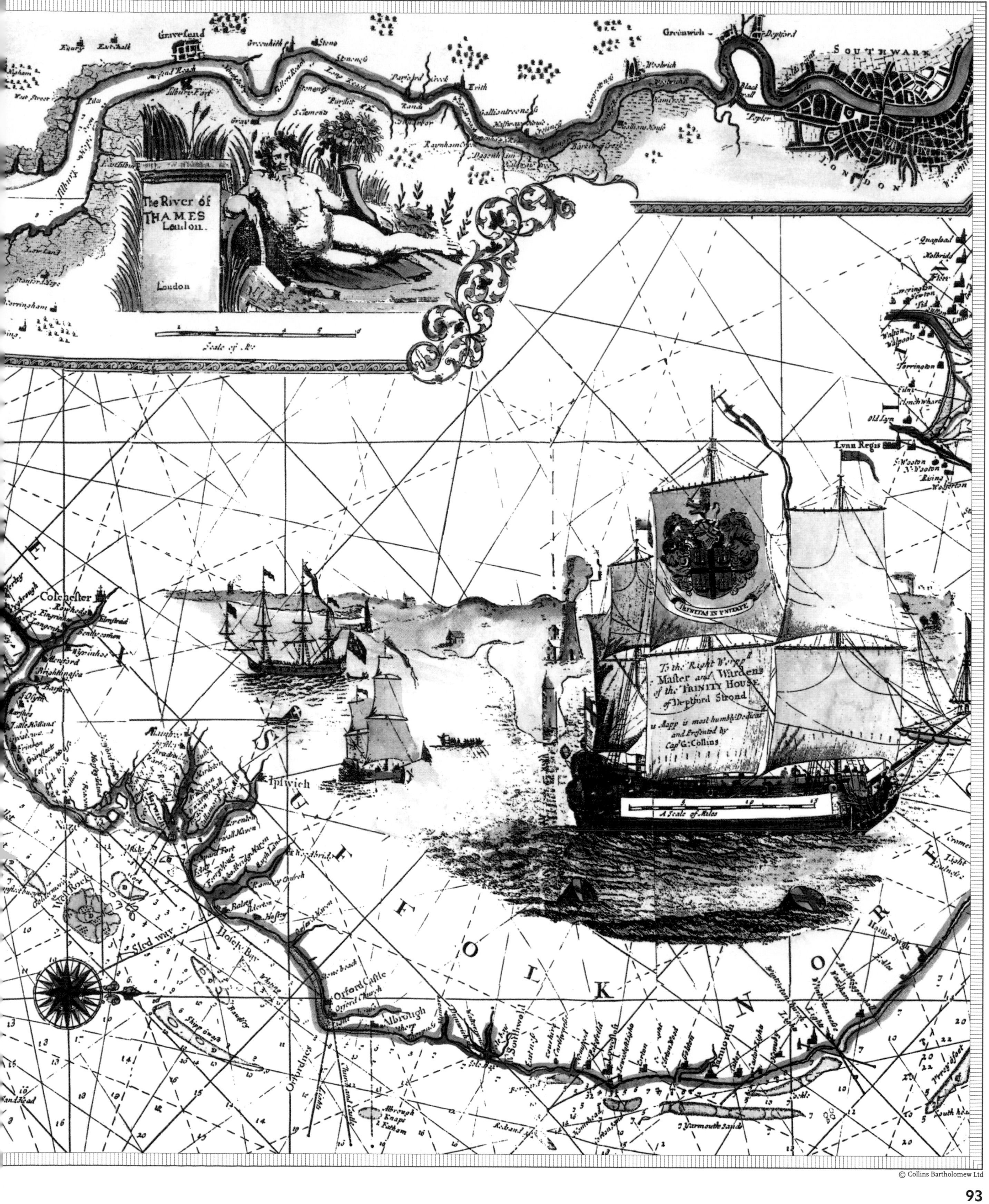
The River of
THAMES
London
London
Gravesend
Greenwich
Deptford
SOUTHWARK
LONDON
Erith
Woolwich
Lynn Regis
Colchester
Ipswich
To the Right Worsp
Master and Wardens
of the Trinity House
of Deptford Strond
this Mapp is most humbly Dedicat
and Presented by
Capt G: Collins
A Scale of Miles
Orford Castle
Albrough
Southwold
Yarmouth Sands
Sled way
S U F F O L K
N O R

BIRD'S-EYE VIEW MAP OF CENTRAL LONDON - 1908

This map shows the central London bridges in 1908. Note the suspension bridge at Lambeth

Bridge. The first bridges were wooden but in 1176 a bridge of nineteen stone arches (with a drawbridge at the Southwark end) was started. At the centre was a chapel dedicated to St Thomas Becket. Buildings on the bridge were first recorded in 1201, and soon it was lined by houses up to seven storeys high. These were demolished in the 18th century and the bridge was pulled down in the 19th century. The engineer Thomas Telford submitted a staggering design in 1801 for a single-span cast-iron bridge, far more ambitious than any existing structure – and just too radical to gain approval.

Cannon Street Railway Bridge is most notable for the two great towers at its northern end, marking the beginning of Cannon Street station, the terminus of the South Eastern Railway which opened in 1866.

Southwark Bridge, between the City and Southwark, has five steel arches and was opened in 1921. It replaced John Rennie's cast-iron bridge of 1819 whose central span far exceeded any other cast iron bridge.

Millennium Bridge, a footbridge designed by Foster and Partners between St Paul's and Tate Modern is a striking, flat suspension bridge which opened briefly in 2000 but then closed until 2002 while the wobble generated by pedestrians walking over it was solved. It was the first new crossing since Tower Bridge, over 100 years before.

Blackfriars Railway Bridge, between Blackfriars and Southwark, was built in 1884–6, with five wrought-iron arches. Next to it are the piers of an earlier railway bridge from 1862–4 that was dismantled in 1984.

Blackfriars Bridge, between Blackfriars and Southwark, was built in 1860–69 and widened in 1907–10. It consists of five wrought iron spans supported on massive, squat piers. It replaced the much more elegant bridge of 1760–69 designed by Robert Mylne. Officially called the William Pitt Bridge it was the third bridge in London to cross the Thames.

Waterloo Bridge, between the Strand and Waterloo, is a reinforced concrete box girder bridge of five spans built 1937–42. It replaced, with much protest, John Rennie's elegant nine-arched granite bridge, once referred to by the sculptor Canova as 'the noblest bridge in the world'. It was opened in 1817 on the second anniversary of the Battle of Waterloo, hence its name.

Hungerford Bridge (rail and footbridge) was opened in 1864, carrying the railway into Charing Cross Station. Long regarded as the ugliest bridge it was greatly enhanced by the addition of footbridges on each side which were opened in 2002 and are formally known as the Golden Jubilee Bridges.

Westminster Bridge, between Westminster and Lambeth was built 1854–62 with seven immensely wide cast-iron arches, and lavishly decorated under the guidance of Sir Charles Barry who had designed the Houses of Parliament next to it. It replaced the beautiful but structurally weak 1750 stone bridge designed by Charles Labelye.

Lambeth Bridge, between Westminster and Lambeth, is a steel-arch bridge, built 1929–32. It replaced a suspension bridge dating from 1862, and from medieval times to around 1750 was the site of a ferry that could take a coach and horses.

Vauxhall Bridge, between Pimlico and Lambeth, was built 1895–1906 and consists of five steel arches. Each river pier is decorated with massive bronze figures representing Pottery, Engineering, Architecture and Agriculture on the upstream side and Science, Fine Arts, Local Government and Education downstream. It replaced the first cast-iron bridge across the Thames, built in 1816.

Grosvenor Railway Bridge carries the main railway line into Victoria Station. First built in 1858–60, it was reconstructed and enlarged in 1963–7 to carry ten railway tracks on steel arches.

Chelsea Bridge, between Chelsea and Battersea, is an unremarkable suspension bridge that was built in 1937 to replace a much-admired Victorian suspension bridge from 1858.

Albert Bridge, between Chelsea and Battersea was opened in 1873, an amalgam of a suspension and cantilever bridge. Its playful design, by R. M. Ordish, restricts its utility as there is a 2 tonne weight restriction on the bridge. It was only just saved from demolition after World War II by conservationists, led by John Betjeman.

Battersea Bridge, between Chelsea and Battersea, was built 1886–90 to the designs of Sir Joseph Bazalgette and consists of five cast-iron spans. It replaced Henry Holland's wooden bridge of 1771–2, now best remembered in the ethereal drawings and paintings of James McNeill Whistler who had a studio in Chelsea.

Battersea Railway Bridge (Cremorne Bridge), between Chelsea and Battersea was built in 1861 to connect the West London Railway to Clapham Junction.

Wandsworth Bridge, between Fulham and Wandsworth, was build 1936–40 with three steel cantilever spans, replacing an earlier bridge from 1873.

Fulham Railway Bridge, completed in 1889, now carries the District line across the river.

Tower Bridge and the Thames, 1931

The working barges and boats of the river Thames have been replaced by pleasure craft and tourist attractions such as HMS Belfast

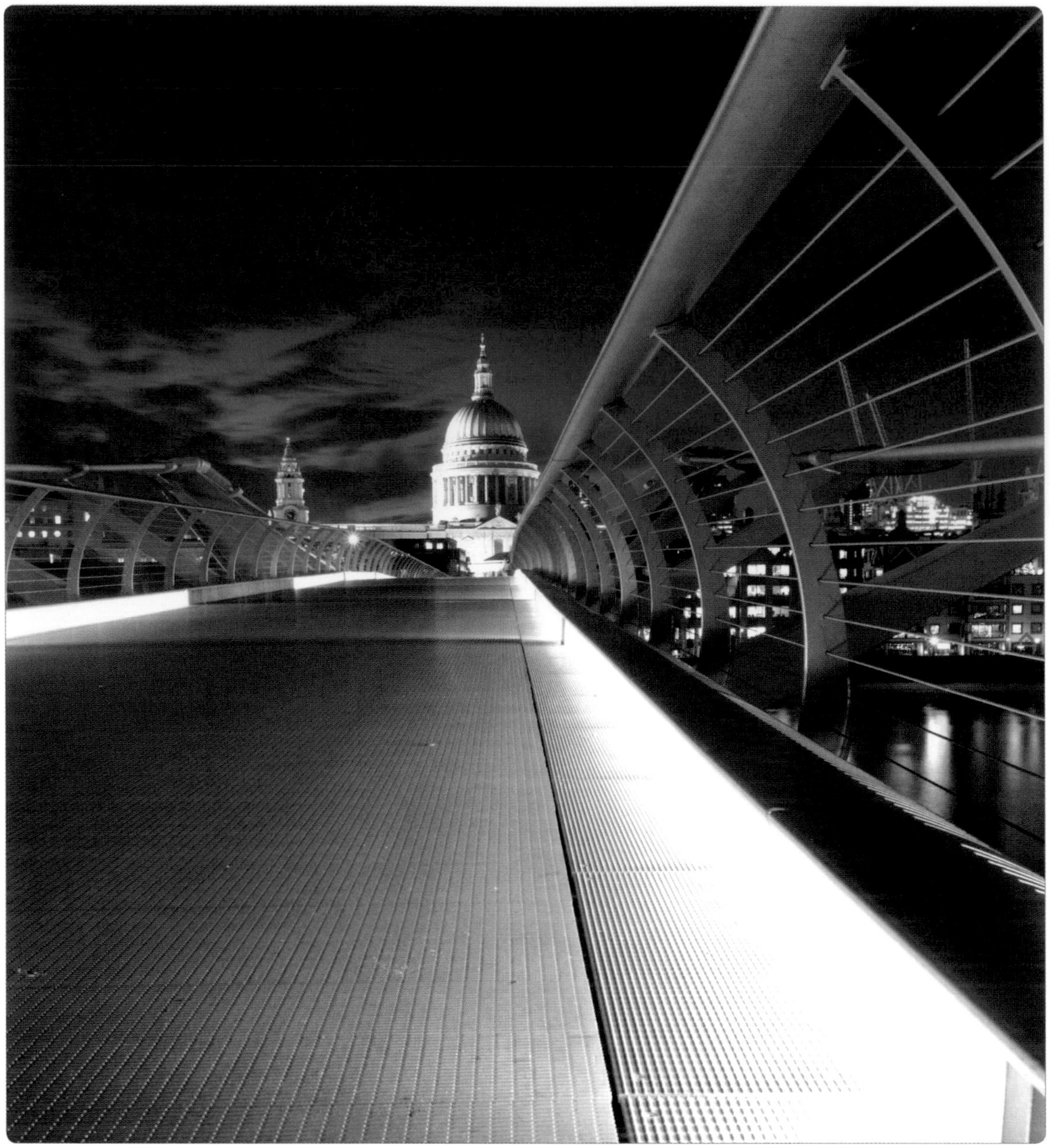

Millennium Bridge

Putney Bridge, between Fulham and Putney, was opened in 1886. Its five granite arches were designed by Sir Joseph Bazalgette. It replaced a wooden bridge dating from 1729, the earliest bridge across the Thames between Kingston and London Bridge.

Hammersmith Bridge, between Hammersmith and Barnes, is a suspension bridge that was built 1883–7 and designed by Sir Joseph Bazalgette. It has survived three attempts by Irish republicans to blow it up. It replaced the first suspension bridge across the Thames, dating from 1827.

Barnes Railway Bridge and Footbridge, between Chiswick and Barnes was built in 1846–9 and strengthened and enlarged in 1891–5, when a footbridge was added. The 1846 structure is no longer used – but it is now the oldest bridge across the Thames downstream from Richmond.

Chiswick Bridge, between Chiswick and Mortlake, is a concrete bridge faced with Portland stone, which was opened in 1933. It marks the finishing point of the Oxford and Cambridge Boat race.

Kew Railway Bridge, between Gunnersbury and Kew, was built in 1864–9, of wrought iron lattice girders.

Kew Bridge, between Gunnersbury and Kew, was built in 1903, on the site of a wooden bridge (1759) and then a stone bridge, designed by James Paine (1789).

Twickenham Bridge, between Twickenham and Richmond, is a three-arched concrete bridge, opened in 1933.

Richmond Railway Bridge was built in 1908 for the railway between Richmond and Windsor. This steel structure replaced an earlier bridge dating from 1848.

Richmond Bridge, between Twickenham and Richmond, was designed by James Paine and built in 1774–7 and is the oldest surviving bridge across the Thames in London. It was widened in 1939.

Kingston Railway Bridge, between Hampton Wick and Kingston stations, was completed in 1863.

Kingston Bridge, between Hampton Wick and Kingston, is a Portland stone bridge of five arches, built 1825–8 and widened in 1914. There has been a bridge over the Thames at Kingston since at least the early 13th century, the first crossing upstream from London Bridge until Putney Bridge opened in 1729.

Hampton Court Bridge, between Hampton and East Moseley, is a three-arched concrete bridge with brick facings, designed by Sir Edwin Lutyens and opened in 1933. It is the fourth bridge at the site, the first dating from 1753.

Tunnels under the Thames

Downstream from the Tower of London there are a number of tunnels, some for pedestrians, some for vehicles and some for trains. The most historic is the Thames Tunnel, from Wapping to Rotherhithe. It was designed by Marc Brunel to provide a way of moving freight from one side of the Thames to the other. Work started in 1825 but it took until 1843 to complete the tunnel (but not the approach routes for horses and carts). It was the first tunnel built under a major river and became a short-lived tourist attraction, visited by 1,000,000 people in its first ten weeks. It was not a commercial success, however, and from 1869 it was used for trains, which it continues to do today. There are also two foot tunnels – between the Isle of Dogs and Greenwich, and North Woolwich and Woolwich – and the Blackwall and Rotherhithe road tunnels. The Blackwall tunnel, opened in 1897 with a second tunnel in 1967, is the last downstream vehicular crossing of the Thames within Greater London.

And when the evening mist clothes the riverside with poetry, as with a veil, and the poorer buildings lose themselves in the dim sky, and the tall chimneys become campanili, and the warehouses are palaces in the night, and the whole city hangs in the heavens, and fairy-land is before us — then the wayfarer hastens home.
James McNeill Whistler writing about the Thames

Composed Upon Westminster Bridge,
September 3, 1802
Earth has not anything to show more fair:
Dull would he be of soul who could pass by
A sight so touching in its majesty:
This City now doth like a garment wear
The beauty of the morning: silent, bare,
Ships, towers, domes, theatres, and temples lie
Open unto the fields, and to the sky,
All bright and glittering in the smokeless air.
Never did sun more beautifully steep
In his first splendour valley, rock, or hill;
Ne'er saw I, never felt, a calm so deep!
The river glideth at his own sweet will:
Dear God! the very houses seem asleep;
And all that mighty heart is lying still!
William Wordsworth

Thames Flood Barrier

Blackfriars Bridge

BRENT

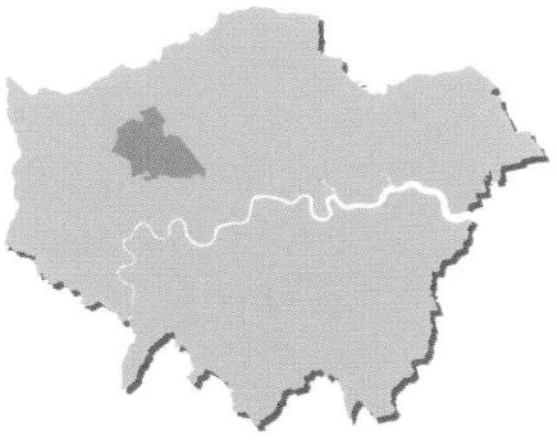

Population	255,500
Area	43 sq. km
Population density	5,940 per sq. km
Area of green space	9.5 sq. km
Jobs in borough	110,000
Average house price	£322,904

The borough of Brent takes its name from the River Brent, in origin a Celtic name meaning 'holy one'. The borough was formed in 1965 from the two municipal boroughs of Wembley and Willesden, both then in Middlesex. Little physical evidence remains of what the area was like before the arrival of the railways from the mid-19th century, the Underground in the early 20th century and the North Circular Road in the 1930s. The speed of change from rural backwater to London suburb was dramatic – the population of Willesden in 1881 was 27,000 and a mere twenty years later it was 115,000. In 1900 Mark Twain stayed at Dollis Hill House in Gladstone Park and remarked that 'I have never seen any place that was so satisfactorily situated, with its noble trees and stretch of country, and everything that went to make life delightful, and all within a biscuit's throw of the metropolis of the world', a rural image now hard to imagine.

The population of the borough continues to grow – one Greater London Authority (GLA) estimate suggests that it will reach 295,400 by 2021, and its ethnic make-up is ever changing. In the 2001 census it was the most diverse borough in London. Only 29 per cent of the population described themselves as white British, while another 7 per cent said they were white Irish. The borough has proved popular with South Asians (27 per cent) and Black Africans or Caribbeans (20 per cent), and by 2021 it is estimated that the South Asian population will make up around a third of the borough. Brent has one of the largest groups of Hindus in the capital, a community which is reflected in the magnificence of the BAPS Shri Swaminarayan Mandir (the 'Neasden Temple'), the largest Hindu temple outside India, a masterpiece of Hindu architecture and sculpture which opened in 1995.

Around 76,000 of the borough's residents commute to other parts of London to work, but 47,000 come into the borough to work, particularly drawn by the Park Royal industrial estate, which covers 750 ha and provides 40,000 jobs. However, the best known feature of the borough is Wembley Stadium.

FAMOUS FOR

The **Welsh Harp Reservoir** and its surrounding marshes and grassland occupy 170 ha on the Brent/Barnet border. It was originally constructed in the 1830s as a reservoir for the Grand Junction Canal, and its name came from a local pub.

In 1937 the Gaumont State cinema opened on **Kilburn High Road**. At the time it was the largest cinema in Europe, with seating for 4,004, and was also used for variety shows. It is now being given a new life as a church for Ruach Ministries.

The original **Wembley Stadium** was built for the 1924 British Empire Exhibition. It had a capacity of 127,000 fans, although it is thought that up to 200,000 watched the first FA Cup final played in the stadium in 1923. The old stadium

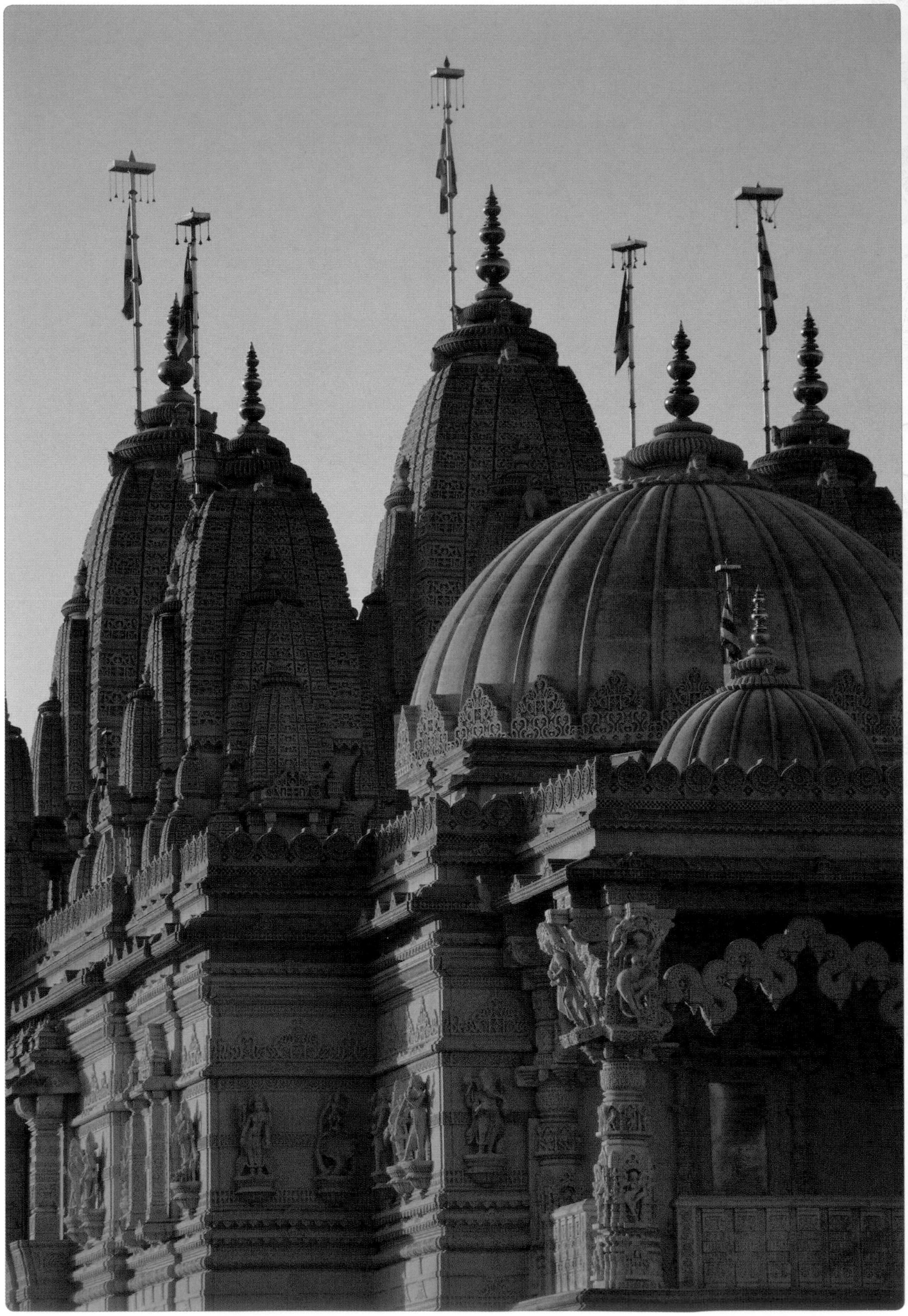

BAPS Shri Swaminarayan Mandir

was demolished in 2003 and the new stadium, with its distinctive soaring arch, was opened in 2007. It can accommodate up to 90,000 spectators.

The **Wembley Arena** was built as the swimming pool for the 1934 Empire Games and was used in the 1948 Olympic Games. It has now been converted into a music venue.

The site of the **Park Royal** industrial estate was for three years (1902–5) the home of the Royal Agricultural Show, and was so named because the Prince of Wales opened the first show at the site. Its location was unpopular with the farming community, so the Show soon moved away.

FAMOUS PEOPLE

A. A. (Alan Alexander) Milne, children's author, including *Winnie the Pooh*, born Kilburn, 1882.
Micheál MacLiammóir (*born* Alfred Wilmore), actor and playwright, founder of the Gate Theatre, Dublin, born Willesden, 1899.
Victor Silvester, ballroom dancer and bandleader, born Wembley, 1900.
Robert Byron, traveller and writer, best known for *The Road to Oxiana*, born Wembley, 1905.
Richard Llewellyn, novelist, best known for *How Green was My Valley*, born Willesden, 1906.
Eric Treacy, bishop of Wakefield and railway photographer, born Willesden, 1907.
Ronald Coase, economist, Nobel Prize winner (1991), born Willesden, 1910.
Richard Baker, newsreader, born Willesden, 1925.
Stanley Sadie, musicologist and music critic, born Wembley, 1930.
Keith Moon, drummer, The Who, born Willesden, 1946.
Roger Diski, a creator of sustainable tourism, born Willesden, 1949.
Twiggy (*born* Leslie Hornby), model, born Neasden, 1949.

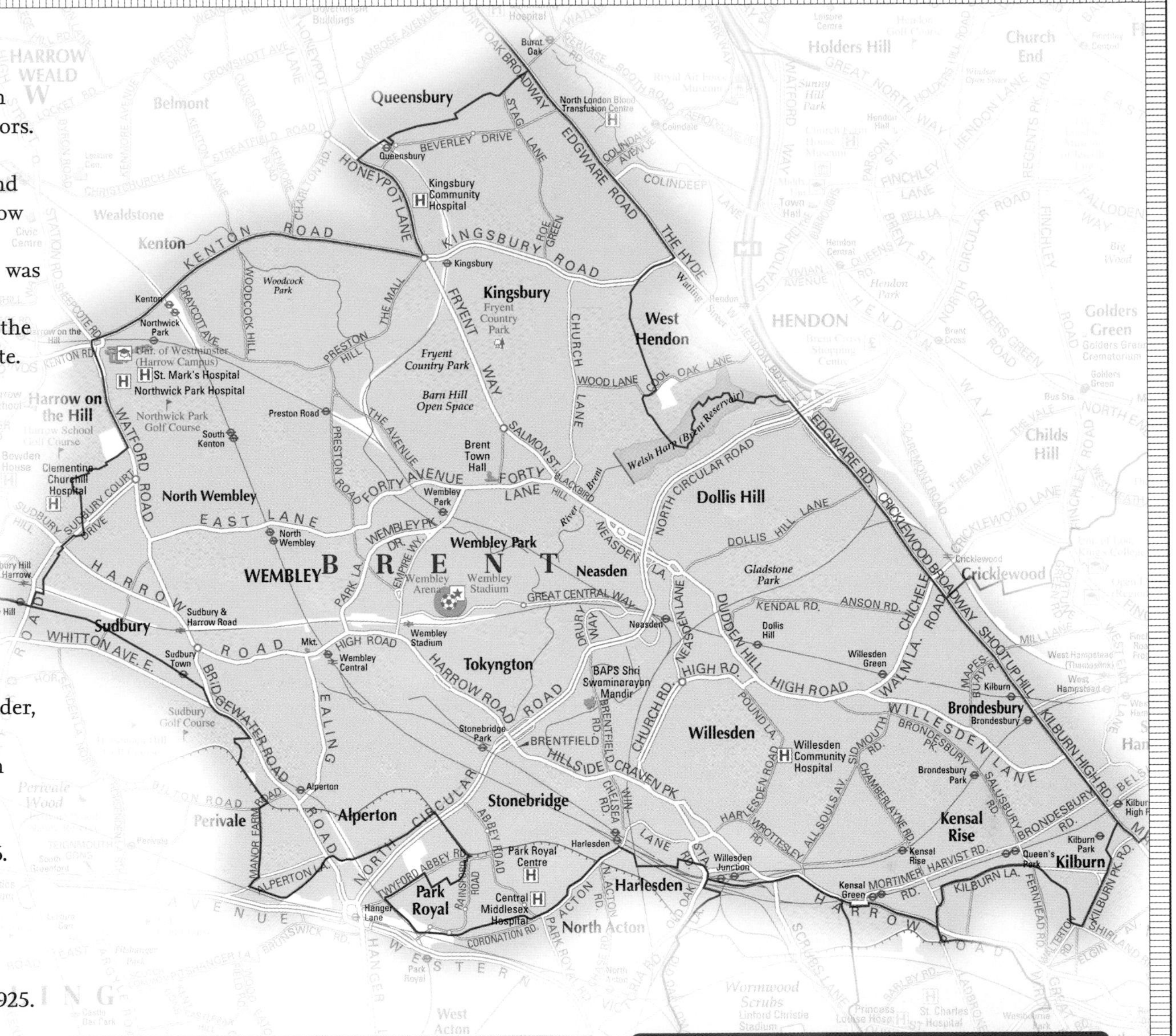

John Bartholomew, Gazetteer of the British Isles (1887)
WILLESDEN.– *par. (ry. stations Willesden Green and Willesden Junction), Middlesex, 7 miles NW. of St Paul's, London, 4383 ac. (81 water), pop. 27,453; the entire par. is a local government district, and contains parts of Kilburn, Kensal Green, Harlesden, &C.; until 1885 a small part of the par. was included in the parl. bor. of Chelsea.*

Wembley Stadium

Former Gaumont State cinema, Kilburn High Road

FOOTBALL IN LONDON

Records of the game being played in London go back a long way. In the 12th century, William Fitz-Stephen reported that ball games were played outside the city walls, players being urged on by teachers, parents and fellow apprentices, and not dissimilar sights can be seen today on Hackney Marshes, the home of Sunday League football, where over sixty football pitches are used by local teams. Football remains the most popular participation sport in London and the city is home to many professional teams, including some of the best in England and Europe. The national centre of English football is also in London, at Wembley Stadium which was rebuilt in 2007 with a capacity of 90,000 (see page 102).

The current form of football emerged in the 19th century, spurred on by the formation of the Football Association (FA) at a meeting held at the Freemasons' Tavern, Great Queen Street on 26 October 1863 and the codification of the laws that followed. All 12 founding members of the FA were London clubs. The popularity of the sport grew quickly and church youth teams and factory teams multiplied, with a few becoming professional teams. The stories behind some of the leading clubs provide insight into the social and industrial development of the city.

Arsenal was started by workers at the great munitions factory, Woolwich Arsenal, and played its first game in December 1886. Initially called Dial Square after one of the factory's workshops, the name Woolwich Arsenal was adopted in 1891 and the club turned professional. It became difficult for the Woolwich area to support a professional team and so in 1913, the club moved north of the river to a new ground at Highbury, albeit with opposition from residents and other local clubs. It dropped 'Woolwich' from its name but the link to Woolwich Arsenal is maintained by the cannon in its crest and its nickname of 'the Gunners'. It moved again, but this time only a short distance, to the Emirates Stadium, in 2006.

Chelsea was founded in 1905 and has a very different origin from most other clubs. Businessman Gus Mears had seen how popular football was in the north of England and thought London could do better. He bought an old athletics ground at Stamford Bridge, on the boundaries of Chelsea and Fulham, as a site for the stadium and then created the team as a commercial operation, signing star players from the start.

Fulham is the oldest of London's leading clubs, having been founded in 1879 as a team linked to St Andrew's Church Sunday School in West Kensington. The team moved to Craven Cottage in 1896 and became professional in 1898. Its ground is on the banks of the Thames and

LONDON FOOTBALL TEAMS IN THE PREMIER LEAGUE AND FOOTBALL LEAGUE IN 2010–11

Football Club	Stadium	Date stadium first used	Current capacity	Nicknames
Arsenal	Emirates Stadium	2006	60,432	The Gunners
Chelsea	Stamford Bridge	1905	42,449	The Blues
Fulham	Craven Cottage	1896	26,400	The Cottagers, The Whites
Tottenham Hotspur	White Hart Lane	1900	36,214	Spurs
West Ham	Boleyn Ground or Upton Park	1904	36,303	The Hammers or Irons
Crystal Palace	Selhurst Park	1924	26,309	The Eagles
Millwall	The Den	1993	20,146	The Lions
Queens Park Rangers	Loftus Road	1917	19,100	The Superhoops
Brentford	Griffin Park	1904	12,763	The Bees
Charlton Athletic	The Valley	1919	27,111	The Addicks
Dagenham and Redbridge	Victoria Road	1917	6000 (2200 seated)	The Daggers
Leyton Orient	Matchroom Stadium	1937	9271	The O's
Barnet	Underhill Stadium	1907	5500	The Bees

Boleyn Ground Stadium (Upton Park)

The Loftus Road Stadium of Queens Park Rangers in Shepherd's Bush

takes its name from a picturesque 'cottage' built there in 1780 by William Craven, 6th Baron Craven of Hampstead Marshall.

Queens Park Rangers was founded in 1882 by the old boys of Droop Street Board School in Queen's Park in North Kensington and were originally know as St Jude's Institute FC. In 1886 they merged with another local team, Christchurch Rangers, and took the name Queens Park Rangers. In their early years they played on a number of grounds in west London, became professional in 1898 and finally settled at Loftus Road, Shepherd's Bush, in 1917. They have remained there ever since, apart from two short periods at White City.

Tottenham Hotspur was founded in 1882 by boys from the Hotspur Cricket Club. It began playing games on Tottenham Marshes and took the name Tottenham Hotspur in 1884. In 1895 the club became professional and it moved to its current ground, White Hart Lane, a former market garden by Tottenham High Road, in 1899. In 1963 it was the first British club to win a major European competition, the European Cup Winners' Cup.

West Ham was created in 1895 by the Thames Iron Works and Shipbuilding Company to further the 'co-operation between workers and management'. The company, based in Canning Town, was the city's largest shipbuilder. In its foundation year it played a night match illuminated by electric light. In 1897 it moved to a new ground, Memorial Gardens, in Canning Town. The company sold the club in 1900 and it was renamed West Ham United, with professional players. In 1904 it moved to Boleyn Castle field in East Ham, better known by many as Upton Park. The nickname 'the Hammers' reflects their shipbuilding origins and is taken from the hammers on their crest, which was that of the company.

Stamford Bridge Stadium *(top)*

White Hart Lane Stadium *(middle)*

The Emirates Stadium, home to Arsenal since 2006 *(bottom)*

The first Football Association Cup Final, four days after completion of the original stadium in 1923

By 1999 the stadium was all-seated and the previously exposed terraces roofed over

The new stadium under construction 2004

The new stadium on completion

BROMLEY

Population	310,200
Area	150 sq. km
Population density	2,068 per sq. km
Area of green space	87 sq. km
Jobs in borough	119,000
Average house price	£301,800

The borough of Bromley is London's largest borough by area, with over half the land area being green belt or open land. The southern part of the borough is in the North Downs and Westerham Heights (245 m) is the highest point in Greater London. The borough takes its name from the town of Bromley, from the Old English meaning 'clearing in a wood where broom grows'. The borough was formed in 1965 from the municipal boroughs of Bromley and Beckenham and the urban districts of Orpington, Penge and the Chislehurst section of Chislehurst and Sidcup.

The area was rural in character until the coming of the railways in the mid-19th century, with settlements serving the agricultural needs of the area – Bromley was the site of a palace of the Bishops of Rochester and was also involved in the growing of hops. A symbol of change was the decision to move the Crystal Palace (used for the 1851 Great Exhibition) from Hyde Park to Sydenham Hill, where an enlarged Crystal Palace opened in 1854 and remained a landmark until it was burnt down in 1936. Areas closer to London, such as Penge, quickly grew into Victorian suburbs, while Beckenham and Bromley grew significantly in the 20th century – in 1851 the population of the borough was 17,000, by 1901 it was 99,500 and by 1951 it was 276,400. The population declined a little thereafter but has been growing strongly again in recent years. In 2007 nearly 88 per cent of the population was white, making it one of the least ethnically diverse boroughs. There is, however, significant variation in the economic wealth, with the south more wealthy than the Cray Valley and some of the areas bordering Inner London boroughs.

Traditionally, there has been little industry in the area and this is reflected in employment patterns – only 3.3 per cent of jobs are in manufacturing whilst the largest share (31 per cent) is in public administration, education and health (compared with a London average of 22 per cent). The borough is popular with commuters and around 77,000 residents work outside the borough, many in central London.

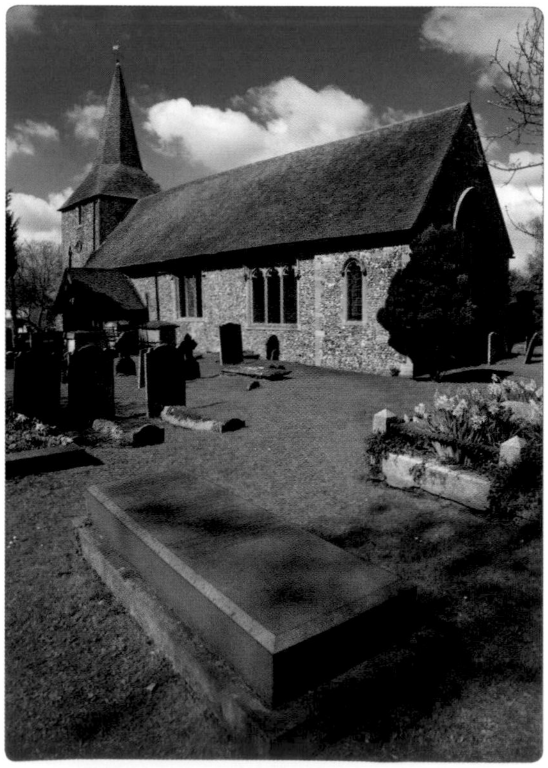

Grave of Charles Darwin's wife, St Mary's Church, Downe

FAMOUS FOR

Charles Darwin lived at **Down House**, near the village of Downe, from 1842 to his death in 1882. It was here that he wrote *On the Origin of Species by Means of Natural Selection*, published in 1859. The house and garden have been restored to reflect the time when Darwin lived there.

Napoleon III, deposed as Emperor of France in 1870, died at Camden Place in **Chislehurst** in 1873, while the Russian anarchist Prince Peter Kropotkin lived in **Bromley** from 1886 to 1914.

In the south of the borough is **Biggin Hill**, the site of an RAF station in World Wars I and II, and which played a vital part in the Battle of Britain in 1940. It is now a civil airport (London Biggin Hill) specialising in private charter flights.

Under **Chislehurst** there is a network of caves covering an area of 6 ha, and up to 30 m below the ground. They were dug out for flint and chalk (used in lime burning and brick making). In more recent times they have been used for munitions storage, mushroom growing, a World War II air-raid shelter and rock concerts.

Crofton Roman Villa in Orpington is the only Roman villa open to the public in London. Inhabited AD 140–400, ten rooms have been excavated.

Orpington is a well-known name among chicken breeders – William Cook from Orpington bred new hybrids in black, white, buff and blue between 1886 and 1905, all named after his home town.

FAMOUS PEOPLE

Thomas Carew, poet, born West Wickham, 1594/5.
William Pitt the Younger, politician, Prime Minster 1783–1801, 1804–6, born Hayes, 1759.
Allan Octavian Hume, civil servant in India and founder of the Indian National Congress, born St Mary Cray, 1829.
Herbert George (H. G.) Wells, novelist, born Bromley, 1866.
Sir Malcolm Campbell, land and water speed record holder, born Chislehurst, 1885.
Maurice Denham, actor, born Beckenham, 1909.
Denis Healey (Lord Healey), Labour politician and Chancellor of the Exchequer, born Mottingham, 1917.
Audrey Lilian (Pat) Barker, novelist and short-story writer, born St Paul Cray, 1918.
Robert (Bob) Monkhouse, comedian and entertainer, born Beckenham, 1928.
Derek Underwood, Kent and England cricketer, born Bromley, 1945.
Dame Antoinette Sibley, ballerina, born Bromley, 1939.
Hanif Kureishi, novelist and playwright, born Bromley, 1954.

There is a memorial bench at Holwood recording the event when ***William Wilberforce*** *visited William Pitt the Younger at his home at Holwood in 1787. He recorded in his diary: 'I well remember after a conversation with Mr. Pitt in the open air at the root of an old tree at Holwood, just above the steep descent into the vale of Keston, I resolved to give notice on a fit occasion in the House of Commons of my intention to bring forward the abolition of the slave-trade'.*

John Bartholomew, Gazetteer of the British Isles (1887)
BROMLEY.– *market town and par., W. Kent, on river Ravensbourne, 8 miles SE. of London by rail, 4725 ac., pop. 15,154; P.O., T.O., 1 Bank, 3 newspapers. Market-day, Thursday. B. was at one time the residence of the Bishops of Rochester. It possesses a college for clergymen's widows, and a medicinal spring strongly impregnated with chalybeate. One mile NW. of the town is* ***Bromley Hill House***.

CHISLEHURST, *par. and vil. with ry. sta., W. Kent, 2½ miles NE. of Bromley and 9 miles SE. of London, 2748 ac., pop. 5341; P.O., T.O.; and P.O. at* ***West Chislehurst***, *1 mile distant; is charmingly situated on a common, about 300 ft. above sea-level. At Camden Place, in vicinity of vil., the Emperor Napoleon III. died in exile, January 1873; his tomb is in a side chapel added to St Mary's Catholic Church.*

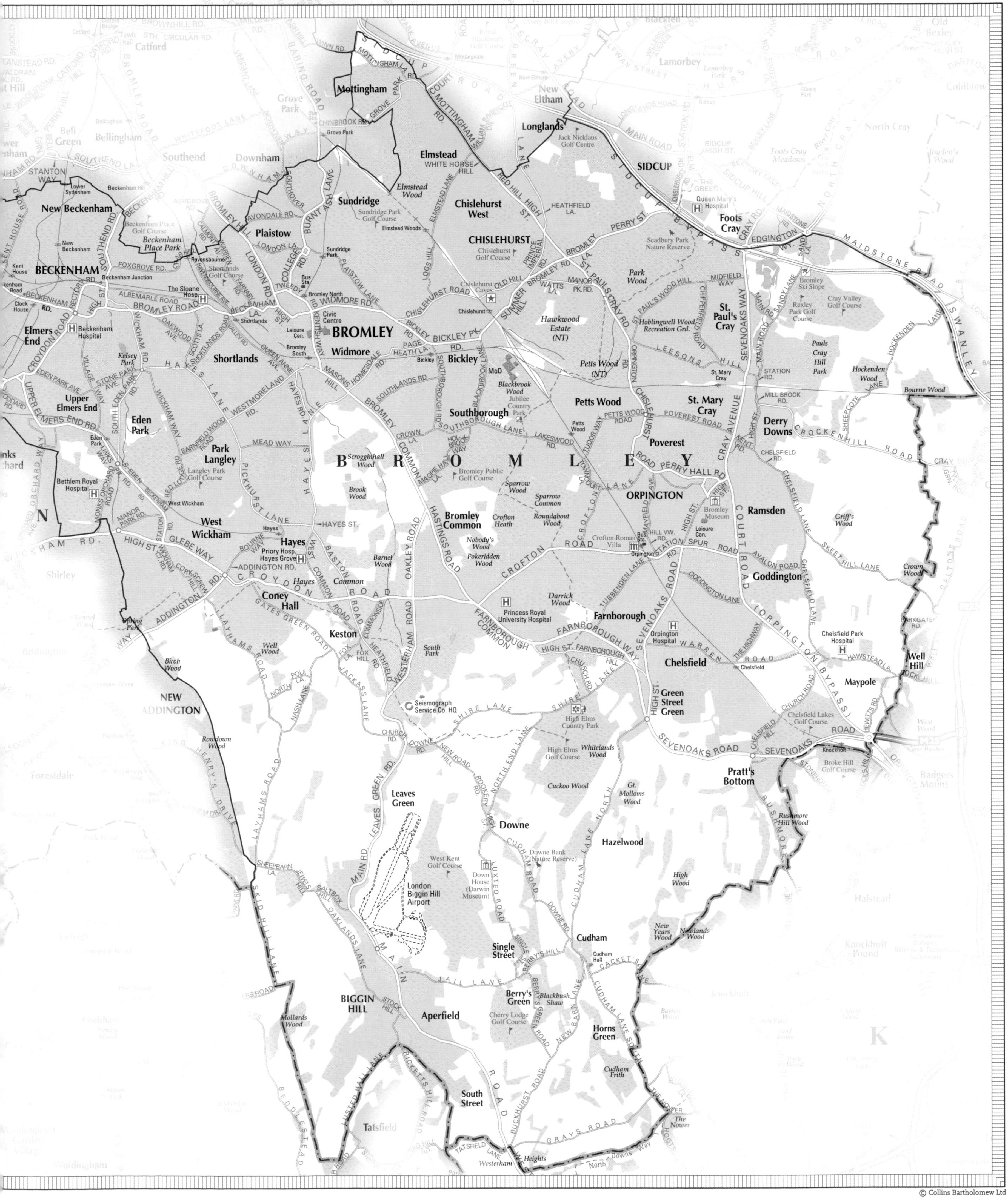
B R O M L E Y
BROMLEY
BECKENHAM
CHISLEHURST
ORPINGTON
SIDCUP
Mottingham
Elmstead
Sundridge
Plaistow
Chislehurst West
New Beckenham
Shortlands
Widmore
Bickley
Elmers End
Upper Elmers End
Eden Park
Park Langley
West Wickham
Hayes
Coney Hall
Keston
Bromley Common
Southborough
Petts Wood
St. Paul's Cray
St. Mary Cray
Foots Cray
Derry Downs
Poverest
Ramsden
Goddington
Farnborough
Chelsfield
Green Street Green
Maypole
Well Hill
Pratt's Bottom
Downe
Leaves Green
Hazelwood
Cudham
Single Street
Berry's Green
BIGGIN HILL
Aperfield
Horns Green
South Street
NEW ADDINGTON
Longlands
New Eltham
Grove Park
Downham
Bellingham
Bell Green
Southend
Catford
Lamorbey
North Cray
Tatsfield
Westerham
Heights
The Nower
Shirley
Forestdale
Badgers Mount
Halstead
Knockholt Pound
London Biggin Hill Airport
Princess Royal University Hospital
Orpington Hospital
Beckenham Hospital
Bethlem Royal Hospital
Chelsfield Park Hospital
Queen Mary's Hospital
Priory Hosp. Hayes Grove
The Sloane Hosp.
Civic Centre
Bromley Museum
Down House (Darwin Museum)
Seismograph Service Co. HQ
High Elms Country Park
Downe Bank Nature Reserve
Scadbury Park Nature Reserve
Hawkwood Estate (NT)
Petts Wood (NT)
Jack Nicklaus Golf Centre
Sundridge Park Golf Course
Chislehurst Golf Course
Shortlands Golf Course
Langley Park Golf Course
Bromley Public Golf Course
Ruxley Park Golf Course
Cray Valley Golf Course
High Elms Golf Course
West Kent Golf Course
Cherry Lodge Golf Course
Chelsfield Lakes Golf Course
Broke Hill Golf Course
Bromley Ski Slope
Chislehurst Caves
SIDCUP BYPASS
MAIDSTONE ROAD
SEVENOAKS WAY
CRAY AVENUE
CROFTON ROAD
SEVENOAKS ROAD
CROYDON ROAD
MAIN ROAD
N
K

THE GREEN SPACES OF LONDON

There is more space in Greater London that is not built on than you might imagine. While some of the areas are urban parks there is also much open countryside, particularly around the outer fringes of the city. The importance of green space has long been recognized whether in the expanses of Royal parks (see page 248) or in the preservation of Epping Forest against encroaching housing in the late 19th century. Today, around 24 per cent of London's land area is made up of domestic gardens while a further 38 per cent is open countryside. Hardly surprisingly, there is much less open space in the Inner London boroughs.

DISTRIBUTION OF SPACE
IN FOUR LONDON BOROUGHS

Gardens are an important habitat in Greater London. In the 2011 Royal Society for the Protection of Birds (RSPB) garden bird survey, the comparison of the 20 most common birds in London and across Britain produced some expected results – woodpigeons and feral pigeons were more common in London than in Britain as a whole. The most surprising bird was the ring-necked parakeet, the 14th most common bird in London but the 39th in Britain (though it would be no surprise to those who look after the Shirley Windmill in Croydon, for the parakeets damaged its sails so badly that they had to be replaced).

RSPB GARDEN BIRD WATCH 2011
MOST COMMON GARDEN BIRDS

Rank	London	UK
1	Starling	House sparrow
2	Woodpigeon	Starling
3	Blue tit	Blackbird
4	House sparrow	Blue tit
5	Blackbird	Chaffinch
6	Feral pigeon	Woodpigeon
7	Great tit	Great tit
8	Robin	Goldfinch
9	Magpie	Robin
10	Goldfinch	Collared dove
11	Collared dove	Long-tailed tit
12	Chaffinch	Dunnock
13	Carrion crow	Magpie
14	Ring-necked parakeet	Greenfinch
15	Long-tailed tit	Coal tit
16	Dunnock	Feral pigeon
17	Coal Tit	Jackdaw
18	Greenfinch	Carrion crow
19	Jay	Song thrush
20	Common gull	Wren

One major contributor to the greenness of London streets is the archetypal London plane tree. It is not a native tree, but a hybrid of two widely separated species – the Oriental plane from southeast Europe and the American plane. First described in 1670, the hybrid was probably originally bred in a nursery in Lambeth. It is a very hardy and long-lived tree that can grow up to 30 m tall and it has a number of features that make it an ideal urban tree. Its leaves provide a dappled shade, it is happy with restricted root space, it can tolerate heavy pruning and it withstands pollution – its shiny leaves are readily washed by rain and it regularly sheds its bark so ensuring that the breathing pores in its trunk do not become blocked (as well as giving the trunk a striking camouflaged look).

Nature reserves

London may not seem the most natural place to find nature reserves, but there are, in fact, many reserves, particularly in the Outer London boroughs. Perhaps the two most significant are the Rainham Marshes Reserve and the London Wetlands Centre.

Rainham Marshes on the northern bank of the Thames at the eastern edge of Greater London are ancient marshlands little changed since medieval times. For more than 100 years they were used as a military firing range and only became an RSPB reserve in 2000. The marshland provides a great habitat for visiting waders and ducks. Among the other species seen here are avocet, lapwing, little egret, ringed plover, marsh harrier, hen harrier and peregrine. The marshes are also home to water voles, frogs, butterflies and dragonflies.

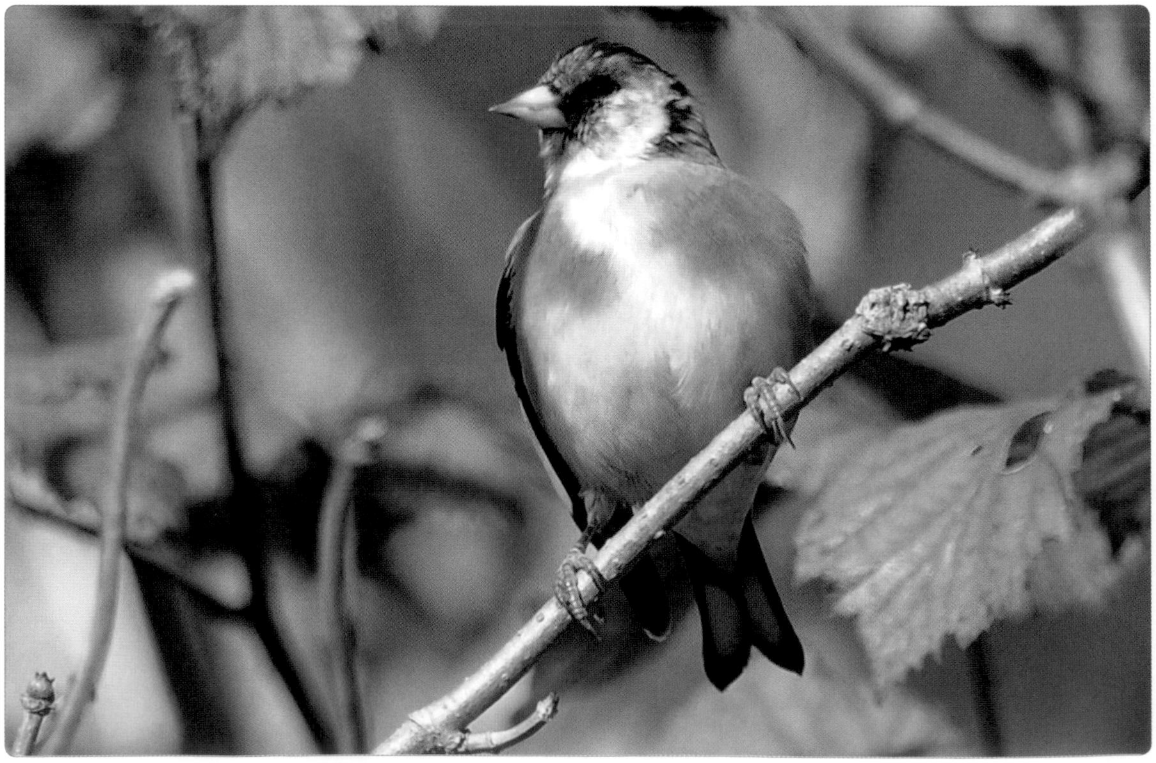

Goldfinch in Rainham Marshes RSPB Reserve

The 42 ha **London Wetland Centre** is said to be the best urban wildlife reserve in Europe. Formerly the site of some small reservoirs located next to the Thames at Barnes, it is a stunning nature haven with walkways weaving amongst lakes, ponds, meadows and reedbeds. It is home to a wide variety of wildlife: 180 species of birds, including kingfisher and bittern, water voles, amphibians, bats, grass snakes, slow worms, butterflies and moths.

The **London Wildlife Trust** has fifty-seven nature reserves across the capital, about half of which are open to the public. Many of them are spread along the southwestern fringe of Greater London from north of Uxbridge down to the North Downs near Biggin Hill. Its most central reserve is Camley Street Natural Park created out of an old coal yard on the banks of the Regent's Canal and close to St Pancras station, providing a hectare of wild space in the city.

Lee Valley Regional Park (Lee Valley Park) contains a wide range of habitats as the River Lea flows down from Hertfordshire to the Thames. It includes East India Dock Basin, the Bow Creek Ecology Park, Walthamstow Marshes and King George V Reservoir. Rammey Marsh in Enfield has a rich collection of marsh flora including bee orchid and pyramidal orchid.

London Wetland Centre

Eco-friendly Information Centre at Rainham Marshes RSPB Reserve

CAMDEN

Population	231,200
Area	22 sq. km
Population density	1,050 per sq. km
Area of green space	5.5 sq. km
Jobs in borough	305,000
Average house price	£601,094

The borough of Camden stretches from the central London areas of Holborn and Bloomsbury up to the open expanses of Hampstead Heath. It was formed in 1965 from the three metropolitan boroughs of Hampstead, Holborn and St Pancras. Camden takes its name from the area of Camden Town, named for the first Earl Camden, who started building here in 1791 – and he took his name from Camden Place in Bromley, so-called after a previous owner, William Camden, author of *Britannia* (1586). Camden only really developed with the coming of the Regent's Canal (and its many canalside industries) in 1821 and then, a little later, with the railways. The parts of the borough close to the centre of London, however, have had a long history of dense occupation, from the elegant squares and terraces of Bloomsbury, developed from the late 17th century onwards to the horrific slums of the 'Rookeries' of St Giles, just off the Tottenham Court Road, notorious for insanitary and overcrowded housing.

On current boundaries, it is estimated that the population of the borough in 1801 was around 97,000, by 1851 it was 270,000 and by 1901 it was 363,000. Since then the dense slums have been cleared and replaced by offices, and the population declined to 161,000 in 1981. It grew quickly thereafter and is now ethnically diverse, with at least 30 per cent of the population coming from black and minority ethnic groups, including a large Bangladeshi community. Indicative of its Inner city status, 86 per cent of the accommodation in the borough is in the form of flats, maisonettes or apartments. The borough contains some of the most desirable residential accommodation in inner London and some great poverty – a boy born in Hampstead has a life expectancy eleven years longer than a boy born near St Pancras.

Over 93 per cent of jobs are in the service sector, the largest area being finance, IT and other business (nearly 40 per cent). Only 16 per cent of the jobs in Camden are held by local residents and over 60 per cent of the jobs are south of the Euston Road. While the commercial sector is a large employee, the borough also contains major hospitals (University College Hospital and the Royal Free Hospital), universities, and national institutions, such as the British Library and the British Museum.

Keats House, Hampstead

FAMOUS FOR

Hampstead Heath, covering 320 ha and rising to 134 m, remains wild with meadows, woods and ponds and also includes Kenwood House and its grounds. Run by the City of London Corporation, it is visited by over 7 million people a year. There is a classic view over London from Parliament Hill.

Sir John Soane lived in **Lincoln's Inn Fields**, where his house is now a museum that bears witness to his great architectural originality. He is buried in **St Pancras Old Churchyard**, where his mausoleum, which he designed, provided the inspiration for the much-loved telephone box.

Keats House in **Hampstead** was where John Keats lived from late 1818 until he left for Rome in 1820. Much of his best verse was composed here, including 'Ode to a Nightingale'.

The **BT Tower** (formerly the Post Office Tower), on Cleveland Street, completed in 1965, was built to contain telecommunication aerials. The tower is 174 m tall and was the tallest building in Britain until 1980. A revolving restaurant on the 34th floor had to close in 1970 after an IRA bomb attack. It remains one of London's most identifiable buildings.

Sir John Soane's mausoleum, St Pancras Old Churchyard

The Roundhouse in **Chalk Farm** was a circular engine shed built in 1847. Its railway life lasted around ten years, but since the 1960s it has become famous as an avant-garde performing arts venue.

FAMOUS PEOPLE

Colley Cibber, actor, writer, and theatre manager, born Bloomsbury, 1671.
Mary Wollstonecraft Shelley (*née* Godwin), writer, author of *Frankenstein*, born Somers Town, 1797.
Sir Julian Huxley, zoologist and philosopher, born Bloomsbury, 1887.
Evelyn Waugh, writer, born West Hampstead, 1903.
Sir Cecil Beaton, photographer and stage designer, born Hampstead, 1904.
Sir John Betjeman, poet, writer, and broadcaster, born Gospel Oak, 1906.
Dame Daphne Du Maurier novelist, born Regent's Park, 1907.
Jean Baptiste de Manio (*known as* Jack de Manio), radio broadcaster, born Hampstead, 1914.
Sir Peter Ustinov, playwright and actor, born Belsize Park, 1921.
Sir Dirk Bogarde (*real name* Derek Niven van den Bogaerde), actor, born in a taxi in Hampstead, 1921.
John Schlesinger, Oscar-winning film and stage director, born Hampstead, 1926.
Graham Hill, racing driver, Formula One World Champion, born Hampstead, 1929.
Dame Elizabeth Taylor, actress, born Hampstead, 1932.
Dusty Springfield (*real name* Mary O'Brien), singer, born West Hampstead, 1939.
Sir Alan Ayckbourn, dramatist, born Hampstead, 1939.
Marianne Faithfull, singer and actress, born Hampstead, 1946
Stephen Fry, actor, writer and comedian, born Hampstead, 1957.

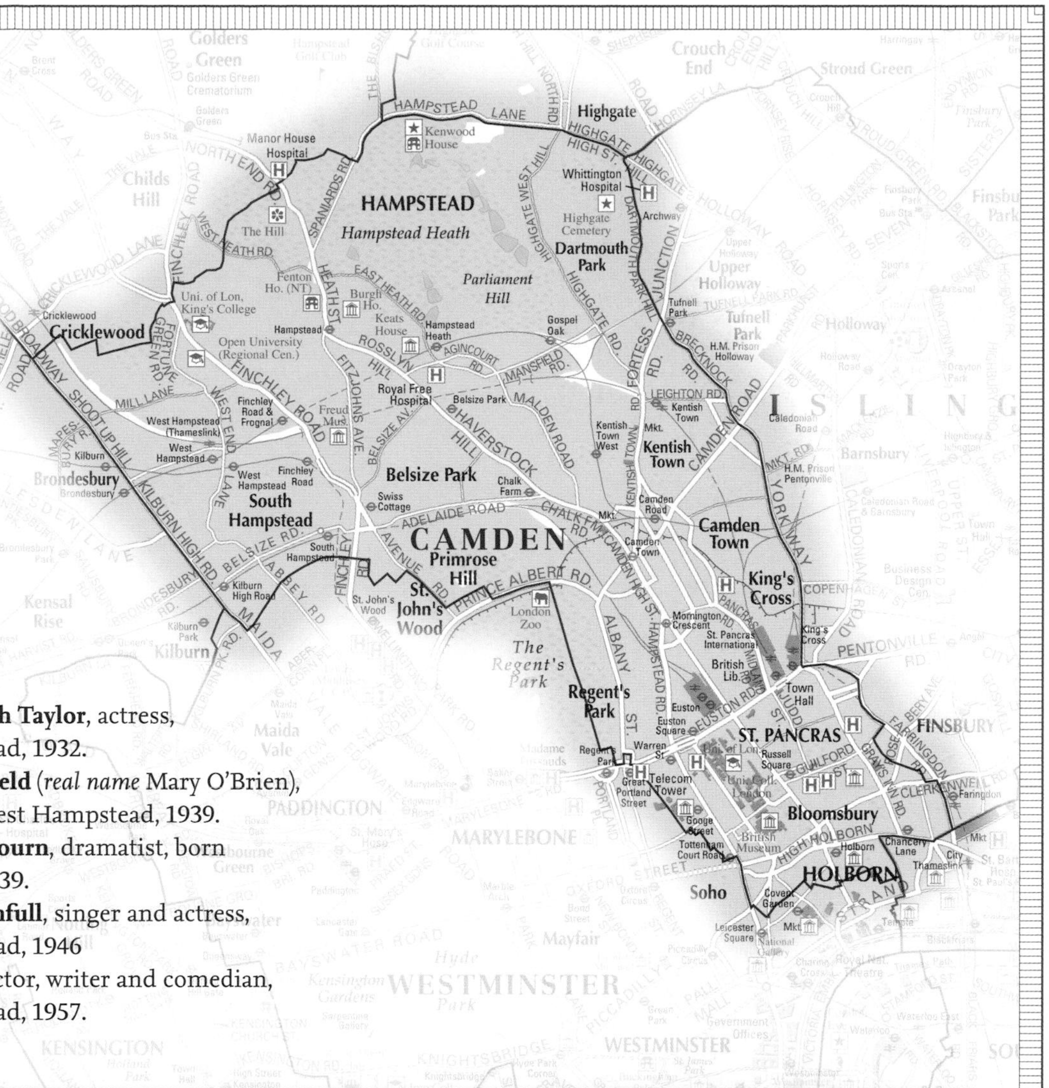

The Regent's Canal at Camden Lock

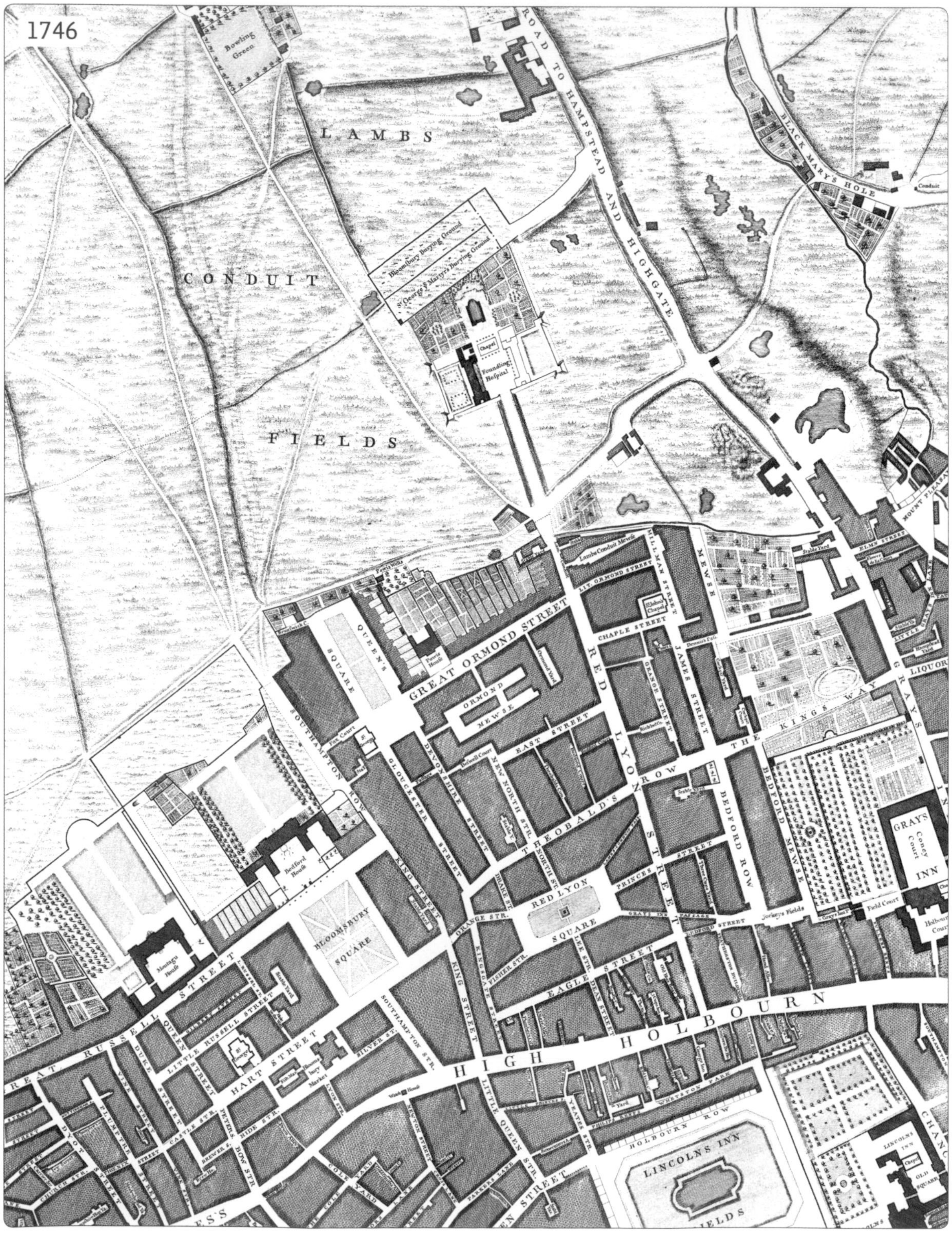

By the middle of the 18th century London's built-up area extended only as far north as Great Ormond Street, as shown in this extract from John Rocque's 1746 *Map of London*.

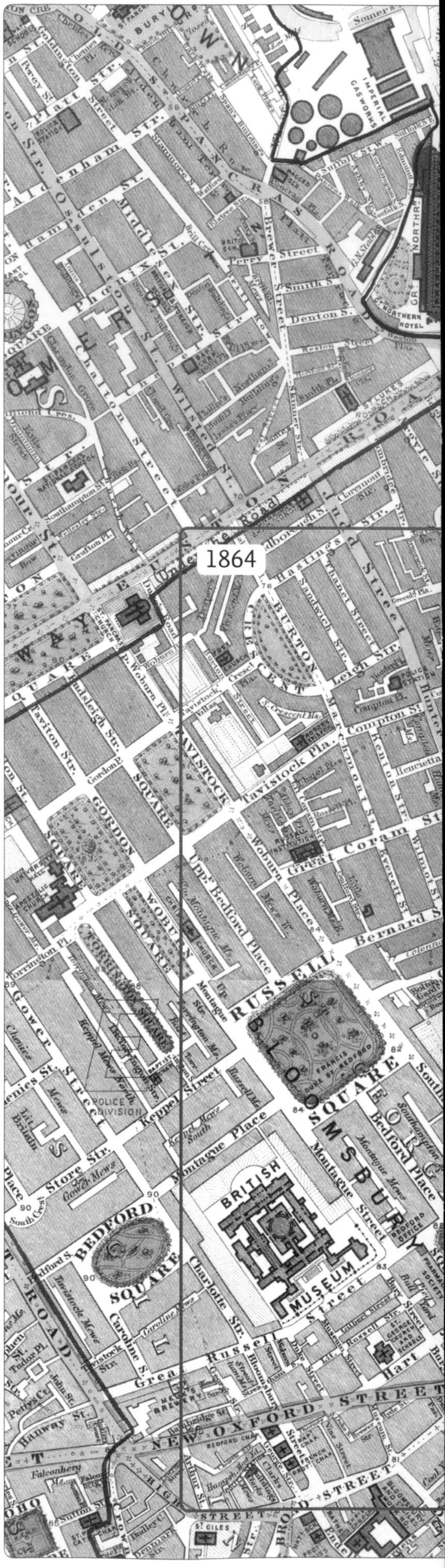

With the growth of the railway in the 19th century the city had expanded greatly with open countryside, such as Lambs Conduit Fields, now completely built over and

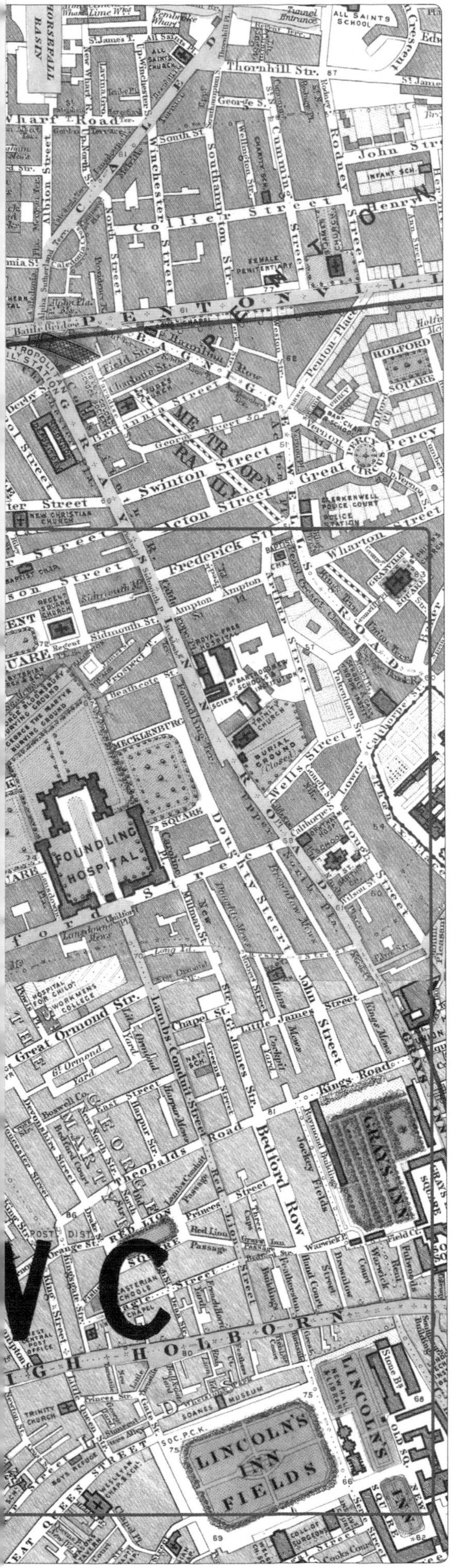

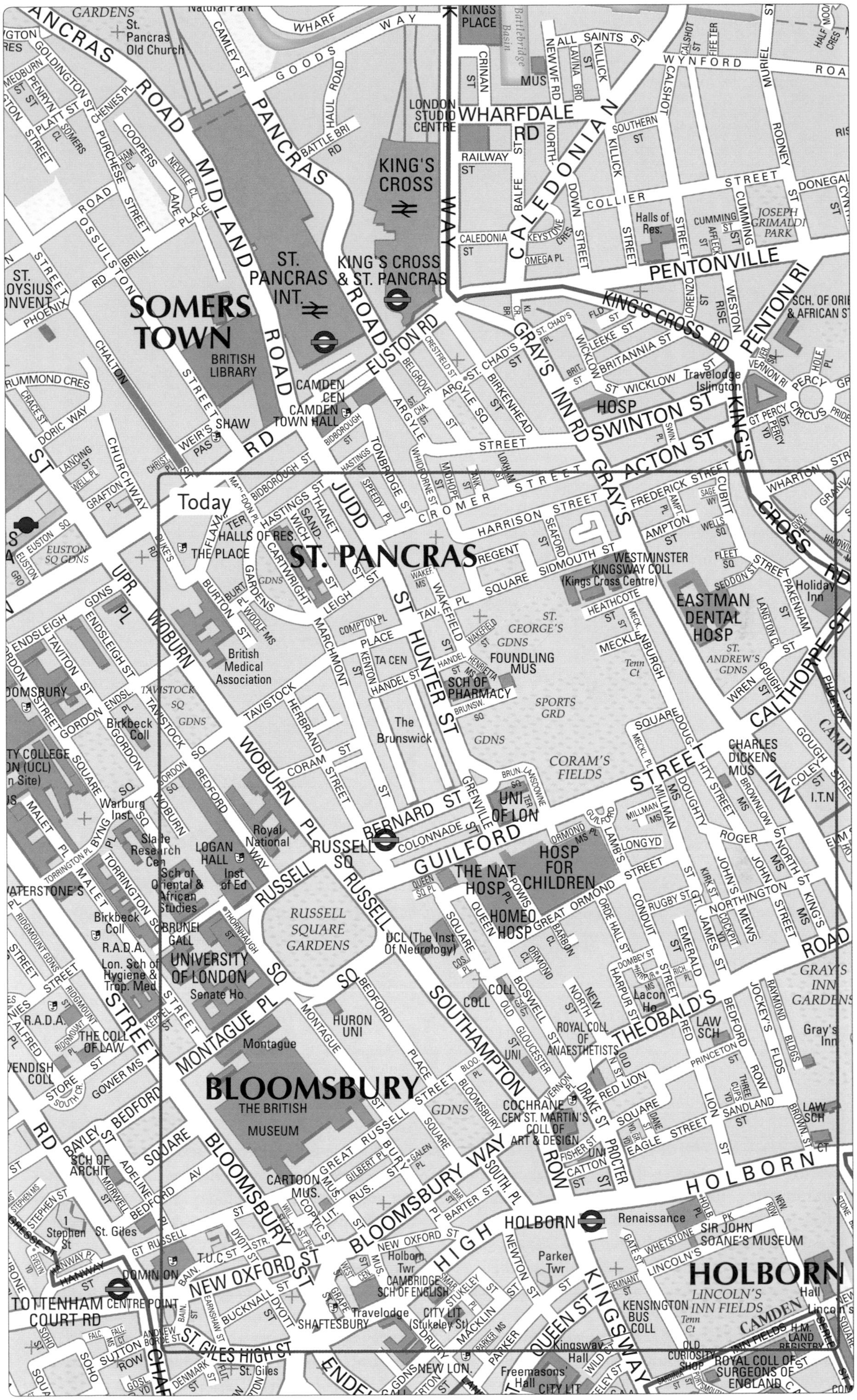

ing's Cross rail terminal completed. The construction f St Pancras terminal is underway as can be seen from he photograph above which dates from this period.

This present-day map shows that, over the centuries, the street pattern has changed very little, with parks and gardens remaining as 'green spaces' within the city.

Middle: *Stanford's Library Map of London*, 1864
Right: Collins Bartholomew mapping

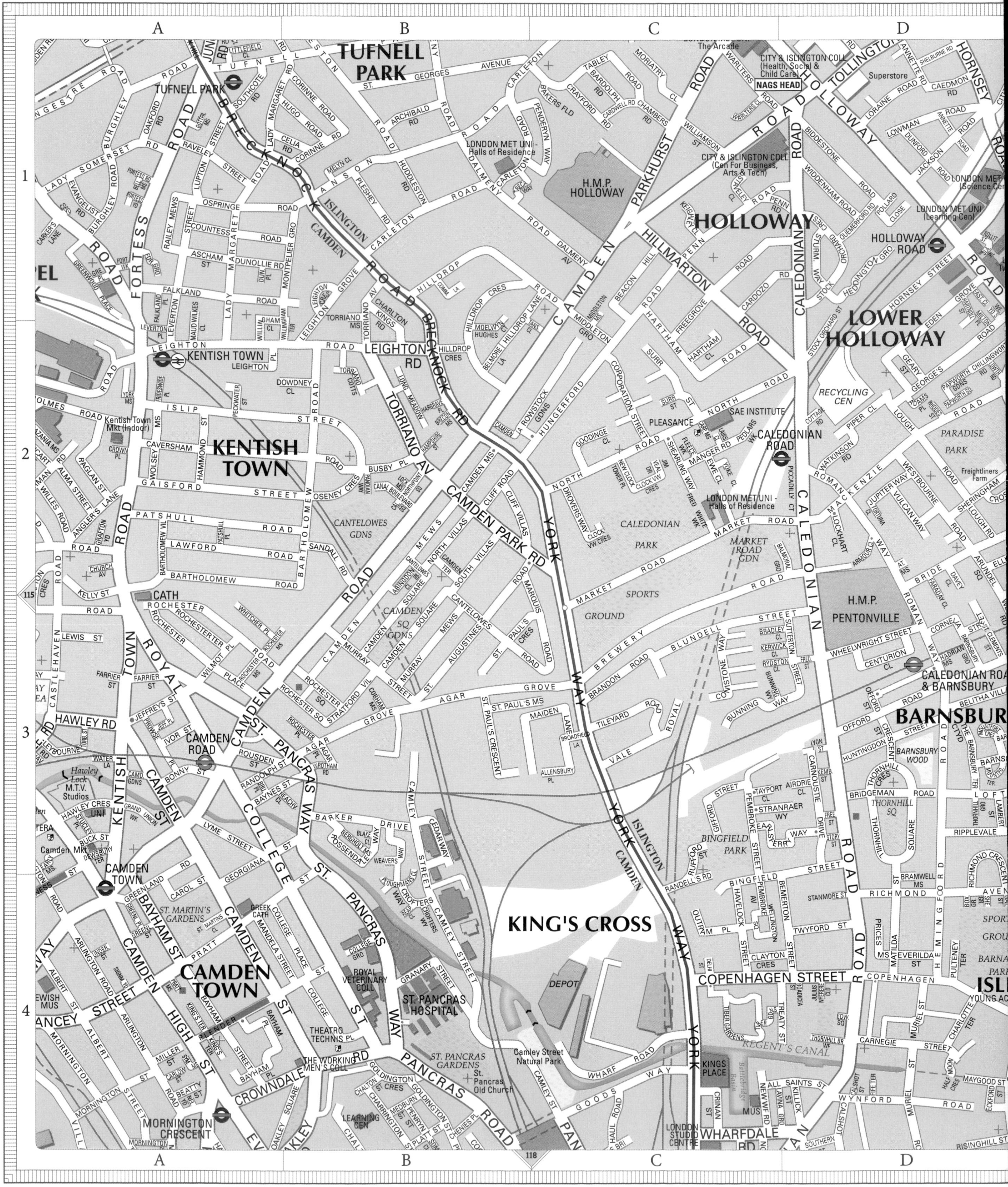
A
B
C
D
1
2
3
4
TUFNELL PARK
HOLLOWAY
LOWER HOLLOWAY
KENTISH TOWN
CAMDEN TOWN
KING'S CROSS
BARNSBURY
H.M.P. HOLLOWAY
H.M.P. PENTONVILLE
CALEDONIAN PARK
CANTELOWES GDNS
CAMDEN SQ GDNS
ST. MARTIN'S GARDENS
ST. PANCRAS GARDENS
ST. PANCRAS HOSPITAL
ROYAL VETERINARY COLL
PARADISE PARK
BARNSBURY WOOD
THORNHILL SQ
BINGFIELD PARK
REGENT'S CANAL
DEPOT
CAMDEN ROAD
CALEDONIAN ROAD
YORK WAY
CAMDEN STREET
KENTISH TOWN ROAD
CAMDEN HIGH ST
ST. PANCRAS WAY
COPENHAGEN STREET
HOLLOWAY ROAD
NAGS HEAD
MORNINGTON CRESCENT
Camley Street Natural Park
St. Pancras Old Church
115
118

E
F
G
H
1
2
3
4
HIGHBURY
CANONBURY
KINGSLAND
DE BEAUVOIR TOWN
HACKNEY
ISLINGTON
DRAYTON PARK
HIGHBURY & ISLINGTON
CANONBURY
ESSEX ROAD
DALSTON KINGSLAND
ANGEL
EMIRATES STADIUM ARSENAL FC
HIGHBURY FIELDS
LONDON MET UNI (Ladbroke Ho)
LONDON MET UNI (Spring Ho)
LAYCOCK ST OPEN SPACE
ESTORICK GALL
CANONBURY TOWER
ISLINGTON TOWN HALL
ALMEIDA
LITTLE ANGEL
KING'S HEAD
BUSINESS DESIGN CEN
N1 Shop Cen
GIBSON SQ GDNS
SPORTS GROUND
ROSEMARY GDNS
ROSEMARY THEATRE & PH
SHOREDITCH
SPORTS GRD PARK
JEWISH BURIAL GRD
KING HENRY'S WK GDN
HOLLOWAY RD
HIGHBURY GROVE
HIGHBURY PARK
ST. PAUL'S ROAD
BALLS POND ROAD
NEWINGTON GRN
ESSEX ROAD
UPPER STREET
LIVERPOOL ROAD
CANONBURY ROAD
NEW NORTH ROAD
SOUTHGATE ROAD
KINGSLAND ROAD
EAGLE WHARF ROAD
Regent's Canal
Kingsland Basin
0
1/4
1/2 Mile
0.25
0.5
0.75 Kilometres
119

A
B
C
D
1
2
3
4
116
287
289
REGENT'S PARK
Cumberland Gate
CAPEL MANOR COLLEGE
CAMDEN
WESTMINSTER
MORNINGTON CRESCENT
HAMPSTEAD ROAD
EVERSHOLT
OAKLEY SQ
SOMERS TOWN
BRITISH LIBRARY
ST. PANCRAS INT.
KING'S CROSS
KING'S CROSS & ST. PANCRAS
WHARFDALE RD
CALEDONIAN
ST. GEORGE'S CATHEDRAL
REGENT'S PARK BARRACKS
EUSTON
Thistle Euston
BUS STA
ST. PANCRAS
EUSTON SQUARE
WELLCOME COLLECTION
BLOOMSBURY
WARREN ST.
GT. PORTLAND ST
REGENT'S PARK
PARK SQUARE GARDENS
ROYAL COLL OF PHYSICIANS
UNIVERSITY COLLEGE LONDON (UCL) (Main Site)
RUSSELL SQUARE GARDENS
RUSSELL SQ
UNIVERSITY OF LONDON
Senate Ho
British Medical Association
CORAM'S FIELDS
FOUNDLING MUS
THE NAT HOSP
HOSP FOR CHILDREN
TOTTENHAM
GOWER
GOODGE ST
BT Tower
UNI OF WESTMINSTER
HEART HOSP
BLOOMSBURY
THE BRITISH MUSEUM
SOUTHAMPTON ROW
HOLBORN
KINGSWAY
TOTTENHAM COURT RD
CENTRE POINT
NEW OXFORD ST
OXFORD CIRCUS
OXFORD ST
JOHN LEWIS
DEBENHAMS
BOND ST
WIGMORE HALL
REGENT ST
LIBERTY
PALLADIUM
HAMLEYS
SOHO
CHARING CROSS
LEICESTER SQ
COVENT GARDEN
ROYAL OPERA HO
STRAND
LONG ACRE
SHAFTESBURY
CARNABY
SOTHEBY'S
FENWICK
NEW BOND
CONDUIT ST
GROSVENOR

E
F
G
H
1
2
3
4
117
131
220
PENTONVILLE
FINSBURY
CLERKENWELL
ST. LUKE'S
BARBICAN
BROAD
HOLBORN
ANGEL
FARRINGDON
BARBICAN
CHANCERY LANE
MOORGATE
OLD STREET
ST. PAUL'S
BANK
MANSION HOUSE
TEMPLE
BLACKFRIARS
CITY THAMESLINK
PENTONVILLE ROAD
CITY ROAD
GOSWELL ROAD
FARRINGDON ROAD
ST. JOHN STREET
CLERKENWELL RD
OLD STREET
BUNHILL ROW
CHISWELL STREET
LONDON WALL
HOLBORN
NEWGATE ST
FLEET STREET
CHEAPSIDE
CORNHILL
VICTORIA EMBANKMENT
NEW BRIDGE ST
ALDERSGATE ST
CHARTERHOUSE ST
HOLBORN VIADUCT
CHANCERY LANE
STRAND
BARTS & THE LONDON Charterhouse
ST. BARTHOLOMEW'S HOSPITAL
ST. PAUL'S CATHEDRAL
London Central Markets (Smithfield)
BUNHILL FIELDS BURIAL GRD
MOORFIELDS EYE HOSP
ROYAL COURTS OF JUSTICE
GUILDHALL SCH OF MUSIC & DRAMA
CITY UNI
SADLER'S WELLS THEATRE
NEW RIVER HEAD
SPA FIELDS PARK
GRAY'S INN GARDENS
City Road Basin
Wenlock Basin
Regent's Canal
THE TEMPLE
BLACKFRIARS MILLENNIUM PIER
H.Q.S. WELLINGTON
H.M.S. PRESIDENT
0
1/4
1/2 Mile
0
0.25
0.5
0.75 Kilometres

THE CEMETERIES OF LONDON

London has always faced the problem of where to bury its dead. In the densely packed medieval city its churchyards were small and quickly became overcrowded – shallow graves were dug above old internments while some coffins were buried under the floors of church buildings, not a wholesome arrangement. The Great Plague of 1665 called for extreme measures and great burial pits were dug to receive the bodies of victims. In his novel *A Journal of the Plague Year*, Daniel Defoe recorded the pit dug at Aldgate: 'As near as I may judge, it was about forty feet in length and about fifteen or sixteen feet broad, and ... it was said they dug it near twenty feet in one part of it, till they could go no deeper for the water' – in two weeks 1,114 bodies were buried.

After the plague, London parishes began to establish burial grounds outside the city. These in turn became grossly overcrowded, becoming targets of the body snatchers who sold newly buried bodies for medical dissection. By 1840, Parliament had sanctioned the building of a ring of major cemeteries around central London: Kensal Green, West Norwood, Highgate, Nunhead, Abney Park, Brompton and Tower Hamlets, each to be run as a commercial operation. Further cemeteries were built later in outer London, run by public bodies, there being objections to profit-making cemeteries.

FAMOUS CEMETERIES

Bunhill Fields, on City Road, was established as a burial ground in the mid-17th century and was where many dissenters and radicals are buried, including John Bunyan, the hymn-writer Isaac Watts, Daniel Defoe and William Blake.

Brompton Cemetery, on Old Brompton Road, was opened in 1840 on 16 ha of land. Its ambitious plan of three chapels linked by colonnades with catacombs was only partially realized. Amongst those buried there are Dr John Snow, who identified how cholera was transmitted by confirming a link between the Broad Street water pump and the disease during the London cholera outbreak of 1854 (see his map on page 12) Others buried include the author George Borrow, Sir Henry Cole, who was the organizer of the 1851 Great Exhibition, the suffragette Emmeline Pankhurst, and, until reburied in South Dakota, Long Wolf, a Sioux chief who died in London in 1892 while with Buffalo Bill's Wild West show.

City of London Cemetery, at Manor Park in Newham, is one of the largest municipal cemeteries in Europe. It opened in 1856 and over half a million burials have taken place there, mainly of people from the East End. It covers around 80 ha and contains well over 11 km of roads, and was the first cemetery to receive a Green Flag Award for its environmental management.

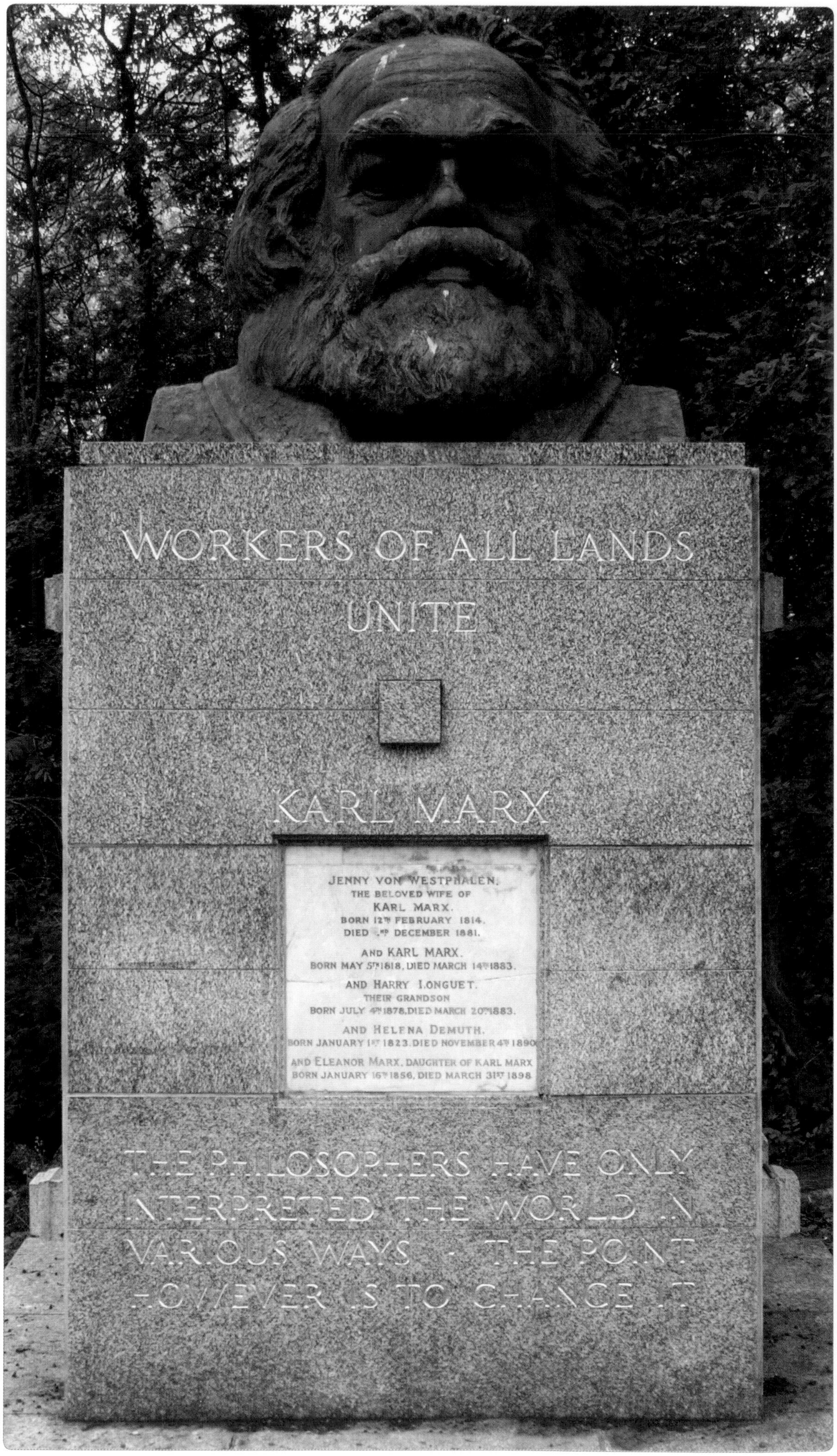

Karl Marx's tomb in Highgate Cemetery

Golders Green Crematorium, built by the London Crematorium Society, was opened in 1902 as London's first crematorium. Cremation at Golders Green was favoured by many creative people including W. S. Gilbert, Bram Stoker, Charles Rennie Mackintosh, Arnold Bennett, Rudyard Kipling, Sigmund Freud, H. G. Wells, George Bernard Shaw, Ivor Novello, Ralph Vaughan Williams, T. S. Eliot and Peter Sellers.

Highgate Cemetery is the most well-known of the commercial cemeteries, established on the hillside at Highgate in 1839 and expanded in 1855. The quality of the buildings and landscaping attracted many burials, and also many living visitors. The most famous grave is that of Karl Marx, while others buried there include George Eliot, Michael Faraday, Christina Rossetti, Douglas Adams and Alexander Litvinenko, the former Russian spy poisoned in 2006. It was here that Elizabeth Siddall, Dante Gabriel Rossetti's wife was buried – at the graveside Rossetti threw in an unpublished book of verse, which, five years' later, he had exhumed so that he could publish the poems.

Kensal Green opened in 1832 and was the first of the great London cemeteries. Covering 22 ha it became one of London's most popular cemeteries and those buried there include Marc and Isambard Kingdom Brunel, W. M. Thackeray, Charles Babbage, Anthony Trollope and Wilkie Collins. In 1914 G. K. Chesterton immortalized the place:

For there is good news yet to hear and fine things to
be seen,
Before we go to Paradise by way of Kensal Green.

Grave of the writer and journalist, Daniel Defoe, at Bunhill Fields

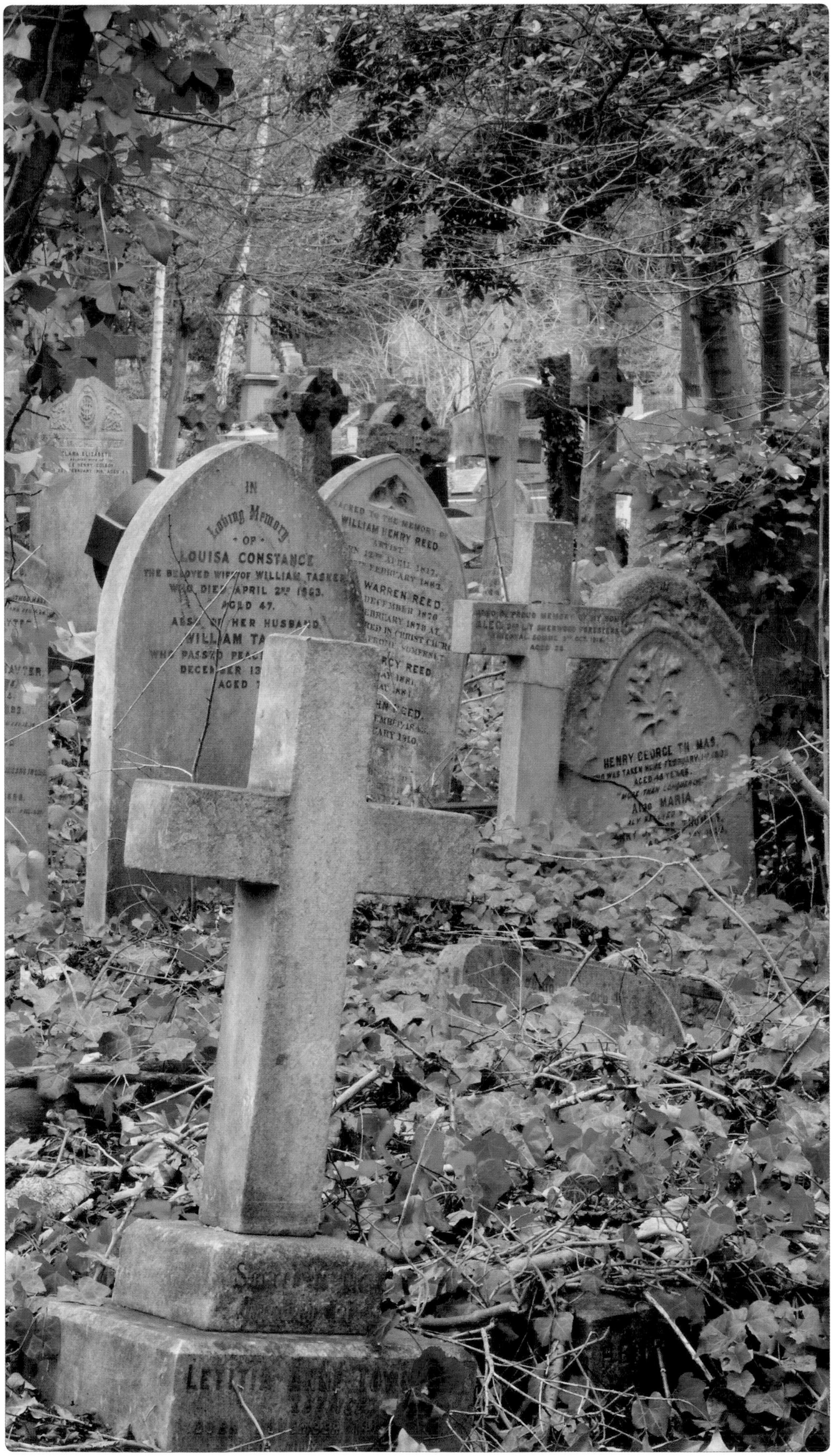

Headstones, Highgate Cemetery

CITY OF LONDON

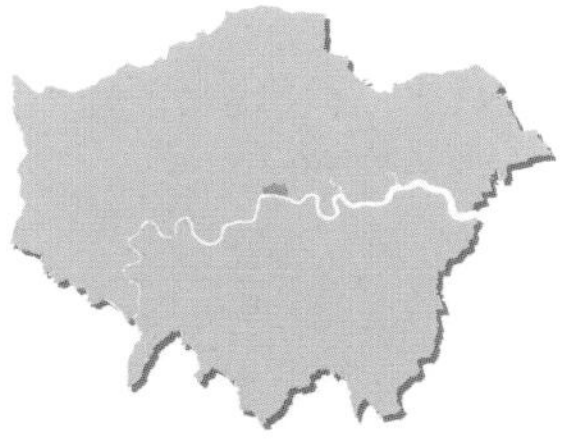

Population	11,500
Area	3 sq. km
Population density	3,800 per sq. km
Area of green space	0.2 sq. km
Jobs in borough	362,000
Average house price	£453,512

The City of London is unlike any other borough in London, or, indeed, any other local authority in Britain. Its boundaries are still little bigger than the walled Roman city of *Londinium* (the main additional area being in the west), although it is responsible for areas outside its boundaries, such as Hampstead Heath and Epping Forest, for markets once in the City but now beyond its boundaries, such as Billingsgate and New Spitalfields, the Port Health Authority, and it has its own police force. While only 11,500 people live within the City, it supports over 362,000 jobs and is one of the world's major financial centres.

The City (or the Square Mile) is the heart of historic London and has been the commercial centre of Britain for well over 1,000 years. Its power has been treated with respect by monarchs and national politicians – it did not become part of London County Council in 1889 and only reluctantly became part of the Greater London Council in 1965. Its system of local democracy is unique in many ways. The City of London Corporation is headed by the Lord Mayor of London and the Court of Aldermen and the Court of Common Council. The City itself is divided into twenty-five historic wards which elect one alderman and a number of Common Councillors depending on the size of the electorate – but unlike anywhere else that electorate includes not just residents but representatives of businesses based in the City.

While the method of government of the City may be from another age, there is no doubting the centrality of the City in the economy of the country. All the signs are that it is recovering from the banking crisis of 2008, a resurgence made physical by the emergence of more skyscrapers to join 30 St Mary Axe (better known as the Gherkin), completed in 2004; these include the Heron Tower (2011) and a number of others culminating in the sixty-three storey Pinnacle (nick-named the Helter Skelter), in Bishopsgate (2013). The City also contains historic buildings of great significance, although almost all date from after the Great Fire. These include St Paul's Cathedral and many surviving Wren parish churches, the Guildhall, which dates from the 15th century onwards and is heart of the City's administration, a number of halls of Livery Companies, the College of Arms, the Mansion House and the Inner and Middle Temples, home to many of London's barristers. Other medieval survivors include the Temple Church, a circular church built in the late 12th century for the Knights Templars, and the Priory Church of St Bartholomew the Great, founded as an Augustinian priory in 1123 and one of London's oldest churches, which is next to St Bartholomew's Hospital, founded in the same year and Britain's longest continuing running hospital.

FAMOUS FOR

The Monument, in Fish Street Hill, close to London Bridge, is 61 m tall and 61 m away from the site of the bakers in Pudding Lane where the Great Fire started in 1666. Designed by Wren, it is a hollow fluted column surmounted by a gilded flaming urn. A climb of 311 steps will bring you to a viewing platform, at a height of around 50 m.

The **Lloyd's Building** houses Lloyd's of London, the world's leading insurance market, whose origins go back to its informal establishment in Edward Lloyd's Coffee House in 1688. Its current building, designed by Richard Rogers (now Lord Rogers) is an uncompromisingly modern building that opened in 1986.

The **Temple Bar**, designed by Wren, used to be the entrance to the City along the Strand, and can now be seen at Paternoster Square by St Paul's Cathedral (though in 1889 it was moved from the Strand to Theobalds Park in Hertfordshire, returning in 2004).

The area to the north of London Wall was badly bombed and in the 1950s and 1960s the **Barbican** estate was built by the City of London Corporation. Its brutalist blocks of low rise and high-rise flats are now listed buildings. The Museum of London is at the Barbican.

In 1441, the former Lord Mayor, Richard Whittington, gifted the land of **Leadenhall** to the City, and shortly thereafter a market developed selling poultry, dairy products, herbs and other foodstuffs. The late 19th-century market building makes for an imposing setting.

The Gherkin and the 16th-century church of St Andrew Undershaft

The Monument

FAMOUS PEOPLE

Thomas Becket (St Thomas of Canterbury), Archbishop of Canterbury, born Cheapside, *c.* 1120.

Sir Thomas More (St Thomas More), Lord Chancellor and martyr, born Milk Street, 1478.

John Milton, poet, born Bread Street, 1608.

Samuel Pepys, diarist and naval official, born Fleet Street, 1633.

Sir John Vanbrugh, playwright and architect, born Nicholas Lane, 1664.

Alexander Pope, poet, born Lombard Street, 1688.

David Ricardo, political economist, born Broad Street, 1772.

Benjamin Gompertz, mathematician and actuary, developed the Gompertz Equation, born Bury Street, 1779.

John Keats, poet, born Moorgate, 1795.

Thomas Hood, poet and humorist, born Poultry, 1799.

Cardinal (Blessed) John Henry Newman, priest and theologian, born Old Broad Street, 1801.

Sir Ebenezer Howard, founder of garden city movement, born Fore Street, 1850.

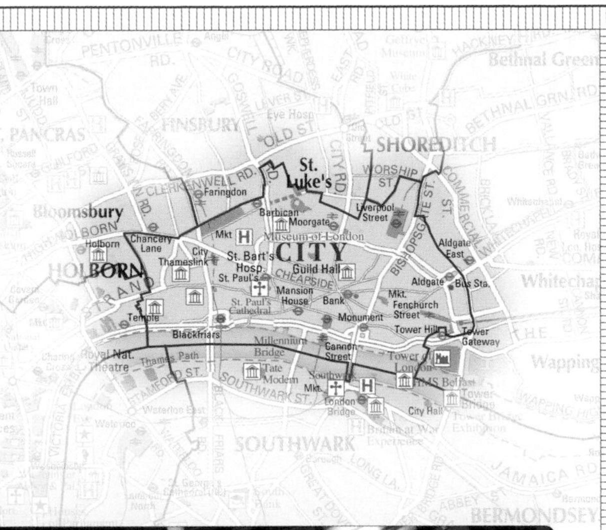

Lloyd's Building

Staple Inn, on High Holborn, a Tudor Inn of Chancery and a reminder of what London looked like before the Great Fire

Looking west from the Dome of St Paul's, as recorded by Thomas Allom in 1846

The same view in the 21st century – while most buildings have changed, the street pattern is easily recognizable

An aerial view of St Paul's Cathedral in 1932

Eighty years on and St Paul's Cathedral still rises above the buildings around it

The Mansion House, the Lord Mayor's official residence, looking west towards Cheapside, around 1926

The Bank of England and the Royal Exchange, mid 1920s

Cheapside, around 1900 – note the horse-drawn double decker omnibus in the foreground. The steeple in the background is St Mary-le-Bow

ROMAN LONDON

It has been suggested that Julius Caesar crossed the Thames in 54 BC at Brentford, marking the first Roman presence in the London area, although the evidence for this is hard to substantiate. What is known is that in the invasion of AD 43 the Roman army forded the Thames within the central London area. By AD 50 they had built a bridge across the river close to the present site of London Bridge and began to build a settlement on the north bank of the Thames. This settlement of *Londinium* grew in importance with the construction of roads (among them Watling Street and Ermine Street) that radiated from the bridge across the new province of Britannia, whose capital at this time was at *Camulodunum* (Colchester). The first town was short-lived, for in AD 60 it was all but destroyed in Queen Boudicca's rising against the Roman occupation. Roman rule was soon restored, with *Londinium* becoming the capital of the province and its commercial hub. By the early 2nd century, *Londinium* supported a population of around 30,000 and contained a forum, amphitheatre and fort. It was at its grandest when Emperor Hadrian visited in AD 122.

Thereafter the size and importance of the city went into decline. It was enclosed by a wall around AD 190–220. The wall, about 5.5 m high and nearly 3 km long enclosing an area of 130 ha, was a massive undertaking – it was built of Kentish ragstone, brought to London by barges from near Maidstone. Fragments of the wall are the most substantial Roman remains left in London. Outside the wall there was a massive protective ditch (or *fossa*) – Houndsditch marks the site of part of this ditch. The decline continued, however, and some areas to the west of the Walbrook were abandoned, as was the forum. After the Romans left in AD 410, it was deserted until Alfred the

An artist's impression of *Londinium* in the 2nd century AD. The sites of some current buildings have been added to provide a guide to the location of the Roman city

A bastion of the City Wall at the Barbican, built on the foundations of the Roman Wall

A section of the Roman Wall at Tower Hill, near the Tower of London (in the background)

Great saw the great defensive value of the city wall and resettled the city within it. In the centuries that followed the wall was much rebuilt. Even today the location of the wall is little different from the boundary of the City of London.

What remains of Roman London today?

The most substantial remains are parts of the Roman wall (frequently with medieval additions) – major sections can be seen close to the Museum of London at London Wall and close to the Tower of London. One notable find is the western gate in the Roman Wall, now contained within an underground car park close to the Museum of London.

The most recent significant discovery was of the site of the Roman amphitheatre, close to the Guildhall. The site was discovered in 1988 and in 2002 it was incorporated within a special gallery in the Guildhall Art Gallery. A line now marks the site of the amphitheatre in the square outside the Guildhall.

The Temple of Mithras was discovered in 1954 close to the banks of the Walbrook. This pagan temple was thought to have been built around AD 240. Its remaining foundations were moved from its original site to Temple Court in Queen Victoria Street where it is open to public view. It is now planned to move it back to its original underground setting in the new Walbrook Square development.

The London Stone, perhaps the most enigmatic and neglected of London's antiquities, is likely to have come from Roman times. The stone is set into the wall of an office building at 111 Cannon Street. Made of limestone, there are no decorations beyond a pair of grooves. It is known to have existed in 1198 and there was a popular belief that it was the Roman milestone from which all measurements were made and so represented the heart of London. It may, equally, just be a stone from a Roman building. Yet more romantic origins have been suggested – that it was brought to London by Brutus of Troy, the great-grandson of Aeneas, who established London in 1100 BC – while William Blake was convinced that it marked the site of Druid executions.

There were many smaller Roman settlements scattered around the Greater London area, such as the Crofton Roman villa at Orpington. In 2010 while work was underway on a new hotel, a significant Roman settlement was also discovered in Syon Park, built around the Roman road from London to Silchester. Over 11,000 artefacts have been excavated by the Museum of London archaeologists.

A
B
C
D
1
2
3
4
119
118
220
ST. PANCRAS
BLOOMSBURY
HOLBORN
CLERKENWELL
STRAND
SOUTHWARK
CITY
WESTMINSTER
LAMBETH
River Thames
King's Reach
THE BRITISH MUSEUM
RUSSELL SQUARE GARDENS
UNIVERSITY OF LONDON
CORAM'S FIELDS
FOUNDLING MUS
GRAY'S INN GARDENS
LINCOLN'S INN FIELDS
SIR JOHN SOANE'S MUSEUM
ROYAL COURTS OF JUSTICE
KING'S COLL LIB
LON SCH OF ECO & POL SCI.
ROYAL OPERA HO
COVENT GARDEN
SOMERSET HOUSE
THE TEMPLE
ST. PAUL'S CATHEDRAL
ST. BARTHOLOMEW'S HOSPITAL
London Central Markets (Smithfield)
NATIONAL GALLERY
NATIONAL THEATRE
ROYAL FESTIVAL HALL
SOUTHBANK CENTRE
TATE MODERN
MILLENNIUM BRIDGE
H.M.S. PRESIDENT
BLACKFRIARS MILLENNIUM PIER
EMBANKMENT PIER
SAVOY PIER
MINISTRY OF DEFENCE
BFI IMAX
LONDON EYE
HOLBORN
FARRINGDON
CHANCERY LANE
RUSSELL SQ
COVENT GARDEN
LEICESTER SQ
CHARING CROSS
EMBANKMENT
TEMPLE
BLACKFRIARS
ST. PAUL'S
BARBICAN
CITY THAMESLINK
FARRINGDON ROAD
CLERKENWELL ROAD
THEOBALD'S ROAD
HOLBORN VIADUCT
KINGSWAY
ALDWYCH
STRAND
FLEET STREET
VICTORIA EMBANKMENT
WATERLOO BRI
BLACKFRIARS BRI
SOUTHWARK STREET
STAMFORD STREET
UPPER GROUND
NEW OXFORD ST
HIGH HOLBORN
SHAFTESBURY
CHANCERY LANE
NEW BR ST
FARRINGDON ST
ALDERSGATE ST
GOSWELL RD
ST JOHN ST
ROSEBERY AV
GRAY'S INN ROAD
SOUTHAMPTON ROW
WHITEHALL
NORTHUMBERLAND AV
ST. MARTIN'S LA
CHARING CROSS RD

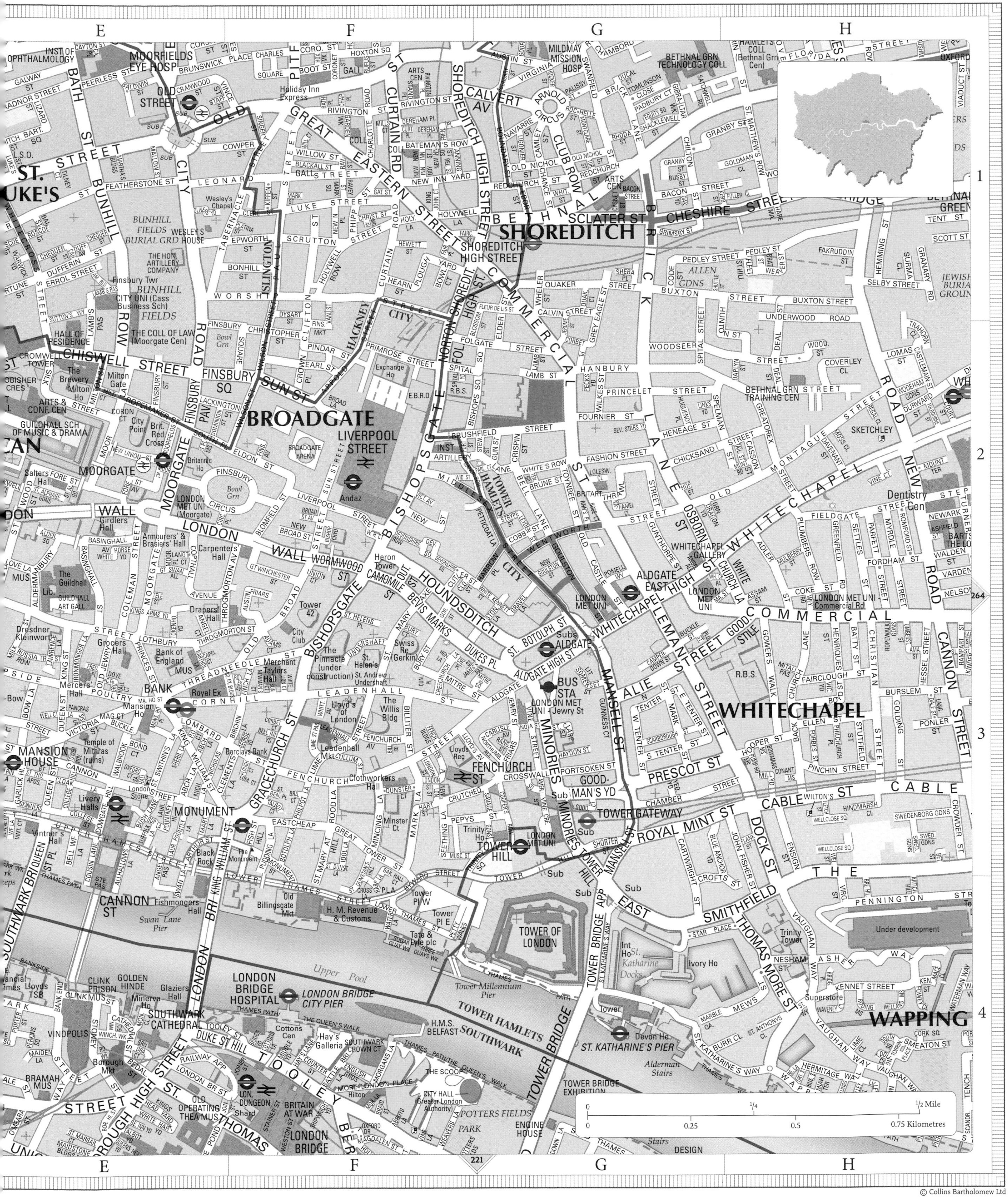
E
F
G
H
1
2
3
4
ST. LUKE'S
SHOREDITCH
BROADGATE
WHITECHAPEL
WAPPING
MOORFIELDS EYE HOSP
OLD STREET
BUNHILL FIELDS BURIAL GRD
WESLEY'S HOUSE
Wesley's Chapel
THE HON. ARTILLERY COMPANY
CITY UNI (Cass Business Sch)
THE COLL OF LAW (Moorgate Cen)
SHOREDITCH HIGH STREET
LIVERPOOL STREET
Exchange Ho
BROADGATE ARENA
MOORGATE
LONDON MET UNI (Moorgate)
FINSBURY CIRCUS
Girdlers Hall
Armourers' & Brasiers' Hall
Carpenters Hall
Drapers Hall
The Guildhall
GUILDHALL ART GALL
GUILDHALL SCH OF MUSIC & DRAMA
Dresdner Kleinwort
Grocers Hall
Bank of England MUS
Merchant Taylors Hall
BANK
Royal Ex
Mercers' Hall
Mansion Ho
Temple of Mithras (ruins)
MANSION HOUSE
CANNON ST
MONUMENT
The Monument
Heron Tower
Tower 42
City Club
The Pinnacle (under construction)
St. Helen's
Swiss Re (Gerkin)
Lloyd's of London
The Willis Bldg
Leadenhall Mkt
Lloyds Reg
FENCHURCH ST
Clothworkers Hall
Minster Ct
Trinity Ho
TOWER HILL
ALDGATE
ALDGATE EAST
BUS STA
LONDON MET UNI - Jewry St
TOWER GATEWAY
WHITECHAPEL GALLERY
LONDON MET UNI
R.B.S.
BETHNAL GRN TRAINING CEN
LONDON MET UNI - Commercial Rd
Dentistry Cen
TOWER OF LONDON
St. Katharine Docks
Ivory Ho
Trinity Tower
Under development
Tower Millennium Pier
TOWER BRIDGE
ST. KATHARINE'S PIER
TOWER BRIDGE EXHIBITION
CITY HALL (Greater London Authority)
POTTERS FIELDS PARK
H.M.S. BELFAST
Hay's Galleria
LONDON BRIDGE HOSPITAL
LONDON BRIDGE CITY PIER
LONDON BRIDGE
LON. DUNGEON
BRITAIN AT WAR
OLD OPERATING THEA MUS
SOUTHWARK CATHEDRAL
VINOPOLIS
CLINK PRISON MUS
GOLDEN HINDE
Borough Mkt
BRAMAH MUS
Billingsgate Mkt
H. M. Revenue & Customs
Tate & Lyle plc
Fishmongers Hall
Swan Lane Pier
Upper Pool
TOWER HAMLETS
SOUTHWARK
CITY
264
221
1/4
1/2 Mile
0
0.25
0.5
0.75 Kilometres

THE LORD MAYOR OF LONDON

The City of London is the oldest continuous municipal democracy in the world. It has had a degree of independence from the Crown since the time of Edward the Confessor. In the late 12th century the office of mayor was created – Henry FitzAilwyn 'of Londonstone' was the first mayor (from 1189 to 1212). King John granted the citizens of London the right to elect their own mayor annually in 1215 (five weeks before he signed the Magna Carta). The title of 'Lord Mayor' was never officially granted but just came into common use from around 1283 – and the earliest reference in written English to 'Lord Mair' is in 1414.

The Lord Mayor is head of the City Corporation and acts as an ambassador for Britain's financial services. The position also carries many other responsibilities including being Chief Magistrate of the City of London and Admiral of the Port of London among other offices. The Lord Mayor's role should not be confused with that of Mayor of London, a position created in 2000. There have been over 700 men but just one woman Lord Mayor since 1189.

The Lord Mayor is elected from, and by, the Court of Aldermen at the end of September each year. On the Friday before the second Saturday in November he is sworn in and the symbols of authority are transferred to him in silence (the Silent Change). The next day by tradition he processes to the Royal Courts of Justice to pledge allegiance to the Crown, a procession now celebrated in the Lord Mayor's Show. The Lord Mayor travels in the spectacular Lord Mayor's Coach, built in 1757 and glistening with gilded carvings and ornate painted panels. Ahead of the state coach in 2010 there were 150 horses, 21 carriages, 20 marching bands, 6,000 people and many floats – indeed the procession stretched for nearly 5 km. In the evening there is a firework display by the Thames and on the following Monday the Lord Mayor hosts the Lord Mayor's Banquet at the Guildhall, held annually for over 400 years and now addressed by the Prime Minister. The Lord Mayor's official residence is the Mansion House, built in 1759 in the heart of the City, next to the Bank of England.

The most well-known Lord Mayor is Richard Whittington, Lord Mayor in 1397, 1398, 1406 and 1419, though fact and folk history are very different. He was born into a wealthy family and was a successful textile and wool merchant and financier before becoming mayor. He was a great benefactor during his lifetime and on his death, his fortune was given to charity. All in all far removed from the stage character of Dick Whittington and his cat setting out to make a fortune, a story that first appeared in the early 17th century and has been embroidered upon ever since.

Lord Mayor and Lord Mayor's Coach, 2010

The Livery Companies

In medieval times those working in particular trades or crafts formed guilds to regulate and control their trade and to provide training and welfare support for their members. In London they became known as 'Livery Companies' because members of each guild wore an identifiable uniform ('livery'). There are now 108 livery companies in the City of London, and while many date from the 15th century or earlier, 31 have been formed since 1926, the most recent to be admitted (in 2008) being the Worshipful Company of Security Professionals. While the companies no longer control their trades, they remain active in charitable and educational work and in general promotion of their trade. Livery members, through the Common Hall, select two Aldermen, one of whom will then be elected Lord Mayor by the Court of Aldermen.

Under half of the Livery Companies now have halls in the City and, as a result of the immense damage caused both by the Great Fire and by the Blitz, few historic halls remain, the oldest being the Apothecaries' Hall in Blackfriars, built in 1672. Perhaps the most impressive is the Stationers' Hall, near St Paul's Cathedral, dating from the late 17th century.

The Livery Companies give an indication of the commercial activities of the City over time. There is an order of precedence for companies, linked to their date of foundation. The list on this page brings the medieval trades of the city to life.

The first 20 Livery Companies in order of precedence

Mercers (merchants in wool, velvet and silk)
Grocers
Drapers
Fishmongers
Goldsmiths
Merchant Taylors
Skinners (fur trade)
Haberdashers
Salters
Ironmongers
Vintners
Clothworkers
Dyers
Brewers
Leathersellers
Pewterers
Barbers
Cutlers
Bakers
Wax Chandlers

Mercers

Grocers

Drapers

Fishmongers

Goldsmiths

Merchant Taylors

Skinners

Haberdashers

Salters

Ironmongers

Vintners

Clothworkers

Plaque at the Church of St Michael Paternoster Royal, founded by Richard Whittington

The Lord Mayor's procession

THE GREAT FIRE OF LONDON

In 1666 London was beginning to recover from the ravages of the Great Plague that closed down the city and killed approaching 100,000 people the previous year. In the early morning of Sunday, 2 September a worker at the Pudding Lane bakehouse of the king's baker, Thomas Farynor, smelled burning and alerted the household. Within an hour the fire quickly spread, being able to leap across the narrow streets between overhanging timber buildings. The Lord Mayor was woken but thought little of it, reportedly saying that 'a woman could piss it out'.

Dawn brought a rather different picture, and when Londoners awoke, the fire had already burnt part of London Bridge. Still residents refused to allow their houses to be pulled down to provide firebreaks, while many, including Samuel Pepys, simply thought that the fire was like many smaller fires seen before. However, fanned by a strong east wind, it jumped whatever firebreaks had been created. In spite of the best endeavours of parish and ward officials, the fire moved faster than the fire-fighters and the city could not be saved. The fire raced west along the waterfront, which was packed with combustibles such as timber, pitch and oil, reaching Three Cranes (present-day Southwark bridge) by the afternoon. Londoners gathered up their possessions and fled by foot, road and river.

The fire burnt all night and gained momentum throughout Monday. Firebreaks at Queenhithe were ineffective, and the fire advanced west towards the Fleet River, and north beyond Cornhill and the Royal Exchange. Belated arrangements were made to check its progress in the northern and western sides of the city with the establishment of Fire Posts, each manned by 130 men with orders to create firebreaks.

By Tuesday morning, even these measures seemed inadequate, and the militia from Middlesex, Hertfordshire and Kent were ordered into the city to prevent riots and fight the fire. But not even the Fleet River served as an effective firebreak: later that day, having destroyed St Paul's, the Guildhall, Custom House, the Royal Exchange and much else, the flames burst out of the City gates, leapt the Fleet and attacked Fleet Street, threatening, for the first time, Whitehall and the Royal residences. Gunpowder was used to clear firebreaks and save the Tower of London.

On Tuesday night all seemed lost for the fire was advancing in a vast arc that stretched from Temple Church in the west, to Smithfield and St Giles Cripplegate in the north and to Leadenhall Market and All Hallows by the Tower in the east. At this point the wind dropped, allowing fire-fighters to control and douse the flames, which they did throughout Wednesday and Thursday, and by Friday they had succeeded in quelling the fire. The devastation was horrific, over 13,000 houses, 87 churches, 52 livery halls and much more besides having been consumed. In all 150 ha within the walls and over 16 ha outside the walls had been devastated.

The rebuilding

There were many who saw London as an insanitary and chaotic city, and the Great Fire provided an opportunity to create a new town. Proposals submitted by Sir Christopher Wren and John Evelyn were radical and elegant, but their solutions quickly succumbed to the practicality of land ownership, so instead the city was rebuilt along the lines of the existing street patterns, but with much widening of streets and two new streets, King Street and Queen Street. Building regulations were radically overhauled – no building in wood was to be allowed and replacement buildings were to be two-storeys in back lanes, three storeys on minor roads and four storeys on the main thoroughfares.

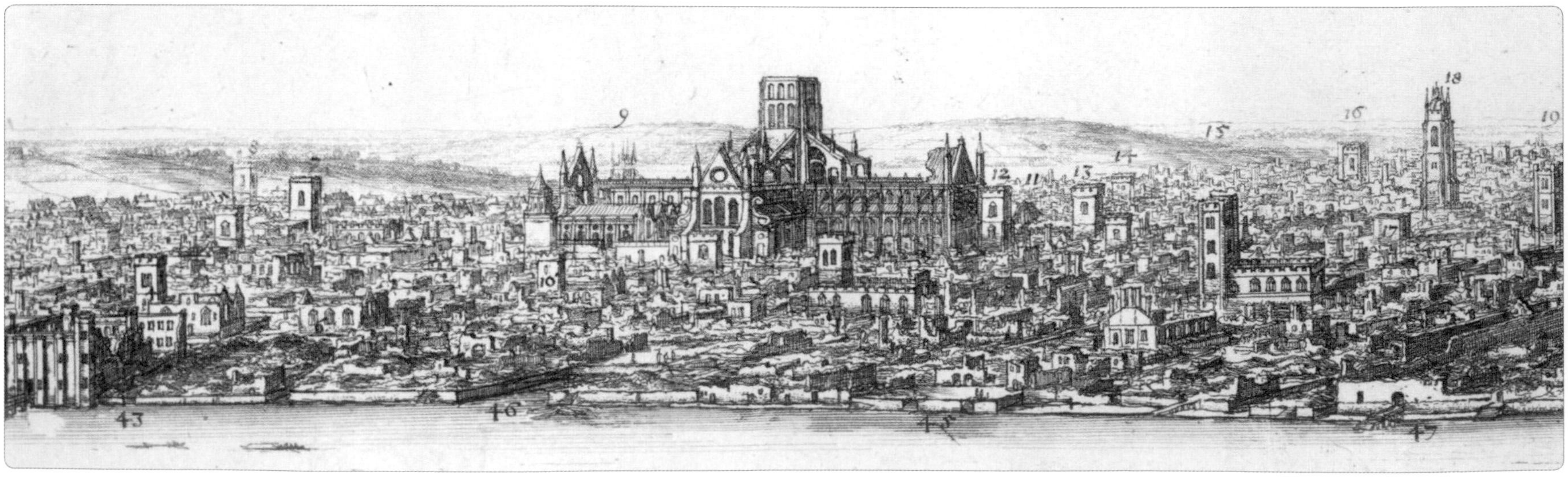

Views of London before and after the fire

The speed of recovery was remarkable; 9,000 houses and some major public buildings were completed by 1671, while work had begun on rebuilding 51 of the 87 destroyed churches, all designed by Sir Christopher Wren (around 25 now remain, many of the others victims of that second great destruction, the Blitz of 1940–41) and finally, the construction of his masterpiece, and the defining building of London, St Paul's Cathedral, constructed between 1675 and 1711. Wren also designed the Monument, built near the site of the Pudding Lane bakehouse, close to London Bridge.

All the sky was of a fiery aspect, like the top of a burning oven, and the light seen above 40 miles round about for many nights. God grant mine eyes may never behold the like, who now saw above 10,000 houses all in one flame; the noise and cracking and thunder of people, the fall of towers, houses, and churches, was like an hideous storm, and the air all about so hot and inflamed that at last one was not able to approach it.

John Evelyn

And among other things, the poor pigeons, I perceive, were loth to leave their houses, but hovered about the windows and balconies, till they some of them burned their wings and fell down.

Samuel Pepys

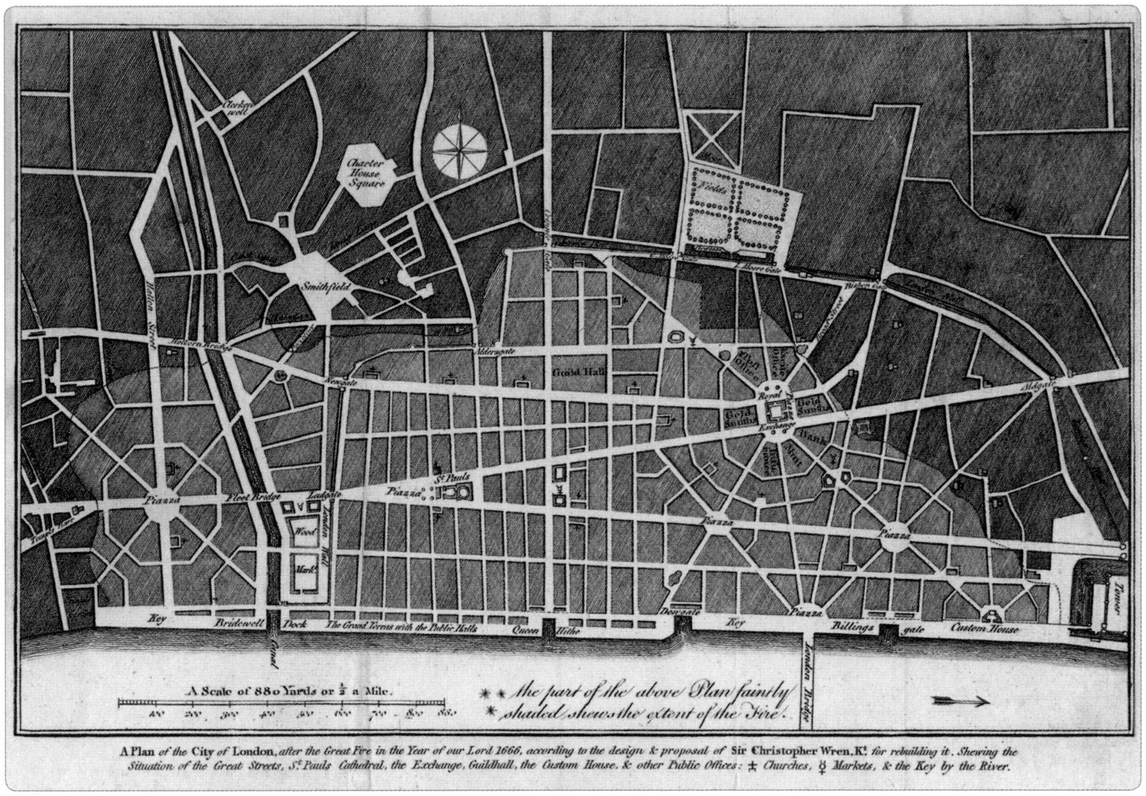

Sir Christopher Wren's 1666 vision for the rebuilding of London

Wenceslaus Hollar's map showing the extent of the Great Fire

CROYDON

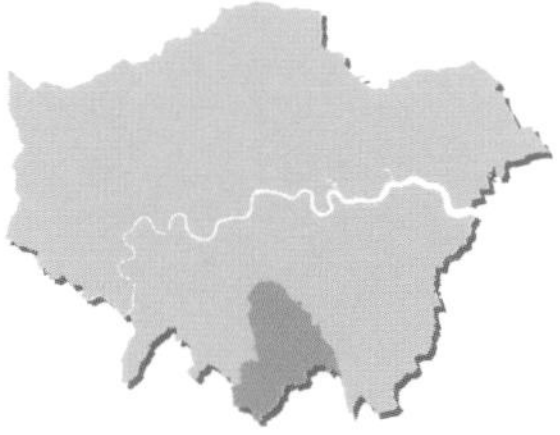

Population	342,800
Area	86 sq. km
Population density	3,986 per sq. km
Area of green space	32 sq. km
Jobs in borough	134,000
Average house price	£234,332

The borough of Croydon takes its name from the town of Croydon, whose Anglo-Saxon name means 'valley where the crocus (wild saffron) grows'; crocus cultivation was started by the Romans who used saffron as a spice and fabric dye. Croydon is located just north of the main routes through the North Downs and developed as a market town under the control of the Archbishops of Canterbury who built a palace here (parts of which can be seen at the Old Palace School). Croydon became a municipal borough of Surrey in 1883, and the current borough was formed in 1965, having grown to include Coulsdon and Purley Urban District to the south. It is the most populous borough in London, and is distinguished from all the other Outer London boroughs by the fact that the town of Croydon is a major financial and commercial centre in its own right, second only to London itself in south-east England.

The population of Croydon grew as the railway network spread out from central London – Norwood developed in the mid-19th century while places in the south of the borough only started growing in the 1930s. In 1851 the population was 21,800, by 1901 it had grown to 141,900 and by 1931 it was 264,400. The Croydon Tramlink, which started operating in 2000, has greatly improved east–west transport links across the Outer London boroughs and has helped reinforce Croydon's commercial domination of the area. Around 78,000 residents work outside the borough but 50,000 people come into the borough to work. Croydon has a more diverse population than its surrounding boroughs.
It was estimated in 2007 that 65 per cent of the population was white, 14 per cent South Asian and 15 per cent black.

Croydon's economy is dominated by the service sector, with 92 per cent of the jobs. Around 30 per cent of all jobs are in the public sector, ahead of the London average, boosted by central government jobs, such as at the UK Border Agency. Many companies have offices here, taking advantage of good facilities at a cheaper price than central London.

FAMOUS FOR

The world's first horse-drawn railway, the **Surrey Iron Railway** opened in 1803 and ran between Croydon and Wandsworth.

Croydon Aerodrome was one of the first airports for London, opening in 1920. Up to the start of World War II, all international flights left from Croydon, and Art Deco buildings from that time survive. It soon became too small, and the last flight was in 1959.

John Whitgift, Archbishop of Canterbury (1583–1604) established the Hospital of the Holy Trinity (better known as the **Whitgift Almshouses**) in 1596. Still in use after over 400 years, the Almshouse provide an oasis of peace right in the centre of Croydon.

Shirley Windmill was built in 1854 and worked until 1893. It has now been restored to working condition, one of only four windmills in Greater London open to the public. In 2010 its sails had to be replaced as they had been badly damaged by rose-ringed parakeets sharpening their beaks on them.

Pickles, a black and white mongrel, is the most famous dog in the borough, for he found the original World Cup Trophy under a hedge in Beulah Hill, **Upper Norwood**, seven days after it had been stolen on 20 March 1966.

Croydon Tramlink

John Bartholomew, Gazetteer of the British Isles (1887)
CROYDON, *parl. and mun. bor., market town, and par., Surrey – par. and bor., 9001 ac., pop. 78,953; 3 Banks, 12 newspapers. Market-days, Thursday and Saturday. C. is 10 miles S. of London Bridge, but forms practically a S. suburb of the metropolis, and contains numerous handsome villas of London merchants. It has 6 stations – Addiscombe Road, Central, East, New, South, West – connecting the town with the main lines and branches of the London, Brighton, and South Coast and South-Eastern Railways. The weekly corn and cattle markets constitute the chief business of the town. There are no mfrs. C. is a place of great antiquity. It has many traces of the Romans. The archiepiscopal palace, of which the chapel and hall still remain, is supposed to have been founded by Lanfranc (1005-1089); it was the occasional residence of his successors until 1757. C. is the capital of E. Surrey, and assizes are held alternately there and at Guildford. It was made a mun. bor. in 1883, and a parl. bor. in 1885; it returns 1 member.*

Croydon Aerodrome, from the cover of *Airways*, 1925

FAMOUS PEOPLE

(Henry) Havelock Ellis, writer and sexologist, born Croydon, 1859.
Cicely Mary Barker, artist and writer of the *Flower Fairies*, born West Croydon, 1895.
Avril Coleridge-Taylor, composer and conductor, born South Norwood, 1903.
(Thomas) Malcolm Muggeridge, journalist and broadcaster, born Croydon, 1903.
Dame Edith Margaret Emily (Peggy) Ashcroft, actress, born Croydon, 1907.
Sir David Lean, film director, born Croydon, 1908.
Bridget Riley, artist, born Norwood, 1931.
Roy Hudd, comedian and writer, born Croydon, 1936.
Allan Ahlberg, children's author, born Croydon, 1938.
Roy Hodgson, footballer and football manager, born Croydon, 1947.
Philip Green, high-street fashion entrepreneur, born Croydon, 1952.
Tracey Emin, artist, born Croydon, 1963.
Sam Taylor-Wood, conceptual artist, and photographer, born Croydon, 1967.
Derren Brown, illusionist, born Croydon, 1971.
Mark Alan Butcher, Surrey and England cricketer, born Croydon, 1972.
Kate Moss, model, born Addiscombe, 1974.

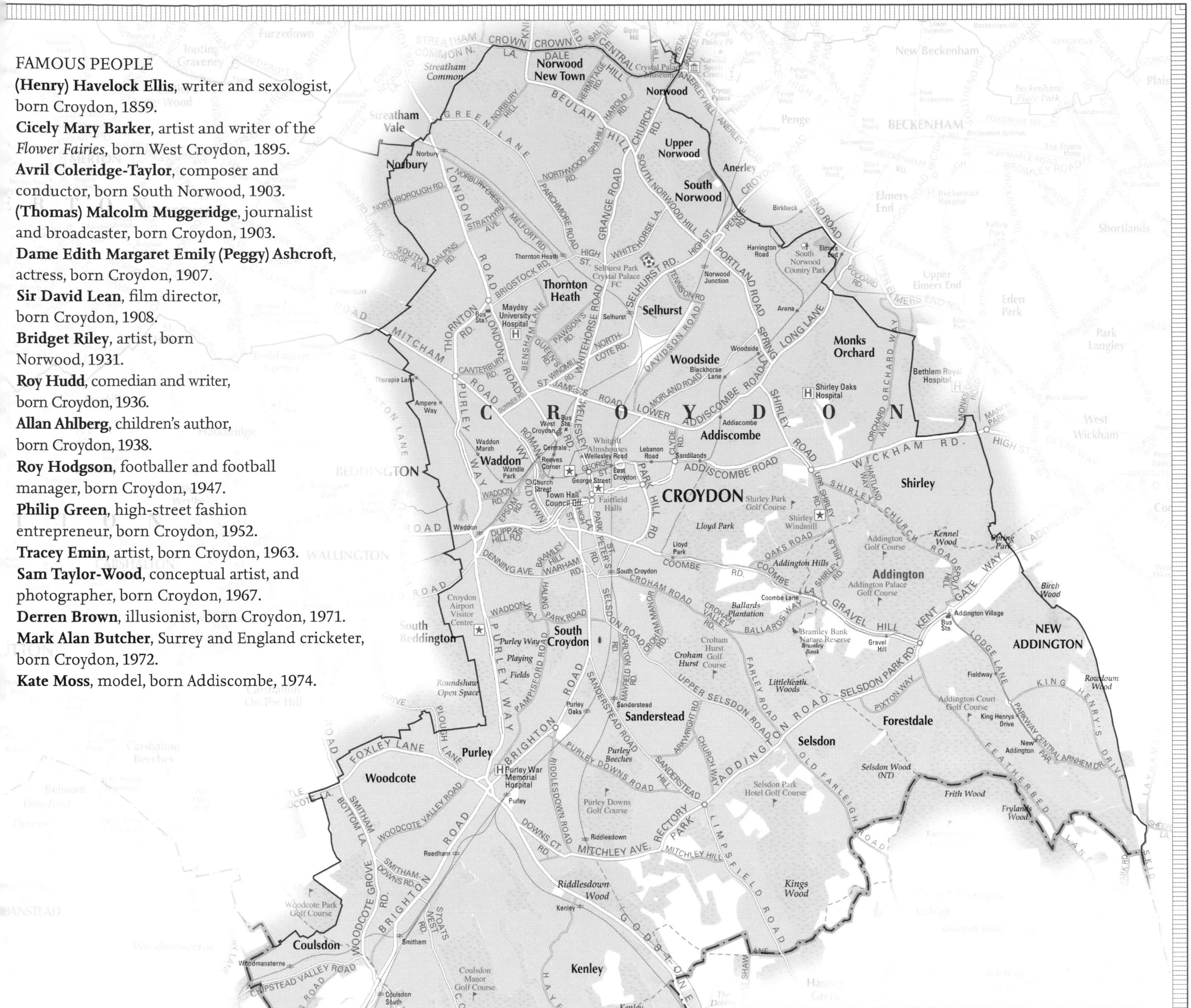

Shirley Windmill,
used for milling flour in the 19th century

PUBLIC TRANSPORT IN LONDON

Efficient and flexible public transport is essential to allow London to function. The rail network brings commuters in from the outer boroughs and from beyond Greater London and this is covered on pages 212–213. All other major forms of public transport come under the umbrella of Transport for London (TfL) and are part of the responsibilities of the Mayor of London. TfL runs some services directly (such as the Underground) and oversees the licensing of others to provide services (such as the bus companies).

TRANSPORT IN LONDON OVERSEEN BY TRANSPORT FOR LONDON (FORECASTS FOR 2011-12)

	Passenger journeys	Distance travelled (km)
London Underground	1133 million	72.4 million
London Buses	2304 million	489 million
London Overground	78 million	4.9 million
Docklands Light Railway	82 million	5.5 million
London Trams	28 million	2.7 million
Totals	3625 million	574.5 million

More information on the London Underground, London Overground (a network of suburban rail routes, including an outer ring around London) and the Docklands Light Railway can be found on page 170.

London buses

About 94 per cent of London residents live within 400 m of a bus service and more passengers are now travelling on the buses than at any time since 1960. Every weekday over 6,800 buses carry 6 million passengers on around 700 different routes. It is one of the largest bus networks in the world.

The iconic red Routemaster bus, with its engine at the front, an open boarding platform at the back and tickets sold onboard by a bus conductor, was introduced in 1956 and was in regular use until 2005. Nearly 3,000 were produced and some continue in service on tourist routes. Current double-decker buses run with just a driver and provide a more comfortable and environmentally efficient service. Recent innovations include the introduction of hybrid electric buses, now with over 100 in use and another 200 planned by the end of 2012, while in 2011 the first zero-emission bus route between Covent Garden and the Tower of London started operation, using hydrogen hybrid buses. Prototypes of a New Bus for London, a hybrid-powered design intended to be a symbolic replacement for the Routemaster, will appear in 2012, and it, too, will have an open rear platform.

The history of the London Omnibus

Slightly surprisingly, the omnibus, as it was once known, was not a London creation – the first horse-drawn omnibus was introduced from France to the streets of London in 1829 by George Shillibeer, a London-born coachbuilder who lived in Paris. His omnibus seated twenty-two within the passenger compartment. Within a few years many others started omnibus services, and, by the 1850s, double-deckers began to appear, with an open upper deck. In the 1880s access to the top deck began to be by a staircase rather than a ladder. At the start of the 20th century the number of horse-drawn vehicles reached a maximum of around 3,700, but motor power was soon to transform their position. In 1905 the London Motor Omnibus Company was formed and within two years the company had 300 buses on the road. Other companies joined in and the very last horse-drawn bus route ended in 1914. A period of great competition ensued – G. K. Chesterton in his 1922 short story 'In the Soul of a Schoolboy'

Mock-up of the New Bus for London in the London Transport Museum (at Covent Garden), 2011

Westminster Bridge traffic in the 1920s, including buses, trams and horse-drawn carts

The iconic Routemaster double-decker bus with its rear open platform

Boarding a bus, from the late 1920s

reflected that his schoolboy 'had a magic and minute knowledge of the Westminster omnibuses, and indeed of the whole omnibus system of London, the colours and numbers of which he knew as a herald knows heraldry. He would cry out against a momentary confusion between a light-green Paddington and a dark-green Bayswater vehicle.'

In 1933 London's buses, trams, trolleybuses and underground railways were brought together under the London Passenger Transport Board to create the system that has grown into today's controlled competitive arrangements.

Trams

The first horse-drawn tram ran on London's roads in 1861, but it took nearly a decade before commercially successful tram routes were introduced. Soon there was a network of services from the suburbs to the edge of central London. From 1901 they began to be powered by electricity and became larger, usually with the upper deck roofed over (so giving a dry journey to everyone). By the 1930s they were beginning to lose out to trolley buses which took their power from overhead cables and did not need tracks. The last tram for nearly fifty years ended its run at New Cross tram depot on 6 July 1952.

However, in 2000 a new tram service started in south London, centred on Croydon. Called the London Tramlink, the route is a mixture of dedicated track and track shared with roads. The network is 28 km long with 39 stops, with each tram carrying a maximum of 208 passengers. It provides a vital east–west transport link in South London from Wimbledon to Beckenham.

The last tram to run to New Cross, 1952

EALING

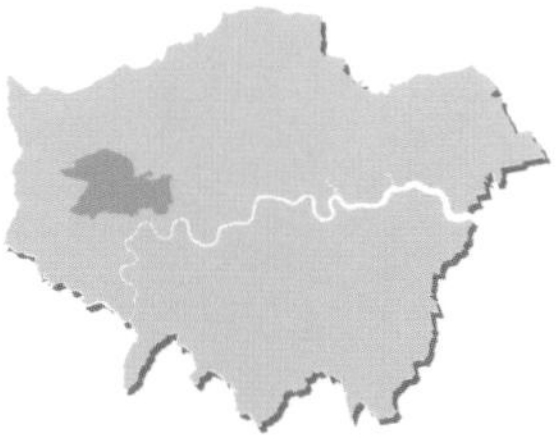

Population	316,000
Area	55 sq. km
Population density	5,745 per sq. km
Area of green space	17 sq. km
Jobs in borough	128,000
Average house price	£258,600

The borough of Ealing takes its name from the long-established settlement of Ealing. The earliest recorded use of the name is as *Gillingas* around AD 700, meaning 'the settlement of the family of Gilla'. Ealing is one of the seven original Saxon villages that make up the main centres of the borough of Ealing, the others being Hanwell, Acton, Southall, Greenford, Perivale and Northolt.

The Art Deco Hoover building, used for the manufacture of vacuum cleaners until the 1980s

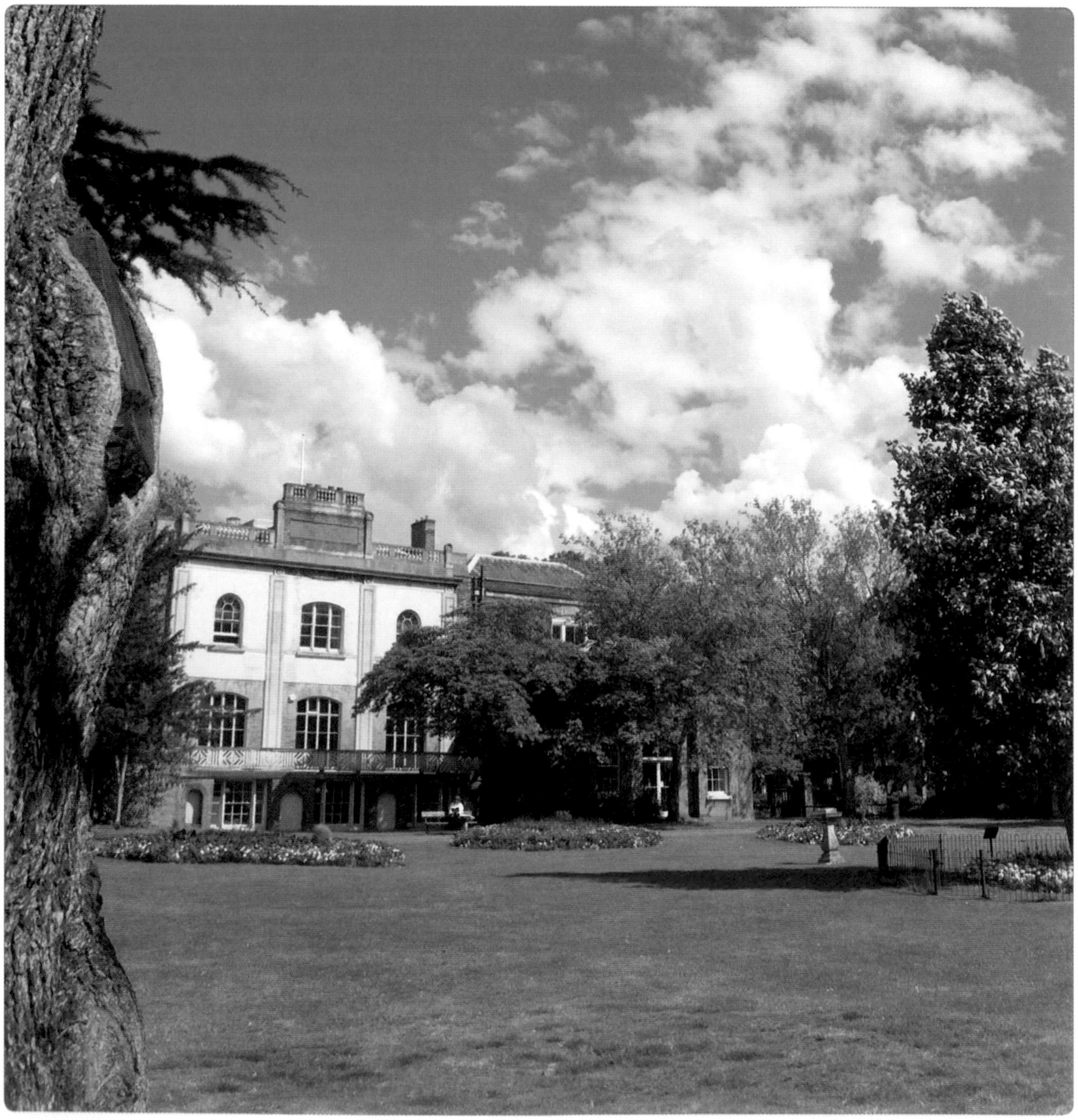

Pitzhanger Manor House

The area remained primarily rural until the coming of the railways in the mid-19th century, spurred on by the construction of Brunel's Great Western Railway that speeds through the heart of the borough. By the 1890s, Ealing was described as the 'Queen of the Suburbs'. Among the developments was Bedford Park, on the boundary with Hounslow, Britain's first garden suburb, designed by Norman Shaw and built 1875–86 and originally popular with artists and writers, including W. B. Yeats and Camille Pisarro.

The current borough of Ealing was created in 1965 from three Middlesex municipal boroughs – Ealing, Acton and Southall. In terms of population, it is the third largest London borough and in area the eleventh largest. Since World War II it has become one of the most diverse boroughs in London. In the 1950s, South Asians began settling in Southall, initially to work in local factories and later at nearby Heathrow airport, and it is now estimated that around 70 per cent of Southall's population is South Asian in origin. It is the largest Sikh community in London. The Gurdwara Sri Guru Singh Sabha in Southall is one of the largest Sikh temples outside India. The present building was completed in 2003, and can accommodate 3,000 worshippers. The borough also contains a long-established Polish community, linked to the arrival of Polish pilots in World War II and émigrés after the war and now much enlarged by Polish workers who came to London after Poland joined the EU.

The area has always been popular with commuters, with its good train and Underground links to central London. Many others come to work in the borough, particularly in the Park Royal industrial estate (which straddles the boundary with Brent) which now provides around 40,000 jobs. Over 9 per cent of the jobs in the borough are in manufacturing (more than double the London average), whilst 24 per cent of jobs are in finance, IT and other business (compared with a London average of nearly 35 per cent). The borough is also the home of the University of West London, formerly Thames Valley University.

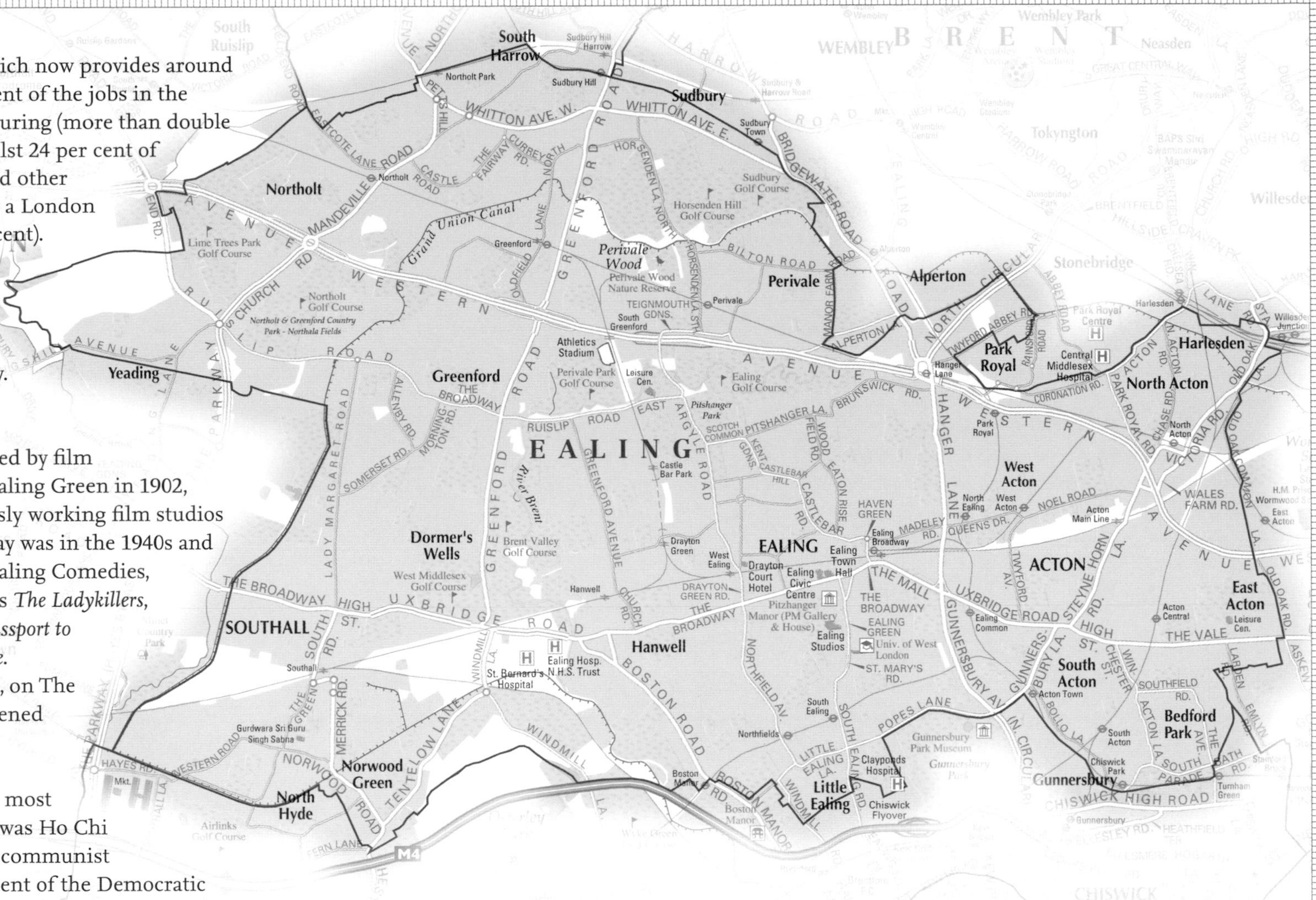

FAMOUS FOR

Ealing Studios, established by film pioneer Will Barker by Ealing Green in 1902, are the oldest continuously working film studios in the world. Their heyday was in the 1940s and 1950s – the time of the Ealing Comedies, including classics such as *The Ladykillers*, *The Lavender Hill Mob*, *Passport to Pimlico* and *Whisky Galore*.

Drayton Court Hotel, on The Avenue at Ealing, was opened in 1894, an imposing building of four storeys and with sixty rooms. Its most famous member of staff was Ho Chi Minh, better known as a communist revolutionary and President of the Democratic Republic of Vietnam, who worked there as a kitchen porter in 1914.

The origin of the Waitrose supermarket chain goes back to a grocer's shop at **263 Acton Hill** in Acton, founded in 1904 by Wallace Waite, Arthur Rose and David Taylor. Taylor did not stay with the business for long, and the two remaining owners coined the name 'Waitrose'.

In the 18th century a number of country houses were built by the wealthy who wished to have a house away from the crowded city. **Pitzhanger Manor** in Ealing, originally a farm house, was rebuilt around 1800 by Sir John Soane, London's most radical architect at that time, for his own use.

The former **Hoover** building, on Western Avenue in Perivale is an iconic Art Deco building designed by Wallis, Gilbert and Partners and completed in 1932. Now converted into a supermarket, not everyone admired it – Nikolaus Pevsner commented in 1951 that it was 'perhaps the most offensive of modernistic atrocities along this road of typical by-pass factories'.

In such a suburban borough, it is a surprise to come across **Perivale Church**, dating from the 13th-century and containing a most unusual 16th-century wooden church tower.

Ealing Studios

FAMOUS PEOPLE

Nathaniel Pearce, adventurer, most notably in Abyssinia, born Acton, 1779.
Sir William Fothergill Cooke, developer of electric telegraphy with Charles Wheatstone, born Ealing, 1806.
Thomas Henry Huxley, biologist and advocate for evolution, nick-named 'Darwin's Bulldog', born Ealing, 1825.
Dorothea Lambert Chambers, tennis player, seven-times Wimbledon champion, born Ealing, 1878.
William (Billy) Smart, circus owner, born Ealing, 1893.
Nevil Shute Norway (*known as* Nevil Shute), novelist and aeronautical engineer, born Ealing, 1899.
Margery Allingham, detective fiction author, born Ealing, 1904.
Dame Cleo (Clementina) Laine, jazz singer, born Southall, 1927.
Brigid Brophy, author and outspoken campaigner, born Ealing, 1929.
Patrick Caulfield, Pop Art painter and printmaker, born Acton, 1936.
Adam Faith, pop singer and actor, born Acton, 1940.

John Bartholomew, Gazetteer of the British Isles (1887)

SOUTHALL, *market town with ry. sta., Hayes par., Middlesex, 3½ miles NW. of Brentford and 9¼ miles W. of London, pop. 3784; P.O., T.O., and P.O. at Southall Green, 1 Bank. Market-day, Wednesday. Southall has trade in cattle.*

HANWELL.– *par., township, and vil. with ry. sta., Middlesex, on river Brent, 7 miles W. of London – par., 1283 ac., pop. 7316; township, 1067 ac., pop. 5178; P.O., T.O.; in vicinity is the Middlesex County Lunatic Asylum, known as Hanwell Asylum; here also is the seat of Hanwell Park.*

THE UNIVERSITIES OF LONDON

At the start of the 19th century, there were only two universities in England, at Oxford and Cambridge, and you could only attend them if you were a member of the Church of England. The first university college established in London was University College in Gower Street, founded by a number of prominent free-thinkers in 1826 to provide a university for Protestants who were not members of the Church of England. Its impressive main building, designed by William Wilkins (who also designed the National Gallery) showed its very serious intent. Its free-thinking credentials did not go un-noticed, and in 1829, Church of England supporters established King's College as an alternative to 'the godless college in Gower Street'. In 1836 the University of London was established, primarily to provide a standard quality of examination, to which colleges could become constituent members. The arrangements developed slowly, but by the early 20th century, nine major university colleges in London were part of the University of London, in addition to a number of smaller institutions.

The next expansion of higher education in London happened in the 1960s with the establishment of the new technological university of Brunel at Uxbridge, and of City University, an advanced college of technology whose origins went back to 1894. A further expansion came in 1992 when a number of former polytechnics became universities. These institutions all had a long history of providing further and higher education to Londoners, and had a fine reputation for providing opportunities for those from more deprived backgrounds. Their change of status resulted in a number of new university names appearing in the capital: East London, Greenwich, Kingston, London Metropolitan, London South Bank, Middlesex, West London, and Westminster. Not all have had an easy time – West London (originally called Thames Valley) and London Metropolitan (itself a merger of North London and London Guildhall) have been through a number of major changes recently, for example. Since 1992, two more universities have been created – Roehampton and the University of the Arts, London. In addition there are many specialist colleges in the capital, particularly for art, drama, music, medicine and veterinary medicine.

In the 21st century, London is one of the world's major academic centres. In the QS World University Rankings in 2010, University College London was 4th, Imperial College 7th, and King's College 21st – no other city had as many institutions in the top 25. There are now over 400,000 students (both full-time and part-time) in London. The institutions themselves vary greatly – while the London School of Economics attracts leading scholars and students from around the world, the University of East London very actively encourages young people from the multi-racial communities of East London to further their education.

LONDON AS A PERCENTAGE OF UK TOTAL STUDENT POPULATION

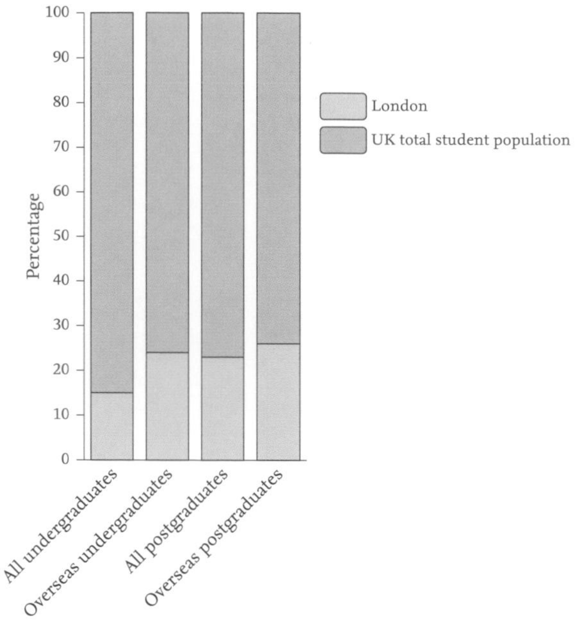

THE TIMES GOOD UNIVERSITY GUIDE 2012 LEAGUE TABLE (COMPILED IN 2011)

Rank	University
3	London School of Economics
4	Imperial College
5	University College London
23	School of Oriental and African Studies
24	King's College London
28	Royal Holloway
37	Queen Mary College
47	City University
50	Goldsmiths College
51	Brunel
79	Roehampton
=82	University of the Arts, London
=94	Middlesex
96	Westminster
97	Kingston
99	Greenwich
113	London South Bank
115	East London
116	London Metropolitan

West London did not take part

Sancte et Sapienter (with holiness and wisdom) motto outside King's College, London

FAMOUS FOR

Brunel University at Uxbridge, is the only English university named after an engineer, Isambard Kingdom Brunel – the university is near Brunel's Great Western Railway.

The **University of East London's** main campus is by the side of the Royal Albert Docks, in jaunty, prize-winning buildings, bringing new life to the area.

Graduates of **Goldsmiths College** have won the Turner prize for contemporary art six times.

University of Greenwich is based in the Old Royal Naval College at Greenwich, one of only two universities in England to form part of a World Heritage Site (the other is Durham).

In 2007 the **Imperial College of Science, Technology and Medicine** became the first college to leave the University of London and become

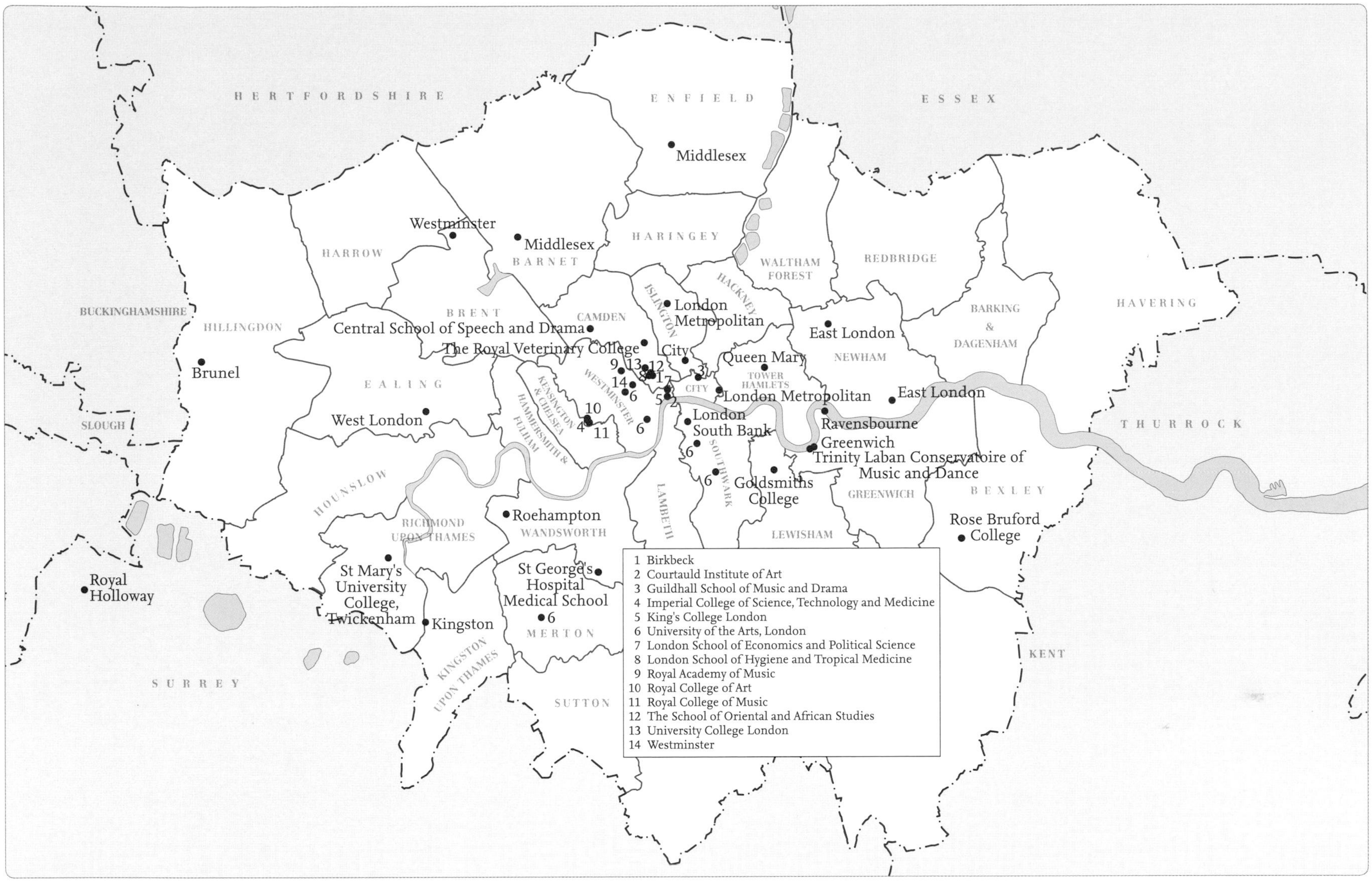

Location of London's universities

independent, 100 years after its foundation. It is Britain's highest rated research university for pure mathematics, chemical, civil, mechanical and aeronautical engineering.

The post-graduate centre for **London Metropolitan University** was designed by Daniel Libeskind, bringing world-renowned architecture to the Holloway Road.

Over 100 languages are spoken on the campus of the **London School of Economics** and 34 past or present world leaders and 16 Nobel laureates have studied or taught there.

The University of the Arts, London brings together the leading art and design colleges in London: Camberwell College of Arts, Central St Martin's College of Art and Design, Chelsea College of Art and Design, London College of Communication, London College of Fashion and Wimbledon College of Art.

In the South Cloister of the main building of **University College London** is the so-called Auto-Icon, a wooden display case containing the skeleton of the 19th century Utilitarian philosopher Jeremy Bentham. He wears his own clothes and hat (which sits on top of a wax image of his head).

University College London was the first British university to teach women, in 1878.

London has always been famous for its teaching hospitals, active long before universities were established in the capital. Their medical schools have now mainly been absorbed into larger institutions: **Imperial College** includes St Mary's, Charing Cross and Westminster hospitals, **King's** includes Guy's and St Thomas's, **Queen Mary** includes St Bartholomew's. **St George's** remains an independent institution.

LARGEST AND SMALLEST NUMBER OF STUDENTS

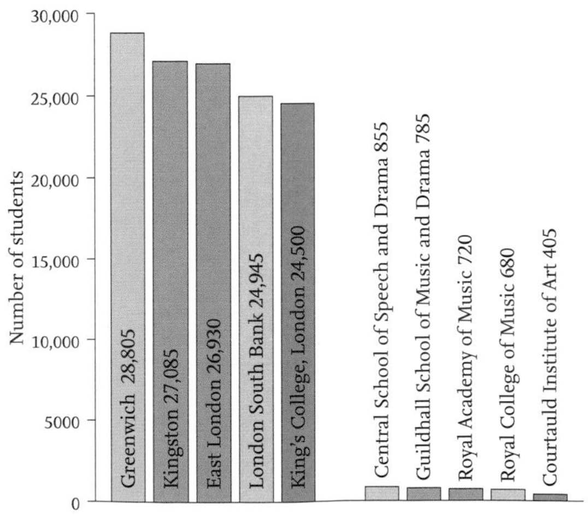

LONDON AS A STUDENT CENTRE

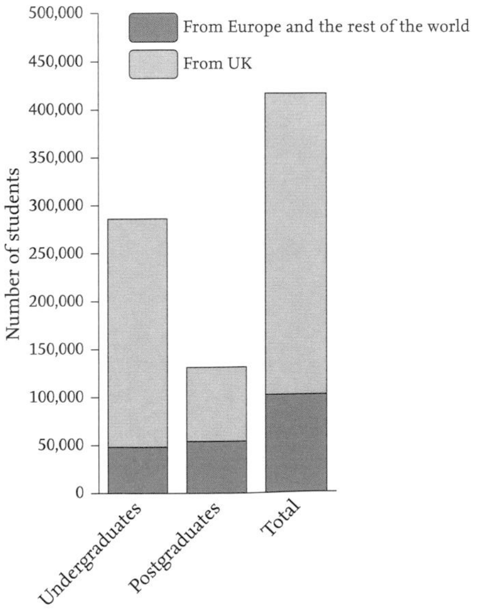

ENFIELD

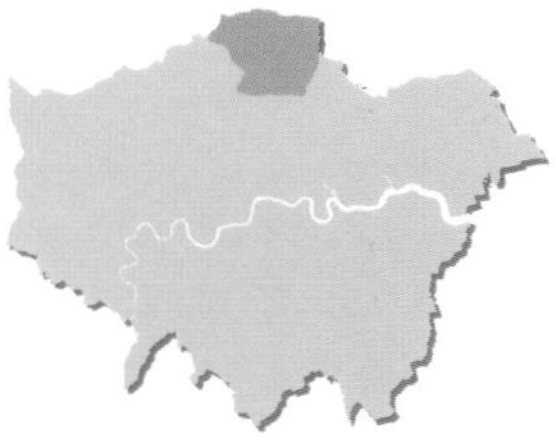

Population	291,200
Area	82 sq. km
Population density	3,551 per sq. km
Area of green space	37 sq. km
Jobs in borough	107,000
Average house price	£266,899

The 17th-century Forty Hall

The borough takes its name from the market town of Enfield, from the Old English meaning 'Ena's field'. Enfield is the most northerly London borough and its northern border with Hertfordshire runs along the M25. The borough was formed in 1965 by bringing together the three Middlesex municipal boroughs of Enfield, Edmonton and Southgate. Historically, settlements developed along the route of the Roman Ermine Street, the road from London to York, and along the valley of the River Lea (or Lee), in the east of the borough, bordering Waltham Forest and Essex.

The northwest of the borough is now green belt and contains part of the great enclosed Royal hunting forest of Enfield Chase, created in 1136 and finally broken up into smaller plots in 1777 – Southgate was at the South Gate to the Chase. The railway arrived in Enfield in 1847 and in Edmonton, in the east of the borough, in 1872, with trams following soon after. This started the growth in the borough's population, which continued into the 1930s, when the Piccadilly line of the London Underground arrived, with its distinctive Art Deco stations at Arnos Grove, Southgate, Oakwood and Cockfosters.

In 1851 the population was 18,900, by 1901 it had grown to 103,000 and by 1951 to 292,100. By 2007, about 71 per cent of the population was white and around 14 per cent black. The borough is home to the largest Cypriot population outside of Cyprus, centred on Palmers Green.

Many industries developed in the Lea Valley, including the Royal Small Arms Factory, established in 1816 at Enfield Lock, and renowned for the Lee Enfield rifle and the Sten and Bren guns (manufacture ceased in 1988 and the site is now used for housing) and the Ediswan electric lightbulb factory, opened in a former jute mill at Ponders End in 1886, the first such factory in Britain. Manufacturing and construction still provides nearly 12 per cent of the jobs in the borough, compared with a London average of just over 7 per cent. The largest sector of employment is public administration, education and health with over 31 per cent of jobs, over a third above the London average. The borough contains the Trent Park campus of Middlesex University.

Enfield Market

FAMOUS FOR

Ponders End Mill is the only independent flour mill in Greater London. The current mill building dates back to the 18th century and a mill was recorded here in the Domesday Book. Owned by the Wright family since 1847, it was converted from water power to electric power at the start of the 20th century.

Forty Hall is a fine Jacobean house, now a museum, that was built in 1632 for Sir Nicholas Rainton, a former Lord Mayor of London. The site of the **Elsyng Palace**, where Henry VIII's children spent much time, has been found in the grounds.

The world's first Automated Teller Machine (ATM) was installed on 27 June 1967 at Barclays Bank in **Enfield**. It was invented by John Shepherd-Brown, who also devised the system of PIN numbers.

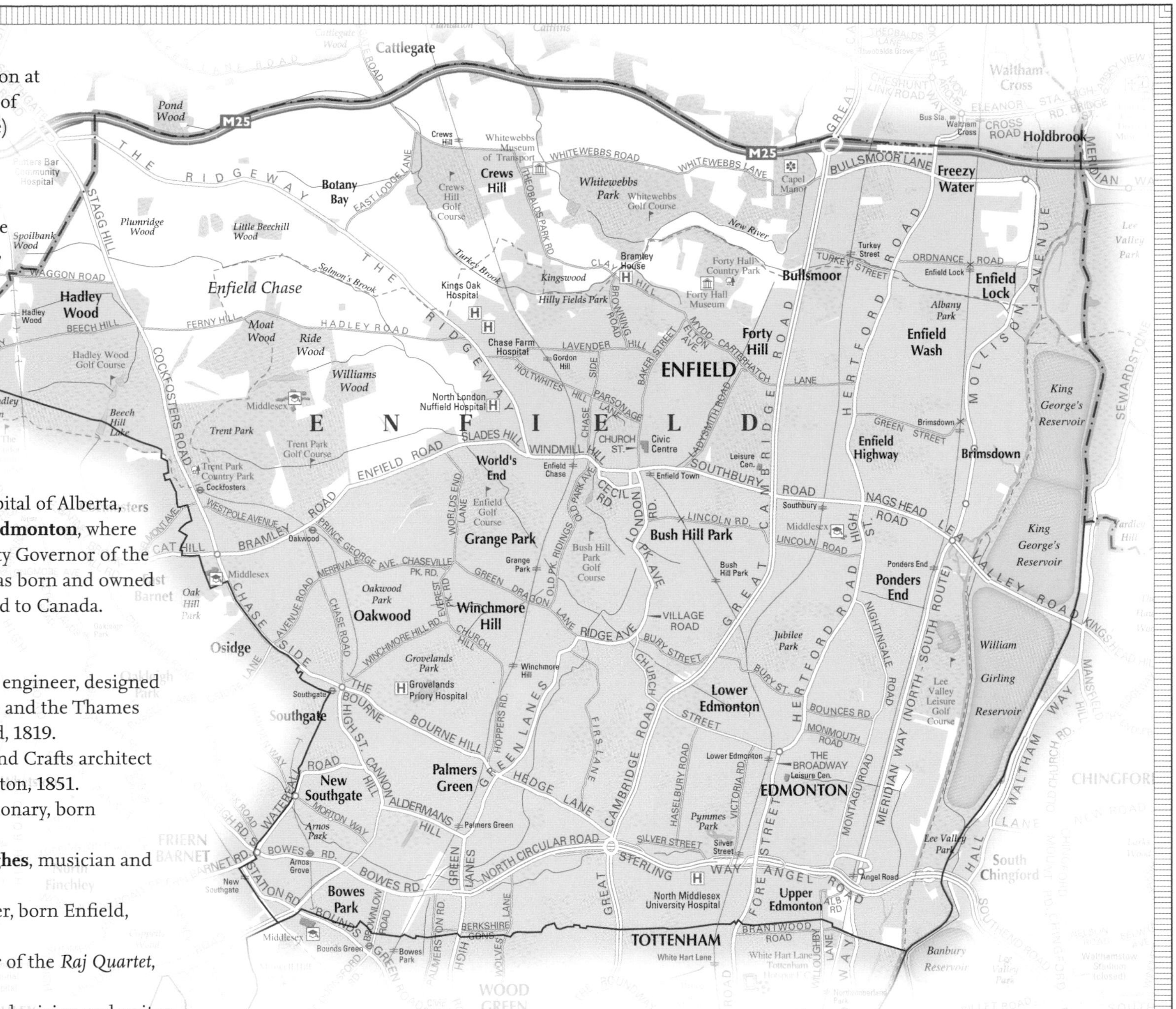

The Underground station at **Arnos Grove** (a corruption of the original Arnold's Grove) was designed by Charles Holden and opened on 19 September 1932. It is regarded as the finest of the many stations he designed, one critic listing it as one of 12 great modern British buildings.

Capel Manor in Enfield is Greater London's only agricultural college. It specializes in horticulture.

Edmonton, now the capital of Alberta, Canada, was named after **Edmonton**, where Sir James Lake, then Deputy Governor of the Hudson's Bay Company, was born and owned an estate. He never travelled to Canada.

FAMOUS PEOPLE

Sir Joseph Bazalgette, civil engineer, designed London's sewerage scheme and the Thames Embankment, born Enfield, 1819.

Arthur Mackmurdo, Arts and Crafts architect and designer, born Edmonton, 1851.

Gladys May Aylward, missionary, born Edmonton, 1902.

Patrick Cairns (Spike) Hughes, musician and writer, born Enfield, 1908.

Norman Lewis, travel writer, born Enfield, 1908.

Paul Scott, novelist, author of the *Raj Quartet*, born Southgate, 1920.

Alexander (Alex) Comfort, physician and writer, born Edmonton, 1920.

Norris and Ross McWhirter, founders of *Guinness Book of Records*, born Winchmore Hill, 1925.

Sir Bruce Forsyth (*born* Bruce Forsyth-Johnson), entertainer, born Edmonton, 1928.

Norman Tebbit (Baron Tebbit), Conservative politician, born Ponders End, 1931.

Simon Mayo, radio presenter, born Southgate, 1958.

Amy Winehouse, singer and songwriter, born Southgate, 1983.

John Bartholomew, Gazetteer of the British Isles (1887)

ENFIELD.– *market town and par. with ry. sta., Middlesex, on New River, 10 m. N. of London, 12,653 ac., pop. 19,104; P.O., T.O.; also P.O., T.O., at* ***Enfield Highway****; P.O., T.O., at* ***Enfield Lock****; and P.O. at* ***Enfield Wash****; 1 Bank, 1 newspaper. Market-day, Saturday. Enfield belonged to the Crown till the time of James I., and has remains of an ancient royal palace.* ***Enfield Chase*** *was disforested in the 18th century, and is now occupied by the villas of London traders.* ***Enfield Lock*** *is the seat of the Government small-arms factory, and gave name to the once famous "Enfield Rifle".*

EDMONTON.– *town and par. (ry. sta. Lower Edmonton), Middlesex, on New River, 7½ miles N. of London, 7483 ac. (86 water), pop. 23,463; P.O., T.O., at Lower Edmonton, and P.O. at Upper Edmonton; has trade in timber by means of the Lea River navigation. The "Bell at Edmonton" has been rendered famous by Cowper's John Gilpin. Charles and Mary Lamb are buried in the church.*

Former Royal Small Arms Factory, Enfield Lock

ROAD TRANSPORT IN LONDON

The origin of London's road network goes back to its foundation by the Romans, for their roads are still some of the main routes out of London, for example:

- **The route from Bishopsgate to Kingsland Road and Stoke Newington and then on to Edmonton follows the route of Ermine Street that ran from London to York.**
- **Going south to Dover, the road from Shooters Hill travels straight though Welling and Crayford following the route of Watling Street (and sections of it are still known by that name) while Watling Street's route north to Shropshire is clearly marked by Edgware Road and Maida Vale straight out to Edgware.**
- **Kennington Park Road and Clapham Road mark the beginning of Stane Street, the Roman route to Chichester.**

The City has mostly kept its medieval street structure, retained after the Great Fire, and as London grew so, too, did its road system, albeit in an unplanned way, with only a few major schemes such as Euston Road (in 1756 as New Road). In the 1860s and 1870s Sir Joseph Bazalgette, the engineer of London's sewage system, turned his attention to the Thames. He built the Victoria and Chelsea Embankments on the north bank, and the Albert Embankment along the south bank, creating the now familiar setting for the Thames with an improved route for traffic and new public gardens.

In the 1920s, major new routes were created away from the centre of the city – the North and South Circular Roads, the Great West Road, and the Western and Eastern Avenues – while the 1980s saw the completion of London's outer orbital motorway, the M25, which encircles all of Greater London apart from North Ockendon in the borough of Havering. A few motorway routes have edged towards London within the M25 (the M11 from Cambridge, the M1 from the Midlands, the M4 from the west and the M3 from the south), but none reach into the heart of the city.

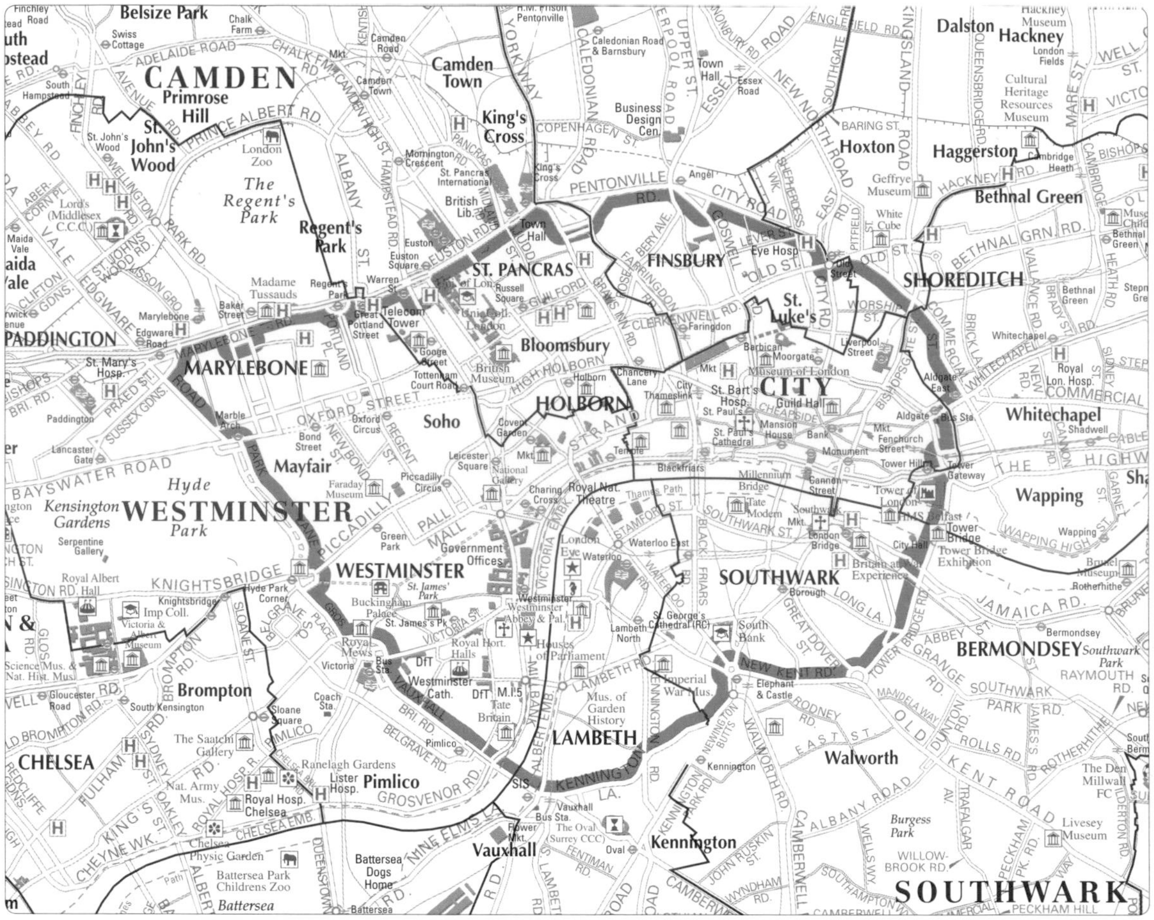

Congestion Charging zone boundary, 2011

Greater London contains under 4 per cent of Britain's total road length, accounts for just over 6 per cent of the vehicle km travelled and has 9 per cent of Britain's cars. Add to that the many people who use London's roads but do not live there, and the inevitable outcome is congestion. It has led to more radical solutions than any other British city.

The **Congestion Charge** was introduced in central London in 2003 and extended westwards in 2007 to include Pimlico, Kensington, Chelsea, Notting Hill and Bayswater. In January 2011 the western area extension was abolished at the instigation of the Conservative Boris Johnson who defeated the initiator of the Congestion Charge, Ken Livingstone, in the 2008 mayoral elections. The purpose is to discourage drivers from using the streets of central London by making a charge and to invest the funds raised in improving public transport. The charge applies between 7 a.m. and 6 p.m. Mondays to Fridays, and the daily charge is now £10. There are no barriers for payment – rather, cameras record the registration plates of all vehicles entering and leaving the congestion charge area. Drivers are responsible for paying the fee in advance or within a day of the journey, or they become liable for a fine, having been identified by their car's registration plate. There are various reductions and exemptions, for example, for low-emission, hybrid and electric cars.

Initially there was a significant reduction in traffic (up to 21 per cent), with reductions in emissions. Over time, traffic has been increasing and congestion has been growing again, in part a result of road works. What is clear, however, is that the situation would have been very much worse if the charge had not been introduced.

Virtually all of Greater London is a **Low Emission Zone (LEZ)**. The zone was established in 2007 and will be fully operational in 2012 and is aimed at reducing the level of particulate emission associated with diesel engines. From 2012 diesel lorries, vans, minibuses and motorized caravans registered before 1 October 2006 will be banned unless fitted with an appropriate filter. The zone is enforced by use of cameras recording vehicle registration plates and there is a £200 a day fine for driving a prohibited vehicle in the zone.

LICENSED VEHICLES IN LONDON
(AND PERCENTAGE OF UK VEHICLES)

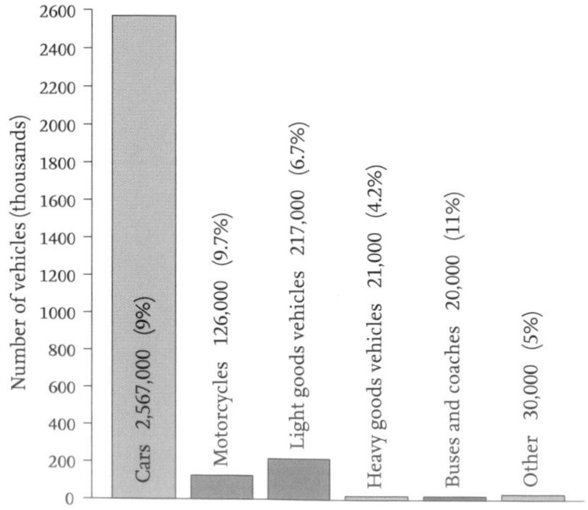

BOROUGHS WHERE MOST AND LEAST VEHICLES OWNED

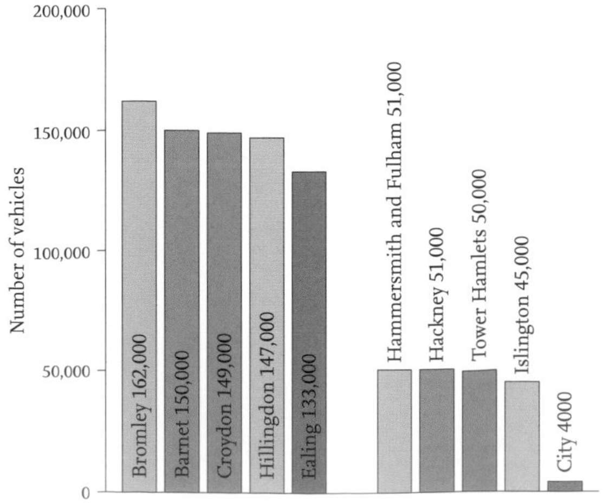

The uniform road surfaces of today are a relatively recent phenomenon, as this map from 1922 shows

Queen Elizabeth II Bridge, just outside Greater London, is the lowest crossing of the Thames and carries the southbound M25 (northbound is in a tunnel)

GREENWICH

Population	226,100
Area	48 sq. km
Population density	4,710 per sq. km
Area of green space	16.5 sq. km
Jobs in borough	80,000
Average house price	£264,426

The borough of Greenwich was formed in 1965 from the metropolitan boroughs of Greenwich and Woolwich (excluding North Woolwich, on the northern bank of the Thames, which was transferred to Newham). In addition to Greenwich (from the Old English 'green harbour' or 'green trading place') and Woolwich, the main settlements are Charlton, Thamesmead, Eltham and Plumstead.

The decision to make Greenwich a Royal Borough (only the fourth in Britain) in 2012, to celebrate the Queen's Diamond Jubilee, reflects the long royal associations with the area. In the early 15th century Duke Humphrey of Gloucester built a great house at Greenwich that was to become a favourite palace of the Tudors. All that now remains is the classical Queen's House built in 1616 for James I's wife. After the Restoration, Greenwich became home to both the Royal Naval Hospital (which later became the Royal Naval College), completed in 1694 and the Royal Observatory, begun in 1675. These buildings are now shared between Greenwich University and the National Maritime Museum and form a UNESCO World Heritage Site.

In 1512 Woolwich was chosen by Henry VIII as a site for a naval dockyard, which was in use until 1869. The Royal Laboratory was also established here, and, in 1671 it became the Royal Arsenal, Britain's major munitions works. In World War I it covered 600 ha and employed 80,000 people. It finally closed in 1994, with the most historic buildings conserved. The Royal Regiment of Artillery, formed in 1719, were originally based at the Arsenal but from the 1780s moved to a new barracks building on Woolwich Common, with an amazing 300 m long façade. Another royal link is with Eltham Palace, much used in the 14th and 15th centuries and restored in the 1930s.

In 1801 the population was nearly 17,000, and, as the Royal Arsenal grew, so did the population, reaching 185,000 in 1901. Since then it has not greatly changed overall although its distribution and ethnic mix has, with over a quarter of the population now coming from non-white communities. The greatest area of growth has been at Thamesmead, a new town created from the 1960s to the east of Woolwich, a development blighted by poor facilities and transport links. The population will continue to increase as transport links are transformed – the Docklands Light Railway now reaches Greenwich and Woolwich, the Jubilee line passes by the O_2 and Crossrail will reach Woolwich and beyond to Abbey Wood. The economy of Greenwich currently relies heavily on the public sector, which provides nearly 40 per cent of jobs (approaching double the London average) while tourism supports 9 per cent of jobs. Higher Education institutions (Greenwich University, Trinity College of Music and Ravensbourne College) bring many students to the borough while the O_2, built on former industrial land on Greenwich Peninsula, brings hundreds of thousands of visitors to its many events staged over the year.

FAMOUS FOR

In 1884 at an international conference in Washington it was agreed that the Prime (or Greenwich) Meridian from which all longitude positions are calculated should pass through the Royal Observatory at **Greenwich** – a brass rail inlaid into the yard outside the Observatory defines its position.

The ***Cutty Sark***, built in Dumbarton in 1869, was designed to bring tea from China as fast as possible. She has been on display in a permanent dry dock at Greenwich since 1954. In 2007, while undergoing conservation work a fire severely damaged the boat, resulting in a five-year restoration programme.

The **London and Greenwich Railway** was the capital's first railway, providing a service between London Bridge and Greenwich by 1838.

On **Shooter's Hill**, one of the highest spots in London at 132 m, is a very unusual building. Severndroog Castle is a triangular brick folly 18 m tall that was built in 1784 after the death of Sir William James by his wife to honour his capture of the pirate fortress of Severndroog on the Malabar coast in South India in 1755.

In 2010 **Ravensbourne** design college moved from Chislehurst to a site adjacent to the O_2 and

Cutty Sark, the 19th-century tea clipper preserved in dry dock at Greenwich

O_2 Arena and Ravensbourne College on the Greenwich Peninsula

into a prize-winning and distinctly edgy building, designed by Foreign Office Architects, which allows for radically modern ways of teaching within.

To cross the **Thames** there are two foot tunnels (at Greenwich and Woolwich) and a car ferry at Woolwich, and, from 2012, a cable car.

FAMOUS PEOPLE

Prince John, Earl of Cornwall, second son of Edward II, born Eltham, 1316.
Henry VIII, King of England and Ireland, born Greenwich, 1491.
Mary I, Queen of England and Ireland, born Greenwich, 1516.
Elizabeth I, Queen of England and Ireland, born Greenwich, 1533.
Richard Lovelace, poet and army officer, born Woolwich, 1617.
Sir George Everest, geodesist and military engineer (Mount Everest was named after him in 1856), born Greenwich, 1790.
Charles George Gordon, army officer ('Gordon of Khartoum', 'Chinese Gordon'), born Woolwich, 1833.
Emily Davison, suffragette who threw herself under the king's horse at Epsom in 1913, born Greenwich, 1872.
Walter de la Mare, poet and writer, born Charlton, 1873.
Edgar Wallace, writer, born Greenwich, 1875.
Frank Murphy, radio manufacturer (founded Murphy Radio Ltd.), born Woolwich, 1889.
Bob Hope, actor, born Eltham, 1903.
Eric Ambler, writer, born Charlton, 1909.
Ruth Khama, wife of Sir Seretse Khama (first president of Botswana), born Eltham, 1923.
Steve Davies, snooker player, born Plumstead, 1957.

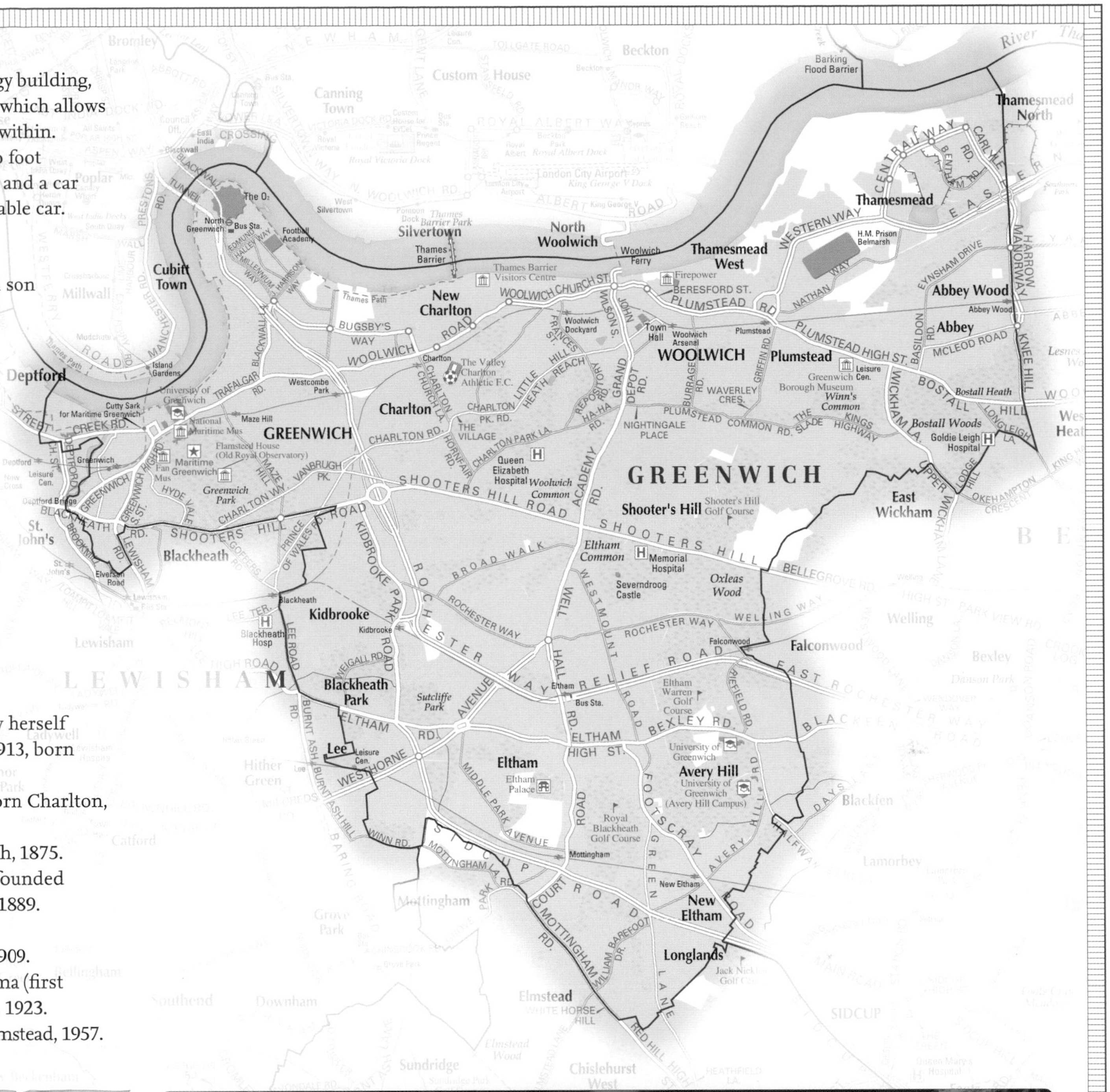

John Bartholomew, Gazetteer of the British Isles (1887)
GREENWICH, *parl. bor. and par., Kent, on river Thames, 4 miles SE. of London Bridge by rail – par., 1741 ac., pop. 46,580; parl. bor. (which includes the pars. of Greenwich, Deptford St Nicholas, Charlton next Woolwich, and Kidbrooke), 3838 ac., pop. 65,411; 1 Bank. Market-days, Wednesday and Saturday. Greenwich possesses several important mfrs. including telegraph works, engineering works, chemical works, &c. The Royal Observatory has a world-wide celebrity; English geographers calculate longitude Greenwich Hospital, now the Royal Naval College, is a splendid edifice built upon the site of a royal palace which was the birthplace of Henry VIII., Queen Mary, and Queen Elizabeth. The bor. returns 1 member to Parliament; it returned 2 members until 1885, when its parl. limits were reduced by the formation of the new parl. boroughs of Deptford and Woolwich.*

The Royal Observatory, Greenwich Park

HAUNTED LONDON

The Tower of London, with its role in history as a place of betrayal, murder and execution, is seen by many as an ideal place for ghosts to roam and they will say that it is the most haunted place in Britain. Similarly, stories from gas-lit back alleys on foggy nights or clear moonlit nights on Hampstead Heath can stimulate the mind to accept paranormal events. Whatever your views on the reality of ghosts, undoubtedly some places in London have atmospheres that do not seem entirely normal or predictable. Here are some of the places that have ghostly reputations.

The Spaniards Inn, Hampstead

Dick Turpin, the romanticized highwayman, featured on a 1926 cigarette card

The Tower of London

As a Royal palace and a Royal prison many famous people in England's history have stayed within its walls, not all of them out of choice. There are victims of Royal murders, so the ghost of Henry VI is said to haunt the Wakefield Tower on 21 May, the anniversary of his murder, as he said his prayers, on that night in 1471. The most shameful murder in the Tower was of the two Royal princes, Richard and Edward, in the Bloody Tower by their uncle the Duke of Gloucester (later Richard III) in 1473 and their terrified ghosts are said to haunt the tower.

During the reign of Henry VIII, the Tower was a place of execution for those who displeased him, and so ghosts of two of his queens (Anne Boleyn and Katherine Howard), Viscountess Rochford (Anne Boleyn's sister-in-law), and Margaret Pole, (Countess of Salisbury and a supporter of Henry's first wife, Catherine of Aragon) are all said to haunt the place. These figures were later joined by ghostly apparitions of Lady Jane Grey (briefly Queen after Edward VI's short reign), the Earl of Essex (Elizabeth I's favourite), Walter Raleigh, and Guy Fawkes as well as an unknown woman in white.

Other haunted historic buildings
Other historic buildings known for ghostly appearances include the Charterhouse, in the City, once a Carthusian monastery. A monk is said to haunt the area, perhaps a victim of Thomas Cromwell's brutal suppression of the monastery, while the headless figure of a later owner, Thomas Howard, Duke of Norfolk, haunts the main staircase where he was arrested prior to his execution in 1572. The Bank of England is said to be haunted by Sarah Whitehead ('The Bank Nun') – her brother worked at the Bank and was executed for forgery in 1811. In life she went to the bank every day to ask for her brother, and in death she returned to the Bank, it is said, still looking for her brother. Sutton House, a large Tudor house in Hackney, is said to be haunted by dogs, an Elizabethan lady and a 19th century headmistress.

Haunted pubs
A number of pubs (quite frequently their cellars) are considered haunted. Spaniards Inn, on Hampstead Heath is said to be haunted by the ghosts of Jack Sheppard, an 18th-century petty criminal and serial prison escapee, and the highwayman Dick Turpin, who can also be encountered on Hampstead Heath riding on his horse, Black Bess. The Grenadier, in Wilton Mews, Belgravia, is alleged to be London's most haunted pub, apparently dating from its time as an officers' mess, though others give this title to the Viaduct Tavern, near the Old Bailey.

Haunted theatres
Theatres, too, abound in stories of ghosts, perhaps the most benign being the ghost of the actor-manager John Baldwin Buckstone at the Theatre Royal, Haymarket, for a sighting of him indicates a successful and long-running show, while a Man in Grey appearing at the Theatre Royal,

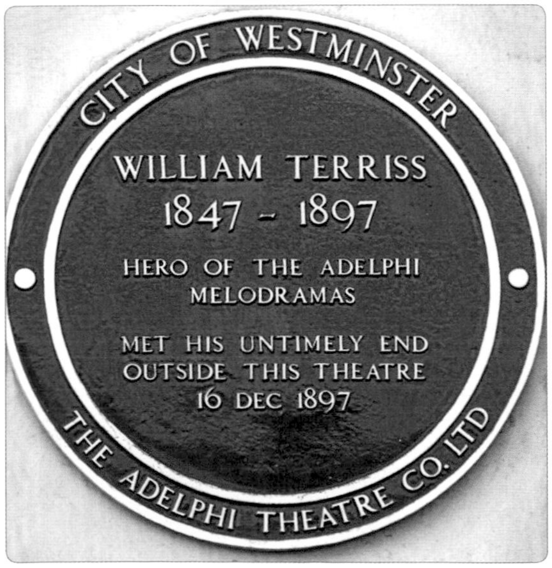

Memorial plaque to William Terriss outside the Adelphi Theatre

50 Berkeley Square, known in Victorian times as the most haunted house in London, but now an antiquarian bookshop

Drury Lane, brings similar good fortune. The Adelphi, though, is said to be haunted by the actor William Terriss, who was murdered at the stage door in 1897 by a fellow actor.

Underground hauntings
The transport system of London, particularly the Underground, is another favoured area. Farringdon Underground station is disturbed by the screams of Anne Naylor, who was murdered there in 1758. The now-closed station at the British Museum is haunted by an ancient Egyptian princess and Aldwych, another closed station, is visited by a female actress from the Royal Strand Theatre, previously on the site, and is normally seen at night by the cleaning staff. Platform 10 of King's Cross station is said to be haunted by Boudicca, whose tomb is allegedly under this platform.

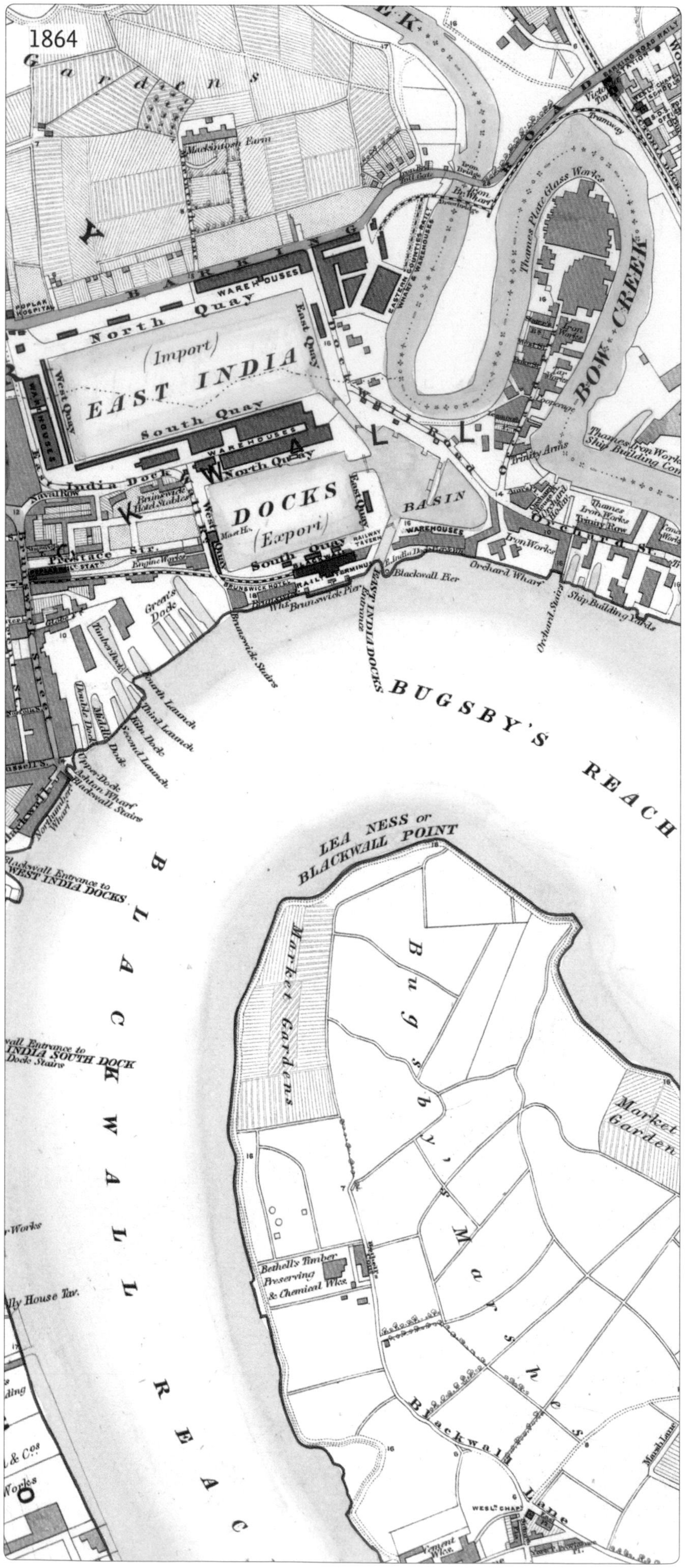

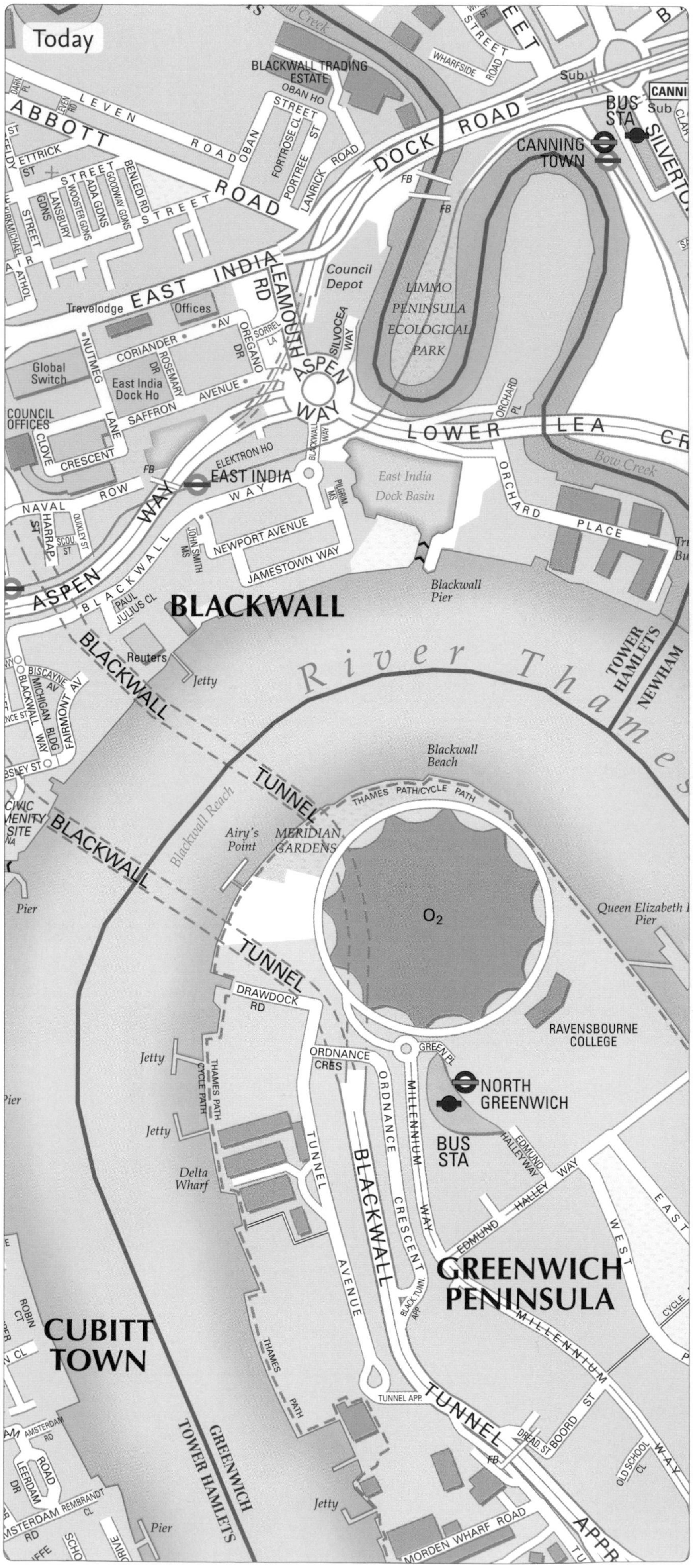

The differences between the detail shown on the 1864 *Stanford's Library Map of London* and the modern-day map are quite dramatic. The East India Docks have been filled in and the area redeveloped, while on the Greenwich Peninsula, Bugsby's Marshes, once pasture land and then the site of heavy industries and a major gas works, now houses The O_2 and the southern entrance to the enlarged Blackwall Tunnel and will see further development of homes and offices.

In the 1930s the peninsula was the site of a large gas works along with other industries

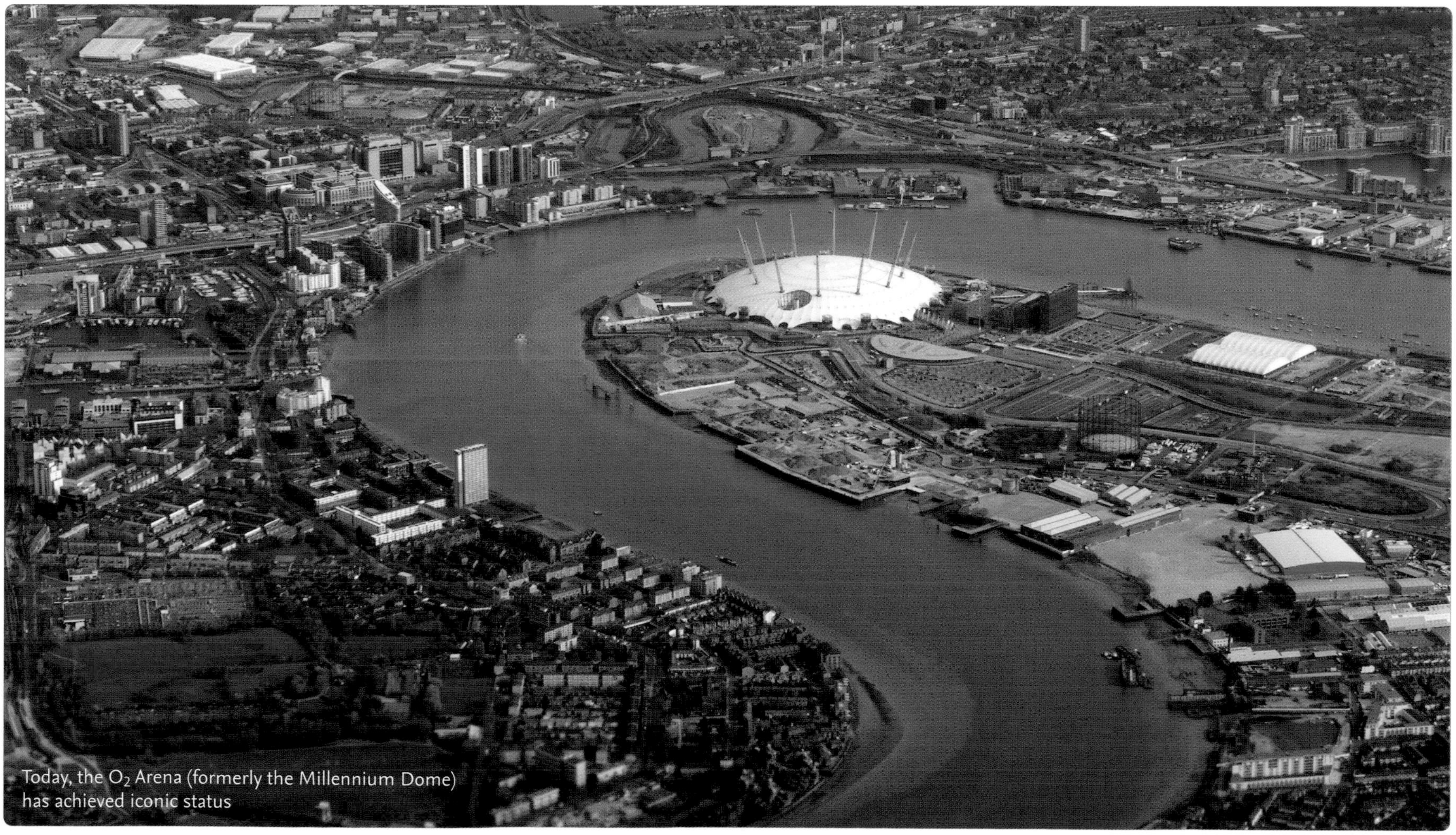

Today, the O_2 Arena (formerly the Millennium Dome) has achieved iconic status

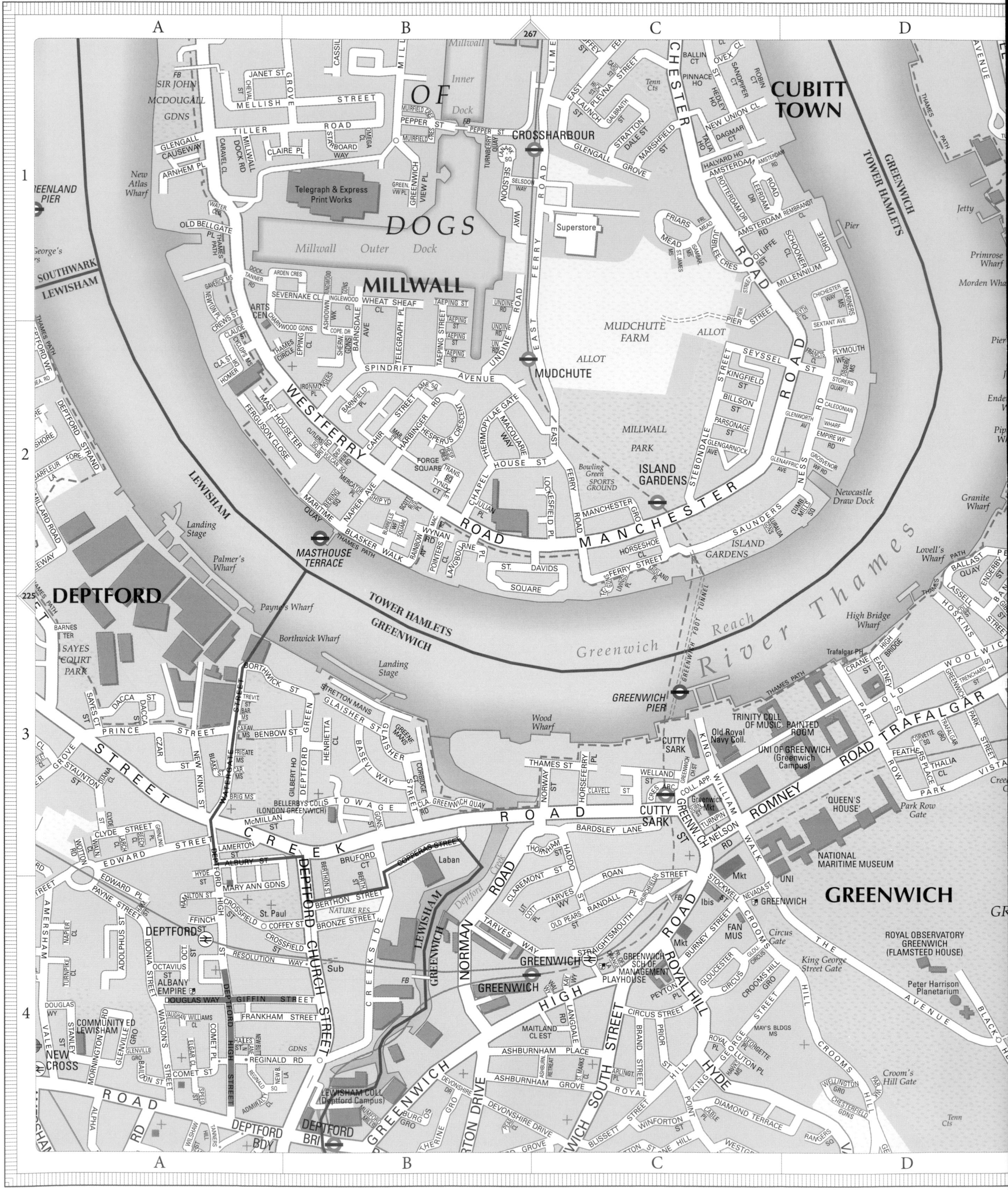
A
B
C
D
1
2
3
4
267
225
CUBITT TOWN
OF
DOGS
MILLWALL
DEPTFORD
GREENWICH
Millwall Inner Dock
Millwall Outer Dock
Telegraph & Express Print Works
CROSSHARBOUR
MUDCHUTE
MUDCHUTE FARM
ALLOT
Superstore
MILLWALL PARK
ISLAND GARDENS
MASTHOUSE TERRACE
GREENWICH PIER
CUTTY SARK
River Thames
Greenwich Reach
TOWER HAMLETS
LEWISHAM
SOUTHWARK
GREENWICH FOOT TUNNEL
SIR JOHN MCDOUGALL GDNS
New Atlas Wharf
Landing Stage
Palmer's Wharf
Payne's Wharf
Borthwick Wharf
Wood Wharf
Lovell's Wharf
High Bridge Wharf
Newcastle Draw Dock
Granite Wharf
Primrose Wharf
Morden Wharf
Jetty
Pier
SAYES COURT PARK
Old Royal Navy Coll.
TRINITY COLL OF MUSIC
PAINTED ROOM
UNI OF GREENWICH (Greenwich Campus)
'QUEEN'S HOUSE'
Park Row Gate
NATIONAL MARITIME MUSEUM
ROYAL OBSERVATORY GREENWICH (FLAMSTEED HOUSE)
Peter Harrison Planetarium
King George Street Gate
Circus Gate
Croom's Hill Gate
FAN MUS
Laban
NATURE RES.
St. Paul
DEPTFORD
NEW CROSS
GREENWICH SCH OF MANAGEMENT
PLAYHOUSE
LEWISHAM COLL (Deptford Campus)
COMMUNITY ED LEWISHAM
BELLERBYS COLLS (LONDON GREENWICH)
WESTFERRY ROAD
MANCHESTER ROAD
EAST FERRY ROAD
CHESTER ROAD
SPINDRIFT AVENUE
CREEK ROAD
PRINCE STREET
EVELYN STREET
DEPTFORD CHURCH STREET
DEPTFORD HIGH STREET
GREENWICH HIGH ROAD
ROYAL HILL
ROMNEY ROAD
TRAFALGAR ROAD
NORMAN ROAD
CREEKSIDE
DEPTFORD BRIDGE
GREENWICH SOUTH STREET

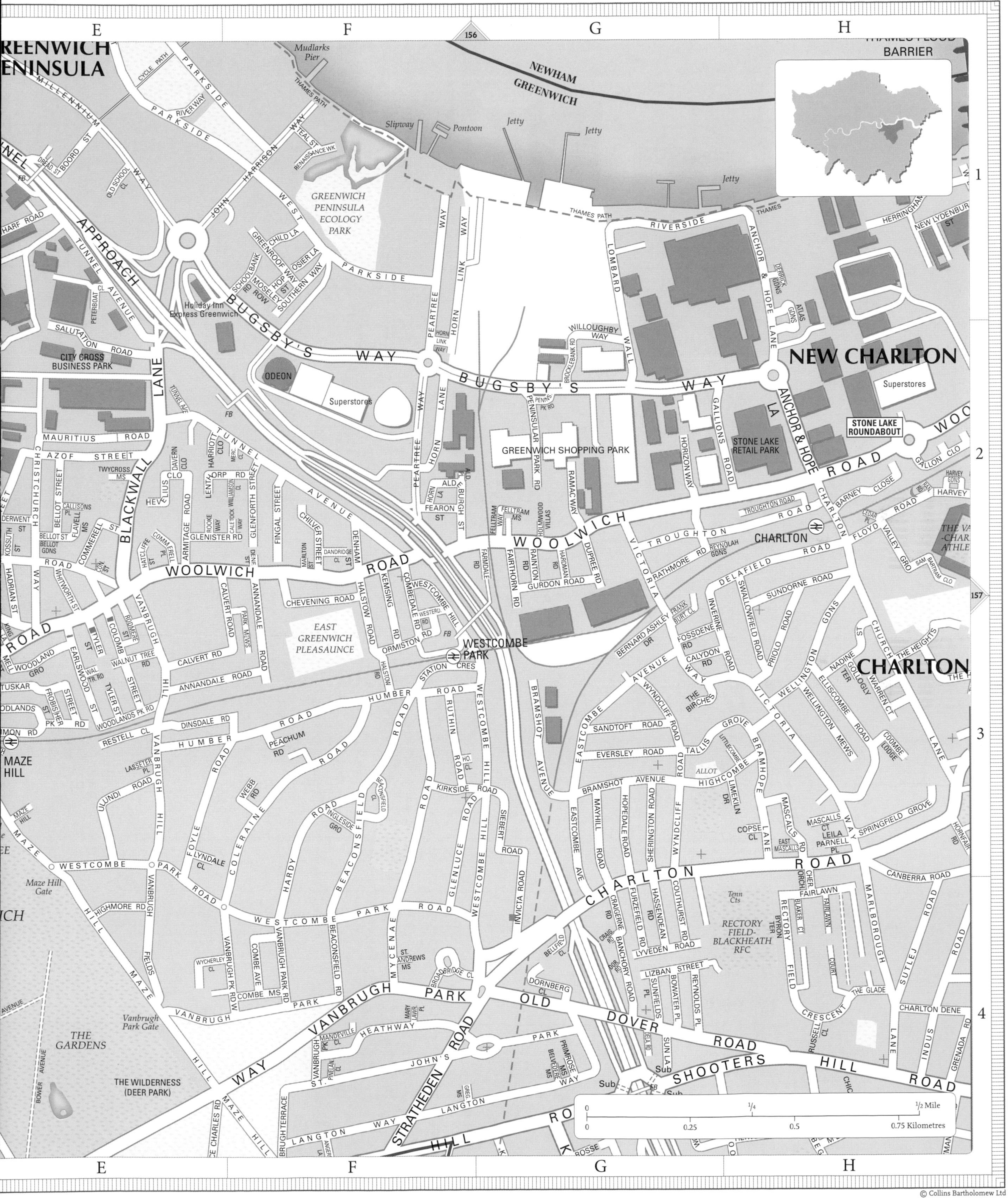
E
F
G
H
GREENWICH PENINSULA
Mudlarks Pier
NEWHAM
GREENWICH
THAMES FLOOD BARRIER
THAMES PATH
Slipway
Pontoon
Jetty
Jetty
Jetty
MILLENNIUM WAY
PARKSIDE
CYCLE PATH
RIVERWAY
TEAL ST
RENAISSANCE WK
JOHN HARRISON WAY
WEST PARKSIDE
OLD SCHOOL CL
BOORD ST
DREADNOUGHT ST
TUNNEL APPROACH
GREENWICH PENINSULA ECOLOGY PARK
CHILD LA
GREENROOF WAY
SCHOOLBANK RD
MOSELEY ROW
HOP ST
OSIER LA
SOUTHERN WAY
PARKSIDE
PEARTREE WAY
HORN LINK WAY
RIVERSIDE
LOMBARD WALL
ANCHOR & HOPE LANE
DERRICK GDNS
ATLAS GDNS
HERRINGHAM
NEW LYDENBURG ST
TUNNEL AVENUE
PETERBOAT CL
Holiday Inn Express Greenwich
BUGSBY'S WAY
SALUTATION ROAD
CITY CROSS BUSINESS PARK
ODEON
Superstores
WILLOUGHBY WAY
BROCKLEBANK RD
NEW CHARLTON
Superstores
BUGSBY'S WAY
PENINSULAR PARK RD
PENNYS PK RD
GREENWICH SHOPPING PARK
HORIZON WAY
GALLIONS ROAD
STONE LAKE RETAIL PARK
ANCHOR & HOPE LA
STONE LAKE ROUNDABOUT
WOOLWICH ROAD
GALLON CL
HARVEY GDNS
HARVEY
BLACKWALL LANE
TUNNEL AVE
FB
MAURITIUS ROAD
AZOF STREET
TWYCROSS MS
CHRISTCHURCH WAY
DAVERN CLO
HARRIOTT CLO
ORP RD
HEVELIUS CLO
LENTHORP RD
ROOKE WAY
CALETOCK WAY
WILLIAMSON CL
GLENISTER RD
GLENFORTH STREET
FINGAL STREET
TUNNEL AVENUE
CHILVER STREET
DENHAM STREET
MARLTON ST
DANDRIDGE CL
ALDEBURGH ST
ALDEBURGH PL
HORN LANE
FEARON ST
FELLTRAM WAY
FELLTRAM MS
VILLAS RD
RAMAC WAY
TROUGHTON ROAD
REYNOLAH GDNS
CHARLTON
BARNEY CLOSE
FLOYD ROAD
CEDAR PL
VALLEY GRO
THE VALLEY
SAM BARTRAM CLO
CALLISONS PL
BELLOT STREET
FLAVELL MS
DERWENT ST
BELLOT ST
BELLOT GDNS
COMMERELL ST
KOSSUTH ST
HATCLIFFE CL
COMMERELL PL
ARMITAGE ROAD
WOOLWICH ROAD
FARMDALE RD
FAIRTHORN RD
RAINTON RD
HARDMAN RD
DUPREE RD
GURDON ROAD
VICTORIA WAY
RATHMORE RD
DELAFIELD ROAD
SUNDORNE ROAD
HADRIAN ST
WHITWORTH ST
ROAD
VANBRUGH HILL
CALVERT ROAD
PARK MEWS
ANNANDALE ROAD
CHEVENING ROAD
KEMSING RD
COMBEDALE RD
WESTCOMBE HILL
HALSTOW ROAD
EAST GREENWICH PLEASAUNCE
ORMISTON RD
WESTCOMBE PARK
STATION CRES
BERNARD ASHLEY DR
FRANK BURTON CL
FOSSDENE RD
CALYDON RD
INVERINE ROAD
SWALLOWFIELD ROAD
PRIOLO ROAD
CHURCH LANE
THE HEIGHTS
CHARLTON
TYLER ST
COLOMB ST
ROAD
WOODLAND GRO
EARLSWOOD ST
WALNUT TREE RD
CALVERT RD
ANNANDALE ROAD
HUMBER ROAD
TUSKAR
FROBISHER PL
WOODLANDS PK RD
DINSDALE RD
RESTELL CL
HUMBER ROAD
PEACHUM RD
RUTHIN ROAD
BRAMSHOT AVENUE
WYNDCLIFF ROAD
AVENUE
THE BIRCHES
WELLINGTON GDNS
NADINE ST
GOLLOGLY TER
ELLISCOMBE ROAD
WARREN CT
WELLINGTON MEWS
COOMBE LODGE
MAZE HILL
EASTCOMBE AVENUE
SANDTOFT ROAD
EVERSLEY ROAD
TALLIS GROVE
LITTLECOMBE
ALLOT
HIGHCOMBE
BRAMHOPE LANE
LIMEKILN DR
LASSETER PL
ULUNDI ROAD
WEBB RD
KIRKSIDE ROAD
BEACONSFIELD ROAD
INGLESIDE GRO
BRAMSHOT AVENUE
MAYHILL ROAD
HOPEDALE ROAD
SHERINGTON ROAD
WYNDCLIFF
COPSE CL
MASCALLS RD
MASCALLS CT
LEILA PARNELL PL
SPRINGFIELD GROVE
EAST MASCALLS
WESTCOMBE PARK ROAD
FOYLE ROAD
LYNDALE CL
COLERAINE ROAD
HARDY ROAD
GLENLUCE ROAD
SIEBERT ROAD
INVICTA ROAD
CHARLTON ROAD
CANBERRA ROAD
FAIRLAWN
Maze Hill Gate
HIGHMORE RD
WESTCOMBE PARK ROAD
CRAIGERNE RD
FURZEFIELD RD
HASSENDEAN RD
COUTHURST RD
Tenn Cts
RECTORY FIELD- BLACKHEATH RFC
RECTORY FIELD CRES
MARLBOROUGH LANE
SUTLEJ ROAD
WYCHERLEY CL
VANBRUGH PK RD W
COMBE AVE
VANBRUGH PARK RD
BEACONSFIELD RD
MYCENAE ROAD
ST. ANDREWS MS
BROADBRIDGE CL
BELLFIELD CL
BANCHORY ROAD
LYVEDEN ROAD
LIZBAN STREET
SUNFIELDS PL
BOWATER PL
REYNOLDS PL
COMBE MS
VANBRUGH PARK
DORNBERG CL
OLD DOVER ROAD
THE GLADE
CHARLTON DENE
Vanbrugh Park Gate
THE GARDENS
VANBRUGH
HEATHWAY
MANDEVILLE CL
PARK
PRIMROSE MS
BELVEDERE MS
SUN LA
SHOOTERS HILL ROAD
INDUS ROAD
GRENADA RD
THE WILDERNESS (DEER PARK)
BOWER AVENUE
MAZE HILL
VANBRUGH HILL
ST. JOHN'S PARK
STRATHEDEN ROAD
LANGTON WAY
Sub
FB
Sub
HILL
CHARLES RD
BRUGHTERRACE
LANGTON WAY
ROSSE
1/4
1/2 Mile
0
0.25
0.5
0.75 Kilometres
156
157
1
2
3
4

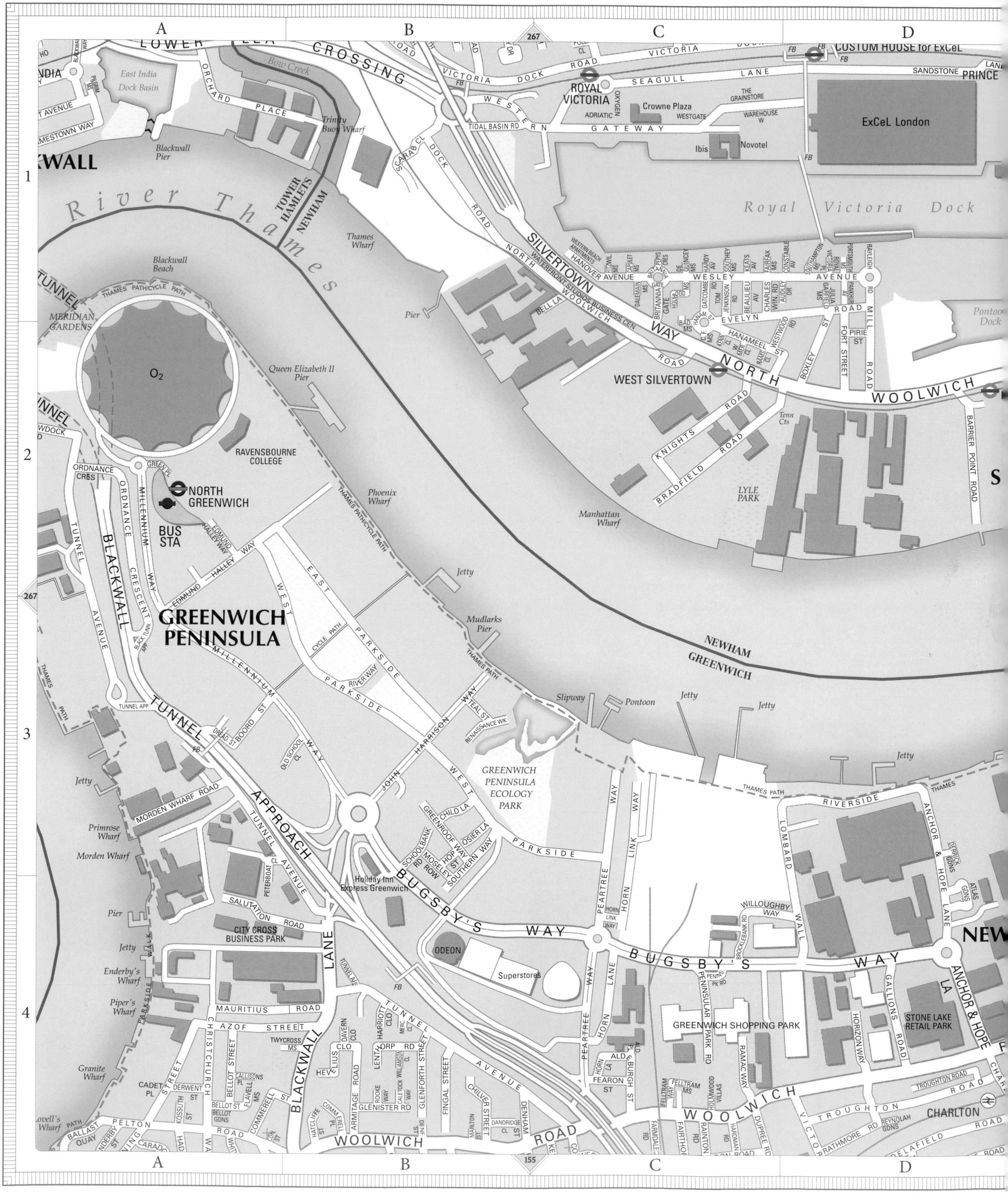
A
B
C
D
1
2
3
4
267
155
River Thames
Bow Creek
East India Dock Basin
Blackwall Pier
TOWER HAMLETS
NEWHAM
Trinity Buoy Wharf
Thames Wharf
Blackwall Beach
MERIDIAN GARDENS
O_2
Queen Elizabeth II Pier
RAVENSBOURNE COLLEGE
NORTH GREENWICH
BUS STA
Phoenix Wharf
Jetty
Mudlarks Pier
GREENWICH PENINSULA
THAMES PATH/CYCLE PATH
EAST PARKSIDE
WEST PARKSIDE
MILLENNIUM WAY
EDMUND HALLEY WAY
BLACKWALL TUNNEL APPROACH
TUNNEL AVENUE
JOHN HARRISON WAY
GREENWICH PENINSULA ECOLOGY PARK
Slipway
Pontoon
NEWHAM
GREENWICH
Primrose Wharf
Morden Wharf
MORDEN WHARF ROAD
Pier
Enderby's Wharf
Piper's Wharf
Granite Wharf
Lovell's Wharf
CITY CROSS BUSINESS PARK
SALUTATION ROAD
Holiday Inn Express Greenwich
BUGSBY'S WAY
ODEON
Superstores
GREENWICH SHOPPING PARK
STONE LAKE RETAIL PARK
MAURITIUS ROAD
AZOF STREET
WOOLWICH ROAD
CHARLTON
ROYAL VICTORIA
CUSTOM HOUSE for ExCeL
ExCeL London
Crowne Plaza
Novotel
Ibis
Royal Victoria Dock
Pontoon Dock
SILVERTOWN WAY
NORTH WOOLWICH ROAD
WEST SILVERTOWN
LYLE PARK
Manhattan Wharf
Tenn Cts
KNIGHTS ROAD
BRADFIELD ROAD
BARRIER POINT ROAD
WESLEY AVENUE
EVELYN ROAD
HANAMEEL ST
RIVERSIDE
ANCHOR & HOPE LANE
LOMBARD WALL
WILLOUGHBY WAY
PEARTREE WAY
HORN LINK WAY
GALLIONS ROAD
HORIZON WAY
Thames Path

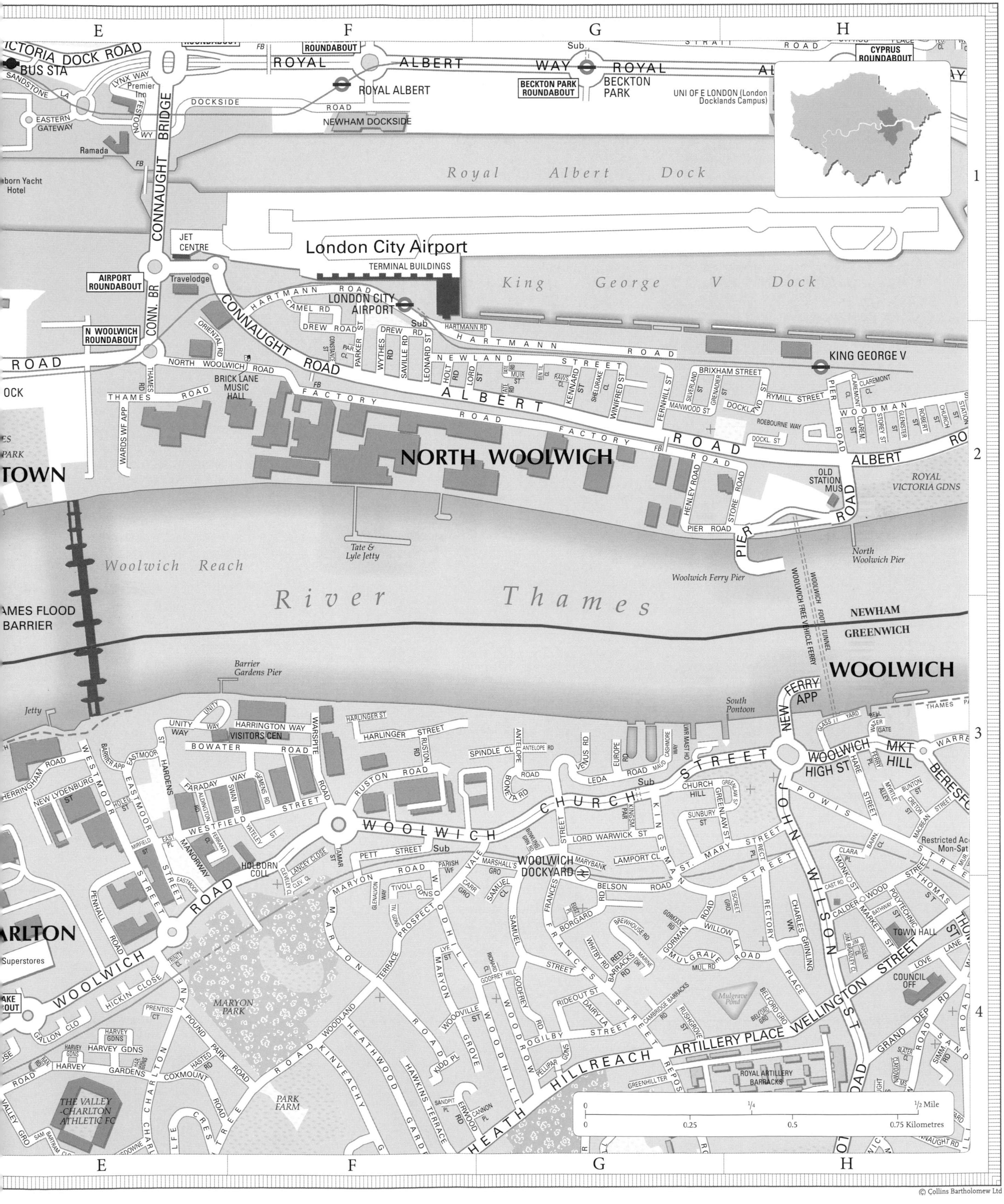

E
F
G
H
1
2
3
4
VICTORIA DOCK ROAD
BUS STA
SANDSTONE LA
LYNX WAY
Premier Inn
EASTERN GATEWAY
FESTOON WY
Ramada
CONNAUGHT BRIDGE
ROYAL ALBERT ROUNDABOUT
ROYAL ALBERT WAY
ROYAL ALBERT
DOCKSIDE ROAD
NEWHAM DOCKSIDE
BECKTON PARK ROUNDABOUT
BECKTON PARK
UNI OF E LONDON (London Docklands Campus)
CYPRUS ROUNDABOUT
Royal Albert Dock
JET CENTRE
London City Airport
TERMINAL BUILDINGS
King George V Dock
AIRPORT ROUNDABOUT
Travelodge
N WOOLWICH ROUNDABOUT
CONN. BR
CONNAUGHT ROAD
HARTMANN ROAD
CAMEL RD
LONDON CITY AIRPORT
DREW ROAD
ORIENTAL RD
NORTH WOOLWICH ROAD
BRICK LANE MUSIC HALL
THAMES RD
THAMES ROAD
WARDS WF APP
NEWLAND STREET
ALBERT ROAD
FACTORY ROAD
KENNARD ST
WINIFRED ST
FERNHILL ST
BRIXHAM STREET
MANWOOD ST
RYMILL STREET
KING GEORGE V
PIER ROAD
WOODMAN ST
NORTH WOOLWICH
HENLEY ROAD
STORE ROAD
OLD STATION MUS
ROYAL VICTORIA GDNS
TOWN
Tate & Lyle Jetty
Woolwich Reach
North Woolwich Pier
Woolwich Ferry Pier
River Thames
THAMES FLOOD BARRIER
NEWHAM
GREENWICH
WOOLWICH FREE VEHICLE FERRY
WOOLWICH FOOT TUNNEL
WOOLWICH
Barrier Gardens Pier
Jetty
South Pontoon
NEW FERRY APP
UNITY WAY
HARRINGTON WAY
VISITORS CEN
BOWATER ROAD
HARLINGER STREET
WARSPITE ROAD
RUSTON ROAD
SPINDLE CL
ANTELOPE RD
VENUS RD
LEDA ROAD
CHURCH STREET
WOOLWICH HIGH ST
MKT HILL
BERESFORD
HERRINGHAM ROAD
NEW LYDENBURG ST
WESTMOOR
EASTMOOR
HARDENS
FARADAY WAY
WESTFIELD STREET
WOOLWICH CHURCH STREET
WOOLWICH ROAD
HOLBORN COLL
PETT STREET
MARYON ROAD
WOOLWICH DOCKYARD
LORD WARWICK ST
LAMPORT CL
KINGSMAN ST
ST MARY STREET
JOHN WILSON ST
POWIS STREET
BELSON ROAD
CHARLTON
Superstores
MARYON PARK
PROSPECT VALE
WOODHILL
SAMUEL ST
FRANCES STREET
WILLOW LA
MULGRAVE ROAD
RECTORY PLACE
CHARLES GRINLING WK
TOWN HALL
THOMAS ST
WELLINGTON STREET
COUNCIL OFF
GRAND DEPOT ROAD
ARTILLERY PLACE
ROYAL ARTILLERY BARRACKS
HILLREACH
HEATH
RIDEOUT ST
OGILBY STREET
WOODLAND TERRACE
HEATHWOOD GARDENS
HAWKINS TERRACE
KINVEACHY
HARVEY GARDENS
CHARLTON LANE
POUND PARK ROAD
COXMOUNT RD
THE VALLEY -CHARLTON ATHLETIC FC
PARK FARM
HICKIN CLOSE
GALLON CLO
1/4
1/2 Mile
0
0.25
0.5
0.75 Kilometres

LONDON'S WORLD HERITAGE SITES

The World Heritage Convention stipulates the creation of a World Heritage List. In a detailed process, properties are inscribed by an intergovernmental twenty-one member elected Committee, only after a preselection, nomination, and evaluation process. Two leading international Non-Governmental Organizations, the International Union for the Conservation of Nature (IUCN) and the International Council on Monuments and Sites (ICOMOS), review and advise on the natural and cultural nominations respectively. The International Centre for the Study of the Preservation and Restoration of Cultural Property provides the Committee with expert advice on conservation of cultural sites. To be included, sites must be of outstanding universal value and meet at least one out of ten selection criteria. London currently has four World Heritage Sites.

THE TOWER OF LONDON

Inclusion criteria: Interchange of values; Significance in human history

The Tower of London is an imposing fortress with many layers of history. Built on the Thames by William the Conqueror to protect his London base and to assert his power over the newly conquered English, it became one of the symbols of royalty in England and is a major reference for the history of medieval military architecture.

The Tower is a complex of fortifications, courtyards and buildings extending over 73,000 m^2. There are many towers in the ensemble and the impressive White Tower, begun around 1078 and completed around nine years later, is the centrepiece. Although a royal residence for centuries, the White Tower was never intended as the main royal palace but rather as a stronghold, a notion reinforced by the formidable curtain walls, moats and ditches successive kings built around it. The Crown Jewels are on display in the Tower of London.

The Water Gate entrance was nicknamed Traitors' Gate because prisoners were brought through it to the Tower. Queen Anne Boleyn, Thomas More, Queen Katherine Howard and Princess Elizabeth, later Elizabeth I, all entered it as prisoners.

The Tower of London

ROYAL BOTANIC GARDENS, KEW

Inclusion criteria: Interchange of values; Testimony to cultural tradition; Significance in human history

Since their creation in 1759, the Royal Botanic Gardens of Kew have made a significant contribution to the study of plant diversity, and this is reflected in the richness of the collections housed there. The first botanic garden at Kew was originally for medicinal plants. Later, internationally renowned architects such as William Chambers and 'Capability' Brown not only created many new buildings, but also remodelled the earlier Baroque gardens to make a pastoral landscape in the English style, establishing a fashion that then spread throughout Europe. The landscape garden designed by William Nesfield – and the iron and glass structure, the Palm House, at its centre – is one of the outstanding features of Kew. As the number of visitors increased, the scientific collections were enriched and glasshouses and spaces were altered to house living plant collections.

Kew's exceptional living collections exemplify the European tradition of collecting and cultivating exotic plants for aesthetic, scientific and economic purposes. This tradition has also led to recording and monitoring of the very rich local biodiversity for over 120 years, including an outstanding range of birds, insects, lichens and fungi; some of the latter have proved to be new to science.

MARITIME GREENWICH

Inclusion criteria: Human creative genius; Interchange of values; Significance in human history; Heritage associated with events of universal significance

The ensemble of buildings at Greenwich, and the park in which they are set, symbolize English artistic and scientific endeavour in the 17th and 18th centuries. The focus of the ensemble is the Queen's House, the work of Inigo Jones, and the first true Renaissance building in Britain, and a striking departure from the architectural forms that preceded it. It was inspired by Italian style, and it was in its turn the direct inspiration for classical houses all over Britain. The Queen's House and its associated buildings have housed the National Maritime Museum since 1937. The complex that was until recently the Royal Naval College was designed by Sir Christopher Wren and Nicholas Hawksmoor and is the most outstanding group of Baroque buildings in Britain. Greenwich Royal Park contains the Old Royal Observatory, the work of Wren and the scientist Robert Hooke.

The Old Royal Observatory is situated on the brow of Greenwich Hill and dominates the landscape. It houses an octagonal room which was used by the Royal Society for meetings and dinners, and this is surmounted by the famous time-ball, which indicates Greenwich Mean Time daily at 13.00.

WESTMINSTER PALACE, WESTMINSTER ABBEY AND SAINT MARGARET'S CHURCH

Inclusion criteria: Human creative genius; Interchange of values; Significance in human history

Westminster Palace is the home of the Houses of Parliament and is an outstanding and complete example of neo-Gothic architecture. The site includes the medieval church of Saint Margaret and Westminster Abbey, where England's sovereigns have been crowned since the 11th century, and is of great historic and symbolic significance.

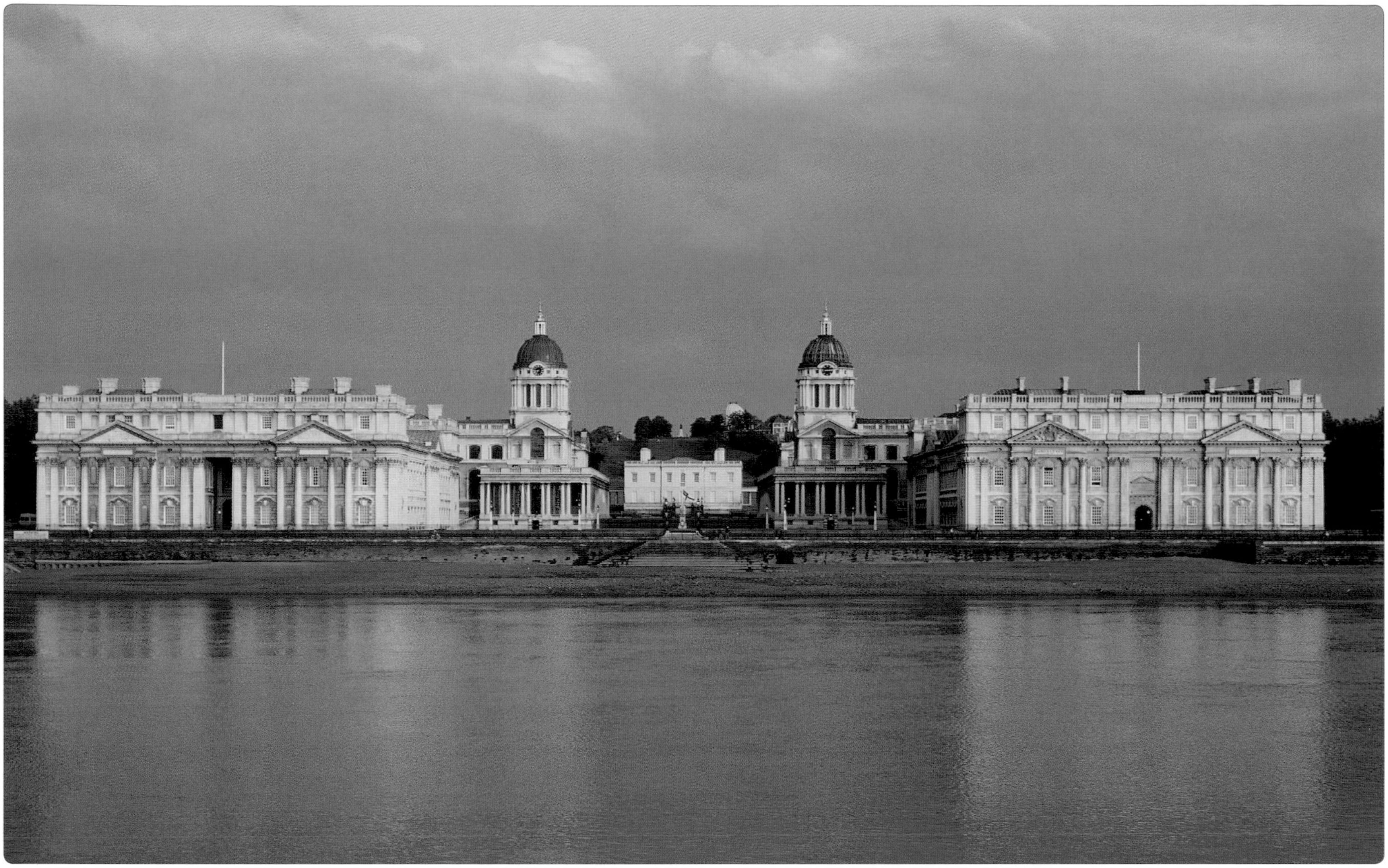

Greenwich from the Thames with the Old Royal Naval College by the river, the Queen's House in the centre, and the Royal Observatory on the hill behind
National Maritime Museum

The construction of a new Westminster Palace by Barry and Pugin began in 1835 after fire destroyed its predecessor. The seat of Parliament, which includes the House of Lords to the south of a central tower and the House of Commons to the north, illustrates in colossal proportions the grandeur of the constitutional monarchy and the principle of the bicameral system.

The site includes Westminster Abbey, a unique construction representing the successive phases of English Gothic architecture and, in the abbey grounds, the charming Perpendicular Gothic church of St Margaret. Rebuilt and remodelled since the fifteenth century, St Margaret's is the Anglican parish church of the House of Commons.

The new Westminster Palace, with the magnificent interiors of the Royal Gallery, House of Lords, Central Lobby, House of Commons, library, and apartments is a vivid symbol of one of the oldest parliamentary institutions in the world. Its façade, situated along the river Thames, is 266 m long; the Victoria Tower, which holds three million archival documents is to the south, and the Clock Tower (Big Ben) to the north.

Temperate House, Kew Gardens

HACKNEY

Population	216,000
Area	19 sq. km
Population density	11,400 per sq. km
Area of green space	4.5 sq. km
Jobs in borough	101,000
Average house price	£314,322

The borough of Hackney is northeast of the City of London and takes its name from the settlement of Hackney ('Haca's high ground', indicating its position above the marshes of the River Lea). The borough was formed in 1965 from the three metropolitan boroughs of Hackney, Shoreditch and Stoke Newington. Shoreditch is just outside the old City walls and was where merchants built larger houses and, being beyond the control of the City authorities, it saw London's first theatres.

Hackney and Stoke Newington remained villages distinct from London until the 19th century. Of the few remaining buildings from these times the most notable are the late medieval tower of St Augustine's Church in Hackney and Sutton House, which is the last surviving Tudor merchant's house in the borough. The area grew rapidly after the railways arrived in the mid-19th century and then the trams a little later – in 1801 the population was 14,600, in 1851 it was 95,000 and by 1901 it had grown to 374,000. New industries established themselves along the Lea Valley, including oil distilling and the manufacturing of paint, chemical dyes and synthetic materials such as shellac.

In the 20th century, deindustrialization and increasingly poor housing stock impoverished the area. It attracted many new arrivals to London, and increased its great racial mix, from the Orthodox Jewish community in Stamford Hill (the largest Hasidic Jewish community in Europe) to Afro-Caribbeans (about 20 per cent of the population) and Turks (5 per cent of the population). Its population shrunk back to around 180,000 in 1981 but since then it has grown considerably. Some areas close to the City, such as Hoxton, have become gentrified, but the fast growth in population has put significant strains on the borough, where around 70 per cent of the population live in rented accommodation. A 2007 survey ranked Hackney as one of the most deprived areas in England, second only to Liverpool.

Parts of Shoreditch benefit from office employment spreading from the City, but most of Hackney benefits less from this than neighbouring boroughs. About a third of the jobs are in finance, IT and other business, just below the average for the whole of London. At nearly 29 per cent, public sector employment is above the London average, but in job numbers well below that in neighbouring Tower Hamlets.

The borough is home to the Geffyre Museum of decorative arts, housed in the early 18th-century Ironmongers' Company Almshouses, and to the Hackney Empire, built in 1901 and now the greatest surviving music hall. Hoxton also has a very lively contemporary art scene. Some of the area around the River Lea is being used for the 2012 Olympic Games – for example the site of the Hackney Wick arena is the Media and Communication Centre.

FAMOUS FOR

Hackney Marsh, the land between the River Lea and the New Hackney Cut, was acquired by London County Council in 1892. It is the centre of the local Sunday football leagues and has over sixty full-sized football pitches.

Homerton College in Cambridge traces its origins back to a college for training Dissenting ministers established on Homerton High Street in 1768.

The two earliest theatres in London were in **Shoreditch**: The Theatre, built by James Burbage in 1576 on the site of the former Augustinian Priory of Holywell and the Curtain Theatre built in 1578.

Fassett Square in **Dalston** was the inspiration for Albert Square in the BBC's 'East Enders'.

Hackney was the name given to a regular horse for hire, so-called because, it is thought, such horses were pastured at Hackney, and from this has come 'Hackney carriage', an archaic name for a taxi, 'hackneyed', for unoriginal or overused and 'hack' for a prolific but uninspired writer.

Hackney Peace Carnival Mural on Dalston Lane, painted in 1985

One of London's most unusual Victorian churches is in **Upper Clapton** – built for the Agapemonite sect as the 'Ark of the Covenant' or 'The Abode of Love' in 1895. The exterior features enormous sculptures of symbolic creatures, while within the magnificent stained glass windows were designed by Walter Crane. It is now the Cathedral of the Nativity of Our Lord of the Georgian Orthodox Church.

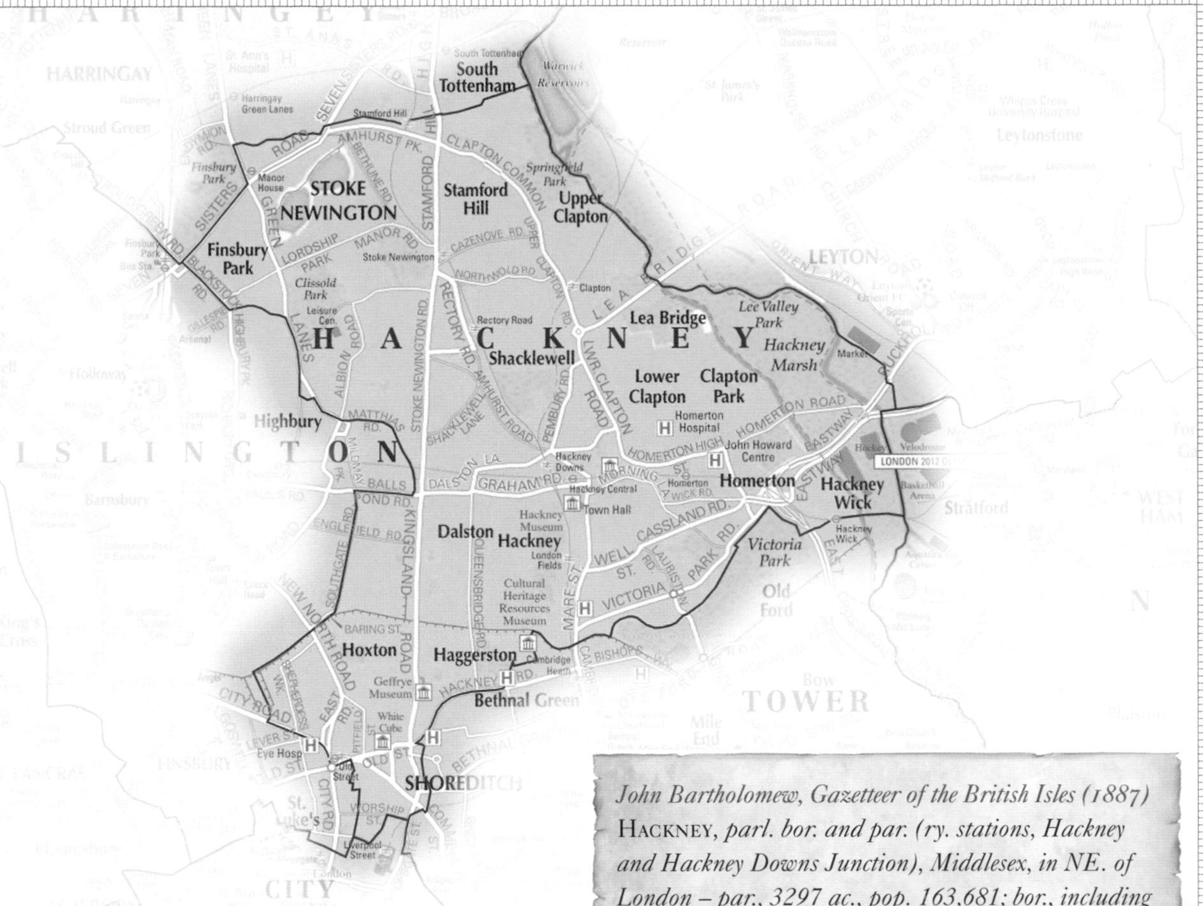

FAMOUS PEOPLE
Edmond Halley, astronomer, after whom the comet is named, born Haggerston, 1656.
Charles Bradlaugh, politician and freethinker, born Hoxton, 1833.
Catherine (Kate) Greenaway, illustrator, born Hoxton, 1846.
Sir Edmund Gosse, writer, born De Beauvoir Town, 1849.
Marie Lloyd (*real name* Matilda Alice Victoria Wood), music-hall entertainer, born Hoxton, 1870.
Jessie (Jessica) Alice Tandy, Oscar-winning actress, born Upper Clapton, 1909.
David Kossoff, actor and broadcaster, born Lower Clapton, 1919.
Arnold Weinstock (Baron Weinstock), industrialist, born Stoke Newington, 1924.
Kray brothers, criminals, **Charles**, born Shoreditch, 1926; twins **Reginald** and **Ronald** born Hoxton, 1933.
Ronald (Ron) Pickering, athletics coach and sports commentator, born Hackney, 1930.
Matt Monro (*born* Terence Richard Parsons), singer, born Shoreditch, 1930.
Marc Bolan (*born* Mark Feld), songwriter, singer and guitarist with T. Rex, born Hackney, 1947.
Paul Boateng (Baron Boateng), Labour politician and cabinet minister, born Hackney, 1951.
Eric Bristow, darts player, born Hackney, 1957.
Phillips Idowu, athlete (champion triple jumper), born Hackney, 1978.

John Bartholomew, Gazetteer of the British Isles (1887)
HACKNEY, *parl. bor. and par. (ry. stations, Hackney and Hackney Downs Junction), Middlesex, in NE. of London – par., 3297 ac., pop. 163,681; bor., including Hackney par. and Stoke Newington par.), 3935 ac., pop. 186,462; Hackney returns 3 members to Parliament – 3 divisions, viz., North, Central, and South, 1 member for each division; its representation was increased from 2 to 3 members in 1885, when its parl. limits were reduced by the formation of the new parl. bors. of Bethnal Green and Shoreditch.*

Hackney Empire Theatre, refurbished in 2004

Hackney City Farm in Haggerston

In the 18th century Hackney was already a densely built-up area although it had retained a number of open areas, as seen on John Rocque's 1746 *Map of London*.

By the mid 19th century these open areas had been fille[d] in, and the Eastern Counties Railway had 'punched' its

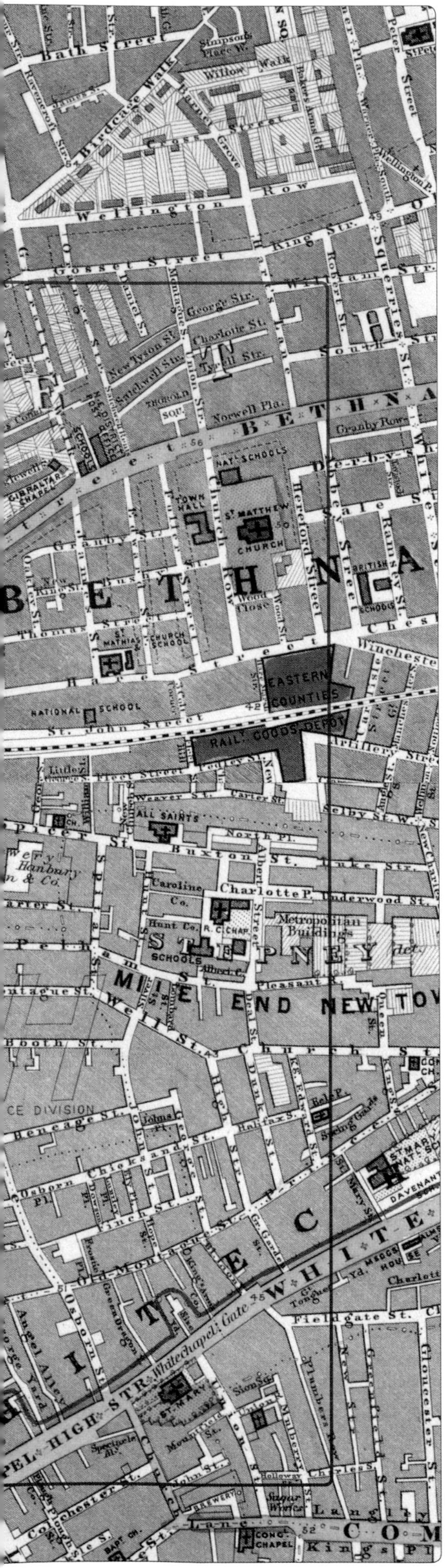

ay through the existing urban street pattern.
tanford's Library Map of London, 1864.

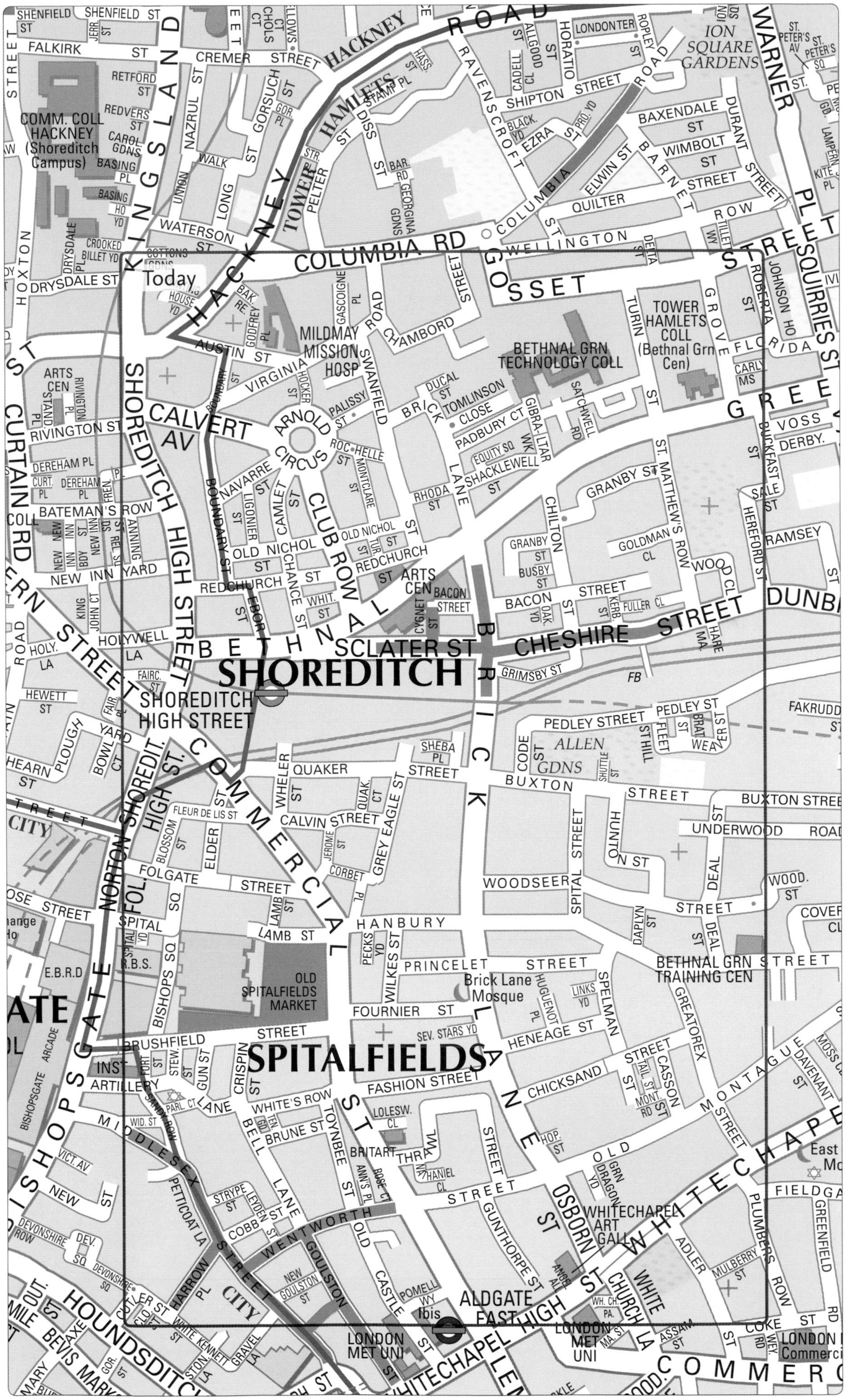

Redevelopment since the 19th century can be seen in the changing street pattern, especially east of Shoreditch High Street on this modern map. Collins Bartholomew mapping

LONDON AT WAR

World War I

The outbreak of war in 1914 coincided with the early development of military aviation. German strategists argued that bombing would undermine morale and force the British to sue for peace. The air raids were initially carried out by Zeppelin airships – the first bomb fell on 30 May 1915, landing in the garden of the Nevill Arms pub in Hackney, although this raid was made by a Zeppelin that reached London as a result of a navigation error. Kaiser Wilhelm II finally authorized the bombing of London in July 1915. Airships dropped 196 tonnes of bombs on London and the surrounding countryside, the most destructive being the raid on 8 September 1915, when a Zeppelin managed to bomb central London, causing significant damage. From 13 June 1917, Germany started to use the Gotha IV, a long-range bomber. Overall 835 Londoners were killed and a further 1,437 injured. The defences developed to counter the attacks, including searchlights, anti-aircraft guns and barrage balloons, were used in the further development of defence plans prior to World War II.

World War II

In the late 1930s the government developed plans for the air defence of London: air raid shelters were built, civil defence training was established, and the evacuation of the city was planned in

German aircraft Heinkel HE III over the Isle of Dogs, Battle of Britain, 1940

The Blitz from the roof of St Paul's Cathedral, December 1940

great detail. In September 1939, about 690,000 children were evacuated from London to safer areas away from the capital. The first bombs were not dropped until September 1940, which was the start of the Blitz, a sustained six-month bombardment of London that produced 71 major raids during which 18,000 tonnes of high explosive bombs were dropped and 20,000 Londoners killed, including many evacuees who had already returned to London. At first German aircraft attacked military and port facilities, but in alleged retaliation for British attacks on German cities, the bombing became more indiscriminate. Londoners were forced to spend sleepless nights in air raid shelters and Underground stations. The bombing cut gas, water and electricity supplies, and brought transport chaos after heavy raids. Large areas of central London were reduced to rubble, particularly around St Paul's Cathedral, which survived the massive raid of 29 December 1940 amidst great devastation all around. Much housing, particularly in the East End, was destroyed – up to 80 per cent of all houses in Silvertown, for example. Yet the Blitz failed to destroy London's economy or undermine London's morale.

In May 1941 the bombing abruptly came to an end with the great raid of 10 May. Over the next three years, London's defences were strengthened and it became a major centre of wartime production, despite its proximity to German bases. The long lull made the renewed assault in the summer of 1944 harder to take. The Allies were mounting ever-heavier attacks on German cities and Germany retaliated with the launch of the rocket-powered flying bombs, first the V1 and then the V2. The first bombs landed in June 1944 and they continued to reach London until the end of the war. The damage was slight when compared with the Blitz, but the attacks were indiscriminate and happened with very little warning, resulting in high casualties. They killed 9,200 and injured another 20,000, with most bombs falling in East and South London, reflecting the range of the weapons.

In total, 29,890 Londoners were killed by enemy action in the capital and 50,507 were injured. At the end of the war the challenge was how best to reconstruct the damaged areas of the city. Not all the town planning decisions made at that time are now seen as successful.

Bomb damage near St Pancras station (*top left*), taken shortly after World War II

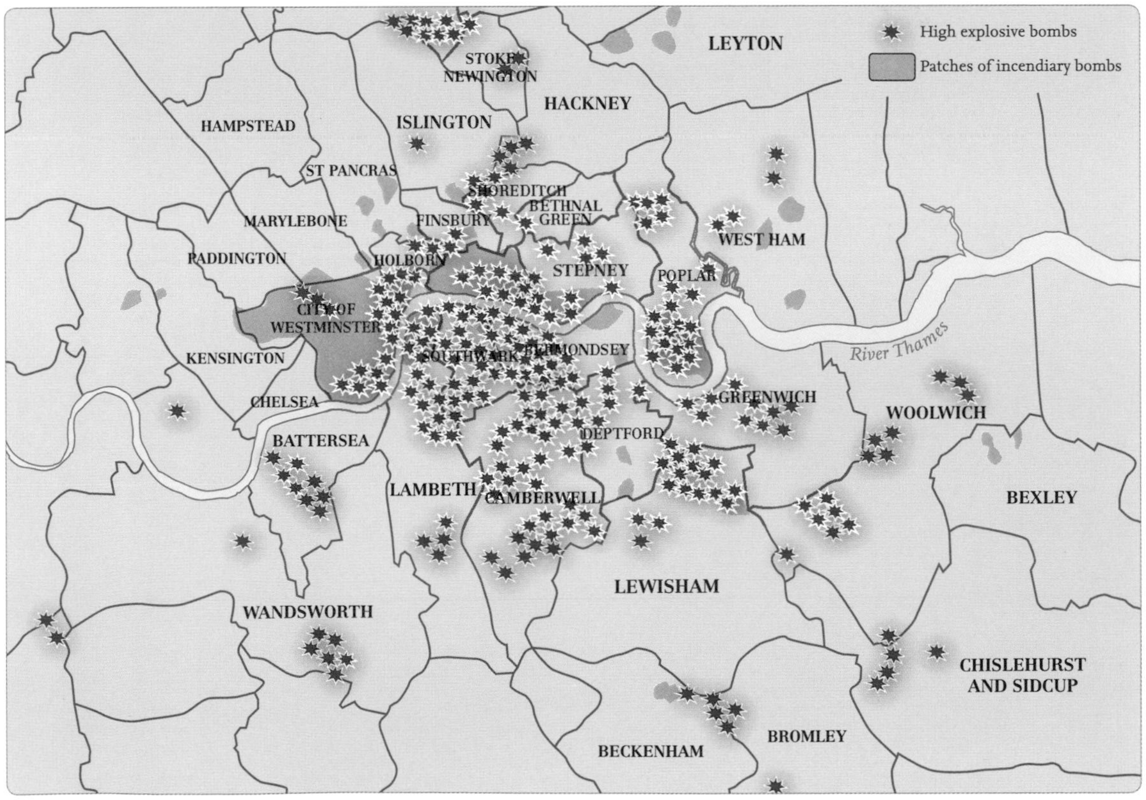

This map shows the scale and spread of the bombing raid on 29 December 1940, at the height of the Blitz

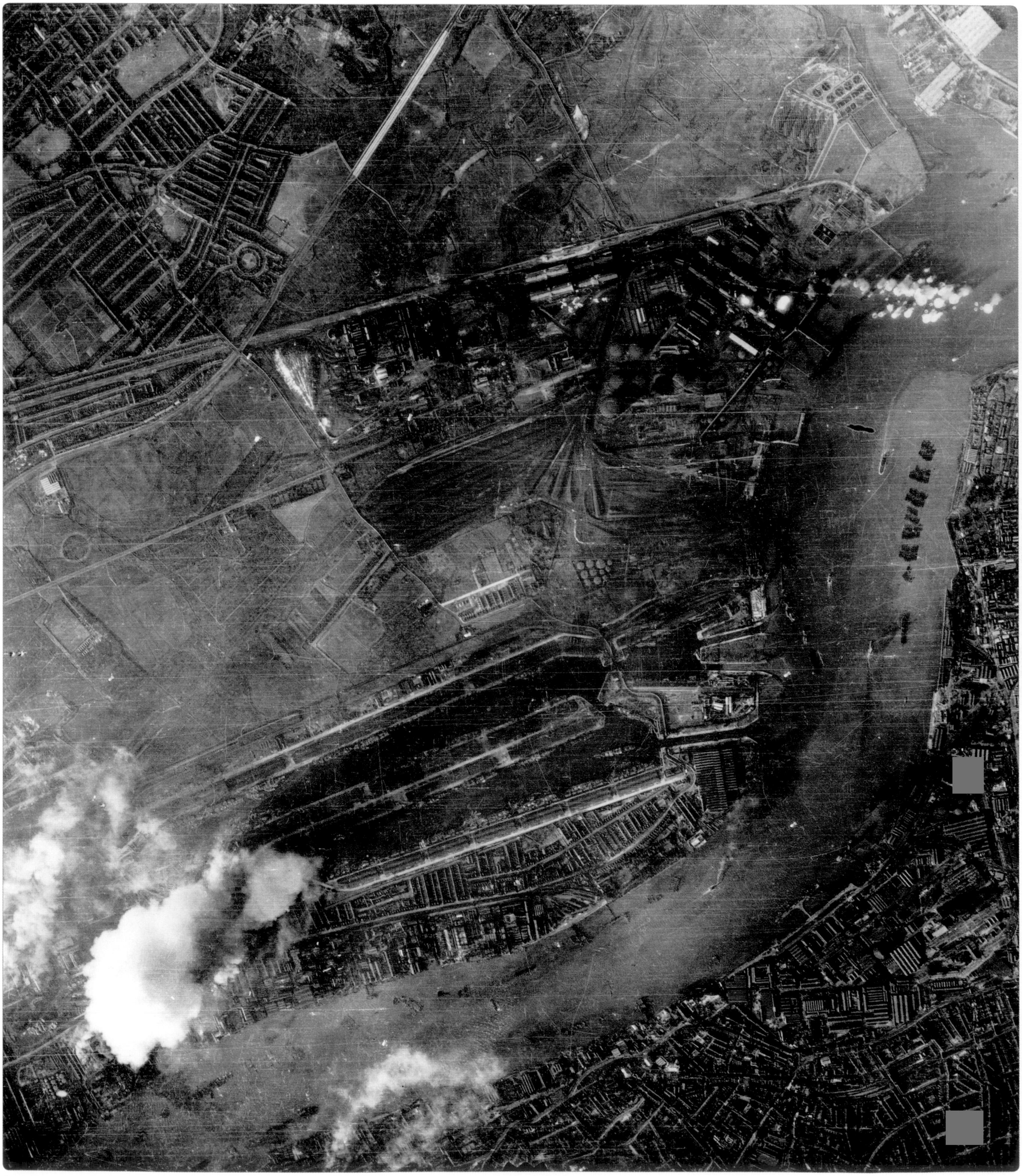

Bombing over Beckton and the Royal Docks; the Woolwich Arsenal can be seen at the bottom right

A service being held in the ruins of St Mary-le-Bow church on Cheapside, which was bombed in the Blitz and which has since been restored

HAMMERSMITH AND FULHAM

Population	169,700
Area	18 sq. km
Population density	9,430 per sq. km
Area of green space	3 sq. km
Jobs in borough	132,000
Average house price	£553,381

The borough of Hammersmith and Fulham has a long frontage along the Thames from Chelsea Creek round the large bend in the river westwards nearly to Chiswick. Northwards it includes Shepherd's Bush, Parsons Green, West Kensington, and Wormwood Scrubs. It was formed in 1965 from the two metropolitan boroughs of Hammersmith (from the Old English, a place with 'a hammer smithy or forge') and Fulham (from the Old English 'land in a river bend belonging to Fulla').

Until the 19th century it was an area of small settlements and farm holdings. The bishops of London had been lords of the manor of Fulham (which included Hammersmith) since the 8th century and Fulham Palace was their official residence until 1973. In the 18th century Fulham also attracted those who wished to escape from the city – Craven Cottage, now a football stadium, was originally one such place, built for Lord Craven. By 1801 the population was only around 10,000. By 1851 it had risen to 30,000, but by 1911, with good railway and Underground links established, the population was 270,000, with most of the area built over, excluding Wormwood Scrubs, which is still an open common of 80 ha. The population declined significantly to 144,000 in 1981 but has been rising again since, although more slowly than many parts of London. The area is popular with students and young adult workers and is not as racially diverse as some London boroughs. Around 22 per cent of the population comes from black and other ethnic minorities, over half of whom have African or Afro-Caribbean roots. In addition 15 per cent of the population come from Europe, North America or the Antipodes, while 5 per cent are of Irish origin.

The employment mix is fairly typical of London apart from increased employment in the media, influenced by the presence of the BBC's Television Centre at White City, the home of BBC Television until 2015. Over recent years, industrial activity has declined, to be replaced by significant growth in office jobs as well as one of the highest rates of self-employment in London, particularly for men. There has also been an increase in retail employment with the Westfield shopping centre in Shepherd's Bush, which was the largest shopping centre in Europe when it opened in 2008.

The borough is home to a number of major sporting venues including three major football stadiums (Chelsea at Stamford Bridge, Fulham at Craven Cottage and Queens Park Rangers at Loftus Road), the Queen's Club (renowned for its pre-Wimbledon tennis competition) and the Hurlingham Club, once the home of polo and croquet. It also has two major performance venues in the Hammersmith Apollo and Shepherd's Bush Empire (both converted cinemas), and the exhibition halls at Olympia in West Kensington bring further visitors to the borough. Half of the Earl's Court exhibition centre is also in the borough, but redevelopment is expected soon at this site.

FAMOUS FOR

Kelmscott House, on the Upper Mall by the Thames at Hammersmith, was the London home and printing and design workshop for William Morris from 1877 to his death in 1896. He named it after his Oxfordshire home at Kelmscott.

Wormwood Scrubs, in addition to being the borough's largest open space, is also the site of Wormwood Scrubs prison; a powerful building that was constructed between 1874 and 1890. The Russian spy, George Blake escaped from here in 1966.

The Dove pub on the Upper Mall at **Hammersmith** is a 17th-century building that became a coffee house in 1796 and later a pub, and has been frequented by literary figures over the centuries.

The Bush Theatre, though small, has vigorously promoted new playwrights since its foundation in 1972 in a room above the Bush pub on **Shepherd's Bush Green**. In 2011 it moved to the former Shepherd's Bush Library nearby on Uxbridge Road.

Inner courtyard of Fulham Palace

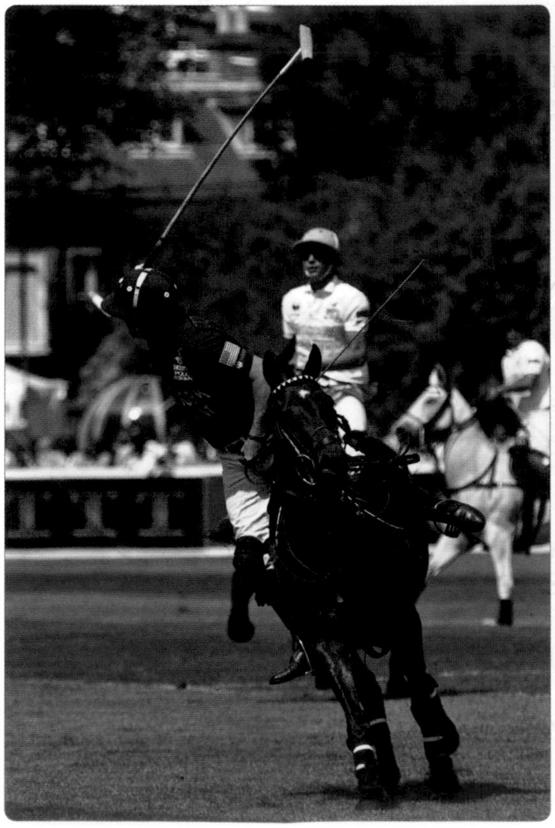

Polo at the Hurlingham Club

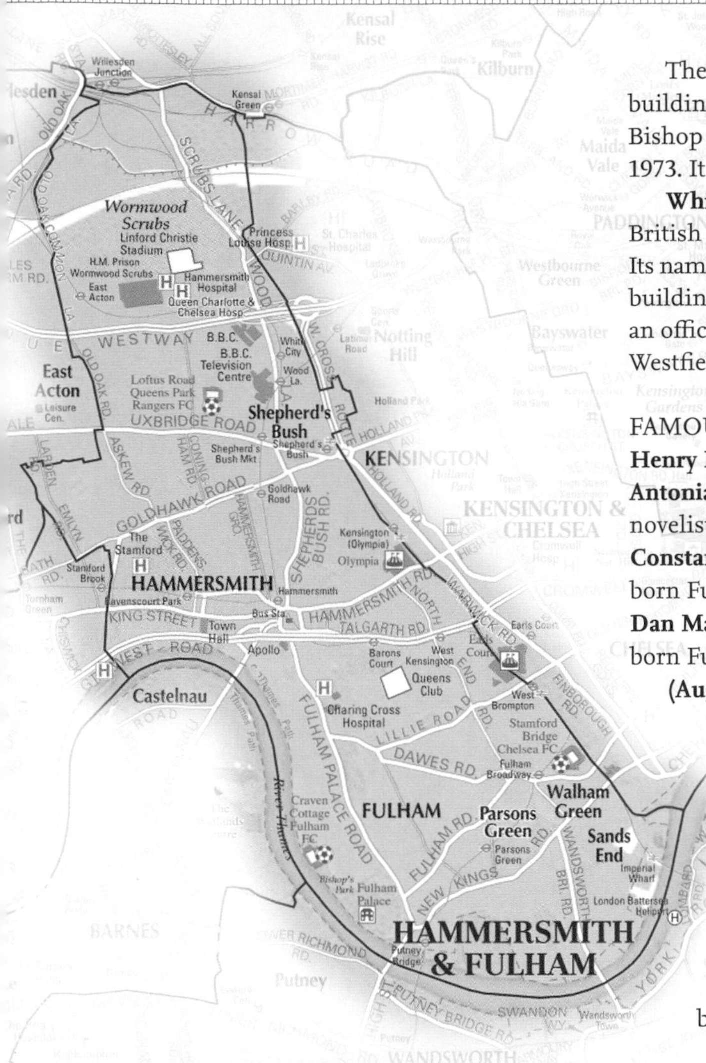

The borough's most important historic building is **Fulham Palace**, built in 1495 for the Bishop of London, and used by the bishop until 1973. It is now a museum.

White City was the site of the 1908 Franco-British Exhibition and the 1908 Olympic Games. Its name came from the whiteness of the exhibition buildings. The Olympic stadium site is now under an office building while other parts are under the Westfield shopping centre.

FAMOUS PEOPLE

Henry Holland, architect, born Fulham, 1745.
Antonia White (Eirene Adeline Hopkinson), novelist, born West Kensington, 1899.
Constant Lambert, composer and conductor, born Fulham, 1905.
Dan Maskell, tennis player and broadcaster, born Fulham, 1908.
(Augustus John) Ruskin Spear, artist and teacher of art, born Hammersmith, 1911.
Eric Porter, actor, born Shepherd's Bush, 1928.
John Osborne, playwright, born Fulham, 1929.
Stirling Moss, racing driver, born West Kensington, 1929.
Gwyneth Dunwoody, Labour politician, born Fulham, 1930.
Janet Street-Porter, media executive and presenter, born Fulham, 1946.
Paul Merton, actor and comedian, born Parsons Green, 1957.
Hugh Grant, actor, born Hammersmith, 1960.
Frank Bruno, boxer and entertainer, born Hammersmith, 1961.
Joe Calzaghe, boxer, born Hammersmith, 1972.
Lawrence Dallaglio, rugby player, born Shepherd's Bush, 1972.
Daniel Radcliffe, actor, born Fulham, 1989.

John Bartholomew, Gazetteer of the British Isles (1887)

HAMMERSMITH, *parl. bor. and par., Middlesex, on river Thames, in W. of London, 2287 ac., pop. 71,939; Hammersmith returns 1 member to Parliament; it was made a parliamentary bor. in 1885. Hammersmith Suspension Bridge across the Thames was erected in 1825–27, at a cost of £80,000; it is 688 ft. long and 20 ft. wide, and was the first suspension bridge erected near London.*

FULHAM, *parl. bor. and par., Middlesex, in W. of London, 1716 ac., pop. 42,900; Fulham returns 1 member to Parliament; it was made a parl. bor. in 1885. Fulham Palace is the residence of the Bishop of London.*

BBC Television Centre, opened in 1960, will cease to be used by the BBC in 2015

THE LONDON UNDERGROUND

The start of the Underground system goes back to 1860 when work began on building an underground route from Paddington station towards Moorgate with the intention of linking the main railway termini with the City. In 1863, this line, the Metropolitan, opened between Paddington and Farringdon. The route was primarily built under main roads using the 'cut and cover' technique, whereby a cutting was dug down from ground level and a tunnel then made by roofing over the cutting. The design of these first stations can now be seen at Baker Street station, where the original design has been reinstated. The trains were pulled by steam engines and, although various ways of suppressing the smoke were used, the journeys were smoky, but proved immediately popular in spite of early critics; *The Times* said that it was 'an insult' to suppose that people would wish to travel 'amid palpable darkness through the foul subsoil of London'.

More lines followed, and the Circle was completed in 1884. Conversion of the lines close to the surface to electricity began in 1905. A different approach to underground railways was introduced in 1890 when the 5-km long City and South London line opened, the world's first underground electric railway. The route ran from King William Street (near London Bridge) to Stockwell in a deep tunnel that required special tunnelling equipment for its

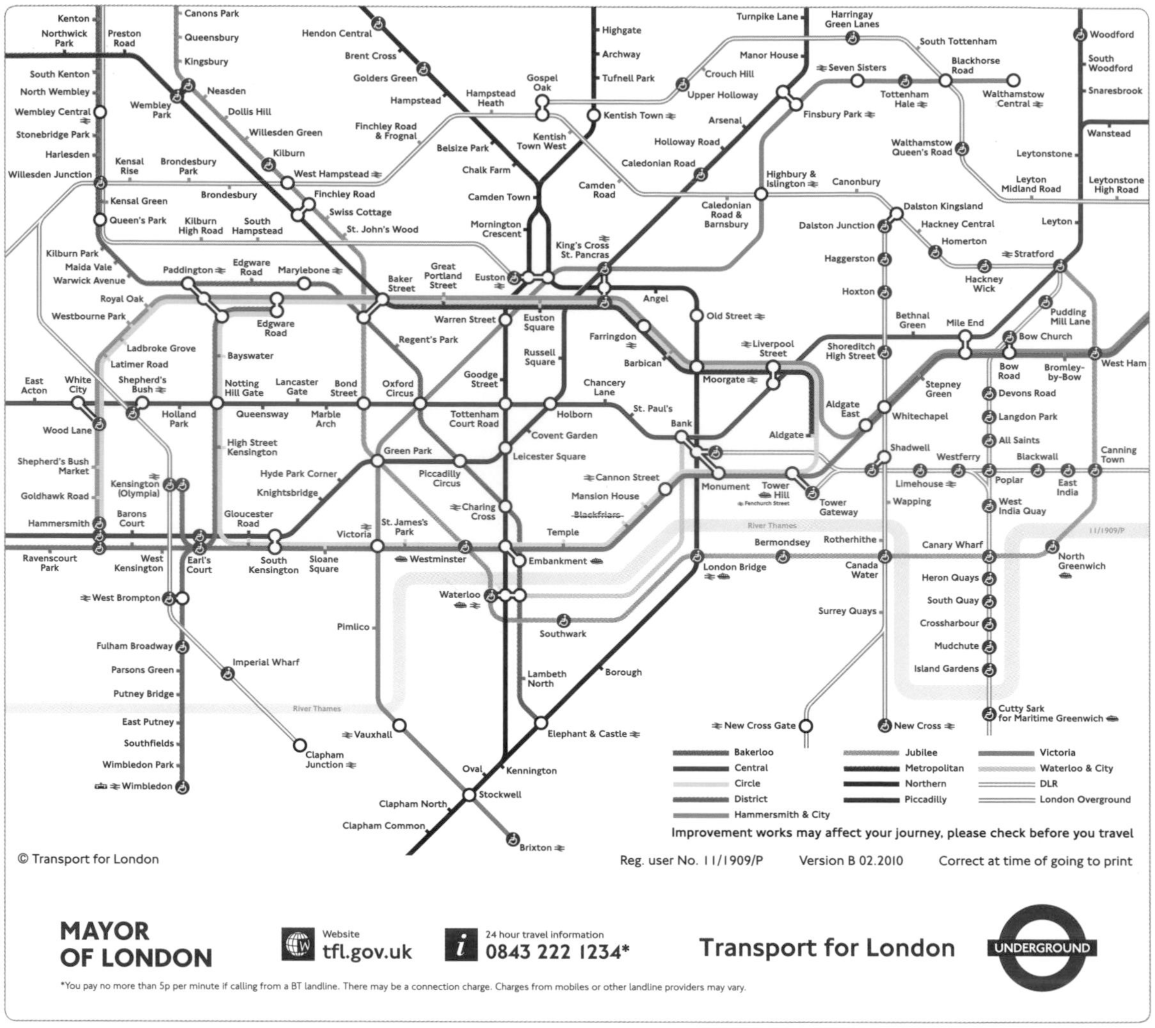

Schematic map of central London showing the Underground, the Docklands Light Railway and the Overground, based on Harry Beck's original 1933 design.

Docklands Light Railway

construction. More deep lines followed, including the central sections of the Piccadilly line, the Central line and the Northern line. Deep stations became possible with the use of lifts and escalators. All these lines were private commercial undertakings and the early development owes much to a Chicago businessman, Charles Tyson Yerkes, who invested heavily in a number of lines from 1900 and built his own power station. He died in 1905 but the lines of his Underground Electric Railway Company formed a significant part of the system that was unified under the London Passenger Transport Board in 1933.

In the 20th century the tube network stretched its tentacles into Outer London and indeed helped to create some of suburban London. The Metropolitan company became a property developer, even coining the term 'Metroland' for its developments in northwest London such those at Pinner and Ruislip. The Piccadilly line extension to Cockfosters in 1933, with its iconic stations designed by Charles Holden, also encouraged suburban developments in the Enfield area. In World War II the tube stations doubled up as mass air raid shelters.

In the 1960s and 1970s two further lines were built – the Victoria line from Brixton across

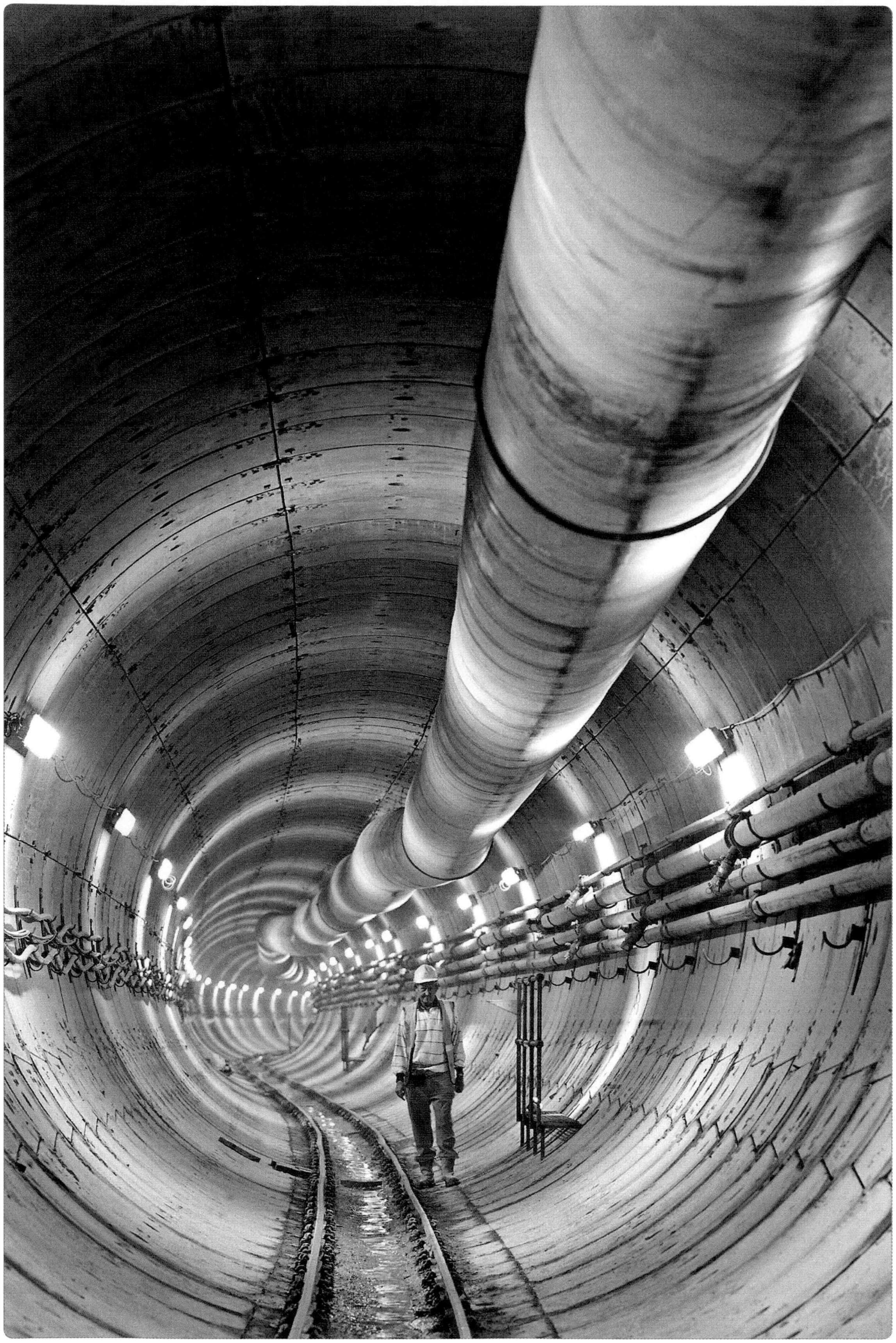

Inspecting a section of the newly built Jubilee line extension in 1997

central London to Walthamstow, and the Jubilee line running from Stanmore via Waterloo and London Bridge to Stratford as a fast link to the Docklands area. In addition the Docklands Light Railway (DLR) opened in 1987 initially to bring convenient public transport to the Docklands. It has been extended a number of times and now has forty stations from Bank in the west, Stratford in the north, Lewisham in the south and Woolwich and Becton in the east. The DLR is not compatible with any other rail system in London.

The London Underground is one of the largest urban transport systems in the world, and opposite are some figures to put that claim into context.

London Underground design

The commercial manager of the Underground, Frank Pick, had a keen sense of the importance of good design. In 1913 he commissioned the typographer Edward Johnson to design a typeface for the Underground – its clean and clear shape continues to look fresh after nearly 100 years. In the 1920s the Underground roundel, as still used for station names and to identify the service, was introduced, and similarly remains in active use today. In the 1920s and 1930s he commissioned the architect Charles Holden to design new stations, creating some of the most striking buildings in Britain from that time, and in 1933 he produced a trial printing of Harry Beck's plan of the network (see page 15) that proved its popularity, and has been in use ever since, although with many modifications along the way.

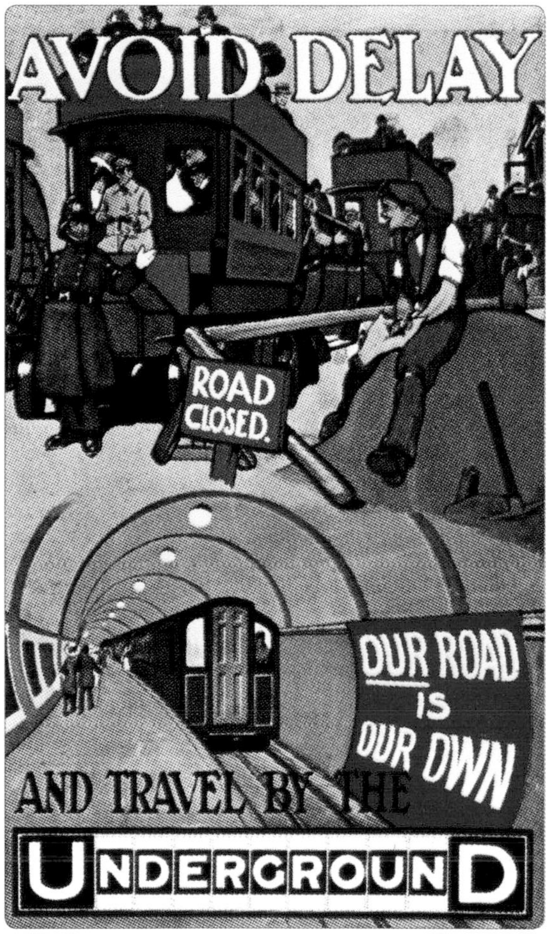

Poster promoting Underground travel in 1910

Total number of passengers	1,133 million
Length of network	402 km
Proportion of network in tunnels	45 per cent
Longest tunnel	East Finchley via Bank to Morden: 27.8 km
Longest line	Central: 74 km
Number of stations	260
Busiest station	Victoria: 77 million passengers per year
Average train speed	33 km per hour
Number of carriages	4,078
Deepest point below sea level	Jubilee line: 32 m

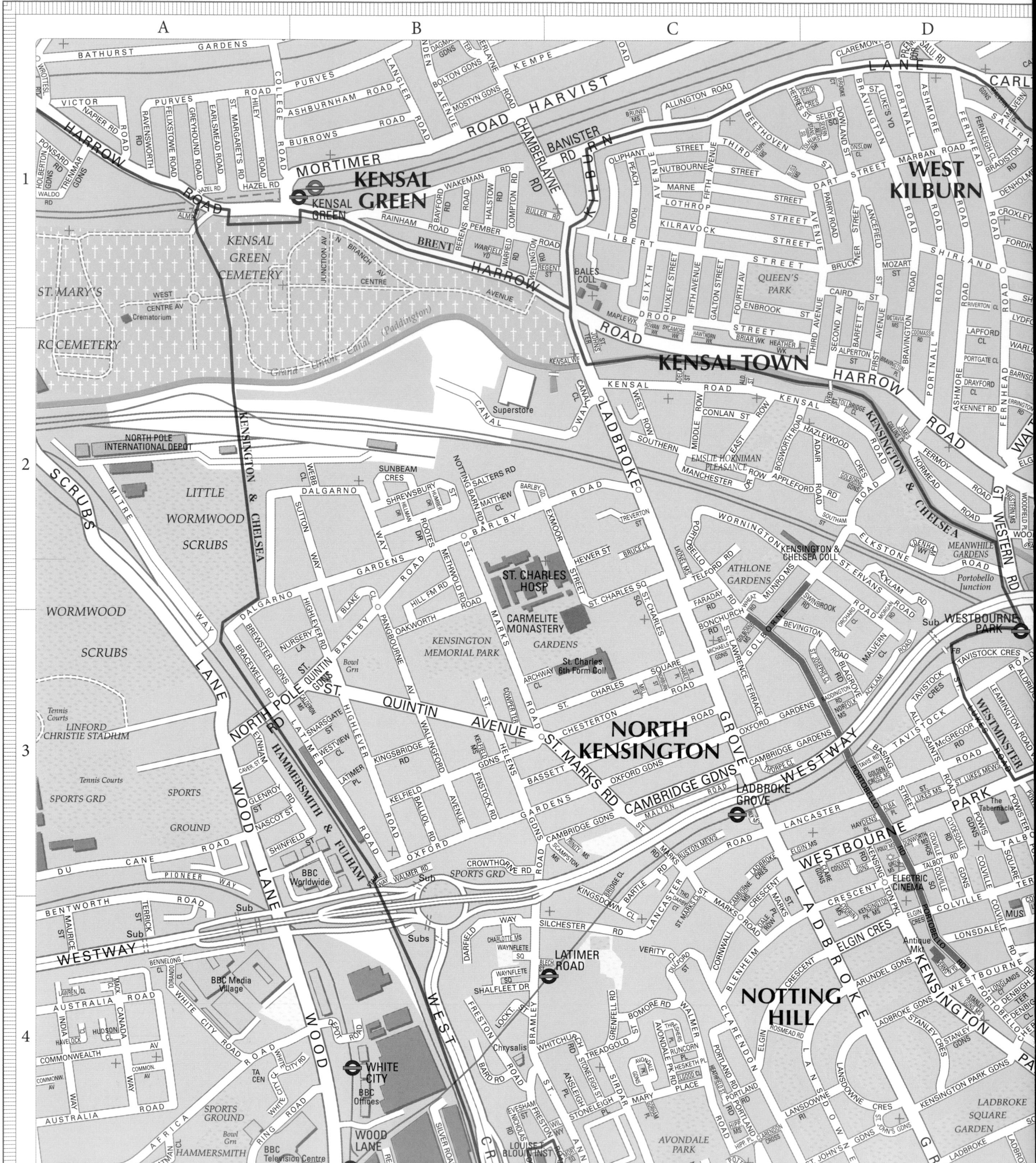
A
B
C
D
1
2
3
4
KENSAL GREEN
WEST KILBURN
KENSAL GREEN CEMETERY
ST. MARY'S RC CEMETERY
KENSAL TOWN
QUEEN'S PARK
NORTH POLE INTERNATIONAL DEPOT
LITTLE WORMWOOD SCRUBS
WORMWOOD SCRUBS
KENSINGTON MEMORIAL PARK
ST. CHARLES HOSP
CARMELITE MONASTERY
ATHLONE GARDENS
EMSLIE HORNIMAN PLEASANCE
KENSINGTON & CHELSEA COLL
NORTH KENSINGTON
LINFORD CHRISTIE STADIUM
SPORTS GROUND
BBC Worldwide
BBC Media Village
BBC Offices
BBC Television Centre
WHITE CITY
WOOD LANE
LATIMER ROAD
LADBROKE GROVE
WESTBOURNE PARK
NOTTING HILL
AVONDALE PARK
HAMMERSMITH PARK
LADBROKE SQUARE GARDEN
ELECTRIC CINEMA
Antique Mkt
The Tabernacle
Superstore
Grand Union Canal (Paddington)
HARROW ROAD
KENSINGTON & CHELSEA
HAMMERSMITH & FULHAM
WESTWAY
SCRUBS LANE
WOOD LANE
LADBROKE GROVE
ST. QUINTIN AVENUE
ST. MARKS RD
WESTBOURNE PARK
KILBURN LANE
174

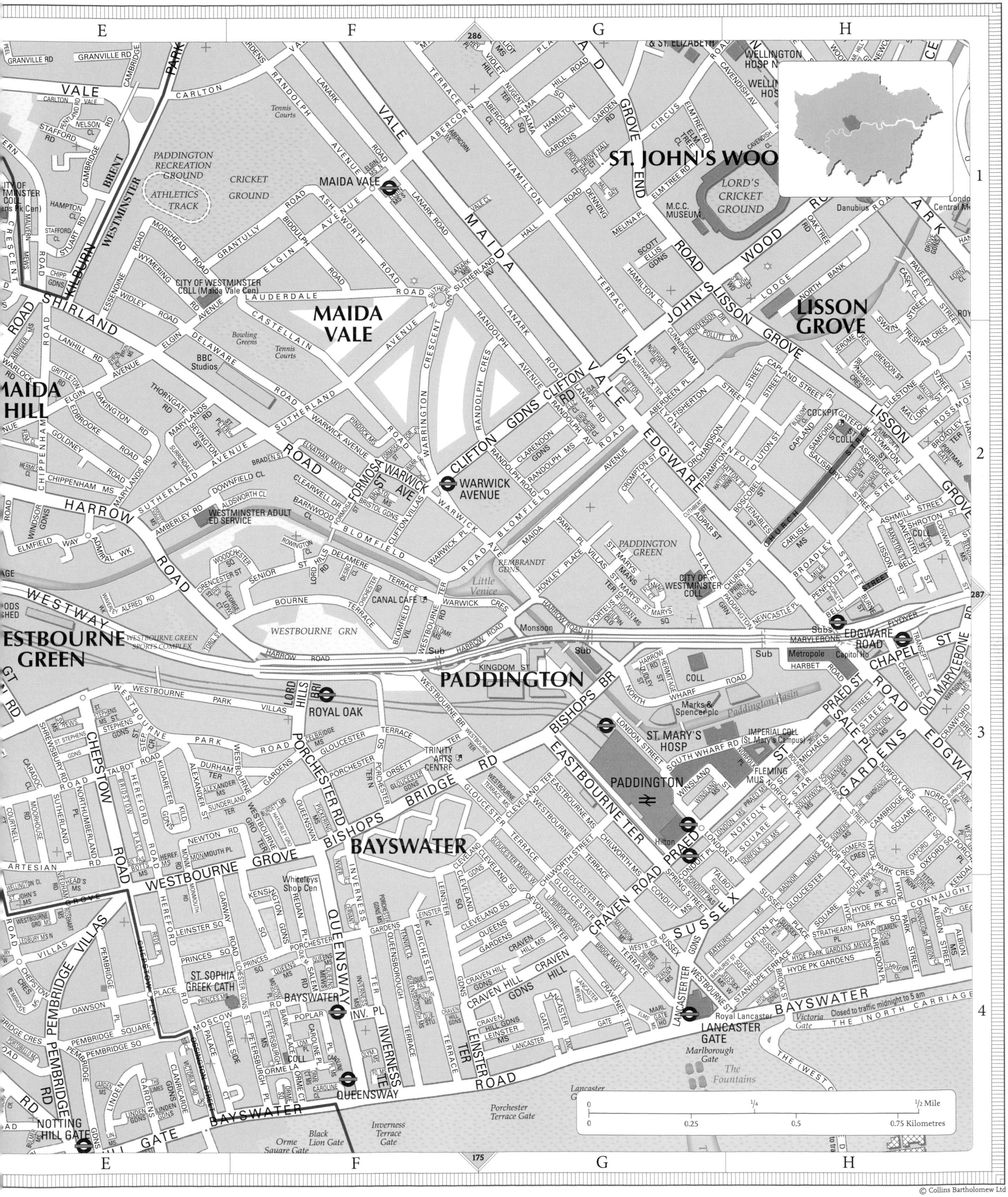
E
F
G
H
286
287
175
1
2
3
4
ST. JOHN'S WOOD
LORD'S CRICKET GROUND
M.C.C. MUSEUM
MAIDA VALE
MAIDA HILL
LISSON GROVE
WESTBOURNE GREEN
PADDINGTON
BAYSWATER
NOTTING HILL GATE
PADDINGTON RECREATION GROUND
ATHLETICS TRACK
CRICKET GROUND
CITY OF WESTMINSTER COLL (Maida Vale Cen)
BBC Studios
WARWICK AVENUE
WESTMINSTER ADULT ED SERVICE
Little Venice
CANAL CAFE
REMBRANDT GDNS
PADDINGTON GREEN
CITY OF WESTMINSTER COLL
ROYAL OAK
TRINITY ARTS CENTRE
ST. MARY'S HOSP
IMPERIAL COLL (St. Mary's Campus)
FLEMING MUS
Marks & Spencer plc
Paddington Basin
EDGWARE ROAD
Metropole
Capitol Ho
Hilton
Whiteleys Shop Cen
ST. SOPHIA GREEK CATH
QUEENSWAY
LANCASTER GATE
Royal Lancaster
Marlborough Gate
The Fountains
Victoria Gate
Closed to traffic midnight to 5 am
Porchester Terrace Gate
Inverness Terrace Gate
Black Lion Gate
Orme Square Gate
WELLINGTON HOSP
0 1/4 1/2 Mile
0 0.25 0.5 0.75 Kilometres

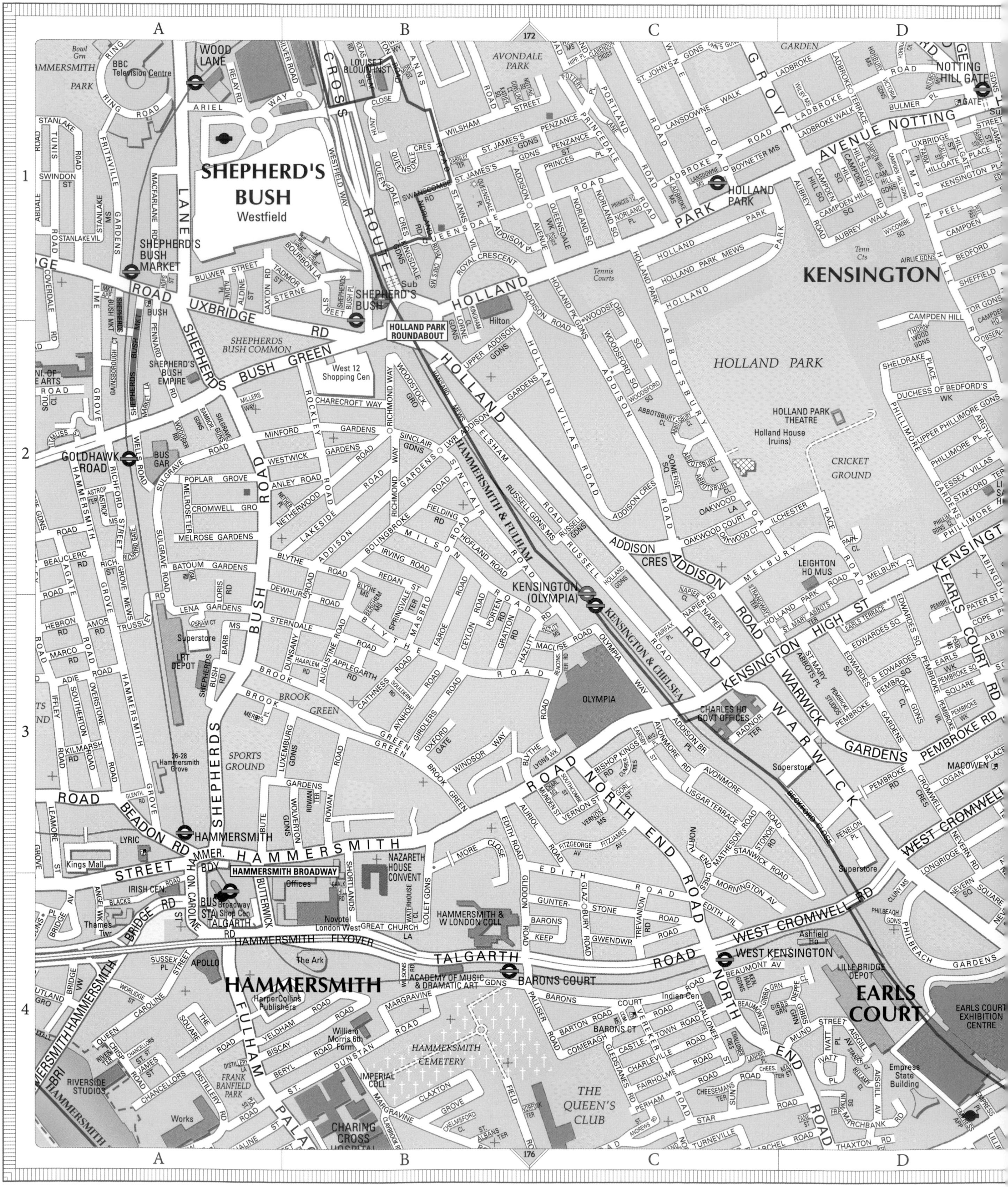
A
B
C
D
1
2
3
4
172
176
SHEPHERD'S BUSH
Westfield
KENSINGTON
HAMMERSMITH
EARLS COURT
HOLLAND PARK
HOLLAND PARK ROUNDABOUT
HAMMERSMITH BROADWAY
WOOD LANE
SHEPHERD'S BUSH MARKET
SHEPHERD'S BUSH
GOLDHAWK ROAD
HAMMERSMITH
KENSINGTON (OLYMPIA)
HOLLAND PARK
NOTTING HILL GATE
WEST KENSINGTON
BARONS COURT
OLYMPIA
BBC Television Centre
HAMMERSMITH PARK
AVONDALE PARK
SHEPHERDS BUSH COMMON
West 12 Shopping Cen
SHEPHERD'S BUSH EMPIRE
HOLLAND PARK THEATRE
Holland House (ruins)
CRICKET GROUND
LEIGHTON HO MUS
CHARLES HO GOVT OFFICES
SPORTS GROUND
BROOK GREEN
LRT DEPOT
Superstore
Kings Mall
LYRIC
NAZARETH HOUSE CONVENT
HAMMERSMITH & W LONDON COLL
Novotel London West
The Ark
APOLLO
HarperCollins Publishers
ACADEMY OF MUSIC & DRAMATIC ART
William Morris 6th Form
HAMMERSMITH CEMETERY
FRANK BANFIELD PARK
RIVERSIDE STUDIOS
IMPERIAL COLL
CHARING CROSS HOSPITAL
THE QUEEN'S CLUB
LILLE BRIDGE DEPOT
EARLS COURT EXHIBITION CENTRE
Empress State Building
Ashfield Ho
Indian Cen
HOLLAND PARK AVENUE
NOTTING HILL GATE
KENSINGTON HIGH ST
HAMMERSMITH ROAD
TALGARTH ROAD
WEST CROMWELL RD
NORTH END ROAD
UXBRIDGE RD
SHEPHERDS BUSH GREEN
HAMMERSMITH FLYOVER
WEST CROSS ROUTE
HAMMERSMITH & FULHAM
KENSINGTON & CHELSEA
FULHAM PALACE RD
SHEPHERDS BUSH ROAD
WARWICK GARDENS
WARWICK ROAD
ADDISON ROAD
EARLS COURT RD
HOLLAND ROAD
PEMBROKE ROAD
BROOK GREEN
BLYTHE ROAD
GOLDHAWK ROAD
ABBOTSBURY RD
CAMPDEN HILL
PHILLIMORE GARDENS
LADBROKE GROVE
ROYAL CRESCENT
QUEENSDALE RD
ST. ANN'S RD
RICHMOND WAY
SINCLAIR RD
RUSSELL ROAD
BEADON RD
KING STREET
ST. PAUL'S

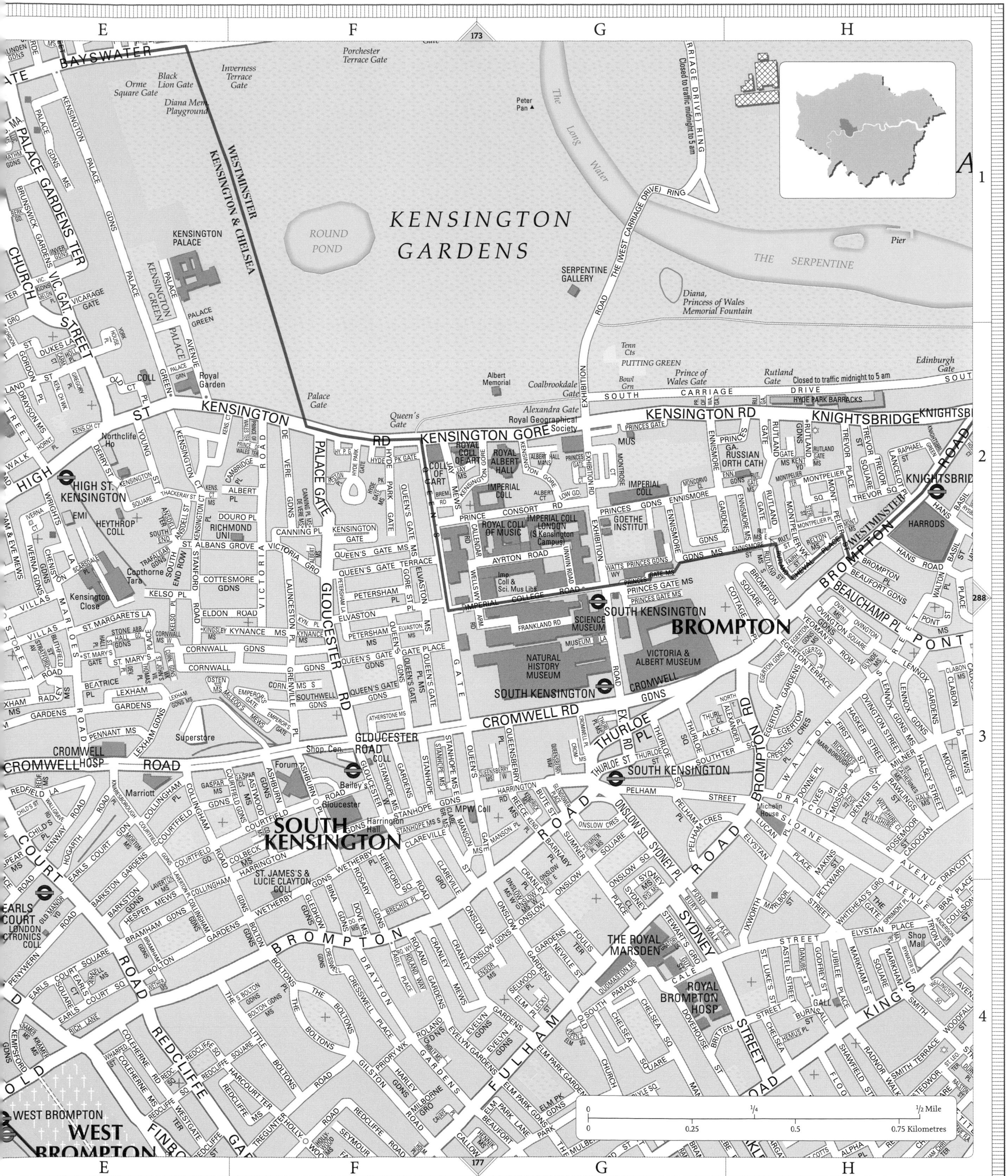
E
F
G
H
173
177
288
1
2
3
4
KENSINGTON GARDENS
ROUND POND
The Long Water
THE SERPENTINE
Serpentine Gallery
Diana, Princess of Wales Memorial Fountain
Porchester Terrace Gate
Black Lion Gate
Orme Square Gate
Inverness Terrace Gate
Diana Mem. Playground
Peter Pan
KENSINGTON PALACE
WESTMINSTER
KENSINGTON & CHELSEA
Albert Memorial
Coalbrookdale Gate
Alexandra Gate
Royal Geographical Society
Queen's Gate
Palace Gate
Prince of Wales Gate
Rutland Gate
Edinburgh Gate
Closed to traffic midnight to 5 am
PUTTING GREEN
Pier
HYDE PARK BARRACKS
BAYSWATER
KENSINGTON RD
KENSINGTON GORE
KNIGHTSBRIDGE
HIGH ST. KENSINGTON
KNIGHTSBRIDGE
HARRODS
ROYAL COLL OF ART
ROYAL ALBERT HALL
IMPERIAL COLL
ROYAL COLL OF MUSIC
GOETHE INSTITUT
RUSSIAN ORTH CATH
SCIENCE MUSEUM
NATURAL HISTORY MUSEUM
VICTORIA & ALBERT MUSEUM
SOUTH KENSINGTON
BROMPTON
CROMWELL RD
GLOUCESTER ROAD
GLOUCESTER RD
QUEEN'S GATE
EXHIBITION RD
BROMPTON ROAD
FULHAM ROAD
SOUTH KENSINGTON
THE ROYAL MARSDEN
ROYAL BROMPTON HOSP
KING'S ROAD
EARLS COURT
WEST BROMPTON
Superstore
Marriott
Michelin House
Shop Mall
0
1/4
1/2 Mile
0.25
0.5
0.75 Kilometres

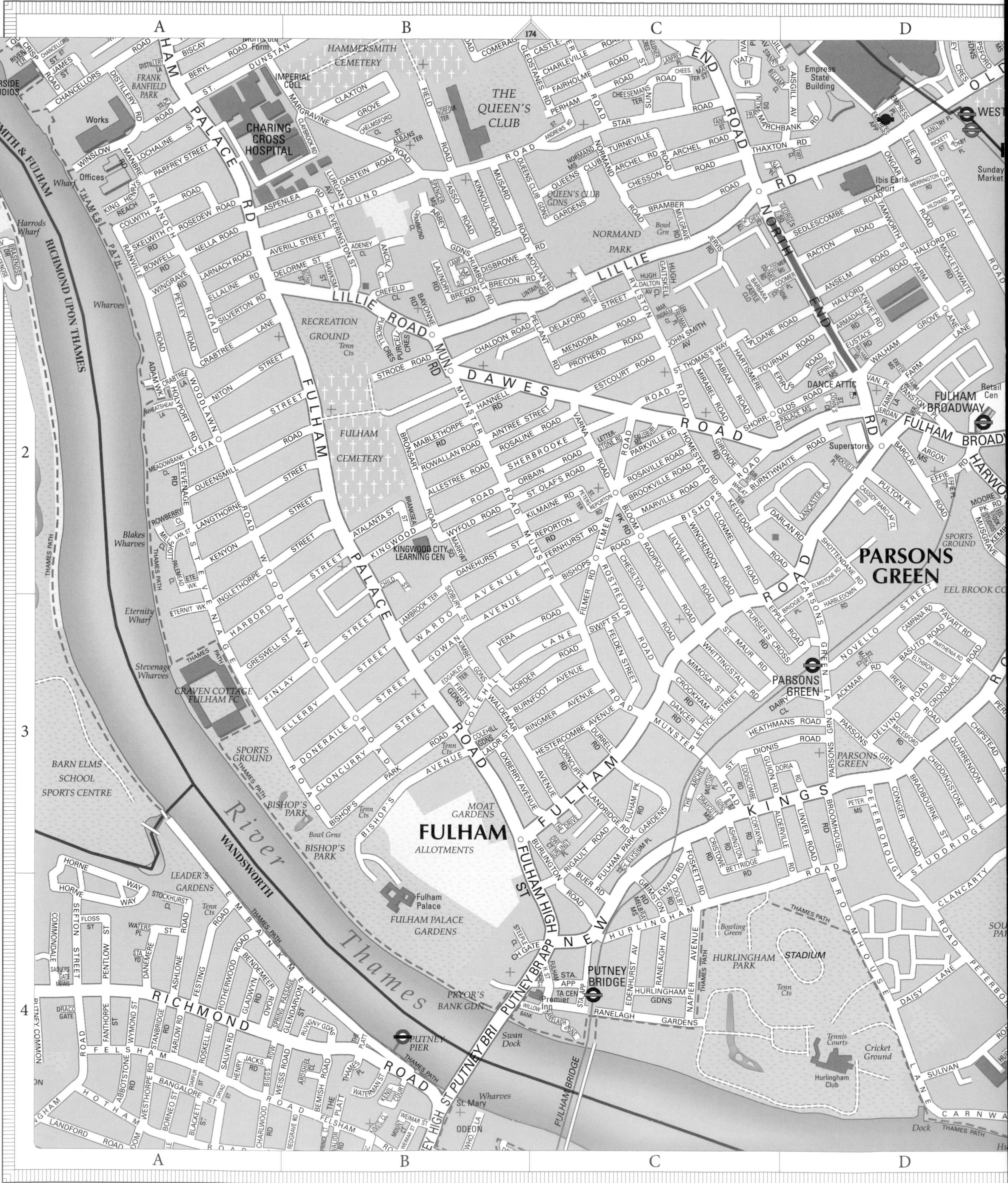
A
B
C
D
174
2
3
4
HAMMERSMITH CEMETERY
THE QUEEN'S CLUB
CHARING CROSS HOSPITAL
RIVERSIDE STUDIOS
HAMMERSMITH & FULHAM
RICHMOND UPON THAMES
WANDSWORTH
NORMAND PARK
RECREATION GROUND
FULHAM CEMETERY
KINGWOOD CITY LEARNING CEN
FULHAM BROADWAY
PARSONS GREEN
CRAVEN COTTAGE FULHAM FC
BARN ELMS SCHOOL SPORTS CENTRE
BISHOP'S PARK
FULHAM
MOAT GARDENS
ALLOTMENTS
Fulham Palace
FULHAM PALACE GARDENS
PUTNEY BRIDGE
PUTNEY PIER
HURLINGHAM PARK
STADIUM
Hurlingham Club
River Thames
FULHAM PALACE RD
LILLIE ROAD
DAWES ROAD
NORTH END RD
FULHAM ROAD
KINGS ROAD
NEW KINGS ROAD
FULHAM HIGH ST
PUTNEY BRIDGE
RICHMOND ROAD
EMBANKMENT
THAMES PATH

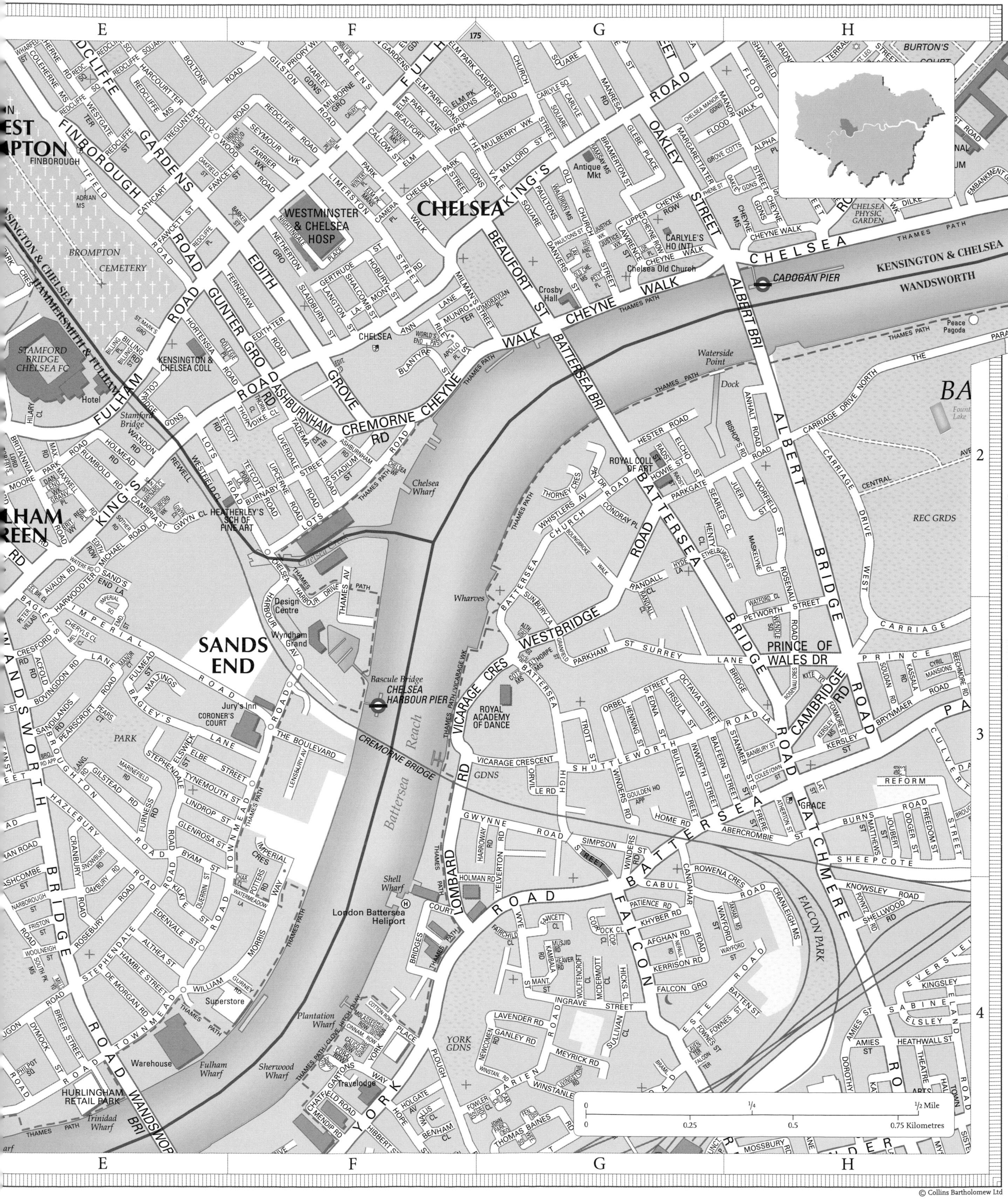
E
F
G
H
175
CHELSEA
SANDS END
WESTMINSTER & CHELSEA HOSP
BROMPTON CEMETERY
STAMFORD BRIDGE CHELSEA FC
KENSINGTON & CHELSEA COLL
HEATHERLEY'S SCH OF FINE ART
Stamford Bridge
Hotel
Antique Mkt
CARLYLE'S HO (NT)
Chelsea Old Church
Crosby Hall
CHELSEA PHYSIC GARDEN
CADOGAN PIER
KENSINGTON & CHELSEA
WANDSWORTH
Peace Pagoda
Waterside Point
Dock
ROYAL COLL OF ART
REC GRDS
PRINCE OF WALES DR
Chelsea Wharf
Wharves
Design Centre
Wyndham Grand
Bascule Bridge
CHELSEA HARBOUR PIER
Jury's Inn
CORONER'S COURT
PARK
ROYAL ACADEMY OF DANCE
CREMORNE BRIDGE
Battersea Reach
Shell Wharf
London Battersea Heliport
FALCON PARK
Superstore
Warehouse
Fulham Wharf
Sherwood Wharf
Plantation Wharf
Travelodge
HURLINGHAM RETAIL PARK
Trinidad Wharf
YORK GDNS
KING'S ROAD
FULHAM ROAD
CHEYNE WALK
CHELSEA EMBANKMENT
BATTERSEA BRI
ALBERT BRI
ALBERT BRIDGE ROAD
BATTERSEA BRIDGE ROAD
WANDSWORTH BRIDGE ROAD
WANDSWORTH BRI
IMPERIAL ROAD
TOWNMEAD ROAD
LOTS ROAD
CREMORNE RD
BATTERSEA HIGH ST
FALCON ROAD
YORK ROAD
LOMBARD RD
WESTBRIDGE ROAD
LATCHMERE ROAD
CARRIAGE DRIVE NORTH
0
1/4
1/2 Mile
0
0.25
0.5
0.75 Kilometres
2
3
4

HARINGEY

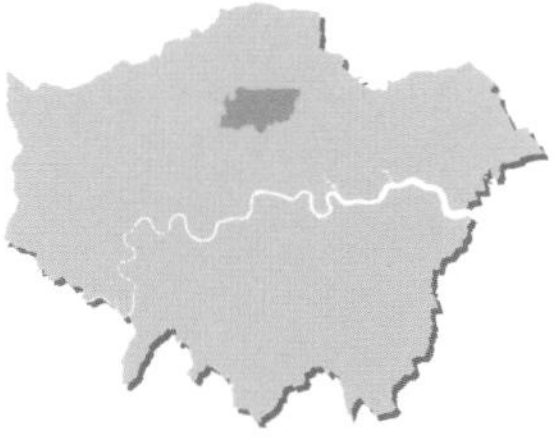

Population	225,500
Area	30 sq. km
Population density	3,551 per sq. km
Area of green space	7.5 sq. km
Jobs in borough	75,000
Average house price	£350,646

The borough of Haringey takes its name from the Old English meaning 'Haering's enclosure'. The style 'Haringey' is more historically accurate than either Hornsey and Harringay, both districts in the borough, which have the same origin. The borough was formed in 1965 from the Middlesex municipal boroughs of Hornsey, Wood Green and Tottenham. It is sometimes regarded as an Inner London borough and sometimes as an Outer London borough. It stretches from the hills of Highgate and Muswell Hill (reaching the height of 120 m) east to the low lands of the Lea Valley. Prior to the arrival of the railways in the mid-19th century, the area was little developed. Tottenham High Road, on the route of the Roman Ermine Street, became lined with houses (Isaak Walton stayed here while fishing on the Lea). All changed with the arrival of railways, with more expensive housing being built on the higher ground in the west and cheaper workers' houses in Tottenham in the east.

Tottenham Hotspur v Roma in 2008, played at White Hart Lane stadium in Tottenham

Its population was 8,800 in 1851 rising to 204,200 in 1901 and 270,200 in 1951. Since then the population has declined, partly as a result of slum clearance schemes, and the ethnic mix of the area has changed greatly. Overall, in 2007, around 66 per cent of the population was white (of whom around a quarter are non-British white) with large black and Asian communities. There is significant variety within the borough, the South Tottenham area having residents from over 100 different ethnic communities, the most diverse area in Britain. It is also London's fifth most deprived borough.

Alexandra Palace plaque commemorating the world's first public television transmissions

Bruce Castle Museum, Tottenham

Alexandra Palace and the BBC transmitter mast

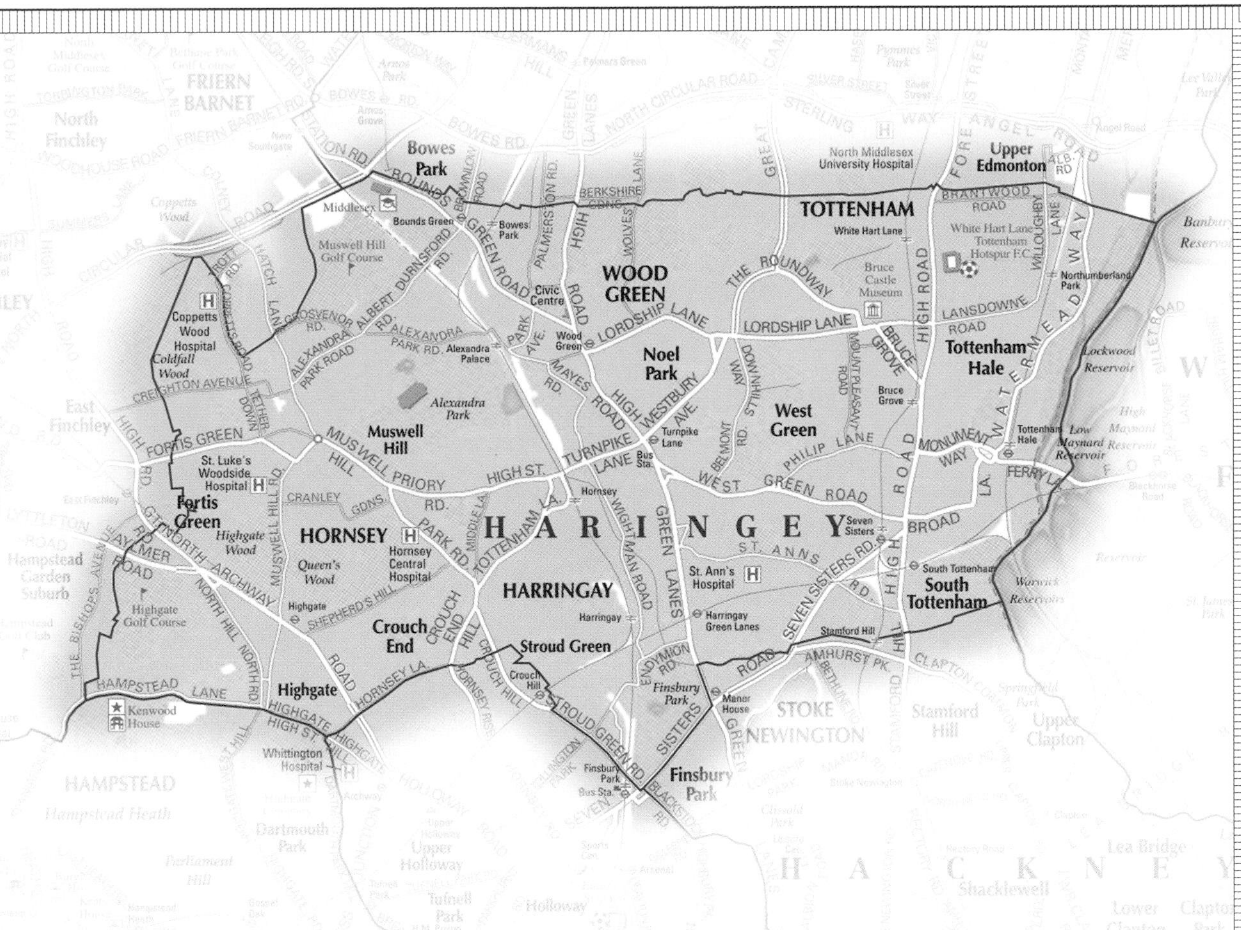

The jobs within the borough are paid significantly below the London average and are concentrated in retail and public administration, with only 18 per cent in finance, IT and other business compared with a London average of 35 per cent. Around 67,000 residents work outside the borough, mainly in central London. The borough is well known as the home of Tottenham Hotspur Football Club, founded in 1882 as Hotspur FC by boys from the local Hotspur Cricket Club and renamed Tottenham Hotspurs in 1884. In 1899 it settled at its present ground, formerly a nursery linked to the White Hart pub on High Road. The ground is referred to as White Hart Lane, even though it is actually on Park Lane.

FAMOUS FOR

Bruce Castle, a much-modified Elizabethan house was at one time a school run by Rowland Hill, the inventor of the postage stamp. It is now Haringey's museum. It was so named in the late 17th century in honour of Robert the Bruce and his family, who owned the manor of Tottenham in the 13th century.

The district of **Seven Sisters** was named after a circle of seven elm trees, on common land known as Page Green. The name is recorded on maps from the 18th century.

Noel Park was built as an early garden suburb between 1881 and 1907 by the Artizans', Labourers' and General Dwelling Company, with over 2,000 visually coherent dwellings built in a number of different styles and sizes.

Alexandra Palace (or Ally Pally) opened in 1873 as a great centre for popular entertainment and education. In 1936 the world's first television service was broadcast from a studio here by the BBC.

Broadwater Farm Estate, between Tottenham and Noel Park, is a large council estate built in the early 1970s. It became a byword for inappropriate design and quickly deteriorated. In October 1985 it was the scene of riots during which PC Keith Blakelock was murdered. Since then great efforts have been made to rehabilitate the Estate.

FAMOUS PEOPLE

Marie Stillman (*born* Marie Spartali), painter and artist's model for the Pre-Raphaelite painters, born Hornsey, 1844.
Alfred Dunhill, manufacturer of pipes and tobacco, born Hornsey, 1872.
Eileen Fowler, fitness instructor, creator in 1954 of the first BBC keep-fit programme, born Tottenham, 1906.
Arthur Bottomley (Baron Bottomley), trade unionist and Labour politician, born Tottenham, 1907.
Mary Treadgold, children's writer and radio producer, born Muswell Hill, 1910.
(Rebecca) Marjorie Proops, advice columnist (agony aunt), born Tottenham, 1911.
Edward (Ted) Willis (Baron Willis), author and screenwriter, best known for *Dixon of Dock Green*, born Tottenham, 1918.
Ralph Harris (Baron Harris of High Cross), economist and free-market polemicist, born Tottenham, 1924.
Leslie Phillips, actor, born Tottenham, 1924.
Barry Took writer and comedian, born Muswell Hill, 1928.
Dave Clark, drummer, the Dave Clark Five, born Tottenham, 1942.
David Lammy, Labour politician, born Tottenham, 1972.

Muswell Hill

LONDON'S THEATRES AND ENTERTAINMENT VENUES

In medieval London, places where plays could be performed were restricted – galleried inns and nobles' houses were two popular locations. In 1574, it was prohibited to build a theatre within the City walls, with the result that a number of playhouses were built in Shoreditch and on the south bank of the Thames at Southwark, where both the Rose and the Globe had close connections with William Shakespeare. An experience of Elizabethan theatre is now offered by the New Globe Theatre, close to the site of the original Globe, which recreates an Elizabethan timber-framed and thatched theatre. It opened in 1997, nearly thirty years after the American director, Sam Wanamaker, began his campaign to recreate the Globe.

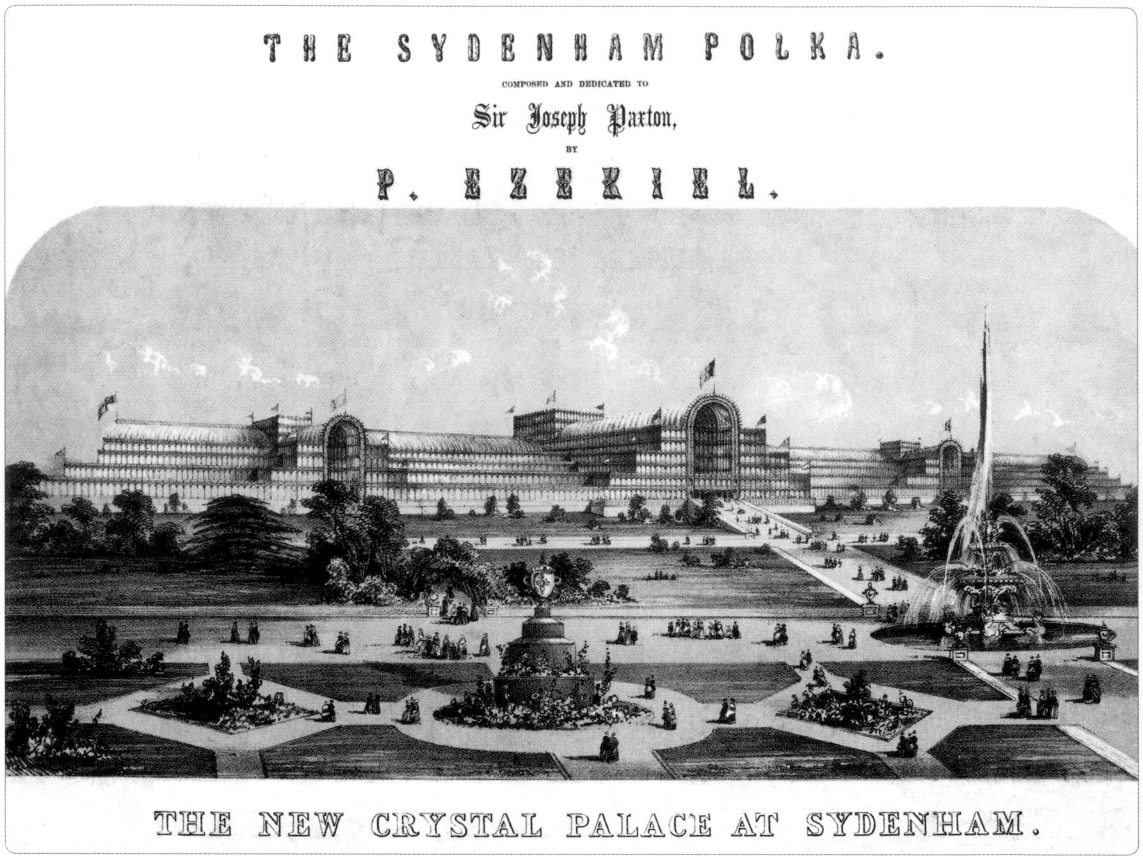

1855 music sheet showing the Crystal Palace at Sydenham and dedicated to the building's designer

All the theatres were closed during the Puritan rule of Cromwell and new theatres began to emerge after the Restoration – the oldest foundation was the Theatre Royal Drury Lane. The first theatre on the site was built in 1663. This building, and some others that followed, fell victims to fire, a great danger in theatres. The present building dates from 1811. Nearby is the Royal Opera House, Covent Garden. The present building dates from 1858 while it took its current title in 1892. However, the first theatre on the site was opened in 1732, with opera becoming the mainstay in the mid-19th century. The late 19th century saw many theatres built in the West End, as the old Bartholomew map shows. More recent theatres include the National Theatre, on the South Bank, the Hammersmith Lyric, the Rose at Kingston and the Ashcroft Theatre at the Fairfield Halls in Croydon.

As well as theatres many music halls were built in the 19th century, particularly in the East End. The home of variety entertainment, the Hackney Empire, which opened in 1901, is a spectacular survivor. The music hall tradition is continued by the Brick Lane Music Hall, now based in a converted church in Silvertown.

The development of multi-purpose public buildings was triggered by the Crystal Palace, built in Hyde Park in 1851 for the Great Exhibition. This massive prefabricated glass building was tall enough to enclose fully grown trees and was visited by over six million visitors at its original site, inspiring dire (and unfulfilled) warnings from Colonel Charles Sibthorp MP: 'That miserable Crystal Palace, the wretched place, where every species of fraud and immorality will be practised. Let the Britisher beware, they will have their food robbed, there will be assassinations, there will be stabbings in the dark'. The Crystal Palace was reassembled and enlarged at Sydenham in South London, reopening in 1854, and it dominated the landscape until it was destroyed by fire in 1936.

Assisted by the proceeds of the Great Exhibition, a Hall of Arts and Sciences was built at South Kensington – a monumental oval hall with a capacity of over 8,000 and notoriously bad acoustics. Its foundation stone was laid by Queen Victoria in 1867, at which point she added 'Royal Albert' to the title, in honour of her Consort, Prince Albert, who had died in 1861. The hall opened in 1871 and remains one of the most used auditoriums in London.

Globe Theatre production of *A Midsummer Night's Dream*

The Alexandra Palace, set in a park on Muswell Hill, was intended to be a North London rival to the Crystal Palace. The original building was the reconstructed exhibition hall from the 1862 International Exhibition, but sixteen days after it opened in 1872, it burnt to the ground. A new building, containing a large hall, concert room, library and theatre, was opened in 1875. While famous as the site of the world's first television broadcast in 1936, it has never really established a clear role. It is now reduced in size following another fire in 1980.

In 1951, the centenary of the Great Exhibition, the Festival of Britain was held on the South Bank. While most of the buildings were designed to be temporary, the Royal Festival Hall, London's premier concert hall, is a stylish reminder of this festival that was designed to refresh the country after the gruelling war and post-war years.

Designed as the exhibition hall for the ill-conceived and unpopular Millennium Experience exhibition in 2000, the striking Millennium Dome, built on derelict land on Greenwich peninsula, looked set for an uncertain future. The building, though, has found a successful new life since 2007 as The O_2, which includes the 20,000-seat capacity O_2 Arena, an eleven-screen cinema and other performance spaces.

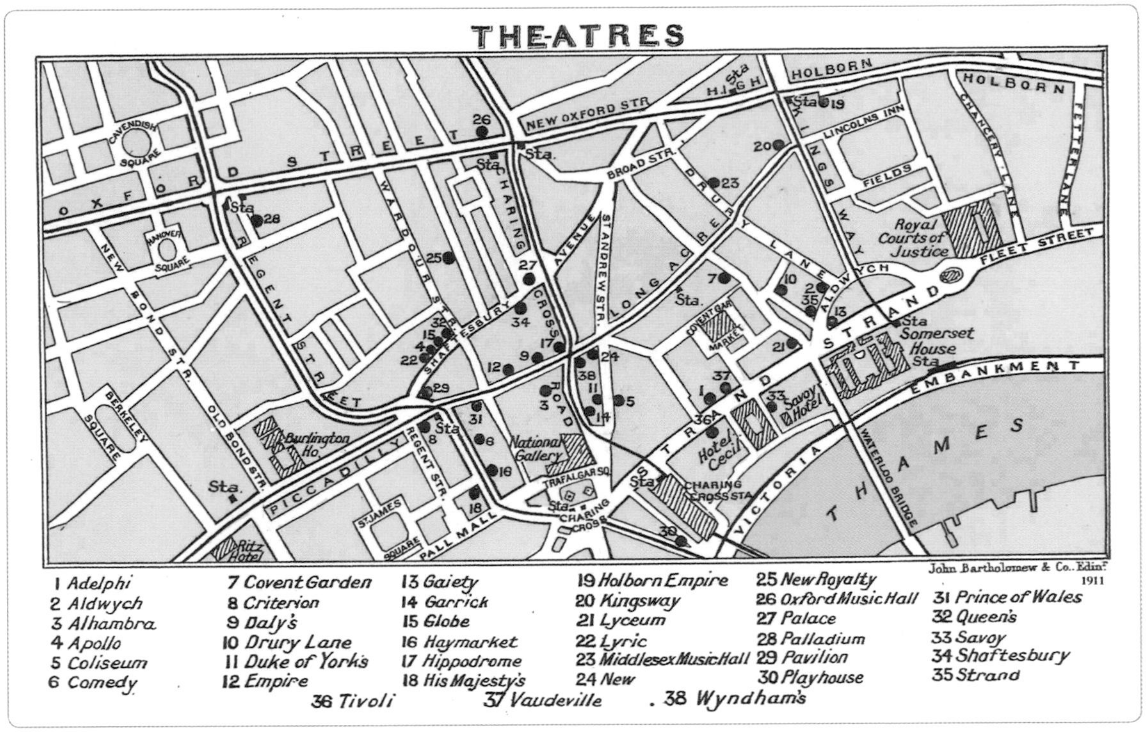

A 1911 Bartholomew map of West End theatres and music halls

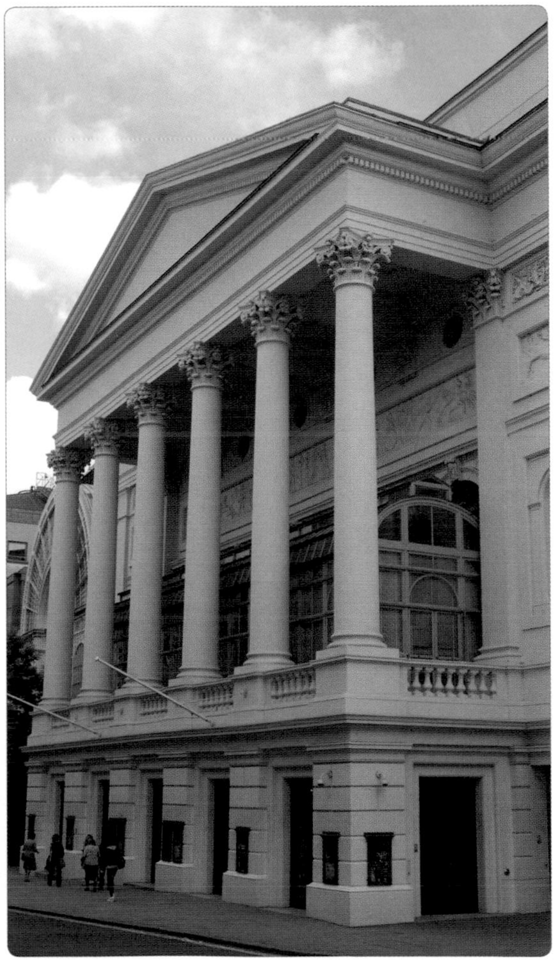

Royal Opera House, Covent Garden

The Royal Albert Hall with Hyde Park beyond

HARROW

Population	228,100
Area	50.5 sq. km
Population density	4,517 per sq. km
Area of green space	17.5 sq. km
Jobs in borough	77,000
Average house price	£290,358

The borough of Harrow takes its name from Harrow on the Hill. The origins of the name Harrow are ancient and uncertain. In the 8th century it was known as *Gumeninga hergae* ('heathen temple of the Gumeningas', an unknown Saxon tribe). The hill at Harrow (124 m high) was then the site of a pagan temple though now topped by a church. The borough of Harrow was formed in 1965 from the municipal borough of Harrow, then in Middlesex. It was the only new London borough that matched the old borough.

Parish church of St Lawrence, Little Stanmore

Until the arrival of the railways in the late 19th century and the Underground in the 20th century, the area was rural, based around a number of settlements including Harrow, Pinner, Stanmore, Wealdstone and Hatch End. The most historic reminder of these times is Headstone Manor, a 14th-century timber-framed house, and its great tithe barn built in 1506, both now part of Harrow Museum. The name of Harrow is widely known on account of Harrow School, founded in 1571 as a free grammar school for thirty poor children by John Lyon, but now a leading public school whose pupils have included Lord Byron, Winston Churchill (and six other British prime ministers) and Jawaharlal Nehru, India's first prime minister.

The population of Harrow was only 5,980 in 1851, growing to 22,690 by 1901. Its real growth (and suburban character) happened in the next 50 years, with the population reaching 217,811 by 1951. Since then it is the ethnic mix of the borough that has changed, making it one of the most diverse boroughs in London. In 2007 around 53 per cent of residents were from minority ethnic groups, with 22 per cent of Indian origin, the second highest level in Britain. This diversity has also made Harrow the most religiously diverse area in the country – 47 per cent Christian, 20 per cent Hindu, 7 per cent Muslim and nearly 7 per cent Jewish along with small communities of Buddhists, Sikhs, Jains and Zoroastrians (the only Zoroastrian centre in Europe meets at the former Art Deco Grosvenor cinema in Rayners Lane).

As would be expected from a suburban borough, over 60,000 residents travel outside the borough to work, while, of jobs within the borough, over 13 per cent (nearly twice the London average) are in manufacturing and construction, and the largest sector (public administration, education and health) accounts for over 27 per cent of jobs.

FAMOUS FOR

Wealdstone, named after an ancient sarsen stone boundary marker between Harrow and Harrow Weald, was the site of Britain's worst civil train crash when the Perth sleeper crashed into a local train at Wealdstone station on 8 October 1952, causing 112 deaths and injuring 340.

Memorial stained glass window, RAF Bentley Priory

From 1856 to 1861 Samuel and Isabella Beeton lived at 2 Chandos Villas, **Hatch End**, and it was here that Isabella wrote *Mrs Beeton's Book of Household Management.*

The highest point in the historic county of Middlesex is 155 m at Bushey Heath, close to the Buckinghamshire border.

RAF Bentley Priory, based in a substantial country house, was the headquarters for Fighter Command and the Royal Observer Corps. The base closed in 2008 and a World War II museum is planned to open there in 2013.

Canons, described by Daniel Defoe as 'the most magnificent [palace] in England … the whole structure is built with such a profusion of expense, and all finished with a brightness of fancy, goodness of judgment; that I can assure you, we see many palaces of sovereign princes abroad, which do not equal it'. Built for the Duke of Chandos, it was completed in 1720, only to be demolished in 1747 as his son could not afford to maintain it. Part of the park remains as does the church of **St Lawrence**, **Little Stanmore**, which gives a flavour of the baroque magnificence of Canons.

In 1717–20 **G. F. Handel** was the Duke of Chandos's composer-in-residence, during which time he composed the eleven Chandos Anthems.

FAMOUS PEOPLE

Dame Ivy Compton-Burnett, novelist, born Pinner, 1884.

(Nora) Sylvia Townsend Warner, writer, born Harrow on the Hill, 1893.

Harrow School

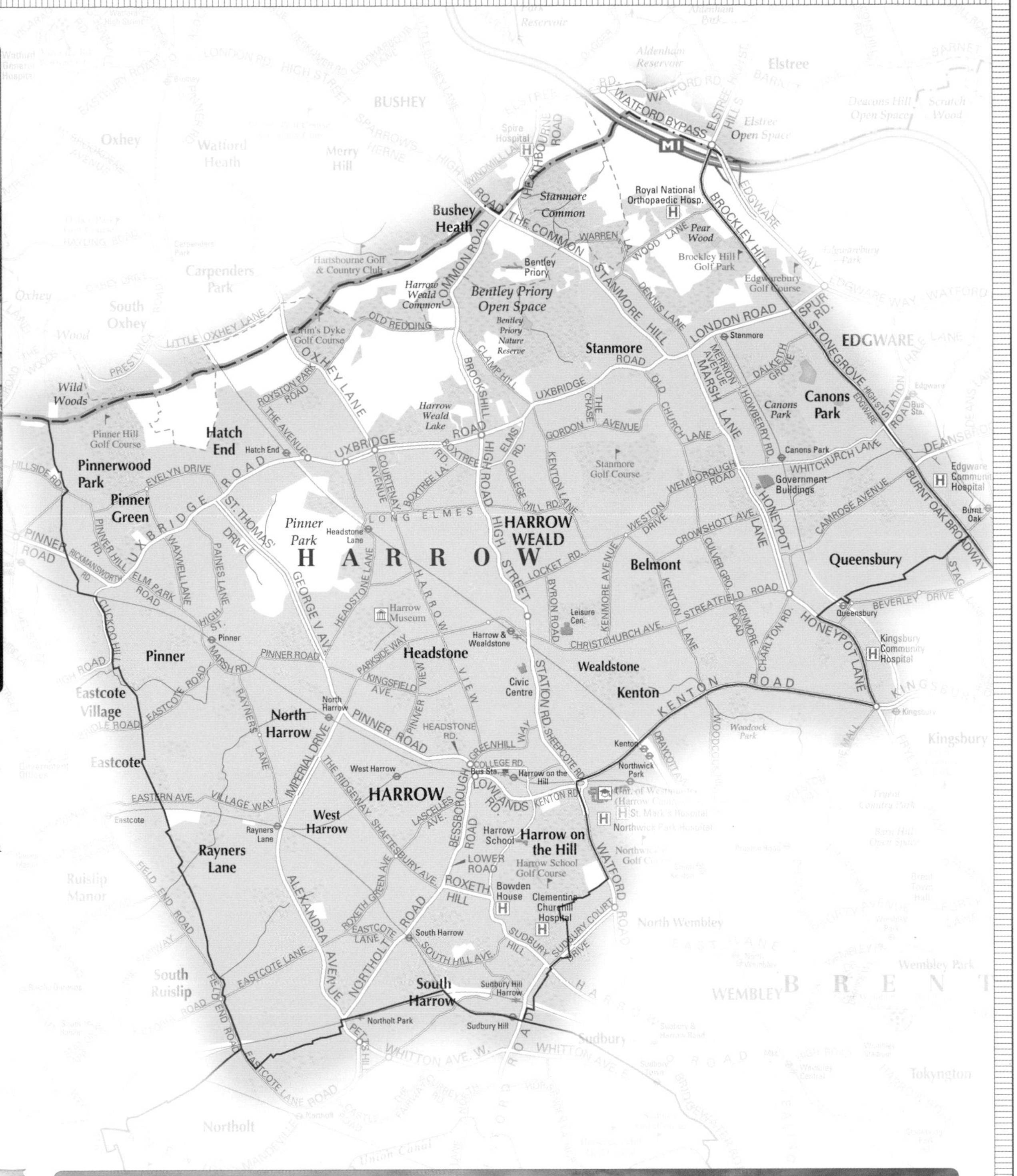

David Gascoyne, poet and essayist, born Wealdstone, 1916.
Sir Patrick Moore, astronomer, born Pinner, 1923.
Sir Roger Bannister, athlete and neurologist, born Harrow, 1929.
John Harris (Baron Harris of Greenwich), Labour and Liberal Democratic politician, born Harrow, 1930.
Ian Robins Dury, singer (with the Blockheads), songwriter, and actor, born Harrow, 1942.
Michael Rosen, poet, born Harrow, 1946.
Clive Anderson, barrister and writer, born Stanmore, 1952.
Theo Walcott, footballer, born Stanmore, 1989.
Dev Patel, actor, born Harrow, 1990.

John Bartholomew, Gazetteer of the British Isles (1887)
HARROW *(or Harrow on the Hill), town and par. with ry. sta., Middlesex, 10 miles NW. of London – par., 10,027 ac., pop. 10,277; town, pop. 5558; P.O., T.O., 1 Bank, 1 newspaper. The celebrity of Harrow is due to its school, which was founded by John Lyon in 1571. The institution is conducted on principles similar to those which regulate Eton College, and, like the latter, Harrow has the honour of being the school at which some very distinguished men have been educated. Members of the governing body are chosen by the Lord Chancellor, the Universities of Oxford, Cambridge, and London, the Royal Society, and the assistant masters of the school. Up to 1837 the education given was exclusively classical; it now embraces every chief department of modern culture.*

Former RAF Bentley Priory

HAVERING

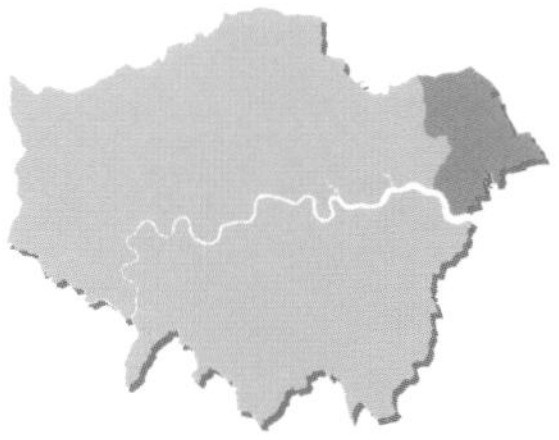

Population	234,100
Area	112 sq. km
Population density	2,090 per sq. km
Area of green space	67 sq. km
Jobs in borough	80,000
Average house price	£224,545

Havering is the third largest London borough in area and one of the least densely populated. A small part, including the village of North Ockendon, lies outside the M25, the only part of Greater London that does so. It takes its name from the Royal Liberty of Havering. Since the time of Edward the Confessor, there was a Royal Palace at Havering, close to the village of Havering-atte-Bower. Havering is from the Old English meaning 'settlement of the family of Haefer' while 'atte-Bower' means 'at the Royal residence'. In 1465 Edward IV granted a charter establishing the Royal Liberty of Havering which covered the area around the Royal Palace, and this charter proclaimed the area's independence from Essex – with its own court and freedom from taxation for its residents. The Royal Palace was in ruins by the 17th century but the Liberty of Havering only became a formal part of Essex in 1892. The 1965 borough of Havering, made up of the municipal borough of Romford and the urban district of Hornchurch covered a similar area to the Liberty, so leading to the borough's name.

Historically Romford was the main settlement and acted as the market town for the surrounding area where the main activities were farming and market gardening. It was only in the 20th century that its population grew significantly, with the construction of major housing estates, such as Gidea Park and Harold Hill, and the arrival of the District line at its Upminster terminus in 1902. In 1901 the population of the borough was 24,900 and by 1951 it was 187,000. It is the least ethnically diverse London borough – in 2007 over 90 per cent of the population was white.

Around two thirds of working residents travel to jobs outside the borough. Within Havering nearly 13 per cent of jobs are in manufacturing and construction, nearly double the London average. However, Romford has now become a major shopping and night-life centre and employment in these sectors provides nearly 29 per cent of jobs. Traditional industries, such as brewing have declined, while Thames Gateway projects by the Thames at Rainham will see new employment opportunities arise.

A 1910 advertisement for Romford Garden Suburb, now known as Gidea Park

FAMOUS FOR

The Royal Palace at **Havering-atte-Bower** was a favourite of many kings and it became the official residence of England's queens until James I. Some stones from its ruins were used to build the Bower House (1729) at Havering-atte-Bower.

Gidea Park was built in 1910–11; around 160 houses were designed by 100 different architects and a further 35 modernistic houses were added in 1934–5. Its original objective was to demonstrate 'the improvement in modern housing and building, due to the advance of Scientific Knowledge, the Revival of Arts and Crafts, and the Progress of the Garden Suburb movement'.

There are two reminders of the agricultural legacy of the area at **Upminster** – a thatched, aisled tithe barn built in 1450 by the Abbey of Waltham (now a Museum of Nostalgia) and Upminster windmill, an eight-sided smock mill built in 1803 and now restored to working order.

Hornchurch takes its name from its parish church (church with horn-like gables) – the carving at the East End of a bull's head with horns plays on the name rather than being the reason for it.

Rainham Marshes by the Thames used to be a military firing range, but, since 2000, has been an RSPB nature reserve, a popular sanctuary for wading birds and ducks. Nearby is **Rainham Hall**, built in 1729 by Captain John Harle, owner of Rainham Wharf. Some restoration work is underway to maintain this little altered house.

Romford Market

The Star Brewery in **Romford** was bought by Edward Ind in 1799. Part of Ind Coope brewers, it was employing 1,000 workers in 1970, but, as the industry rationalized, it was closed in 1993, the site now being The Brewery shopping centre.

FAMOUS PEOPLE

Sir Anthony Cooke, educator and humanist, tutor to Edward VI, born Gidea Hall, 1505/6.
Francis Quarles, poet, born at Stewards manor house, Romford, 1592.
William Derham, academic, President of St John's College Oxford, born Upminster, 1702.
Mary Benton, headmistress, South Hampstead High School, and educational reformer, born Hornchurch, 1855.
William Strang (first Baron Strang), diplomatist, born Rainham, Essex, 1893.
Sir (James) Gordon Reece, television producer and public relations consultant (coached Margaret Thatcher), born Romford, 1929.
Imogen Heap, singer, composer, songwriter, born Romford, 1977.
Frank Lampard, footballer, born Romford, 1978.

John Bartholomew, Gazetteer of the British Isles (1887)

ROMFORD, *market town and par., Essex, 6 miles SW. of Brentwood and 12 miles NE. of London by rail – par., 7224 ac., pop. 9050; town, 1159 ac., pop. 7176; P.O., T.O., 1 Bank, 1 newspaper. Market-day, Wednesday. Romford is the capital of the liberty of Havering-atte-Bower, and a local government district. It has large corn and cattle markets, gardening and brewing, and is noted for its ale.*

HORNCHURCH.– *par. and vil., S. Essex, between rivers Rom and Ingerburn, 2 miles SE. of Romford, 6784 ac. and 138 tidal water and foreshore, pop. 2824; P.O., T.O.; has iron-founding and mfrs. of steam engines, boilers, agricultural implements, bricks, tiles, drain pipes, &c.*

UPMINSTER, *par. and vil. with ry. sta., Essex, 3 miles SE. of Romford, 3375 ac., pop. 1202; P.O.; near vil. is Upminster Hall, seat.*

RAINHAM.– *par. and vil. with ry. sta. and quay, Essex, 5 miles SE. of Barking, 3253 ac., pop. 1253; P.O., T.O.; 2 miles NE. of sta. is Rainham Lodge, seat.*

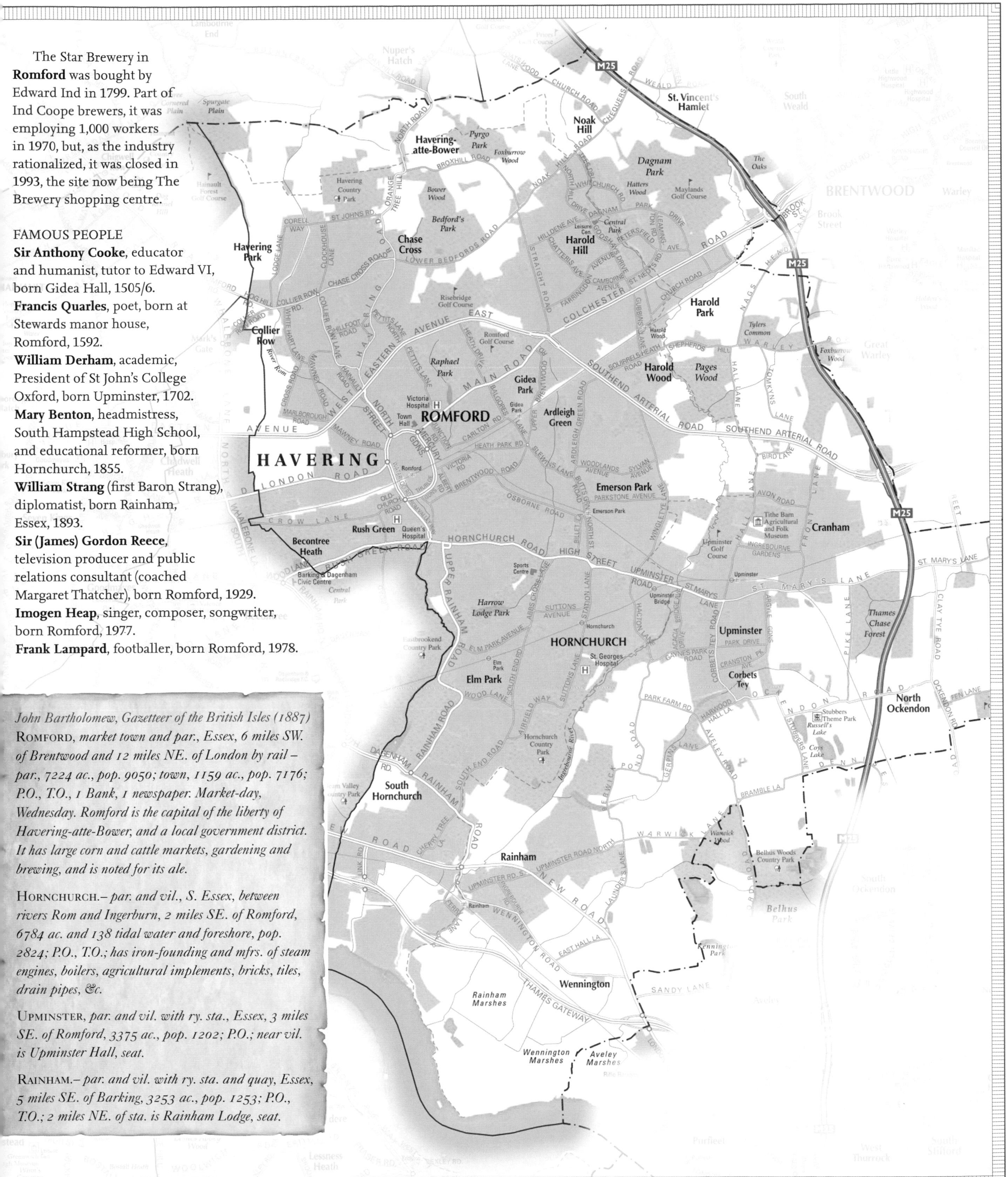

GREEN LONDON

At the Crossness Sludge Incinerator, sewage sludge is burnt, generating some electricity, rather than dumped at sea, as used to happen

London, as a densely populated conurbation, faces many environmental challenges to restrict waste and improve its carbon footprint.

London's carbon footprint

Contrary to many expectations, the estimated carbon emissions per head of population is lower in London than any other region of Britain. It is estimated at 6 tonnes of carbon dioxide per year per person, compared with a figure of 8 tonnes per person per year in Scotland and Wales. The overall contribution by various sectors is also lower than you might expect.

Various factors influence this – it is more efficient for people to live close together, to be relatively close to their places of work and to use public transport to make most journeys, in contrast to those living in detached houses in a scattered rural community at a significant distance from regularly needed supplies and services. In 2008 London's emissions from industry and commercial use were 20,648,000 tonnes (11.5 per cent of UK total), from domestic use 16,470,000 tonnes (11 per cent of UK total) and from transport 8,120,000 (8 per cent of UK total) – and for reference London's population is 12.5 per cent of the UK total. Within Greater London there are some variations – the carbon dioxide emitted per person per year varies from 4 tonnes in Hackney, Harrow, Lewisham, Redbridge and Waltham Forest to 10 tonnes in Tower Hamlets and 14 tonnes in Westminster.

PERCENTAGE OF HOUSEHOLD WASTE RECYCLED IN 2009/10

London's record on recycling

However, London does not fare so well on recycling. The city has the lowest percentage of recycled household waste of any area in Britain, although, at 32 per cent in 2009/10, it was up from 9 per cent ten years earlier. The map shows percentages across the boroughs, where fairly wide variations can be seen. The challenge is large – London produces 2.6 million tonnes of organic waste each year, much of which is not recycled, and 280,000 tonnes of plastic, much of which ends up in landfill.

Recycling rates in the more densely populated Inner London boroughs are mostly lower than in the outer boroughs. However, ambitious targets have been set by the Mayor to raise the percentage of material recycled to 45 per cent in 2015 and 60 per cent by 2031, and to scrap all landfill by 2025. Reaching these targets will require major changes in the ways of doing things both for Londoners and for the collection services of their borough councils. Options will include some conventional solutions, such as the large new waste incinerator at Belvedere on the southern bank of the Thames in Bexley. It was completed in 2011 and is expected to handle half a million tonnes of waste a year, much of it brought to the plant on barges from central and west London.

Barclays cycle hire scheme

'Boris bikes'

This is the informal name for the Barclays cycle hire scheme arranged by Transport for London. It is named after Boris Johnson, the cycling Mayor of London when the scheme was introduced – though the scheme was actually a creation of his predecessor, Ken Livingstone. The principle is simple – in central London there are bike-docking stations from where you can borrow a bicycle and then return it to any other docking station. There is a small access fee and then the first half hour is free; after which you will need to pay a fee, from £1 for one hour to £35 for six hours and £50 for a day. In April 2011 the most westerly docking station was at Kensington Olympia, the southernmost at Kennington Road Post Office, the most easterly in Whitechapel and the most northerly at Camden Town, and there are plans to expand the service.

Away from central London there is a network of cycle routes throughout Greater London, including Greenways, designed to meet the needs of walkers, cyclists and horse riders. Many of these routes are traffic free and run through Royal Parks (such as at Richmond Park), alongside canals (such as Regent's Canal) or along rivers (such as the Wandle Trail which follows the river Wandle from Croydon to Wandsworth).

Cleaner transport

Transport for London has started to use hybrid buses and on one route is using hydrogen fuel cells to power buses. Electric cars and vans are also being encouraged, and electric charging points are appearing on London streets. One of the more innovative schemes to provide a cleaner transport solution is the 1.1 km cable car crossing of the Thames between The O_2 on Greenwich Peninsula and the Royal Victoria Docks and the ExCel centre, which is planned to carry up to 2,500 people an hour.

Mayor Boris Johnson and Arnold Schwarzenegger try the Barclay's cycle hire scheme

Charging point for electric cars

HILLINGDON

Population	262,500
Area	116 sq. km
Population density	2,263 per sq. km
Area of green space	57 sq. km
Jobs in borough	197,000
Average house price	£256,124

Terminal 5 at Heathrow Airport, opened in 2008

The borough of Hillingdon takes its name from the town of Hillingdon, from the Old English, meaning 'hill of a man named Hilda', a slightly surprising choice given the greater importance of Uxbridge in the borough. It was formed from the municipal borough of Uxbridge and the three urban districts of Hayes and Harlington, Ruislip–Northwood and Yiewsley and West Drayton. It is the second largest borough by area and one of the least densely populated. It is effectively divided by the Great Western Railway. The area to the north is a mixture of prosperous residential areas and open countryside and the south is dominated by Heathrow Airport and settlements such as West Drayton and Harlington, once major centres for food processing and the recording industry.

The area's agricultural past can be seen in small medieval churches (for example at Hayes, Harefield and Uxbridge) and great aisled barns at Harmonsdworth, built in the 15th century, and at Manor Farm Ruislip, built in the 13th century and possibly the oldest timber-framed building in London. The railways arrived in the mid-19th century, but the population grew slowly, from 18,700 in 1851 to 32,500 in 1901. All changed in the 20th century with the population reaching 217,600 by 1951, spurred on by the growth of the London Underground, which encouraged the development of much suburban housing, for example in Ruislip and Northwood. The population has continued to grow, becoming more ethnically diverse, with just under three-quarters of residents being white by 2007.

The economy of the borough is dominated by Heathrow Airport (see page 190), with over 35 per cent of jobs in transport and communications compared with just over 7 per cent for London generally. It also means that Hillingdon is the only Outer London borough where there is a major net inflow of workers, with over 111,000 travelling into the borough but only 52,000 residents leaving for work. The borough is also home to RAF Northolt, once the home for a number of Battle of Britain squadrons (including the Polish Fighter Squadron) and now the base of the Royal Squadron, and to Brunel University at Uxbridge, founded in 1966, its technological focus indicated by naming it after the great Victorian engineer Isambard Kingdom Brunel.

FAMOUS FOR

Harefield Hospital is one of the largest centres in the world for heart and lung transplants. Britain's first heart-lung transplant was performed here by a team led by Sir Magdi Yacoub.

Penguin Books, established in 1935 by Allen Lane, moved from the crypt of Holy Trinity Church, Marylebone Road to new offices and warehouse in **Harmondsworth** just opposite what was then a small airstrip at Heathrow in 1937. It was from here that Penguin paperbacks revolutionized the world of publishing. The company moved away in 2004.

Harmondsworth Barn, known as the 'Cathedral of Middlesex', dates back to the 1420s and it is thought that 95 per cent of its current timber frame dates from then. It is 158 m long, 11 m wide and 11 m high and is one of the largest medieval barns in Britain.

Uxbridge was an important market town for surrounding parts of Middlesex and Buckinghamshire and well placed to serve the needs of London. Its large Market House, built in 1789, shows the importance at that time of the corn trade – the ground floor was originally entirely open, providing space for farmers and merchants to trade, while the first floor was used to store grain and as a charity school. Behind the Market House is the medieval church of St Margaret, dominated by the large south aisle, built around 1450.

FAMOUS PEOPLE

Sir William Dickson, air force officer, first Chief of Defence Staff, born Northwood, 1898.
Bernard Miles (Lord Miles), actor and theatre manager, born Uxbridge, 1907.

British Airways regeneration of Harmondsworth Moor, near Heathrow

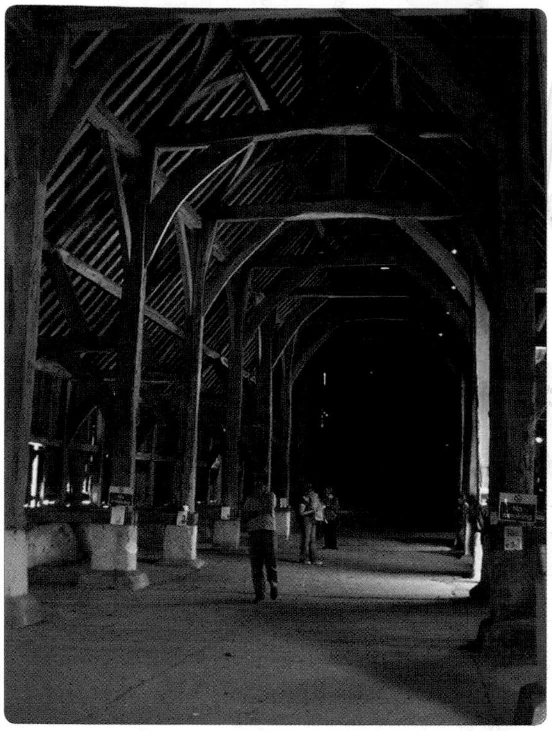

The great medieval barn at Harmondsworth

Roger Hilton, artist, born Northwood, 1911.
Lana Morris, actress, born Ruislip, 1930.
Peter Levi, poet and scholar, born Ruislip, 1931.
Donald (Don) James Thompson, Olympic gold medal winner (50 km walk), born Hillingdon, 1933.
Derek Jarman, film director, artist and gardener, born Northwood, 1942.
Ronnie Wood, rock guitarist, the Rolling Stones and the Faces, born Hillingdon, 1947.
Sue Cook, broadcaster, born Ruislip, 1949.
Jane Seymour (*born* Joyce Frankenburg), actress, born Hillingdon, 1951.
Ray Wilkins, footballer and football coach, born Hillingdon, 1956.
Glen Hoddle, footballer and football manager, born Hayes, 1957.
Andy Serkis, actor, born Ruislip, 1964.
Kwame Kwei-Armah (*born* Ian Roberts), actor, born Hillingdon, 1967.
Tony Lee, graphic novelist, born Hayes, 1970.

John Bartholomew, Gazetteer of the British Isles (1887)
UXBRIDGE, *market town and township, Hillingdon par., Middlesex, on W. border of co. and on river Colne, 16 miles NW. of London by rail – township, 99 ac., pop. 3346; town (containing also part of Hillingdon township and part of Cowley par.), 496 ac., pop. 7669; P.O., T.O., 2 Banks, 2 newspapers. Market-days, Thursday and Saturday. Uxbridge is supposed to have been founded by Alfred, and was the scene of negotiations between Charles I. and the Parliament in 1645. It is well built, and contains an ancient church and a spacious corn exchange. Iron-founding, brick-making, and brewing are carried on, and there is an extensive traffic in corn and flour. Uxbridge gives the title of earl to the Marquis of Anglesey.*

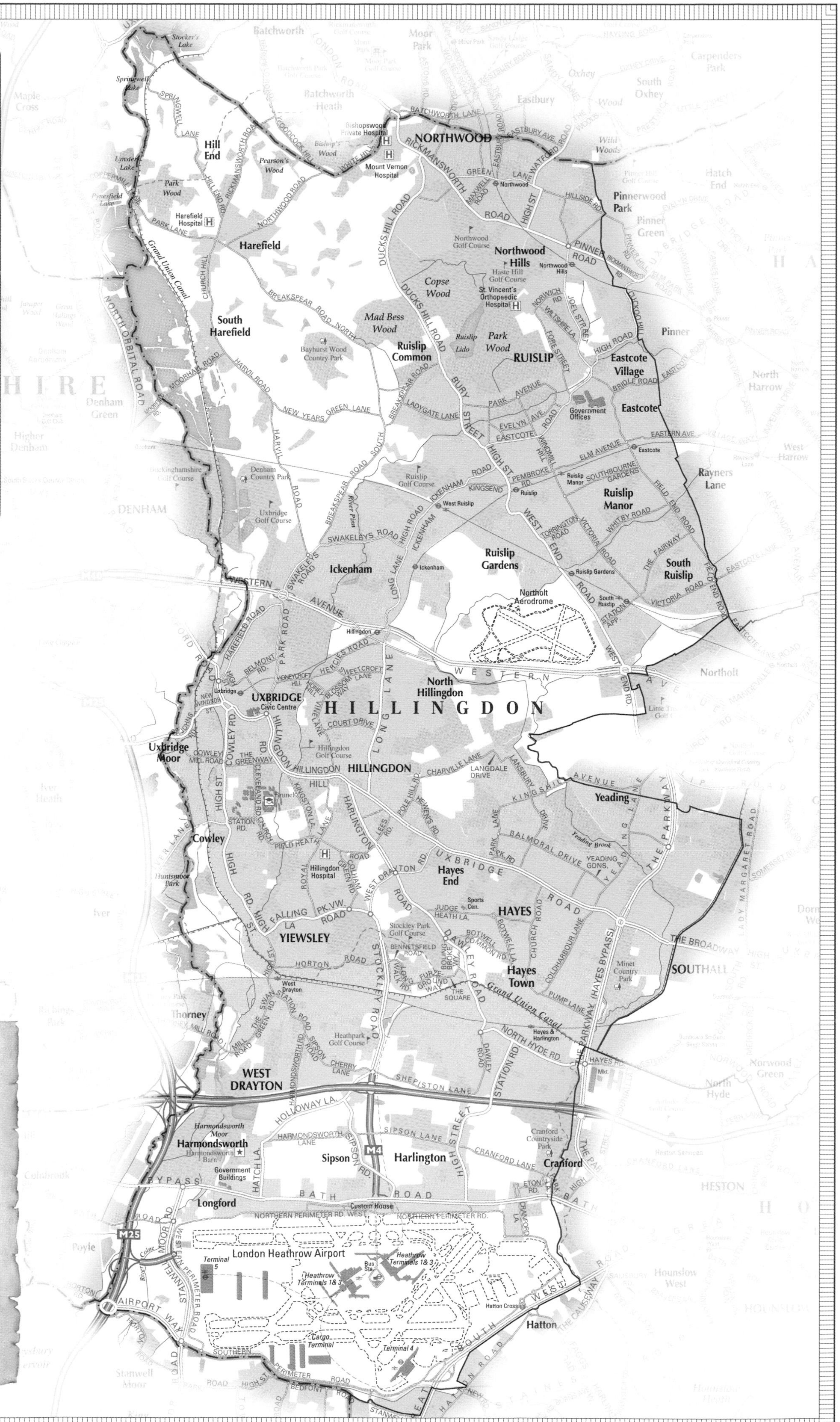

LONDON'S AIRPORTS

Terminal 5B, part of the new Terminal 5 complex at Heathrow Airport

London is served by five major airports and in 2010 over 127 million passengers passed through them. Only two airports, Heathrow and London City, are within the boundaries of Greater London, and both are looked at in more detail below. The three other major London airports at Gatwick, Stansted and Luton are in Sussex, Essex and Bedfordshire respectively. Each is served by a direct rail link to the capital.

London Heathrow Airport

Heathrow is London's leading airport, handling more international passengers than any other airport in the world (although Atlanta is the world's busiest, with its mixture of domestic and international passengers). Its origins go back to 1930 when the aircraft maker, Richard Fairey, purchased 60 ha of Hounslow Heath as a private airstrip to test his planes. During World War II, it was decided to build a large RAF station at the site and work started in 1944 on the star-shaped arrangements of runways. However, the war ended before it was completed and the airfield was no longer needed by the RAF. On 1 January 1946 it officially became London's civil airport, with the passenger terminals being ex-military marquees set up (with no heating) along the northern perimeter of the airfield. By the end of the first year 63,000 passengers had used the airfield. By 1951 passenger numbers had increased more than tenfold and by 1955 the control tower and first terminal buildings had been built in the centre of the airport, linked by a tunnel under the runway.

LONDON'S AIRPORTS

Airport	Passengers 2010	Aircraft movements	Destinations	Airlines	Distance from central London (km)
Heathrow	65.7 million	449,220	176	89	24
Gatwick	31.5 million	233,652	200	90	45
Stansted	18.8 million	155,000	140	12	64
Luton	8.7 million	99,071	90	13	56
City	2.8 million	75,878	35	11	10

An aeroplane coming in to land at City Airport, with the O_2 and the towers of Canary Wharf in the background on the left and the Gherkin on the right

This description of Heathrow from London Transport's *Visitor's London* in 1958, recalls the early days of the airport: *It is already an impressive and fascinating sight. There are public enclosures, including terraced gardens, where the visitor is given a running commentary on departures and arrivals, and children have such amusements as pony rides, a miniature railway, and sand pits. There are also conducted tours of the airport including, during the summer, London Transport's conducted coach tours from Victoria Coach Station.*

By 1969 there were three main terminal buildings in the centre of the airfield. A fourth terminal was opened on the southern perimeter in 1986, and a fifth terminal opened on the western perimeter in 2008. In 2010 a decision to build a third runway was reversed by a new Conservative government, and the airport continues to operate at around 98 per cent of capacity. It remains vulnerable to scheduling problems when unexpected circumstances occur: in 2010 it had problems with the vagaries of snow, volcanic ash and industrial disputes. The airport is linked to central London by an express railway route that takes 15 minutes to Paddington station, and by the London Underground Piccadilly line (about 45 minutes to central London).

London City Airport

London City is close to the centre of London and was one of the first major redevelopments within the former Royal Docks, which had recently closed. Initially proposed in 1981, permission was granted in 1985 and it opened in 1987. It has a single runway on the site of former warehouses next to the main docks. Because of its position it can only be used by quiet aircraft that can handle the relatively short runway. As it is close to Canary Wharf and the City, it predominately serves the business community. There are plans, opposed by local residents, to increase the number of annual aircraft movements from 80,000 to 120,000, but remained with its night-time, Saturday afternoon and Sunday morning closures. It is linked to central London by the Docklands Light Railway.

London's former airfields

Hendon became London's first 'Aerodrome' in 1911 but was taken over by the War Office in World War I. In the inter-war period it was renowned for its annual RAF Display and is now the site of the RAF Museum. Croydon, which was London's main international airport before World War II, closed in 1959, unable to compete with Heathrow, and all that remains is the terminal building and control tower. Heston operated as a commercial airport between 1931 and 1947. It was closed because it was too close to Heathrow and now partly lies under the M4 motorway.

A poster for Hendon Aerodrome from 1910

HOUNSLOW

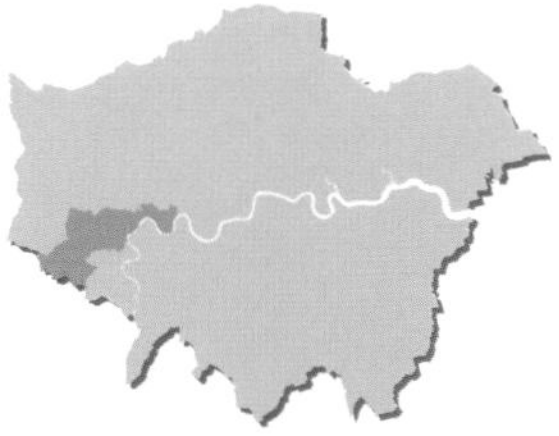

Population	234,200
Area	57 sq. km
Population density	4,110 per sq. km
Area of green space	23 sq. km
Jobs in borough	138,000
Average house price	£314,128

The borough of Hounslow takes its name from the town of Hounslow, first recorded in the Domesday Book, from the Old English, most likely meaning 'mound of the hound (or of a man called Hund)'. The borough was formed in 1965 from three distinct councils: Brentford and Chiswick municipal borough, centred on these two historic communities on the north bank of the Thames, Heston and Isleworth municipal borough, now to the east of Heathrow Airport and historically covering much of Hounslow Heath and the grand houses of Isleworth, and Feltham Urban District, to the south of Heathrow. Compared with other outer London boroughs its 1851 population of 23,100 was large, boosted by the importance of Brentford as a Middlesex market town. By 1901 the population was 85,700, after which it grew rapidly, encouraged by further extensions of the Underground and the building of the Great West Road, which stimulated both housing and industry. By 1951 the population was 211,900.

Osterley Park, the 18th-century country retreat of the Child family

The population of the borough declined after 1951, returning to 1951 levels by 2001. Since then it has grown by 10 per cent. By 2007 it was estimated to be the fifth most ethnically diverse London borough, with around 27 per cent of the population being of Asian origin. The west of the borough is now dominated by Heathrow Airport, for, although the airport itself is in Hillingdon, many of the support activities linked to it are in Hounslow, with over 13 per cent of jobs in the borough linked directly to the transport sector, nearly twice the London average. Brentford is an important commercial centre – industries originally grew up along the Great West Road and it is now home to the headquarters of pharmaceutical giant GlaxoSmithKline and the satellite broadcaster BSkyB.

The borough is also home to some of Britain's finest 18th-century country houses: Chiswick House, the great Palladian building designed by its owner, the Earl of Burlington, in 1729, and two dramatic alterations by Robert Adam of earlier buildings, Syon Park and Osterley Park, as well as the Jacobean Boston Manor and the Chiswick house of the painter, William Hogarth.

Waterside housing development at Brentford Dock on the River Thames

The Gillette Building, part of the 1930s development along the Great West Road

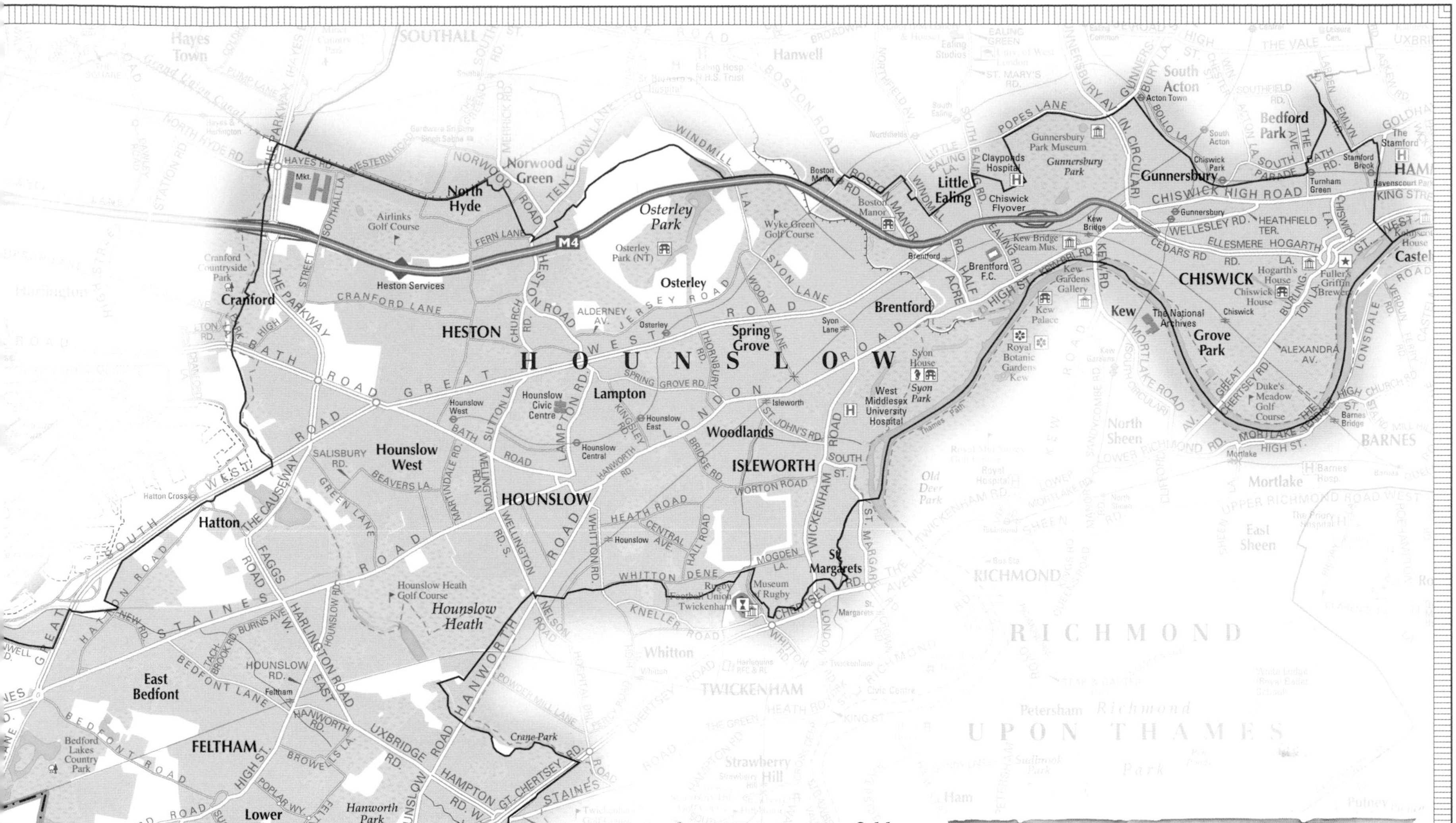

On 30 September 1959, Jayne Mansfield, the curvaceous Hollywood star, opened the **Chiswick Flyover**, an elevated dual carriageway of nearly 2.5 km between Chiswick and the open countryside beyond Brentford, the first major such construction in London. Originally designed for 40,000 vehicles a day it now carries around 100,000.

In 1876 Vincent van Gogh lived in **Isleworth**. He taught at a boarding school and assisted the local Congregational minister, preaching his first sermon in October.

John Bartholomew, Gazetteer of the British Isles (1887)
HOUNSLOW, *town and ry. sta. (Hounslow and Whitton), Heston and Isleworth pars., Middlesex, 2½ miles SW. of Brentford and 9 miles SW. of Hyde Park Corner, London, pop. 10,459; P.O., T.O., and P.O., T.O. at Hounslow Heath, 1 Bank, 1 newspaper; has extensive military barracks for both cavalry and infantry. The mfr. of gunpowder is largely carried on, as is also carriage-building and brickmaking. The local gardens send considerable supplies to the London market. The heath, which is notorious in the annals of highway robbery, stretches 5 m. westwards, and is partly enclosed*

BRENTFORD, *market town, S. Middlesex, 10½ miles W. of London by rail, at influx of river Brent to the Thames, pop. 11,810; P.O., T.O., 3 Banks. Market-day, Tuesday; is divided by river Brent into two parts, Old and New B.; has gin-distilleries, brewery, malt-kilns, soap works, &c. Brentford is a very ancient place, and was the scene of a Danish defeat (1016) and of a Royalist victory (1642). It is the co. town of Middlesex, being the place where the elections are held.*

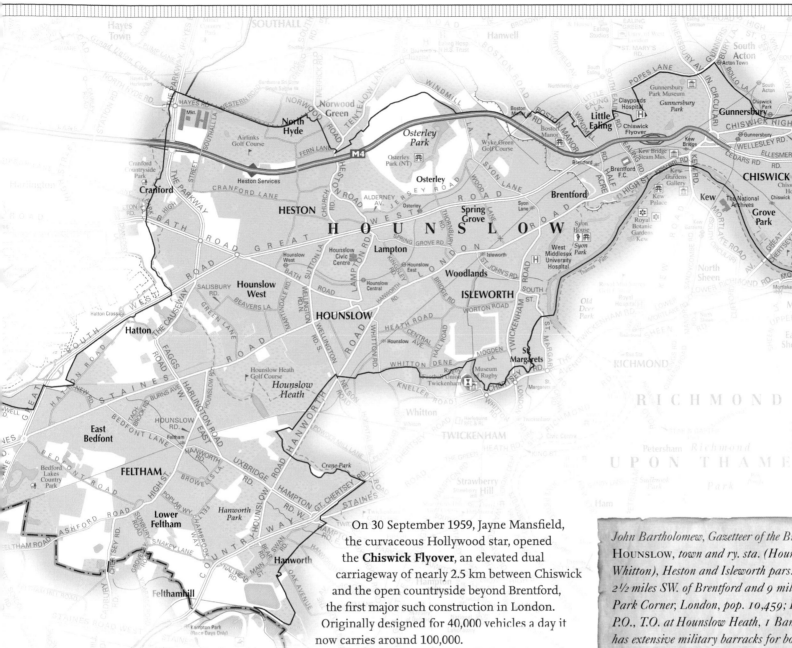

FAMOUS FOR

Hounslow Heath has played a vital part of the mapping of Britain. In 1784 William Roy, the father of the Ordnance Survey, established a highly accurate 27,404.72 ft (about 8 km) baseline on Hounslow Heath, then flat and wild countryside, for the triangulation survey of Britain. The ends of the baseline are marked by up-turned cannon barrels at King's Arbour, Heathrow (now close to a runway at Heathrow Airport) and the former Hampton Court Poor House near Bushy Park.

The **Grand Junction Canal** was built between 1794 and 1805 and connected the Thames at Brentford with the Midland canal network at Braunston in Northamptonshire, linking London and the Midlands for the first time. It was renamed the Grand Union Canal in 1929.

Two airports close to Heathrow were closed in 1946. The **London Air Park** (visited by the Graf Zeppelin in 1931 and 1932) is now the site of Hanworth Park and **Heston Airport** (to which Neville Chamberlain returned to after his ill-fated visit to see Hitler in Munich in 1938) is now partly under the M4 Heston Services.

FAMOUS PEOPLE

Henry Fox, first Baron Holland of Foxley, politician, born Chiswick, 1705.
Charles Holland, actor, born Chiswick, 1733.
(Kathleen) Kaye Webb, children's publisher and journalist, born Chiswick, 1914.
Charles Hawtrey, actor, born Hounslow, 1914.
Ronald Chetwynd-Hayes, author, born Isleworth, 1919.
(Elsie Ethel) Irene Thomas, quiz panellist and radio personality, born Feltham, Middlesex, 1920.
John Entwistle, musician, bass guitarist, The Who, born Chiswick, 1944.
Phil Collins, musician, born Chiswick, 1951.
Mel Smith, actor, born Chiswick, 1952.
Sebastian Coe, athlete and politician, born Chiswick, 1956.
Kim Wilde, singer, born Chiswick, 1960.
Patsy Kensit, actress, born Hounslow, 1968.
Jimmy Carr, comedian, born Isleworth, 1972.

GREAT LONDON HOUSES

As the capital city, London always attracted the rich and powerful, and those who wished to display their prestige through the lavish houses they built.

There were many grand townhouses in the centre of London, but few survive today. Northumberland House, on the corner of Trafalgar Square and the Strand was the Jacobean home of the Dukes of Northumberland until it was demolished in 1874 to make way for Northumberland Avenue. Devonshire House, on Piccadilly, was designed by William Kent for the Duke of Devonshire and built in 1740, complete with lavish interiors, but was demolished in the 1920s. Other fine houses have been put to different use; Burlington House, also on Piccadilly, has at its heart an 18th-century house designed by Colen Campbell for Lord Burlington but is now much enlarged as the home of the Royal Academy of Arts. Other sites have changed use but retained their names – for example, Somerset House was built in the 1820s as government offices on the site of the Duke of Somerset's house. Yet other were victims of the Blitz – for example the Jacobean Holland House, of which a small part remains in Holland Park, or Montague House once on Portman Square. As London developed, many aristocrats aspired to a

15th-century Great Hall at Eltham Palace, childhood home of Henry VIII

Charlton House, one of the finest Jacobean mansions in London

country estate close to town and many splendid houses were also built on the outskirts of London; some remain but some were demolished as a result of shrinking family fortunes – the gravest losses being Wanstead House and Canons, at Edgware.

Medieval houses

Parts of three medieval Episcopal palaces remain within Greater London: Lambeth Palace, on the banks of the Thames across the river from Westminster is the main residence of the Archbishop of Canterbury; the Old Palace at Croydon, one of his summer palaces, is now part of the Old Palace School; and Fulham Palace, the former palace of the Bishop of London. Lambeth Palace dates from the early 13th century onwards and has been through much restoration and rebuilding. The Gate House dates from the very late 15th century while the Great Hall was converted into a library in the 19th century.

Eltham Palace, in southeast London was, from 1295 until the reign of Henry VIII, a popular Royal Palace with its Great Hall dating from around 1480. Much of it was pulled down in the 17th century after it was sold by the Royal Family. In 1931 it was bought by Stephen and Virginia Courtauld – the Great Hall was restored and around it they built a new house with high quality Art-Deco interior designs. The Great Hall of Crosby Hall, built 1466–75 by the city merchant, Sir John Crosby, still survives. Originally in Bishopsgate, it was moved in 1910 to Chelsea to the site of Sir Thomas More's garden, as More had once owned it. At that time it formed part of an International Student Hostel, but is now incorporated within a re-created Tudor palace built for a wealthy businessman.

Jacobean houses

Two Jacobean buildings of distinction are Ham House in Richmond and Charlton House in Charlton. Ham House was built in 1610 and from 1637 was occupied by the Earls of Dysart for the next 300 years. It was at the centre of Restoration politics, and the house and garden was redesigned in the late 17th century to reflect this. The lavish period decorations give a unique image of luxury living at that time. Charlton House was built between 1607 and 1612 for Adam Newton, Dean of Durham and tutor to James I's son, Prince Henry, and is one of the finest buildings of this period in Britain. It is now owned by Greenwich borough, and while the grounds are open, access to the house is limited. Other Jacobean houses of note include Boston Manor in Brentford and Bruce Castle in Tottenham. Also in Greenwich, and designed in 1616 is a house that is revolutionary – The Queen's House, designed by Inigo Jones as part of Greenwich Palace, the first Palladian house in Britain and immensely influential on British house design.

Spencer House, central London's only surviving 18th-century private palace

Chiswick House, one of the finest examples of neo-Palladian architecture in London

The 18th century

In central London very few major houses of this period survive in anything like their original form. Spencer House, in St James's, is one – built for Earl Spencer between 1756 and 1766 as his townhouse by John Vardy and James 'Athenian' Stuart, the house was used by the family until the 1920s, and it has recently been restored to its original appearance. It has a grandeur that was reproduced in many other townhouses. Outside central London there are many buildings from this time. Chiswick House, built by the Earl of Burlington in 1729, was inspired by Roman architecture and the buildings of Antonio Palladio in 16th-century Italy. Designed effectively as a pavilion to show off his works of art and his taste, it is an exquisite and restrained building that became a talking point of Georgian society and influenced many architects. Set in classically landscaped gardens close to the Thames, it provides a peaceful haven, now just a short distance away from the Great West Road. Fairly close by are two of Robert Adam's masterpieces. At Syon House, a large 16th-century house built on the site of Syon Abbey at Isleworth, Robert Adam created some of his grandest interior designs for the Duke of Northumberland from 1762 onwards. He developed his style further at

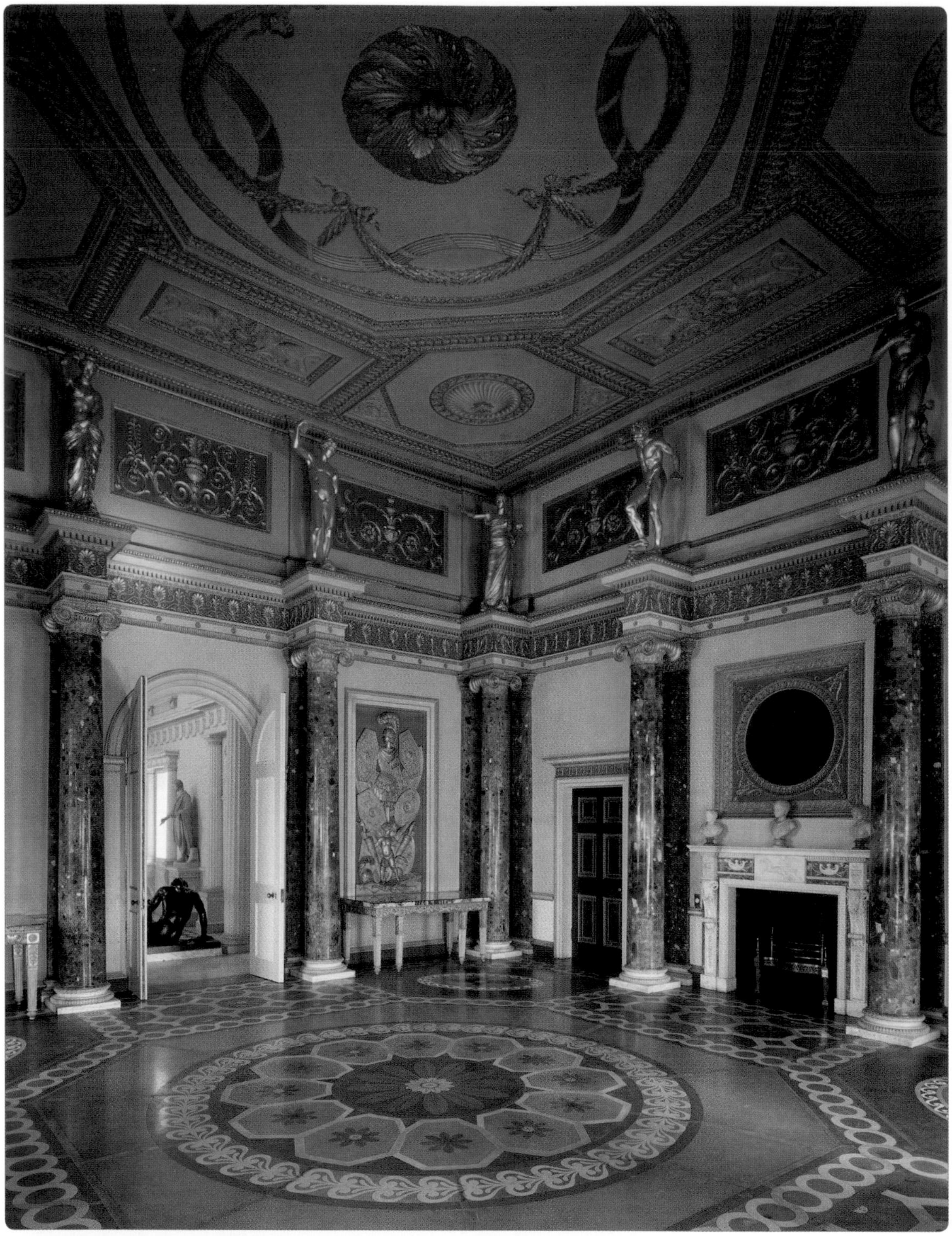

The Ante Room at Syon House, one of Robert Adam's most original designs

Osterley Park, where he dramatically reconstructed an Elizabethan house (built by Sir Thomas Gresham, the founder of the Royal Exchange) between 1761 and 1776 for Francis Child, from a wealthy banking family. He modified the external look of the house by inserting a great portico into the fabric of the building and designed all the internal details down to the furniture and fittings, making it one of the best examples of his great design skills.

Kenwood House, set in the northeast of Hampstead Heath at Highgate, was remodelled by Robert Adam for the Earl of Mansfield, who was Lord Chief Justice 1756–88. His design for the library is one of his most accomplished creations. The house contains a superlative art collection, bequeathed to the nation by Lord Iveagh in 1927, and outdoor concerts are performed in the grounds.

Predicting a change in taste is the extraordinary Gothic revival Strawberry Hill, designed as his own house by the writer and collector Horace Walpole, on a site overlooking the Thames in Twickenham. Built between 1750 and 1776, it was the first major domestic building to embrace the developing Gothic style and it was to have significant influence on architectural design in the 19th century. It was restored and re-opened to the public in 2010.

The 19th and 20th centuries

Apsley House, at Hyde Park Corner, was built in the 1770s but came into its own after 1815 when it became the home of the Duke of Wellington who carried out many modifications, including the great portico that overlooks Hyde Park Corner and the Waterloo Gallery. It provides a snapshot of European taste at that time. As the century developed, tastes changed towards the Gothic and three houses stand out as supreme and influential examples among the many buildings of this period. The Red House at Bexleyheath, designed by Philip Webb for the designer and poet William Morris in 1860, reflects the needs of a contemporary family and the re-imagining of

Kenwood House, remodelled in the 18th century

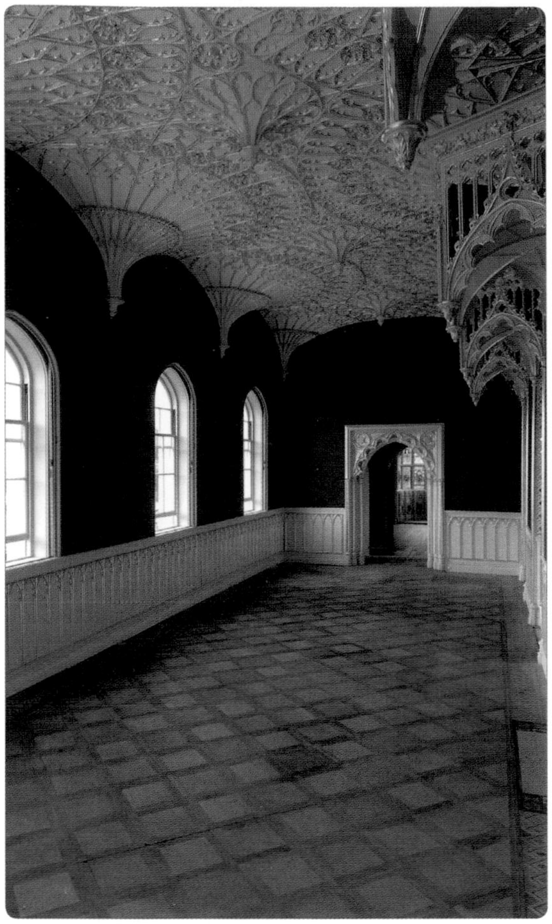

The restored Gallery at Strawberry Hill, Horace Walpole's main room for entertaining

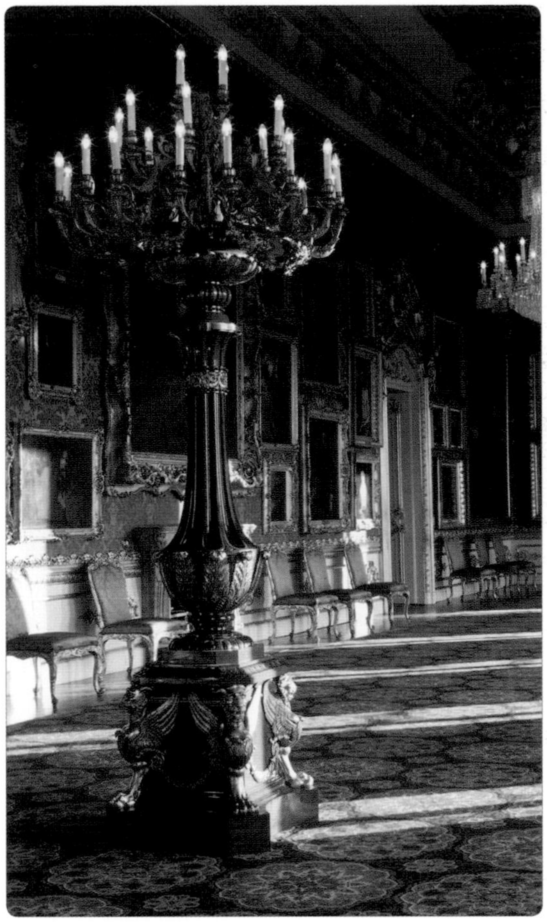

Waterloo Gallery, Apsley House

Leighton House, Holland Park

medieval arts and crafts. It had great influence on the Arts and Crafts movement of the late 19th century and was described by the Pre-Raphaelite artist, Edward Burne-Jones as the 'the beautifullest place on earth'. Leighton House in Holland Park was built for the artist Lord Leighton from 1866 and contains sumptuous medieval and Moorish-influenced décor within. Tower House, also in Holland Park, was designed by the flamboyant architect William Burgess in 1878, for his own use, and is regarded as one of the finest houses of the period, with lavish and complex medieval-inspired decoration. The first two are open to the public but the third remains a private home.

The most recently built London house owned by the National Trust is 2 Willow Road, overlooking Hampstead Heath. This house, designed by the architect Erno Goldfinger for his own use, was completed in 1939 and provides a fascinating opportunity to see a little modified Modernist house of the 1930s that remained in the family until the National Trust became the owner.

Modernist architecture at 2 Willow Road, Hampstead

ISLINGTON

Population	191,800
Area	15 sq. km
Population density	12,800 per sq. km
Area of green space	2 sq. km
Jobs in borough	206,000
Average house price	£415,206

The borough of Islington takes its name from the Anglo-Saxon settlement of Islington (in Old English 'Gisla's Hill'), when Islington was a forested area to the north of the City of London. In the 18th century the land was used for dairy farming to supply the City and from the 19th century it became a fast-growing area of housing. The borough of Islington was formed in 1965 from the metropolitan boroughs of Islington and Finsbury, which bordered the City. It stretches from Clerkenwell and Finsbury through Islington and Highbury, and up to Holloway and Tufnell Park.

Clerkenwell is the most historic part of the borough – it takes its name from the Clerk's Well in Farringdon, where London's parish clerks performed an annual series of mystery plays based around biblical stories. Clerkenwell was also the site of the Priory of St John of Jerusalem and the late medieval St John's Gate, formerly an entrance gate to the priory remains, now used again by the Order as its UK headquarters. Close by is the Carthusian 'Charter House', which, after the dissolution of the monasteries became a private house and then a school. City residents came to enjoy the gardens, spring waters and the entertainments provided by Sadler's Wells Theatre, founded by Thomas Sadler in 1683.

Clerkenwell became an area of breweries and printing workshops with, at is heart, Clerkenwell Green, long known as a centre of radicalism. However, as the 19th century progressed the area became overcrowded and slums developed. It is estimated that the population of the borough was around 65,000 in 1801, rising to 405,300 in 1901 but declining to 157,000 in 1981. Today, around 25 per cent of the population come from black and ethnic minority communities which include significant populations of Turks, Kurds and Cypriots. Many parts of Islington have now become highly desirable areas to live in, with the streets and squares of early 19th-century houses having been restored from the dilapidation that affected the area in the early 20th century.

The business activities of the City extend into the borough and over 43 per cent of all jobs are in finance, IT and other business, well over the average for London as a whole. With a resident population of 192,000 and around 206,000 jobs in the borough, many workers commute into Islington to work. The borough is home to cultural institutions such as Sadler's Wells Theatre in Clerkenwell, the Almeida Theatre in Islington, the City University, the Holloway Road campus of London Metropolitan University (including a dramatic graduate centre, designed by Daniel Libeskind), as well as Arsenal Football Club at the Emirates Stadium. It also houses two of London's prisons at Pentonville and Holloway.

FAMOUS FOR

One of the oldest buildings in Islington is **Canonbury Tower**, built in the early 16th century by the Priory of St Bartholomew's, Smithfield, who owned the manor of Canonbury. After the dissolution of the monasteries, it was lived in by Thomas Cromwell before his downfall, and later Sir Francis Bacon in the 17th century and Oliver Goldsmith in the 18th century.

New River Head in **Clerkenwell** was the original London end of the New River, a man-

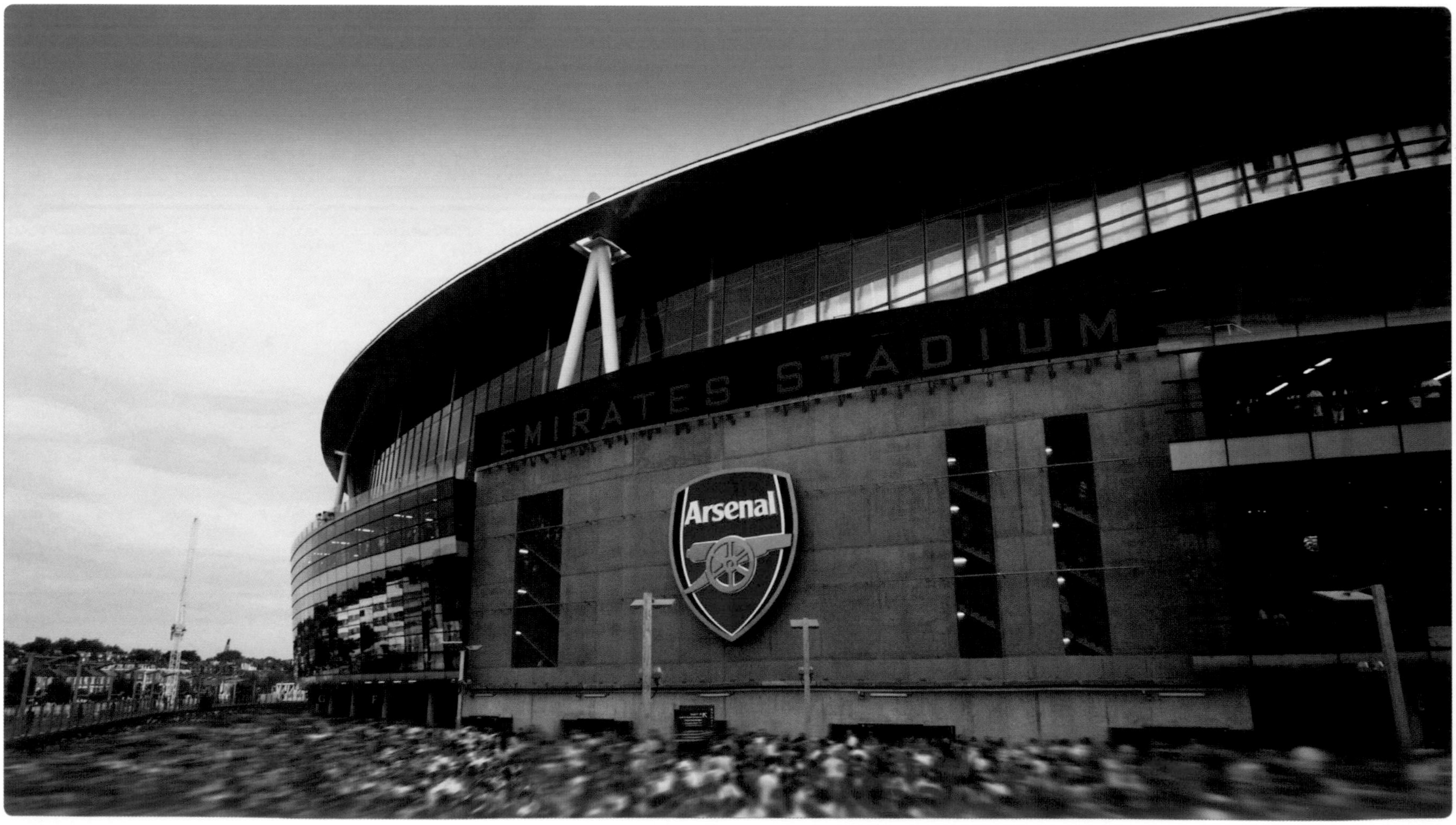

Emirates Stadium, the largest football club stadium in London

made river that comes from Hertfordshire and first brought drinking water to London in 1633.

John Wesley (1703–91), the founder of Methodism, lived near **Bunhill Fields** on the City Road. His house, now the Wesley House Museum, is next to Wesley's Chapel, built in 1778 and one of Methodism's most revered buildings.

Dadabhai Naoroji (1825–1917) was a Parsi from Bombay, where he was a teacher and politician. Moving to England, he was elected as Liberal MP for **Finsbury** in 1892, the first Asian MP in the House of Commons.

The Diary of a Nobody, by George and Weedon Grossmith retells the life of a city clerk living in **Upper Holloway** in the 1890s, capturing and caricaturing the customs and manners of the new middle class.

Clerkenwell Green's reputation for radicalism continued into the 20th century; in 1902–3, Vladimir Lenin produced Iskra (*The Spark*), a Russian Marxist paper, in a former school, now the Marx Memorial Library.

FAMOUS PEOPLE

John Wilkes, radical politician, born Clerkenwell, 1725.
Thomas Curson Hansard, printer and publisher, born Clerkenwell, 1776.
John Stuart Mill, philosopher and economist, born Pentonville, 1806.
Edward Lear, landscape painter and writer, born Upper Holloway, 1812.
Sir Arthur Wing Pinero, playwright, born Islington, 1855.
Sir Charles Scott Sherrington, physiologist, Nobel laureate, born Islington, 1857.
Mary Henrietta Kingsley, traveller and writer, born Islington, 1862.
(John) Robertson Hare, actor, born Islington, 1891.
Gerald Walcan-Bright (*performing name* Geraldo), bandleader, born Islington, 1904.
Charles Hill (Baron Hill of Luton), doctor, politician, and broadcaster, born Islington, 1904.
Kenneth Williams, actor and comedian, born Islington, 1926.
Sir Julian Critchley, Conservative politician, born Islington, 1930.
Laurence Marks, sitcom writer, born Islington, 1948.
John Hegley, poet and musician, born Newington Green, 1953.
Joe Cole (Joseph John Cole), footballer, born Islington, 1981.

John Bartholomew, Gazetteer of the British Isles (1887)
ISLINGTON, *parl. bor. and par. with ry. sta., Middlesex, in N. of London, 2½ miles N. of St Paul's, 3107 ac., pop. 282,865. Market-days, Tuesday, Wednesday, and Thursday; was a country vil. at the beginning of the 19th century; the Agricultural Hall, the largest building of the kind in London (capable of holding 50,000 people), is situated in the par. Islington returns 4 members to parl. (4 divisions – namely, North, West, East, and South – 1 member for each division); it was made a parl. bor. in 1885.*

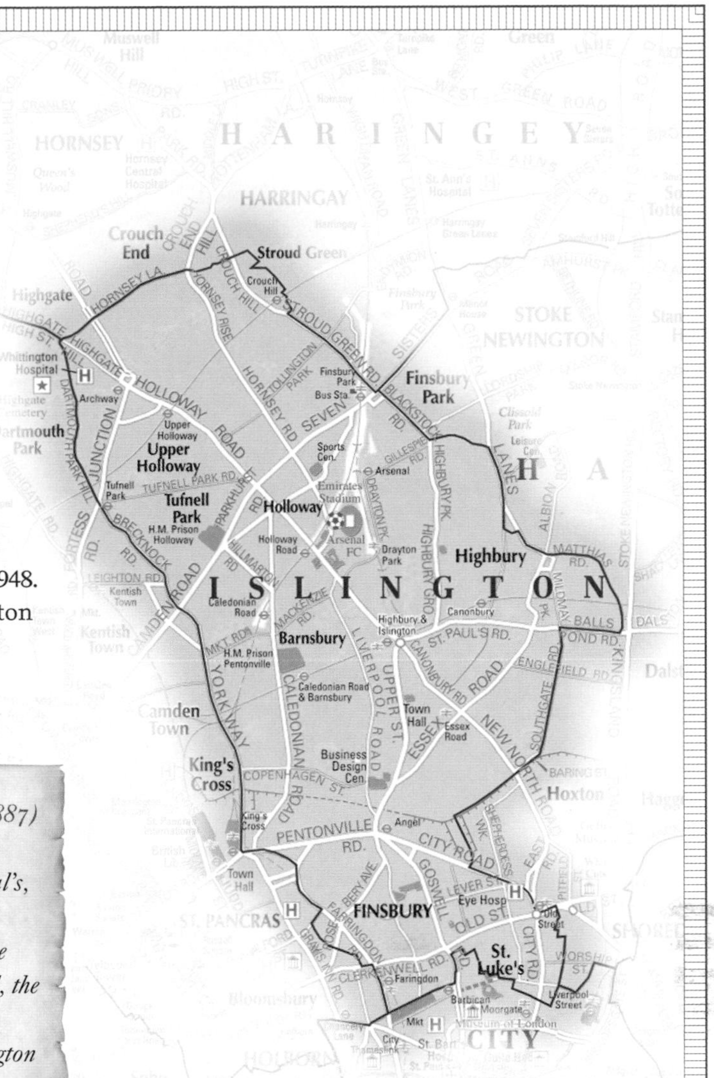

Wesley's Chapel

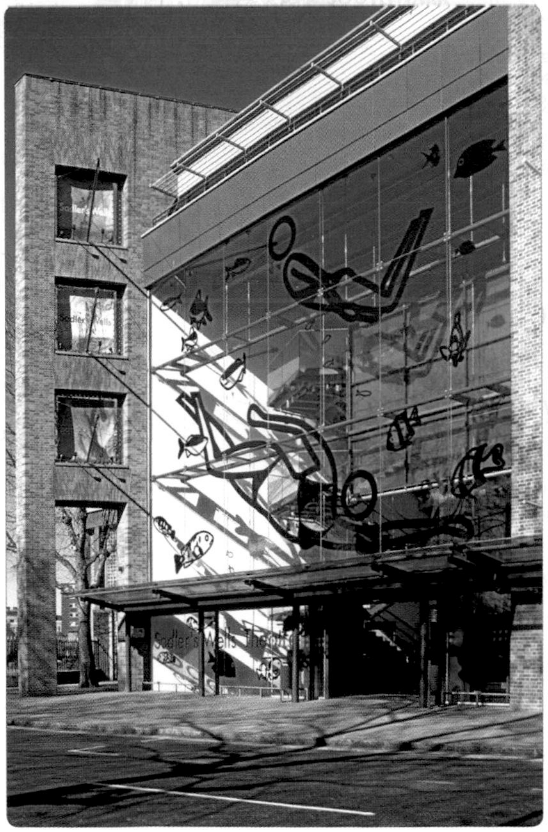
Sadler's Wells Theatre, Clerkenwell

EATING AND DRINKING IN LONDON

One of the significant sectors of the London economy that both Londoners and visitors enjoy is eating and drinking. One survey undertaken in 2008 estimated that the restaurant trade employed over 143,000 people and the pub and bar trade over 49,500 people, together generating over £10 billion a year. Add to that the jobs and revenue generated by the 134,000 hotel rooms currently available, from the grandeur of the Ritz and the Savoy to budget hotels in Outer London (and a target of adding a further 40,000 rooms by 2031) and there is no doubting the importance to the economy. There is more to it than that, however, because eating and drinking adds so much to the vibrancy of life in a city.

Brewing and the pubs of London

Beer has been a standard drink for Londoners for much of the city's history, not least because it provided a safer drink than water until the water supplies of London were put on a more reliable footing after the cholera outbreaks in the mid 1850s.

Brewing was a major industry and London gave the world a particular brew, porter, so named because of its popularity with the market porters. In more recent years, most of the old breweries have closed, their sites being too valuable for the making of beer, most recently Young's brewery in Wandsworth. The London tradition is still maintained by Fuller's brewery at Chiswick (calling one of their beers London Pride says much about the city). Although the large breweries may have gone, a late 20th century and early 21st century trend is the advent of microbreweries, and their attached pubs have become popular places to drink handcrafted artisan ales. There are also many historic pubs scattered around London, perhaps the most venerable being Ye Olde Cheshire Cheese in Fleet Street, for the cellars of the building certainly date from medieval times – and Dr Johnson, Voltaire and Dickens are all said to have drunk here. The most historically significant pub is the George on Borough High Street in Southwark. While the building that Shakespeare and possibly Chaucer knew was burnt down in 1676, the existing building gives a flavour of what a galleried inn would have been like – and it is not hard to see how theatres borrowed the design. There are a number of old pubs along the Thames, from the Dove at Hammersmith to the Mayflower at Rotherhithe and the Trafalgar at Greenwich, while many Victorian pubs, some still with their drink stalls and elaborately etched glass decorations, remain. More recently the city has seen the growth of wine bars, often as part of a restaurant, and the difference between bar and eating-place has become less distinct.

Eating out

Much has changed in our expectations over the last 100 years – the *Baedeker Guide to London* in 1900 advised visitors that:

English cookery, which is as inordinately praised by some epicures and bons vivants as it is abused by others, has at least the merit of simplicity, so that the quality of the food one is eating is not so apt to be disguised as it is on the Continent. Meat and fish of every kind are generally excellent in quality at all the better restaurants, but visitors accustomed to Continental fare may discern a falling off in the soups, vegetables, and sweet dishes.

London has a few traditional foods, a legacy of earlier times when there was less variety but still a demand for prepared food from those working long hours or without cooking facilities where they lodged. Thus developed Victorian London's answer to fast food: jellied eels and pie and mash. Eels became increasingly popular in the 19th century, in part because they were one of the few fish that still thrived in the polluted Thames – even so they were cooked in gelatine to counter the pollution, and absorbing some gelatine, they became jellied eels. Frequently used in pies, they were sold by street hawkers or in pie shops, where they were served with mash and liquor sauce (made from the liquor the eels are cooked in and flavoured and coloured with parsley). Manzes, in Peckham, is an outstanding survivor of a traditional pie shop. Today's city workers, tourists and pre-theatre visitors prove that there is still a high demand for fast food, catering to the needs of those in a hurry. Traditional fish and chips, a very British meal, are available and there is a more recent abundance of chain restaurants serving pizza, pasta and burgers all across the city, including many themed eateries catering for family diners.

The Bibendum Restaurant at Michelin House, Chelsea

Riverside eating and drinking in Richmond

Food stalls in the Stables Market, Camden

The relatively recent proliferation of restaurants is enlivened by the many cuisines that new residents of London have brought with them, making London the city with the greatest variety of restaurants in the world. African, Oriental, Mexican, and Middle-Eastern restaurants are all well represented, as are cuisines from all over Europe. In contrast are some restaurants that have been operating for more than 200 years – Rules in Maiden Lane by Covent Garden and Simpson's Tavern in Cornhill both have their origins in the 18th century, but longevity is not a necessary feature in this important sector. Atmosphere, fine views, music or speciality cuisine are all features that attract the consumer. The result is a wide range of restaurants from the grandeur of the Café Royal, through the art nouveau Michelin building that now houses Bibendum, to new and chic minimalist restaurants.

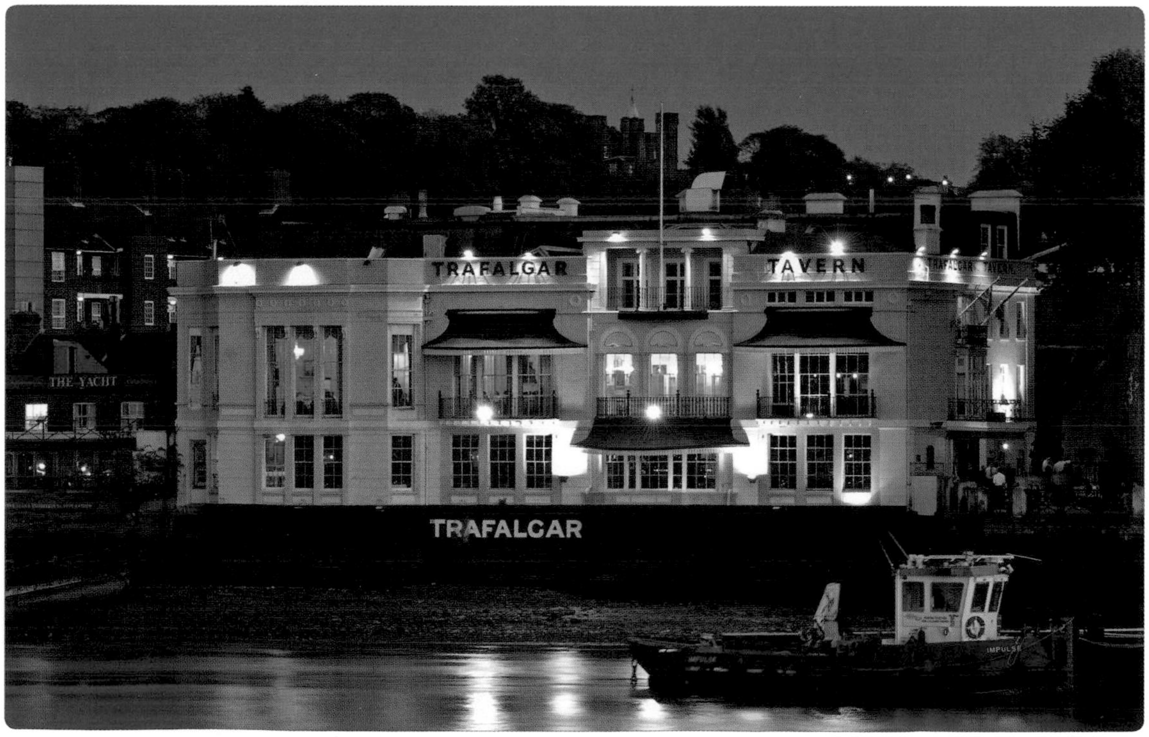

Trafalgar Tavern, popular with 19th-century politicians and writers

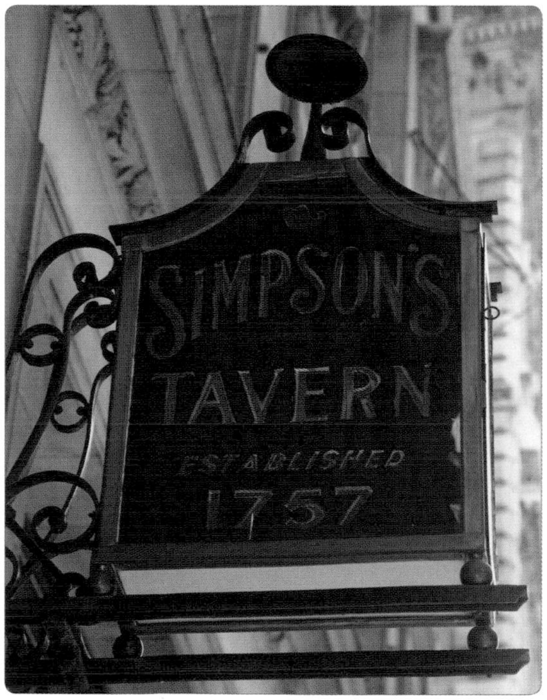

A traditional English 'chop house' tucked away down an alleyway in the City

KENSINGTON AND CHELSEA

Population	166,700
Area	12 sq. km
Population density	13,890 per sq. km
Area of green space	2 sq. km
Jobs in borough	129,000
Average house price	£1,036,158

The Royal Borough of Kensington and Chelsea stretches from the Thames at Chelsea, through Kensington and Holland Park to Notting Hill and beyond to North Kensington and Kensal Town. It is the most densely populated local authority in Britain, with some of Britain's most expensive housing in Chelsea and South Kensington and with areas of real deprivation in the north of the borough. It was formed in 1965 from merging the metropolitan borough of Chelsea (from the Old English for 'chalk landing place') and the Royal Borough of Kensington (from the Old English for 'settlement of Cynesige's people').

Chelsea, with its position on the Thames, developed earlier than Kensington. In 1520 Thomas More built a large house (later called Beaufort House) and others then followed. In the 19th and first half of the 20th century, Chelsea was home to many famous artists and writers. Kensington began to be popular in the 17th century – Holland House (whose ruins survive after it was bombed in World War II) was the first of the Kensington estates. Kensington's prosperity was confirmed when William III moved to what became Kensington Palace in 1689. The rest of the area remained fairly agricultural until the mid 19th century.

By 1871 the District line began to serve many places in the borough and housing development happened at great speed, from the grand houses of Belgravia, through the substantial terraces of Kensington and Notting Hill Gate to workers' houses in Notting Hill and Kensal Town. The result shows in the population figures. In 1801 the population was 22,000, in 1851 it was 69,000 and by 1891 it had risen to 258,000. Thereafter it declined to about half that level in 1981 since when it has grown again. The population is diverse with 50 per cent being White British, 26 per cent being white but not of British origin and 24 per cent from a wide range of other ethnic backgrounds.

Tourism accounts for around 20 per cent of jobs (nearly three times the London average), influenced by the museums of South Kensington and the many hotels and shops in the borough. It is estimated that visitors spend £3 billion annually in the borough, with nearly half of this being spent in shops, from the classic London department stores of Harrods, Harvey Nichols and Peter Jones to niche shops on the King's Road. In South Kensington and Earls Court, many houses have been converted into hotels, with the borough providing around 11,500 hotel beds. In addition to the main museums other attractions include the Royal Hospital, whose noble building designed by Sir Christopher Wren welcomed its first military veterans ('Chelsea Pensioners') in 1689, the Royal Palace of Kensington, the Saatchi Gallery and the spectacular Victorian Leighton House, while special events such as the Chelsea Flower Show in May and the Notting Hill Carnival in August bring many visitors to the borough.

FAMOUS FOR

The great national museums in **South Kensington** – the Natural History Museum, the Science Museum and the Victoria and Albert Museum – attract over 8.5 million visitors a year.

The **Chelsea Physic Garden** was established by the Apothecaries' Company in 1676 on Cheyne Walk. Still an active botanical garden, it was from here in 1732 that cotton plant seedlings were sent to the new colony of Georgia, so starting the American cotton plantations.

The Electric Cinema on **Portobello Road** is London's oldest surviving cinema, having opened in 1910. After a period of closure in the 1990s it has since been restored back to its original elaborate design.

Chelsea Old Church, which dated from the 13th century, was severely damaged by bombs in World War II. Now reconstructed, the least

Central Hall of the Natural History Museum

damaged part was the chapel on the south side rebuilt in 1528 by Sir Thomas More as his private chapel.

The Royal Court Theatre on **Sloane Square** opened in 1888 and has had a long history of promoting new drama and shocking the rather staid surroundings in which it sits.

FAMOUS PEOPLE

James Gillray, caricaturist, born Chelsea, 1756.

Elizabeth Gaskell novelist and short-story writer, born Chelsea, 1810.

Victoria, Queen of the United Kingdom of Great Britain and Ireland, born Kensington Palace, 1819.

Beatrice Stella Campbell (*performing name* Mrs Patrick Campbell), actress, born Kensington, 1865.

Beatrix Potter, artist and children's author, born South Kensington, 1866.

Howard Carter, archaeologist and artist, born Brompton, 1874.

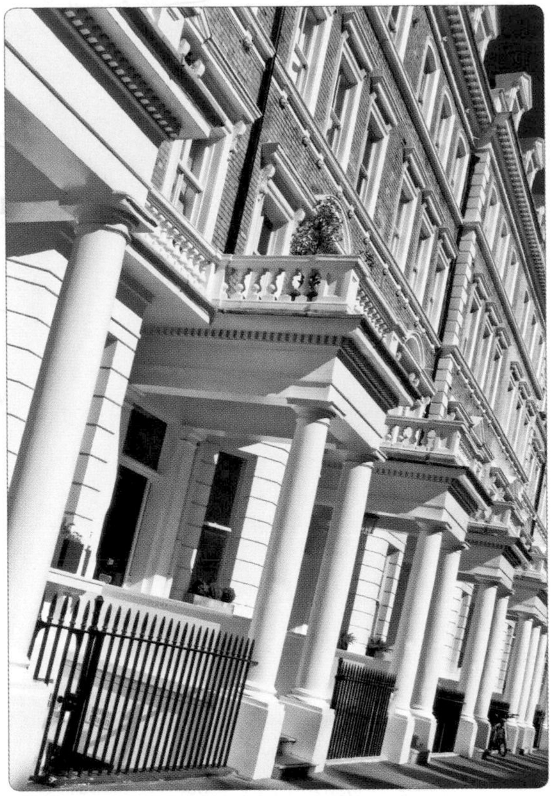

Grand Victorian terraces provide desirable London addresses

Portobello Road Market, Notting Hill

The Provence-inspired L'Occitane Garden, Chelsea Flower Show 2010

Kensington Palace

Leonard Sidney Woolf, author and publisher, born Kensington, 1880.
Sir Thomas Sopwith, engineer and aircraft designer, born Kensington, 1888.
John Nash, painter and printmaker, born Kensington, 1893.
Harold Macmillan (Earl of Stockton), Conservative politician, Prime Minister 1957–63, born Knightsbridge, 1894.
Sir John Gielgud, actor and theatre director, born South Kensington, 1904.
John Snagge, radio broadcaster, born Chelsea, 1904.
Hugh Gaitskell, Labour politician, leader of the Labour Party 1955–63, born Kensington, 1906.
Sir Terence Rattigan, playwright, born Kensington, 1911.
Mary Leakey, archaeologist and paleoanthropologist, born Knightsbridge, 1913.
Jon Pertwee, actor, born Kensington, 1919.
Rosalind Franklin, crystallographer, helped discover the structure of DNA, born Notting Hill, 1920.
Patrick Lichfield (Thomas Patrick John Anson, 5th Earl of Lichfield), photographer, born Chelsea, 1939.
Andrew Lloyd Webber (Baron Lloyd Webber), composer and theatre director, born South Kensington, 1948.

John Bartholomew, Gazetteer of the British Isles (1887)
KENSINGTON.– *parl. bor. and par. with ry. sta., Middlesex, in W. of London, 2190 ac., pop. 163,151; contains the South Kensington Museum, the gardens of the Horticultural Society, the Kensington Gardens (300 acres), which extend to Hyde Park, and Kensington Palace (the property of the Crown since the time of William III.), in which Queen Victoria was born. Kensington parl. bor. is divided into 2 divisions – viz., North and South–1 member for each division; it was made a parl. bor. in 1885.*

CHELSEA, *parl. bor. and par. with ry. sta., on river Thames, Middlesex, 796 ac., pop. 88,128; was formerly a vil. 2 miles W. of London, but now forms part of the metropolis. In the 16th century C. was the residence of Queen Catherine Parr, Sir Thomas More, the Princess Elizabeth, Sir Hans Sloane, and many of the nobility. In the 18th century it was a favourite resort of pleasure-seekers from the capital, the principal attractions being Ranelagh and Cremorne Gardens. C., however, is chiefly famous for its hospital for invalid soldiers, built by Sir Christopher Wren (1682-1690) on the site of King James's College. It has also a Royal Military Asylum, for the education of children connected with the army. Chelsea returns 1 member to Parliament; it returned 2 members till 1885, when its parliamentary limits were reduced by the formation of the new parliamentary boroughs of Fulham, Hammersmith, and Kensington.*

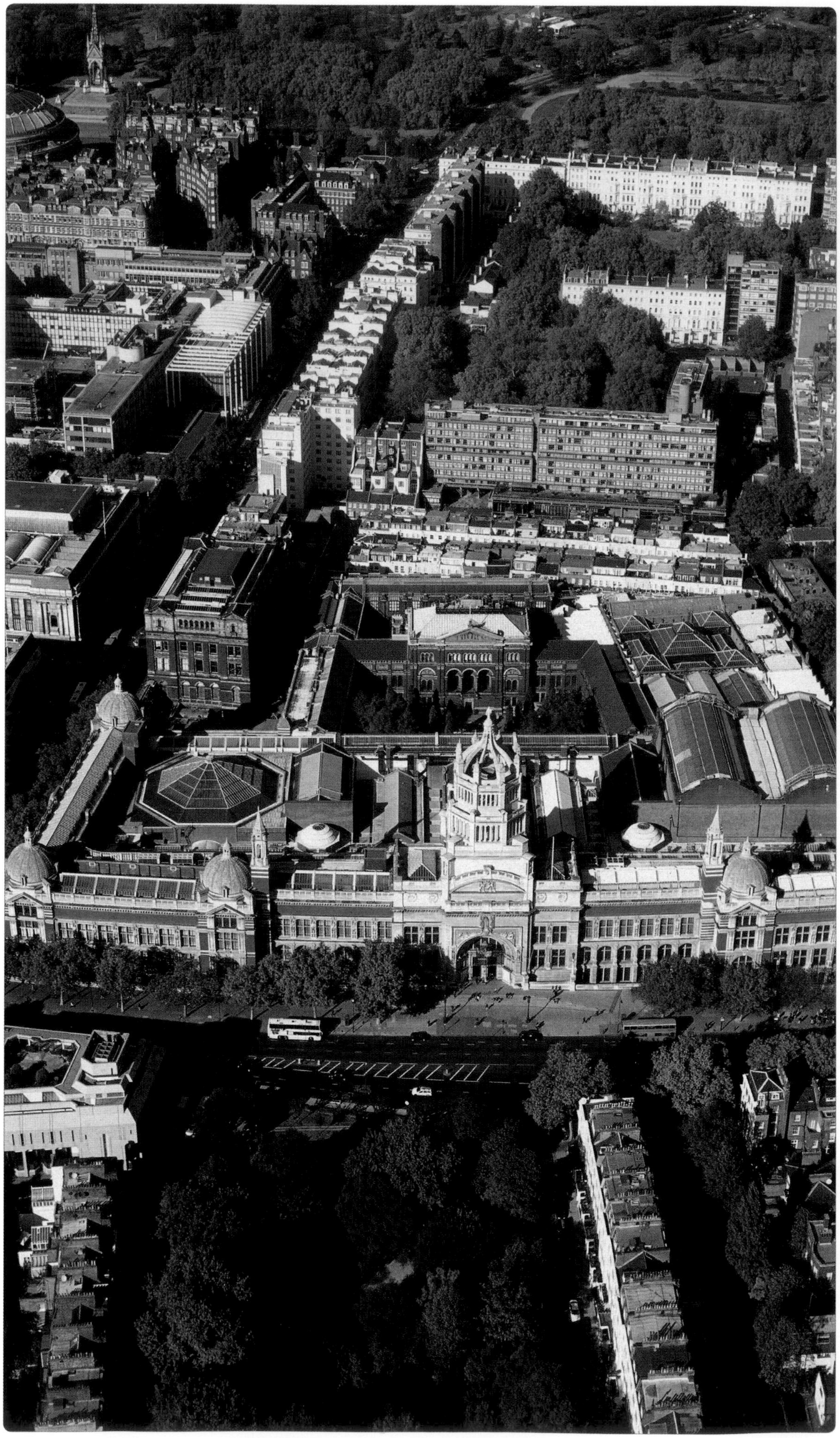

The Victoria and Albert Museum at South Kensington. At the top left can be seen the Royal Albert Hall and the Albert Memorial (both in the City of Westminster)

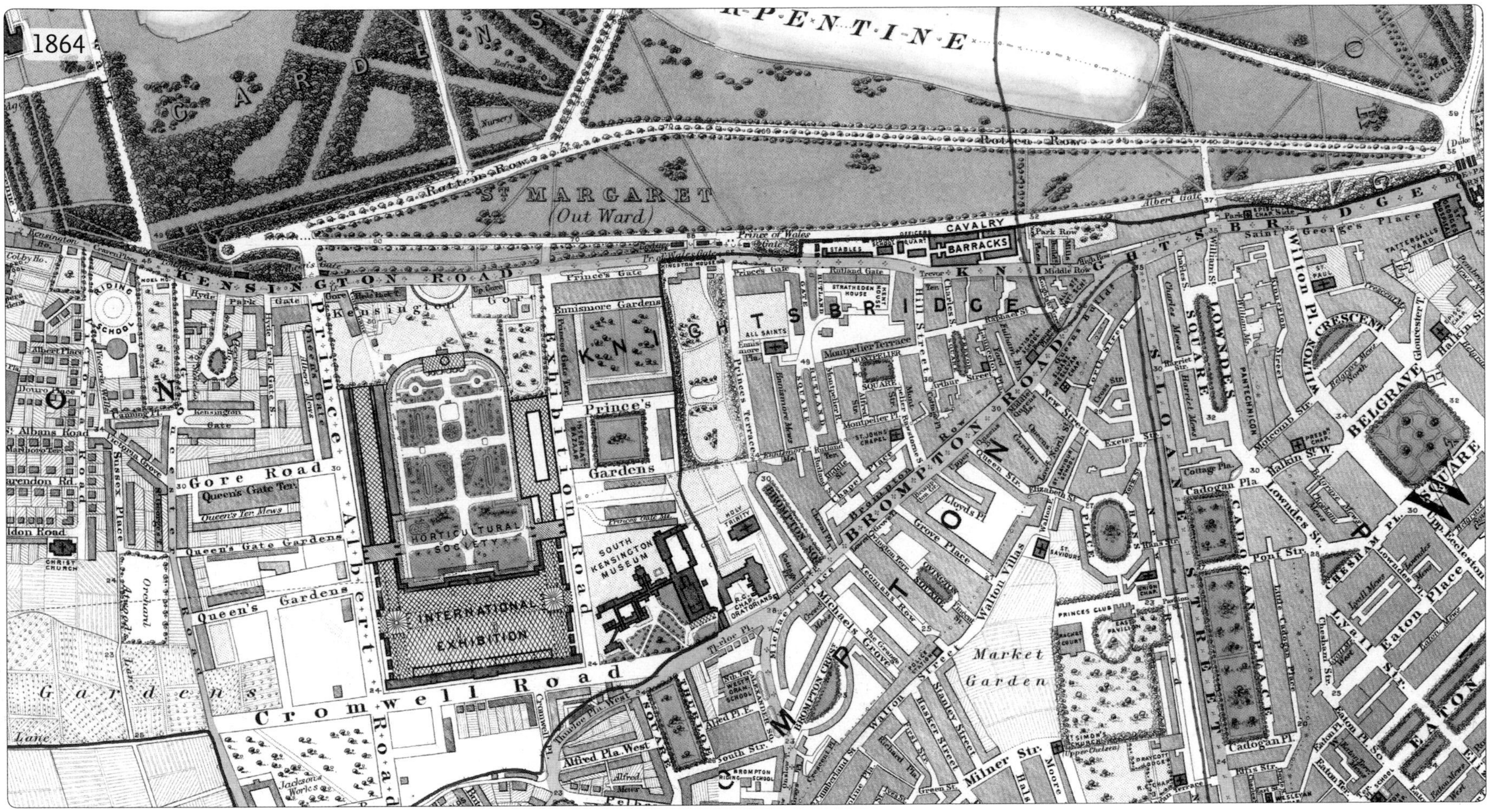

In the 19th century a hint of the future of the Brompton area can be seen with the location of the South Kensington Museum and the 1862 International Exhibition beside the gardens of the Royal Horticultural Society. *Stanford's Library Map of London*, 1864.

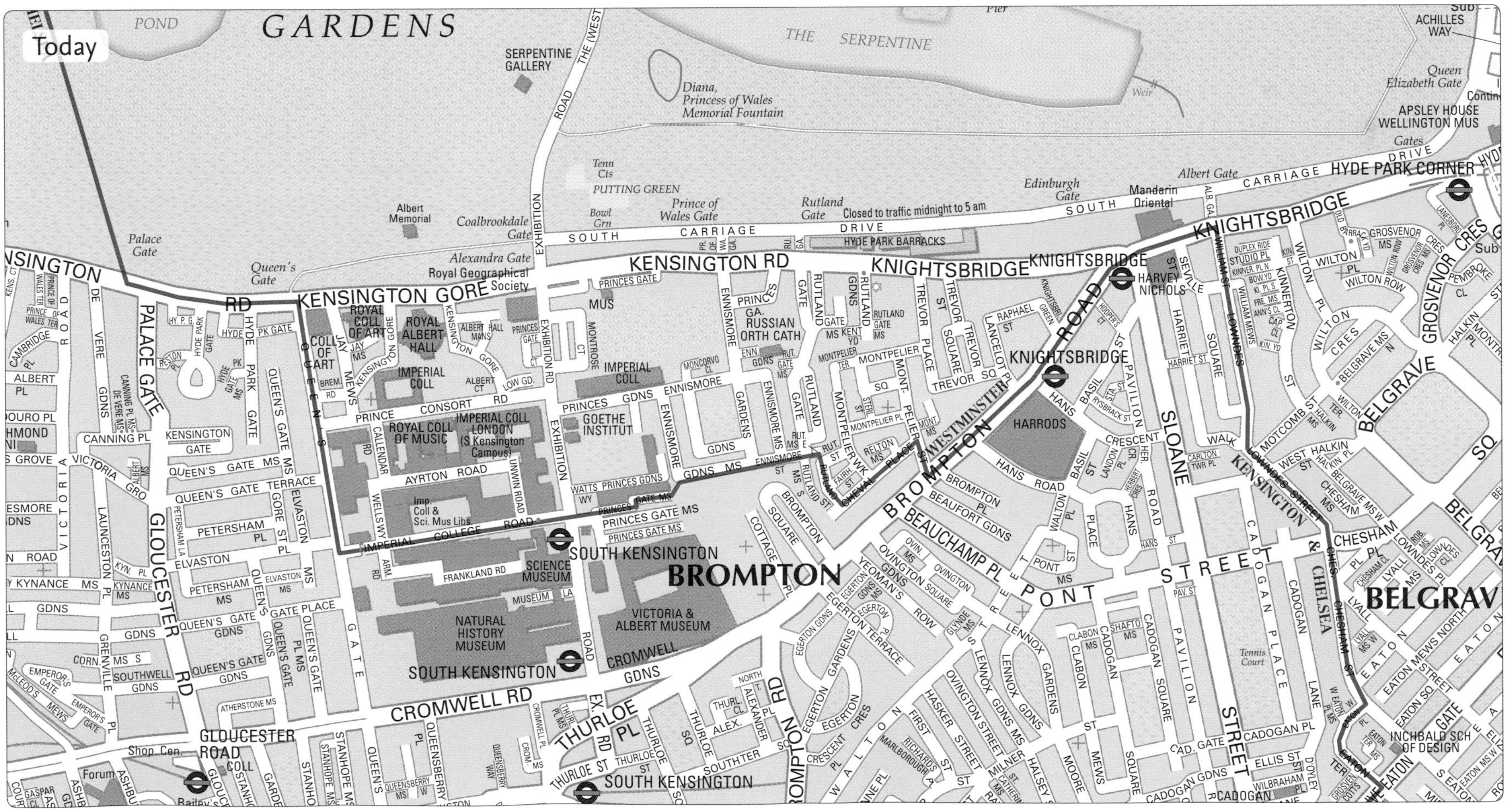

The Natural History Museum was built on the site of the International Exhibition and today most of the land between Kensington Gore and Cromwell Road is occupied by museums and colleges, and the Royal Albert Hall. Collins Bartholomew mapping

LONDON'S FESTIVALS

Throughout the year there are festivals and regular events that add to the vibrancy of the city. Some, like Trooping of the Colour or the Lord Mayor's Show (see page 132–133), are rooted in the history of the capital. Others celebrate the multicultural city of today – such as the Notting Hill Carnival or the London Mela – or promote the artistic, creative and sporting energy of the city, such as the Proms, the London Film Festival or the London Marathon (see page 236–237). A few major festivals have been selected below, and there are many other celebrations throughout the Greater London area ranging from the Brick Lane Curry Festival to the Tooting Spring Market Festival.

The **London Parade Festival** includes a series of concerts and events that take place between Christmas and New Year and is dominated by the New Year's Day Parade. For what is now a tradition, it has had a short history – the first parade, then called the Lord Mayor of Westminster's Big Parade, took place in 1987. The Parade now features marching bands, cheerleaders, dancers, decorated floats from London boroughs and much more – in 2011 there were over 8,500 performers and half a million spectators on the 3 km route from the Ritz Hotel on Piccadilly to Parliament Square.

The **Chelsea Flower Show** takes place in May in the grounds of the Royal Hospital Chelsea, the home for army veterans designed by Sir Christopher Wren. The show, organized by the Royal Horticultural Society, is renowned the world over for its display of flowers and garden designs. The show has been held at Chelsea since 1913 and is now attended by 157,000 visitors, a number limited by the size of the site. Also in May, the **A Baishakhi Mela** is held in the Banglatown area around Brick Lane, to celebrate the Bangladeshi New Year. It is the largest such celebration outside Bangladesh, with crowds enjoying music, dancing and food, in one of the capital's largest outdoor events.

The **Trooping the Colour** is held on Horse Guards Parade in Whitehall on the monarch's official birthday in early June. This military ceremony involves soldiers from the Foot Guards and the Household Cavalry parading in the presence of the monarch. First undertaken in 1748, its original purpose was to carry (troop) the flags (colours) through all the ranks of soldiers so that they would recognize the flags in battle.

The **Notting Hill Carnival** takes place on three days over the August Bank Holiday weekend and is now Europe's largest street festival, celebrating Caribbean traditions with steel bands, reggae music, spectacular floats and costumes, and hundreds of Caribbean food stalls. It is now attended by over a million people, having grown

Notting Hill Carnival costume

Last Night of the Proms, Royal Albert Hall

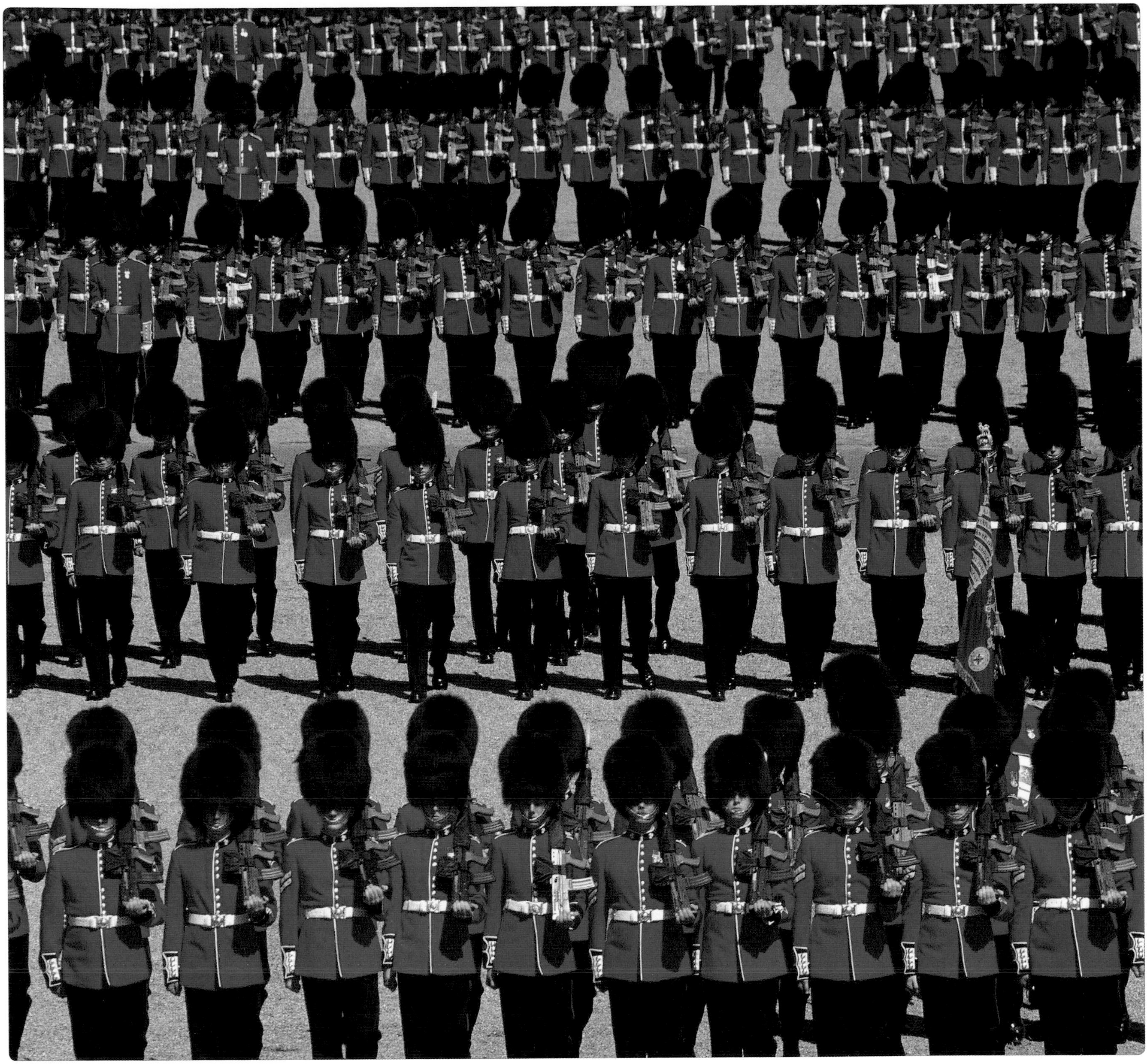

Trooping the Colour on Horse Guards Parade

dramatically from the first Carnival held in 1964 as a way for Afro-Caribbeans to celebrate the traditions of the many Trinidadians who had settled in the area and had been victims of race riots in 1958.

The Proms (the Henry Wood Promenade Concerts) is a series of over 100 concerts held between July and September every year, mainly in the Royal Albert Hall but also in a number of other venues, and frequently described as the largest classical music festival in the world. The Last Night of the Proms has become a great patriotic musical occasion, greatly encouraged by the 'promenaders', the regular attendees who stand in an area at the front of the auditorium where there are no seats and where they can 'promenade'. The first series of Promenade concerts was held in 1895 under the direction of Henry Wood, and he continued to direct them until his death in 1944, by which time the BBC had taken over their running and they had established a permanent home in the Royal Albert Hall.

The **Mayor's Thames Festival** is a weekend festival in September focused on the river from Westminster Bridge to Tower Bridge with music, dance, river races, street arts and food, concluding with a magnificent fireworks display. The festival was first held in 1997. The **London Mela**, currently held in September in Gunnersbury Park, West London, is a free festival inspired by the cultures of South Asia, with a diverse mixture of classical and modern music, dance, crafts, food and a funfair, attended by approaching 100,000 people in 2010.

ROYAL LONDON

There has always been a contrast between the pageantry of Royal London and the commercial development of the capital, and it goes back nearly 1,000 years to the time when Edward the Confessor established himself at Westminster and built both a palace and St Peter's Monastery (soon to become Westminster Abbey). It was here that he was buried in January 1066. From this time onwards the centre of government and the monarchy was focused on Westminster as a distinct community separate from the walled City of London. While the Norman Tower of London (see page 258) provided a Royal bastion just outside the City walls, the monarchs in the succeeding centuries lived in a number of palaces in and around London, either close to the Thames (as at Richmond and Greenwich) or close to royal hunting forests (as at Havering-atte-Bower, Eltham and Henry VIII's flamboyant Nonsuch Palace, once sited in Cuddington, on the Surrey borders).

Buckingham Palace

For matters of government, power rested at the Palace of Westminster, the only remaining part of which is Westminster Hall, now incorporated into the Houses of Parliament. Originally built by William II in 1097, it was modified over the years, most spectacularly during the reign of Richard II, by the addition of the hammerbeam roof, which has the widest span of any such roof in the country.

It is from the time of Henry VIII that much of the fabric of Royal London comes, particularly from the fall from grace of Cardinal Wolsey. The cardinal's Westminster home, York Place, became Henry's Whitehall Palace. All that remains is the Banqueting House on Whitehall, a beautiful Palladian building designed by Inigo Jones for James I in 1619 (and from which Charles I walked out of to his execution in January 1649). The remainder of the palace burnt down in 1698 and the area is now government offices.

The cardinal's Hampton Court Palace also came to Henry, and this building, sitting by the Thames in spacious grounds is perhaps the most palatial of all the royal buildings of London with its imposing Tudor courtyards and the elegant additions designed by Sir Christopher Wren for William and Mary after 1689. William and Mary also purchased the house now known as Kensington Palace and enlarged it. It remained the main Royal residence in central London until George III moved to Buckingham Palace in 1762. Kensington Palace from then on provided apartments for members of the Royal Family.

Henry VIII also built St James's Palace, which, from the destruction of Whitehall Palace until the move to Buckingham Palace, became the central London heart of the monarchy. It remains a Royal Palace today and within its grounds are Clarence House, still a Royal residence, and the former Royal buildings of Lancaster House and Marlborough House.

It is Buckingham Palace that now defines the Royal presence in London. The house was originally built for the Duke of Buckingham in 1702–5. Sited at the end of The Mall it was one of the grandest private houses in London, and, indeed, the Duchess, as an illegitimate daughter of James II, had Royal pretensions. In 1762 George III purchased it from the Duke's family and it became his main residence in London.

George IV initiated a major expansion of the palace, amidst much argument over costs, and his building works were not completed by the time Queen Victoria moved there in 1837. The familiar front of the palace facing The Mall was added over the existing front in 1913. Within the Palace are a total of 600 rooms, including many state rooms used for ceremonial occasions. It sits in 18 ha of garden, part of which was once a mulberry orchard established by James I to encourage a silk industry.

The ceremony of Changing the Guard at Buckingham Palace takes place every morning at 11.30 a.m. from May to July (and every alternate day for the rest of the year) in a tradition that dates back over 300 years. Changing the Guard also takes place at St James's Palace and at Horse Guards Parade.

Royal and State occasions bring great pageantry to London – whether in annual events such as the Trooping the Colour on Horse Guards Parade in June, or the State Opening of Parliament (usually in October), or special occasions such as receiving visiting heads of state or Royal Family occasions, such as the wedding of the Duke and Duchess of Cambridge, celebrated in great style on 29 April 2011.

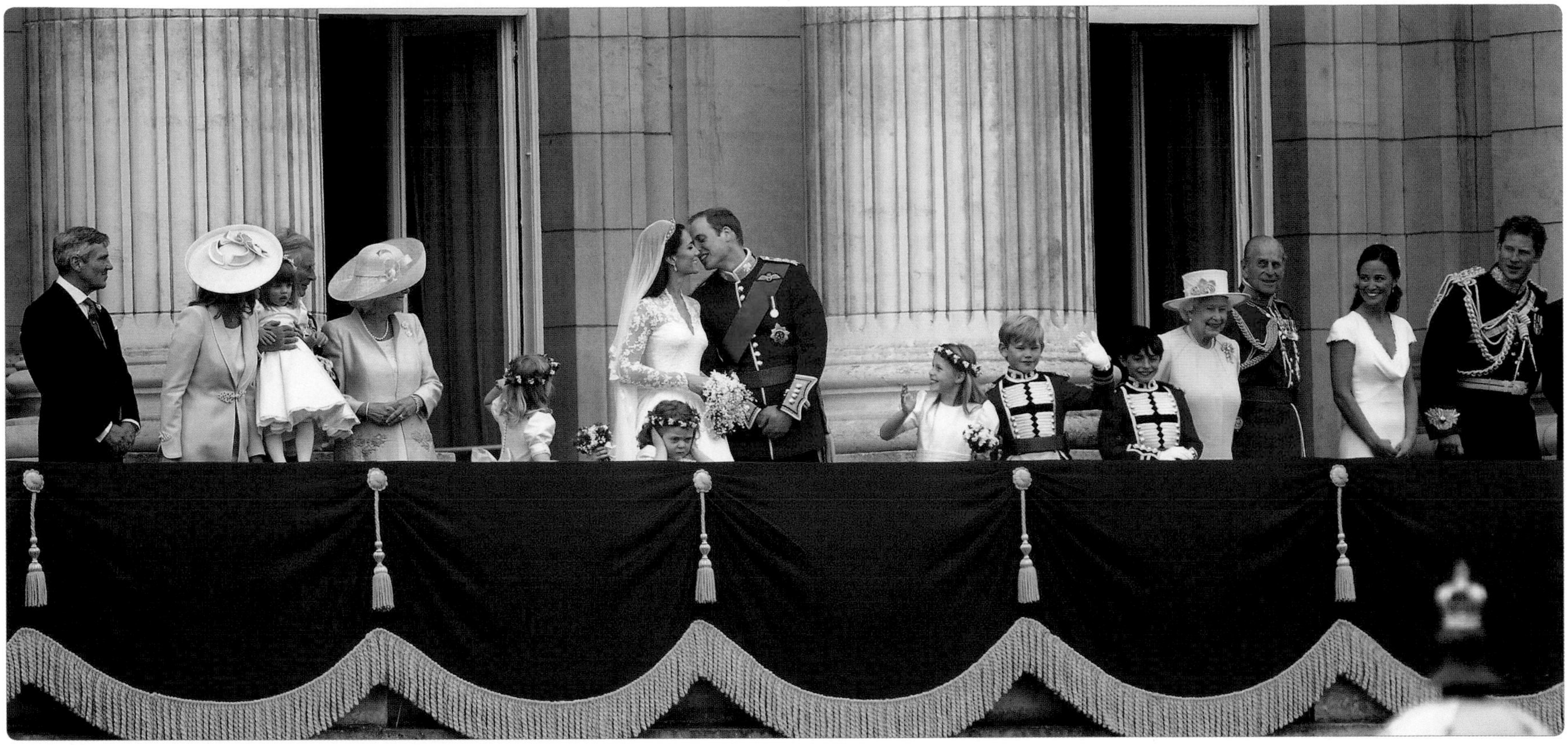

The wedding of the Duke and Duchess of Cambridge, 2011

Hampton Court Palace

KINGSTON UPON THAMES

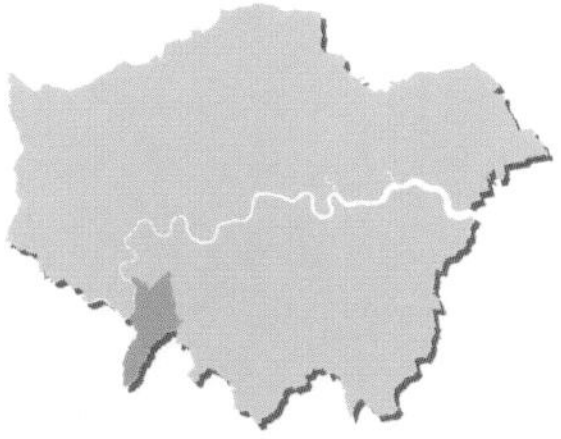

Population	166,700
Area	37 sq. km
Population density	4,505 per sq. km
Area of green space	14 sq. km
Jobs in borough	84,000
Average house price	£327,609

The Royal Borough of Kingston upon Thames has the distinction of being the oldest Royal borough in the country, its earliest surviving Royal charter being that granted by King John in 1208. Indeed Kingston (meaning 'king's estate') was the place of coronation for seven Saxon kings including Athelstan in AD 924 and Ethelred in AD 978. The coronation stone, thought to be used in the ceremonies, is now sited outside the Kingston Guildhall. Kingston owed this importance to the fact that it was the lowest point at which the Thames could be forded. Later, until 1729, its bridge was the first bridge upstream of London Bridge. It became an important market town and was the county town of Surrey (and still contains the headquarters of Surrey County Council though now no longer in Surrey). The area developed with the coming of the railways, but, as Kingston initially resisted the railway, the 1838 line went south to what is now part of Surbiton but was initially called Kingston on Railway. The current borough was formed in 1965 combining three municipal boroughs of Surrey: Kingston-upon-Thames, Surbiton, and Malden and Coombe.

After the City of London, Kingston has the smallest population of any London borough. Its fastest growth came at the start of the 20th century – in 1891 its population was 44,100 and by 1951 it was 143,500. By 2001 it was only 147,295 but since then it has grown at twice the average rate for London. In 2007 around 80 per cent of the population was white, and the two largest ethnic groups were Tamils and Koreans. New Malden has the largest community of South Koreans in Europe.

Kingston used to support a number of traditional industries, such as brewing, malting and tanning. In the 20th century there was a major aeronautics industry producing such iconic planes as the Sopwith Camel, the Hawker Hurricane and the Harrier. Manufacturing ceased in 1992 and now the area is a centre for the service sector, with over 94 per cent of jobs in services, including those working for Kingston University which was formed in 1992 and now has over 20,000 full-time students.

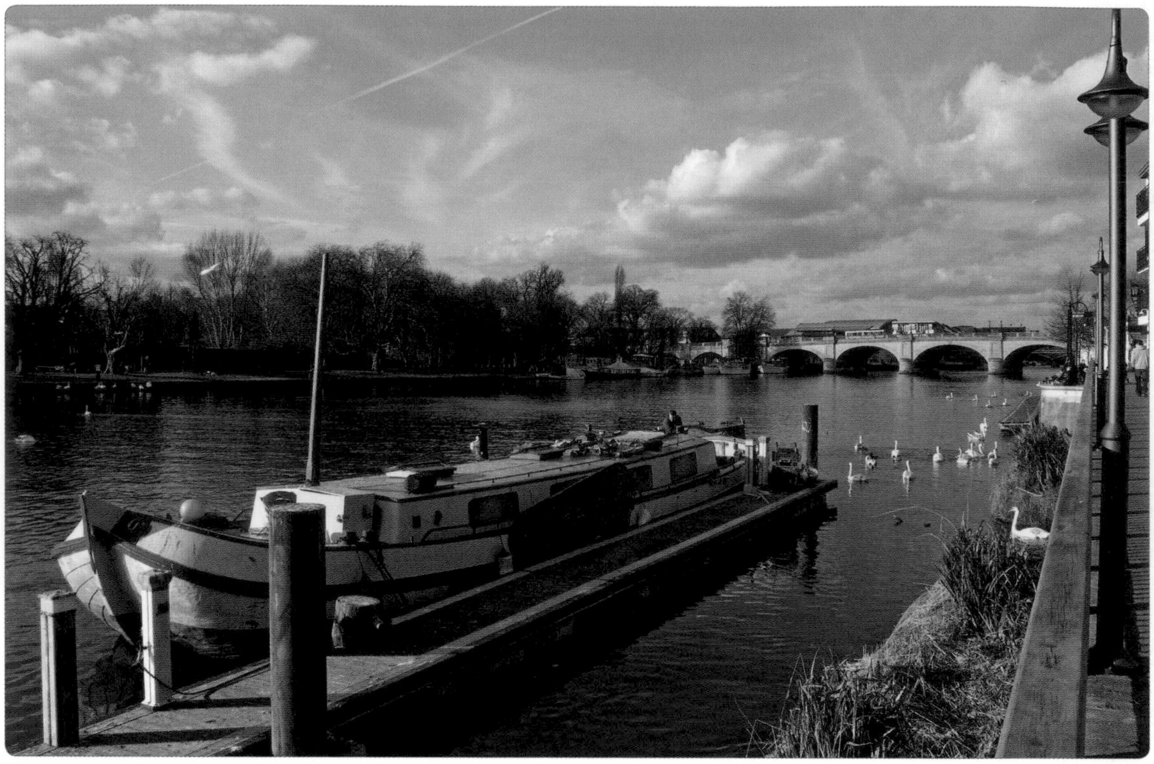

Houseboat at Kingston Bridge

FAMOUS FOR

Eadweard Muybridge was born in Kingston in 1830 but moved to America, where he became a renowned experimental photographer. In later life he returned and left his photographic collection and equipment to Kingston Museum. He chose the spelling of Eadweard to match that used on Kingston's coronation stone.

Kingston once had a thriving river fishery – and this is the reason for the three salmon depicted on the borough's coat of arms.

Kingston is home to one of Britain's newest theatres. The **Rose Theatre** opened in 2008 and seats 900 people in a circular auditorium, interpreting the design of the Elizabethan Rose Theatre in Southwark for the 21st century.

In 1761 a Senegalese boy was brought from Africa and presented to Sir John Philipps of Kingston. He was given the name **Cesar Picton**. He became a family retainer and then was given the means to become an independent businessman, owning Picton House in

The circular auditorium of the Rose Theatre

Kingston as well as a wharf and a malthouse. He died aged 89 a wealthy man.

Burnt Stub Hall at Chessington is so named because it was built on the site of an earlier house razed in the Civil War. It was here that Chessington Zoo opened in 1931, and it is now part of the **Chessington World of Adventures** theme park, leading a new life as 'Hocus Pokus Hall'.

FAMOUS PEOPLE

John Cleland, author of *Fanny Hill*, born Kingston upon Thames, 1710.
Thomas Daniell, landscape painter and printmaker, born Kingston upon Thames, 1749.
Eadweard James Muybridge (*formerly* Edward James Muggeridge), developer of motion photography, born Kingston upon Thames, 1830.
William Henry Heinemann, publisher, born Surbiton, 1863.
John Galsworthy, novelist and playwright, born Kingston Hill, 1867.
(Violette) Muriel Box [*née* Baker], screenwriter and film director, born New Malden, 1905.
(Francis) Roy Plomley, radio broadcaster, born Kingston upon Thames, 1914.
John Newton Cooper, racing car engineer, creator of the Mini Cooper, born Kingston upon Thames, 1923.
Sir Anthony Caro, sculptor, born New Malden, 1924.
Sir Terence Conran, designer, born Kingston upon Thames, 1931.
Max Clifford, PR consultant, born Kingston upon Thames, 1943.
Lynne Truss, writer, born Kingston upon Thames, 1955.
Debbie McGee, entertainer, born Kingston upon Thames, 1958.
Julian Clary, entertainer, born Surbiton, 1959.

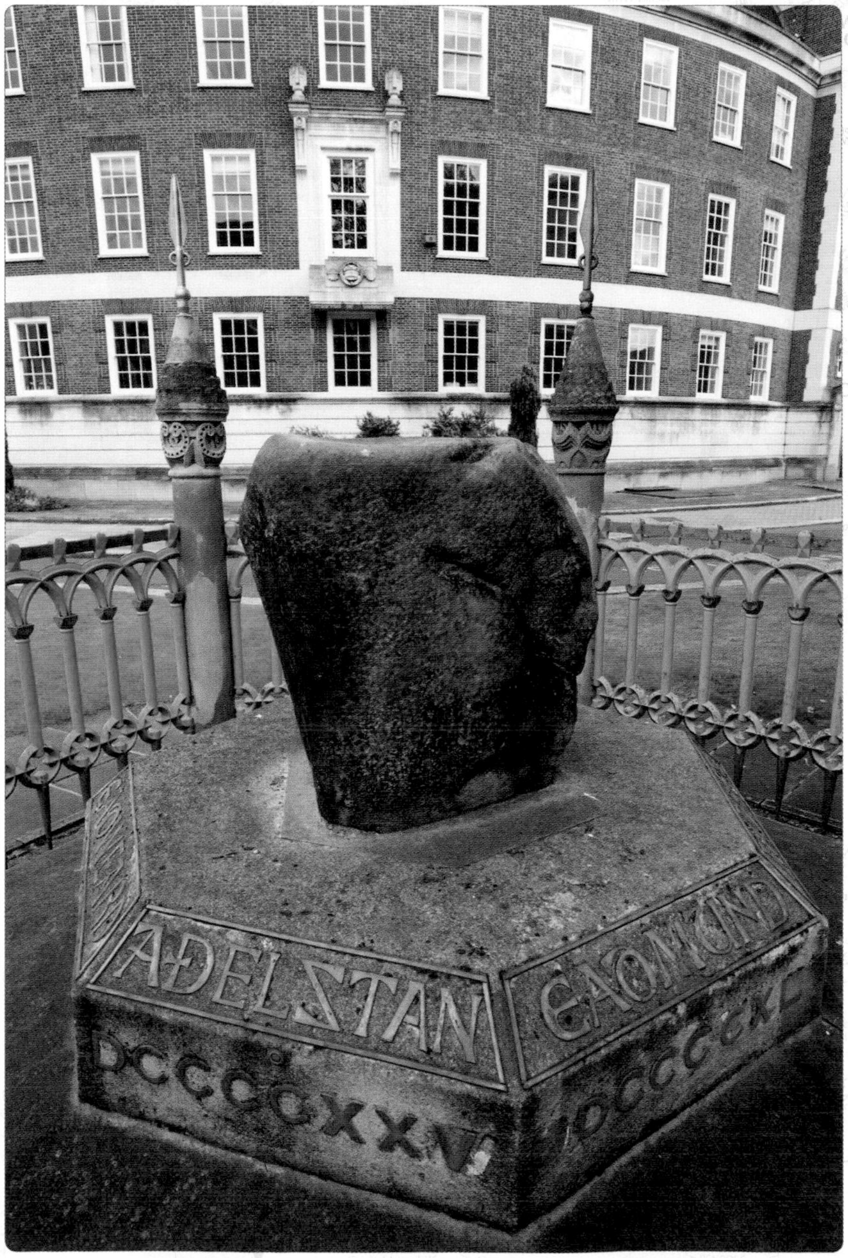

Coronation Stone outside the Guildhall, Kingston upon Thames

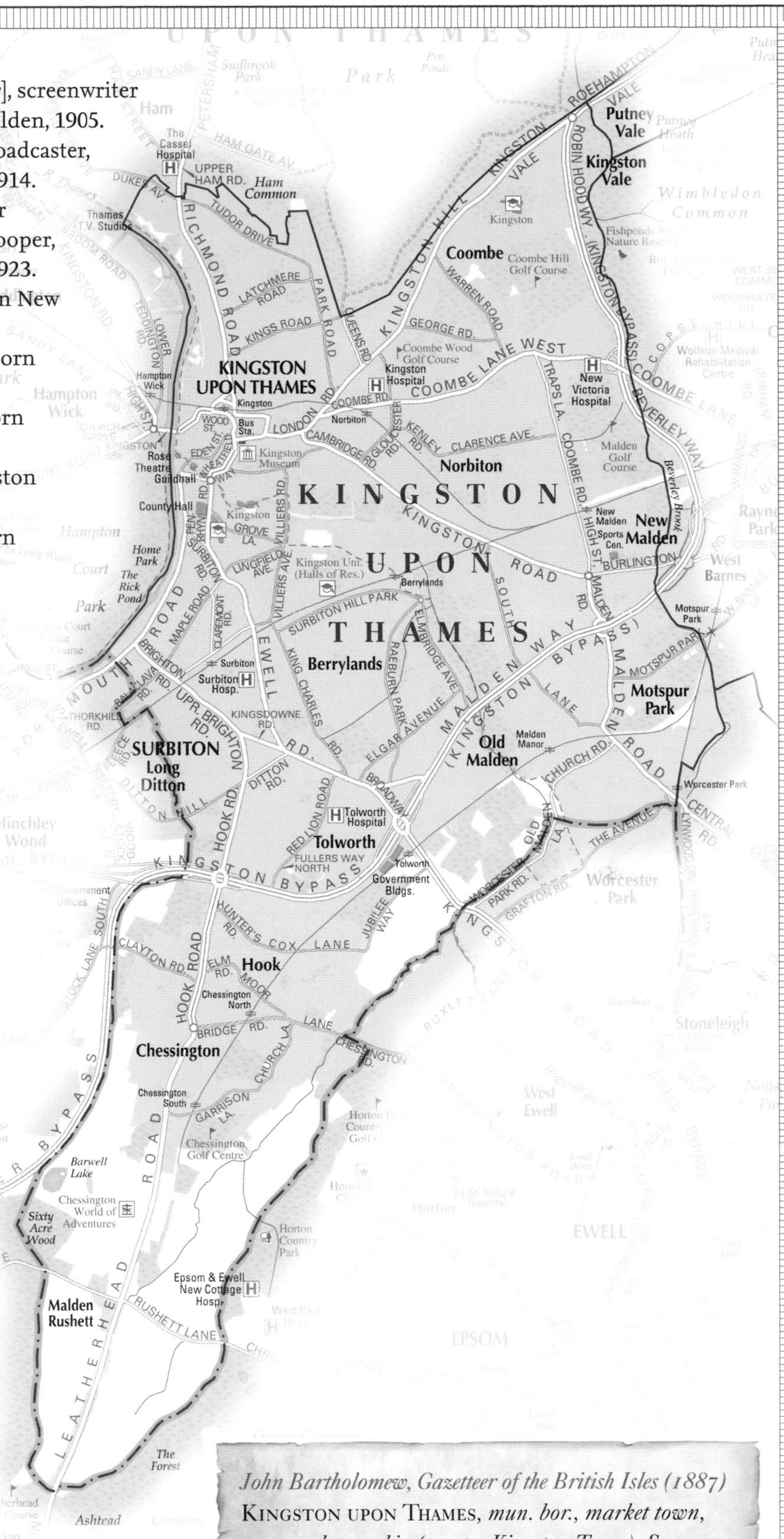

John Bartholomew, Gazetteer of the British Isles (1887)
KINGSTON UPON THAMES, *mun. bor., market town, par., and township (ry. sta. Kingston Town), Surrey, 5 miles S. of Richmond, and 12 miles SW. of Waterloo sta., London, by rail–par., 7229 ac., pop. 35,829; township, 4824 ac., pop. 33,560; bor., 1085 ac., pop. 20,648; 2 Banks, 2 newspapers. Market-day, Saturday. Several Saxon kings were crowned here, the first being Athelstane, in 924. In ancient times the place was important through its ford, and afterwards its bridge across the Thames. Kingston is now chiefly known as a place of residence for London business men, and its trade entirely consists in supplying the wants of a suburban resort.*

LONDON'S RAILWAYS

The first railway in London was the horse-drawn Surrey Iron Railway from Wandsworth to Croydon – it opened in 1803 and was only used for the transport of freight until it closed in 1846. Passenger steam railways arrived in 1836 with the London & Greenwich Railway, a 6-km route from London Bridge to Greenwich. The developments that followed initially focused on mainline termini built in a ring around central London: Euston in 1838, Bishopsgate in 1840 (replaced by Liverpool Street in 1874), Paddington in 1841, Waterloo in 1848, King's Cross in 1852, Victoria in 1860, St Pancras in 1868, with just Charing Cross (1864), Cannon Street (1866) and Holborn Viaduct (1874) terminating in central London. The last mainline terminus to be built was Marylebone (1899) and by this time much of the suburban network in use today was completed. This rapid development transformed great areas of London – many buildings were demolished and local areas transformed, some for ever ending up on the wrong side of the tracks, but without the railways, London would never have developed at the speed it did. The rail infrastructure shown in the 1908 map of railway routes (page 215) is close to today's

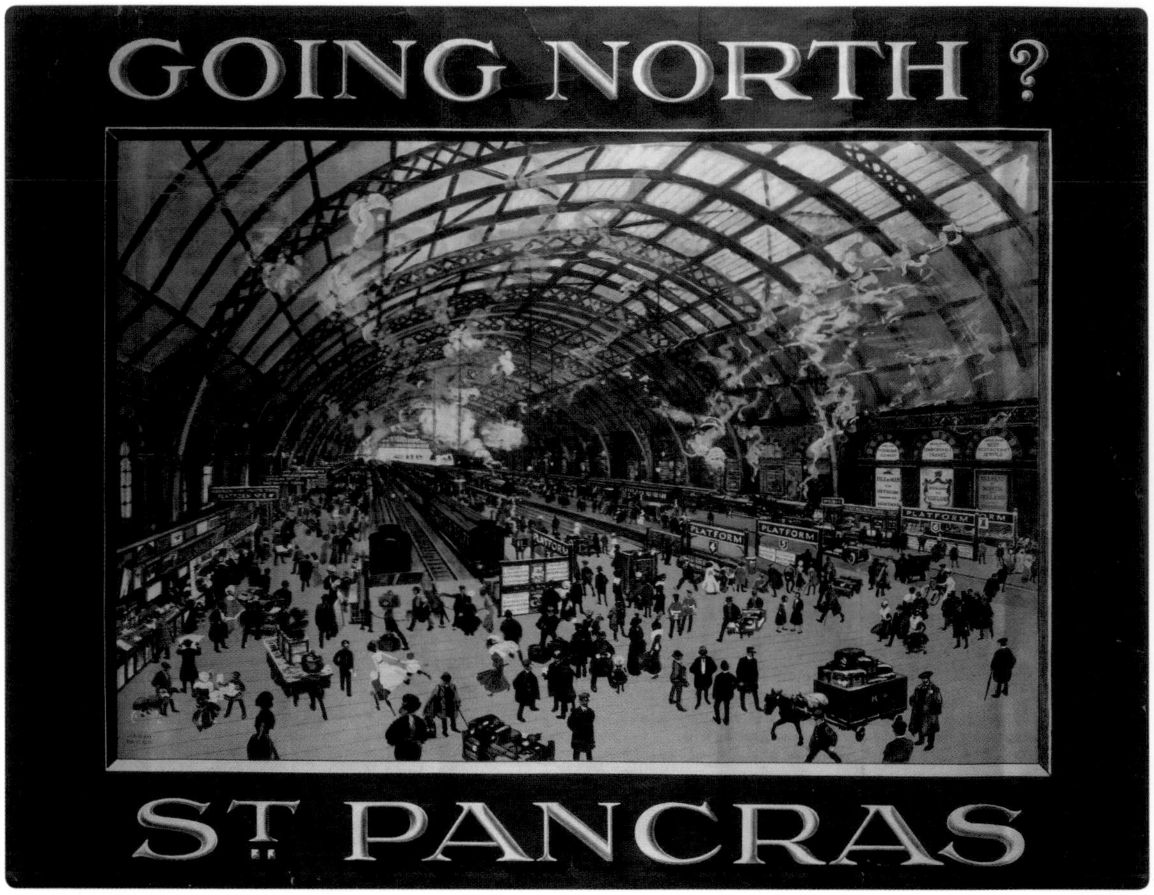

Poster advertising train travel, 1910

St Pancras International station and the recently restored former Midland Hotel. To the left is the British Library and to the right is King's Cross station

network, for intensive use ensured that no significant Beeching cuts were required in the 1960s, in stark contrast to the rest of Britain.

As with all areas of Britain, train use has been increasing in London over recent years. Between 1995/6 and 2005/6 passenger journeys within London grew by 15 per cent while travel in and out of London grew by 52 per cent. After 2006 travel within London declined until 2009/10 when it was stimulated by Transport for London accepting rail use on the Oyster card scheme. Over 2 million rail journeys a week are now made by passengers using Oyster cards.

2009–10 LONDON RAILWAY JOURNEYS

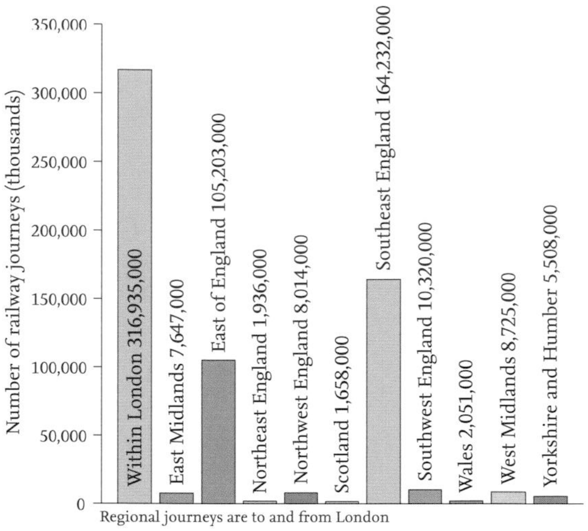

London's railway stations are also among the busiest in Britain – eight of the top ten stations in Britain are in London and just over half the top fifty stations are in the Greater London area. The busiest station in Britain is Waterloo, used by over 86 million passengers a year, followed by Victoria (70 million), Liverpool Street (51.5 million) and London Bridge (49 million). The 10th busiest station in Britain was the suburban East Croydon station (20 million) while Wimbledon saw over 14 million passengers a year. Three recent developments have had or will have a significant impact upon London's rail network.

Eurostar trains to Paris and Brussels

Eurostar started to operate trains through the Channel Tunnel to Paris and Brussels in 1994, initially using Waterloo station and then in 2007 transferring to St Pancras, once a 19 km tunnel to Dagenham and a 2.5 km tunnel under the Thames near Swanscombe had been completed. The service now carries around 9.5 million passengers a year and takes under two hours to Brussels and just over two hours to Paris. Its arrival at St Pancras stimulated a major refurbishment: its spectacular Victorian train shed (the largest single-span structure in the world when it was built) has been restored, and after many years of neglect the former Midland Grand Hotel, designed by Sir George Gilbert Scott in 1867 and one of the classic Victorian buildings of London, has been reopened.

The London Overground

In 2007 Transport for London took over the running of a number of suburban train routes which it rebranded as the Overground. One of the key objectives was to create an outer London circle, the last link being a new route from Clapham Junction to Surrey Quays. With new rolling stock and modernized stations, the Overground is set to see significant increases in passenger numbers.

Crossrail

This is the next major railway development. It will provide new train routes from Heathrow and Maidenhead in the west under central London in two 21 km tunnels, and then terminating at Shenfield in Essex and Abbey Wood beyond Woolwich. The route will take full-size trains that will carry more than 1,500 passengers. Construction started in 2009, with the central section planned to open in late 2018. In total there will be 118 km of new track and thirty-seven stations, with eight in central London (including Paddington, Tottenham Court Road and Liverpool Street) and a station at Canary Wharf.

Charing Cross Station at the northern end of Hungerford Bridge

Eurostar, the high-speed passenger rail service from St Pancras to Paris and Brussels

Paddington station in the 1920s

Paddington station, 2009

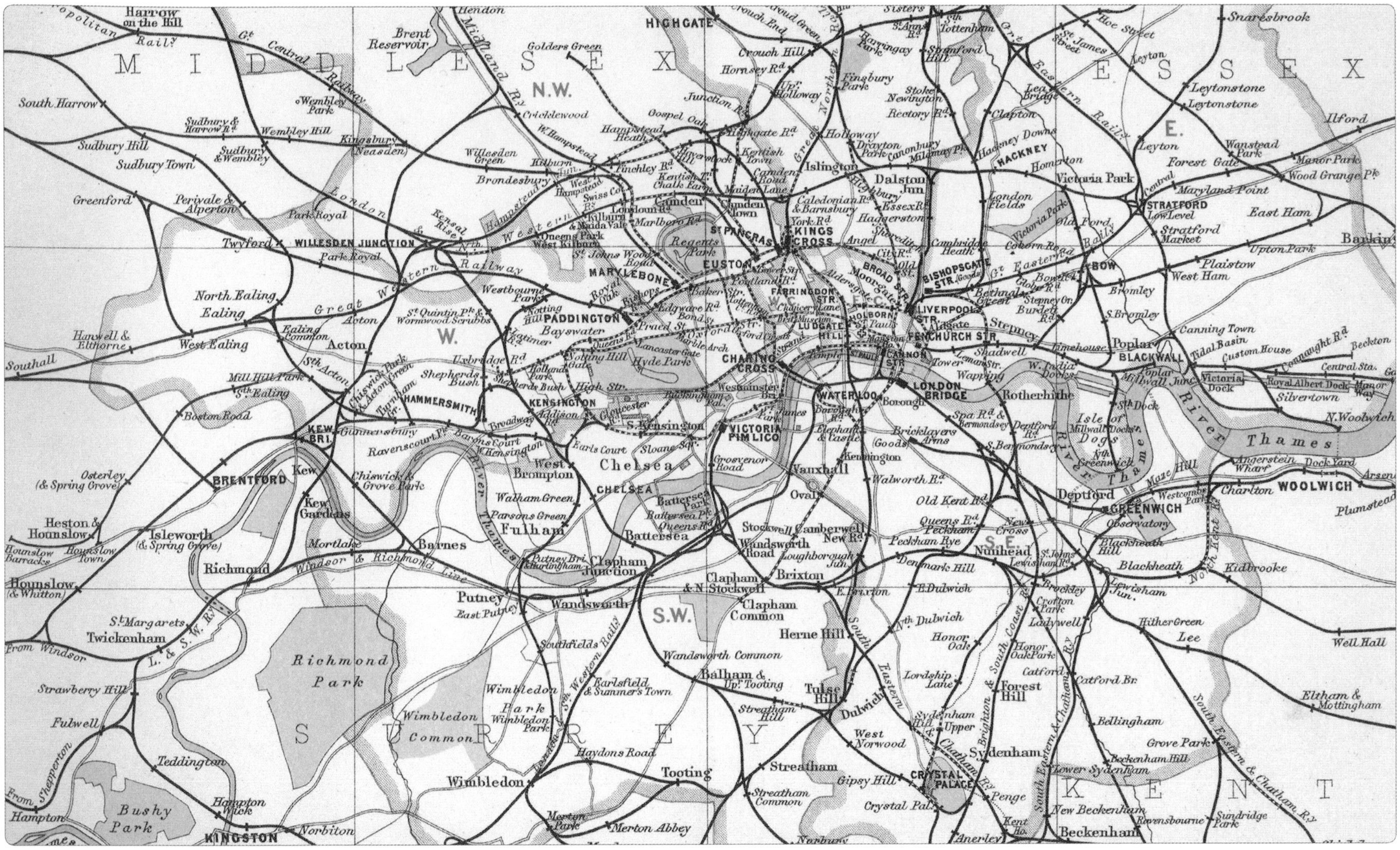

A railway map of London from Bartholomew's 1908 *Handy Reference Atlas of London & Suburbs*

King's Cross station, around 1930

LAMBETH

Population	283,300
Area	27 sq. km
Population density	10,500 per sq. km
Area of green space	5 sq. km
Jobs in borough	149,000
Average house price	£337,009

London Eye

The borough of Lambeth includes the south bank of the Thames from Vauxhall to the Southbank Centre and then stretches south in a narrow strip incorporating Kennington, Stockwell, Clapham, Brixton, Norwood and Streatham. It was formed in 1965 when the metropolitan borough of Lambeth took in the areas of Clapham and Streatham from neighbouring Wandsworth and it takes its name from Lambeth (from the Old English 'lamb's landing place') across the Thames from Westminster.

Its long, narrow shape basically matches that of the traditional parish of Lambeth, which belonged to the Archbishop of Canterbury from 1190 and whose palace at Lambeth remains his official home. Until the 18th century the area was little developed. Its fortunes began to change when new bridges were built across the Thames, first at Westminster in 1750, and then at Blackfriars and Vauxhall, stimulating much new house building, as still seen on parts of Kennington Road. As a result the population in 1801 of around 34,000 grew to 158,000 in 1851 before the full impact of the railways had arrived and to 357,000 in 1901 as the suburban railway network brought areas such as Streatham and Norwood into commuting distance. The population continued to grow for the next thirty years and then declined, shrinking to 244,000 in 1981.

It is one of London's most diverse boroughs – around 36 per cent of the population are from black and ethnic minorities. The roots of the Caribbean community go back to the first Jamaicans who arrived on MV *Empire Windrush* in 1948, many of whom settled in Brixton. Lambeth was classed as the 14th most deprived local authority in England in 2010 and contains great disparities of wealth within it. Nearly twenty years after the Brixton riots of 1981, the Coldharbour Lane area of Brixton is still the most deprived area in the borough. The largest employment sector is public administration, education and health, providing nearly 35 per cent of all jobs, boosted by the headquarters of MI6 by Vauxhall Bridge. There is a very marked geographical distribution of jobs, with nearly half of all jobs in the borough being in the South Bank area, which includes the head offices of major companies like Shell and ITV.

Many visitors to the borough go no further than the area around the South Bank of the Thames, home to the Hayward Gallery, the Royal Festival Hall, the National Theatre, the BFI IMAX, the London Eye, and the Old Vic theatre. The railway terminus of Waterloo is in Lambeth, as is the Oval cricket ground.

Secret Intelligence Service (SIS) headquarters (MI6 Building) on the Albert Embankment

FAMOUS FOR

The **London Eye** opened in 2000 and quickly became one of the city's most popular attractions, with over 3 million people a year enjoying the views to up to 40 km away as the wheel slowly revolves – it takes 30 minutes for one revolution and the top is 135 m above the ground.

The **Old Vic** theatre in Waterloo was established in 1818, but its reputation for staging drama came around 100 years later under the direction of Lilian Baylis. The National Theatre was established here in 1963 before moving to its new building on the South Bank in 1976.

In 2011, after a major restoration, **Brixton Windmill** opened to the public. Built in 1816,

Brixton Academy

the windmill on Brixton Hill thrived until the 1860s by which time it was surrounded by new housing, a poignant reminder of a rural past.

The **Garden Museum**, recently redesigned, is based in St Mary's Church by Lambeth Palace. The graveyard contains the tomb of John Tradescant (father and son), the great 17th century plant collectors, after whom the genus *Tradescantia* is named.

The **Brixton Academy** is one of London's major music venues. It opened in 1983 in the former Astoria theatre and cinema in Brixton, built in 1929.

The first **Vauxhall** car was made by the Vauxhall Iron Works in 1903 at their works on Wandsworth Road, though two years later car manufacture moved to Luton. The griffin symbol used by the company was that of the Norman Falkes de Breauté, whose house, 'Falkes Hall', gave its name to the area.

FAMOUS PEOPLE

Sir Arthur Sullivan, composer and conductor, born Lambeth, 1842.
John James Sainsbury, founder of Sainsbury's, born Lambeth, 1844.
Sir Joseph Nathaniel Lyons, caterer, founder of Lyons Coffee Houses, born Kennington, 1847.
Sir Aston Webb, architect (Admiralty Arch, front of Buckingham Palace), born Clapham, 1849.
Arthur Rackham, painter and illustrator, born Lambeth, 1867.
Bernard Law Montgomery (Viscount Montgomery of Alamein), army officer, born Kennington, 1887.
Herbert Stanley Morrison (Baron Morrison of Lambeth), Labour politician, born Brixton, 1888.
Sir Norman Hartnell, fashion designer, born Streatham, 1901.
Graham Sutherland, painter and printmaker, born Streatham, 1903.
Max Wall (*real name* Maxwell George Lorimer), comedian and actor, born Brixton, 1908.
Tommy Trinder, comedian, born Streatham, 1909.
George Brown (Baron George-Brown), Labour politician, born Lambeth, 1914.
Joan Littlewood, theatre director and writer, born Stockwell, 1914.
Sir Kingsley Amis, writer, born Clapham Common, 1922.
Ronnie Biggs, Great Train robber, born Lambeth, 1929.
Ken Livingstone, Labour politician, first Mayor of London, born Lambeth, 1945.
David Bowie (David Robert Jones), rock musician, born Brixton, 1947.
Naomi Campbell, model, born Streatham, 1970.

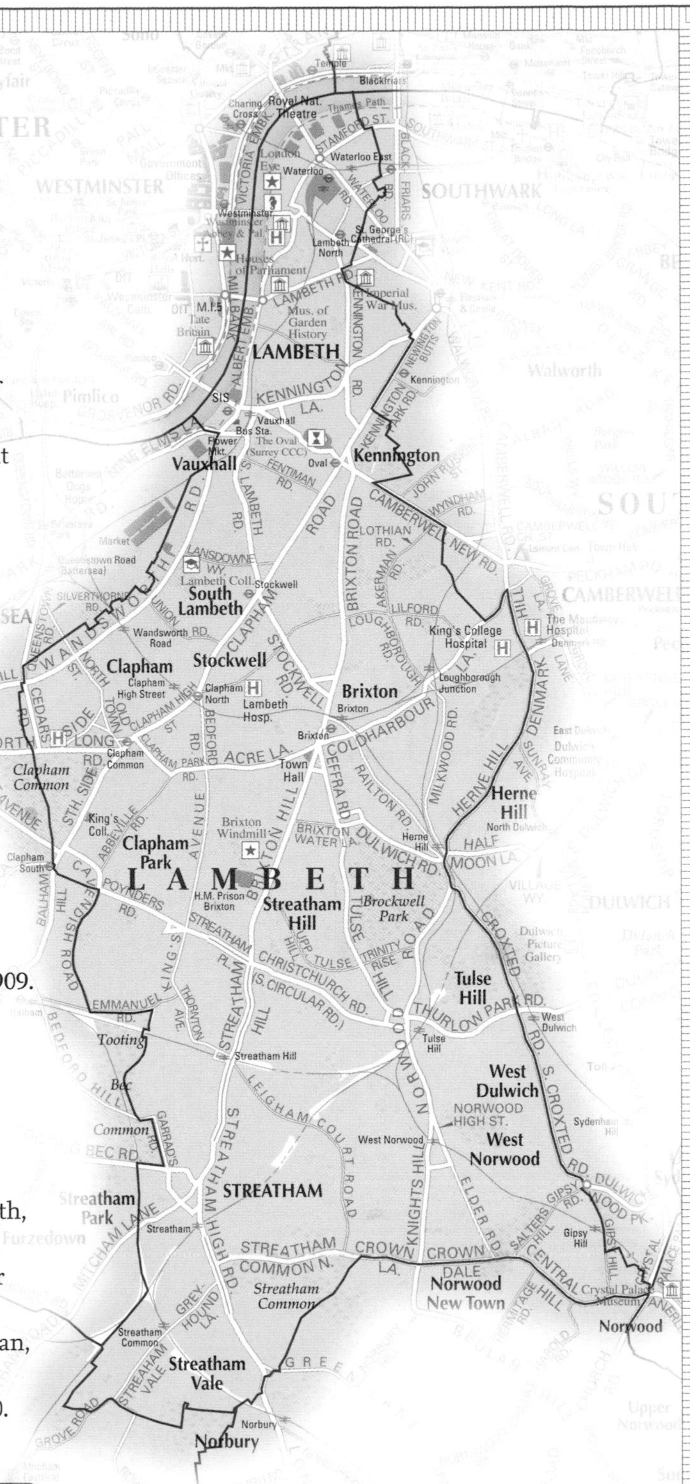

The Oval in August 2009 during the deciding Test Match of the Ashes series, which England won

John Bartholomew, Gazetteer of the British Isles (1887)
LAMBETH, *parl. bor. and par., Surrey, on r. Thames, in SW. of London, 3942 ac., pop. 253,699. Lambeth Palace (1197) has for centuries been the official residence of the Archbishops of Canterbury; the library contains records of the see dating from the 13th century. St Thomas' Hospital is situated on the Thames, opposite the Houses of Parliament. Lambeth Bridge is 1040 ft. long, with 3 spans of 280 ft. each. The bor. returns 4 members to Parliament (4 divisions–viz., North, Kennington, Brixton, and Norwood, 1 member for each division); the old parl. bor. of Lambeth (which included parts of Camberwell and Lambeth pars. and the whole of Newington par.) returned 2 members until 1885.*

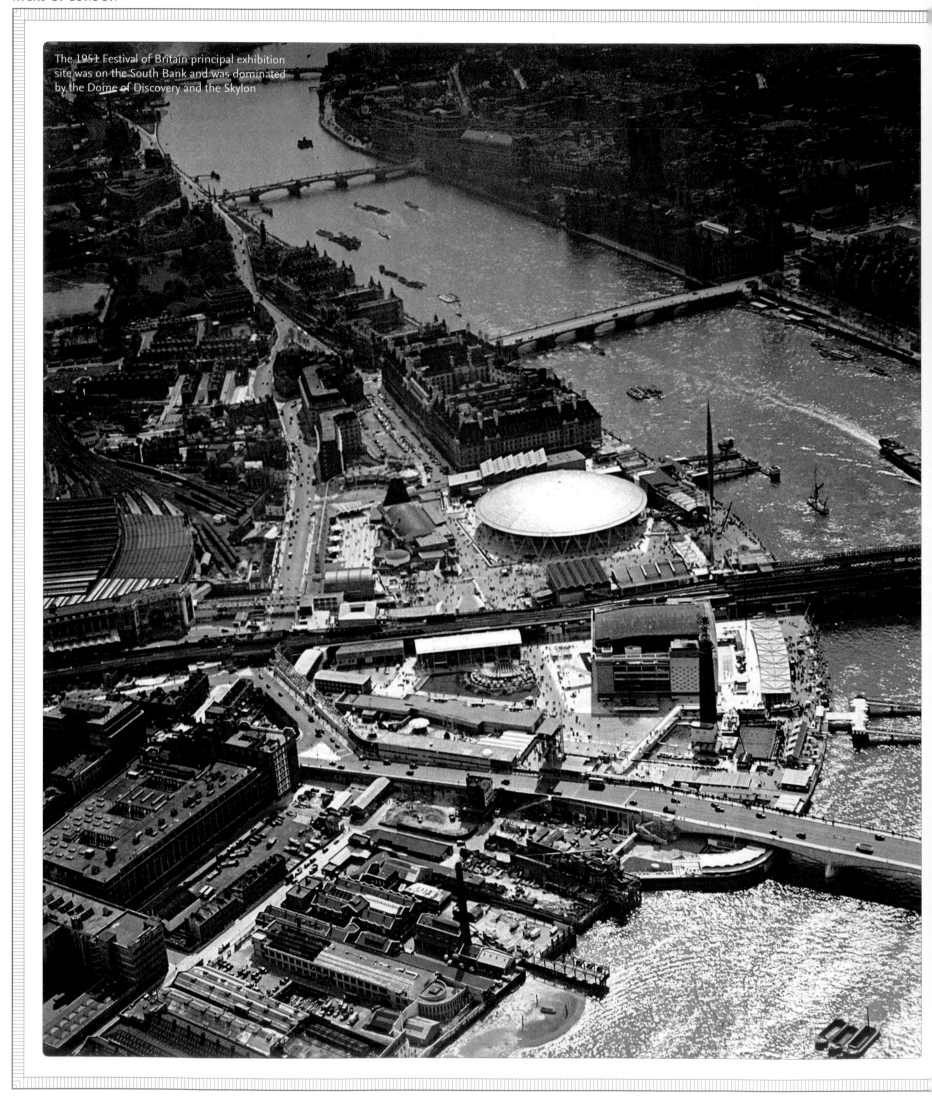

The 1951 Festival of Britain principal exhibition site was on the South Bank and was dominated by the Dome of Discovery and the Skylon

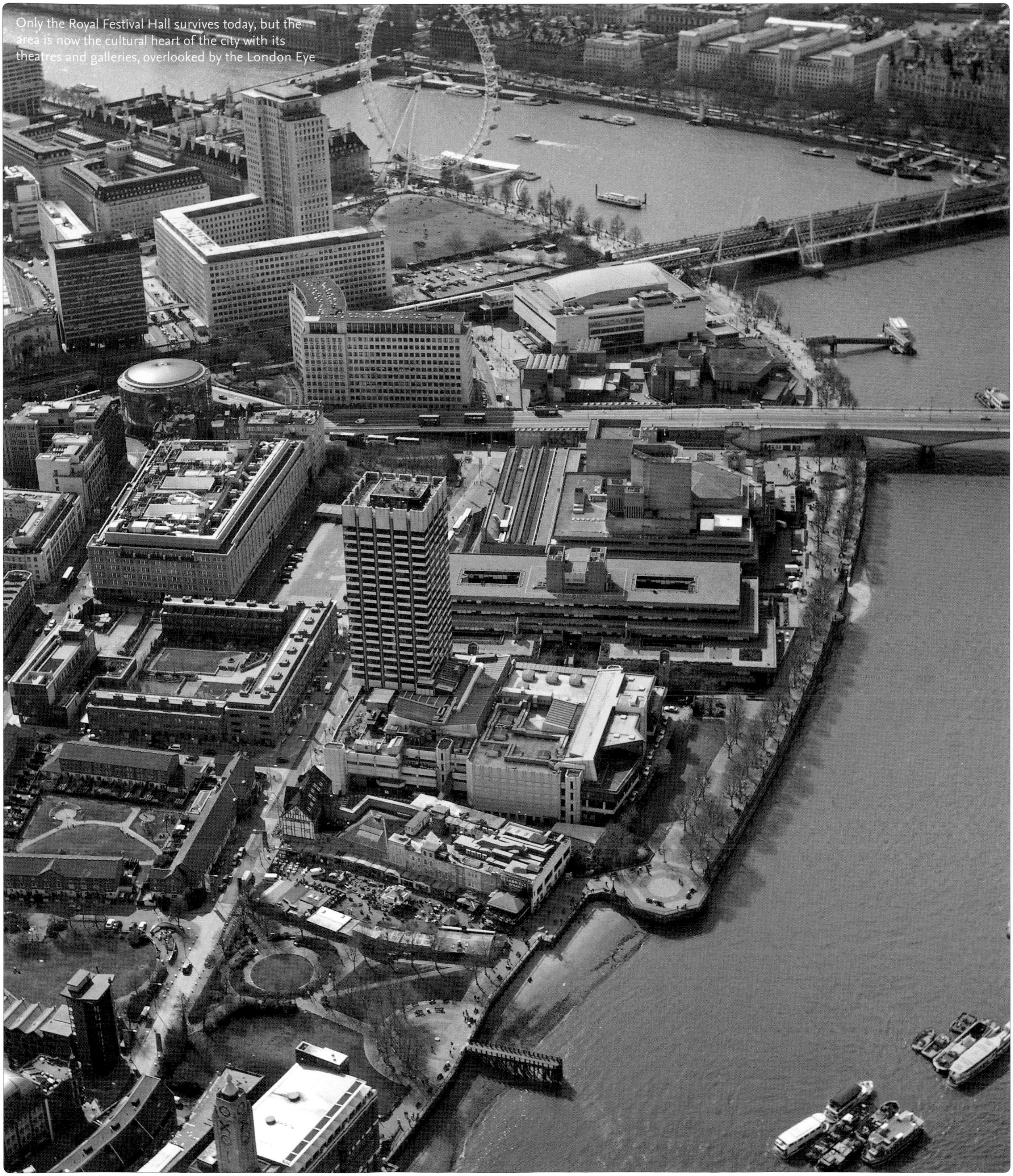

Only the Royal Festival Hall survives today, but the area is now the cultural heart of the city with its theatres and galleries, overlooked by the London Eye

A
B
C
D
1
2
3
4
119
223
289
STRAND
SOUTHWARK
LAMBETH
THE BORO
NEWING
WALW
VICTORIA EMBANKMENT
WESTMINSTER
LAMBETH
CITY
SOUTHWARK
River Thames
King's Reach
BLACKFRIARS
BLACKFRIARS MILLENNIUM PIER
TEMPLE
EMBANKMENT
CHARING CROSS
EMBANKMENT PIER
WATERLOO
WATERLOO EAST
SOUTHWARK
LAMBETH NORTH
ELEPHANT & CASTLE
KENNINGTON
WESTMINSTER
BLACKFRIARS BRI
WATERLOO BRI
WESTMINSTER BRI
LAMBETH BRI
HUNGERFORD BRI
MILLENNIUM BRIDGE
SOUTHWARK BRIDGE
WHITEHALL
PARLIAMENT ST
MILLBANK
STAMFORD ST
UPPER GROUND
THE CUT
UNION STREET
SOUTHWARK STREET
WESTMINSTER BR ROAD
BOROUGH ROAD
ST. GEORGE'S ROAD
LAMBETH ROAD
KENNINGTON ROAD
KENNINGTON LANE
KENNINGTON PARK ROAD
NEWINGTON BUTTS
NEWINGTON CAUSEWAY
WALWORTH ROAD
LONDON ROAD
LAMBETH PALACE ROAD
ALBERT EMBANKMENT
TATE MODERN
NATIONAL THEATRE
ROYAL FESTIVAL HALL
SOUTHBANK CENTRE
LONDON EYE
County Hall
HOUSES OF PARLIAMENT
St. Stephen's Tower (Big Ben)
WESTMINSTER ABBEY
ST. THOMAS' HOSP
LAMBETH PALACE GDNS
Lambeth Palace
ARCHBISHOP'S PARK
GERALDINE MARY HARMSWORTH PARK
IMPERIAL WAR MUS
TATE BRITAIN
MINISTRY OF DEFENCE
H.M. TREASURY
CABINET OFFICE
BANKSIDE PIER
BANKSIDE GALLERY
SHAKESPEAR GLOBE THEA
LONDON SOUTH BANK UNI
LON COLL OF COMMUNICATIONS
THE YOUNG VIC
THE OLD VIC
BFI IMAX
MILLBANK MILLENNIUM PIER
WESTMINSTER MILLENNIUM PIER
WATERLOO MILLENNIUM PIER
SAVOY PIER
Cleopatra's Needle
VICTORIA TOWER GARDENS
LAMBETH WK OPEN SPACE
H.M.S. PRESIDENT
H.Q.S. WELLINGTON MASTER MARINERS'
SOMERSET HOUSE
Sea Containers Ho
IBM
London Television Centre
DEPOT

E
F
G
H
264
224
1
2
3
4
MONUMENT
CANNON ST
TOWER HILL
TOWER GATEWAY
ROYAL MINT ST
TOWER OF LONDON
Upper Pool
LONDON BRIDGE HOSPITAL
LONDON BRIDGE CITY PIER
TOWER HAMLETS
SOUTHWARK
TOWER BRIDGE
ST. KATHARINE'S PIER
WAPPING
TOWER BRIDGE EXHIBITION
CITY HALL (Greater London Authority)
POTTERS FIELDS PARK
DESIGN MUSEUM
Pool of London
Lower Pool
Cherry Garden Pier
King's Stairs
Wapping Old Stairs
SOUTHWARK CATHEDRAL
BOROUGH HIGH ST.
TOOLEY STREET
LONDON BRIDGE
GUY'S HOSP
BERMONDSEY STREET
DRUID STREET
JAMAICA ROAD
BERMONDSEY
LONG LANE
GREAT DOVER STREET
TOWER BRIDGE RD
OLD KENT RD
BRICKLAYER'S ARMS ROUNDABOUT
GRANGE ROAD
SPA ROAD
BERMONDSEY SPA GDNS
SOUTHWARK PARK ROAD
Bricklayer's Arms Distribution Centre
MANDELA WAY
DUNTON ROAD
PATERSON PARK
SURREY SQUARE PARK
ROLLS ROAD
LEATHERMARKET GARDENS
TABARD GARDENS
KING'S COLLEGE (Hall Of Residence)
SOUTHWARK COLL
0
1/4
1/2 Mile
0.25
0.5
0.75 Kilometres

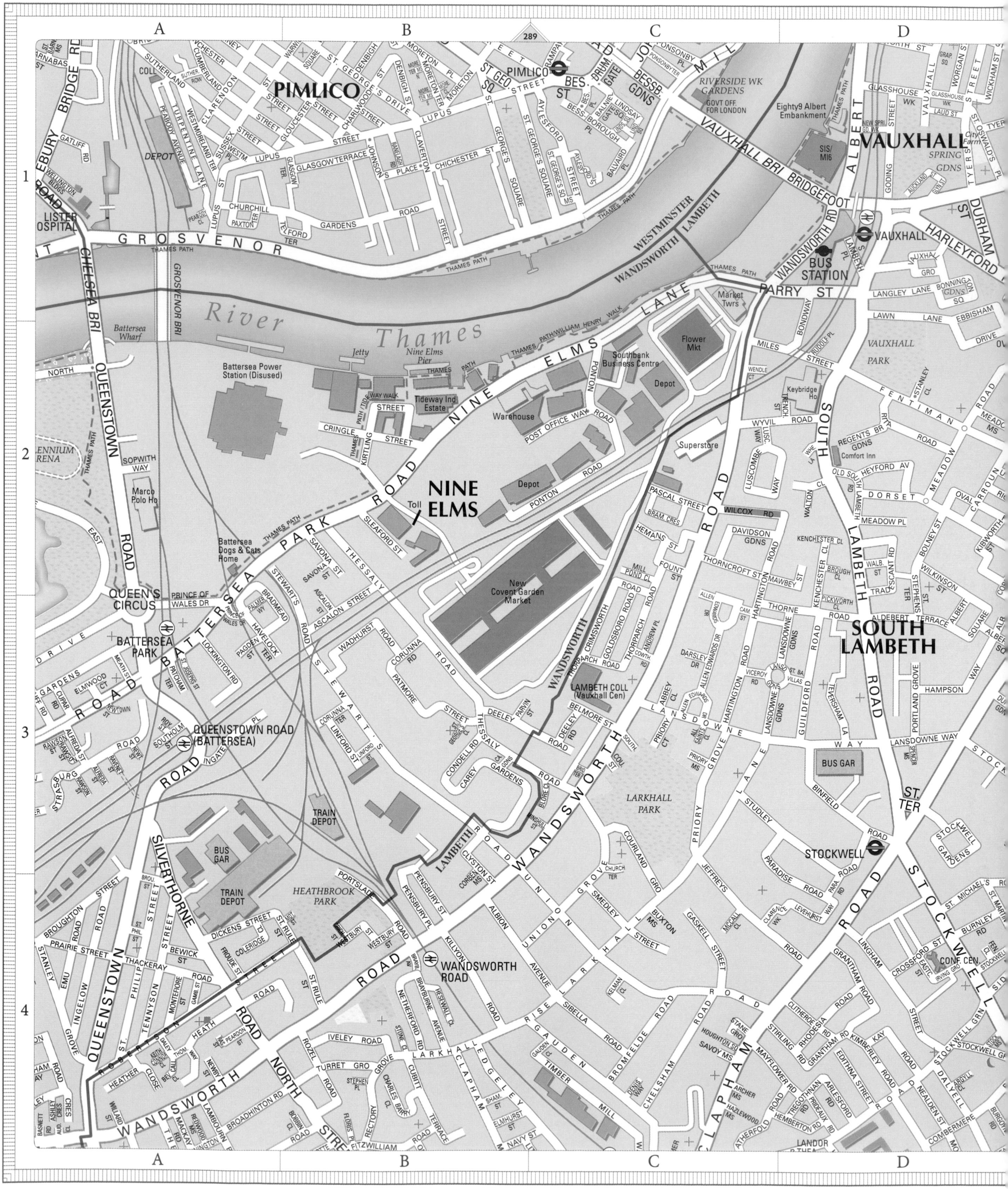
A
B
C
D
1
2
3
4
289
PIMLICO
Pimlico
VAUXHALL
Vauxhall
NINE ELMS
SOUTH LAMBETH
River Thames
Battersea Power Station (Disused)
New Covent Garden Market
Flower Mkt
Battersea Dogs & Cats Home
Battersea Wharf
Nine Elms Pier
Jetty
Tideway Ind Estate
Southbank Business Centre
Market Twrs
Warehouse
Depot
Superstore
Marco Polo Ho
Keybridge Ho
Comfort Inn
Eighty9 Albert Embankment
SIS/MI6
GOVT OFF. FOR LONDON
RIVERSIDE WK GARDENS
BUS STATION
Toll
QUEEN'S CIRCUS
BATTERSEA PARK
QUEENSTOWN ROAD (BATTERSEA)
WANDSWORTH ROAD
STOCKWELL
LAMBETH COLL (Vauxhall Cen)
BUS GAR
TRAIN DEPOT
HEATHBROOK PARK
LARKHALL PARK
VAUXHALL PARK
SPRING GDNS
CONF. CEN.
THAMES PATH
GROSVENOR ROAD
GROSVENOR BRI
CHELSEA BRI
CHELSEA BRIDGE RD
VAUXHALL BRIDGE
VAUXHALL BRIDGEFOOT
ALBERT EMBANKMENT
WANDSWORTH RD
NINE ELMS LANE
BATTERSEA PARK ROAD
QUEENSTOWN ROAD
SILVERTHORNE ROAD
WANDSWORTH ROAD
SOUTH LAMBETH ROAD
CLAPHAM ROAD
STOCKWELL ROAD
LANSDOWNE WAY
LARKHALL LANE
PRIORY GROVE
UNION ROAD
PARRY ST
HARLEYFORD ROAD
DURHAM ST
FENTIMAN ROAD
THESSALY ROAD
STEWART'S ROAD
PONTON ROAD
POST OFFICE WAY
CRINGLE STREET
KIRTLING STREET
PRINCE OF WALES DR
LUPUS STREET
ST. GEORGE'S DRIVE
ST. GEORGE'S SQUARE
CLAVERTON STREET
CHURCHILL GARDENS
ROAD NORTH
HEATHBROOK
ROBERTSON STREET

E
F
G
H
220
224
1
2
3
4
KENNINGTON
CAMBERWELL
STOCKWELL
KENNINGTON PARK
THE OVAL
SURREY CCC
OVAL
BURGESS PARK
Kart Track
BURGESS BUSINESS PARK
SURREY GDNS
FARADAY GARDENS
MYATT'S FIELDS PARK
MOSTYN GDNS
SLADE GDNS
MAX ROACH PARK
KING'S COLLEGE HOSPITAL
MAUDSLEY HOSPITAL
DENMARK HILL
CAMBERWELL GREEN
GREEK CATHEDRAL
SOUTHWARK COLL
CAMBERWELL COLL OF ARTS
WILLIAM BOOTH COLL
CITY & GUILDS OF LONDON ART SCH
GASWORKS GALLERY
BRIXTON ACADEMY
LOUGHBOROUGH JUNCTION
Butterfly Walk Shop Cen
BLUE ELEPHANT
WHITE BEAR
DEPOT
Superstore
SPORTS GRD
BUS GAR
CAMBERWELL NEW ROAD
CAMBERWELL ROAD
CAMBERWELL CHURCH ST
DENMARK HILL
KENNINGTON ROAD
KENNINGTON LANE
BRIXTON ROAD
ALBANY ROAD
WALWORTH ROAD
CHAMPION PK
LOUGHBOROUGH ROAD
COLDHARBOUR LANE
VASSALL ROAD
WYNDHAM ROAD
JOHN RUSKIN STREET
COOKS ROAD
CAMBERWELL GROVE
0
1/4
1/2 Mile
0
0.25
0.5
0.75 Kilometres

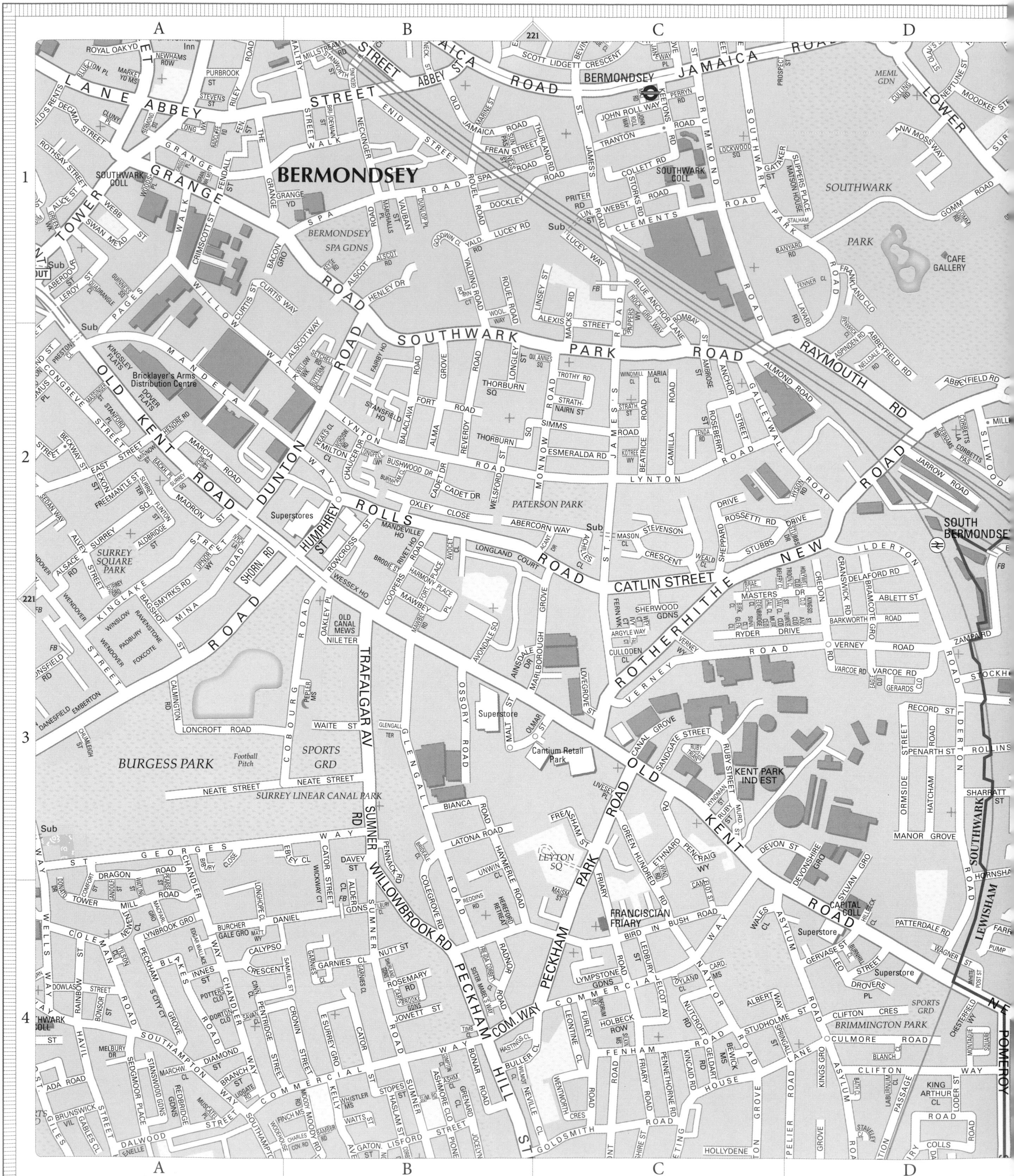
A
B
C
D
1
2
3
4
221
BERMONDSEY
SOUTHWARK PARK
PARK
CAFE GALLERY
BERMONDSEY SPA GDNS
SOUTHWARK COLL
Bricklayer's Arms Distribution Centre
SURREY SQUARE PARK
PATERSON PARK
BURGESS PARK
Football Pitch
SPORTS GRD
SURREY LINEAR CANAL PARK
LEYTON SQ
FRANCISCIAN FRIARY
KENT PARK IND EST
Cantium Retail Park
Superstores
Superstore
CAPITAL COLL
BRIMMINGTON PARK
SOUTH BERMONDSEY
JAMAICA ROAD
ABBEY STREET
GRANGE ROAD
TOWER BRIDGE ROAD
SPA ROAD
SOUTHWARK PARK ROAD
LYNTON ROAD
ROLLS ROAD
OLD KENT ROAD
DUNTON ROAD
CATLIN STREET
ROTHERHITHE NEW ROAD
RAYMOUTH RD
ORB STREET
VERNEY ROAD
ILDERTON ROAD
TRAFALGAR AV
WILLOWBROOK RD
PECKHAM PARK ROAD
PECKHAM HILL ST
COMMERCIAL WAY
ST GEORGES WAY
LOWER ROAD
DRUMMOND ROAD
CLEMENTS ROAD
BLUE ANCHOR LANE
CANAL GROVE
GLENGALL ROAD
NEATE STREET
LONCROFT ROAD
ASYLUM ROAD
CLIFTON WAY
LEWISHAM WAY

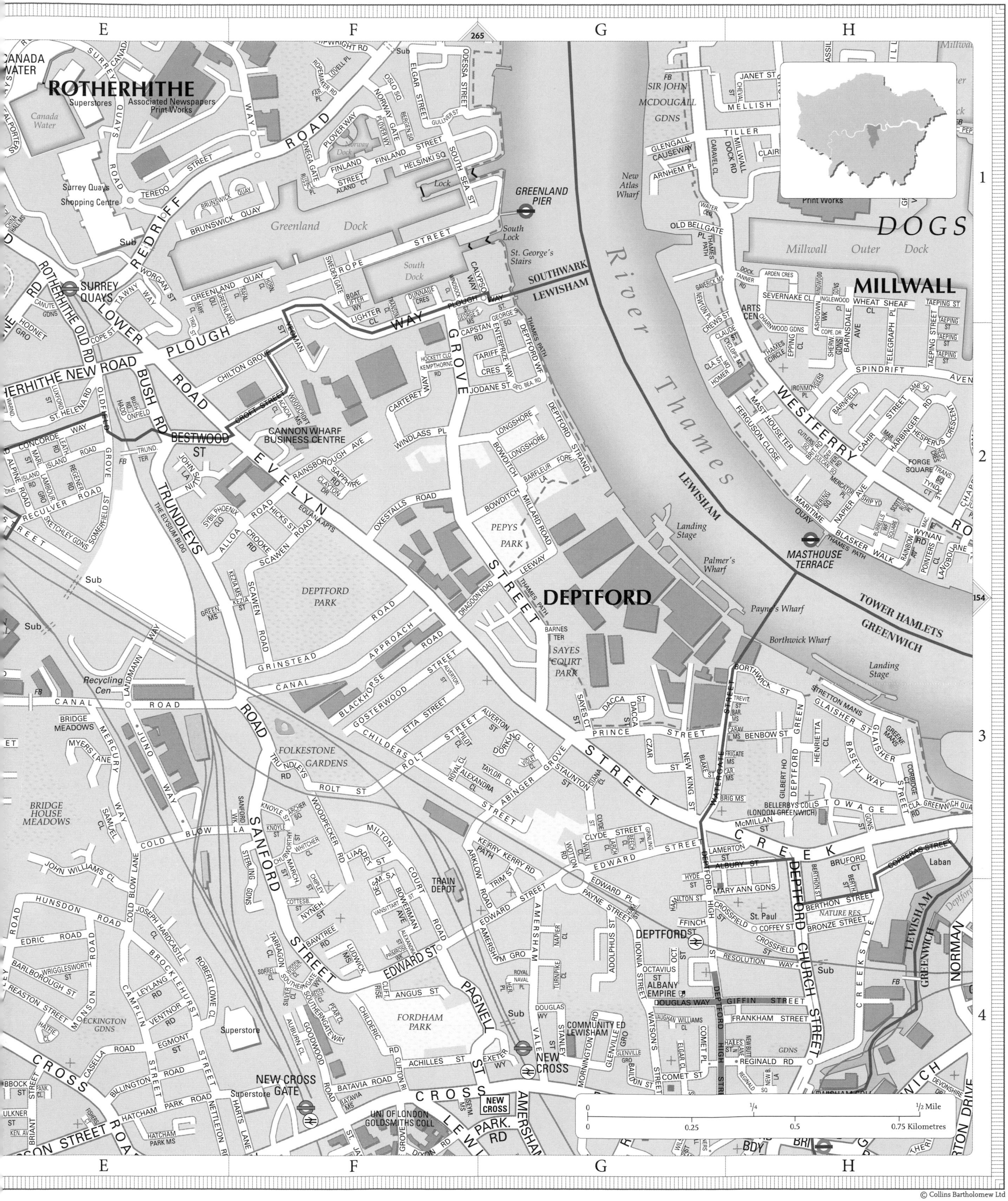
E
F
G
H
1
2
3
4
265
154
ROTHERHITHE
DEPTFORD
MILLWALL
DOGS
CANADA WATER
Canada Water
Superstores
Associated Newspapers Print Works
Surrey Quays Shopping Centre
SURREY QUAYS
GREENLAND PIER
Greenland Dock
South Dock
Norway Dock
South Lock
St. George's Stairs
New Atlas Wharf
SIR JOHN MCDOUGALL GDNS
Millwall Outer Dock
River Thames
Landing Stage
Palmer's Wharf
Payne's Wharf
Borthwick Wharf
MASTHOUSE TERRACE
SOUTHWARK
LEWISHAM
TOWER HAMLETS
GREENWICH
CANNON WHARF BUSINESS CENTRE
PEPYS PARK
DEPTFORD PARK
SAYES COURT PARK
FOLKESTONE GARDENS
BRIDGE HOUSE MEADOWS
BRIDGE MEADOWS
Recycling Cen.
TRAIN DEPOT
FORDHAM PARK
ECKINGTON GDNS
Superstore
NEW CROSS GATE
NEW CROSS
DEPTFORD
St. Paul
ALBANY EMPIRE
COMMUNITY ED LEWISHAM
UNI OF LONDON GOLDSMITHS COLL
BELLERBYS COLLS (LONDON GREENWICH)
NATURE RES.
Laban
SALTER ROAD
LOWER ROAD
REDRIFF ROAD
PLOUGH WAY
EVELYN STREET
GROVE STREET
PRINCE STREET
CREEK ROAD
DEPTFORD HIGH STREET
DEPTFORD CHURCH STREET
WESTFERRY ROAD
DEPTFORD STRAND
GRINSTEAD ROAD
CANAL APPROACH
CANAL ROAD
OXESTALLS ROAD
TRUNDLEYS ROAD
SANFORD STREET
ROLT STREET
ABINGER GROVE
EDWARD STREET
AMERSHAM VALE
NEW CROSS ROAD
LEWISHAM WAY
PAGNELL ST
CROSS
AMERSHAM
0
1/4
1/2 Mile
0.25
0.5
0.75 Kilometres

LONDON'S MARKETS AND SHOPS

London's markets arose out of the need to provide food and other goods for the people of the city. They first developed around Cheapside and, as the city grew, particular trades and markets developed in certain areas – the markets may have gone, but the City street names of Poultry, Bread Street, Milk Street, Fish Street Hill and Cornhill are a reminder to today's traders of earlier commodity markets. Among the survivors of markets established in medieval times are Smithfield, Leadenhall, Billingsgate and Borough markets. From the 17th century onwards, many new markets, including Covent Garden, were established, and as the city spread, so markets sprung up in the newly developing areas. Among the most well-known of the many other markets today are Bermondsey, Brick Lane, Brixton, Camden Lock, Camden Passage, Columbia Road Flower Market, Petticoat Lane, Portobello Road, Shepherd's Bush, Southall, Strutton Ground (in Victoria) and Walthamstow, one of Europe's longest street markets. Some markets specialize in food, clothes or antiques and most have special opening times and days. Other markets, though once general markets, have now become wholesale markets: Billingsgate (fish), Smithfield (meat), New Covent Garden (fruit and vegetable) and New Spitalfields (vegetables and flowers).

Covent Garden was originally a 'Convent Garden' owned by Westminster Abbey and was established as a market in 1670 to serve the new housing nearby. It became London's main fruit and vegetable market, providing a great contrast to the neighbouring Royal Opera House. The market moved to more spacious surroundings at Nine Elms in 1973 and the old market building, sitting in the middle of a square, is now a very popular shopping area and meeting place.

Billingsgate Market existed before 1327, for in that year Edward III granted it a charter prohibiting any other market to set up within a day's walk (around 10 km). Originally a general market, it became exclusively a fish market in the 16th century. The Old Billingsgate Market building in Lower Thames Street, built in 1876, is no longer a fish market, for Billingsgate Market moved to Poplar in 1982, where it is now Britain's largest inland fish market, selling around 25,000 tonnes of fish a year.

Smithfield, outside the City walls, was London's livestock market from the 10th century onwards, with cattle and sheep being driven on the hoof from many parts of England. The sale of live animals moved to Islington in the 1850s, but the meat market, one of Europe's most modern, has stayed on the same site and operates out of modernized Victorian market halls, selling 120,000 tonnes of produce a year.

Harrods, one of the world's largest and most famous department stores

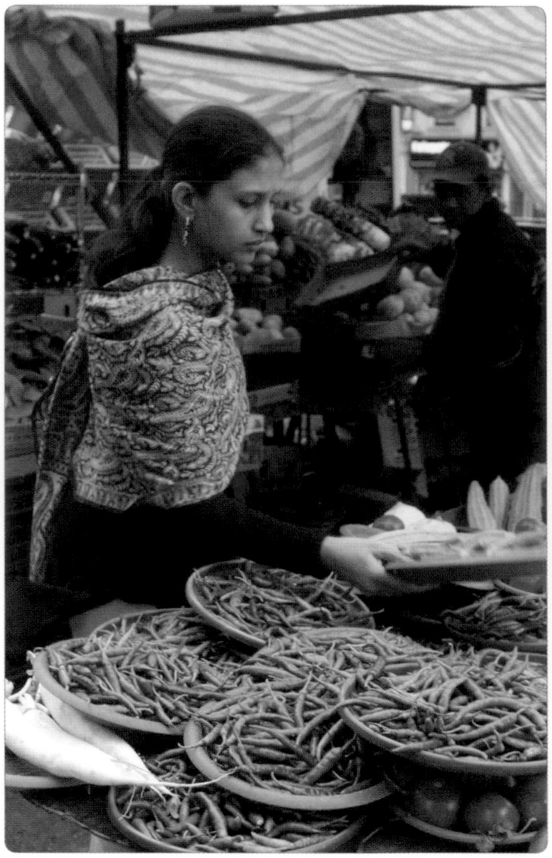
Whitechapel Market, Tower Hamlets

Covent Garden in the 1920s

From the 13th century, there was a market in Borough High Street, close by the southern end of London Bridge. In 1755, **Borough Market** was established on its present site and it became one of the largest food markets in Victorian London. It has had a recent renaissance as a retail market for high quality British and international food, with many producers having stalls.

London's shops

Shops first developed around markets and then moved west with the spread of the city. Many were established in the area around St James's Palace to meet the needs of the Royal Court, a function still performed by some shops in Mayfair. It was here that a Royal footman, William Fortnum, and Hugh Mason established their grocery shop in 1707. William Hamley's toyshop, then called 'Noah's Ark', was founded in 1760, while Hatchard's bookshop dates from 1797.

As the 19th century advanced, many of the famous London shops came into existence. Benjamin Harvey founded a store in 1813, and in 1820 his daughter and her husband, Colonel Nichols, began to run Harvey Nichols. Harrods was founded in 1849, John Lewis in 1863, Peter Jones in 1871 in Hackney and in 1877 at its present site on Sloane Square, Liberty's in 1874 and Selfridges in 1909.

As London's middle classes grew, so did the demand for consumer goods, not least to decorate their new houses. Shop owners realized that public transport could bring them customers more easily – William Whiteley started his department store in Westbourne Grove, close to Paddington station. By the 1890s he employed 6,000 staff at his 'immense symposium of the arts and industries of the world'. The first purpose-built department store was Bon Marché in Brixton, which opened in 1877, while the ultimate store, Selfridges, opened in Oxford Street in 1909, bringing an American style to British retailing.

Grocery chains also developed – J Sainsbury was established as a dairy in Drury Lane in 1869 and by 1914 had grown to 115 branches. Waitrose was founded in Acton in 1904, while Woolworths and Marks and Spencer also both brought their own retailing style to London at the start of the 20th century.

The shops of central London remain a vibrant part of London's economy, but more for visitors than residents, many of whom now shop at the large covered shopping malls, once just in Outer London, but coming ever closer to the centre, for example at Shepherd's Bush and Stratford.

Covent Garden has become popular for shopping and street entertainment since the early 1980s

Porters outside Billingsgate fish market mid 1920s – in the background on the right is the Monument

LEWISHAM

Population	264,500
Area	35 sq. km
Population density	7,560 per sq. km
Area of green space	8 sq. km
Jobs in borough	75,000
Average house price	£239,766

The borough of Lewisham is to the south of the Thames, with a short river frontage at Deptford. It includes New Cross, Lewisham, Blackheath, Catford, Forest Hill and Sydenham, and was formed in 1965 from the metropolitan boroughs of Lewisham and Deptford, taking the name of the town of Lewisham (from the Old English 'the settlement of Liof').

Though both the main settlements are on the River Ravensbourne, a site of watermills since the Domesday Book, they have very different histories. Deptford, originally a fording place across the Ravensbourne on the London to Canterbury road, really developed after Henry VIII selected it as one of his naval dockyards in 1513. As ships grew in size it became less suitable as a boatyard and instead became the main victualling centre for the navy until the yard closed in 1869. Thereafter, until 2000, it was used as a commercial dock. A few buildings remain from its period of prosperity; the most distinguished is the baroque St Paul's Church, designed by Thomas Archer in 1712–30. Lewisham was a small market town until the arrival of the railways, and later trams, in the latter part of the 19th century, when it and the surrounding settlements developed as residential areas for workers in central London. The population grew from 52,000 in 1851 to 185,000 in 1901, and it now has a growing and diverse population, with one in four people under 19 and over 40 per cent of residents from black or ethnic minority communities.

The largest employment sector is public administration, education and health which provides nearly 39 per cent of all jobs (compared with a London average of 22 per cent). The borough is primarily residential and many residents work in other areas of London. Lewisham is now a terminus for the Docklands Light Railway. Goldsmiths' College, part of the University of London is in New Cross and is internationally renowned for its creative art courses (Lucien Freud, Antony Gormley and Damien Hirst are among its alumni) and the Laban, one of the world's finest dance training institutions, has a stunning new building at Creekside designed by Herzog and de Meuron (who also designed Tate Modern). In Forest Hill is the Horniman Museum, which opened in 1901 in an art nouveau building designed by C. H. Townsend to house the collection of biological specimens and artefacts from around the world amassed by the tea merchant, Frederick John Horniman, which he gave to the people of London.

The Laban dance centre at Creekside, which won the Stirling architecture prize in 2003

FAMOUS FOR

It was in **Deptford** that Queen Elizabeth I knighted Sir Francis Drake in 1581, and that the playwright Christopher Marlowe was murdered in a drunken brawl in 1593.

The Kentish rebels led by Wat Tyler in the Peasants' Revolt of 1381 and the followers of Jack Cade's rebellion in 1450 both camped on open ground at **Blackheath**.

Blackheath Football Club is the oldest Rugby Union club in the world, having been founded in 1858 at the Princess of Wales pub in Blackheath. It was also here that the first English international team was organized, for a match against Scotland on 25 March 1871. The club now plays at the Rectory Field within the neighbouring borough of Greenwich.

Dietrich Bonhoeffer, the distinguished theologian who was executed for his resistance to Hitler in 1945, was pastor of the German Evangelical Church in **Forest Hill** from 1933 to 1935.

In the 1640s medicinal springs were found at Wells Park in **Sydenham**, and their bitter waters were very popular until the 19th century.

Sydenham became a popular place to live after the Crystal Palace was re-erected in the area. Camille Pissarro's 1871 painting 'The Avenue, Sydenham' (in the National Gallery) catches the feel of the area in those prosperous times.

FAMOUS PEOPLE

Frederick William Lanchester, car and aircraft designer and engineer, born Lewisham, 1868.
James Elroy Flecker, poet and playwright, born Lewisham, 1884.
Leslie Howard (*born* Leslie Howard Steiner), actor and film director, born Forest Hill, 1893.
Sir Dudley Stamp, geographer, born Catford, 1898.
James Robertson Justice, actor, born Lewisham, 1907.
Patience Strong (*born* Winifred Emma May) author and poet, born Catford, 1907.
Ernest William [Jim] Swanton, cricket commentator, born Forest Hill, 1907.
Ronald Frederick (R. F.) Delderfield, author and playwright, born New Cross, 1912.
Sir Denis Thatcher, businessman and husband of Margaret Thatcher, born Lewisham, 1915.
Thomas Patrick Keating, artist, restorer, and admitted faker, born Forest Hill, 1917.
Bill Wyman (*born* William George Perks), bass guitarist with the Rolling Stones 1962–92, born Lewisham, 1936.
Ginger Baker (Peter Edward Baker), rock drummer, especially with Cream, born Lewisham, 1939.
Sid Vicious (*real name* Simon John Beverley; *formerly* Simon John Ritchie), rock musician, born Lewisham, 1957.

Mosaic artwork, Horniman Museum entrance

Ben Elton, writer and comedian, born Catford, 1959.
Alexander McQueen, fashion designer, born Lewisham, 1969.
Jude Law, actor, born Lewisham, 1972.

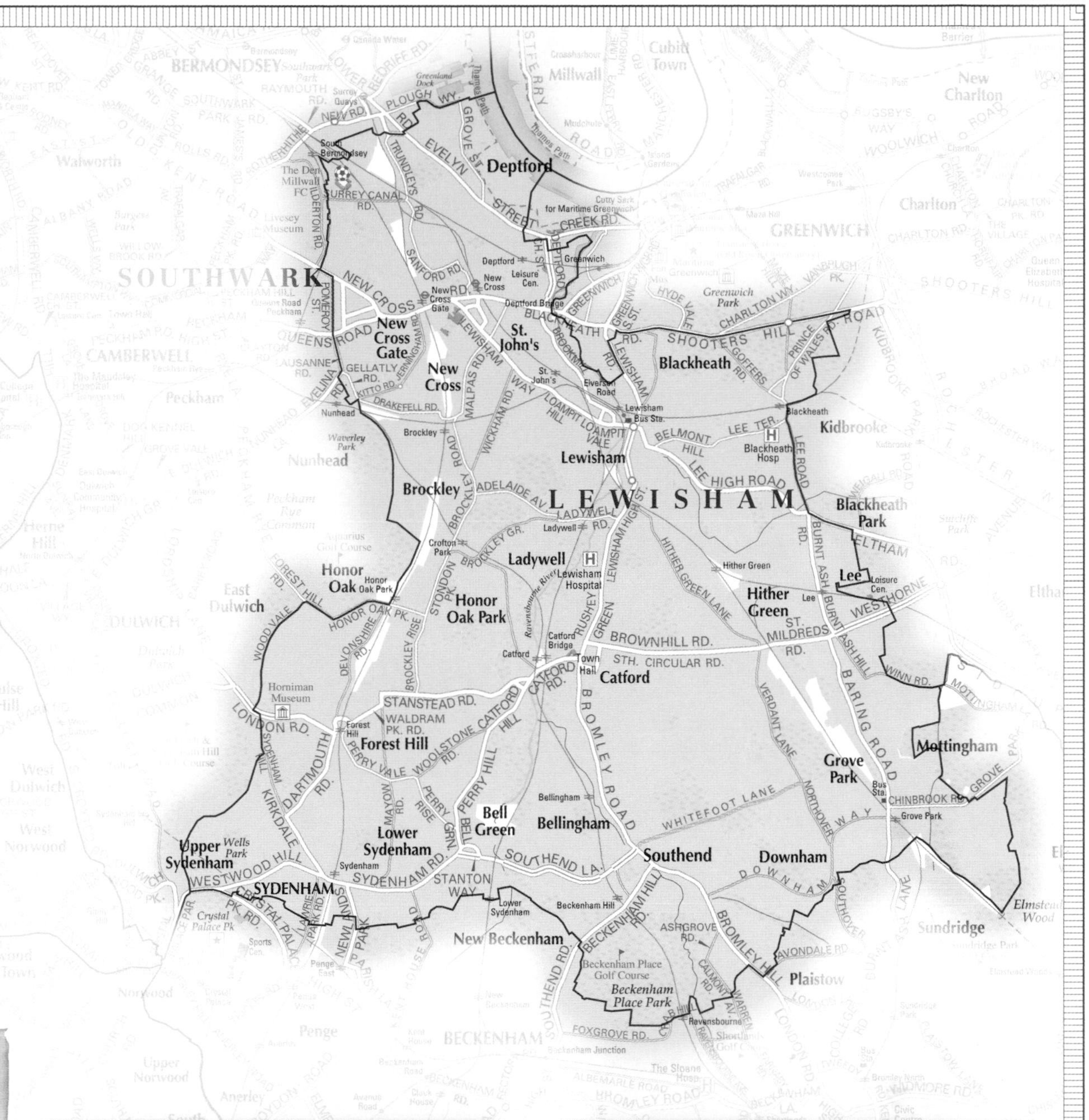

John Bartholomew, Gazetteer of the British Isles (1887)
LEWISHAM, *parl. bor., par., and SE. suburb of London with ry. sta. (Lewisham Junction), Kent, on river Ravensbourne, 4 miles SE. of St Paul's – par., 5774 ac., pop. 53,065; pad. bor. (including also the par. of Lee), 7012 ac., pop. 67,500; 1 Bank; has large nurseries. Lewisham returns 1 member to Parliament; It was made a parl. bor. in 1885.*

DEPTFORD.– *parl. bor., consisting of the par. of Deptford St Paul, Kent and Surrey, on Ravensbourne rivulet and river Thames, 3 miles SE. of London Bridge by rail and immediately W. of Greenwich, 1575 ac., pop. 76,752. Deptford has engineering works, some mfrs. of earthenware, soap, and chemicals, and, in the neighbourhood, excellent market gardens. The old naval dockyard was discontinued in 1869; it was filled up and converted into a foreign cattle-market, which was abolished in 1873. The royal victualling-yard, the most important in the kingdom, is still maintained. The corporation of Trinity House have at D. an hospital for master mariners. Of Sayes Court, which figures in Scott's Kenilworth, and which was the residence of Peter the Great while he was studying shipbuilding at D., only the garden now remains. D. returns 1 member to Parl.; it was made a parl. bor. in 1885.*

All Saints' Church, Blackheath, consecrated in 1858

The clock tower of the Horniman Museum, Forest Hill

HOUSING IN LONDON

There are over 3.4 million households in London. The city has some of the most expensive houses in the world but also has a higher percentage of council housing than Britain as a whole. The scale of housing disparity was reinforced in April 2011 when it was revealed that a Ukrainian billionaire had paid £135 million for a three-storey penthouse apartment at One Hyde Park, reputedly London's most exclusive new development. The different types of household tenure give an indication of some of the variations, both between London and the rest of Britain and between different areas of London.

TYPES OF HOUSING TENURE IN LONDON IN 2009

Housing type	Number	Percentage of total	UK percentage of total
Owned outright	715,000	21	31
Purchased on a mortgage	1,046,000	31	36
Rented from local authority	536,000	16	11
Rented from housing Association	310,000	9	8
Private landlord	690,000	20	12
Other private rented	118,000	4	3

As one would expect there are great variations across the boroughs:
Owned outright: from 9 per cent (Tower Hamlets) to 38 per cent (Bexley);
Purchased on a mortgage: from 15 per cent (Westminster) to 44 per cent (Sutton);
Rented from a local authority: from 2 per cent (Bromley) to 34 per cent (Southwark);
Rented from a private landlord: from 6 per cent (Havering) to 34 per cent (Newham).

Belgrave Square, one of the grandest 19th-century squares in London

How London's housing has changed
Prior to the Great Fire of London in 1666, most London houses were timber-framed and built very close together – the Ancient House in Walthamstow provides a surviving example of such housing. After the Great Fire, under the terms of the London Building Act of 1667, buildings had to be built of brick or stone and over the succeeding years further regulations were applied. Examples can be seen in Fournier Street in Spitalfields and in a house built in 1710 on Bankside in Southwark.

As London grew, building started on open land and this produced the planned streets of elegant Georgian brick terraces that appeared in Bloomsbury and Mayfair, punctuated by open squares – Russell Square and Grosvenor Square for example. This development of a formal urban landscape continued into the 19th century with the great terraces of Belgravia and then South

The annual *Metro-Land* magazine encouraged people to move to the suburbs in the 1920s

Terraced housing on the Becontree Estate, the largest public housing development in London

The partial collapse of Ronan Point tower block in Newham, 1968

Kensington, while they reached their most triumphant expression in the monumental stucco terraces that John Nash designed for Regent's Park in the early 19th century.

As the growth of the city continued, the need for housing for the new middle class increased, and across London developments of terraces of smaller Victorian brick houses stretched ever outwards. These were followed by the development of garden suburbs, such as Bedford Park and Hampstead Garden Suburb, with planned green space and private gardens providing an enhanced environment. Some of these features were used in the commercial suburban spread of London after World War I, typified by the development of 'Metroland' adjacent to the Metropolitan rail line out to Ruislip, Uxbridge and Amersham.

But while housing for the better off in London improved, the city also had many slum areas, vividly described in the works of Charles Dickens and the evocative engravings of the French artist Gustav Doré. The cholera outbreaks of the 1850s reinforced the need for improvements to be made. Charitable housing societies began to build model housing for workers. They were followed by larger organizations including the Peabody Trust (established by George Peabody, a London-based American banker). After the formation of the London County Council in the late 1880s, it, too, started to provide housing for rent. After World War I, it was building major estates both within central London and on open sites at the edge of London – such as the 27,000-home Becontree Estate in Dagenham and the 9,000-home St Helier Estate in Sutton.

Council-provided housing continued after World War II to replace damaged and destroyed housing and to clear slums, though one solution, the tower block, proved unpopular and disrupted once socially coherent communities. After the partial collapse of twenty-two-storey Ronan Point block of flats in 1968, further developments involved only low-rise buildings. New building of council housing went into a major decline in the 1980s as a result of government policies (including giving the tenants the right to buy their homes), and housing associations have been unable to fill the growing shortfall in social housing. From the 1980s onwards, private housing (particularly in the form of flats) have formed a major part of the redevelopment of the Docklands and the Thames riverside. An alternative approach is provided by the Peabody Trust's BedZed low carbon houses at Beddington in South London.

Residential building in the Docklands. Large areas of the Docklands were developed for residential use in the 1980s

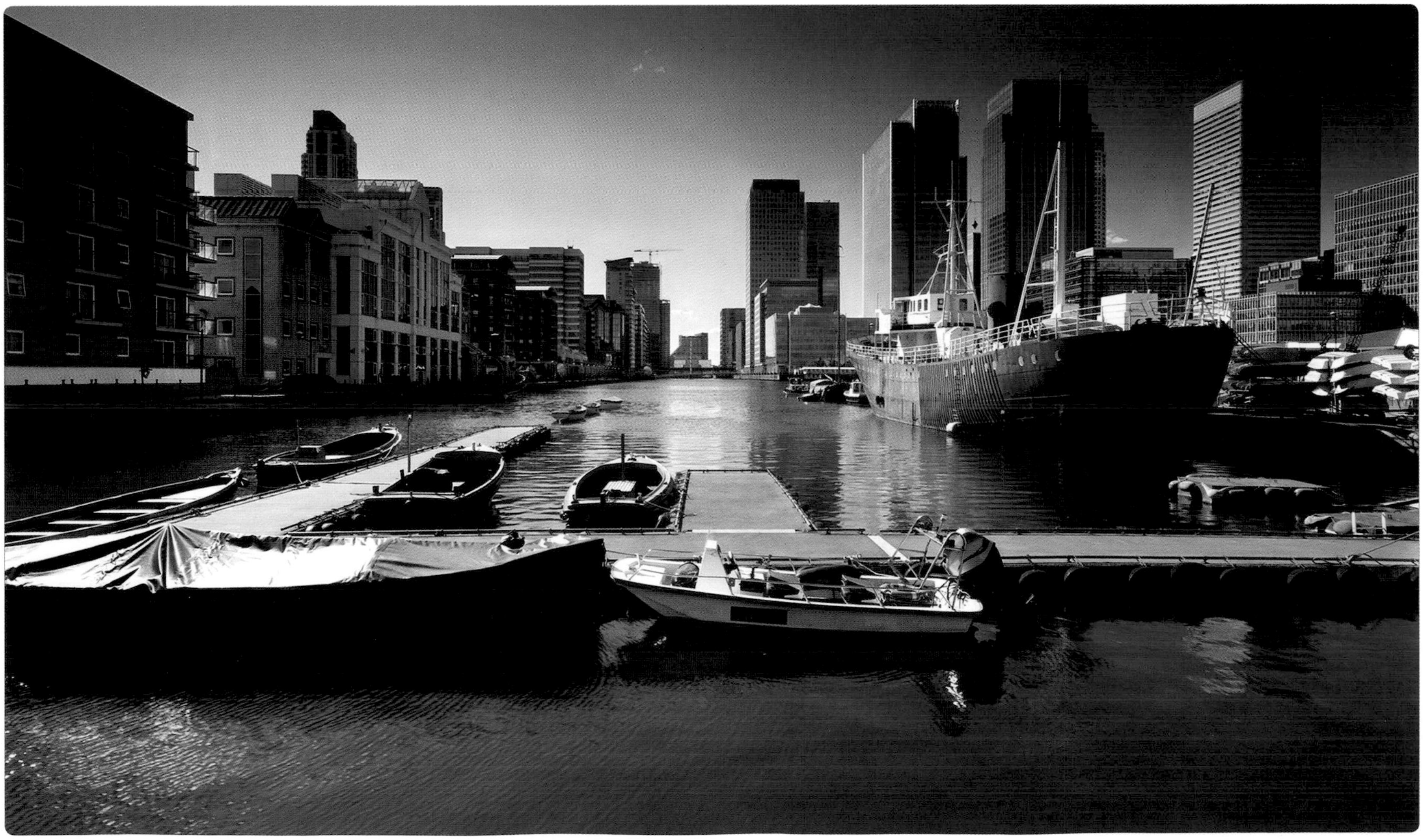

New apartment buildings, on the left, form part of the Canary Wharf development

MERTON

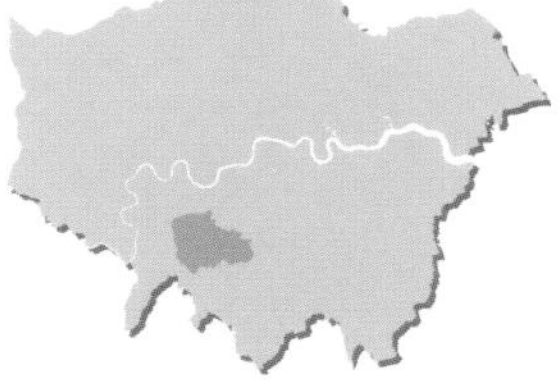

Population	206,400
Area	38 sq. km
Population density	5,452 per sq. km
Area of green space	13 sq. km
Jobs in borough	79,000
Average house price	£365,097

The borough of Merton takes its name from the Anglo-Saxon settlement of Merton ('farm by the pool'), sited by the banks of the Wandle, close to where the Roman road from London to Chichester crossed the river. The borough was formed from the municipal boroughs of Mitcham and Wimbledon, and Merton and Morden Urban District, all traditionally part of Surrey.

Snuff Mill and the River Wandle, Morden Hall Park

The main settlements had a long history before becoming London suburbs in the 19th and 20th centuries. Merton was the site of a large and powerful Augustinian priory, founded in 1114. Henry VI's coronation was held there and Thomas Becket and Nicholas Breakspear (who became the only English pope) were educated there. Only the foundations of the chapter house remain, hiding under a new road. The area around Mitcham was farmed in Roman times, and, until suburban housing was built from the 19th century onwards, was a major centre of lavender and watercress cultivation. Morden remained a village until the arrival of the City and South London Railway (now the Northern line) in 1926, while Wimbledon was connected to central London by train in 1838 and really developed in the late 19th century. The growth in population shows this change – in 1851 the population was 7,300, in 1901 it was 63,300, and in 1931 it was 154,300. The current population is more diverse than many London boroughs –73 per cent of the population in 2007 was white, nearly 12 per cent south Asian, and 8 per cent black.

Many small industries such as snuff and tobacco were based by the side of the Wandle, and with the arrival of the Huguenots in the late 17th century came textile bleaching and printing. By the late 19th century both William Morris and Liberty's produced textiles at Merton Abbey Mills, now the site of a popular weekend market and craft fair. Today around 64,000 residents travel outside the borough to work. Within the borough, 25.6 per cent of jobs are in the retail, hotels and restaurant sector (compared with a London average of 21 per cent) and 11.5 per cent in manufacturing and construction (compared with a London average of 6 per cent). For two weeks in late June, however, all attention is focused on the borough for the All England Tennis Club's Championships at Wimbledon (see page 234).The Championships celebrated its 125th anniversary in 2011.

Prize presentation at the Wimbledon Tennis Championships, 2010

FAMOUS FOR

Lord Nelson lived at **Merton Place** from 1801 until his death. The house was demolished in 1823 – the Nelson Arms pub on Merton High Street is on the site of the lodge gates and entrance to Merton Place.

John Innes, a city merchant, laid out the residential area of **Merton Park** from the 1860s, a precursor of the garden suburb. His name is now better known for garden compost created by the John Innes Horticultural Institution which he founded, and which was based in Merton Park until 1948.

The **Baitul Futuh Mosque** in Morden opened in 2003 and is one of the largest purpose-built mosques in Europe. It is able to accommodate around 3,000 worshippers of the Ahmadiyya Muslim Community, a sect not recognised by other branches of Islam.

Wimbledon and Putney Commons provide 460 hectares of open woodland, scrubland, heathland and recreation areas, featuring a great variety for flora and fauna. In the centre of Wimbledon Common is a restored hollow-

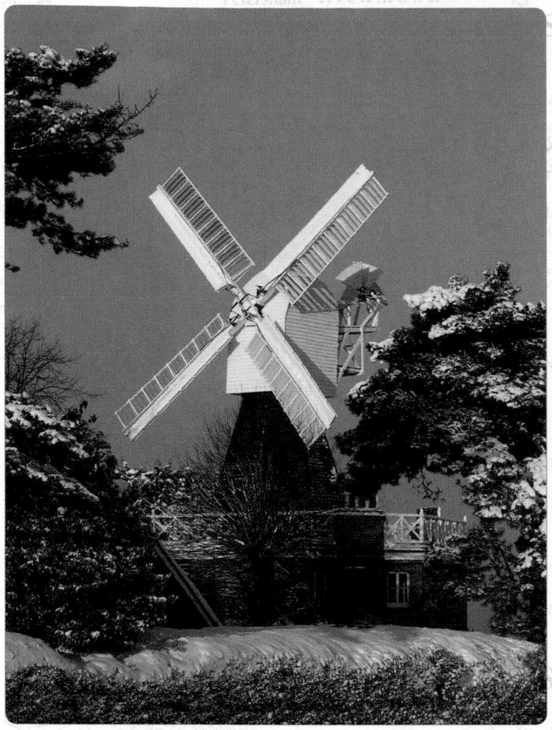

Wimbledon Windmill, restored as a museum on Wimbledon Common

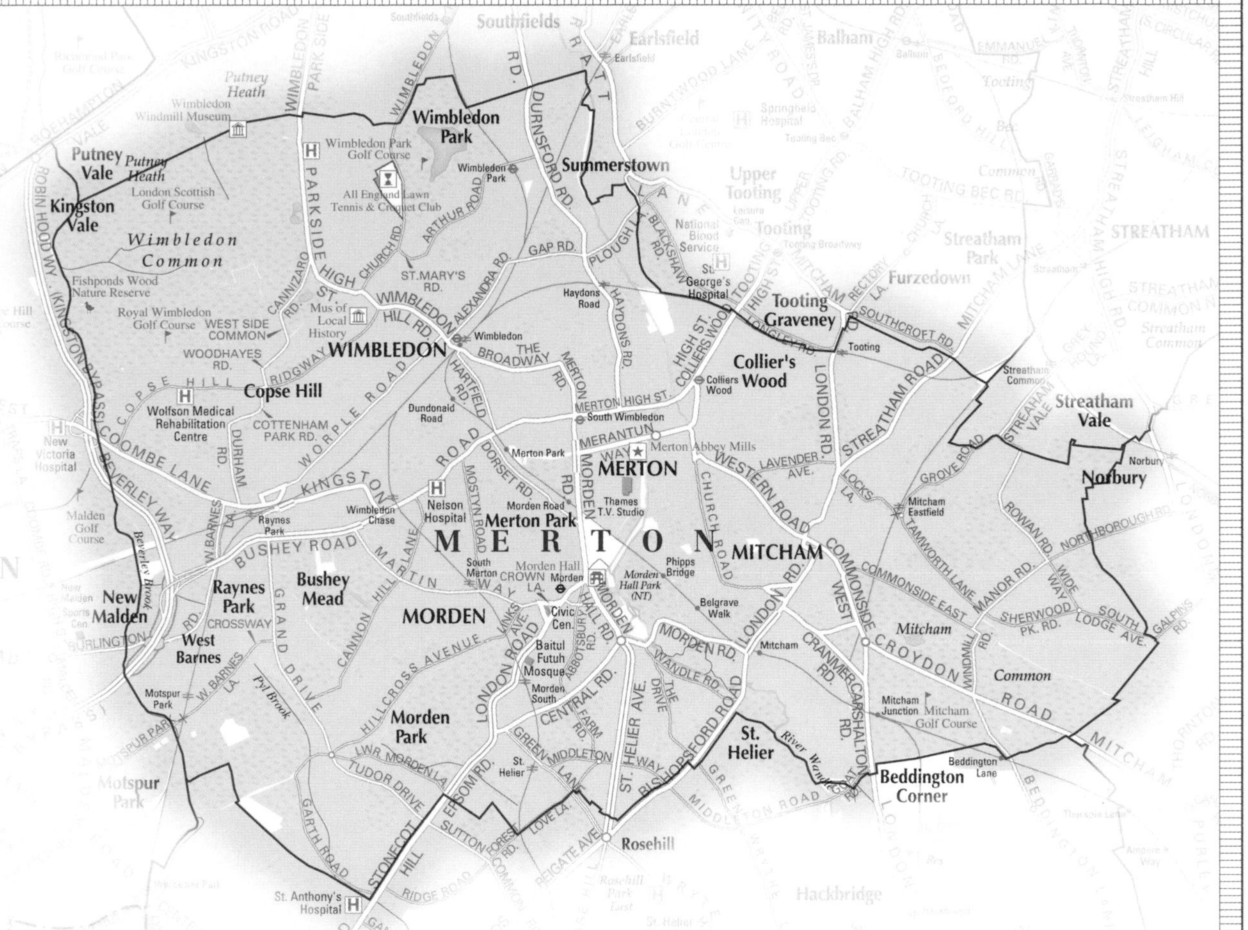

post windmill, built in 1817, and a windmill museum.

The **Wat Buddhapadipa** in Wimbledon is the only Thai Theravada Buddhist temple in Europe. The Uposotha Hall is of a traditional Thai design and was inaugurated by the elder sister of the King of Thailand in 1982.

Mitcham Eastfields railway station opened in 2008 – the first new suburban railway station in south London since World War II.

FAMOUS PEOPLE

Georgiana, **Duchess of Devonshire** [*née* Spencer], political hostess, born Wimbledon, 1757.

Sibyl, **Lady Colefax** [*née* Halsey], hostess and interior decorator, born Wimbledon, 1874.

Robert Graves, poet, born Wimbledon, 1895.

Georgette Heyer, romantic novelist, born Wimbledon, 1902.

Lancelot Lionel Ware, founder of Mensa, born Mitcham, 1915.

John Randall Bratby, artist, born Wimbledon, 1928.

Annie Ross, jazz singer and actress, born Mitcham, 1930.

Raymond Briggs, writer and illustrator, born Wimbledon Park, 1934.

Oliver Reed, actor, born Wimbledon, 1938.

Alex Stepney, footballer (goalkeeper), born Mitcham, 1942.

Benjamin (Ben) John Pimlott, historian and political commentator, born Merton, 1945.

Alan Pardew, footballer and football manager, born Wimbledon, 1961.

Alec Stewart, Surrey and England cricketer, born Merton, 1963.

Fay Ripley, actress, born Wimbledon, 1966.

The Nelson Arms, Merton High Street

John Bartholomew, Gazetteer of the British Isles (1887)

WIMBLEDON, *town and par., Surrey, at the NE. extremity of Wimbledon Common, 7½ miles SW. of Waterloo Station, London, by rail, 3220 ac. (47 water), pop. 15,950. Good residences, chiefly modern villas, are numerous, many families having been attracted to Wimbledon by the salubrity of the climate, Wimbledon Common being the most breezy bit of open country adjoining London. There is a golfing course on the Common, where also the annual competition of the National Rifle Association is held in July. At the S. of the Common there was formerly an entrenched camp.*

MERTON, *par. and vil. (ry. sta. Wimbledon and Merton), Surrey, on river Wandle, 3½ miles SW. of Clapham Junction and 7¼ miles SW. of Waterloo sta., London, 1765 ac., pop. 2480; has remains of a priory (1115). which became a factory for calico printing; Merton Place, where Lord Nelson lived from October 1801 to May 1803, has been pulled down.*

SPORTING LONDON

Sport has always played an important part in London life. Some traditional sports only remain in street names – Newington Butts (near the Elephant and Castle) is named after the archery butts of a medieval shooting ground. Others, such as boxing have a long history – the first rules of boxing were devised by Jack Broughton, a Wapping waterman, in 1743. While football and the Olympics are looked at elsewhere in the book, there are many other hallowed sporting sites.

Twickenham Rugby Football Stadium

The Rugby Football Union (RFU) was formed after a meeting of twenty-one rugby clubs at the Pall Mall Restaurant in 1871. After thirty years the RFU felt the need for a national stadium and a former market garden in Twickenham was purchased in 1907. The stadium opened in 1909, being referred to by some as the 'Cabbage Patch'. It has been modified and enlarged many times since then. The current stadium was completed in 2009 and accommodates 82,000 spectators, making it the largest dedicated Rugby Union stadium in the world.

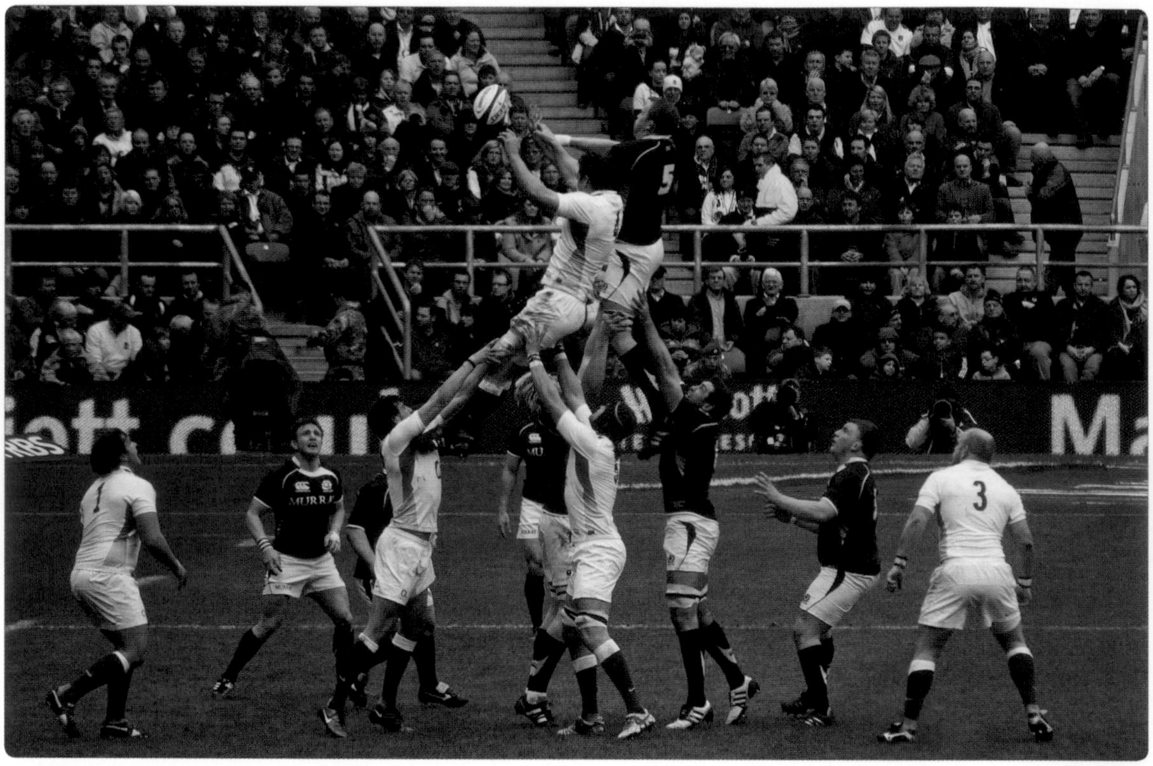

England against Scotland at Twickenham, 2011

England against Scotland at Twickenham in the 1920s

Lord's Cricket Ground

Cricket was a popular sport in 18th-century London. Enthusiasts from the Star and Garter Tavern in Pall Mall played cricket on fields in Islington, but they wished for a private ground. They asked the help of Thomas Lord, who took out a lease on some land in Marylebone in 1787, and his ground became the home of the Marylebone Cricket Club (the MCC). Lord moved the ground further out as London expanded, settling on its current site, some former duck ponds, in St John's Wood in 1814. The ground can now accommodate around 32,000 spectators in a range of buildings including the iconic Victorian Pavilion and the unashamedly modern Media Centre that opened in 1999.

The Oval Cricket Ground

The Oval in Kennington is the home of Surrey County Cricket Club. It opened in 1845 on the site of a former market garden, on land leased from the Duchy of Cornwall. The ground saw the first Test match against Australia in 1880 and, more surprisingly, it was the site of the first football international (between England and Scotland) in 1870. The ground now holds 23,500 spectators and was renamed the Kia Oval in 2011.

Wimbledon

In 1868 the All England Croquet Club was established off Worple Road, Wimbledon. In 1875, tennis was introduced to the club and quickly proved popular – in 1877 the club was renamed the All England Croquet and Lawn Tennis Club and the first Wimbledon tennis tournament was held. In 1922 the club, now the All England Lawn Tennis and Croquet Club, moved to its present site at Church Road. There are nineteen grass tournament courts and twenty-two grass practice courts. The Centre Court seats 15,000 spectators and from 2009, benefited from a retractable roof to allow play to continue when it rains.

The Hurlingham Club

The Hurlingham Club is on the banks of the Thames at Fulham and has been home to a number of sports. The club was established in 1867 to promote pigeon shooting – live pigeons were released for shooting up to 1905. Polo was played there from 1874, shortly after the sport was introduced from India, until 1939, and the British governing body of the sport remains the Hurlingham Polo Association. Croquet then replaced polo, and the club became the headquarters of the Croquet Association from 1959 to 2002. Through all these changes, the Hurlingham Club has remained a private members' club.

Greyhound racing

Whilst there is no horse racing within Greater London, there are some greyhound racing tracks, whose origins go back to the 1920s, when the sport arrived from the USA. Three London tracks continue to operate – at Wimbledon, Crayford and Romford. Haringey was the largest stadium, operating from 1927 to 1987 with a capacity of 50,000, while Walthamstow Stadium ('the Stow'), perhaps London's most famous track, closed in 2008.

Centre Court, with its retractable roof, Wimbledon

The Media Centre at Lord's Cricket Ground

1875 depiction of the Oxford and Cambridge Boat Race course, the same course that is used today

Rowing

Competitive rowing on the Thames has a long history – the oldest annual sporting event in Britain is Doggett's Coat and Badge race over 7.25 km (4.5 miles) between London Bridge and Cadogan Pier, first rowed in 1715. In 1829 the first Oxford and Cambridge Boat Race was held at Henley and it was not until 1845 that the current course of 6.78 km (4 miles and 374 yards) from Putney to Mortlake was established. Over 250,000 spectators crowd along the banks of the Thames to watch this annual event.

The London Marathon

The London Marathon has become one of the most recognized sporting events held in London and yet was only thirty years old in 2011. Its origins go back to two runners, Chris Brasher and John Disley, who took part in the 1979 New York Marathon, and then promoted the idea for holding such an event in London. The first London Marathon was run on 29 March 1981. On the day 7,055 runners started the race and 6,255 finished on a spectacular route from Blackheath to Constitution Hill by Buckingham Palace. The race caught the imagination of both runners and spectators. For the 1982 event there were more than 90,000 applications by runners (and 16,350 starters) and it has grown ever since. In 2011 there were over 125,000 applicants and 35,643 runners. The Men's event was won by the Kenyan Emmanuel Mutai in 2 hours, 4 minutes and 40 seconds, breaking the previous London Marathon record by half a minute. The Women's event was won by the Kenyan Mary Keitany as the second-fastest runner in a time of 2 hours 19 minutes and 19 seconds; Britain's Paula Radcliffe holds the record at 2 hours, 15 minutes and 25 seconds.

The route of the London Marathon, which is 42 km and 195 m (26 miles and 365 yd) long, has remained basically unchanged since its inception. It starts at Blackheath, above Greenwich, and then heads east through Charlton and Woolwich before turning west to Greenwich and along the southern side of the Thames through Rotherhithe until it crosses the river at Tower Bridge. From there it heads east again to the Isle of Dogs and Canary Wharf and then back to Tower Hill and along Upper Thames Street to Blackfriars and the Embankment, through Parliament Square and down Birdcage Walk to Buckingham Palace with the finish in the Mall. The first London Marathon finished at Constitution Hill, and from 1982 to 1993 it finished at Westminster Bridge.

One distinctive feature of the London Marathon is that more than three-quarters of the runners take part to raise funds for charities, with a good number of runners gaining extra attention by running in fancy dress. In 2010 charities raised £50.6 million as a result of donations by runners. In addition the London Marathon distributes its surplus to charity, primarily to help support community sports facilities around London.

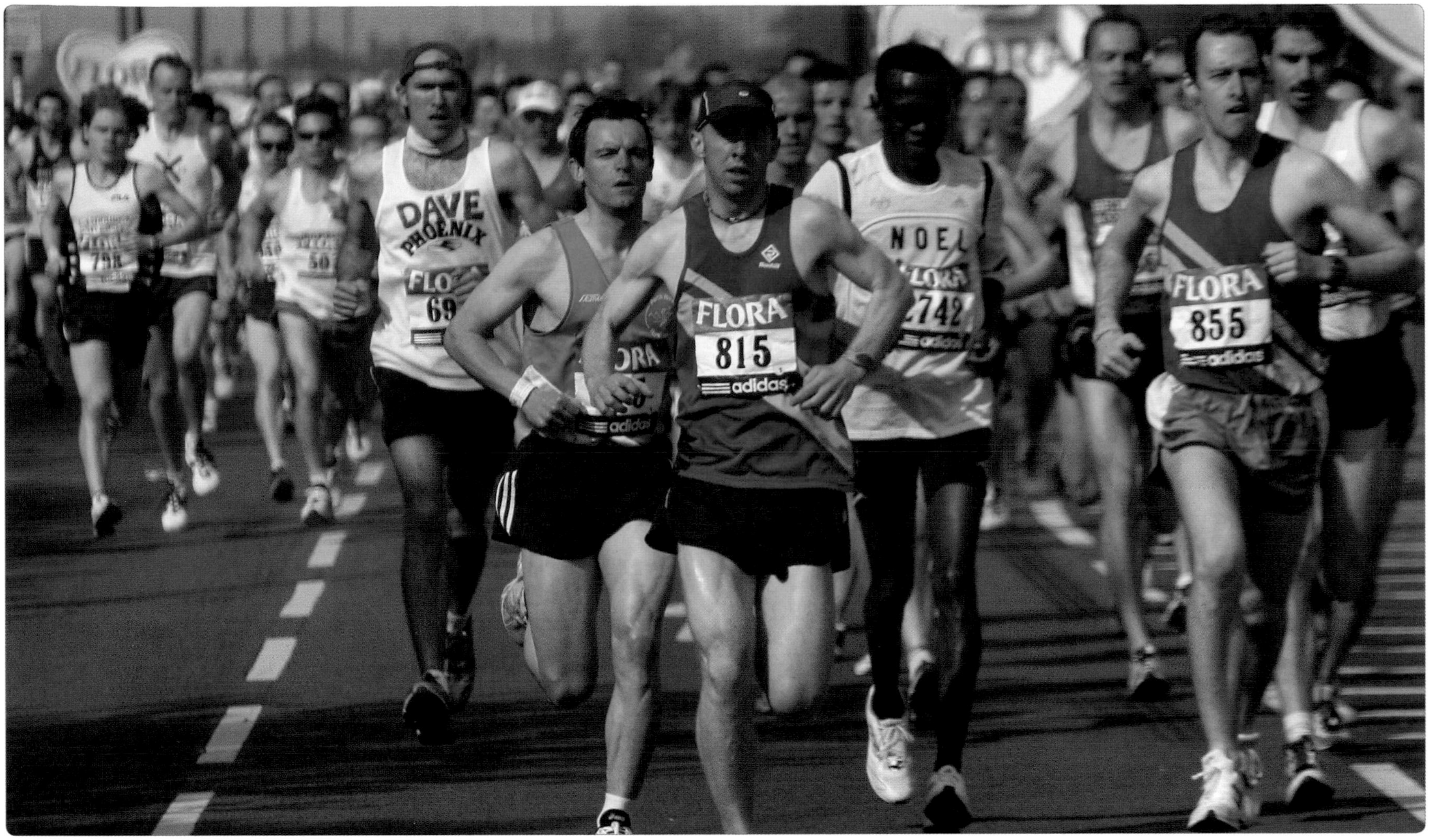

Runners in the London Marathon in 2007

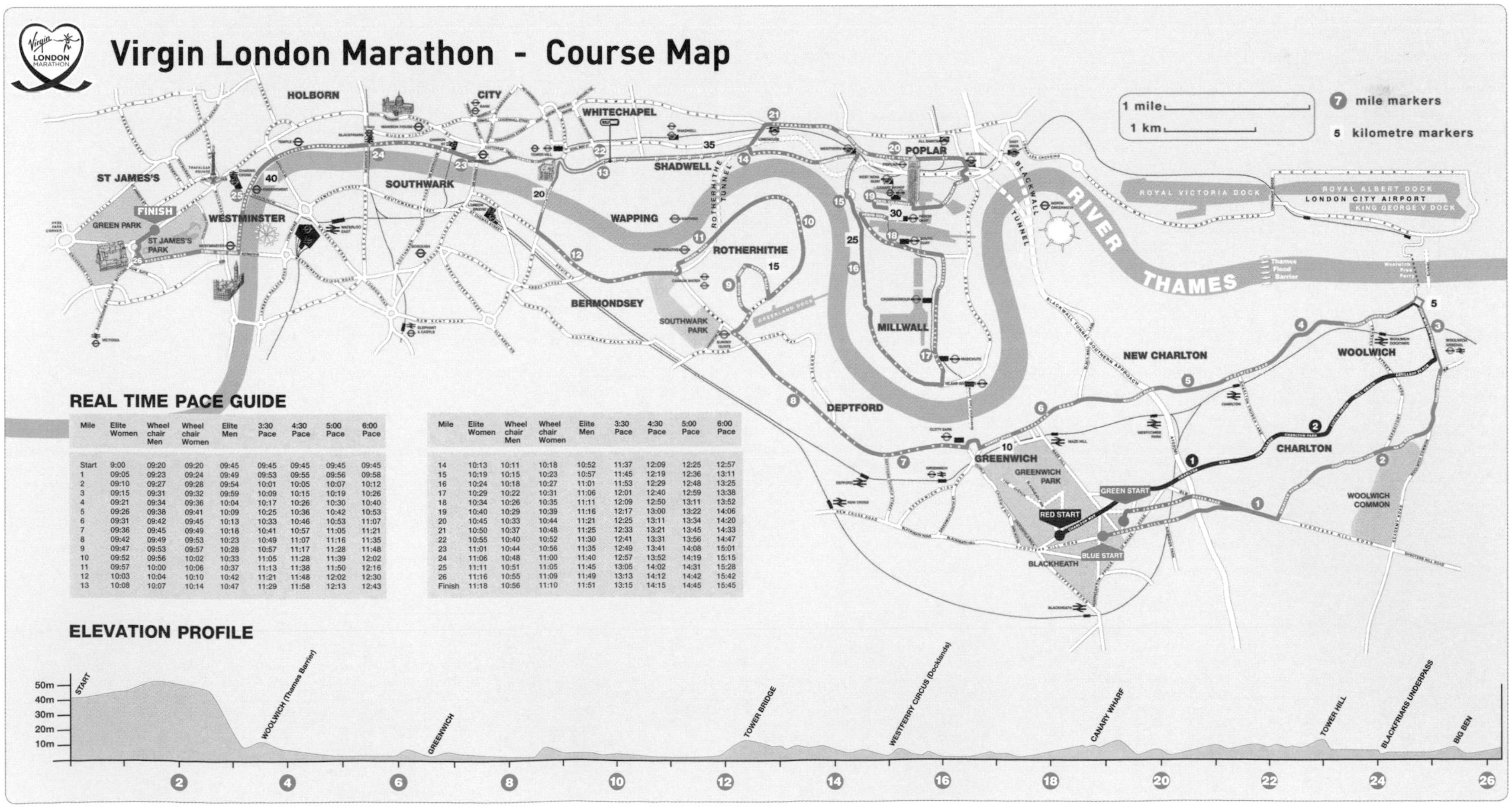

Mile	Elite Women	Wheel chair Men	Wheel chair Women	Elite Men	3:30 Pace	4:30 Pace	5:00 Pace	6:00 Pace
Start	9:00	09:20	09:20	09:45	09:45	09:45	09:45	09:45
1	09:05	09:23	09:24	09:49	09:53	09:55	09:56	09:58
2	09:10	09:27	09:28	09:54	10:01	10:05	10:07	10:12
3	09:15	09:31	09:32	09:59	10:09	10:15	10:19	10:26
4	09:21	09:34	09:36	10:04	10:17	10:26	10:30	10:40
5	09:26	09:38	09:41	10:09	10:25	10:36	10:42	10:53
6	09:31	09:42	09:45	10:13	10:33	10:46	10:53	11:07
7	09:36	09:45	09:49	10:18	10:41	10:57	11:05	11:21
8	09:42	09:49	09:53	10:23	10:49	11:07	11:16	11:35
9	09:47	09:53	09:57	10:28	10:57	11:17	11:28	11:48
10	09:52	09:56	10:02	10:33	11:05	11:28	11:39	12:02
11	09:57	10:00	10:06	10:37	11:13	11:38	11:50	12:16
12	10:03	10:04	10:10	10:42	11:21	11:48	12:02	12:30
13	10:08	10:07	10:14	10:47	11:29	11:58	12:13	12:43

Mile	Elite Women	Wheel chair Men	Wheel chair Women	Elite Men	3:30 Pace	4:30 Pace	5:00 Pace	6:00 Pace
14	10:13	10:11	10:18	10:52	11:37	12:09	12:25	12:57
15	10:19	10:15	10:23	10:57	11:45	12:19	12:36	13:11
16	10:24	10:18	10:27	11:01	11:53	12:29	12:48	13:25
17	10:29	10:22	10:31	11:06	12:01	12:40	12:59	13:38
18	10:34	10:26	10:35	11:11	12:09	12:50	13:11	13:52
19	10:40	10:29	10:39	11:16	12:17	13:00	13:22	14:06
20	10:45	10:33	10:44	11:21	12:25	13:11	13:34	14:20
21	10:50	10:37	10:48	11:25	12:33	13:21	13:45	14:33
22	10:55	10:40	10:52	11:30	12:41	13:31	13:56	14:47
23	11:01	10:44	10:56	11:35	12:49	13:41	14:08	15:01
24	11:06	10:48	11:00	11:40	12:57	13:52	14:19	15:15
25	11:11	10:51	11:05	11:45	13:05	14:02	14:31	15:28
26	11:16	10:55	11:09	11:49	13:13	14:12	14:42	15:42
Finish	11:18	10:56	11:10	11:51	13:15	14:15	14:45	15:45

London Marathon course map *(courtesy of the London Marathon)*

NEWHAM

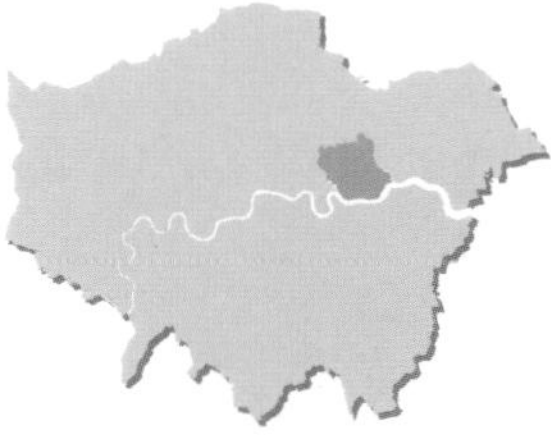

Population	241,200
Area	37 sq. km
Population density	6,519 per sq. km
Area of green space	9 sq. km
Jobs in borough	80,000
Average house price	£202,795

The borough of Newham (with its specially created name) was formed in 1965 from the Essex county boroughs of West Ham and East Ham plus North Woolwich. Prior to the 19th century, Stratford was the main town serving a number of villages and market gardening was a major activity. Thereafter the area changed beyond recognition, with the arrival of the railways, the Royal Docks, major industries and residential developments. The main railway to East Anglia reached Stratford in 1839. There followed a network of lines (most recently including the Docklands Light Railway and the Jubilee line) that encouraged much housing development. Stratford also became a major railway engineering centre, and today is the site of the Eurostar maintenance centre.

The next spur to development was the 1844 Metropolitan Building Act which prohibited 'harmful trades' within London. However, there were no such restrictions in West Ham and many industries came, led by Samuel Silver's waterproof garment factory, hence the name Silvertown. Further east the Beckton gas works opened in 1870, providing gas to all of London, while Beckton was also the site of Europe's largest sewage works. The Royal Docks were developed as the port of London's trade grew. Changing trading patterns and the onset of containerization led to their decline from their peak in the 1950s to complete closure in 1981. Since then much work has been done to regenerate the area, including the building of London City Airport, the ExCel exhibition centre and a new campus for the University of East London. Around Stratford there is further reconstruction with the creation of the Olympic Park (see page 240).

The area only started to grow in the mid-19th century, with its population of 24,900 in 1851 growing to 338,500 in 1901 and 454,100 in 1931. With industrial decline and terrible damage during World War II (85 per cent of Canning Town's housing was destroyed), its population declined but since 1981 has been growing again. It is now one of the most diverse boroughs in London –39 per cent of the population was white in 2007, with 34 per cent Asian and 20 per cent black. With good transport links to the City, 69 per cent of working residents have jobs outside the borough.

Stratford International, transport hub of the 2012 Olympics, and the restored 1933 steam locomotive *Robert*

FAMOUS FOR

The **Royal Docks** were built in three stages – the Victoria Dock in 1855, the Albert Dock in 1888 and the King George V Dock in 1921. They formed the largest enclosed docks in the world and ships of 30,000 tonnes could berth at the King George V docks.

The **Theatre Royal Stratford East** opened in December 1884 and gained international prominence when Joan Littlewood's Theatre Workshop was based there from the 1950s. It was refurbished and extended (completed 2001), and continues to play a vibrant part in the multicultural life of Stratford.

Newham is one of three London boroughs where voters have, since 2002, directly elected a mayor (the other two are Hackney and Lewisham).

On 16 May 1968, a gas explosion in one flat in **Ronan Point**, a new 23-storey block in Canning Town, caused the corner of the block to collapse, killing four people and injuring seventeen. It put an end to prefabricated building techniques and cemented the public's dislike of high-rise blocks.

Waves of hedges, Thames Barrier Park

London City Airport

Three Mills, on the River Lea was recorded as a site of tidal mills in the Domesday Book. House Mill, built in 1776 on this site, is the largest surviving tidal mill in Britain. It has recently been restored while the adjacent distillery, of a similar age, is now a major film and television studio.

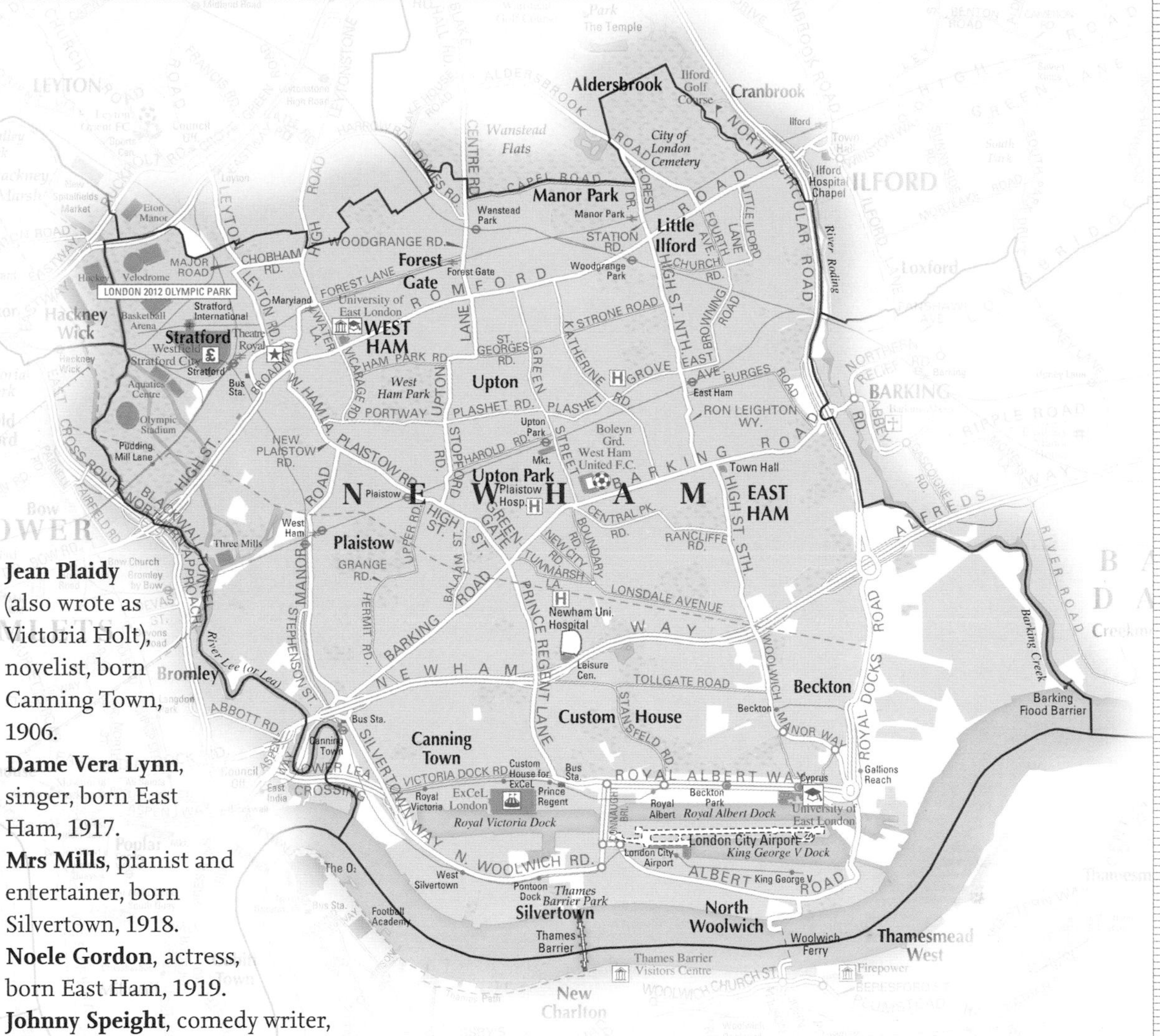

FAMOUS PEOPLE

George Edwards, ornithologist and artist, born West Ham, 1694.

Gerard Manley Hopkins, poet, born Stratford, 1844.

William Hillman, bicycle and motor vehicle manufacturer, born Stratford, 1848.

Alice Cornwell, goldmine owner (*known as* 'Princess Midas') and Australian newspaper proprietor, born West Ham, 1852.

Cecil Jackson-Cole, businessman and founder of Oxfam and Help the Aged, born Forest Gate, 1901.

Dame Anna Neagle, actress and film producer, born Forest Gate, 1904.

Mary Renault, novelist, born West Ham, 1905.

Jean Plaidy (also wrote as Victoria Holt), novelist, born Canning Town, 1906.

Dame Vera Lynn, singer, born East Ham, 1917.

Mrs Mills, pianist and entertainer, born Silvertown, 1918.

Noele Gordon, actress, born East Ham, 1919.

Johnny Speight, comedy writer, born Canning Town, 1920.

Honor Blackman, actress, born Plaistow, *c.* 1925.

Jermaine Defoe, footballer, born Beckton, 1982.

Christine Ohuruogu, Olympic gold medal winning athlete, born Newham, 1984.

Halls of residence, University of East London Docklands Campus

John Bartholomew, Gazetteer of the British Isles (1887)

STRATFORD.– *town (ry. stations Stratford and Stratford Market), West Ham par., Essex, 3½ m. NE. of Liverpool Street sta., London, and within the parl. limits of West Ham, pop. 36,455. Stratford is situated on the navigable river Lea (here crossed by a bridge leading to Bow), and on the fork of the railway which proceeds in two lines to Cambridge and Colchester. It has remains of a Cistercian abbey founded in 1135, a fine town hall (1868), extensive works in connection with the Great Eastern Railway, chemical works, and other industrial establishments.*

WEST HAM, *parl. bor., par., and local government dist., Essex, on N. bank of river Thames, opposite Greenwich, and in E. of London, 4667 ac., pop. 128,953; contains Stratford town and has several industrial establishments in connection with the Victoria Docks; ship-building, silk-printing, brewing, leather-cloth mfr., &c., See STRATFORD. West Ham returns 2 members to Parliament (2 divisions – viz., North and South, 1 member for each division); it was made a parl. bor. in 1885.*

THE OLYMPICS

In 2005, London was chosen to host the Olympic Games in 2012. It previously hosted the Games in 1908 and 1948. The size of the Games now requires an immense infrastructure to support the two-week event, and while London's first two Games left little lasting legacy, the 2012 Games brought dramatic changes to the Lower Lea Valley, which was an unloved, former industrial area around the River Lea just to the west of Stratford. The map shows the area after the development of the Olympic Park, which provided a massive stimulus to the local communities, especially within the borough of Newham, which contains the majority of the 2.5 sq. km Olympic Park.

The Olympic legacy

The Olympic Park will become a major urban park, to be named the Queen Elizabeth Olympic Park. The River Lea will have been cleaned and widened and its natural floodplain reinstated to provide a new wetland environment for bird life. Within the park, which is being planted with many native tree species, the main sports facilities created for the Games will remain. The main

The finish of the marathon in the White City Stadium, 1908 Olympic Games

2012 Olympic Stadium

Programme from the 1948 Olympic Games

stadium will become the football stadium for the local West Ham team as well as retaining its athletics facilities, while two of the most striking buildings – the Aquatics Centre and the Velodrome – will have a continuing sporting life, and new playing fields for community use will be included in the park.

The Olympic Village will be converted into housing and further housing will be built within the park. It is planned to provide up to 11,000 new homes by 2030 and up to 18,000 jobs in the park and the related Westfield Stratford City shopping centre (the largest urban shopping centre in Europe when it opened in 2011). All residents will also benefit from the improved transport links on the Dockland Light Railway, the Jubilee line and the Overground (and, in time, from Crossrail as well). Boris Johnson, the Mayor of London waxed lyrical about the potential:

Not since Georgian England has London seen such an ambitious and comprehensive vision for a new district. Our plans seek to combine the classical best of this city with the greatest benefits of modern urban living… deliberately designed to capture the most attractive features of the Georgian age, to ensure our own Elizabethan age sets London up for generations to come.

Other Olympic sites

In addition to the Olympic Park, various other venues were chosen for events in the capital: Earls Court (volleyball), ExCel exhibition centre by the Royal Docks (boxing, fencing, judo, table tennis, taekwondo, weightlifting, wrestling), Greenwich Park (equestrian events), Hampton Court Palace (road cycling time trial), Horse Guards Parade (beach volleyball), Hyde Park (triathlon, marathon swimming), Lord's Cricket Ground (archery),

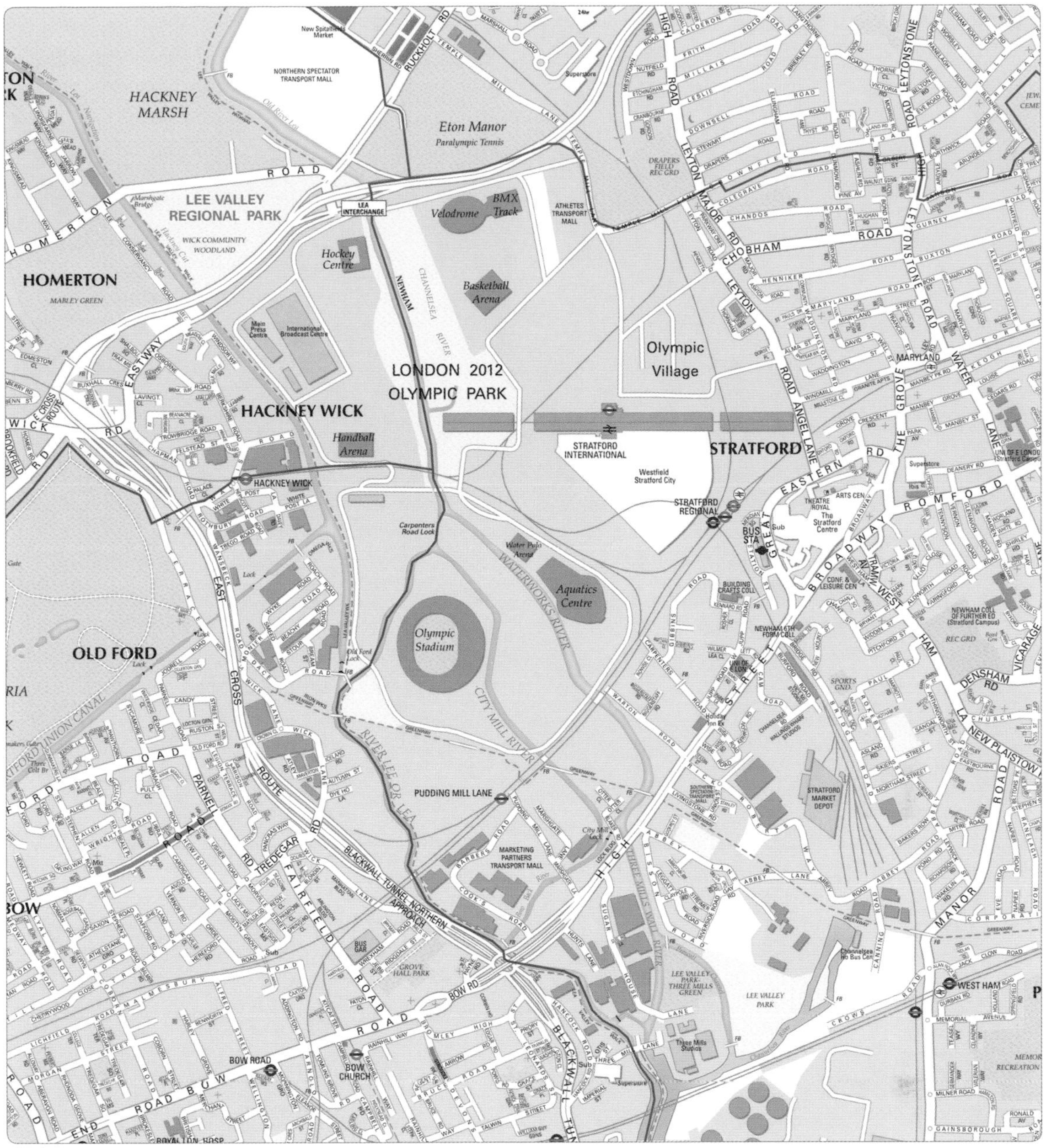

London 2012 Olympic Park

North Greenwich Arena (part of the O_2 Arena) (artistic gymnastics, trampoline, basketball), The Mall (start and finish of marathons and cycling road races), Royal Artillery Barracks, Woolwich (shooting), Wembley Arena (badminton, rhythmic gymnastics), Wembley Stadium (football), and Wimbledon (tennis).

Previous London Olympics

The 1908 Games were originally to be held in Rome, but an eruption of Mount Vesuvius in 1906 required the Italian government to redirect funds to that crisis, and so, with 18 months' notice, the event was moved to London. The Games were held in a specially constructed stadium at White City. The stadium contained the running track and a cycling track and, in the centre a swimming pool, so that most events could take place within one stadium that could seat around 70,000 people. It was the first Olympics to hold a formal Opening Ceremony and also the first Games to award Gold, Silver and Bronze medals. There were 110 events and athletes from twenty-two countries competed. After the Games, the stadium had a number of uses including athletics, greyhound racing, football, boxing and speedway. It was demolished in 1985 to make way for new office buildings.

London was originally chosen to host the 1944 games, which were cancelled because of World War II, and instead hosted the 1948 games. Known as the 'Austerity Games' as all of Europe was still recovering from the war, no new buildings were built. Both Wembley Stadium and the Empire Pool (now the Wembley Arena) were used and athletes were put up in army camps or college buildings. There were 136 events with athletes coming from fifty-nine nations.

REDBRIDGE

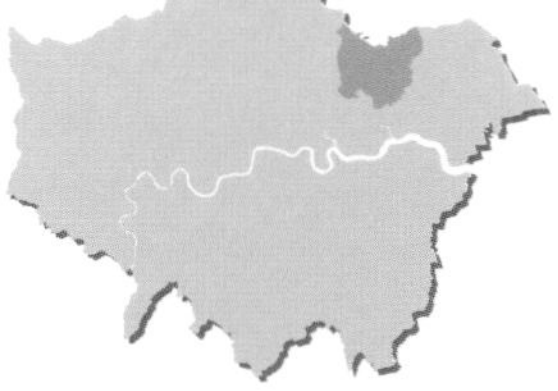

Population	267,700
Area	57 sq. km
Population density	4,697 per sq. km
Area of green space	23 sq. km
Jobs in borough	79,000
Average house price	£256,857

The borough was created in 1965 from the municipal boroughs of Ilford, and Wanstead and Woodford, both then in Essex. It takes its name from the area called Redbridge, after an old redbrick bridge over the River Roding, demolished in 1921. The name appears on maps from 1746.

The area was once well wooded with Epping Forest to the north and Hainault Forest to the east, while the areas around Ilford and Wanstead were agricultural with settlement going back to Roman times, for Ilford was on the Roman road to Colchester. In the 18th century, some City merchants built grand houses in the area, most magnificently at Wanstead (see page 244) and more long-lastingly, Valentines Mansion, near Gants Hill. A hundred years ago, Ilford was described as 'all sky and turnips'. It was, however, the arrival of the railways that transformed the area: in 1851 the population was 9,900, by 1901 it was 77,600 and by 1951 it was 270,900.

Population growth was initially fuelled by skilled workers moving out of the East End, but in recent years the ethnic mix of the borough has changed – in 2007 around 58 per cent of the borough was white with nearly 25 per cent of Asian origin. One estimate has suggested that by 2026 minority ethnic groups will make up nearly 60 per cent of the borough. Earnings by residents are slightly above the London average and it is consistently one of the best London boroughs for educational achievement.

This image of a suburban borough is reinforced by the fact that around 62 per cent of working residents commute to jobs outside the borough, while the largest sector within the borough (over 34 per cent) work in public administration, education and health, more than 50 per cent above the London average. There is now little manufacturing in the borough, although it was home to the eponymous photographic film manufacturer Ilford until 1976, and to the electronics and communications equipment company, Plessey, who arrived in 1923 at Ilford and ceased all production in 2001.

FAMOUS FOR

The oldest building in Redbridge is the **Ilford Hospital Chapel**, a 14th century building that was once part of the Hospital of St Mary the Virgin and St Thomas of Canterbury, founded c. 1145 by Adelicia, Abbess of Barking, to look after thirteen aged and infirm men.

Snaresbrook Crown Court

The digging of brick clay around **Ilford** has yielded many fossils of woolly mammoths. The largest British mammoth skull (complete with tusks) was found in Ilford in 1864 and is now in the central hall of the Natural History Museum in South Kensington. Its tusks are nearly 3 m long.

During World War II, the communications equipment manufacturer Plessey moved from its Ilford factory into the tunnels of the Central line between **Redbridge** and **Wanstead** stations to provide protection from bombing.

Winston Churchill was MP for **Epping** (1924–45) and then for the new seat of **Woodford** (part of the old Epping seat) from 1945 to his retirement in 1964.

Snaresbrook Crown Court in now the largest Crown Court centre in Britain. The building it occupies was originally the Infant Orphan Asylum, established by the Congregationalist minister Andrew Reed with Royal patronage. Renamed the Royal Wanstead School, it closed in 1971.

When it is completed in 2018, the **Crossrail** route will go through Ilford, with journey times of 15 minutes to the West End and 30 minutes to Heathrow.

The Hospital Chapel of St Mary the Virgin and St Thomas of Canterbury, Ilford

FAMOUS PEOPLE

Sydney Smith, author, cleric and wit, born Woodford, 1771.

George Edmund Street, architect, designer of the Royal Courts of Justice on The Strand, born Woodford, 1824.

Sir Charles Tilston Bright, telegraph engineer, laid first transatlantic telegraph cable, born Wanstead, 1832.

Robert Kindersley (Baron Kindersley), merchant banker, organiser of the National Savings movement, born Wanstead, 1871.

Stanley Morison, typographer, creator of the typeface 'Times New Roman' for *The Times*, born Wanstead, 1889.

Sidney Bernstein (Lord Bernstein), businessman, creator of entertainment group Granada, born Ilford, 1899.

Cardinal John Carmel Heenan, Archbishop of Westminster, 1963–75, born Ilford, 1905.

Eva Hart, survivor of RMS *Titanic*, died 1996, born Ilford 1905.

Kathleen Raine, poet and literary scholar, born Ilford, 1908.

Raymond Baxter, broadcaster and writer, born Ilford, 1922.

Kenny Ball, jazz trumpeter and band leader, born Ilford, 1930.

Sir Ian Holm, actor, born Goodmayes, 1931.

Dame Maggie Smith, actress, born Ilford, 1934.

Kathy Kirby (*born* Kathleen O'Rourke), singer, born Ilford, 1938.

Ken Campbell, actor and director of experimental theatre, born Ilford, 1941.

Noel Edmonds, television entertainer, born Ilford, 1948.

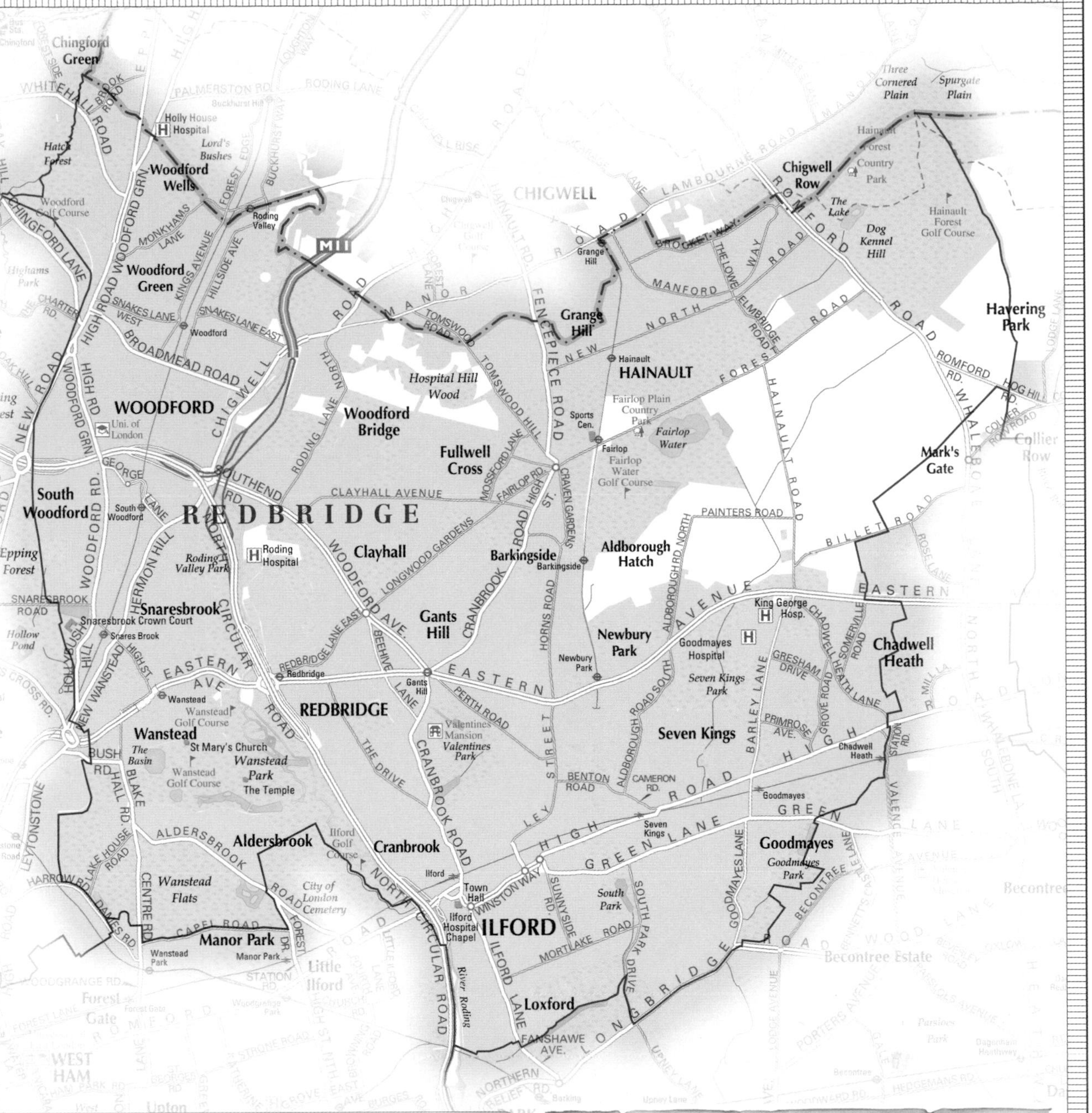

Charlie Brown's roundabout at the southern end of the M11, one of the busiest intersections in London. The name comes from the renowned Limehouse publican, Charlie Brown, who died in 1932. Six years later one of his sons moved to the Roundabout Tavern, which was soon referred to as 'Charlie Brown's'. The pub was demolished in 1972 – but the name lives on.

John Bartholomew, Gazetteer of the British Isles (1887)

ILFORD, *(or Great Ilford), town and ry. sta., Barking par., S. Essex, on river Roding, 3½ miles NE. of Stratford and 7 miles NE. of London by rail, pop. 4397; P.O., T.O.; contains St Mary's Hospital, founded in time of Henry II., and refounded by Queen Elizabeth in 1572; here is the Ilford Paper Mill.*

WANSTEAD, *town and par., Essex – par. (partly in town of Leyton), 2002 ac. (51 water), pop. 9414; town, 1½ mile NW. of Ilford and 7 miles NE. of London, 1072 ac., pop. 5362. Wanstead is a local government dist., and contains many fine residences.*

WOODFORD.– *par. and ry. sta., Essex, 4½ miles NE. of Stratford by rail, 2146 ac., pop. 7154; P.O., T.O., 1 newspaper; is a local government district, and contains many fine mansions, villas, and other residences. Woodford Bridge, Woodford Green, and Woodford Wells are vils. in the par.*

WANSTEAD HOUSE – A LOST BUILDING

It is quite hard to imagine that Wanstead was once the site of one of Britain's greatest country houses. Some vestiges of this greatness remain in Wanstead Park, administered by the City of London Corporation as part of Epping Forest. The only building that remains is 'The Temple', now used by park rangers but which was once a garden banquet room, but never a temple. What then is the story of this lost house?

The manor of Wanstead came into prominence when Edward VI gave it to his Lord Chancellor Richard Rich, who rebuilt the manor as his country estate. At his death, it was bought by Robert Dudley, Earl of Leicester, who entertained Elizabeth I there, as did his stepson the Earl of Essex. James I was also a frequent visitor but thereafter it fell on harder times. In 1667 it was bought by Josiah Child, a director of the East India Company, who lavished his attention on the gardens. His grand baroque monument can be seen in St Mary's Church, Wanstead.

In 1704 the estate passed to Sir Richard Child, who commissioned Colen Campbell to replace the old house with a magnificent Palladian design. Its clean, Roman-inspired lines were a dramatic break with the traditional English country houses of the time and it had immense

The grandeur of Wanstead House, as recorded in the late 18th century

The Temple at Wanstead Park

Interior of St Mary's Church, Wanstead

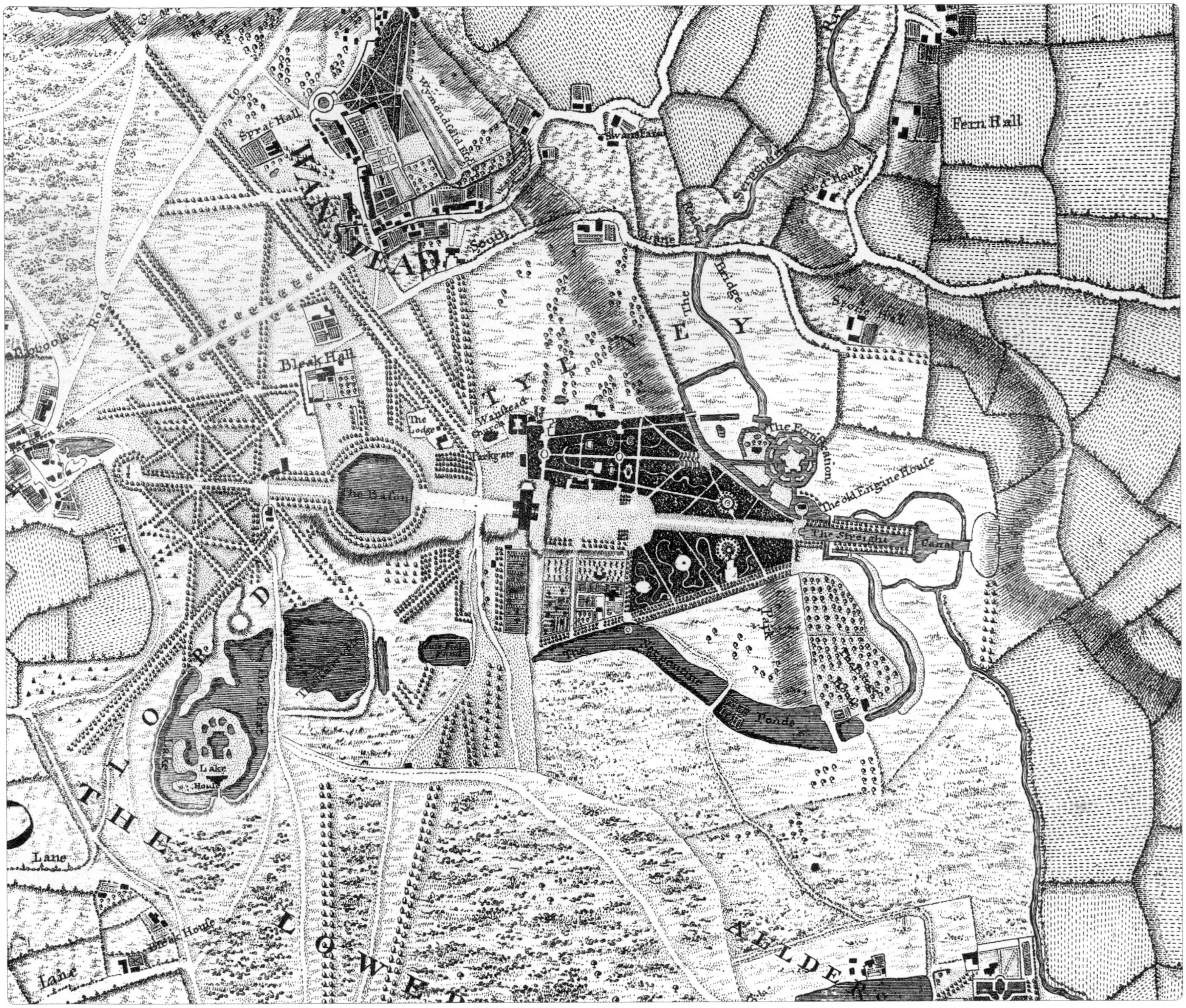

Extract from Rocque's map showing Wanstead House and gardens 1744-46

influence on future house designs, though few were so large – it was 76 m wide and 23 m deep with over seventy rooms. Building started in 1715 and was completed in 1720. Thereafter Child lavished more attention on the grounds so that, according to Daniel Defoe 'it looks all like one planted garden as far as the eye can see'.

Sir Richard Child, who gained the title Earl Tylney, grew extremely wealthy through both his inheritance and directorship of the East India Company. His son enhanced Wanstead and entertained lavishly and on his death in 1784, the estate passed to his nephew, Sir James Long. It was he who commissioned Thomas Hardwick to rebuild St Mary's Church, a very fine classical building that has survived with little change. Sir John's daughter, Lady Catherine inherited the estate and became one of the wealthiest people in Britain. However, marriage to the Duke of Wellington's nephew, William Pole-Wellesey, in 1812, was disastrous. His extravagance and gambling debts quickly ran through Lady Catherine's wealth, and in 1822 his creditors seized the estate and started to sell the contents. To raise further funds, they then sold the house in 1824 on condition that it was 'removed from the face of the Earth by Lady Day 1825'. Parts of the building were re-used elsewhere including a fireplace surround in George Washington's house at Mount Vernon and a portico attached rather uncomfortably to Hendon Hall. The site of the house now lies under Wanstead golf course.

Lady Catherine died in 1825 but William survived until 1857, one obituary commenting that he was: 'Redeemed by no single virtue, adorned by no single grace, his life has gone out, even without a flicker of repentance.'

The Conservators of Epping Forest bought the park in 1882 as an addition to Epping Forest. Maintained in a less formal manner than in its heyday, the park has been a popular open space ever since.

RICHMOND UPON THAMES

Population	189,000
Area	59 sq. km
Population density	3,203 per sq. km
Area of green space	30 sq. km
Jobs in borough	84,000
Average house price	£509,330

The borough of Richmond upon Thames is the only borough to straddle the river, having been created in 1965 from parts of Surrey (Ham, Petersham, Richmond, Kew, Mortlake and Barnes) south of the Thames and parts of Middlesex (Hampton, Twickenham and Teddington) on the north side. It was named Richmond upon Thames to distinguish it from the town of Richmond in North Yorkshire. Richmond itself took its name from the great Royal Palace of Richmond, once known as the Palace of Shene, but renamed after his North Yorkshire earldom of Richmond by Henry VII when he rebuilt it in 1499. The borough has over 34 km of river frontage on the Thames and around half the borough is open space. It has long attracted those who wished to live away from the city of London or to be near the Royal palaces of Richmond, Hampton Court and Kew. With the arrival of the railways some areas, particularly in Barnes and Twickenham, saw significant housing development. However, the borough maintains the prosperous nature of its constituent settlements, being the least deprived and one of the least ethnically diverse London boroughs. Its population in 1851 was 28,800, in 1901 it was 103,700 and in 1951 it rose to 202,200, after which the population declined until 1991 when it started growing again.

The character of the borough is defined by its historic buildings and by its open spaces. While Richmond Palace fell into ruins during the Civil War, with just a restored gatehouse now remaining, there are still many fine Queen Anne houses grouped around Richmond Green. Other distinguished buildings include the fine palace of Hampton Court, and Ham House, a magnificent unchanged 17th-century house and garden. Marble Hill at Twickenham was built for Henrietta Howard, mistress of George II in 1728 whilst White Lodge in Richmond Park was built as a hunting lodge for George II in 1727, and Strawberry Hill was Horace Walpole's 18th century gothic fantasy. Open spaces include Richmond Park, London's largest park, covering 1,000 ha. It was originally enclosed as a deer park for Charles I and remains home to around 600 red and fallow deer.

Ham House

Almost two-thirds of working residents travel out of the borough to work and an above average number of residents work from home. The mixture of jobs within the borough mainly reflects the London average, although, with all its tourist attractions over 12 per cent of jobs are in this sector compared with a London average of 8 per cent.

FAMOUS FOR

The **London Wetland Centre** in Barnes is a 42-ha nature reserve by the Thames consisting of lakes, ponds, meadows and reed beds, home to over 180 species of bird and many small mammals.

The **Royal Botanic Gardens** at Kew is a World Heritage Site (see page 158).

Garrick's Temple, by the Thames at Hampton, was built in 1756 by the great actor and theatre manager, David Garrick, to celebrate the genius of Shakespeare.

White Lodge, Richmond Park

The Star and Garter was originally the name of a hotel on **Richmond Hill**. In 1916 it became a home for disabled ex-servicemen and a magnificent new building was erected as a memorial to those who died in the World War I. In 2013 the Royal Star and Garter Home moves to Surbiton.

A former cabbage field is now the home of English Rugby Union in the form of the **Twickenham Stadium** (see page 234).

The strangely named **Castelnau** area of Barnes takes its name from Castelnau-de-Lez near Montpellier in France, ancestral home of the Huguenot Boileau family who developed the area.

FAMOUS PEOPLE

Arthur Dee, physician and writer on alchemy, born Mortlake, 1579.
Arthur Cayley, mathematician, born Richmond, 1821.
Sir Arthur Bliss, composer, born Barnes, 1891.

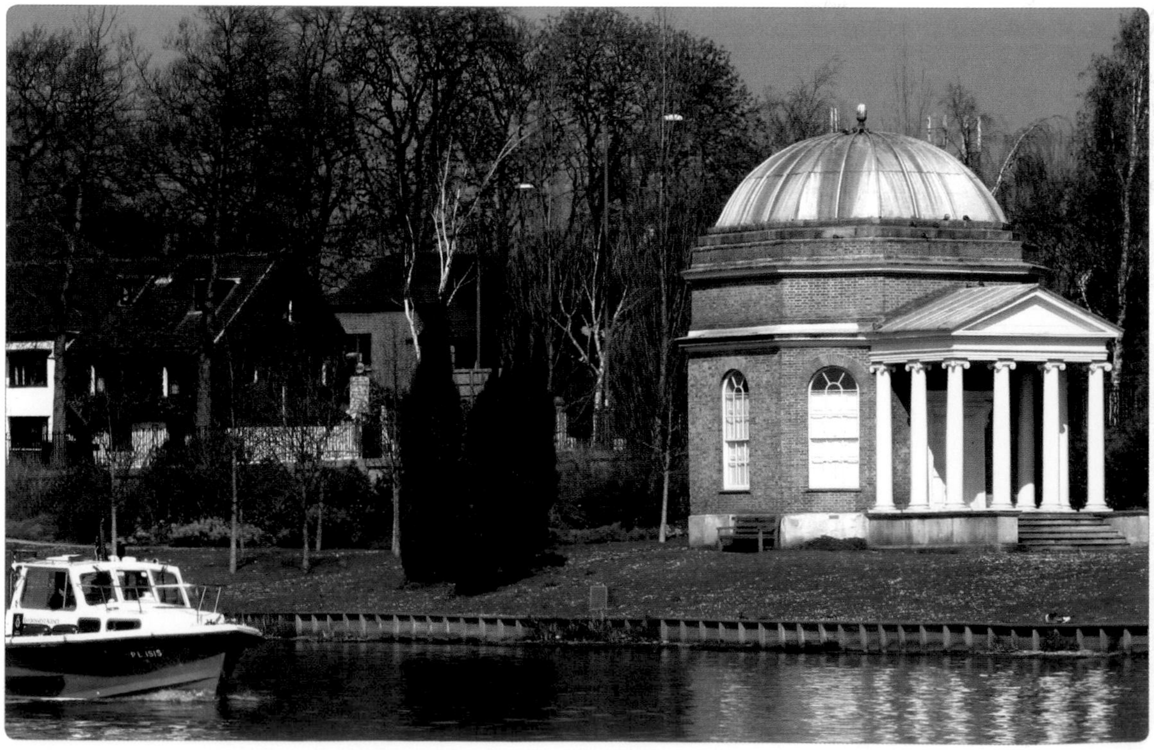

The Temple to Shakespeare by the Thames at Hampton, built by David Garrick, the great 18th-century actor and theatre manager

Edward VIII, King, 1936; abdicated 1936 and then became Duke of Windsor, born White Lodge, Richmond Park, 1894.
Robert Cedric Sherriff, playwright and scriptwriter, born Hampton Wick, 1896.
Sir Noël Coward, playwright and composer, born Teddington, 1899.
John Bertram Phillips, biblical translator and Christian theologian, born Barnes, 1906.
Imogen Holst, musician, born Richmond, 1907.
Dame Celia Johnson, actress, born Richmond, 1908.
Richard Dimbleby, radio and television broadcaster, born Richmond, 1913.
Lynn Chadwick, sculptor, born Barnes, 1914.
(George) Eric Newby, travel writer and adventurer, born Barnes, 1919.
(Anthony) Colin Bruce Chapman, racing car designer and manufacturer, born Richmond, 1928.
Brian May, guitarist and song writer, born Hampton, 1947.
Keira Knightley, actress, born Teddington, 1985.

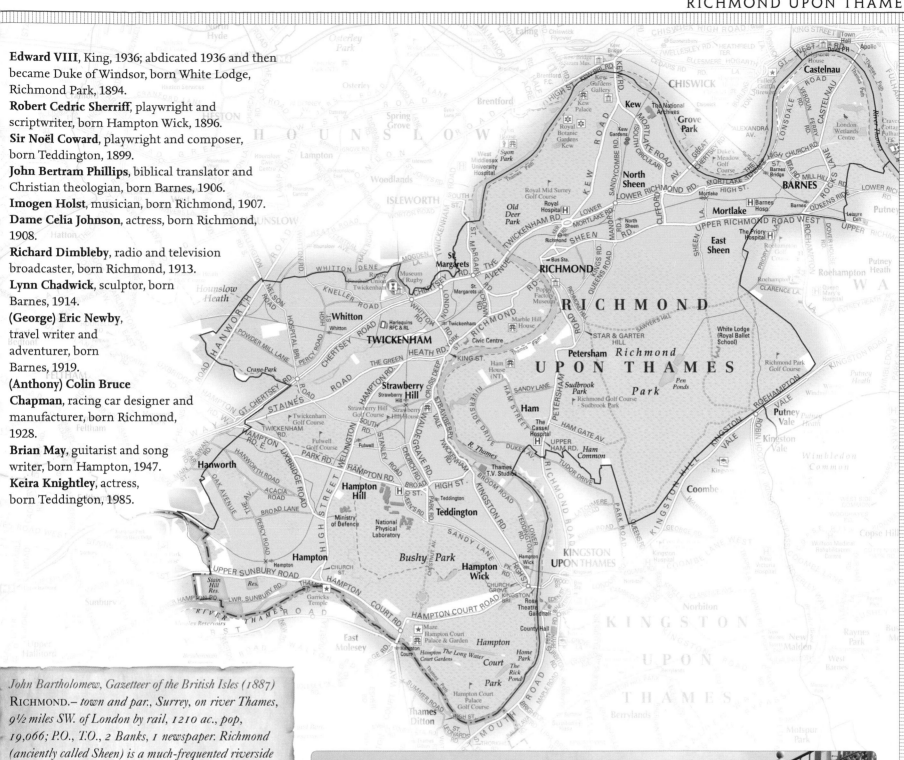

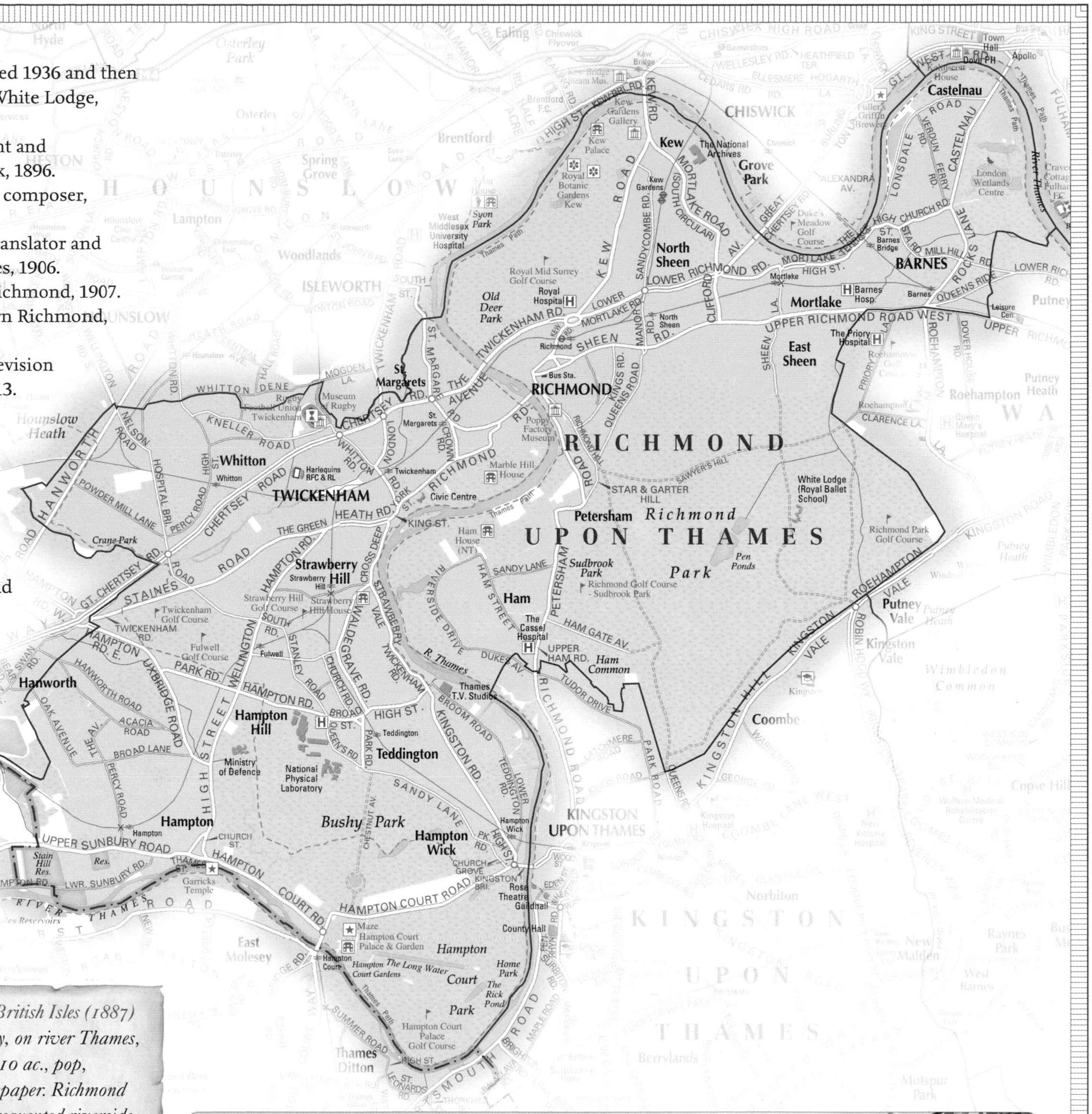

> *John Bartholomew, Gazetteer of the British Isles (1887)*
> RICHMOND.– *town and par., Surrey, on river Thames, 9½ miles SW. of London by rail, 1210 ac., pop, 19,066; P.O., T.O., 2 Banks, 1 newspaper. Richmond (anciently called Sheen) is a much-frequented riverside resort. It occupies a site of remarkable beauty, on the slope of Richmond Hill, which rises somewhat abruptly from the right bank of the Thames, here crossed by a handsome 5-arch bridge leading to Twickenham. Its scenery combines all the charms of wood, meadow, and water, and the prospect from the summit of the hill is very fine. Richmond Palace was for many centuries a favourite residence of the English monarchs, and Edward III., Henry VII., and Elizabeth died in it. Richmond Park, formed by Charles I., is enclosed by a wall 8 miles in length, has red and fallow deer, excellent timber, and 2 fine sheets of water (the Pen Ponds). Richmond has market gardens and nursery grounds, and some small industries; but it depends chiefly on the gentry resident in the vicinity and on the crowd of summer visitors.*

Richmond Lock, the furthest lock downstream on the Thames

THE ROYAL PARKS

The eight Royal Parks, covering over 2,000 ha, were created by the monarchy and are London's most historically important parks. In 2010 it was proposed that direct administration of the parks by the government be transferred to the Greater London Authority following the 2012 Olympics.

Bushy Park (445 ha) is probably the least well-known Royal Park. It is adjacent to and provides a setting for Hampton Court Palace. Its most dramatic feature is the Chestnut Avenue, a 1.5 km avenue of horse chestnut and lime trees designed by Sir Christopher Wren to provide a formal approach to the palace from Teddington. Near to the palace is the 'Diana' fountain, named after the Roman goddess of hunting (but actually showing Diana's nymph, Arethusa), moved to this site in 1713 by Wren.

The Green Park (19 ha) is a tranquil park of mature trees and grassland positioned between the commercial activities of Piccadilly and the formality of Buckingham Palace and The Mall. It was purchased by Charles II in 1667 to provide a link between Hyde Park and St James's and he enclosed it the following year. He took a daily walk (a 'constitutional') in the park, now remembered by the name of Constitution Hill for the road on its southern boundary.

Greenwich Park (74 ha) is the oldest of the enclosed Royal parks. In 1427 the park land was inherited by Henry V's brother, Duke Humphrey of Gloucester and the park and the palace built there became a Royal favourite up to the time of James II. Henry VIII (both of whose daughters were born at Greenwich) enclosed the park and introduced deer. Within the park is the Queen's House, the Royal Observatory and the former Royal Naval College. The park, which is part of the Greenwich World Heritage Site, was designated as the backdrop for the 2012 Olympics equestrian events.

Hyde Park (142 ha) was purchased from Westminster Abbey by Henry VIII in 1536 as a hunting ground and around 100 years later Charles I opened the park to the public. In the 1730s Queen Caroline had The Serpentine created by damming the Westbourne stream, and the present plantings and layout date from the 1820s. In 1851 it was the site of the Great Exhibition and from 1872 at Speaker's Corner people have been able freely to address the public on any topic. The park is the site of the Diana, Princess of Wales Memorial Fountain, opened in 2004 and the 7 July Memorial to the fifty-two people who died in the London Bombings of 7 July 2005.

Kensington Gardens (111 ha), adjacent to Hyde Park, were originally the private gardens of Kensington Palace, with public access only coming in the late 18th century. The gardens are now best known for the flamboyant Victorian gothic Albert Memorial that was erected in honour of Queen Victoria's husband and completed in 1876, the statue of Peter Pan commissioned by the author J. M. Barrie in 1912, and the Diana, Princess of Wales Memorial Playground which opened in 2000.

The Regent's Park (197 ha, including Primrose Hill) is the largest of the central London parks. Originally another hunting park for Henry VIII, it owes its current appearance (and name) to the Prince Regent, who, in 1811, had the park redesigned by John Nash as the site for a new Royal palace. The palace was not built, but Nash designed the great terraces that look over the park and created sites for villas within the park. One villa was occupied by the Zoological Society, a development that grew into the park's best-loved feature – London Zoo. The park also has an open-air theatre and plenty of grass areas for sports.

Richmond Park (over 1,000 ha) is the largest of the royal parks, indeed the largest urban park in Europe. Originally part of Edward I's Manor of Shene, the park was enclosed with walls by Charles I, who then stocked it with red and fallow deer. Its untamed landscape of hills, woodlands and grassland brings the countryside into London. The Isabella Plantation is a woodland garden that was created in the 1950s.

St James's Park (23 ha) was originally the site of St James's leper hospital and was purchased by Henry VIII for his new palace of St James's and as another hunting park. Charles II opened the park to the public and its current layout was designed by John Nash in the 1820s. Close to Westminster, Whitehall and Buckingham Palace, it provides a green backdrop to the centre of Britain's government and monarchy, and is widely used by tourists and those who work nearby.

Richmond Park in winter, a touch of wild countryside in London

The Serpentine, Hyde Park

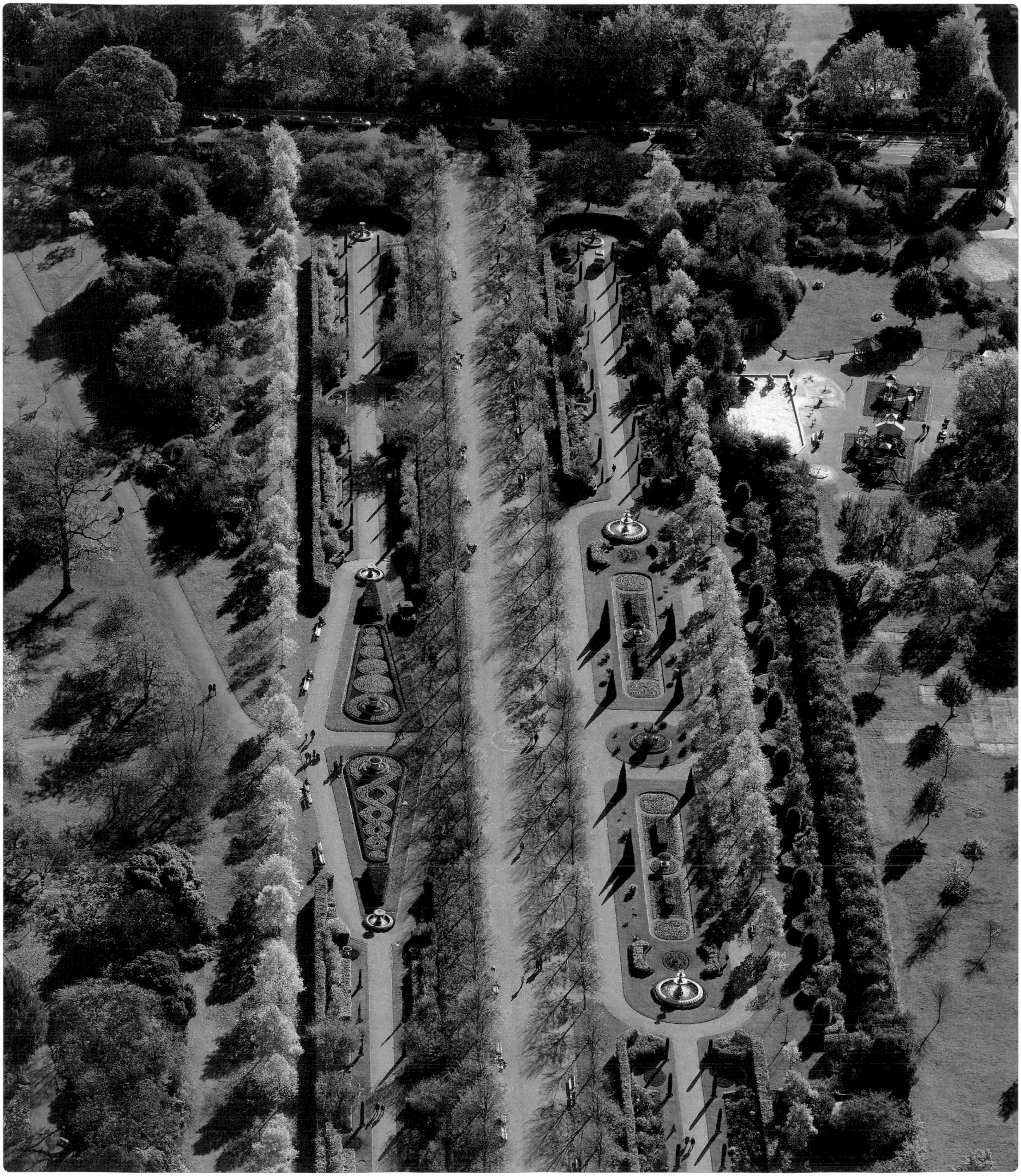

Formal planting in The Regent's Park

SOUTHWARK

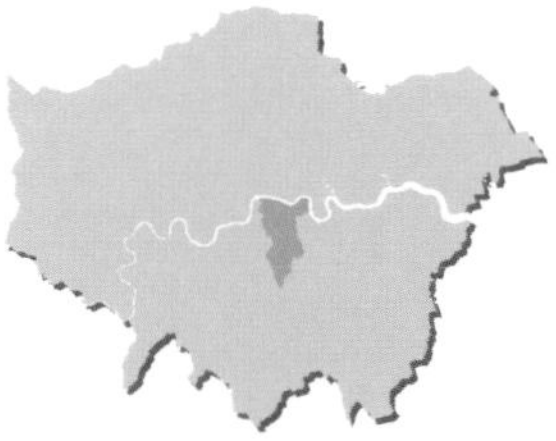

Population	285,600
Area	29 sq. km
Population density	9,850 per sq. km
Area of green space	4 sq. km
Jobs in borough	236,000
Average house price	£339,256

The borough of Southwark takes its name from the settlement of Southwark, from the Old English 'southern fortifications', indicating its defensive position at the southern end of London Bridge. It was formed in 1965 from the metropolitan boroughs of Southwark, Bermondsey and Camberwell.

The area was first settled in Roman times and it thrived in the medieval period as a place beyond the reach of the City of London authorities. It was from the Tabard Inn on Borough High Street that Chaucer had his pilgrims start their journey to Canterbury and close by the Rose and the Globe theatres were built by the 1590s. In the 18th century the agricultural villages of Peckham, Camberwell and Dulwich started to grow. Soon industries (particularly food processing) started close to the docks of Bermondsey and Rotherhithe, while the traditional Bermondsey industry of leather processing declined. As the railways developed, so the southern parts of the borough became urbanized (with the exception of Dulwich Village). Southwark had become densely populated by the start of the 20th century, increasing from 114,900 in 1801 to 578,000 in 1901, and thereafter declining. The population reached its lowest point in 1981 (209,700) and has been rising since. The population is diverse, with nearly 20 per cent of the population of Black African or Black Caribbean origin, while in the borough's schools only one quarter of pupils are white British.

The area close to the Thames, and to the major commuting terminus of London Bridge station, has attracted many financial companies, so that 43 per cent of the borough's jobs are in finance, IT and business, well above the average for London as a whole. There has been much recent office development here, most spectacularly in London's tallest building, the 310 m Shard. City Hall, the home of the Mayor of London and the London Assembly is by the Thames close to Tower Bridge. Also along the river are the Tate Modern (converted from the former Bankside power station), the Millennium Bridge (the newest, pedestrian-only, bridge across the Thames), HMS *Belfast*, the reconstructed Globe Theatre, Southwark Cathedral and Tower Bridge. Additional tourist attractions include the Imperial War Museum London, and the Dulwich Picture Gallery which was Britain's first public art gallery.

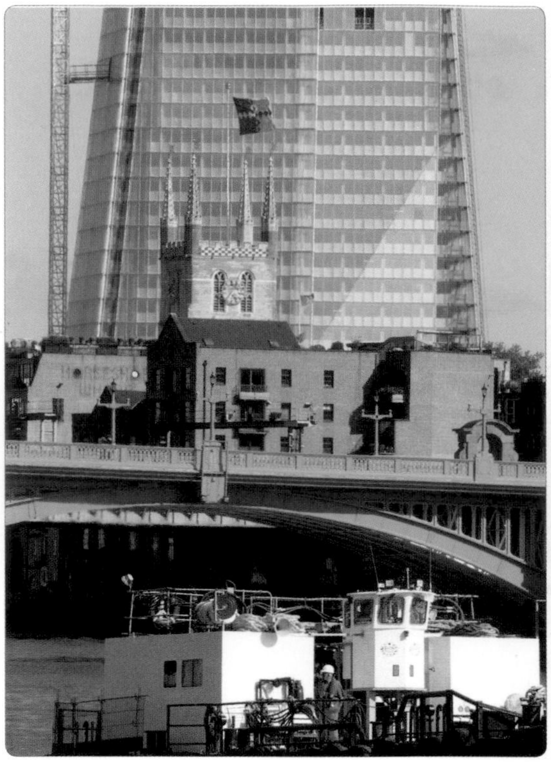

The tower of Southwark Cathedral, now dwarfed by the Shard, London's tallest building

HMS *Belfast* and Tower Bridge

FAMOUS FOR

Southwark Cathedral is one of the largest medieval buildings in London. The current building was originally an Augustinian priory, founded in 1106, which became known as St Mary Overy ('over the river'). After the Dissolution of the Monasteries in 1536, it became a parish church until it was raised to the status of the cathedral of the new diocese of Southwark in 1905. Next to the church the monks established a hospital, now known as St Thomas' Hospital, named in honour of St Thomas Becket.

Borough Market, close to London Bridge and Southwark Cathedral, is one of London's oldest food markets. There has been a market on Borough High Street since the 13th century. Once primarily a wholesale market, it is now home to over 130 stalls selling an exceptional range of quality foods.

The **Millennium Bridge**, a pedestrian bridge between St Paul's Cathedral and Tate Modern, had a most inauspicious opening in 2000 – its innovative suspension design could not manage the large number of people crossing the bridge and it started to wobble. Within days it closed but it has since been modified and now provides a great way to cross the river.

The **Globe Theatre** was originally built in Southwark in 1599. The theatre burnt down in 1613 and was quickly rebuilt, only to be closed down by the Puritans in 1642 and demolished two years later. Today's **Shakespeare's Globe** is a reconstruction, on a different site, of what the original Globe Theatre might have been like. It was opened in 1997.

The area around **Newington** is commonly referred to as the '**Elephant and Castle**'. The name comes from a pub that was established there in the mid-18th century on the site occupied by a blacksmith and cutler – the coat of arms of the Worshipful Company of Cutlers includes the image of an elephant with a castle on its back.

John Bartholomew, Gazetteer of the British Isles (1887)
SOUTHWARK, *parl. bor., Surrey, on river Thames, opposite London city, 1990 ac., pop. 221,946. Southwark returns 3 members to Parliament (3 divisions - viz., West Southwark, Rotherhithe, and Bermondsey, 1 member for each division); its representation was increased from 2 to 3 members in 1885.*

SOUTHWARK BRIDGE, *between Blackfriars Bridge and London Bridge, is an iron bridge 708 ft. long, the centre arch having a span of 402 ft.*

SOUTHWARK PARK, *near the Surrey Commercial Docks, covers an area of 63 ac.*

FAMOUS PEOPLE

John Harvard, clergyman and benefactor of Harvard University, born Southwark, 1607.
Thomas Guy, bookseller and founder of Guy's Hospital, born Southwark, *c.*1644.
Charles Babbage, mathematician and inventor of the 'Difference Engine', the precursor of the computer, born Newington, 1791.
Michael Faraday, chemist, physicist and inventor, born Southwark, 1791.
Samuel Palmer, artist, born Newington, 1805.
Robert Browning, poet, born Camberwell, 1812.
Joseph Chamberlain, industrialist and Liberal and Unionist politician, born Camberwell, 1836.
Alfred Marshall, economist, born Bermondsey, 1842.
Stanley Robert Mullard, electrical and radio engineer and industrialist, born Bermondsey, 1883.
Boris Karloff (*born* William Henry Platt), actor, particularly in horror films, born East Dulwich, 1887.
Sir Charles ('Charlie') Chaplin, comic actor and Hollywood star, born Walworth, 1889.
Enid Blyton, children's book author, born East Dulwich, 1897.
Phyllis Pearsall, creator of the *London A-Z Street Atlas*, born Dulwich, 1906.
Sir Michael Caine, actor, born Rotherhithe, 1933.
Tommy Steele (*born* Thomas Hicks), rock and roll singer and actor, born Bermondsey, 1936.
Rio Ferdinand, footballer, captain of England, born Peckham, 1978.

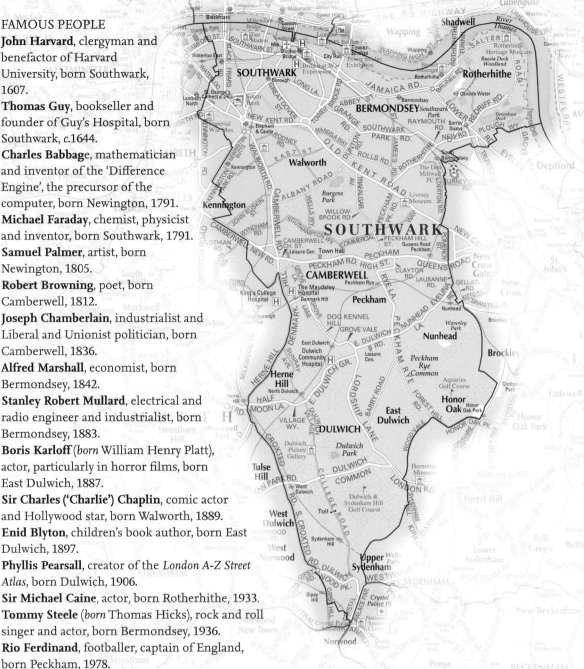

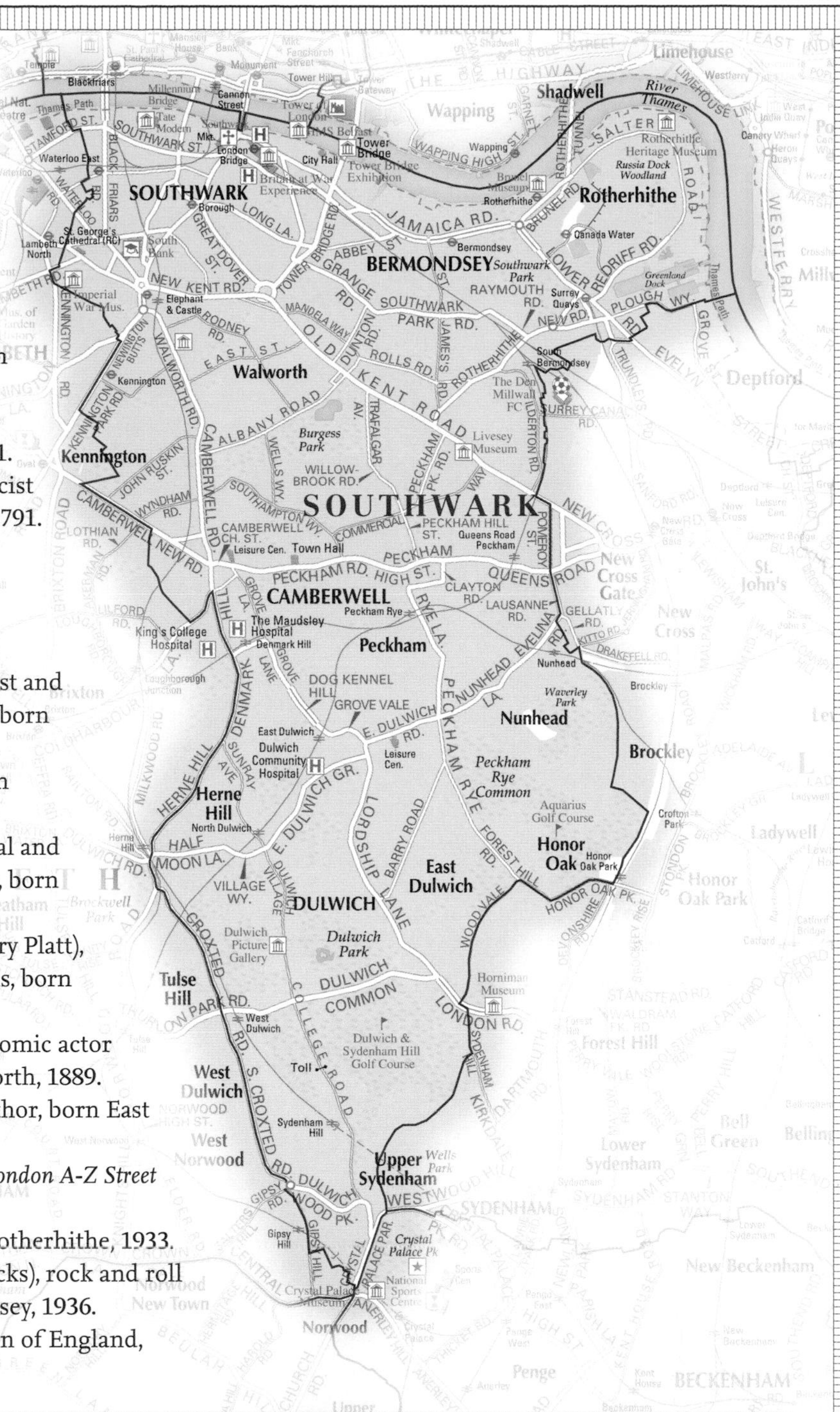

Robert Morris's interactive installation in the Turbine Hall of the Tate Modern, 2009

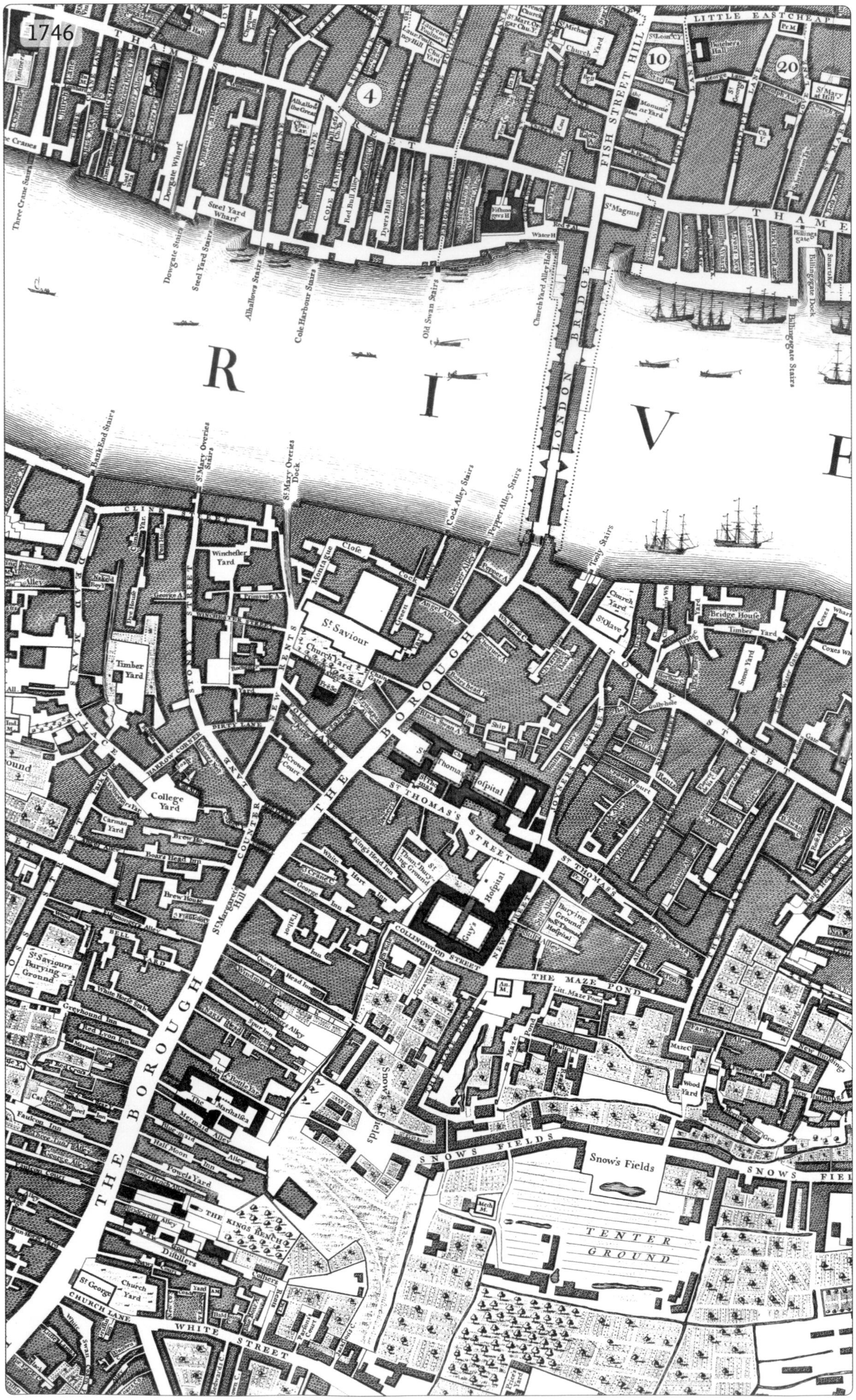

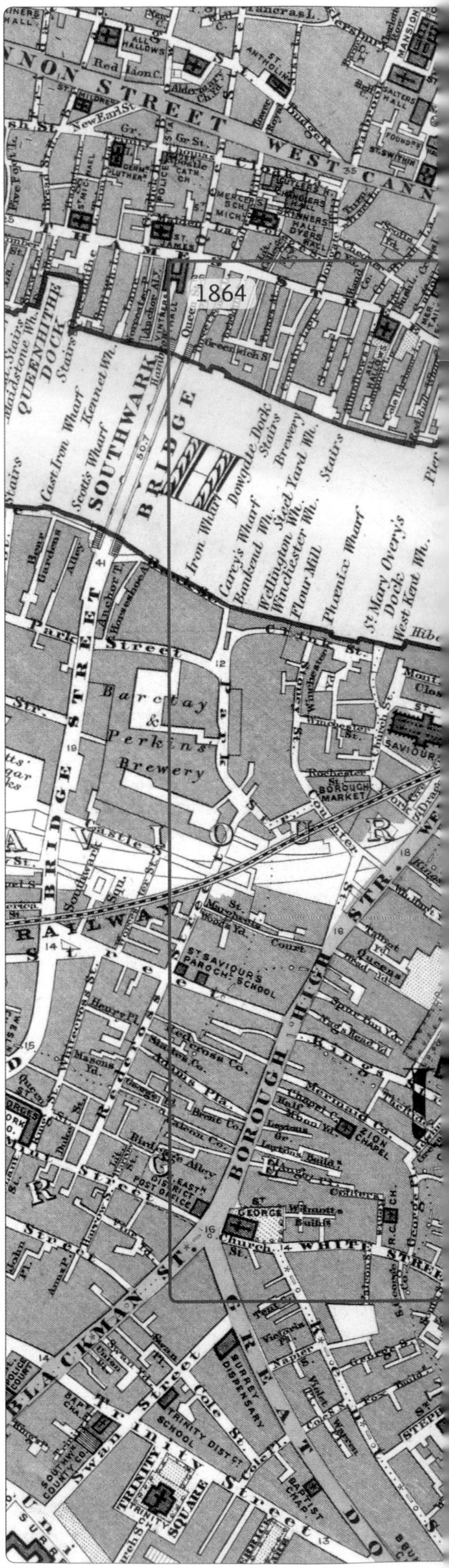

These three maps, although illustrating the developments that have taken place on the south bank of the river, also show the three versions of London Bridge that have spanned the river since medieval times.

The 600 year-old bridge on the 1746 map was lined with shops and houses until 1762 and then was replaced in the early 19th century by a five-arched road bridge. This bridge was built slightly upstream of the old one and in 1968 was sold, to be re-assembled at Lake Havasu City, Arizona, USA. The current three-span bridge, opened in 1973, replaced it.

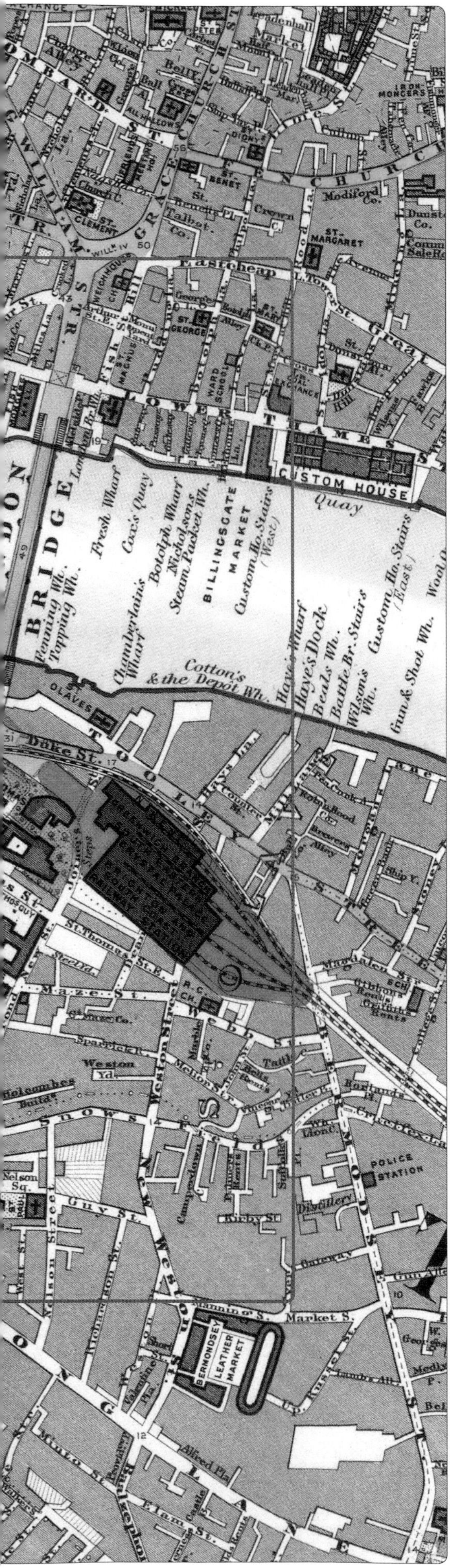

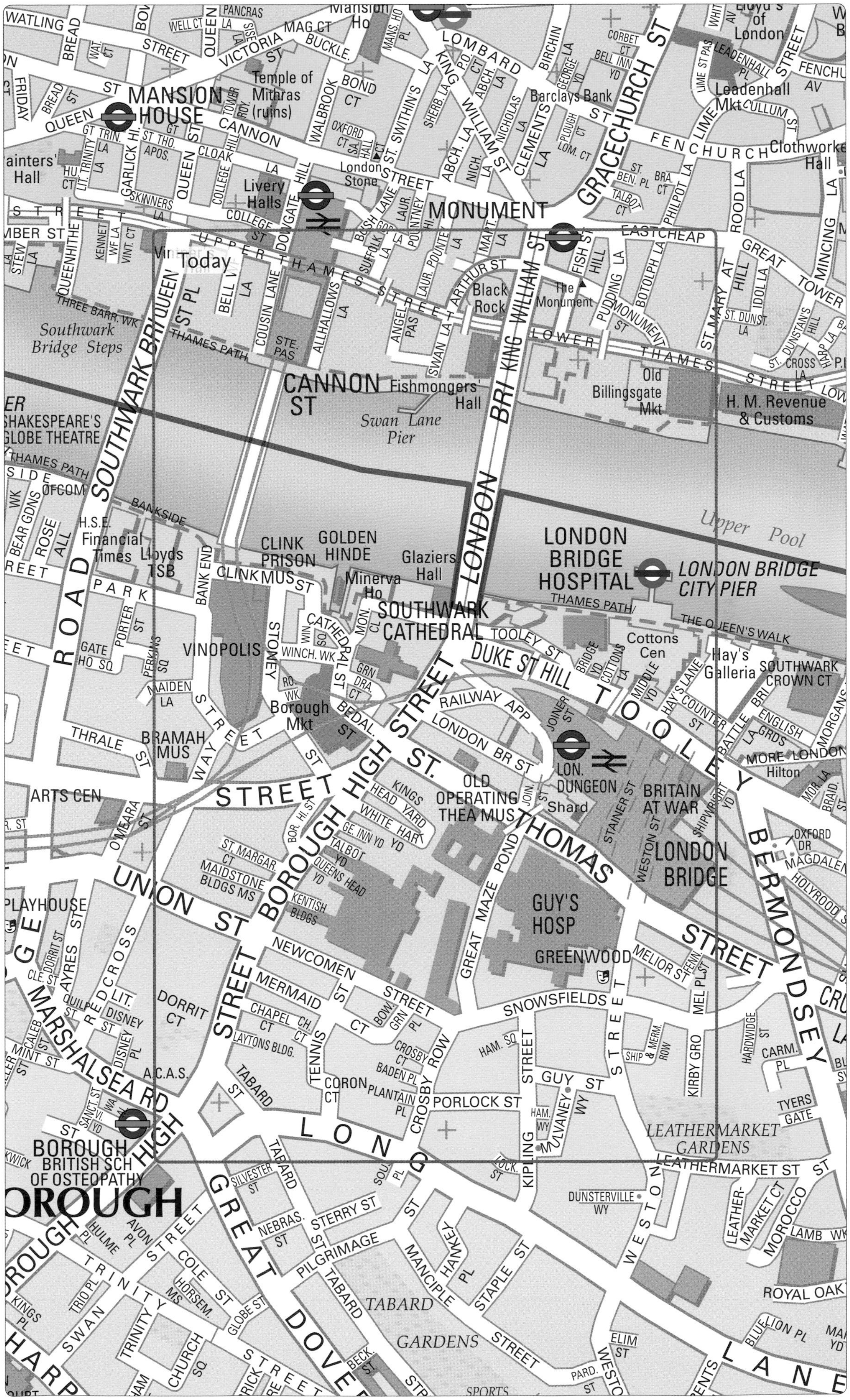

Left: Extract from John Rocque's *Map of London*, 1746
Middle: Extract from *Stanford's Library Map of London*, 1864
Right: Collins Bartholomew mapping

LONDON'S ART GALLERIES

TOP LONDON ART GALLERIES 2010 VISITOR NUMBERS

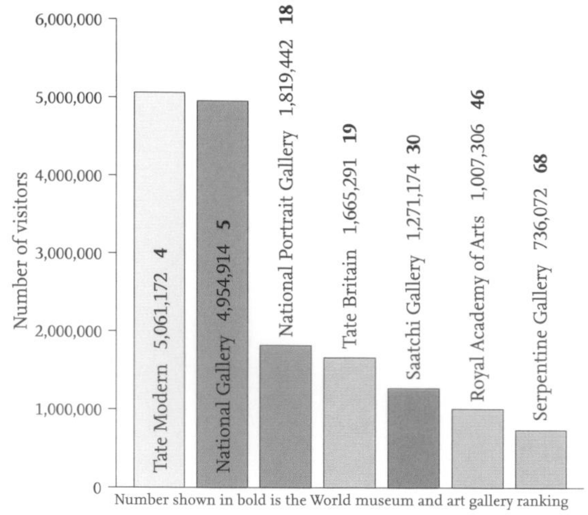

Number shown in bold is the World museum and art gallery ranking

London is the home of Britain's most important national collections of art and the newest major gallery in London, the Tate Modern, is also the most popular. The Dulwich Picture Gallery, by contrast, was Britain's first public art gallery to be housed in a purpose-built building. It was designed by Sir John Soane in 1811 and contains features that have influenced gallery design ever since. As well as many public galleries (many of which are free), London is also home to a large private art market, with both major international auction houses (such as Sotheby's and Christies) and many galleries selling art and decorative arts, both historical and contemporary.

Tate Modern opened in 2000 in the very imaginatively converted but unlikely setting of Bankside power station, a massive brick building on the South Bank of the Thames, now directly linked across the river by the Millennium Bridge to St Paul's Cathedral. The gallery houses the Tate Gallery's collection of international modern and contemporary art. In addition it holds major exhibitions and a special commission each year to fill the vast internal space that was once the turbine hall of the power station.

The **National Gallery**, in its prime position by Trafalgar Square, opened in 1838 in its current building, designed by William Wilkins. The origins of the collection go back to the 1824 purchase of an accumulation of art collected by the banker John Julius Angerstein, and the gift in 1826 of pictures by the collector and painter Sir George Beaumont on condition that a suitable building could be provided. It now comprises the national collection of western European art from the 13th to the 19th centuries, with particular strengths in early Italian art.

Saatchi Gallery

Tate Modern; the new Globe Theatre (Shakespeare's Globe) is on the left. The construction of the Tate Modern extension began in 2010 above the three underground oil tanks originally used by the power station

National Gallery, Trafalgar Square

The **National Portrait Gallery** is just behind the National Gallery and was originally to consist of portraits of 'those persons who are most honourably commemorated in British history as warriors or as statesmen, or in the arts, in literature or in science'. After over forty years in temporary homes, the current gallery opened in 1896. The collection now contains 160,000 portraits from Tudor times to the present day, including many iconic images from Henry VIII to Lucien Freud.

Tate Britain features British art from 1500 onwards including about 300 paintings by J. M. W. Turner that he left to the nation. The annual Turner Prize for contemporary art is exhibited at the gallery. The Tate Gallery was founded in 1897 after a benefaction from Henry Tate, who made a fortune from sugar refining. It was to be a national gallery of British art and it also became the national collection of modern and contemporary international art. This part of the collection is now housed at Tate Modern. The Tate Gallery, on Millbank, overlooking the Thames, became Tate Britain.

The **Saatchi Gallery** is a gallery of contemporary art that shows works from the major collection of Charles Saatchi, and contains many iconic works by contemporary British artists. It opened in 1985 and in 2008 it moved to the Duke of York Headquarters on the King's Road by Sloane Square. In 2010 it was announced that the gallery would be gifted to the nation.

The **Royal Academy of Arts** at Burlington House on Piccadilly and the **Serpentine Gallery** in Hyde Park have a regular series of special exhibitions but do not have permanent collections on display. The Royal Academy of Arts also has an annual Summer Exhibition of works by members. Each summer the Serpentine Gallery commissions a temporary pavilion from a leading architect.

Smaller collections of great quality include the **Wallace Collection** in Manchester Square, which has a superb collection of French 18th century paintings, furniture and porcelain as well as Franz Hals' 'Laughing Cavalier', all displayed in a London townhouse. The **Courtauld Gallery** in Somerset House displays a small but internationally important collection of European art, while the **Dulwich Picture Gallery** contains a world renowned collection of European Old Masters from the 17th and 18th centuries. **The Queen's Gallery**, at Buckingham Palace, hosts a series of special exhibitions drawn from the great wealth of the Royal Collection while the **Guildhall Art Gallery**, in the City, has important collections of London pictures and paintings by the Pre-Raphaelites and the **Whitechapel Gallery**, further east, has had a long tradition of exhibiting international contemporary art since its foundation in 1901.

SUTTON

Population	192,200
Area	44 sq. km
Population density	4,368 per sq. km
Area of green space	14 sq. km
Jobs in borough	72,000
Average house price	£240,045

The borough of Sutton takes its name from the main settlement in the borough and comes from the Old English for 'southern farmstead', originally in contrast to Mitcham and Morden to the north. The borough was formed in 1965 by combining the municipal boroughs of Sutton and Cheam, and Beddington and Wallington, with Carshalton Urban District.

Until the mid-19th century the area was agricultural with a number of settlements on the edge of the North Downs and on the River Wandle. Traditional activities included the commercial growing of lavender and watercress. The area started to change with the arrival of railways. Sutton developed after the railway to Epsom reached it in 1847, while other settlements, such as Carshalton, did not really develop until the 1930s. In 1851 the population of the whole area was around 6,300. By 1911 it had grown to 53,400 and by 1951 it reached 176,150. It is not a particularly diverse area, with 85 per cent of residents identified as white in 2007, nor is it an area of significant population growth.

As with most Outer London boroughs, many residents work outside the borough, with over 52,000 leaving Sutton for work. Within the borough the largest job sector is finance, IT and business (31.5 per cent of jobs) while nearly 12 per cent of jobs are in manufacturing and construction compared with a London average of just over 7 per cent.

It is now hard to appreciate that Sutton was once the site of the most extravagant of Henry VIII's palaces, Nonsuch, at Cuddington on the Surrey border. The building of this flamboyant Renaissance palace began in 1538, its name a reminder of Henry's ambition – that nonesuch should compare with it. It was in use up to the Civil War but during the Restoration, Charles II gave it to his mistress Barbara Villiers, who, in 1682, demolished it and sold the stone to pay her gambling debts. We now just need to use our imagination when visiting the site of the palace in Nonsuch Park.

FAMOUS FOR

Beddington Zero Energy Development (BedZED) provides a glimpse of the future. It was Britain's first carbon-neutral housing project involving around 100 homes and some workspaces and was completed in 2002 for the Peabody Trust. Even though not all the green technology worked, there have been dramatic reductions in energy and water use compared with conventional houses.

Carew Manor (or Beddington Place), now a school, contains a magnificent late medieval Great Hall, spanned by an arch-braced hammer beam roof. It was built in the 16th century for the Carew family. Sir Francis Carew, who died in 1611, is thought to have been the first person in Britain to plant orange trees successfully.

The great racing enthusiast, the Earl of Derby, had an estate in **Carshalton** called 'The Oaks'. It was here that the Earl and his friends planned the two classic Epsom races –The Oaks (first run in 1779) and The Derby (first run in 1780). The house was demolished in the 1950s.

In the centre of **Cheam** is a rare survivor – Whitehall is a 16th-century timber-framed weatherboard house, one of the finest examples in Outer London. It has been restored and is now a museum.

Wallington is the centre of a once flourishing lavender growing industry, commemorated in a sculpture depicting 'English lavender' in the town centre. Carshalton Lavender, a community organization, continues the tradition, with 1.2 ha of lavender at Carshalton Beeches.

FAMOUS PEOPLE

Cyril Frederick (Bob) Danvers-Walker, newsreel commentator and radio and television broadcaster, born Cheam, 1906.
Elsie May Widdowson, nutritionist, born Wallington, 1906.
Alec Clifton-Taylor, architectural historian and lecturer, born Sutton, 1907.
Quentin Crisp (*real name* Dennis Charles Pratt), writer and actor, born Sutton, 1908.
Penelope Keith, actress, born Sutton, 1940.
Angus Calder historian, writer and poet, born Sutton, 1942.
Sir John Major, Conservative politician, Prime Minister 1990–97, born Carshalton, 1943.
Jeff Beck, guitarist, born Wallington, 1944.
James Hunt, racing driver, Formula One champion in1976, born Sutton, 1947.
Paul Greengrass, film director and screenwriter, born Cheam, 1955.

John Bartholomew, Gazetteer of the British Isles (1887)
WALLINGTON, *township and vil. with ry. sta., Beddington par., Surrey – township, 823 ac., pop. 3007; vil., 2½ miles SW. of West Croydon sta.; P.O., 1 newspaper; the township contains Upper Wallington, vil., P.O.; is the site of a Roman station, and has yielded many Roman relics.*

BedZED, the low-energy housing development in Hackbridge

Carshalton Lavender

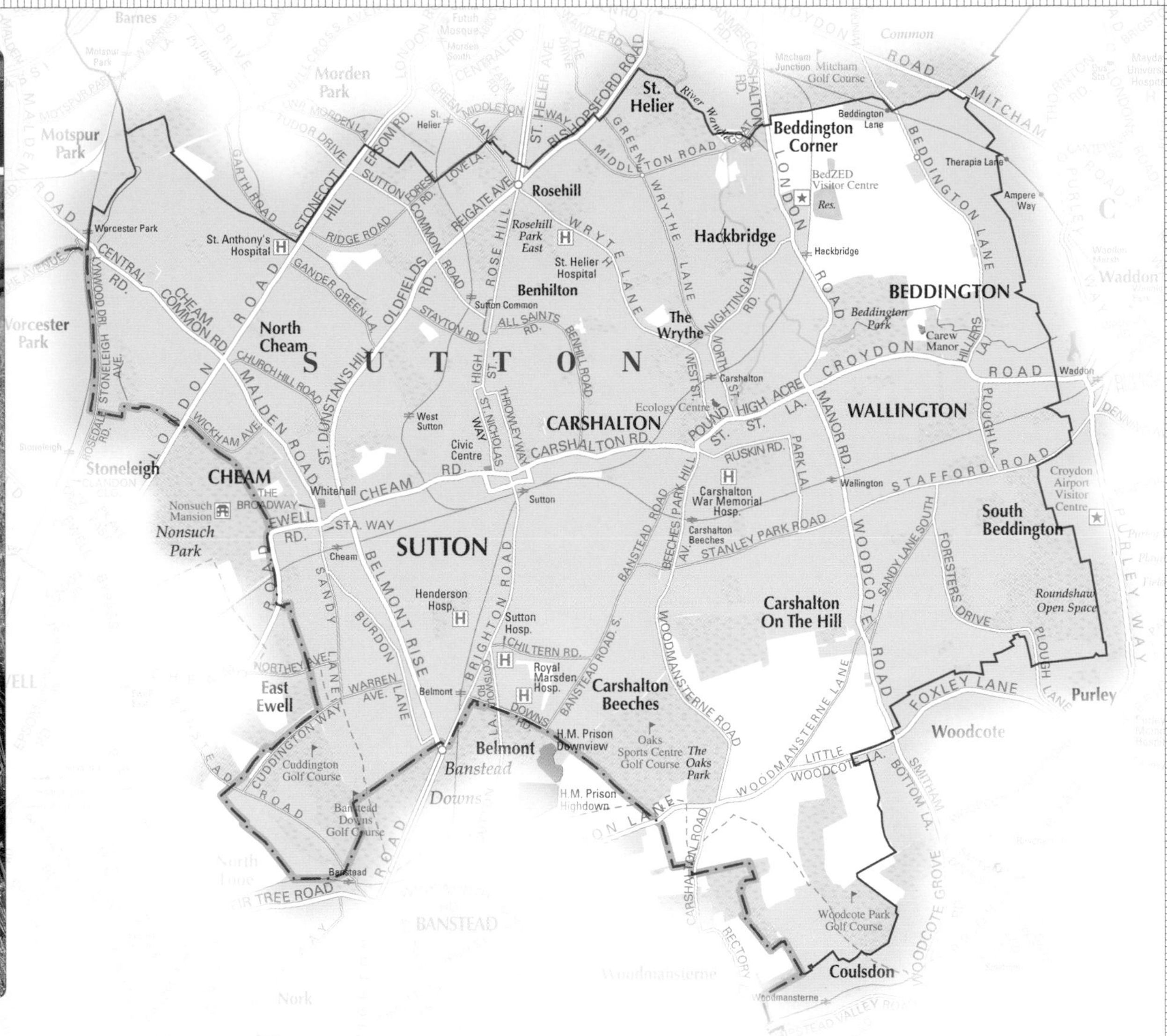

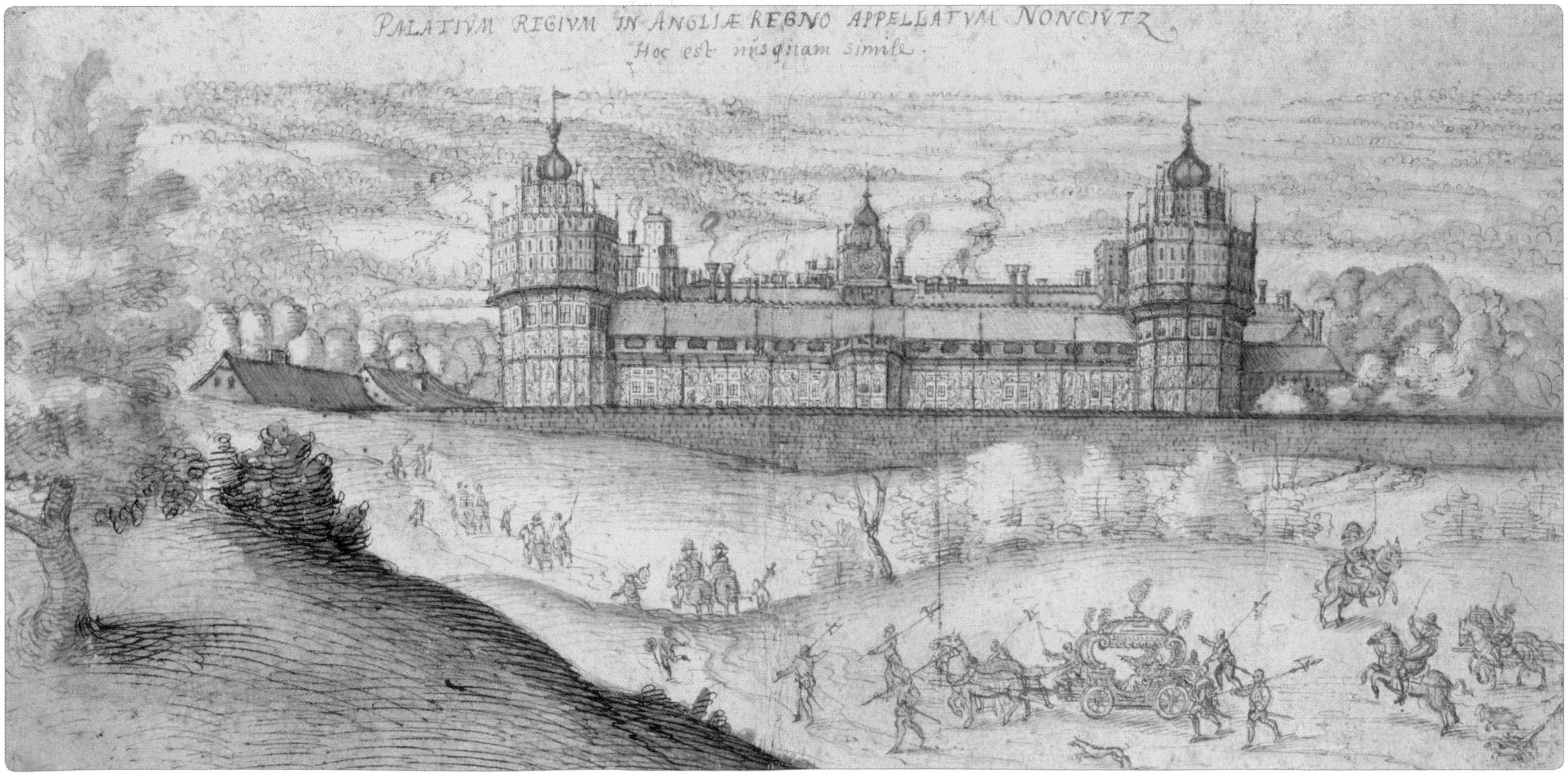

Nonsuch Palace, Henry VIII's magnificent palace, built near Cheam, as seen *c.*1582. The site of the palace is in Nonsuch Park, jointly run by the London borough of Sutton and Epsom & Ewell Borough Council in Surrey. The 'Nonsuch Mansion' identified on the map is a different building and is not built on the site of Nonsuch Palace.

THE TOWER OF LONDON

The Tower of London is by far the most significant military building in London, indeed, some would say in Britain. It provides a potent symbol of the imposition of Norman rule over England's largest settlement and of the autocratic and sometimes violent rule of British monarchs for the following 500 years.

William the Conqueror selected the site of the Tower, just beyond and downstream of the city walls, on the one hand to protect the city from attack from the river, and on the other to impose his authority on the city, an authority given massive physical presence by the White Tower, the central Keep of the castle. It was designed by a military prelate, Gundulf, bishop of Rochester, who was renowned for building both cathedrals and castles, and building started around 1078. By the standards of the time it was a huge structure, built using some unfamiliar materials, most strikingly Caen limestone from France. The tower was a royal palace, the oldest surviving in Europe. From the mid 12th century it became known as the White Tower, it is thought because it was whitewashed. This building then gave its name to the whole complex of the Tower of London which was somehow less threatening than the great moated castle that the Tower had become by the reign of Edward I at the end of the 13th century. In and amongst all the military swagger, within the White Tower is the king's private chapel, dedicated to St John, a perfect and serene example of Norman architecture once used by William the Conqueror. The military strength of the Tower only once failed, during the Peasant's Revolt in 1381. When Richard II came out of the Tower to speak to the rebels at Mile End, Wat Tyler and some others broke into the Tower, ransacking rooms, assaulting the Queen Mother and executing courtiers.

Over its life the Tower has been used as a fortress (it is still garrisoned by a Constable, usually a retired general, and the Yeomen Warders), a royal palace, a prison, a mint (until the Royal Mint was built outside its walls in 1810), a treasury (established because of the security of the Tower, which remains the home of the Crown Jewels), an observatory (until the observatory was built at Greenwich in 1675) and for 500 years until 1835, a royal menagerie (all the animals, apart from the ravens, were moved in 1836 to the Zoological Gardens in Regent's Park after a lion attacked a soldier), the Royal Armouries, a home for the National Archives, a major tourist attraction and a World Heritage Site.

In the public mind it is most remembered as a place of murder and execution. Its most treacherous time was in the late 15th century, when Edward IV was murdered there in 1471, his brother, the Duke of Gloucester, forcibly drowned in a butt of Malmsey in 1478 and his sons, Edward V and the Duke of York ('the Princes in the Tower') murdered in the Bloody Tower by order of their uncle Richard III in 1483. Richard's reign ended two years later, and the Tudor dynasty came to power and they used the Tower as a royal palace. Only with the coming of the Reformation did Henry VIII and his successors use the tower again as a prison and place of execution. Among the many victims were Sir Thomas More (1535),

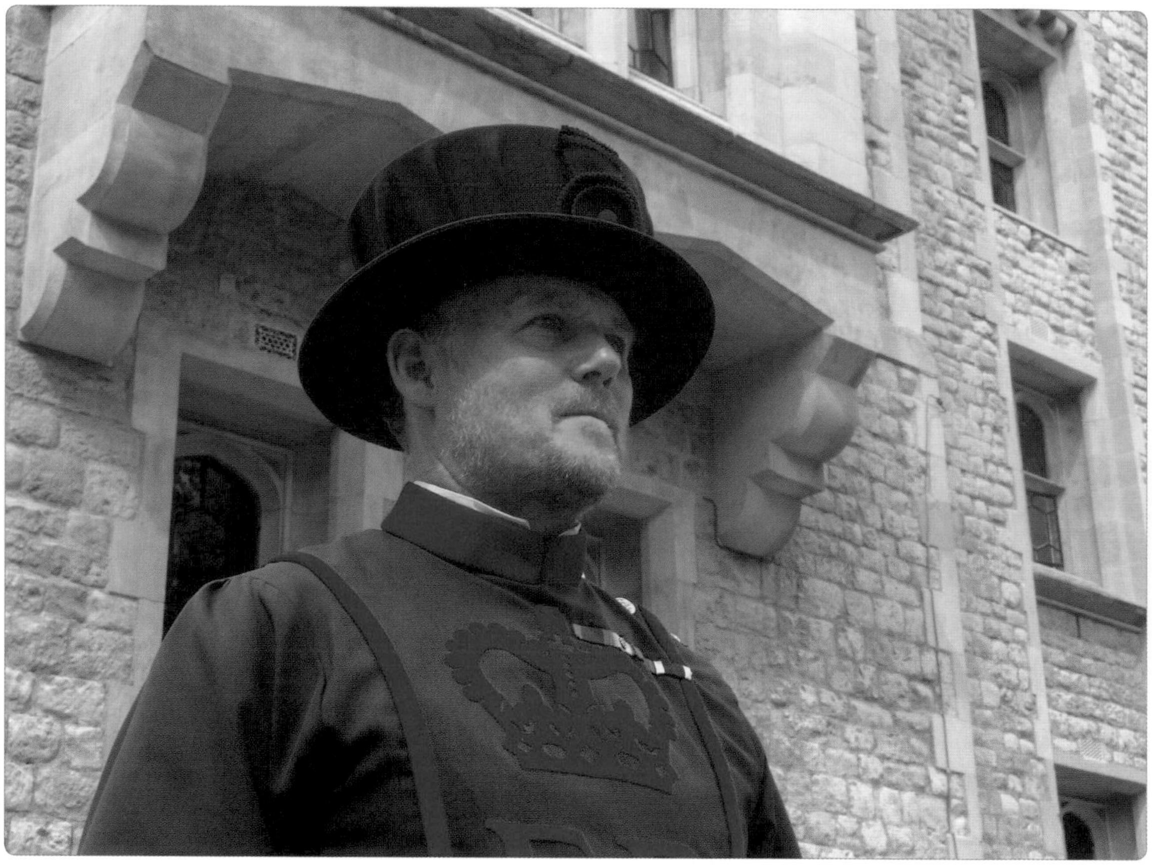

Yeoman Warder, ceremonial guardian of the Tower of London

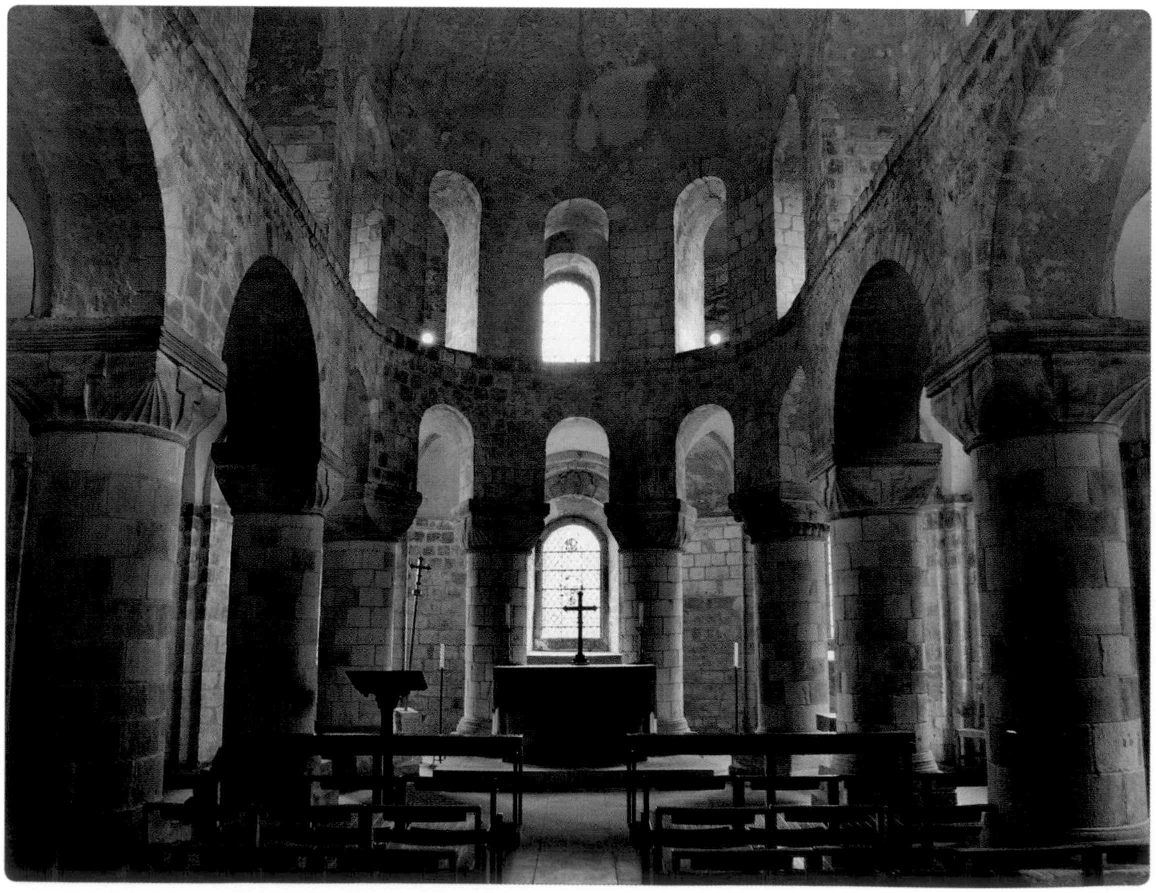

St John's Chapel in the White Tower, one of the best preserved Norman churches in Britain

Tower of London, 2010

Anne Boleyn (1536), Thomas Cromwell (1540), Margaret Pole, Countess of Salisbury (1541), Katharine Howard (1542), Lady Jane Grey (1554), Robert Devereux, Earl of Essex (1601), Duke of Monmouth (1685), and the Jacobite Simon, Lord Fraser of Lovat (1747). Charles II was the last monarch to stay in the Tower, which he did on the night before his coronation in 1661.

After all this *Visitor's London*, a 1958 guide, commented that:

you will perhaps feel that Merrie England and the Good Old Days were not so merry and not so good … but before he leaves the Tower the wise visitor will restore his sense of proportion … he will say good afternoon to the tower's Ravens, which hop tamely and happily where so much savage tragedy has been enacted.

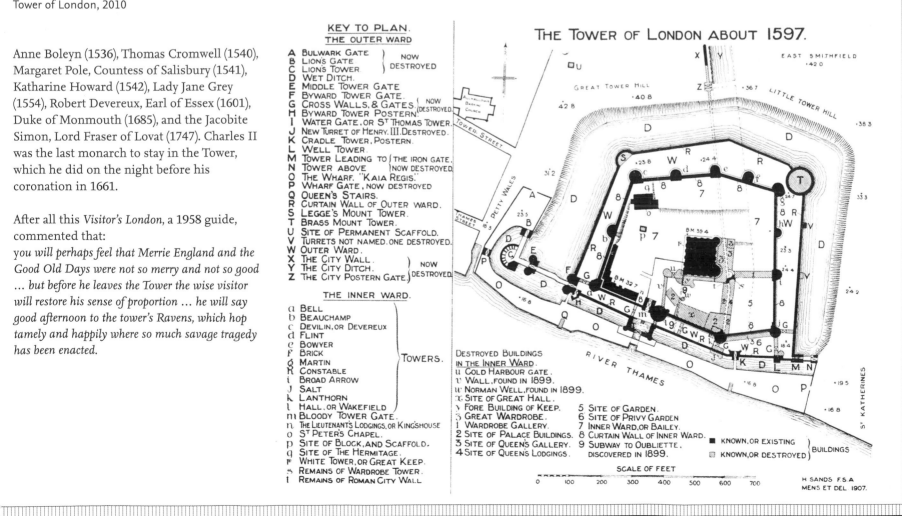

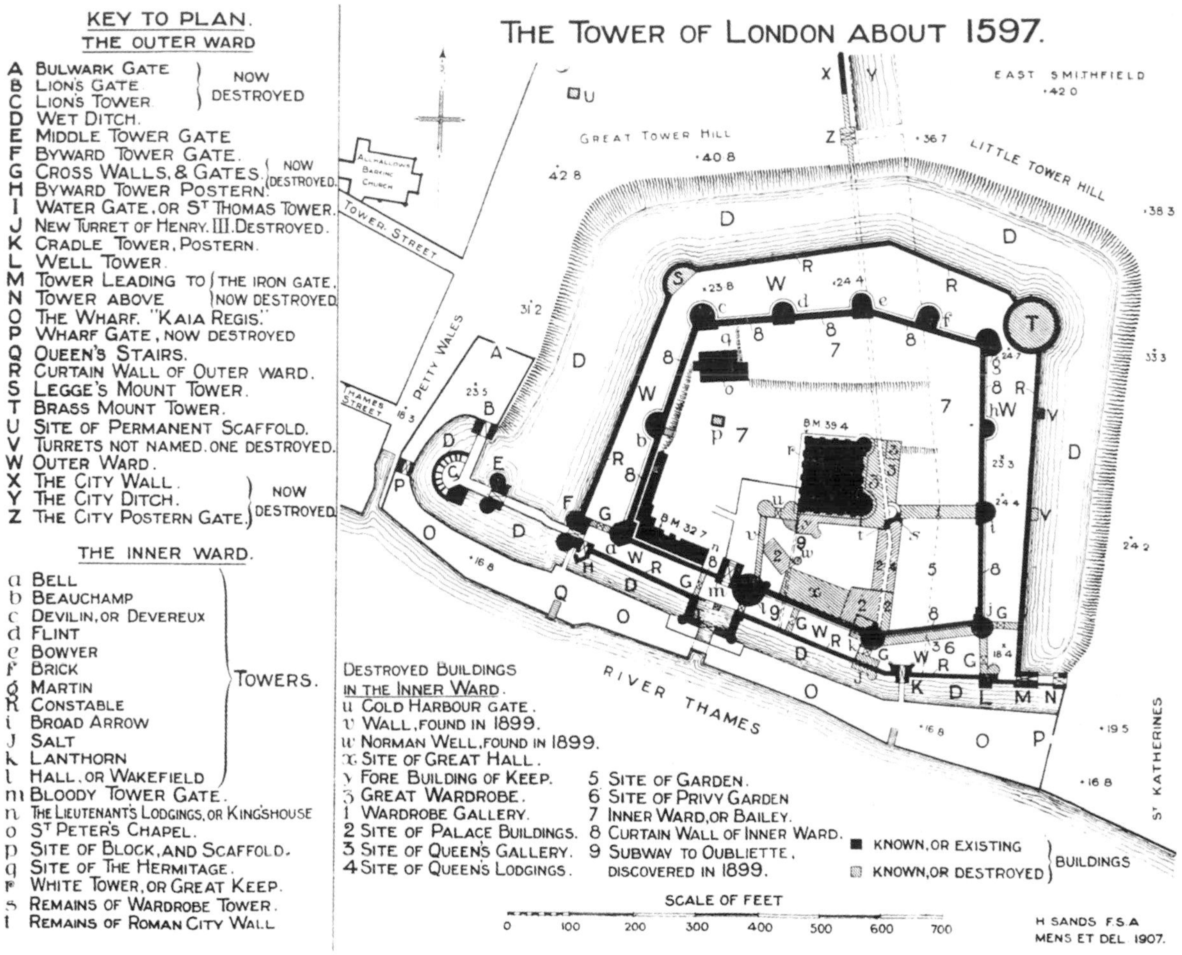

TOWER HAMLETS

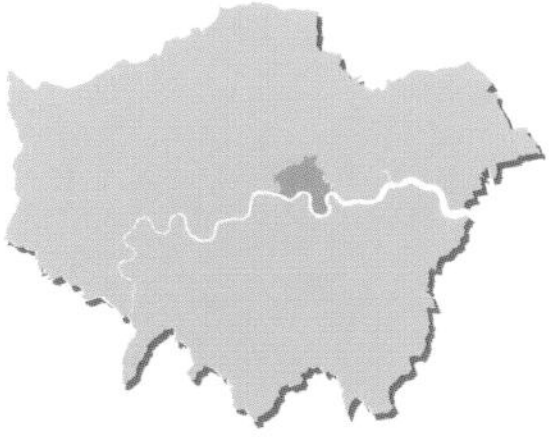

Population	234,800
Area	25 sq. km
Population density	9,400 per sq. km
Area of green space	3.75 sq. km
Jobs in borough	217,000
Average house price	£333,241

The name Tower Hamlets was used from the 16th century to describe settlements to the east of the Tower of London in which the Lieutenant of the Tower could raise a guard. It was brought back into use in 1965 for this new borough made up of the metropolitan boroughs of Bethnal Green, Poplar and Stepney. Being close to the City of London and bordering the Thames, the area has a long history – indeed in 1801, it is estimated that its population was nearly 131,000 growing to a peak of 585,000 in 1891. By then it had become a byword for overcrowding, insanitary housing and criminality. The population declined after 1891, with slum clearance, wars and industrial decline, until it reached around 140,000 in 1961. Since then the process has been dramatically reversed, the old East End communities changed with the growth of a large Bangladeshi population (about two-fifths of the total London Bangladeshi population and 30 per cent of the borough's residents) and by much private housing for City workers.

Tower Hamlets contains communities intimately connected with London's East End and its Cockney traditions – Bethnal Green, Shoreditch, Whitechapel, Stepney, Poplar, Millwall and Bow – but it is also an area that has seen immense change. The former docks area around the Isle of Dogs has become a major business and financial centre, based around Canary Wharf and linked to central London by the Docklands Light Railway and the Jubilee line. The Brick Lane area of Spitalfields, originally occupied by French Huguenots who fled France in the 1690s, and then by a large Jewish immigrant population in the early 20th century, is now home to the Bangladeshi community in an area long associated with the textile trade. Many workers commute into Tower Hamlets, with around 113,000 jobs in the borough in the finance, IT and other business sectors. There is a great contrast between these workers and those who actually live in the borough – male life expectancy in Stepney Green is 72 compared with an average for Kensington and Chelsea of 82, while areas in Bow and Bromley by Bow are amongst the most deprived in Britain.

Columbia Road Flower Market

Brick Lane, 'curry capital' of London

Brushfield Street, Spitalfields

The Tower of London is the most well-known landmark, whilst other significant buildings include Tower Bridge (though actually looked after by the City of London Corporation) and the Baroque churches of Nicholas Hawksmoor at Spitalfields, Wapping and Limehouse. Scattered through the area are a few buildings that predate the major changes caused by the development of the docks in the 19th century, including one of London's oldest pubs, 'The Prospect of Whitby', which dates from 1520.

FAMOUS FOR

In 1888, there were six murders in the slums of **Whitechapel** that gripped the nation, all allegedly committed by 'Jack the Ripper'. The crimes were never solved, but the conspiracy theories continue to this day.

Canary Wharf was where boats bringing goods from the Canary Islands docked. The docks closed in the 1960s and in the 1980s the area was redeveloped, its greatest symbol being One Canada Square, fifty storeys and 235 m tall, the highest building in London from 1991 until overtaken by the Shard, in Southwark, in 2010.

The **Whitechapel Art Gallery** opened in 1899 in a striking art nouveau building designed by C. H. Townsend and is devoted to exhibitions of modern art.

Life in the slums ('Rookeries') of Old Nichol in **Shoreditch** were described in Arthur Morrison's *A Child of the Jago* (1896), just as they were being replaced by London County Council's first housing estate, the Boundary Estate.

Queen Mary, University of London, started out as the People's Palace, founded on the **Mile End Road** in 1887 to bring education to the people of the East End. It has since become one of London's leading universities.

FAMOUS PEOPLE

John Dollond and his son Peter, silk weavers, manufacturers of optical and scientific instruments, born Spitalfields, 1707 and 1731.
John Newton, slave trader, Church of England clergyman and hymn writer, born Wapping, 1725.
Mary Wollstonecraft *(married name* Godwin*)*, author and advocate of women's rights, born Spitalfields, 1759.
Sir John Robertson, Australian politician, premier of New South Wales five times, born Bow, 1816.
Elizabeth Garrett Anderson, physician, born Whitechapel, 1836.
Sir William Henry Perkin, chemist, created first synthetic dye, mauveine, born Shadwell, 1838.
Mabel Lucie Attwell, illustrator, born Mile End, 1879.
Elsie and Doris Waters, comedians (known as their characters, Gert and Daisy), Elsie, born 1893, Doris, born 1899, and **Jack Warner**, actor and their brother, born 1895, Poplar.
Bud Flanagan *(real name* Chaim Reuben Weintrop*)*, comedian and singer, born Spitalfields, 1896.
Sir Charles Clore, businessman, born 1904, Mile End, 1904.
Joshua (Joe) Alexander Loss, bandleader, born Spitalfields, 1909.
Ronald (Ronnie) Scott, jazz saxophonist and nightclub owner, born Stepney, 1927.
Lionel Bart *(formerly* Begleiter*)*, song-writer and composer of musicals, born Whitechapel, 1930.
Des O'Connor, singer, born Stepney, 1932.
Arnold Wesker, playwright, born Bethnal Green, 1932.
Helen Shapiro, singer, born Bethnal Green, 1946.
Ashley Cole, footballer, born Stepney, 1980.

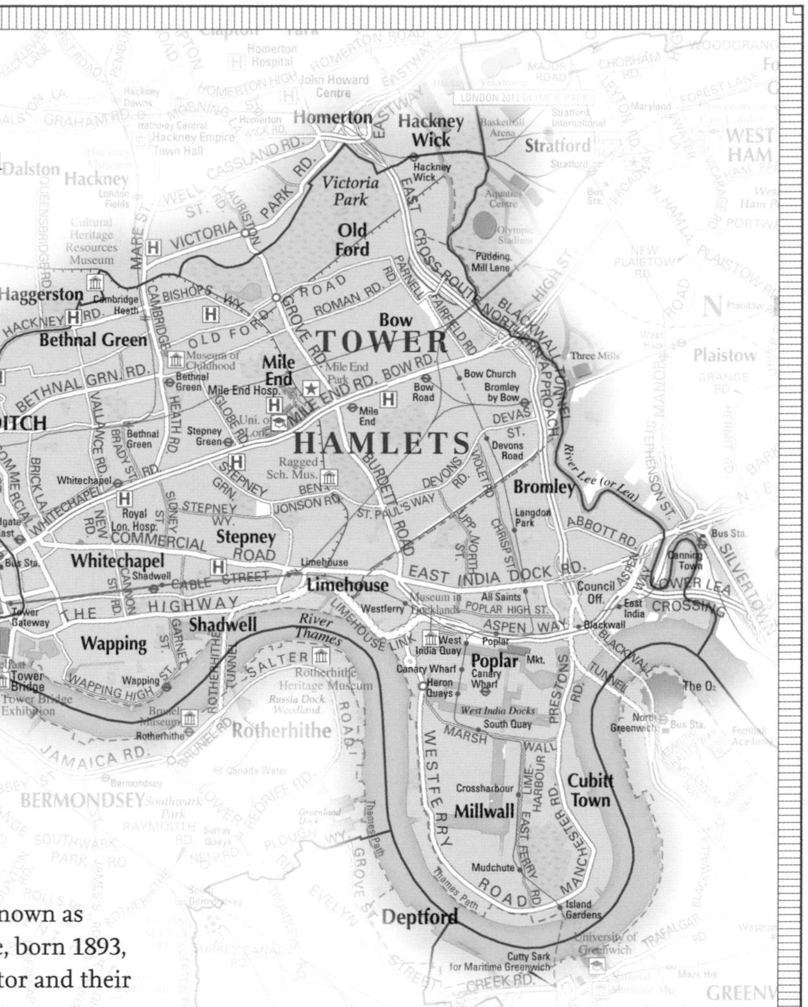

Canary Wharf, 2009

In 1932, Millwall and the Isle of Dogs was a busy docks area with rows of terraced housing

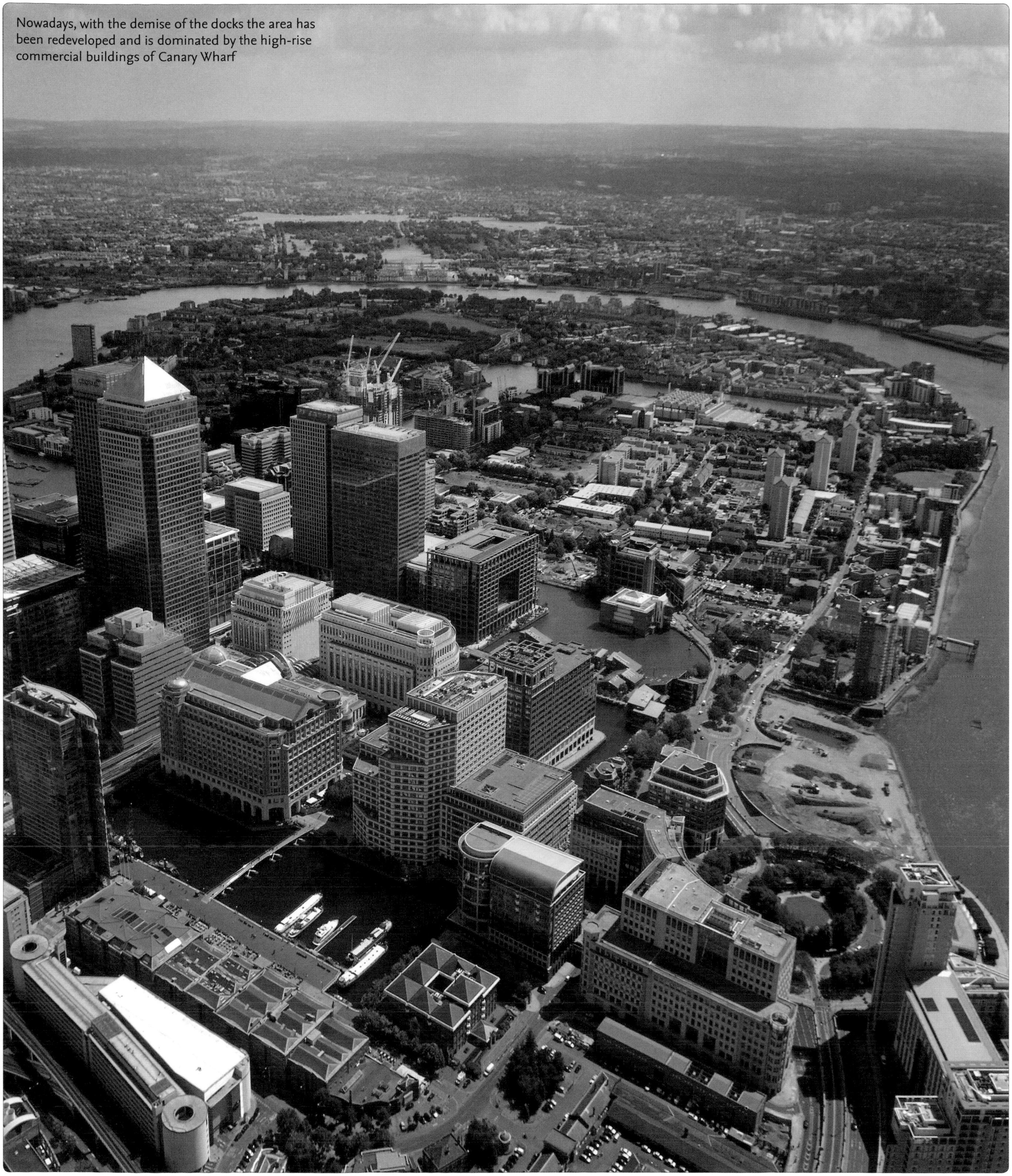

Nowadays, with the demise of the docks the area has been redeveloped and is dominated by the high-rise commercial buildings of Canary Wharf

A
B
C
D
1
2
3
4
131
221
BROADGATE
SPITALFIELDS
WHITECHAPEL
WAPPING
SHADWELL
LIVERPOOL STREET
OLD SPITALFIELDS MARKET
Brick Lane Mosque
JEWISH BURIAL GROUND
WHITECHAPEL
ROYAL LONDON HOSP
East London Mosque
WHITECHAPEL ART GALL
ALDGATE EAST
ALDGATE
FENCHURCH ST
TOWER GATEWAY
TOWER HILL
TOWER OF LONDON
St. Katharine Docks
ST. KATHARINE'S PIER
TOWER BRIDGE
TOWER BRIDGE EXHIBITION
CITY HALL (Greater London Authority)
H.M.S. BELFAST
LONDON BRIDGE CITY PIER
Tower Millennium Pier
POTTERS FIELDS PARK
DESIGN MUSEUM
Tobacco Dock
Under development
Shadwell Basin
WAPPING
Wapping Old Stairs
Wapping New Stairs
Upper Pool
The Pool
Lower Pool
Cherry Garden Pier
King's Stairs
KING'S STAIRS GARDENS
BRUNEL MUSEUM
SHADWELL
COMMERCIAL ROAD
COMMERCIAL STREET
WHITECHAPEL ROAD
WHITECHAPEL HIGH ST
MILE END RD
CABLE STREET
THE HIGHWAY
WAPPING HIGH ST
WAPPING LANE
JAMAICA ROAD
BERMONDSEY STREET
TOWER HAMLETS
SOUTHWARK
CITY

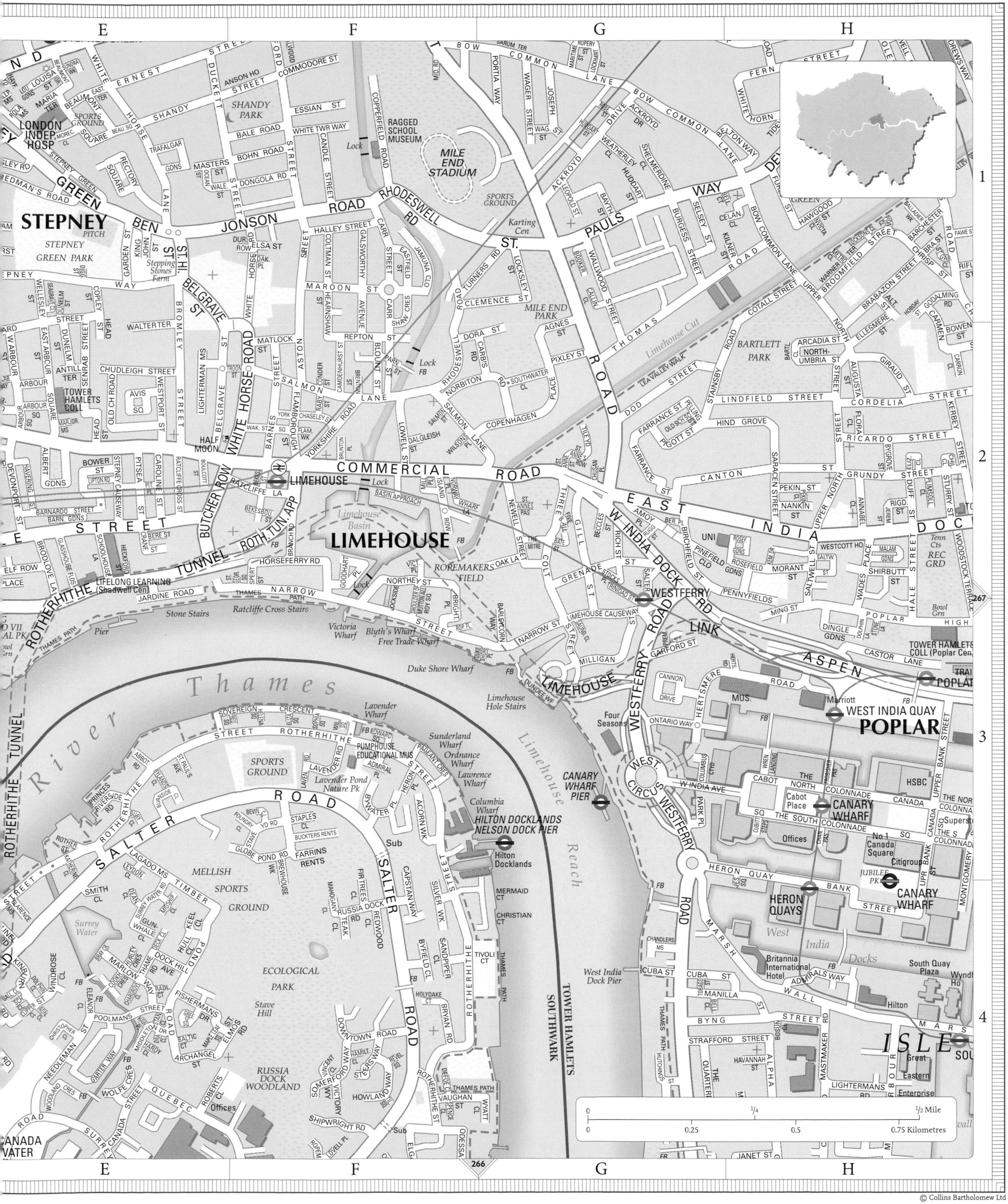
E
F
G
H
1
2
3
4
STEPNEY
STEPNEY GREEN PARK
LONDON INDEP. HOSP
SHANDY PARK
RAGGED SCHOOL MUSEUM
MILE END STADIUM
SPORTS GROUND
Karting Cen
MILE END PARK
BARTLETT PARK
LIMEHOUSE
Limehouse Basin
ROPEMAKERS' FIELD
TOWER HAMLETS COLL
HALF MOON
Stepping Stones Farm
LIFELONG LEARNING (Shadwell Cen)
Stone Stairs
Ratcliffe Cross Stairs
Victoria Wharf
Blyth's Wharf
Free Trade Wharf
Duke Shore Wharf
Limehouse Hole Stairs
River Thames
Limehouse Reach
WESTFERRY
WEST INDIA QUAY
POPLAR
CANARY WHARF
HERON QUAYS
CANARY WHARF PIER
HILTON DOCKLANDS NELSON DOCK PIER
Hilton Docklands
West India Docks
West India Dock Pier
Four Seasons
Marriott
MUS.
HSBC
Citigroup
No 1 Canada Square
Cabot Place
JUBILEE PK
Offices
South Quay Plaza
Britannia International Hotel
Hilton
ISLE
TOWER HAMLETS COLL (Poplar Cen)
Tenn Cts
REC GRD
Bowl Grn
UNI
SPORTS GROUND
PUMPHOUSE EDUCATIONAL MUS
Lavender Wharf
Sunderland Wharf
Ordnance Wharf
Lawrence Wharf
Columbia Wharf
Lavender Pond Nature Pk
MELLISH SPORTS GROUND
Surrey Water
ECOLOGICAL PARK
Stave Hill
RUSSIA DOCK WOODLAND
CANADA WATER
TOWER HAMLETS
SOUTHWARK
COMMERCIAL ROAD
EAST INDIA DOCK RD
ROTHERHITHE TUNNEL
SALTER ROAD
ROTHERHITHE STREET
NARROW STREET
LIMEHOUSE LINK
ASPEN WAY
WESTFERRY ROAD
WESTFERRY CIRCUS
BURDETT ROAD
ST. PAULS WAY
JONSON ROAD
BEN JONSON ROAD
WHITE HORSE ROAD
SALMON LANE
COPENHAGEN PLACE
BOW COMMON LANE
DEVONS ROAD
THOMAS ROAD
HERON QUAY
MARSH WALL
UPPER BANK STREET
THE NORTH COLONNADE
THE SOUTH COLONNADE
CANADA SQ
Limehouse Cut
LEA VALLEY WALK
THAMES PATH
0
1/4
1/2 Mile
0
0.25
0.5
0.75 Kilometres
266
267

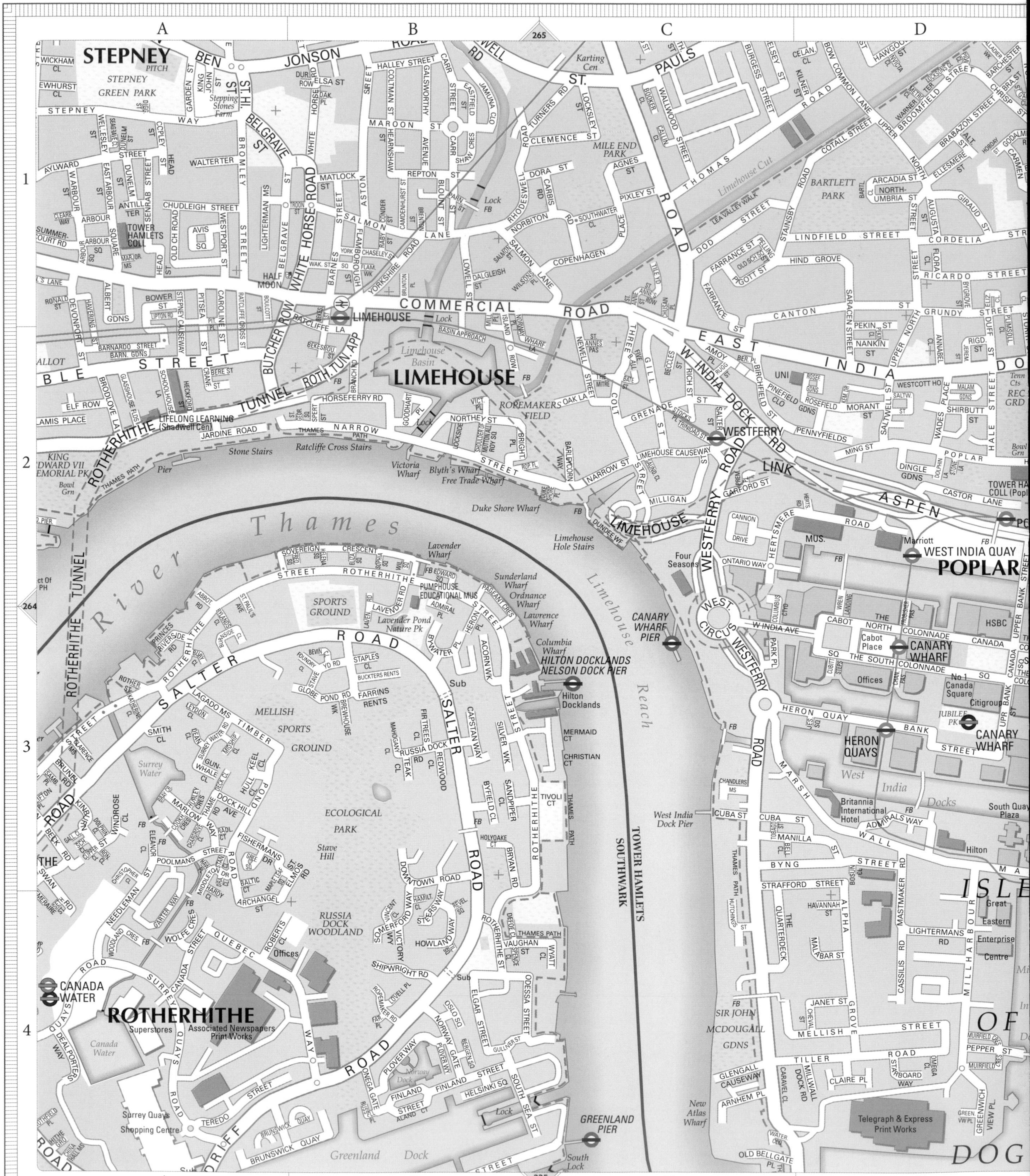
A
B
C
D
265
1
2
3
4
264
225
STEPNEY
LIMEHOUSE
POPLAR
ROTHERHITHE
River Thames
Limehouse Reach
STEPNEY GREEN PARK
Stepping Stones Farm
MILE END PARK
BARTLETT PARK
Limehouse Cut
Limehouse Basin
ROPEMAKERS FIELD
TOWER HAMLETS COLL
COMMERCIAL ROAD
EAST INDIA DOCK RD
LIMEHOUSE
WESTFERRY
WEST INDIA QUAY
CANARY WHARF
HERON QUAYS
CANADA WATER
SALTER ROAD
ROTHERHITHE STREET
ROTHERHITHE TUNNEL
Stone Stairs
Ratcliffe Cross Stairs
Victoria Wharf
Blyth's Wharf
Free Trade Wharf
Duke Shore Wharf
Limehouse Hole Stairs
Lavender Wharf
Sunderland Wharf
Ordnance Wharf
Lawrence Wharf
Columbia Wharf
HILTON DOCKLANDS NELSON DOCK PIER
CANARY WHARF PIER
Four Seasons
SPORTS GROUND
PUMPHOUSE EDUCATIONAL MUS
Lavender Pond Nature Pk
MELLISH SPORTS GROUND
ECOLOGICAL PARK
Stave Hill
RUSSIA DOCK WOODLAND
Surrey Water
Canada Water
Associated Newspapers Print Works
Superstores
Surrey Quays Shopping Centre
Greenland Dock
GREENLAND PIER
South Lock
TOWER HAMLETS
SOUTHWARK
West India Dock Pier
SIR JOHN MCDOUGALL GDNS
New Atlas Wharf
Telegraph & Express Print Works
West India Docks
Britannia International Hotel
Cabot Place
Canada Square
Citigroup
HSBC
Hilton
South Quay Plaza
Great Eastern Enterprise Centre
ISLE OF DOGS
WEST INDIA AVE
WESTFERRY CIRCUS
WESTFERRY ROAD
ASPEN WAY
MARSH WALL
POPLAR

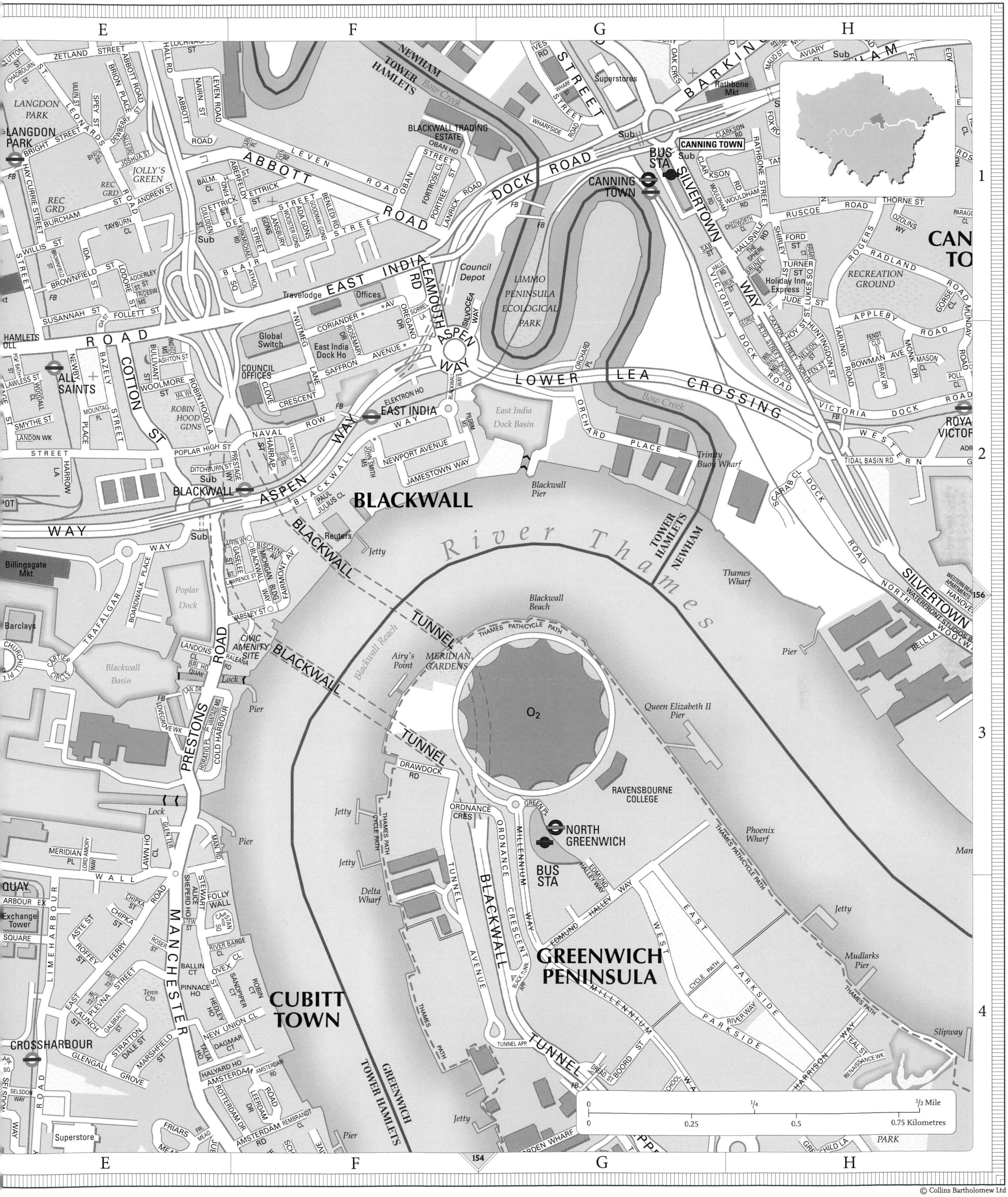
E
F
G
H
1
2
3
4
154
156
LANGDON PARK
ALL SAINTS
BLACKWALL
EAST INDIA
CANNING TOWN
NORTH GREENWICH
CROSSHARBOUR
BLACKWALL
GREENWICH PENINSULA
CUBITT TOWN
River Thames
Bow Creek
TOWER HAMLETS
NEWHAM
GREENWICH
LIMMO PENINSULA ECOLOGICAL PARK
East India Dock Basin
Poplar Dock
Blackwall Basin
O2
RAVENSBOURNE COLLEGE
MERIDIAN GARDENS
Airy's Point
Blackwall Beach
Blackwall Pier
Trinity Buoy Wharf
Thames Wharf
Queen Elizabeth II Pier
Phoenix Wharf
Delta Wharf
Mudlarks Pier
Billingsgate Mkt
Rathbone Mkt
Superstores
Superstore
Global Switch
East India Dock Ho
COUNCIL OFFICES
Council Depot
Travelodge
Offices
Reuters
Barclays
Holiday Inn Express
RECREATION GROUND
JOLLY'S GREEN
REC GRD
ROBIN HOOD GDNS
CIVIC AMENITY SITE
BLACKWALL TRADING ESTATE
EAST INDIA DOCK ROAD
ASPEN WAY
LOWER LEA CROSSING
ABBOTT ROAD
LEVEN ROAD
COTTON ST
PRESTONS ROAD
MANCHESTER ROAD
BLACKWALL TUNNEL
SILVERTOWN WAY
VICTORIA DOCK ROAD
ORCHARD PLACE
MILLENNIUM WAY
EDMUND HALLEY WAY
WEST PARKSIDE
EAST PARKSIDE
TUNNEL AVENUE
BLACKWALL AVENUE
ORDNANCE CRESCENT
THAMES PATH/CYCLE PATH
0
1/4
1/2 Mile
0.25
0.5
0.75 Kilometres

LONDON DOCKS

Until the start of the 19th century, most ships coming to London either unloaded at wharves along the banks of the Thames or moored in the river, ideally in the Upper Pool section of the Pool of London between the Tower of London and London Bridge, and discharged their cargos into lighters to take the goods to shore. As the Thames became more congested, secure, enclosed docks off the main waterway were needed. The London Docks, in Wapping, opened in 1801, quickly followed by the West India Docks on the Isle of Dogs (1802-6), the East India Dock at Blackwall in 1806 and the Surrey Commercial Docks from 1805. These docks secured London's place as a major deep-water port. Further docks included St Katharine Docks (1828), next to Tower Bridge, followed by the three stages of the Royal Docks (Royal Victoria, 1855, Royal Albert, 1880 and King George V in 1921) and by Millwall Docks in 1868. By the end of the 19th century the docks were handling a third of all British imports and many industries had developed close to the wharves to use raw materials shipped in. The docks (combined under the Port of London Authority in 1909, and including Tilbury Docks) were badly damaged during World War II, but increased their activity thereafter, handling a record 62.8 million tonnes of goods in 1964. However, there was to be a very swift change in fortune. The docks furthest upstream were becoming too small for larger boats and started closing – East India Dock in 1968, St Katharine and London Docks in 1969 and Surrey Commercial Docks in 1970. In June 1968, the first container ship docked at Tilbury and a shipping revolution began. In 1978 London's first custom-built container dock opened at Tilbury and by 1981 the last of the operating docks, the Royal Docks, closed. The London Docklands Development Corporation was set up in that year to spearhead the redevelopment of 22 square km of Docklands, which enabled Canary Wharf and London City Airport to emerge and open up a once hidden area of London.

The Royal Docks in the 1950s were a hive of activity with ships lining all the quays

By the end of the 20th century the Royal Docks were closed and the area had been redeveloped as the site of London City Airport.

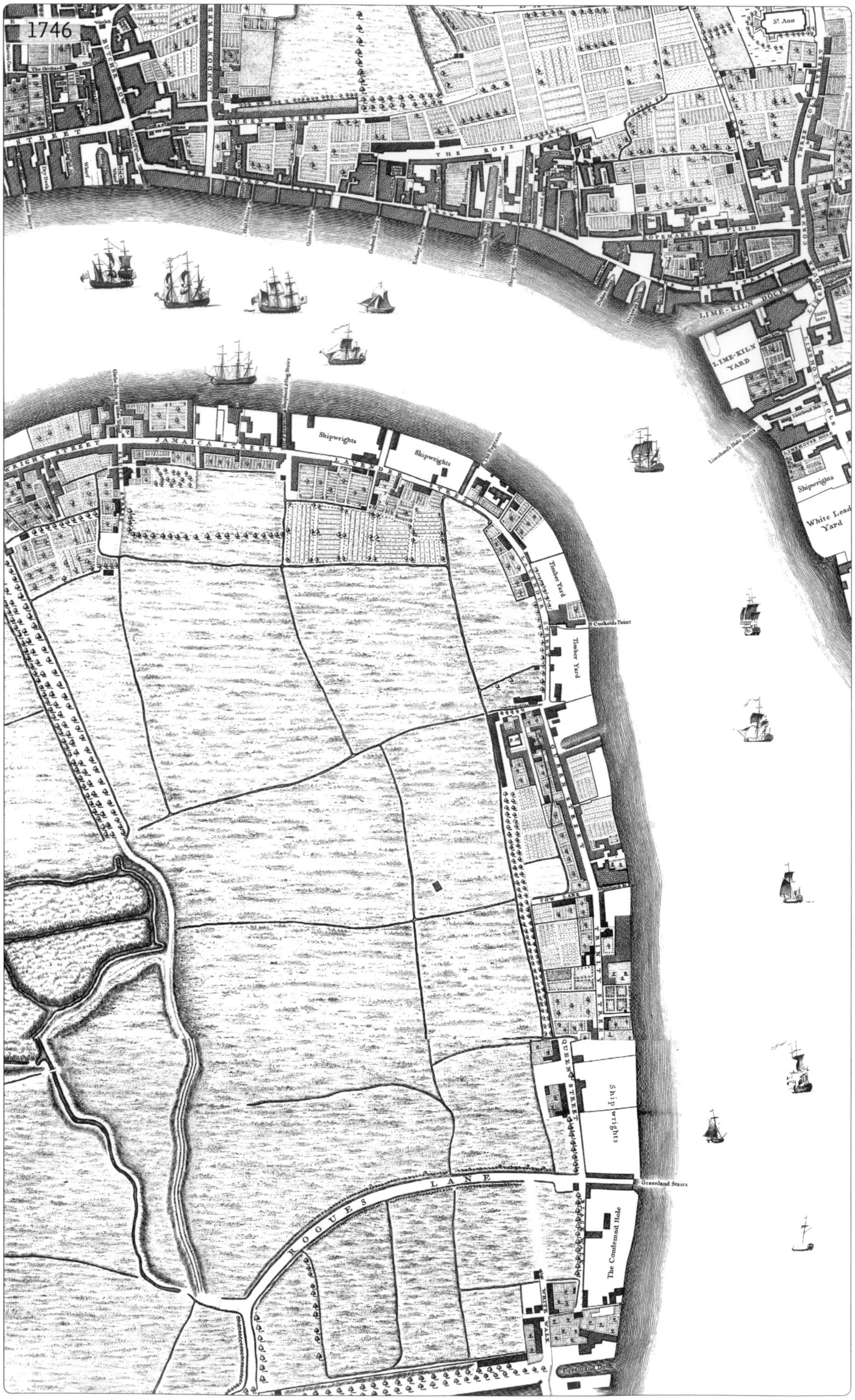

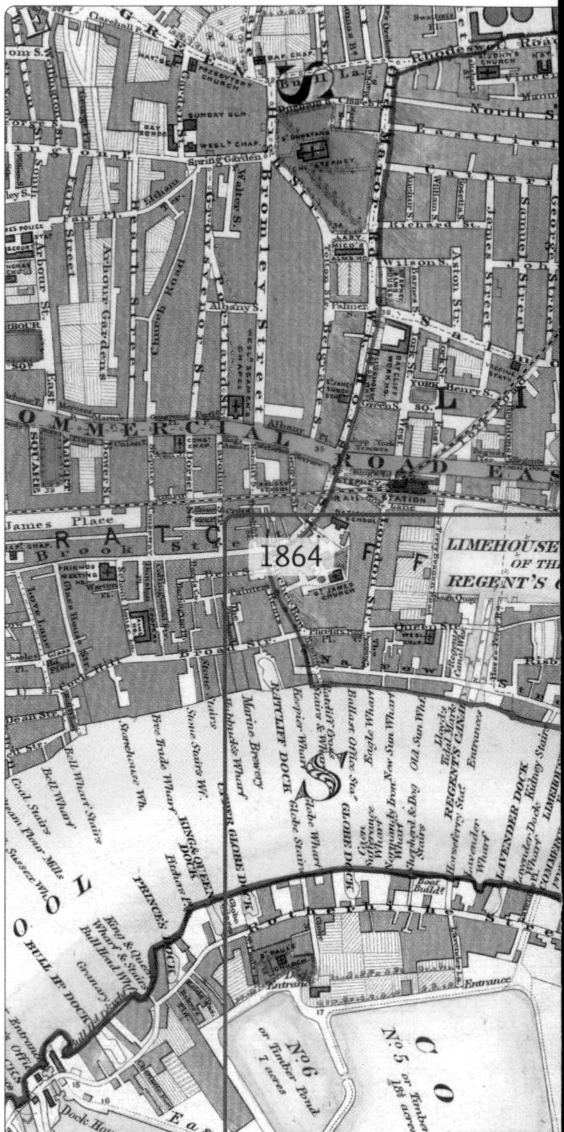

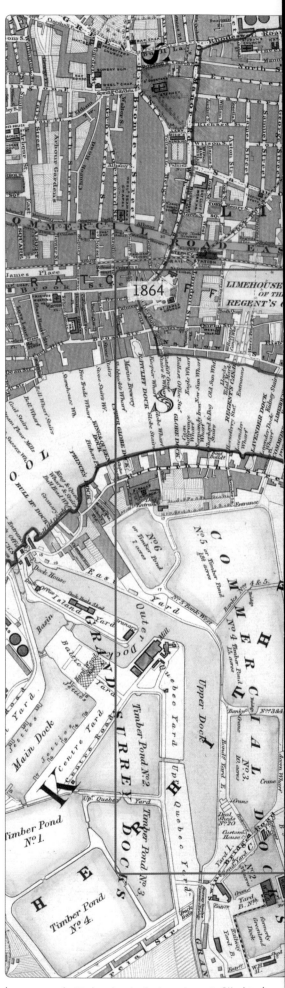

The amount of change that has taken place in the Docklands area of London is well illustrated by these three maps. In the mid 18th century ships moored along the river banks, but by the middle of the next century vast enclosed docks had been constructed to deal with the huge increase in trade and to accommodate the much larger vessels. Today the docks have been infilled to be replaced by modern housing developments, open areas and walkways.

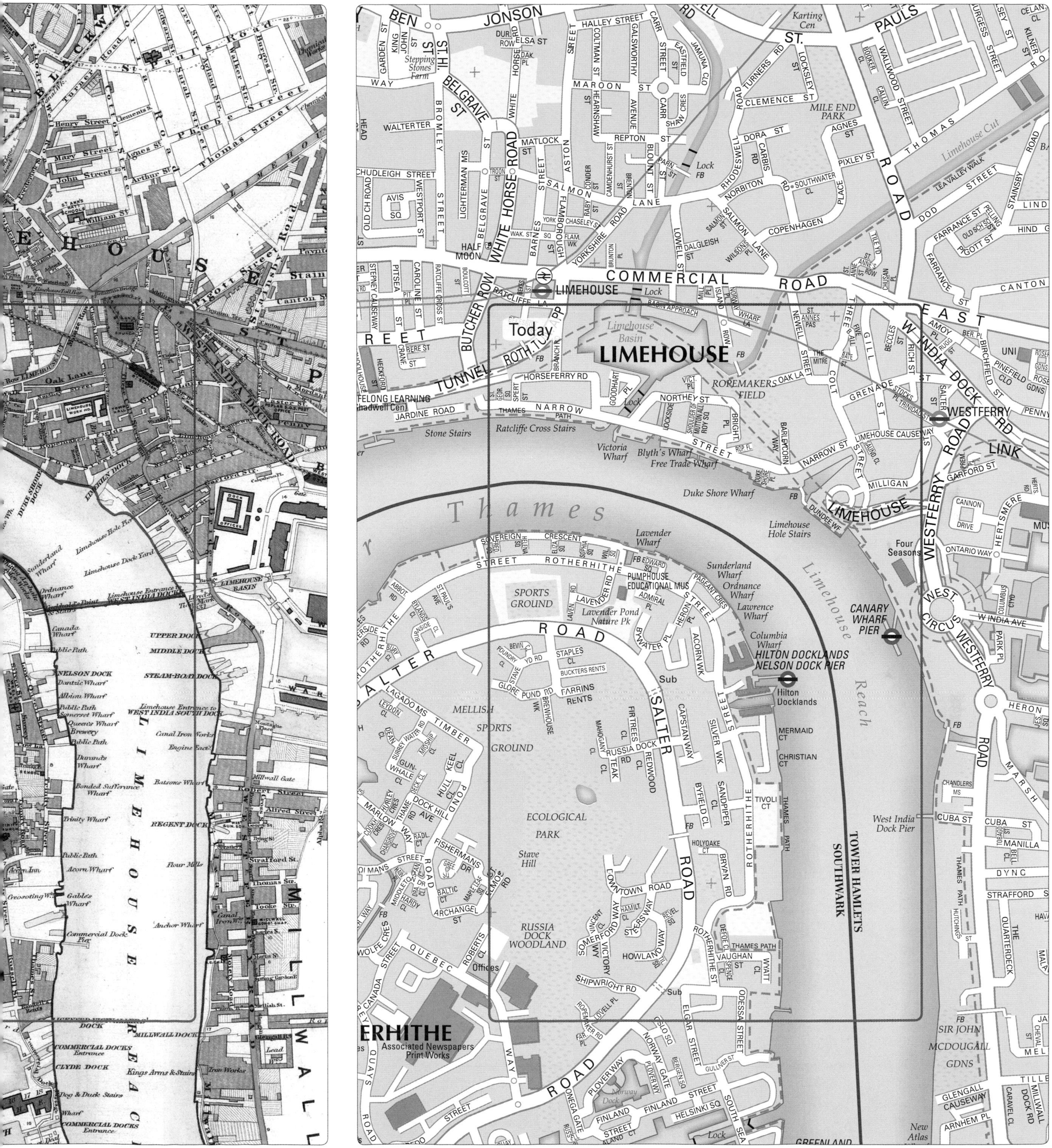

Left: Extract from John Rocque's *Map of London*, 1746
Middle: Extract from *Stanford's Library Map of London*, 1864
Right: Collins Bartholomew mapping

WALTHAM FOREST

Population	224,300
Area	39 sq. km
Population density	5,751 per sq. km
Area of green space	13 sq. km
Jobs in borough	69,000
Average house price	£220,300

The borough of Waltham Forest takes its name from the Royal forest whose remnants are now known as Epping Forest. 'Waltham' comes from the Essex town of Waltham Abbey ('woodland village') and not from the borough's main settlement of Walthamstow, which was once known as Wilcomestowe and has a different origin. The main settlements are Walthamstow, Chingford and Leyton, each with evidence of medieval churches. Epping Forest once ran through the whole borough and up to the 19th century it was an area of agriculture in which wealthy London merchants had country houses. All changed with the arrival of the railways. The Lea Valley, on the western boundary of the borough became industrialized while villages quickly became suburbs. More of the borough would have been developed but for the Commoners of Epping Forest who wished to protect their rights, leading to the Epping Forest Act of 1878. This protected the remaining forest under the administration of the City of London Corporation, who continue to manage it today.

Walthamstow Market

The population growth in the 19th century was dramatic – from 10,800 in 1851 to 154,100 in 1901 and 255,700 in 1911. While one study suggests that the current population is 20,000 larger than that given above, it still has not returned to the level of 100 years ago. The ethnic mix of that population has changed dramatically however. In 2007 it was estimated that nearly 63 per cent of the population were white, 15 per cent Asian and 15 per cent black, with the third largest Muslim population in London.

At the start of the last century the Lea Valley and Walthamstow was the home to new technological industries – the first British car was made by Frederick Bremer in 1894 in a workshop at Connaught Road, Walthamstow while Edwin Alliott Vernon Roe built the first all-British aeroplane (powered by an engine made in Tottenham) under the railway arches at Walthamstow Marshes. A century later, manufacturing is not an important part of the borough's economy – the largest provider of employment is now public administration, education and health (32 per cent of jobs), while 63,000 residents work outside the borough, almost equal to the total number of jobs within Waltham Forest.

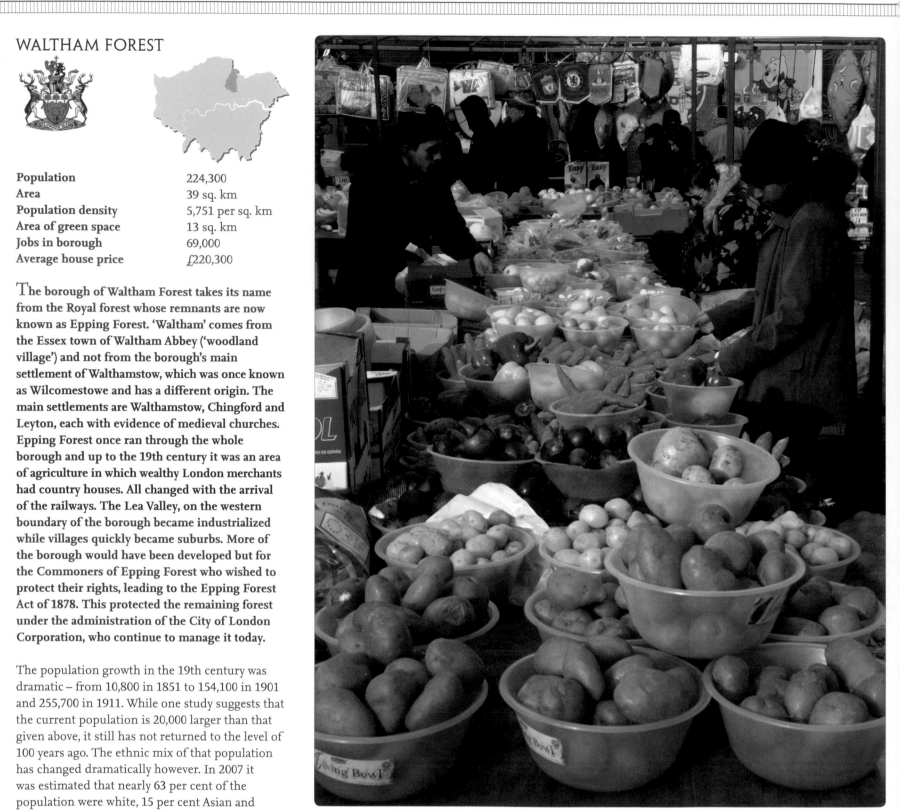

FAMOUS FOR

Queen Elizabeth's Hunting Lodge in Chingford was actually built by Henry VIII in 1543 as a 'Grand Standing' from which he and his guests could watch hunting parties in Epping Forest. Elizabeth I repaired it in 1589 and in 1604 it was converted into a house. It is now owned by the City of London Corporation.

Walthamstow Market is one of the longest daily (Tuesday to Saturday) street markets in Europe. Started in 1885, around 500 stalls line both sides of Walthamstow High Street for around 1 km.

William Morris was born in Walthamstow in 1834 and from 1848 to 1856 the 18th-century Water House was the family home. It now houses the **William Morris Gallery**, a world-renowned museum devoted to his work.

Eton Manor in Leyton forms the northern end of the 2012 Olympic Park. It will house temporary swimming training pools and will host Wheelchair Tennis in the Paralympics.

In 1991 Spitalfields Market, established in 1682, moved to Leyton. Run by the City of London

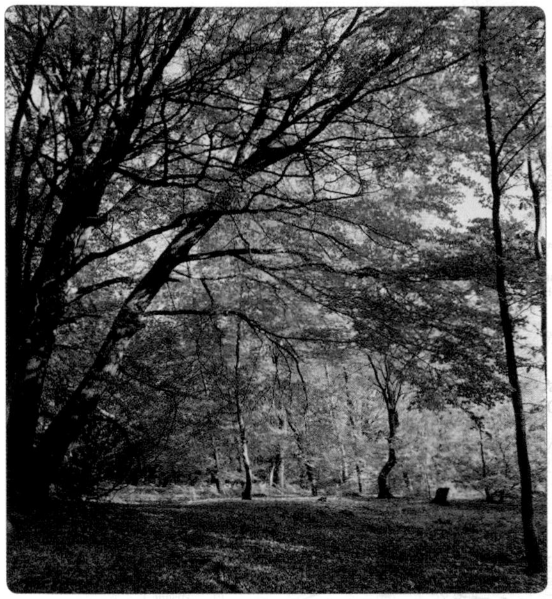

Epping Forest

Corporation, **New Spitalfields Market** is Britain's largest horticultural wholesale market and offers a greater variety of exotic fruit and vegetables than any other market in Europe.

The **Lee Valley Regional Park** was established in 1966. It stretches down the Lea Valley from Ware in Hertfordshire to the East India Dock on the Thames and encourages recreational use and wildlife conservation along this once-industrial valley.

In 1968 **Walthamstow Central** Underground station was opened. It is the northern terminus of the Victoria Line, the first deep-level line built across central London since the early 20th century.

Walthamstow Stadium closed in 2008 but for seventy-five years it was an iconic greyhound racing track.

FAMOUS PEOPLE

William Morris, designer, author, and visionary socialist, born Walthamstow, 1834.
John Kemp Starley, inventor of a recognisably modern bicycle, born Walthamstow, 1855.
Alfred Joseph Hitchcock, film director, born Leytonstone, 1899.
Sir Frederick Pontin, founder of holiday camps, born Walthamstow, 1906.
Sir George Edwards, aircraft designer and industrialist (original architect of Concorde project), born Walthamstow, 1908.
Fanny Cradock, television chef, born Leytonstone, 1909.
Roy Ullyett, cartoonist and caricaturist, born Leyton, 1914.
Sir John Pritchard, conductor, born Walthamstow, 1918.
Sean MacStiofáin (*born* John Stephenson), Irish republican, born Leytonstone, 1928.
Sir Derek Jacobi, actor, born Leytonstone, 1938.
Steve Bell, political cartoonist, born Walthamstow, 1951.
Graham Gooch, cricketer, born Leytonstone, 1953.
Jonathan Ive, designer of the iMac and other Mac products, born Chingford, 1967.
David Beckham, footballer, born Leytonstone, 1975.

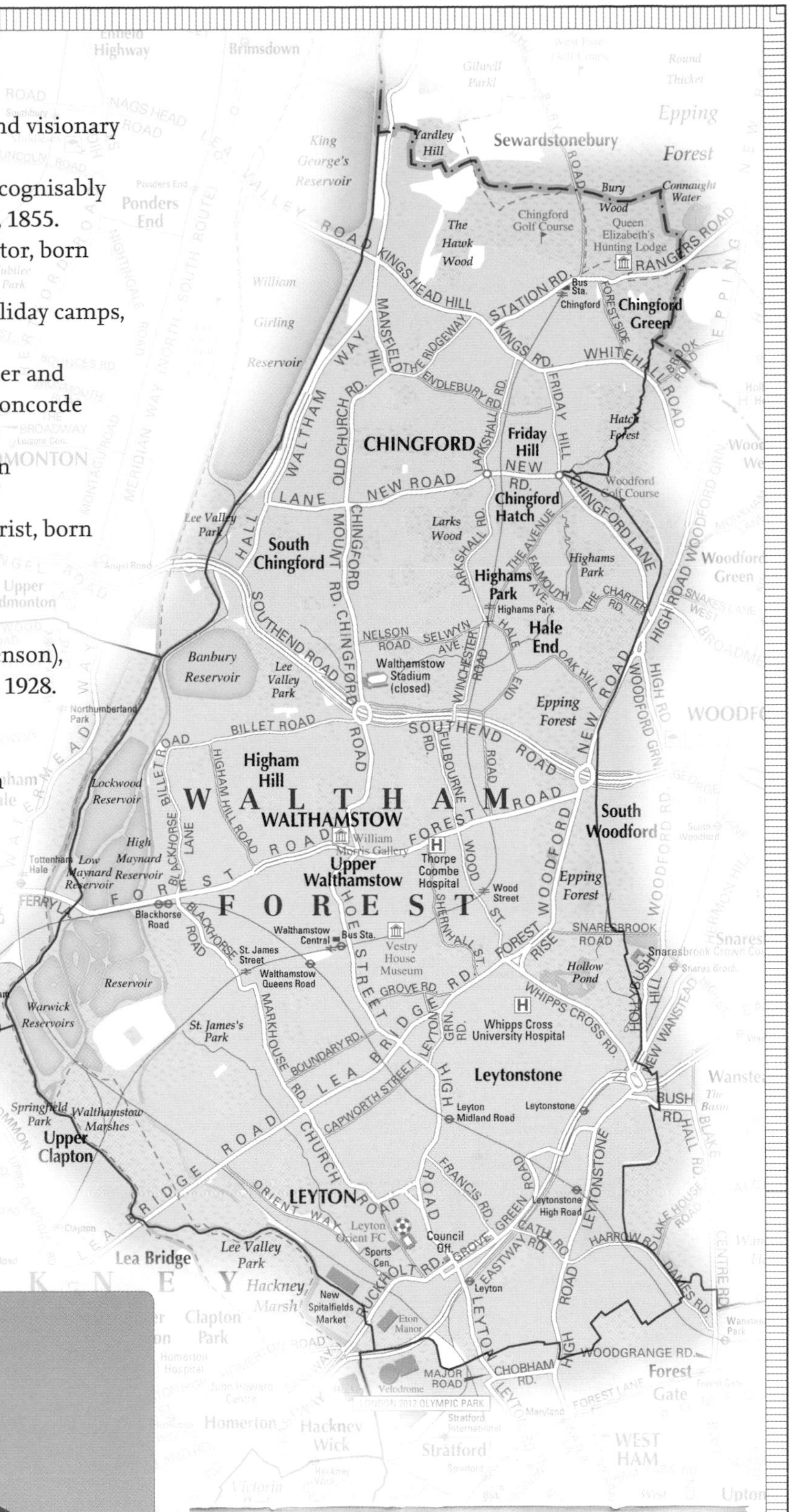

The Ancient House, Walthamstow

Walthamstow, par. and ry. sta., Essex, in SW. of co., 6 miles NE. of Liverpool Street Station, London, by rail, 4374 ac., pop. 21,715; the rapid growth of the population of Walthamstow is due to its proximity to London.

Leyton.– town and par. with ry. sta., Essex, 1 mile N. of Stratford, and 5¼ miles NE. of Liverpool Street sta., London – par. (Low Leyton), 2370 ac., pop. 23,016; town (comprising Low Leyton par. and part of Wanstead par.), 2577 ac., pop. 27,068; P.O., T. O.; is an ancient place, and has yielded many relics of the Roman occupation. Many fine suburban residences are here. Leyton is a local government dist.

WANDSWORTH

Population	286,600
Area	35 sq. km
Population density	8,190 per sq. km
Area of green space	8 sq. km
Jobs in borough	125,000
Average house price	£439,342

The borough of Wandsworth, on the south bank of the Thames, is Inner London's most populous borough. It was formed in 1965 from the metropolitan boroughs of Battersea and Wandsworth (excluding Clapham and Streatham, which became part of Lambeth). It takes its name from Wandsworth (Old English 'enclosure of a man called Waendel'), from which also comes the name of the River Wandle that flows from Croydon to the Thames at Wandsworth. It was this river that stimulated the development of Wandsworth as many textile mills were built along its banks. Prior to the arrival of the railways in the mid 19th century the area was primarily agricultural with settlements either on the Thames, as at Battersea or Putney, or on the main coaching roads out of London, as at Balham and Tooting. The construction of Putney Bridge in 1729 (the first bridge upstream from London Bridge), led to the creation of large estates by the aristocracy who wished good access to London; a number are now incorporated into the grounds of Roehampton University.

Once the railways came in 1850, the whole area changed radically. In 1851 the population was around 30,000 but by 1901 it was 306,000 and by 1931 it was 405,000. Thereafter the population shrunk back to 252,000 in 1981 since when it has started growing again. Around 48 per cent of residents are in the age range 25 to 39, the highest proportion in the country, and it is less ethnically diverse than many inner London boroughs. The borough contains a great range of housing stock, both in terms of size and quality. One quarter of the borough is open green space, such as Wandsworth Common and Putney Heath, while one third is residential accommodation. Over 130,000 people living in the borough work elsewhere in London, and there are a similar number of jobs within the borough. Over 31 per cent of jobs are in the public sector, much higher than the London average, boosted by Roehampton University, a collection of long-established colleges that became a full university in 2004, and St George's, University of London, a major medical school based at St George's Hospital in Tooting.

Its most symbolic building is the former Battersea Power Station, while Clapham Junction railway station (really in Battersea) is one of Europe's busiest stations, with 2,000 commuting trains each day using sixteen platforms, and the railways, rather than the Underground, provide the most important transport links to central London.

FAMOUS FOR

Battersea Power Station, a massive brick building designed by Sir Giles Gilbert Scott which started generating electricity in 1933. It was completed in 1955 and stopped all generation in 1983. Since then there have been a number of unfulfilled schemes to reuse the building.

St Mary's Church in **Putney** was the scene in 1647 of the Putney Debates among the radical group called the Levellers over the future form of democracy in England after the Civil War.

The Ram Brewery in **Wandsworth** was

Refurbished Battersea Dogs and Cats Home, 2011

Battersea Power Station in 1949, before it was completed, with one chimney still to be built

John Bartholomew, Gazetteer of the British Isles (1887)
WANDSWORTH, *parl. bor. and par., Surrey, on river Wandle, at its influx into the Thames, 5 miles SW. of Waterloo Station, London, by rail – par., 2433 ac., pop. 28,004; bor. (including also the pars. of Tooting-Graveney, Streatham, and Putney), 8148 ac., pop. 68,792. Wandsworth is mentioned in Domesday Book, and became a seat of several important manufactures introduced by refugee Frenchmen after the revocation of the Edict of Nantes; the present industries include oil-mills, dye-works, paper-works, calico printing, hat making, corn mills, brewing, vinegar making, &c. There are 3 ry. stations – Wandsworth, Wandsworth Common, and Wandsworth Road. The Surrey County Lunatic Asylum, the Royal Hospital for Incurables, and the Boys' Home Reformatory, are here. Wandsworth returns 1 member to Parliament; it was made a parl. bor. in 1885.*

regarded as the oldest continuously operating brewery site, from the 1580s until it was closed in 2006, with Young's beer now being brewed in Bedford.

Battersea had a radical reputation at the start of the 20th century – in 1913 John Archer became the first black Mayor in Britain, while in 1922 Shapurji Saklatvala was elected as a Communist Party MP.

The new US Embassy will leave Grosvenor Square in central London and relocate to **Nine Elms** in 2016. Designed to give maximum protection against terrorist attacks, it is also going to spearhead the redevelopment of this area.

In the 83 ha **Battersea Park**, a Peace Pagoda was built in 1985, one of over eighty around the world built by Buddhists as a place where all people can search for world peace.

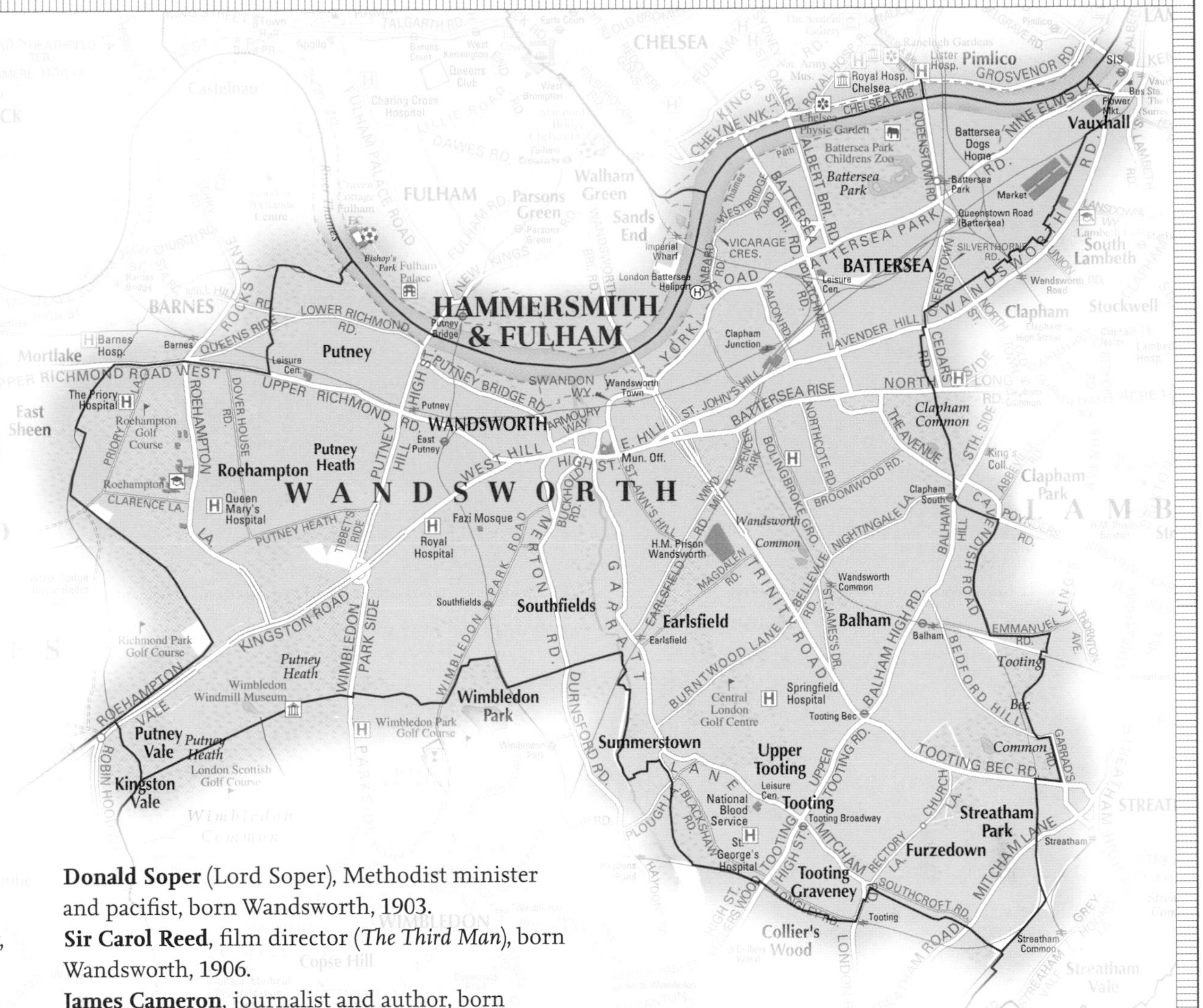

FAMOUS PEOPLE

Thomas Cromwell, Earl of Essex, royal minister and adviser to Henry VIII, born Putney, *c.* 1485.

Edward Gibbon, historian, author of *The History and the Decline and Fall of the Roman Empire*, born Putney, 1737.

William George Pye, scientific instrument and radio manufacturer, born Battersea 1869.

Captain Lawrence Oates, Antarctic explorer, member of ill-fated Scott expedition, born Putney, 1880.

Clement Attlee (Earl Attlee), Labour Prime Minister, 1945–51, born Putney, 1883.

Dame Margaret Rutherford, actress, born Balham, 1892.

John Bingham Morton (*pseud.* Beachcomber), humorous journalist, born Tooting, 1893.

Donald Soper (Lord Soper), Methodist minister and pacifist, born Wandsworth, 1903.

Sir Carol Reed, film director (*The Third Man*), born Wandsworth, 1906.

James Cameron, journalist and author, born Battersea, 1911.

Julian Symons, crime fiction writer, born Battersea, 1912.

Norman Parkinson, society and fashion photographer, born Roehampton, 1913.

Jimmy Hill, footballer and commentator, born Balham, 1928.

Sir Robin Knox-Johnston, explorer, born Putney, 1939.

Ainsley Harriott, celebrity chef, born Balham, 1957.

Railway lines close to Clapham Junction

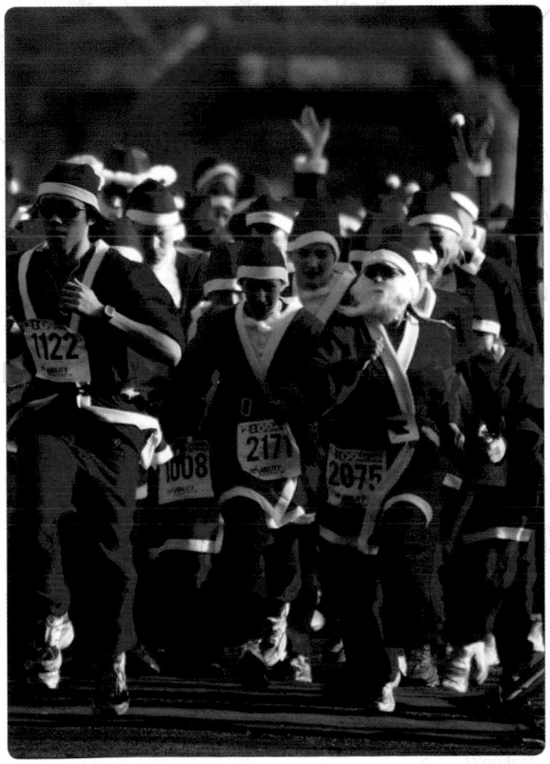

Charity Santa Run in Battersea Park

RELIGIONS OF LONDON

London is a multi-cultural city and one manifestation of cultural difference is religion. While overall statistics of the number of believers are just estimates, they do give a flavour of the religious mix of the city and also the distribution of these believers around London. The nationwide *Annual Population Survey* published in 2010 indicates the following overall distribution.

RELIGIOUS BELIEVERS AS A PERCENTAGE OF THE TOTAL POPULATION OF LONDON

Christian	58.5%
Muslim	12.2%
Hindu	4.8%
Jewish	2.2%
Sikh	1.5%
Buddhist	1%
Any other religion	1.9%
No religion	18.1%

Christianity

Christianity reached London during the Roman times and has played a central part in the development of the city, leaving its mark in buildings, in street and area names and in many institutions. It is also a living faith and there are many in London who express their faith through church attendance across a large number of different Christian denominations, some with formal structures, such as the Roman Catholic Church and the Church of England, some with a more local organization such as Methodism and the United Reformed Church, and some independent Evangelical churches, many of which have grown out of immigrant communities.

Major Christian buildings form part of the landscape of central London. Westminster Abbey was founded in the 10th century, enlarged by Edward the Confessor, the first English king to be buried at Westminster, and then rebuilt by Henry III and his successors, and completed by the building of Henry VII's Lady Chapel (where the Royal tombs can be found) and the west towers in 1745. Coronations have been held here since 1066 and it has been used for many royal occasions over the centuries. Other notable pre-Reformation churches include Southwark Cathedral, St Bartholomew the Great in Smithfield and the Temple Church. Many churches were lost in the Great Fire, including Old St Paul's Cathedral, leading to a concentrated period of church building under Sir Christopher Wren, culminating in the completion of St Paul's Cathedral in 1710. As houses spread beyond the City, churches followed, and London has many 18th and 19th century churches – St Martin in the Fields being a great 18th century church and All Saints, Margaret Street an example of a high Victorian church. Many churches were lost during

The Chancel Screen, Westminster Abbey

World War II and others have changed in use as the number of Christians declined, while new churches are still being built to meet new needs.

Islam

Islam first arrived in London in the 19th century, but the number of believers only grew significantly after World War II with immigration from the Indian subcontinent. It is now the second largest religion in London and is widely distributed with particularly large communities in Tower Hamlets (on some estimates 40 per cent of the population), Newham, Waltham Forest and Westminster. The first purpose-built mosque in London was the Fazl mosque in Southfields, built by the Ahmadiyya Muslim Community in 1926. There are now many mosques spread through London, the London Central Mosque (by Regent's Park) and the East London Mosque in Whitechapel being among the oldest and largest. Perhaps the most unusual mosque is the Brick Lane Mosque for the building it uses was built as a French Huguenot church in 1745, since when it has been a Methodist church, a Jewish synagogue and now, since 1976, a mosque to serve the community of 'Banglatown'.

Hinduism

Hinduism came to London in the 19th century with students and scholars from India, but a large community did not settle until after World War II, with immigration from the Indian subcontinent and, later, with the arrival of Indians expelled from Kenya in 1972. The largest numbers of Hindus are in the boroughs of Harrow, Brent and Redbridge, and about half the Hindus in Britain live in London. The most spectacular of the Hindu temples is the BAPS Shri Swaminarayan Mandir in Neasden.

Judaism

Jewish communities are well established in London and approaching 60 per cent of British Jews live in the city, particularly in the boroughs of Brent, Camden and Hackney. In the 19th century the position of the established community was boosted by emancipation and then grew significantly with many Jewish immigrants coming from Eastern Europe to the East End. As the new arrivals became more established, they moved north to Stamford Hill (with a large Hassidic community) and Golders Green.

Sikhism

The Sikh community in London also grew with immigration from the Indian subcontinent and is very much a feature of the west London boroughs of Ealing, Hillingdon and Hounslow and also Redbridge. The Gurdwara Sri Guru Singh Sabha in Southall is one of the largest Sikh temples outside India.

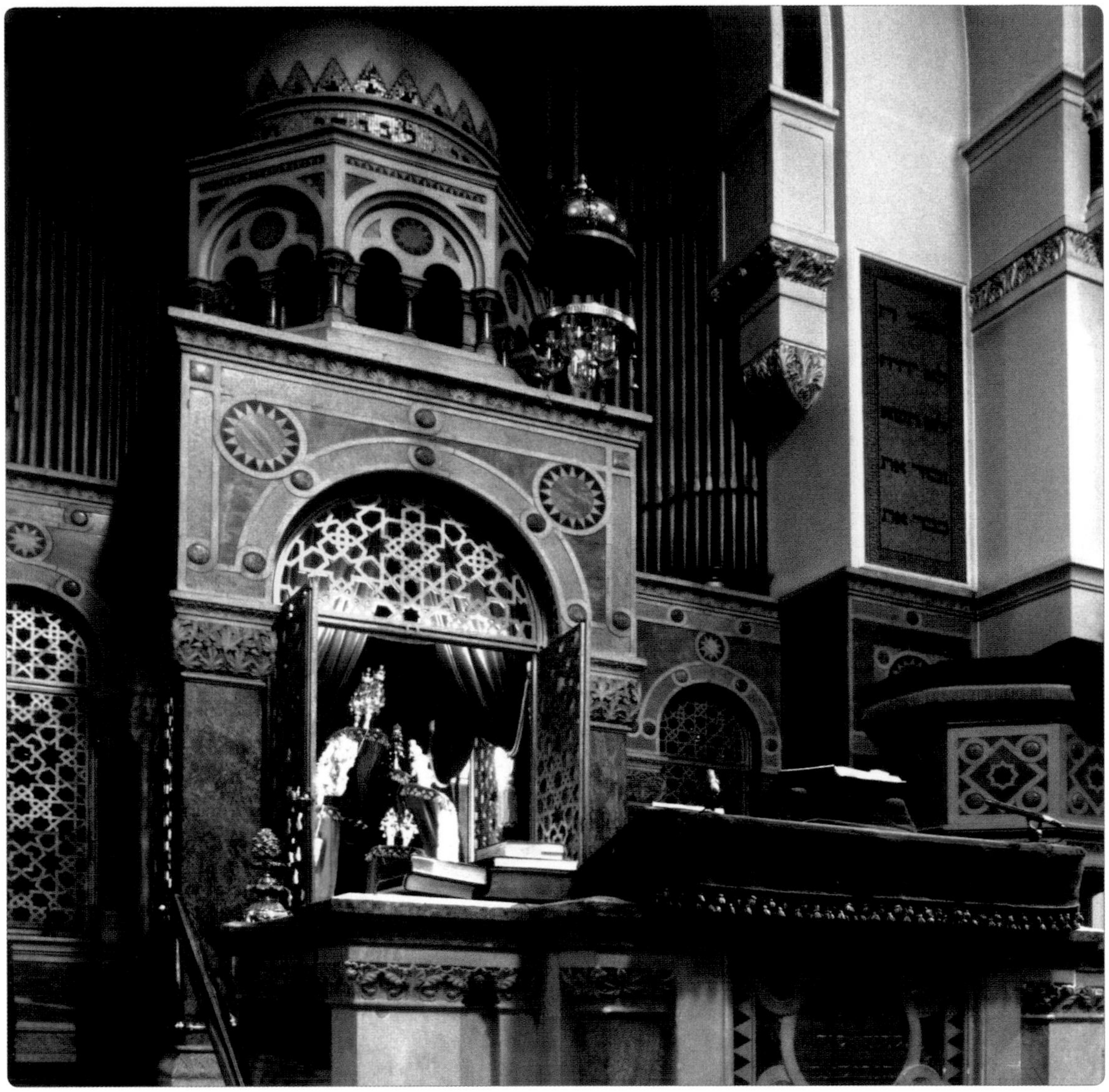

West London Synagogue, near Marble Arch, is a centre of Jewish life in central London

London Central Mosque

Wat Buddhapadipa in Wimbledon, the first Thai Buddhist temple in the UK

CITY OF WESTMINSTER

Population	249,400
Area	22 sq. km
Population density	11,340 per sq. km
Area of green space	5 sq. km
Jobs in borough	640,000
Average house price	£736,691

The City of Westminster was created in 1965 by merging together the old City of Westminster with the metropolitan boroughs of St Marylebone and Paddington. Its name describes the 'west minster' that became Westminster Abbey. Edward the Confessor undertook to restore it after he became king in 1042. Not only did he restore the abbey (which was consecrated on 28 December 1065, eight days before he died), but he also built a royal palace next to it, an act of great significance, because Westminster became the centre of royal power and justice, distinct from the commercial power of the City of London. A settlement soon grew up around the abbey and palace to meet the needs of the court and, in time, of Parliament. The setting of Westminster Abbey (the current building dates from the 13th century) and the Houses of Parliament owes much to 19th century improvements, including the creation of Parliament Square and Victoria Street, in the process clearing slums that had developed.

The City of London spread west from the 17th century onwards and the areas of Covent Garden, St James's and Soho were built up. In the 19th century the development moved west to Paddington and Bayswater and north through Marylebone to St John's Wood. By 1801 the population within the current City of Westminster boundaries was 220,000 and it reached a peak in 1881 at 493,000, encompassing the grandeur of Belgrave Square and the squalor of the slums of Lisson Grove in Marylebone. Thereafter, many people moved further away from the centre to escape the overcrowded conditions and the population went into a long decline to 164,000 by 1981. Since then there has been significant growth (around 20 per cent in the last ten years). It has also become much more diverse – around half the population is White British, with a wide range of other ethnic groups including a large Arab community and many people from Eastern Europe.

There are very wide disparities in the wealth of residents, with the borough having very exclusive housing in Mayfair and Belgravia while deprivation is a major issue in West Kilburn and parts of North Paddington. More people come in to work in Westminster than live there, with over 600,000 jobs of which 39 per cent are in finance, IT and other business, boosted by many company head offices. Around 102,000 jobs are in the public sector (clearly influenced by the needs of the national government and by seven major higher education institutions), while 13 per cent are in tourism. It is estimated that 30 million visitors a year come to Westminster, which also has 40 per cent of London's hotel rooms. The Lord's Cricket Ground in St John's Wood and the rail termini of Paddington, Charing Cross, Victoria and Marylebone are also in Westminster.

Allies, the statue of Franklin D. Roosevelt and Winston Churchill in New Bond Street

FAMOUS FOR

Nationally important religious buildings including Westminster Abbey, Westminster Cathedral, Westminster Central Hall, St Martin in the Fields, St Sophia Greek Orthodox Cathedral and the London Central Mosque among many others.

William Caxton established the first printing press in England next to Westminster Abbey in 1476.

Broadcasting House, the headquarters of the BBC in Portland Place

The Royal Arcade, built in 1879 to connect Old Bond Street and Albemarle Street, Mayfair

Trafalgar Square was first laid out in 1840 under the guidance of Sir Charles Barry. Nelson's Column, at 51 m tall, dominates the square and was completed in 1842; the bronze lions at its base, created by Sir Edwin Landseer, were installed in 1867.

Gerrard Street was built in the late 17th century and has a long history as a place of coffee houses and restaurants. In the 1950s Chinese from Hong Kong began to settle and it has now become the centre for London's Chinese community, complete with many Chinese restaurants and food shops.

The Royal Courts of Justice on the **Strand** are the most senior courts for civil cases, while the Supreme Court, established in 2009, is in the former Middlesex Guildhall building on **Parliament Square** (the Central Criminal Court – the Old Bailey – is in the City).

Marble Arch was designed by the architect John Nash in 1828 as the main entrance to Buckingham Palace and celebrates Britain's victories at the battles of Trafalgar in 1805 and Waterloo in 1815. Built of white Carrara marble, it is based on the triumphal Arch of Constantine in Rome. It was moved to the northeast corner of Hyde Park in 1851, when a new east front was added to the palace (not because it was too narrow for royal coaches).

FAMOUS PEOPLE

Edward I, King of England and Lord of Ireland, born Westminster, 1239.
Francis Bacon (Viscount St Albans), philosopher, scientist and statesman, born the Strand, 1561.
Anne, Queen of Great Britain and Ireland, born St James's Palace, 1665.
James Francis Edward Stuart (The Old Pretender), born St James's Palace, 1688.
William Pitt (Earl of Chatham, Pitt the Elder), politician, Prime Minister 1766–8, born Westminster, 1708.
Horatio (Horace) Walpole, author and patron of the arts, born Westminster, 1717.
William Blake, artist and poet, born Soho, 1757.
Joseph Mallord William Turner, artist, born Covent Garden, 1775.
Peter Mark Roget, physician and creator of *Roget's Thesaurus*, born Soho, 1779.
Viscount Palmerston (Henry John Temple), politician, Prime Minister 1855–8 and 1859–65, born Westminster, 1784.
Sir Charles Barry, architect, born Westminster, 1795.
William (Wilkie) Collins, author, born Marylebone, 1824.
Richard D'Oyly Carte, theatre impresario, born Soho, 1844.
Robert Baden-Powell (Baron Baden-Powell), founder of Boy Scouts and Girl Guides, born Paddington, 1857.
Constance Markievicz (*née* Gore-Booth), Irish republican, first woman elected as MP, born Pimlico, 1868.
Lilian Baylis, theatre manager, born Marylebone, 1874.
William (Billy) Edward Cotton, bandleader, born Westminster, 1899.
Alan Turing, mathematician and computing pioneer, born Paddington, 1912.
Ian Fleming, author, born Mayfair, 1908.
Sir Hardy Amies, fashion designer, born Maida Vale, 1909.
Sir Alec Guinness, actor, born Marylebone, 1914.

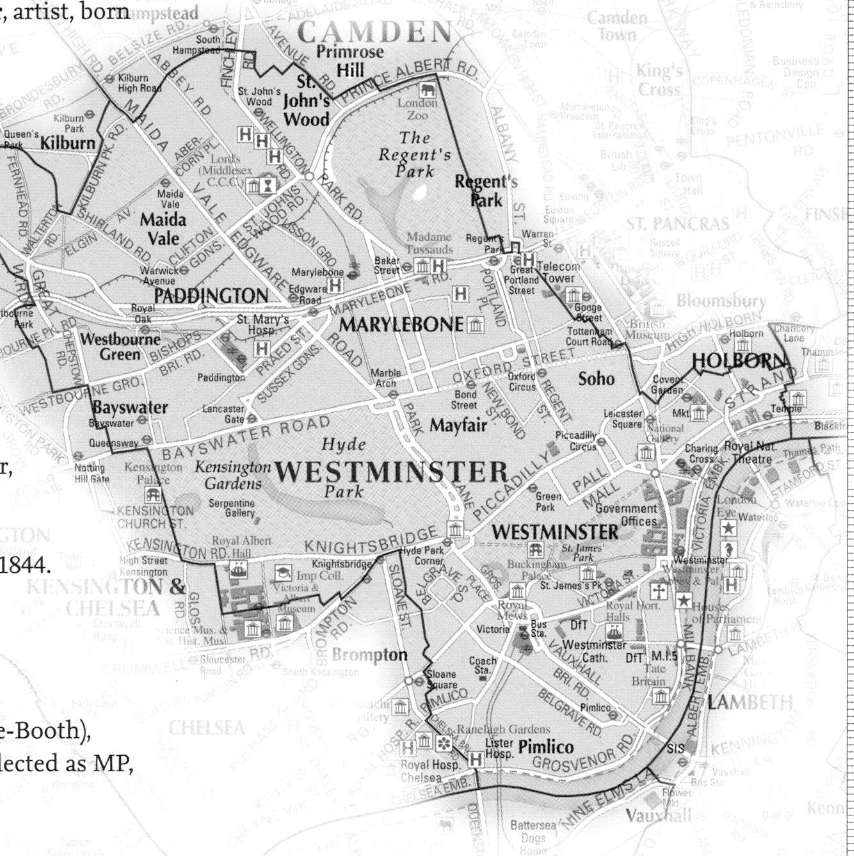

John Bartholomew, Gazetteer of the British Isles (1887)
WESTMINSTER.– *parl. bor. and city, Middlesex, on N. bank of river Thames, in W. of London, 2546 ac., pop. 229,238. The parl. limits include the pars. of St James Westminster, St Margaret and St John the Evangelist Westminster, St George Hanover Square. St Anne Soho, St Martin in the Fields, &c. Westminster is the seat of government and the residence of royalty, and contains, besides Westminster Abbey, the Houses of Parliament, St James's Palace, Buckingham Palace, &c. It was formerly separated from the city of London by Temple Bar. It owes its origin to a market and fair granted to the abbot and convent of Westminster Abbey in 1259. It was made a separate diocese at the suppression of religious houses, but was re-incorporated with the diocese of London in 1550. It was made a parl. bor. in the time of Edward VI.*

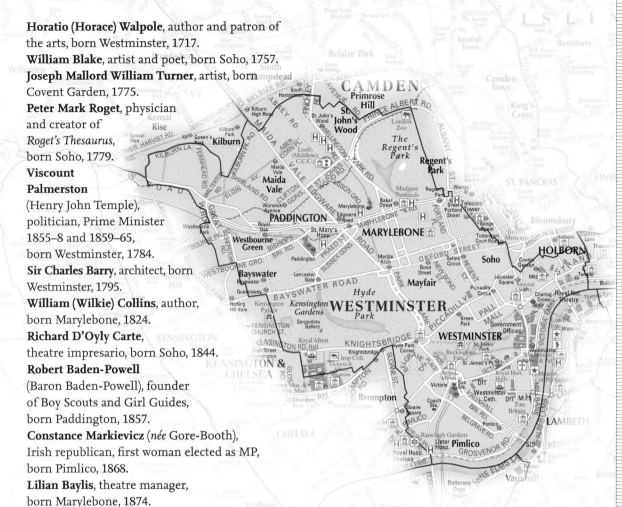

Piccadilly Circus. On the left of the picture is the Shaftesbury Memorial Fountain, designed by Alfred Gilbert, to honour the 7th Earl of Shaftesbury, a noted social reformer and philanthropist. Commonly called Eros, in the mistaken belief that the winged figure represented the Greek god of love rather than Anteros, god of selfless love, or, to some, the Angel of Christian Charity.

Regent Street, 1920

Regent Street, Christmas 2008

Westminster Abbey and the Houses of Parliament, 1931

Westminster Abbey and the Houses of Parliament, 2011

Fountains in Trafalgar Square, around 1865. Note the National Gallery (*left*) and St Martin-in-the-Fields (*centre*).

Fountains in Trafalgar Square, 2009

Trafalgar Square and the Admiralty Arch, 1937

Trafalgar Square and the Admiralty Arch, 2010

THE CENTRE OF GOVERNMENT

The area of Westminster and Whitehall is the heart of the British government, home to both the Houses of Parliament and the main government ministries, and has been so for nearly 1,000 years.

The Palace of Westminster

The selection of Westminster as the centre of Government goes back to Edward the Confessor, the last Saxon king of England, who built a royal palace next to the abbey he was restoring. The Norman kings then developed the Palace of Westminster as the centre of their administration – Westminster Hall (with later modifications) was built by William II. In the 16th century, Henry VIII moved to the Palace of Whitehall and Parliament joined the administrators at the Palace of Westminster. The House of Commons began to meet in the former royal chapel of St Stephen's, with the Speaker's Chair replacing the altar and the stalls on either side of the chapel becoming the two opposing sides of the house, a layout still maintained. In 1834 the old Palace of Westminster was almost completely destroyed by fire, leaving only Westminster Hall and the Jewel Tower. A design competition for its replacement was won by Charles Barry and Augustus Welby Pugin. The competition specified that the building should be in a 'gothic or Elizabethan' style, and it was Pugin's great love of gothic detail that made the resulting building so successful. The building began in 1837 and was finally completed in 1858, when the clock tower, commonly named after its largest bell, Big Ben, was finished. During World War II, the Commons chamber was severely damaged by an incendiary bomb and was rebuilt in a less ornate style while keeping to the spirit of the original. Since then, further offices have been provided for MPs in Portcullis House, opened in 2001 to mixed reactions, and next to it in Norman Shaw House (originally New Scotland Yard, the headquarters of the Metropolitan Police before it moved to Victoria Street).

The Palace of Whitehall

The area between Westminster and Trafalgar Square used to be the Royal Palace of Whitehall, created by Henry VIII around the former home of Cardinal Wolsey. The only building that survived a fire in 1695 was the Banqueting House, built for James I by Inigo Jones in 1619–22, its original purpose brought to an end in 1649 when Charles I walked from this building to his execution. William III had already moved away to St James's Palace before the fire, and thereafter Whitehall became the site of government ministries.

Whitehall today

Most of the Government ministries are on Whitehall, as can be seen on the street map of the area. Other departments are nearby in Victoria Street, Marsham Street and Petty France. The grandest is the Foreign and Commonwealth Office. The original gothic design was rejected by Parliament and the next Venetian-inspired design was thrown out by the prime minister, and we

HM Treasury, the Foreign and Commonwealth Office, Downing Street, St James's Park and Buckingham Palace

now have an ornate Italianate building. One side of the building lines Downing Street, and on the other is a relatively diminutive row of Georgian terrace houses that now make up 10 Downing Street, home of the prime minister and of the regular Cabinet Meetings. Next door, 11 Downing Street, is the home of the Chancellor of the Exchequer, while 12 Downing Street is used by the prime minister's press office. The houses were originally built by Sir George Downing in the 1680s and have been much modified since. Until 1989 it was possible to walk down Downing Street, but now security gates protect the street from casual observers.

Other buildings of note include Horse Guards, an 18th-century building still used by the army and guarded by the Household Cavalry, Dover House (the Scotland Office), originally an 18th-century private house, the Old Admiralty, completed in 1726, and the oldest government building in Whitehall and Admiralty Arch, between the Mall and Trafalgar Square, commissioned by Edward VII in 1910 as a memorial to Queen Victoria.

Monuments and statues

The most significant monument is the Cenotaph, designed by Sir Edwin Lutyens and completed in 1920, as a memorial to those who died in World War I. Inscribed 'The Glorious Dead' it is the national focus of remembrance for all who have died in both World Wars and other recent conflicts. In 2005 it was joined by a memorial to The Women of World War II. There are a number of other less distinguished military statues in Whitehall, while in Parliament Square there is an impressive statue of Winston Churchill, erected in 1973, along with several 19th-century British prime ministers, and Abraham Lincoln.

Home Office, Marsham Street

House of Lords Chamber, Houses of Parliament. The throne is only used when the monarch opens Parliament.

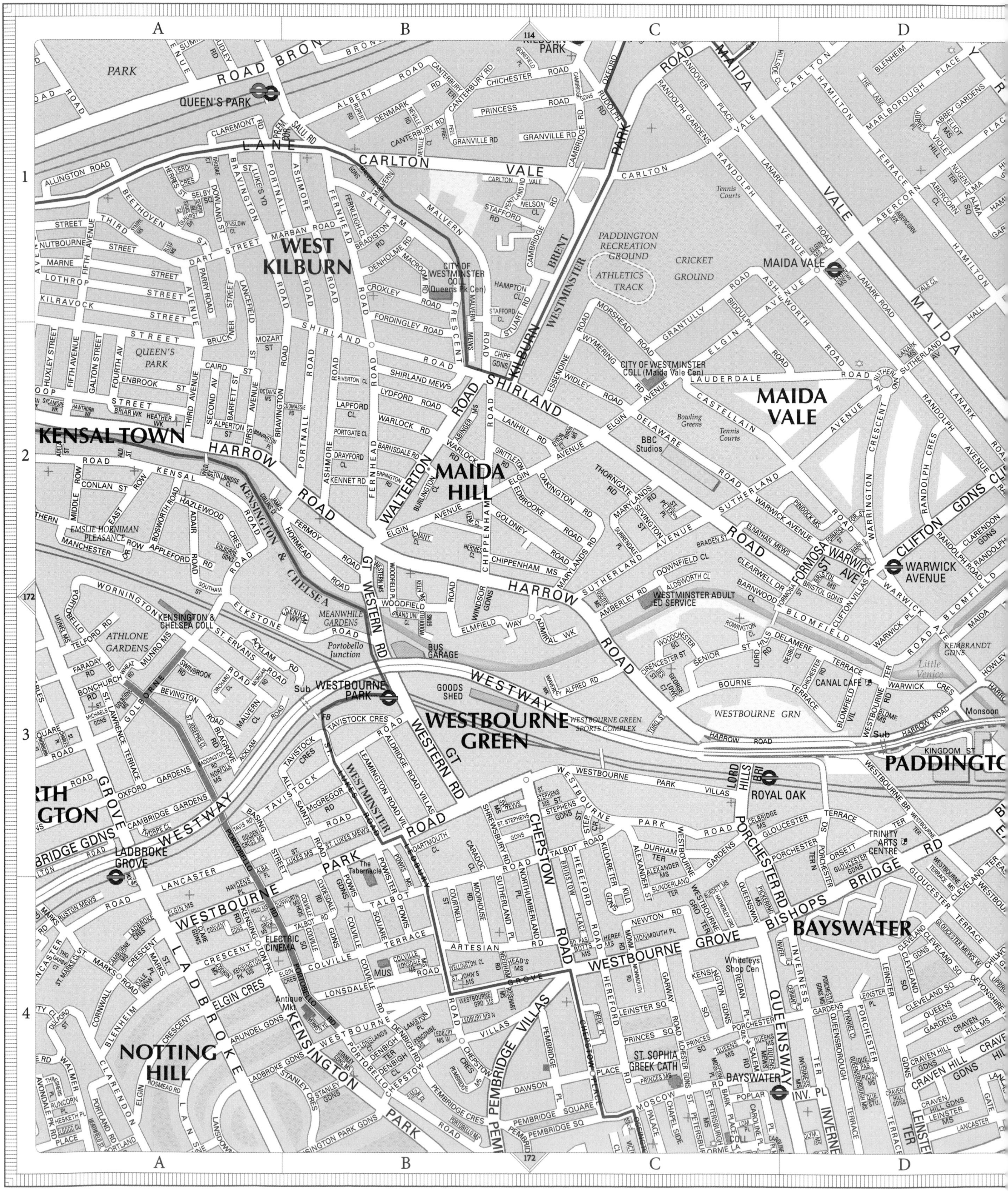
A
B
C
D
1
2
3
4
114
172
WEST KILBURN
KENSAL TOWN
MAIDA HILL
MAIDA VALE
WESTBOURNE GREEN
PADDINGTON
BAYSWATER
NOTTING HILL
QUEEN'S PARK
MAIDA VALE
WARWICK AVENUE
WESTBOURNE PARK
ROYAL OAK
LADBROKE GROVE
BAYSWATER
PADDINGTON RECREATION GROUND
CRICKET GROUND
ATHLETICS TRACK
CITY OF WESTMINSTER COLL (Queens Pk Cen)
CITY OF WESTMINSTER COLL (Maida Vale Cen)
BBC Studios
KENSINGTON & CHELSEA COLL
ATHLONE GARDENS
MEANWHILE GARDENS
Portobello Junction
BUS GARAGE
GOODS SHED
WESTBOURNE GREEN SPORTS COMPLEX
WESTMINSTER ADULT ED SERVICE
EMSLIE HORNIMAN PLEASANCE
CANAL CAFE
Little Venice
TRINITY ARTS CENTRE
Whiteleys Shop Cen
ST. SOPHIA GREEK CATH
ELECTRIC CINEMA
Antique Mkt
The Tabernacle
WESTWAY
HARROW ROAD
SHIRLAND ROAD
ELGIN AVENUE
KILBURN PARK
CARLTON VALE
KENSINGTON & CHELSEA
WESTMINSTER
WESTBOURNE GROVE
BISHOPS BRIDGE RD
QUEENSWAY
PORCHESTER RD
LADBROKE GROVE
PORTOBELLO RD
CHEPSTOW ROAD
PEMBRIDGE VILLAS
KENSINGTON PARK ROAD

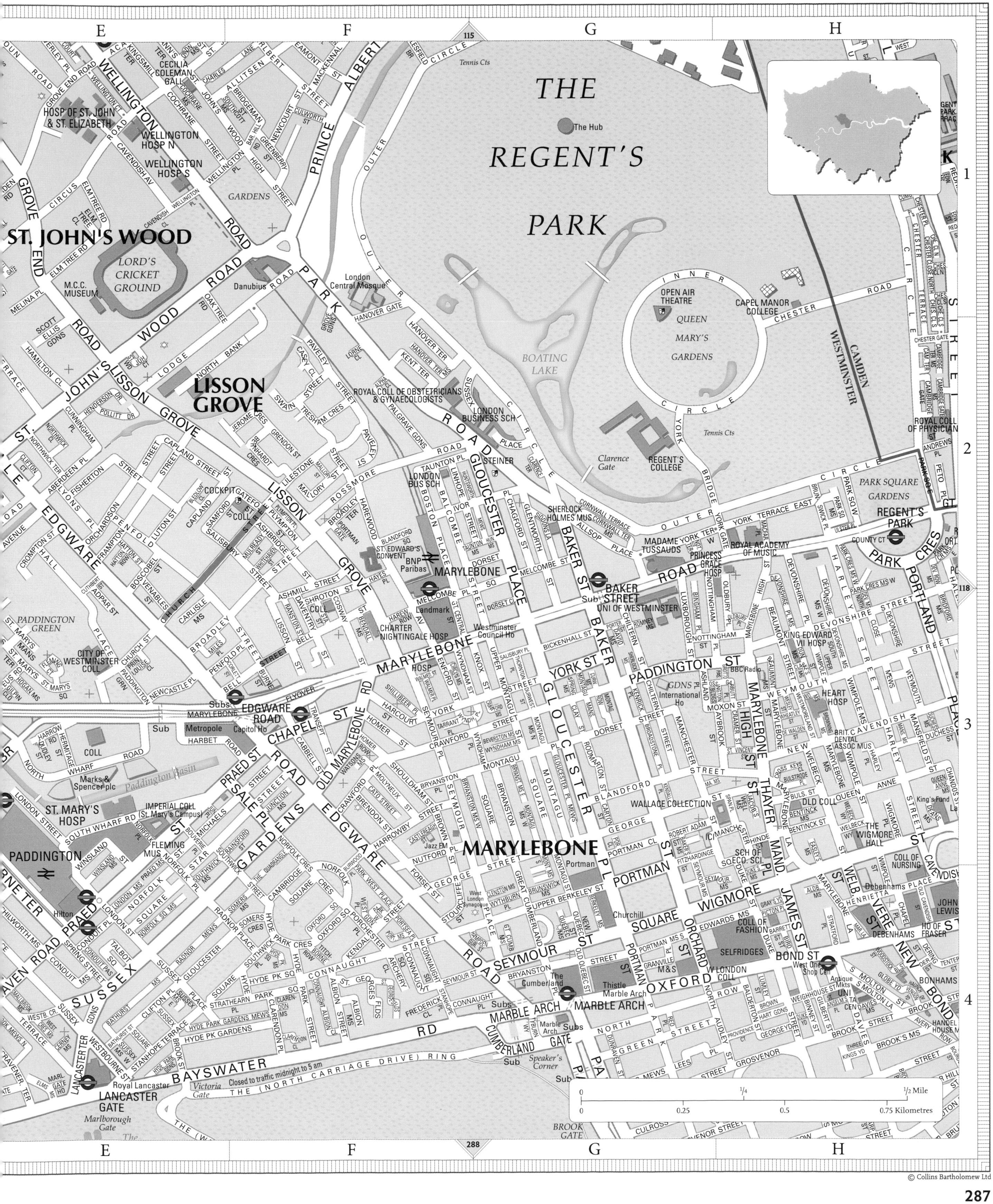
THE REGENT'S PARK
The Hub
Tennis Cts
BOATING LAKE
OPEN AIR THEATRE
QUEEN MARY'S GARDENS
INNER CIRCLE
OUTER CIRCLE
CAPEL MANOR COLLEGE
REGENT'S COLLEGE
Clarence Gate
PARK SQUARE GARDENS
ROYAL COLL OF PHYSICIANS
REGENT'S PARK
ST. JOHN'S WOOD
LORD'S CRICKET GROUND
M.C.C. MUSEUM
HOSP OF ST. JOHN & ST. ELIZABETH
WELLINGTON HOSP N
WELLINGTON HOSP S
London Central Mosque
LISSON GROVE
ROYAL COLL OF OBSTETRICIANS & GYNAECOLOGISTS
LONDON BUSINESS SCH
STEINER
SHERLOCK HOLMES MUS
MADAME TUSSAUDS
ROYAL ACADEMY OF MUSIC
PRINCESS GRACE HOSP
BAKER STREET
UNI OF WESTMINSTER
MARYLEBONE
ST. EDWARD'S CONVENT
BNP Paribas
Landmark
CHARTER NIGHTINGALE HOSP
Westminster Council Ho
KING EDWARD VII HOSP
HEART HOSP
BRIT. DENTAL ASSOC
PADDINGTON GREEN
CITY OF WESTMINSTER COLL
EDGWARE ROAD
Metropole
Capitol Ho
Paddington Basin
Marks & Spencer plc
ST. MARY'S HOSP
IMPERIAL COLL (St. Mary's Campus)
FLEMING MUS
PADDINGTON
Hilton
WALLACE COLLECTION
MARYLEBONE
Portman
Jazz FM
West London Synagogue
Churchill
SELFRIDGES
COLL OF FASHION
M&S
LONDON COLL
SCH OF ECO. SCI
OLD COLL
THE WIGMORE HALL
COLL OF NURSING
Debenhams
JOHN LEWIS
HO OF FRASER
BOND ST
West One Shop Cen
Antique Mkts
The Cumberland
Thistle Marble Arch
MARBLE ARCH
Speaker's Corner
BAYSWATER ROAD
Closed to traffic midnight to 5 am
THE (NORTH CARRIAGE DRIVE) RING
Victoria Gate
Royal Lancaster
LANCASTER GATE
Marlborough Gate
BROOK GATE
CAMDEN
WESTMINSTER
0 1/4 1/2 Mile
0 0.25 0.5 0.75 Kilometres
E F G H
1 2 3 4
115 118 288

A
B
C
D
1
2
3
4
287
175
177
HYDE PARK
KENSINGTON GARDENS
ROUND POND
THE SERPENTINE
The Long Water
The Fountains
Marlborough Gate
Lancaster Gate
Peter Pan
Bird Sanctuary
THE (WEST CARRIAGE DRIVE) RING
Closed to traffic midnight to 5 am
SERPENTINE GALLERY
Diana, Princess of Wales Memorial Fountain
Pier
Weir
BROOK GATE
GROSVENOR GATE
Marriott Grosvenor House
Albert Memorial
Coalbrookdale Gate
Alexandra Gate
Queen's Gate
Palace Gate
Prince of Wales Gate
Rutland Gate
Edinburgh Gate
Albert Gate
Mandarin Oriental
SOUTH CARRIAGE DRIVE
HYDE PARK BARRACKS
WESTMINSTER
KENSINGTON & CHELSEA
KENSINGTON RD
KENSINGTON GORE
KNIGHTSBRIDGE
HARVEY NICHOLS
HARRODS
Royal Geographical Society
ROYAL ALBERT HALL
ROYAL COLL OF ART
IMPERIAL COLL
ROYAL COLL OF MUSIC
IMPERIAL COLL LONDON (S Kensington Campus)
GOETHE INSTITUT
SCIENCE MUSEUM
NATURAL HISTORY MUSEUM
VICTORIA & ALBERT MUSEUM
SOUTH KENSINGTON
BROMPTON
GLOUCESTER ROAD
CROMWELL RD
BROMPTON ROAD
SLOANE STREET
SLOANE SQ
PETER JONES
CADOGAN HALL
Saatchi Gallery
Michelin House
THE ROYAL MARSDEN
ROYAL BROMPTON HOSP
KING'S ROAD
FULHAM ROAD
THE BOLTONS
BURTON'S COURT
NATIONAL ARMY MUSEUM
ROYAL HOSPITAL CHELSEA
ST. JAMES'S & LUCIE CLAYTON COLL
MPW Coll
Harrington Hall
Bailey's
Gloucester
Forum
Shop Mall

E
F
G
H
1
2
3
4
118
220
222
MAYFAIR
PICCADILLY CIRCUS
THE GREEN PARK
ST. JAMES'S
ST. JAMES'S PARK
BUCKINGHAM PALACE GARDENS
BUCKINGHAM PALACE
WESTMINSTER
VICTORIA
PIMLICO
BELGRAVIA
NATIONAL GALLERY
TRAFALGAR SQ
CHARING CROSS
EMBANKMENT
WESTMINSTER ABBEY
HOUSES OF PARLIAMENT
St. Stephen's Tower (Big Ben)
ST. THOMAS' HOSP
LONDON EYE
County Hall
River Thames
TATE BRITAIN
VICTORIA TOWER GARDENS
LAMBETH BRI
WESTMINSTER BRI
HORSEFERRY ROAD
VAUXHALL BRIDGE RD
MILLBANK
WHITEHALL
THE MALL
BIRDCAGE WALK
CONSTITUTION HILL
STRAND
HAYMARKET
REGENT ST
PICCADILLY
GROSVENOR PLACE
BUCKINGHAM PALACE ROAD
VICTORIA ST
GROSVENOR RD
HYDE PK. CORNER
GREEN PARK
ST. JAMES'S PARK
PIMLICO
0 1/4 1/2 Mile
0 0.25 0.5 0.75 Kilometres

LONDON IN THE FUTURE

London has always been a city of change and there can be little doubt that it always will be – the two commentators below could as easily have been talking about the transformation of the Southwark skyline by the Shard as about their own times.

So rapidly indeed are these improvements taking place around us, that the absence of a few months from London, produces revolutions in sites, and alterations in appearances, that are almost miraculous, and cause the denizen to feel himself a stranger in his own city.
Thomas Shepherd and James Elmes, *Metropolitan Improvements; or London in the Nineteenth Century*, 1827.

Hurricanes of 'development' have swept over districts that for one reason or another had survived… and in a year these parts have been so transformed that recent tenants lose their way in them.
James Bone, *The London Perambulator*, 1925

The changes can indeed be fast. We have seen how the area around Stratford was transformed for the 2012 Olympics and wait to see the long-term impact of this on the regeneration of this area of East London.

The London skyline

The familiar look of central London is changing with the emergence of a series of new skyscrapers in the City, Southwark and Canary Wharf. Ever since 30 St Mary Axe was given the nickname 'the Gherkin' by Londoners, every new landmark building needs such a name so the skyline is to be graced by a shard, a pinnacle or a helter skelter, a cheese grater, a walkie-talkie and a boomerang. The Shard, by London Bridge station in Southwark is the tallest of this next generation of skyscrapers, containing a mixture of offices, a hotel, and at the top, exclusive apartments. It is 310 m high with seventy-two usable floors and fifteen radiator and ventilation floors at the top (by contrast One Canada Square in Canary Wharf, the Shard's predecessor as London's highest building is 235 m high and has fifty floors). The tapering tower, designed by Renzo Piano, is an emphatic addition to London's skyline. Its name, the Shard, has an intriguing origin for it was originally used by English Heritage as criticism – a shard of glass stabbing the historic heart of London. Following next in construction is the Pinnacle, which, at 288 m, will be the highest building in the City with sixty-three floors, primarily of office space. A large number of new skyscrapers are planned for the Canary Wharf area, mostly for office use, and Croydon will also see more tall buildings, led by Saffron Tower, a forty-five-storey residential block, while work is also under way on Britain's tallest residential block, forty-nine-storey St George Wharf Tower, on the banks of the Thames at Nine Elms. Property development proposals are always affected by commercial pressures, however, so that not all the buildings that have been approved will actually appear.

Visitors to London will soon be afforded this incredible view of the tower blocks of Canary Wharf from London's newest skyscraper, the Shard. The pyramid-roofed skyscraper of One Canada Square in this picture was the tallest building in the UK until the Shard surpassed it in 2010.

An artist's impression of the Pinnacle, which will be the tallest building in the City

Energy

London will always require its energy supplies to come from its hinterland, whether that energy is produced by conventional means or from renewable sources. There are opportunities for small-scale generation, either domestically or for particular commercial buildings, but there is not space for large-scale renewable generation in London. Instead London has to adopt ways of reducing consumption through innovative building design, district heating schemes and less energy-consuming lifestyles. One attempt at this can be seen in the Peabody Trust's Beddington Zero Energy Development (BedZED) in South London. Not all the technology used has worked, however, which indicates that practical solutions that people will accept are not going to be easy to find.

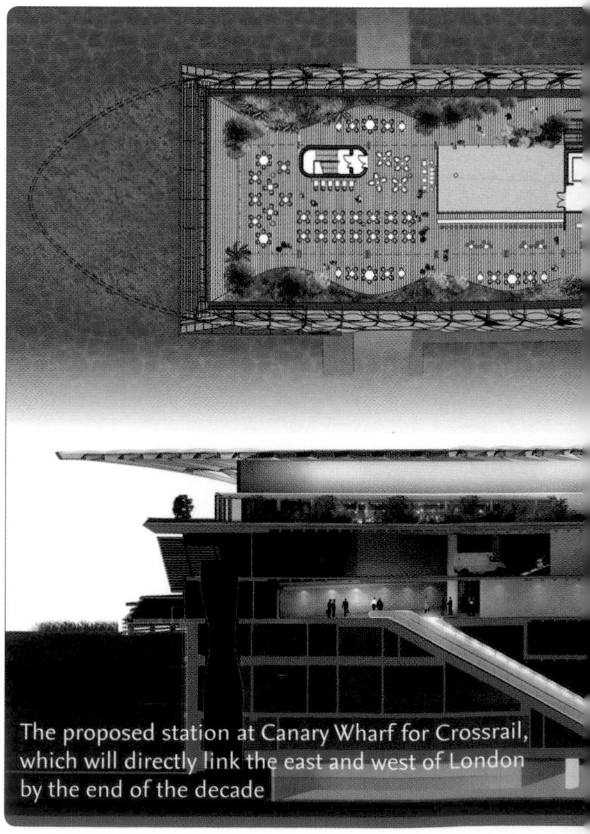

The proposed station at Canary Wharf for Crossrail, which will directly link the east and west of London by the end of the decade

Transport

Many more people travel by public transport in London than in other major British cities, but congestion and pollution will still always be a challenge for London. Among the changes that will be seen in the years ahead is much greater use of electric vehicles (in 2011 Transport for London started its first hydrogen fuel-cell-powered bus route). The Mayor of London has launched a scheme to create 1,300 publicly accessible charging points by 2013 and to prioritize boosting the number of electric and hybrid vehicles in London to 100,000. Other innovations that may have wider implications are the driverless 'pods' (or Personal Rapid Transport system) used at Heathrow to take passengers from Terminal 5's car park to the terminal – each battery-powered 'pod' can take four adults and their luggage on a 3.8 km concrete guideway – and a cable car crossing of the Thames by the Greenwich peninsula.

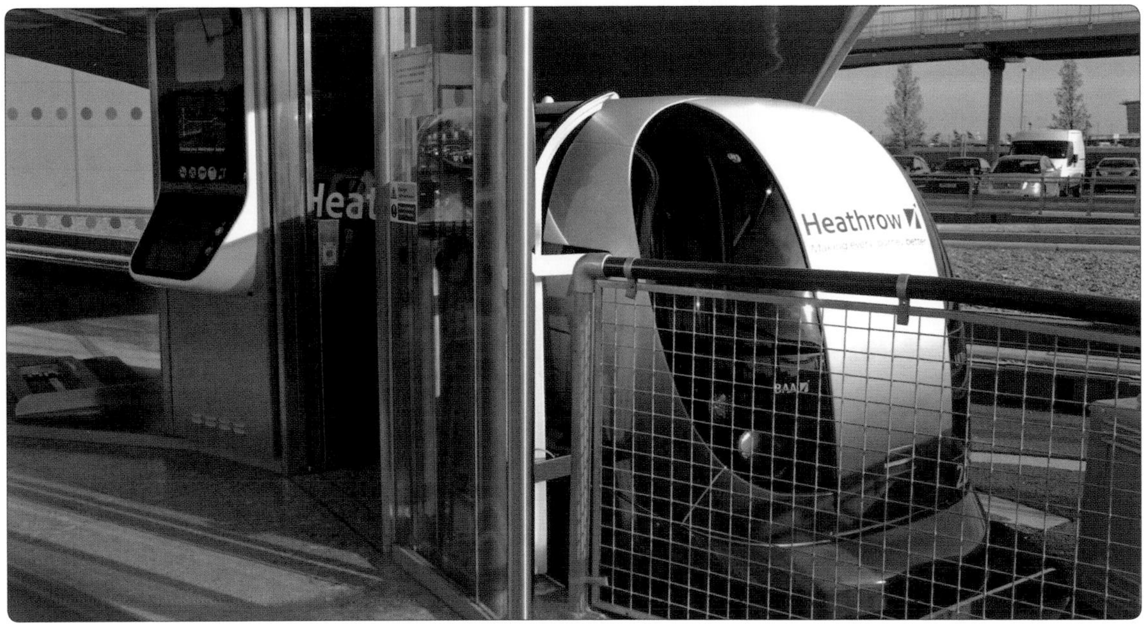

The world's first commercial Personal Rapid Transport (PRT) system uses programmed pods along a dedicated guideway to reduce congestion on airport roads. It is designed to be 70 per cent more energy efficient than traditional airport buses and is currently being tested at Heathrow airport.

The planned cable car crossing of the Thames between the Royal Docks and the Greenwich Peninsula

Population

In the last twenty years London's population has grown significantly and now includes people from more countries in the world than ever before. Estimated to have a population of 7.81 million in 2011, it is expected to rise to 8.37 million in 2021 and 8.89 million in 2031 – meaning that a further million people will need housing, employment and support services. The population will become increasingly diverse - a further six boroughs are expected to have a majority black and ethnic minorities population by then. With a growing population, a major challenge will be to lessen the inequalities that are so readily apparent in London, shown at its most extreme in Tower Hamlets which combines Canary Wharf with its international banking headquarters and exclusive accommodation with some of the worst deprivation in Britain. Facing up to these challenges while maintaining London as one of the world's financial centres and the political and economic heart of Britain will ensure that London learns from its history and keeps on changing for the better.

LONDON PLACE NAMES AND THEIR MEANING

Not all London place names are mysterious – **Highgate** actually does refer to a 'high gate' (probably a *toll-gate*) – but many are. London place-names have histories of different lengths. New ones are created from time to time; **Highgate's** history goes back to 1354; **Hendon's** ('high hill') to 959; **London's** to 115. Many changes can take place in the course of time: *Londinium* has become **London**; *Tidwulf's tree* has become **Elstree**; *St. Vedast's Lane* has become **Foster Lane**. In some cases, the cumulation of changes of form has led to amazing changes of meaning: today's **Cannon Street** began life as, in effect, 'candlemaker street'. Fortunately, the written records of these changes are copious enough to allow us to parade before you an ordered sequence of well-preserved fossils that preceded the place-name's latest form, like the well-attested evolution of the horse from *Eohippus* to *Red Rum*.

For reasons of space this appendix concentrates on the names of London's rivers and districts (or 'villages'), and the names of streets in its old City. They are listed in alphabetical order; after each map name comes its history given as clearly and succinctly as necessary. Each such history has one or more of the following parts in the following order:

Name: 'meaning of the name as it might have appeared to those who coined it' [history of the forms of the name: analysis of the parts of the name (with their individual meanings); additional information] *cross-references to other relevant* **Names.**

Off-putting conventions have been avoided; **bold-face** means 'name listed in this appendix'; ? means 'perhaps'; ‹ means 'from'. The analysed parts of each name come from Old English (in use till about 1100) unless otherwise specified.

A

Abchurch Lane [1291–92 (*Abbechirchelane*); by the church of *St. Mary Abchurch*]

Acton: 'oak-tree estate' [1181 (*Acton(e)*): *āc* 'oak' + *tūn* 'estate, home farm']

Acton Common ‹ **Acton**

Aldermanbury: 'alderman's manor; aldermen's manor' [c.1130 (*Aldremanesburi*), 1336 (*Aldermannebury*): *(e)aldermann* 'elder, chief; alderman' + *burh* 'stronghold, fortified manor']

Aldersgate *see* **Aldersgate Street**

Aldersgate Street: 'street of Ealdred's gate' [1303 (*Aldresgatestrete*): *Ealdre(d)* (name) + *geat* 'gap; gate' + *strǣt* '(paved) road, street' (‹ Latin)]

Aldgate: 'ale gate' [c.1095 (*Ealsegate*), 1275 (*Alegate*): *ealu* 'ale' + *geat* 'gap; gate'; City gate previously called *Æst Geat* 'east gate']

Aldgate Street: 'ale-gate street' [13th C. (*Alegatestrat*), c.1600 (*Aldgate street*); now **Aldgate**] ‹ **Aldgate**

The Artillery Ground [named officially in 1746; the 'Old Artillery Ground' near Spitalfields is mentioned in the diary of Samuel Pepys (1633–1703)]

Ashford: 'Eccel's ford' [1042–66 (*Echelsford*), 1062 (*Exforde*), 1488 (*Assheford*): *?Ecceles* (from name) + *ford* '(river-)ford']

B

The Bailey [c.1166 (*Bali*), 1298 (*le Bail*), 1431–32 (*la Baillye*), 1444-45 (*Old Bailey*): Middle English *bail, bailey* 'outermost wall or court (as of a castle), bailey' (‹ Old French); sited just west of the City wall; now *Old Bailey*]

Baker Street [after William *Baker*, 18th-century property-developer of land here that he acquired from W.H. Portman]

Balham: 'Bælga's village; Bælga's river-bend land' [957 (*Bælgenham*), 1472 (*Balam*): *?Bælgen* (from name ?‹ *bealg* 'rounded') + *hām* 'settlement, village' or *hamm* 'river-bend land']

Banstead: 'bean-place' [675 (*Benstede*), 1062 (*Bænstede*), 1198 (*Banstede*): *bēan* 'bean' + *stede* 'place, stead']

Barbican Street [1348–49 (*Barbecanstret*), 1377 (*Barbycanstret*): Middle English *barbican* 'outer fortification, typically with a tower' [‹ Middle French ‹ Medieval Latin ‹ Persian) + *strǣt* '(paved) road, street' (‹ Latin)]

Barking: 'Berca's folk' [c.730 (*Bercingum*), 1086 (*Berchinges*): *Berc(a)* (name) + *-ing(as)* 'followers of']

Barnes: 'barns' [1086 (*Berne*), 1222 (*Bernes*), 1387 (*Barnes*): *bern* 'barn' (‹ *bere* 'barley' + *ærn* 'building for the stated purpose')]

Barnet: 'burnt (site)' [c.1070 (*Barneto*): *bærnet* 'burnt'; area cleared for settlement by burning part of the former Middlesex and Hertfordshire woodland]

Basinger Lane, Basing Lane: 'Basing('s) lane' [1279–80 (*Basingelane*), 1324 (*Basingeslane*), 1544 (*Basinglane*): *Basing* (attested local surname, perhaps originally from *Basing* in Hampshire) + *lane* 'lane'; now part of **Cannon Street**] *compare* **Bassishaw Street**

Bassishaw Street: 'the Bas(s)ings' manor street; Bassishaw-ward street' [1279 ((the street of) *Basingeshawe*), c.1600 (*Bassings hall streete*): *Bas(s)ing(a)s* 'followers of Bas(sa)' (perhaps as in *Basing*stoke in Hampshire) + *haga* 'hedge; enclosure, property; town house' + *strǣt* '(paved) road, street' (‹ Latin); *Bassishaw* was also the name of a ward of the City of London; now *Basinghall Street*] *compare* **Basinger Lane**

Battersea: 'Beadurīc's (high) ground' [c.1050 (*Batrices ege*): *Batric* (name) + *ēg* 'high ground']

Battersea Park ‹ **Battersea**

Bayswater Road ‹ **Bayswater**: 'Bayard's watering place' [1380 (*Bayards Watering Place*): *?Baynardus*, henchman of William the Conqueror]

Bearward Lane, Berewards Lane: 'bear-keeper's lane' [1285 (*Berewardeslane*), 1417 (*Berwardeslane*): Middle English *berewarde* 'bearward, bear-keeper' (‹ *?beraweard*) + *lane* 'lane']

Beckenham: 'Biohha's village' [862 (*Biohhahema mearc*), 1086 (*Bacheham*): *Biohha* (name) + *hām* 'settlement, village' (+ *mearc* 'boundary, landmark')]

Beddington: 'Beadda's folk's estate' [675 (*Bedintone*), c.905 (*Beaddinctun*), 1229 (*Bedington*): *Bead(da)* (name) + *-ing* '-follower of' + *tūn* 'estate, home farm']

Bedfont: 'hollow spring' [1086 (*Bedefunt, Bedefunde*): *?byde(n), bede(n)* 'hollow (place), depression' + *funta* 'spring' (‹ Celtic ‹ Latin)]

Belleyetteres Lane: 'bell-maker's lane' [1306 (*Belleyetterslane*), 1421 (*Belleterlane*), 1667 (*Billiter Lane*); mainly *Billiter Lane* till the 19th century, but now **Billiter Street**] *see* **Billiter Street**

Bercher's Lane: 'barber's lane' [1193–95 (*Bercheuere lane*), 1260 (*Berchervereslane*), 1300 (*Berchenereslane*), 1372–73 (*Berchereslane, Bercherlane*), 1386 (*Birchenlane*), 1493–94 (*Birchinlane*): ?Middle English *berdcherver(e)* 'barber' (‹ *?beardceorfere* ‹ *beard* 'beard' + *ceorfere* 'carver') + *lane* 'lane'; now *Birchin Lane*]

Bermondsey: 'Beornmund's (high) ground' [1086 (*Bermundeseye*): *Beornmund* (name) + *ēg* 'high ground']

Bethnal Green: 'Blitha's-corner green' [13th C. (*Blithehale*), 1443 (*Blethenalegreene*): *Blithe(n)* (from name) + *halh* 'corner/nook of land' + *grēne* '(village) green']

Beverley Brook ‹ **Beverley**: 'beaver rivulet' [693 (*Beferiþi*): *beofor* 'beaver' + *rið* 'stream' + *-ig* (diminutive)]

Bexley: 'box(-tree) lea/grove' [c.780 (*Bixle*): *?byxe* (variant of *box* 'box-tree') + *lēah* 'grove; meadow, lea']

Bexleyheath ‹ **Bexley**

Billingsgate: 'Belling's gate' [c.1205 (*Bæl☒es☒ate*), c.1250 (*Bellinges-☒ate*): *Belling* (name) + *geat* 'gap; gate'; the *gate* presumably gave access to the Thames]

Billiter Street: 'bell-maker street' [1298 *Bel☒eterslane*), 1349 *Belle☒eterestret*): Middle English *belleyetere* 'bell-founder' + *strǣt* '(paved) road, street' (‹ Latin)] *see also* **Belleyetteres Lane**

Bishopsgate *see* **Bishopsgate Street**

Bishopsgate Street: 'street of the bishop's gate' [1275 (*Bis(s)hopesgatestrete*): *biscop* 'bishop' (‹ Late Latin ‹ Greek *episcopos*) + *geat* 'gap; gate' + *strǣt* '(paved) road, street' (‹ Latin); a gate in the north-eastern part of the City wall was built by order of Erkenwald, Bishop of London 675-693]

Blackheath [1166 (*Blachedefeld*); from the dark colour of the peat thereon]

Blackheath Common ‹ **Blackheath**

Borough Road [*burh* 'stronghold, fortified manor'; from (the) *Borough* (of *Southwark*)] *see* **Southwark**

Bowyer Row [1359 (*Bowiarresrowe*): Middle English *bowiar* 'bowyer, (archery) bow-maker' + *rǣw* 'row' (of trees or houses); now *Ludgage Street* east of **Ludgate**]

Bread Street [1163–70 (*Bredstrate*): *brēad* 'bread' + *strǣt* '(paved) road, street' (‹ Latin); from the baking and selling of *bread* here]

Brent: 'Holy One' [c.974 (*Brægentan*): Latin *brigantiā* 'holy one' (‹ Celtic)]

Brentford: '(*River*) *Brent ford*' [705 (*Bregunt ford*), 1222 (*Brainford*): **Brent** + *ford* '(river-)ford'] ‹ **Brent**

Bridge Street [1193–1212 (*vicus de ponte*), 1226–27 (*Brygestrate*); after **London Bridge**; later *Fish Street*; now *Fish Street Hill*]

Brixton: 'Brihtsige's stone' [1062 (*Brixges stane*), 1279 (*Brixistane*): *Brihtsige* (?name) + *stān* 'stone']

Broad Street [c.1212 (*Bradestrate*), 1513 (*Brodestrete*): *brād* 'broad, wide' + *strǣt* '(paved) road, street' (‹ Latin)]

Bromley: 'broom (-plant) lea/grove' [862 (*Bromleag*): *brōm* 'broom' + *lēah* 'grove' meadow, lea']

Brompton: 'broom (-plant) estate' [1294 (*Brompton*): *brōm* 'broom' + *tūn* 'estate, home farm']

Buckingham Palace [?1825: originally *Buckingham House*; built 1703 for John Sheffield, Duke of *Buckingham*; remodelled about 1825 by Nash for George IV]

Bucklersbury: 'Buckerel's manor' [1343 (*Bokerellesbury*), 1477 (*Bokelersbury*): *Bukerel, Bucherel(l)* (attested surname) + *burh* 'stronghold, fortified manor']

Budget Row, Budge Row: 'budge-fur row' [1342 (*Bogerowe*), 1383–84 (*Bugerowe*), 1553–54 (*Bouge Rowe*), 1591 (*Budgerowe*): Middle English *bugee, boge* 'fur of lamb, rabbit or kid' (?‹ French) + Middle English *rowe* ‹ *rǣw* 'row' (of trees or houses); near the skinner's district]

Bull's Cross, Bulls Cross [1540 (*Bellyscrosse*), 16th C. (*Bulls Cross*): ?(Gilbert) *Bolle* (name attested locally in 1235) + *cros* 'cross' (‹ Old Irish ‹ Latin)]

Bunhill Fields: 'bone-hill fields' [1544 (*Bonhilles*), 1567 (*Bonhill Field*), 1799 (*Bunhill Fields Burying Ground*): *bān* 'bone' + *hyll* 'hill' + *feldas* 'fields'; perhaps from the transfer here of *bones* from St. Paul's charnel house for burial; also *Tindals Burying Ground* (1746)]

Bushy Park, Bushey Park (Middlesex) [1650 (*Bushie Park*), 1667 (*Bushey Park*): *?busc* 'bush, shrub' + (ge)*hǣg* 'enclosure']

Butchery [1349 (*Bocherie*)] *see* **Shambles**

C

Camberwell: [1086 (*Cambrewelle*): ? + *well(a)* 'well; spring']

Camden ‹ **Camden Town**

Camden Town [1795; after Charles Pratt, Earl *Camden* of *Camden* Place in Kent, local landowner]

Candlewick Street [1241 (*Kandelwiccestrate*), 14th C. (*Candelwikstrete, etc.*): ‹ *Candelwrichstrete* 'candlemaker street' (by folk etymology); now **Cannon Street**] *see* **Cannon Street**

Cannon Street: 'candlemaker street' [c.1185 (*Candelwrichstrete*), 1480 (*Canɤngesstrete*), 1664 (*Cannon-street*): *?Candelwyrhta* 'candle-wright, chandler' + *strǣt* '(paved) road, street' (‹ Latin)] *compare* **Candlewick Street**

Canonbury: 'canon's manor' [1373 (*Canonesbury*): Middle English *canoun* 'canon' [‹ Old Northern French ‹ Latin) + *burh* 'stronghold, fortified manor'; after the *canons* of St. Bartholomew's in **Smithfield**, granted land here in 1253]

Carshalton 'cress well-spring farm' [1086 (*Aultone*), 1235 (*Cresaulton*), 1279 (*Carshaulton*): *cærse* '(water-) cress' + *ǣwell, ǣwiell* 'spring; well-spring, (stream-) source' (‹ *éa* 'stream' + *well(a), wiell(a)* 'well, spring') + *tūn* 'estate, home farm']

Carter Lane [1295 (*Carterestrate*), 1349 (*Cartereslane*): Middle English *carter(e)* (‹ *crǣt* + *-ere*) + *strǣt* '(paved) road, street' (‹ Latin) or *lane* 'lane']

Caterham 'hill-fort village' [1179 (*Catheham*), 1200 (*Katerham*), 1372 (*Caterham*): ?Celtic *cater* 'hill-fort' (‹ Latin) + *hām* 'settlement, village']

Chancellor's Lane [1227 (*Newestrate*), 1278–79 (*Converslane*), 1338 (*Chauncellereslane*), 1454 (*Chauncerylane*): *Newestrate* 'new street'; *Converslane* 'converts' lane' (after the *Domus Conversorum* founded here in 1231–32 by Henry III for Jewish *converts* to Christianity); *Chauncellereslane, Chauncerylane* (from the subsequent use of the *Domus* as seat of the *Chancery* and perhaps office of the *Chancellor*); now *Chancery Lane*]

Charing Cross: 'turning-point cross' [c.1000 (*Cyrringe*), 1360 (*La Charryngcross*): *cierring* 'bend' (in a river or road) + *cros* 'cross' (‹ Old Irish ‹ Latin); from the *cross* put here in 1291 by Edward I to mark the last stage in the funeral procession of his first Queen, Eleanor of Castile, from Harby in Nottinghamshire to Westminster Abbey] *compare* **Waltham Cross**

Charlton: 'peasants' farmstead; peasants' (part of) estate' [1086 (*Cerletun*): *ceorla* '(free) peasants'' + *tūn* 'estate, home farm']

Charlton (Middlesex): 'Cēolrēd's folk's estate' [1086 (*Cerdentone*), 1550 (*Charleton*), 1594 (*Charleton al. Chertington*):

?*Cēolrēd* (name, with *d/l* confusion) + *-ing* '-follower of' + *tūn* 'estate, home farm']
Cheam '(tree-) stump village; (tree-) stump river-bend land' [675 (*Cegeham*), 933 (*Cheham*): ?*cege* (tree-) stump; underbrush' + *hām* 'settlement, village' or *hamm* 'river-bend land']
Cheapside: 'market-side' [1436 (*Chapeside*): *cēap* 'market; trade' + *sīde* 'side'; formerly *Westcheap*] *see also* **West Cheap**
Chelsea: 'chalk landing-place' [789 (*Celchyth*), 1214 (*Chelchee*): *cealc* 'chalk, lime; limestone' (‹ Latin) + *hȳð* 'landing place, harbour']
Chessington: 'Cissa's folk's hill' [1086 (*Cisendone*), 1279 (*Chessingdone*): *Cis(sa)* (name) + *-ing* '-follower of' + *dūn* 'hill']
Chicken Lane, Chick Lane [1181–89 (*Chikenslane*), 1540–41 (*Cheke Lane*): *cicen* 'chicken' + *lane* 'lane'; where *chickens* were reared and sold]
Chigwell: 'Cicca's folk's spring/well' [1086 (*Cingheuuella*), 1158 (*Chigwell*, etc.): *Cicc(a)* (name) + *-ing* '-follower of' + *wella, wiella* 'well; spring']
Chigwell Row ‹ **Chigwell**
Chingford: 'shingle-ford' [1086 (*Cingefort*): ?*cinge(l)* 'shingle' + *ford* '(river-)ford']
Chipping Barnet: 'market Barnet' [1329 (*Chepyng Barnet*), 1628 (*Chipping Barnet al. High Barnet*): *cēping, cī(e)ping* 'market' + **Barnet**; also *High Barnet*] ‹ **Barnet**
Chislehurst: 'gravel hill' [973 (*Cyselhyrst*), 1159 (*Chiselherst*): *cisel, ceosel* 'gravel; flint; pebble' + *hyrst, herst* 'hill(ock); copse']
Chiswell Street: 'gravel street' [13th C. (*Chysel strate*), 1458 (*Cheselstrete*), late 16th C. (*Chiswell Street*): *cisel, ceosol* 'gravel; flint; pebble' + *strǣt* '(paved) road, street' (‹ Latin); perhaps from the character of the local soil]
Chiswick: 'cheese farm' [c.1000 (*Ceswican*): *ciese* 'cheese' + *wīc* 'farm or harbour of the stated kind']
City Road ‹ the City (of **London**)
Clapham: 'hill village' [c.880 (*Cloppaham*): ?*clop* (perhaps from a Germanic word cognate with *hill* and *culminate*) + *hām* 'settlement, village']
Clapham Common ‹ **Clapham**
Clapton: 'hill estate' [1339 (*Clopton*), 1593 (*Clapton*): ?*clop* (*see* **Clapham**) + *tūn* 'estate, home farm']
Clarence House [built 1825 for William IV when Duke of *Clarence*]
Clay Hill [1524 (*Clayhyll*): ?*Clay, Cleye* (local surnames) + *hyll* 'hill']
Clerkenwell: 'clerics' well; scholars' well [c.1150 (*Clerkenwell*): Middle English *clerken(e)* 'clerics', scholars' (‹ *clerc* ‹ Latin ‹ Greek) + *well(a)* 'well, spring']
Cock Lane [c.1200 (*Cockeslane*), 1543 (*Coklane*): *cocc* 'cock' + *lane* 'lane'; perhaps from *cock*fighting here]
Coleman Street: 'Coleman's street' [1181–83 (*Colemanestrate*): ? (St. Stephen) *Coleman* (variant name, recorded in 1276, of the former church of St. Stephen here) + *strǣt* '(paved) road, street' (‹ Latin)]
Cordwainer Street [1216–17 (*Corueiserestrate*), 1230 (*Cordwanere-strete*): Middle English *corviser, cordwaner* 'cordwainer: leather-merchant; shoemaker' (‹ Old French ‹ Old Spanish *cordovano* 'cordovan'); now *Bow Lane* and *Garlick Hill*)
Cornhill: 'hill where corn is grown; hill where corn is sold' [1055 (*Cornehulle*): *corn* 'corn' + *hyll* 'hill']
Counter's Creek: 'countess's creek' [after the *Countess* of Oxford, wife of the Earl of Oxford (after whom *Earl's Court* was named)]
Cowley: 'Cofa's lea/grove' [959 (*Cofenlea*), 1086 (*Covelie*), 1294 (*Cowelee*): *Cofen* (from name) + *lēah* 'grove; meadow, lea']
Cranford: 'crane-ford; heron-ford' [1086 (*Cranforde*): *cran* 'crane; heron' + *ford* '(river-)ford']
Crayford: '(River) Cray ford' [1322 (*Crainford*): Celtic *crai* ?'fresh, new; clean, pure' + *ford* '(river-)ford']
Cricklewood: 'crinkled wood' [1294 (*le Crikeldwode*), 1509 (*Crykyll Wood*): ?dialectal *crickled* 'bent' (perhaps related to *crinkled*) + *wudu* 'wood']
Cripplegate: 'low gate' [991–1002 (*Cripelesgate*): *crypel* (as in *cripple*, ‹ *crēopan* 'creep') + *geat* 'gap; gate'; in some dialects *cripplegate* still has a similar meaning]
Crooked Lane [1278 (*la Crokedelane*)]
Croydon: 'saffron valley' [809 (*Crogedene*): *croh* 'saffron + *denu* 'valley']
Crudrun Lane, Godrun Lane: 'Gēdrūn('s) lane' [1180–92 (*Godrun lane*), c.1206–7 (*Godruneslane*), 1349 (*Gother lane*), 1472 (*Gutterlane*): *Gōdrūn, Guðrún* (woman's name) + *lane* 'lane'; now *Gutter Lane* [by folk etymology)]
Crutched Friars: 'be-crossed friars' [1405 (*le Crouchedfrerestrate*): Middle English *crutched* 'crossed' (‹ Latin) + Middle English *freres* 'friars' (‹ Old French ‹ Latin *fratres* 'brothers') (+ *strǣt* '(paved) road, street' (‹ Latin); after the insignia of the Augustinian *Friars* of the Holy Cross, whose house here was found in 1298]

D

Dagenham: 'Dæcca's village' [695 (*Dæccenham*), 1499 (*Dagnham*): *Dæccen* (from name) + *hām* 'settlement, village']
Dalston: Dēorla's estate' [1294 (*Derleston*), 1581 (*Darleston*), *Dēorla* (name) + *tūn* 'estate, home farm']
Dartford: '(River) Darent ford' [1086 (*Tarenteford*), 1089 (*Darenteford*), c.1100 (*Derteford*): Celtic *Darent* 'oak river' + *ford* '(river-)ford']
Deptford: 'deep ford' [14th C. (*Depeford*): *deop*'deep' + *ford* '(river-)ford']
Dicer's Lane, Dicer Lane: 'ditcher's lane' [1275 (*Diceresłane*, *Dikereslane*), 1411–12 (*Diserlane*): *dīc* 'ditch; dyke' + *-ere* '-er: -maker; -worker' + *lane* 'lane'; spellings with *Dicer-* and *Diser-* may show Norman-French influence; later *Rose Street*]
Dollis Brook ‹ **Dollis Farm** (Hendon): 'share of land' [?Middle English *dol* ‹ *dāl* 'share']
Dowgate: 'dove-gate' [1244 (*Douegat*), c.1600 (*Dowgate*): ?*dūfe* 'dove, pigeon' + *geat* 'gap; gate'; a former water*gate* and wharf that gave its name to a street now called *Dowgate Hill*]
Down, Downe: 'hill' [1316 (*Doune*): *dūn* 'hill']
Dulwich: 'dill-marsh' [967 (*Dilwihs*), 1210–12 (*Dilewisse*): *dile* 'dill' (the herb) + *wisce* 'marshland' (not *wīc* as in **Greenwich**)]
Dulwich Common ‹ **Dulwich**

E

Ealing: 'Gilla's folk' [c.700 (*Gillingas*), c.1170 (*Yllinges*), 1553 (*Elyng*): *Gill(a)* (name) + *-ingas* '-followers of, -people of']
Earl's Sluice [after the first *Earl* of Gloucester, bastard son of Henry I (1086–1135) and lord of the manor of **Camberwell** and **Peckham**]
East Acton [1294 (*Estacton*): *ēast* 'east' + **Acton**] ‹ **Acton**
East Barnet [c.1275 (*Est Barnet*): *ēast* 'east' + **Barnet**] ‹ **Barnet**
East Dulwich [1340 (*Est Dilewissh*): *ēast* 'east' + **Dulwich**] ‹ **Dulwich**
East Molesey ‹ **Molesey**
East Smithfield [1229 (*Estsmethefeld*), 1272 (*Est Smythefeld*): *ēast* 'east' + **Smithfield**] ‹ **Smithfield**
Eastcheap, East Cheap: 'east market' [c.1100 (*eastceape*): *ēast* 'east' + *cēap* 'market; trade'; former site of a meat-market]
Ebbgate: 'ebb-tide gate' [c.1190 (*Ebbegate*): *ebb(a)* 'ebb, low tide' + *geat* 'gap; gate'; a former water*gate*; now *Swan Lane*]
Edgware: 'Ecgi's weir' [c.975 (*Æcges Wer*): *Æcge* (name) + *wer* 'weir']
Edgware Road [1574 (*Edgware High Waie*)] ‹ **Edgware**
Edmonton: 'Ēadhelm('s) (folk's) estate' [1086 (*Adelmetone*), 1211 (*Edelmintone*), 1214 (*Edelmeston*), 1369 (*Edmenton*): *Ēadhelm* (name) (+ *-ing* '-follower of' or *–es* '-'s') + *tūn* 'estate, home farm']
Elbow Lane: 'old Bow Lane' [1343 (*Eldebowelane*), c.1600 (*Elbow lane*): *eald* 'old' + *boga* '(archery) bow; arch, arched bridge' + *lane* 'lane'; *Elbow(e)* ‹ *Eldebowe* (by folk etymology, as the lane has a bend); now *College Street*]
Elstree: 'Tidwulf's tree' [785 (*Tiðulfes treow*), 1188 (*Tidulvestre*), 13th C. (*Idulfestre*), 1320 (*Idelstre*), 1487 (*Illestre*), 1598 (*Elstre*): *Tidwulf* (name) + *treow* 'tree']
Eltham: 'Elta's village' [1086 (*Elteham*): *Elte* (from name) + *hām* 'settlement, village']
Enfield: Ē(a)na's field' [1086 (*Enefelde*), 13th C. (*Enesfeud*), 1293 (*Enfeld*): *Ē(a)na* (name) + *feld* 'field']
Enfield Highway [14th C. (*Alta Via*), 1610 (*the kings highe way leading from Waltham Cross toward London*)] ‹ **Enfield**
Epsom: 'Ebbi's village; Ebbi's river-bend land' [933 (*Ebesham*), 973 (*Ebbesham*), 1086 (*Evesham*), 1404 (*Epsam*): *Eb(bi)* + *hām* 'settlement, village' or *ham(m)* 'river-bend land']
Erith: 'gravel landing' [695 (*Earhyð*), 1610 (*Eryth*): *ēar* 'gravel; mud, earth' + *hȳð* 'landing-place, harbour']
Esher: 'ash (-tree) district' [1005 ((to) *Æscæron*), 1062 (*Esshere*): *æsc* 'ash(-tree)' + *scearu* 'share, district; boundary']
Euston [after *Euston* in Suffolk, seat of the Duke of Grafton, lord of the manor of **Tottenham Court** when the *Euston* Road was built (1756–75)]
Ewell: 'well-spring' [675 (*Euuelle*), 1066 (*Æwelle*): *ǣwell, ǣwiell* 'spring; well-spring, (stream-) source' (‹ *ēa* 'stream' + *well(a), wiell(a)* 'well, spring')]

F

Faitour Lane: 'layabouts' lane' [1292 (*Faytureslane*), 1568 (*Feter Lane*): Middle English *faitour* 'vagrant; beggar' (‹ Anglo-French ‹ Old French ‹ Latin) + *lane* 'lane'; now *Fetter Lane*]
Falcon [(*Falcon Brook*): after the *Falcon* Inn, near Clapham Junction]
Farnborough: 'fern hill' [1180 (*Ferenberga*), 1242 (*Farnberg*): *fearn* 'fern, bracken' + *beorg* 'hill, mound; barrow']
Feltham: 'field village; mullein (-plant) village' [969 (*Feltham*), 1086 (*Feltehā*): *feld* 'field' or *felte* (name of various plants, such as *mullein, marjoram, couch grass*) + *hām* 'settlement, village']
Fenchurch Street [1377–78 (*Fancherchestret*), 1510 (*Fanchurche Strete*)] ‹ **Fenchurch**: 'fen church' [1337 (*Fanchurche*): *fenn* 'fen, marsh' + *cirice* 'church' (‹ Late Greek)]
Finameur Lane, Finamour Lane [1316 (*Fynamoureslane*), c.1600 (*Finimore lane or fiue foote lane*): *Finamour* (attested local surname, of French origin) + *lane* 'lane'; later *Fye Foot Lane*]
Finchley: 'finch lea/grove' [c.1208 (*Finchelee*): *finc* 'finch' + *lēah* 'grove; meadow, lea']
Finks Lane [1231–45 (*Finkeslane*), 1305–6 (*Fynghis Lane*), 1326 (*Fyncheslane*): *Fink* (attested local surname ‹ *finc* 'finch') + *lane* 'lane'; by the church of *St. Benet Fink* (same surname); now *Finch Lane*]
Finsbury: 'Fin's stronghold' [1231 (*Vinisbir'*), 1535 (*Fynnesbury*): *Fin* (‹ *Vin* name, perhaps Scandinavian) + *burh* 'stronghold, fortified manor']
Finsbury Fields ‹ **Finsbury**
Fleet Lane [1544 (*Fletelane*): *Flete* (name of river or person) + *lane* 'lane'] ‹ **River Fleet**
Fleet Street [1271–72 (*Fletestrete*): (River) *Flete* + *strǣt* '(paved) road, street' (‹ Latin)] ‹ **River Fleet**
Foot's Cray: 'Fot's (property by the River) Cray' [c.1100 (*Fotescræi*), 1210 (*Fotescraye*): *Fot* (name) + *Cray* (river-name)] *see* **Crayford**
Foster (Vedast) Lane: 'St. Vedast's Lane' [1271 (*Seint uastes lane*), 1321 (*Seint Fastes lane*), 1337 (*Fasteslane*), 1359 (*Fasterslane*), 1428 (*Foster lane*); by the church of *St. Vedast*]
Friday Street [1138–60 (*Fridaiestraite*): *Frīgdæg* 'Friday' + *strǣt* '(paved) road, street' (‹ Latin); from a fish-market there on *Fridays* or a person called *Friday*]
Friern Barnet: 'friars' burnt (site)' [1235 (*le Bernet, la Barnate*), 1274 (*Frerennebarnethe, Frerebarnet*, etc.): Middle English *freren* 'friars" (‹ Old French ‹ Latin) + *bærnet* 'burnt'; formerly held by the monastic order of Knights of St. John of Jerusalem] *see* **Barnet**
Fulham: 'Fulla's river-bend land' (c.705 (*Fulanham*), c.895 (*Fullanhamme*): *Ful(l)an* (from name) + *hamm* 'river-bend land']

G

Giltspur Street [1547 (*Gyltesporestrete*); the *gilt spur(s)* were made there or displayed on a local signboard; also *Knyghtryders Strete* (1547)]
Godliman Street [?after *Godalming* (in Surrey, formerly a leather-tanning centre); the Cordwainers' Hall was near this street] *compare* **Cordwainer Street**
Golden Lane: 'Golda's lane' [1291–92 (*Goldinelane*), 1317 (*Goldenlane*): ?*Goldine* (from woman's name *Golda*, attested nearby in 1245) + *lane* 'lane']
Golders Green: 'Le Godere's green; Godyer's green' [1612 (*Golders Greene*), 1790 (*Groles or Godders Green*): (John le) *Godere* or (John) *Godyer* (names in 14th C. records) + *grēne* '(village) green'; the surname *Golder* is not attested]
Gracechurch Street: 'grass-church street' [1284 (*Garscherchestrate*), 1437 (*Gracechirche strete alias Graschirche strete*): *græs* 'grass' + *cirice* 'church' (‹ Late Greek) + *strǣt* '(paved) road, street' (‹ Latin); after the nearby church of *St. Benet Gracechurch*, perhaps thatch-roofed or grass-surrounded]
Gray's Inn Fields ‹ **Gray's Inn**: 'Gray's dwelling-place' [1396 (*Grays Inn in Holborne*): (Reginald de) *Gray* (died 1308; owner of the property) + *inn* 'dwelling, lodging'; formerly called *Portpoole Manor*]
Great Stanmore: 'great stony pool' [793 (*Stanmere*), 1392 (*Great(e) Stanmare*): Middle English *grēat* 'big' (‹ Old English *grēat* 'thick, bulky') + *stān* 'stone' + *mere* 'pool'; *Great* by contrast with *Little Stanmore (Whitchurch)*]
Green Hill Green, Greenhill Green (Middlesex, near Harrow) ‹ **Greenhill** [1334 (*Grenehulle*), 1563 (*Grenehill*), 1675 (*Green Hill*); ? after the local family *de Grenehulle, de Grenhulle* or *de Grenehill*]

The Green Park [because embellished with *greenery* (lawns and trees) rather than flowers]
Greenford: 'green (river-)ford' [845 (*Grenan Forda*): *grēne* 'green' + *ford* '(river-)ford']
Greenwich: 'green harbour' [964 (*Grenewic*): *grēne* 'green' + *wīc* 'farm or harbour of the stated kind']
Gresham Street [1845; after the nearby *Gresham* College (founded 1579 by Sir Thomas Gresham); previously *Lad Lane* and *Cateaton Street*]

H

Hackney: 'Haca's (high) ground' [1198 (*Hakeneia*): *Hacan* (from name) + *ēg* 'high ground']
Hackney Marsh [1397 (*Hackenemershe*)] ‹ **Hackney**
Hackney Wick: 'Hackney farm' [1294 (*…atte Wyk in Hakeney*): **Hackney** + *wīc* 'farm or harbour of the stated kind'] ‹ **Hackney**
Hammersmith: 'hammer smithy' [1294 (*Hamersmyth*): *hamor* 'hammer' + *smiđđe* 'smithy']
Hampstead: 'settlement, homestead' [959 (*Hemstede*): *hām* 'settlement, village' + *stede* 'place, stead']
Hampstead Heath [1543 (*Hampstede Heth*)] ‹ **Hampstead**
Hampton: 'river-bend estate' [1086 (*Hammtone*): *hamm* 'river-bend land' + *tūn* 'estate, home farm']
Hampton Court: 'Hampton manor' [1476 (*Hampton Courte*): **Hampton** + Middle English *court(e)* 'manor' (‹ Old French)] ‹ **Hampton**
Hampton Court Park ‹ **Hampton Court**
Hanwell Common ‹ **Hanwell**: 'cock well' [959 (*Hanewelle*): *hana* 'cock(erel)' + *well(a)* 'well, spring']
Hanworth: 'cock's ward' [1086 (*Haneworde*), 1254 (*Hanesworth*): *hana* 'cock(erel)' (perhaps used as a personal name) + *worđ* 'ward, enclosure']
Harefield: 'army field' [1086 (*Herefelle*), 1206 (*Herefeld*), 1223 (*Harefeld*): *here* 'army' + *feld* 'field']
Haringey: 'Haering's enclosure' [1201 (*Haringeie*)] *see* **Hornsey**
Harlington: 'Hygered's folk's estate' [831 (*Hygereding tun*), 1362 (*Herlyngdon*), 1521 (*Harlyngton*), 1535 (*Hardington al. Harlington*): *Hygered* (name, with *d/l* confusion) + *-ing* '-follower of' + *tun* 'estate, home farm']
Harmondsworth: 'Heremōd's ward' [1086 (*Hermodesworde*), 1408 (*Hermesworth*): *Heremōd* (name) + *worđ* 'ward, enclosure']
Harrow: 'heathen shrine' [767 (*Gumeninga Hergae*), 825 (*Hearge*), 1234 (*Herewes*), 1347 (*Harwo*), 1369 (*Harowe*), 1398 (*Harowe atte Hille*): (*Gumeninga* 'Guma's folk('s)' +) *hearg* 'heathen sacred place or temple' (+ *hyll* 'hill')]
Harrow on the Hill [1426 (*Harrowe on the Hill*)] ‹ **Harrow**
Hatton: 'heath estate' [1086 (*Hatone, Haitone*): *hǣđ* 'heath' + *tūn* 'estate, home farm'; near **Hounslow** Heath]
Havering: 'Hæfer's folk' [1086 (*Haueringas*): *Hæfer* (name) + *-ingas* '-followers of, -people of']
Haverstock Hill ‹ Haverstock: 'cattle (live)stock; Stock's cattle' [1627 (*Haverstocke*): ?*aver(ia)* 'cattle' (which may have grazed there) (‹ Late Latin) + *stocc* 'livestock' or *Stock* (name of local family orginally from *Stock* in Essex)]
Hayes: 'brushwood' [1177 (*Hesa*), 1610 (*Heys*): ?*hæse* 'brushwood(-land)']
Heathrow: 'heath-side row' [c.1410 (*La Hetherewe*): *hǣđ* 'heath' + *rǣw* 'row' (of trees or houses)]
Hendon: 'high hill' [959 (*Hendun*): *hēan* (‹ *hēah* 'high') + *dūn* 'hill']
Heston: 'brushwood farm' [1123–33 (*Heston(e)*): ?*hæse* 'brushwood(-land)' + *tūn* 'home farm, estate']
High Holborn: 'high (part of the River) Holborn' ‹ **Holborn**
Highbury: 'high stronghold' [1274 (*Neweton Barrewe*), c.1375 (*Heybury*), 1548 (*Newington Barowe al. the manor of Highbury*): *Neweton/Newington* (as in **Stoke Newington**) + *Barrewe/Barowe* (after the landholder Thomas de *Barewe*) + *hēah* 'high' + *burh* 'stronghold, fortified manor'; called *high* because higher than **Canonbury** or *Barnsbury*]
Highgate: 'high (toll-)gate' [1354 (*Le Heighgate*): *hēah* 'high' + *geat* 'gap; gate']
Hillingdon: 'Hilda's hill' [c.1080 (*Hildendune*), 1086 (*Hillendone*), 1274 (*Hylingdon*): *Hilden* (from name, probably short for *Hild(rīc)*, *Hild(wulf)*, etc.) + *dūn* 'hill']
Hogsmill River: 'Hogs' mill river' [1638] ‹ **Hogs Mill** [1535 (*Hoggs Myll*), 1564 (*Hoggesmyll*): after (the family of John) *Hog* (attested 1179 in **Merton**)]
Holborn: 'valley stream' [959 (*Holeborne*): *holh* 'valley, hollow' + *burna* 'stream, brook'; former name of (the upper part of) the **River Fleet**]
Holloway: 'valley way' [1307 (*Le Holewey…*), 1553 (*Holoway…*): *holh* 'valley, hollow' + *weg* 'road, way']
Homerton: 'Hūnburh('s) estate' [1343 (*Humburton*), 1581 (*Hummerton*): *Hūnburh* (woman's name ? ‹ *hūne* 'horehound' + *burh* 'stronghold') + *tūn* 'estate, home farm']
Honey Lane [c.1200 (*Hunilane*), 1274–75 (*Honylane*): Middle English *hony* (‹ *honig* 'honey') + *lane* 'lane'; from bee-keeping here]
Hook: 'hook (of land)' [1227 (*Hoke*), 1680 (*Hook*): *hōc* 'hook, bend, spit' (of land, as by a river)]
Hornsey: 'Haering's enclosure' [1201 (*Haringeie*), 1243 (*Haringesheye*), 1524 (*Harnesey*), 1564 (*Hornsey*): *Haering* (name) + (ge)*hæg* 'enclosure'; **Haringey** and *Harringay* have the same origin]
Hosier Lane [1328 (*Hosiereslane*), 1338 (*Hosierlane*)]
Houndsditch: 'dog's ditch' [1502 (*Hundesdich*), 1550 (*Houndesdyche*): *hund* 'dog, hound' (probably not a personal name as in **Hounslow**) + *dīc* 'ditch; dyke'; after the City of London ditch *Houndsditch* (1275 *Hondesdich*), into which dead dogs and rubbish were discarded]
Hounslow: 'Hund's mound; Hund's barrow' [1217 (*Hundeslawe*), 1341 (*Houndeslowe*): *Hund* (name) + *hlaw* 'mound, mount; burial mound']
Hoxton: 'Hoc's estate' [1086 (*Hochestone*): *Hoc* (name) + *tūn* 'estate, home farm']
Hubbard Lane [1231 (*vicus Sancti Andreæ*), 1252–65 (*venella Sancti Andree Hubert*); by the church of *St. Andrew Hubbard*; now **Philpot Lane**] *see* **Philpot Lane**
Hyde (Middlesex, near Hendon): 'hide of land' [1281 (*la Hyde*): *hīd* 'enough land to support a family' (generally believed to have been 120 acres)]
Hyde Park: 'park at Hyde (in the manor of Ebury)' [1204 (*Hida*), 1543 (*Hide Park*): *hīd* (as in **Hyde**) + Middle English *park* 'park' (‹ Old French)] *compare* **Hyde**

I

Ickenham: 'Ticca's village' [1086 (*Tichehā*), 1176 (*Tikeham*), 1203 (*Tikenham, Ikeham*), 1236 (*Ikenham*): *Ticcan* (from name, with loss of initial *T* through merger with final *t* of preceding *æt* 'at') + *hām* 'settlement, village']
Ilford: '(River) Hyle ford' [1086 (*Ilefort*), 1300 (*Hyleford*): *Hyle* '? trickling stream; ?still stream' (former name of the **River Roding**) + *ford* '(river-)ford'] *see also* **River Roding**
Isle of Dogs [1365 (*marsh of Stebenhithe*), 1593 (*Isle of doges ferm*), 1799 (*Popular Marshes or Isle of Dogs*); of unknown origin, the present name is probably derogatory]
Isleworth: 'Gīslhere's ward' [695 (*Gislheresuuyrth*), 1231 (*Istleworth*): *Gīslhere* (name) + *worđ* 'ward, enclosure']
Islington: 'Gisla's hill' [c.1000 (*Gislandune*): *Gislan* (from name) + *dūn* 'hill']
Ivy Lane [13th C. (*Yvi lane*), 1280 (*Ivilane*); perhaps from *ivy* on nearby houses; previously *Alsies Lane*]

J

Jewry Street: 'street where Jews live' [1366 (*la Porejewerie*); also *Jewry*; previously **Poor Jewry**]

K

Kennington: 'Cæna's folk's estate' [1086 (*Chenintune*), 1263 (*Kenyngton*): *Cæn(a)* (name) + *-ing* '-follower of' + *tūn* 'estate, home farm']
Kensal Green: 'king's-wood green' [1253 (*Kingisholte*), 1367 (*Kyngesholt*), 1550 (*Kynsale Grene*): *cyning* 'king' + *holt* 'wood, holt; thicket' + *grēne* '(village) green']
Kensington: 'Cynesige's folk's estate' [1086 (*Chenist'*), 1235 (*Kensington*): *Cynes(ige)* (name) + *-ing* '-follower of' + *tūn* 'estate, home farm']
Kensington Gardens ‹ **Kensington Palace**
Kensington High Street ‹ **Kensington**
Kensington Palace ‹ **Kensington**
Kentish Town: 'Kentish estate; Le Kentiss(h)'s estate' [1208 (*Kentisston*), 1278 (*Le Kentesseton*), 1294 (*La Kentishton*), 1488 (*Kentisshtowm*): *Kentish* (‹ *Kent* (place-name) or *Le Kentiss(h)* (name or nickname)) + *tūn* 'estate, home farm']
Keston: 'Cyssi('s) stone('s folk's boundary)' [862 (*Cystaninga mearc*), 1086 (*Chestan*), 1205 (*Kestan*): *Cyssi* (name) + *stān* 'stone' (+ *-inga* '-followers' of' + *mearc* 'boundary, boundary marker')]
Kew: 'quay on a neck of land' [1327 (*Cayho*): Middle English *kai* 'quay' (‹ Old French ‹ Celtic) + *hōh* 'neck/spur of land']
Kew Gardens ‹ **Kew**
Kidbrook: 'kite brook' [1202 (*Ketebroc*): *cēta* ‹ *cȳta* 'kite (bird)' + *brōc* 'brook']
Kilburn: 'royal stream; cows' stream; kiln stream' [c.1130 (*Cuneburna*), 1181 (*Keleburne*): *cyne-* 'royal' or *cȳna* 'cows' or *cyln* 'kiln' + *burna* 'stream, brook']
King Edward Street [1843: after *King Edward* (VI) (1537–53), who endowed Christ's Hospital school here; previously **Stinking Lane**] *see* **Stinking Lane**
King William Street [built 1829: after *King William* (IV) (1765–1837), who opened it]
Kings Cross: 'the King's cross-roads' [from a statue of *King* George IV at a cross-roads here from 1830 to 1845; formerly *Bradford (bridge), Battlebridge*]
King's End [1550 (*Kings End*): owned then by *King's* College Cambridge, but perhaps already so called after the *King* family prominent locally since at least 1296]
Kingsbury: 'the King's stronghold' [1044 (*Kynges Byrig*): *cyning* 'king' + *burh* 'stronghold, fortified manor']
Kingsland: 'the King's land' [1395 (*Kyngeslond*)]
Kingston: 'the King's demesne' [838 (*Cyninges tun*): *cyning* 'king' + *tūn* 'estate, home farm']
Kingston Hill ‹ **Kingston**
Kingston upon Thames ‹ **Kingston, River Thames**
Knightrider Street: 'knight's street' [1322 (*Knyghtridestrete*): *cniht* 'youth; servant, soldier; knight' + *ridere* 'knight; rider' + *strǣt* '(paved) road, street' (‹ Latin); *knight* and *rider* overlapped in meaning for a time]
Kyroun Lane: 'Cynrūn('s) lane' [1259 (*Kyrunelane*), 1275 (*Kyroneslane*): ?*Cynrūn* (woman's name) + *lane* 'lane'; later *Maiden Lane*]

L

La Riole [1331 (*la Ryole, la Rioloe*), 1455–56 (*le Royall*): *La Ryole* (name of house here ‹ *La Réole* wine-exporting town in Bordeaux); later *Royal Street* (*Royal* ‹ *Réole* by folk etymology); now *College Hill*]
Ladle Lane [c. 1300 (*Ladelane*): Middle English *ladel* 'ladle' (‹ *hlædel*) + *lane* 'lane'; *ladles* may well have been made here]
Laleham: 'withe village; withe river-bend land' [1042–66 (*Læleham*): *lǣl* 'twig, withe' + *hām* 'settlement, village' or *hamm* 'river-bend land']
Lambard's Hill: 'Lambert's rise' [1283 (*Lamberdeshul, Lambardeshull*), 1645 (*Lambert-Hill*), 1659–60 (*Lambeth Hill*): *Lambert, Lamberd* (surname) + *hyll* 'hill'; hill in such London street names means 'steep street'; now *Lambeth Hill* (*Lambeth* ‹ *Lambert* by folk etymology)]
Lambeth: 'lambs' landing-place' [1088 (*Lamhytha*), 1312 (*Lambhehithe*): *lamb* 'lamb' + *hȳđ* 'landing-place, harbour']
Lambs Conduit Fields ‹ Lamb's Conduit [?1577: (William) *Lamb(e)* (name of the conduit's builder) + Middle English *conduit* 'aqueduct' (‹ Anglo-French ‹ Old French ‹ Medieval Latin]
Lampton: 'lamb farm' [1376 (*Lampton feld*), 1438 (*Lamtonfeld*), 1611 (*Lambton*), 1633 (*Lampton*): *lamb* 'lamb' (with *b* as *p* before *t*) + *tūn* 'estate, home farm' (+ *feld* 'field')]
Leadenhall Street: 'street of the lead(-roofed) hall' [1605 (*Leaden Hall Street*): after *Leadenhall* (a large local house)]
Lee: 'lea/grove' [1086 (*Lee*): *lēah* 'grove; meadow, lea']
Les(s)nes(s) Heath ‹ Les(s)nes(s): 'pasture promontory' [1086 (*Lesneis*): *lǣs* 'pasture; meadow' + *nǣs* 'headland, promontory, cape'; from its projection into the **Erith** Marshes]
Leveroune Lane: 'Lēofrūn's lane' [1233 (*Le Vrunelane*), 1331 (*Lyveroneslane*), 1353 (*Leverounelane*), 1604 (*Lither lane al. Liver lane*), 1682 (*Leather Lane*): ?*Lēofrūn* (woman's name) + *lane* 'lane'; now *Leather Lane*]
Lewisham: 'Liof's village' [862 (*Liofshema mearc*), c.1060 (*Liofesham*): *Liof* (name) + *hām* 'settlement, village' (+ *mearc* 'boundary, landmark')]
Leyton: '(River) Lea demesne' [c.1050 (*Lugetune*): **Lea** + *tūn* 'estate, home farm'] ‹ **River Lea**
Leytonstone: 'Leyton (at the) stone' [1370 (*Leyton atte Stone*), 1426 (*Leyton Stone*): **Leyton** + *stān* 'stone' (from the reputed site here of a Roman milestone)] *see* **Leyton**
Lime Street: 'street where (quick)lime was burnt and sold' [1170–87 (*Limstrate*): *līm* '(quick)lime' + *strǣt* '(paved) road, street' (‹ Latin)]
Limehouse: '(quick)lime-kilns' [1367 (*Le Lymhostes*), 1547 (*Lymehouse*): *līm* '(quick)lime' + *āst* 'oast, kiln']
Lincoln's Inn Fields ‹ Lincolns Inn: 'Lincoln's dwelling-place' [1399 (*Lincolnesynne*): *Lincoln* (name) + *inn* 'dwelling, lodging'; after Thomas de *Lincoln*, owner of related property

elsewhere, and Henry de Lacy, Earl of *Lincoln* (died 1311), lawyers' patron]
Little Britain [1329 (*Brettonstrete*), 1547 (*Britten Strete*), c.1600 (*little Brittain streete*): after (Robert le) *Bretoun*, local landowner (attested 1274) (+ Middle English *strete* ‹ *strǣt* '(paved) road, street' (‹ Latin)]
Little Chelsea [1655 (*Little Chelcy*)] ‹ **Chelsea**
Liverpool Street [after R.B. Jenkinson, 2nd Earl of *Liverpool*, Prime Minister 1812–27]
Lombard Street [1318 (*Lumbardstret*): *Lumbard* 'Lombard' + *strǣt* '(paved) road, street' (‹ Latin); after the *Lombards* (north Italians, often early bankers) there]
London [115 (*Londinium*), 150 (*Londinion*), c.380 (*Lundinium*), 962 (*Lundene*), 12th C. (*Lundres*), 1205 (*Lundin*); origin unknown]
London Bridge [10th C. (*Lundene brigc*): *Lundene* 'London' + *brycg* 'bridge'] ‹ **London**
London Wall [1547 (*London Walle*); after the former city *wall*; previously also called *Babeloyne* 'Babylon' (1385–86)] ‹ **London**
Long Ditton: 'long ditch estate' [1086 (*Ditune*), 1233 (*Ditton*), 1242 (*Longa Dittone*): *lang* 'long' + *dīc* 'ditch; dyke' + *tūn* 'estate, home farm']
Long Lane [1530 (*Long Lane*)]
Lothbury: 'Lotha's manor' [1293 (*Lotheberi*): *Hloþa* (name) + *burh* 'stronghold, fortified manor']
Loughton: 'Luh(h)a's folk's estate' [1062 (*Lukintone*), 1200 (*Lucheton'*), 1331 (*Lughton*), 1338 (*Loughton*): *Luh(ha)* (name) + *-ing* '-follower of' + *tūn* 'estate, home farm']
Lower Clapton ‹ **Clapton**
Lower Norwood ‹ **Norwood**
Lower Sydenham ‹ **Sydenham**
Lower Tooting ‹ **Tooting**
Ludgate: 'postern gate; low gate' [1164–79 (*Ludgate*): *ludgeat* 'back gate' or 'low gate' (?‹ *lud-* ‹ *lūtan* 'bow (head), lower' + *geat* 'gap; gate')]

M

Malden: 'cross hill' [1086 (*Meldon(e)*), 1225 (*Maldon*): *mǣl* 'sign; cross' + *dūn* 'hill']
Mark Lane: 'Martha's lane' [c.1200 (*Marthe-lane*), 1481 (*Markelane*): ?*Marthe* 'Martha' + *lane* 'lane'; formerly also *Mart Lane*]
Marlborough House [built 1709–11 by Wren for John Churchill (1650–1722), first Duke of *Marlborough*]
Mart Lane ‹ **Mark Lane**
Marylebone: '(St.) Mary's stream; (St.) Mary('s) by the stream' [1453 (*Maryburne*): *Mary* (name) + French *le* 'the' (17th-C. insertion) + *burna* 'brook, stream'] *see also* **Tyburn Street**
Mayes Brook [after (Richard le) *May* (attested 1314) or his family]
Merton: 'pool(-side) estate' [967 (*Mertone*): *mere* 'pool' + *tūn* 'estate, home farm']
Mile End: 'mile's end' [1288 (*La Mile Ende*): *mīl* 'mile' (‹ Latin) + *ende* 'end, edge; district'; from its being a *mile* from **Aldgate**]
Milk Street [c.1140 (*Melecstrate*), 1153–67 (*Milkstrete*): *meoluc, milc* 'milk' + *strǣt* '(paved) road, street' (‹ Latin); from the selling of *milk*, and perhaps also the *milk*ing of cows, here]
Mill Hill [1547 (*Myllehill*): *myln* 'mill' (‹ Latin) + *hyll* 'hill']
Minchen Lane [1360 (*Mynchenelane*)] *see* **Mincing Lane**
Mincing Lane: 'nuns' lane' [12th C. (*M(e)ngenelane*): *mynecenu* 'nuns' + *lane* 'lane'; formerly also **Minchen Lane**] *see also* **Minchen Lane**
Mitcham: 'big village' [1086 (*Michelham*), c.1150 (*Micham*): *micel* 'big, large, great' + *hām* 'settlement, village']
Molesey: 'Mūl's (high) ground' [675 (*Muleseg*), 967 (*Muleseye*): *Mūl* (name) + *ēg* 'high ground']
Monument Street [after its *Monument* (built 1671–7) commemorating the Great Fire of London (1666)]
Moor Fields: 'marsh fields' [*mōr* 'marsh, moor' + *feld* 'field'; now *Moorfields*]
Moorgate: 'marsh gate' [*mōr* 'marsh, moor' + *geat* 'gap; gate']
Morden: 'marsh hill' [969 (*Mordune*), 1204 (*Moreden*): *mōr* 'marsh, moor' + *dūn* 'hill']
Moselle, Moselle Brook [previously *Campsborne* (1608)] ‹ **Muswell Hill**
Mottingham: 'Mod(da)'s folk's river-bend land' [973 (*Modinga hammes gemǣro*), 987 (*Modinga hæma mearc*), 1044 (*Modingeham*), 1206 (*Modingh'*): ?*Mod(da)* (name) + *-inge-, -inga-* '-followers' of' + *hamm* 'river-bend land']
Mugwell Street: 'Muc(c)a's well street' [c.1200 (*Mukewellstrete*), 1279 (*Mogewelstrete*), 1544 (*Mugwellstrete*), c.1600 (*Monkeswell Streete*): ?*Muc(c)a* (name) + *well(a)* 'well; spring' + *strǣt* '(paved) road, street' (‹ Latin); later called *Monkwell Street*, probably through folk etymology]
Muswell Hill: 'moss-spring hill' [c.1155 (*Mosewella*), 1535 (*Muswell*), 1631 (*Mussel Hill*): *mēos* 'moss' + *wella* 'well; spring' + *hyll* 'hill']
Mutton Brook: 'Mordin's brook' [1574 (*Mordins Brook*), 1819 (*Mutton Brook*): ?*Mordin* (name) + *brōc* 'brook']

N

Necklinger, Neckinger: 'noose; bend' [from (the Devil's) *Neckercher* 'the Devil's neckerchief' (former slang name for 'hangman's noose') or from the stream's sinuosity]
Needler Lane, Needler's Lane [1400–01 (*Nedlerlane*), 1403 (*Nedelerslane*), c.1600 (*Needlers lane, Needlars lane*): Middle English *nedlere* 'needler: needle-maker; needle-seller' + *lane* 'lane': now *Pancras Lane*]
New Bond Street [1732 (*New Bond Street*): after Sir Thomas *Bond*, developer of land in the area]
New Cross: 'new cross-roads' [?from the junction of the Old Kent Road with a road leading to **Dartford** in Kent]
New River [1625 (*the Newe River*); engineered 1609–13]
Newham [London borough comprising west **Barking**, **West Ham**, *East Ham* and **Woolwich** north of the Thames]
Newington (Middlesex): 'new estate' [1086 (*Neutone*), 1255 (*Newinthon*); another name for **Stoke Newington**] *see* **Stoke Newington**
Newington (Surrey): 'new estate' [c.1200 (*Neuton*), 1258 (*Neweton*): *nīwe 'new'* + *tūn* 'estate, home farm'; *-ing-* probably from the *-an* of Old English "*æt Þǣm nīwan tūne*" ('at the new estate')]
Newington Green [1480 (*Newyngtongrene*): **Newington** + *grēne* '(village) green'] ‹ **Newington** (Middlesex)
North End (Hampstead): 'the north end of Hampstead' [1741–45: *nor* 'north' + *ende* 'end, edge; district']
Northolt: 'north corner' [960 (*(æt) norð healum*), 1086 (*Northala*), 1610 (*Northolt*): *norð* 'north' + *halh, healh*]
Northwood [1435 (*Northwode*): *norð* 'north' + *wudu* 'wood'; north of **Ruislip**]
Norwood: 'north wood' [1176 (*Norwude*): *norð* 'north' + *wudu* 'wood'; north of **Croydon**]
Norwood Common ‹ **Norwood**

O

Old Broad Street [eastern part of the former **Broad Street**; contrasted with the later *New Broad Street*] ‹ **Broad Street**
Old Change: 'old trading-place' [1297–98 (*Chaunge*), 1316 17 (*Eldechaunge*), 1393 (*Oldechaunge*): *eald* 'old' + ?Middle English *chaunge* 'change; merchants' meeting place' (‹ Anglo-French ‹ Old French ‹ Latin ‹ Celtic); this *change* may have been the royal mint formerly here]
Old Dean's Lane [1257 (*Eldedeneslane*), 1513 (*Eldens lane* alias *Warwik lane*): *eald* 'old' + Middle English *deen* 'dean' (‹ Middle French ‹ Late Latin) + *lane* 'lane'; after a former *Dean* of St. Paul's; now **Warwick Lane**]
Old Fish Street [1230–40 (*Westfihistrate*), 1272–73 (*Fihstrate*), 1293–94 (*Old Fistrete*); probably from a *fish*-market there; now **Knightrider Street**] *see also* **Knightrider Street**
Old Fish Street, Old Fish Street Hill [c.1600 *Old Fishstreete Hill*); *hill* in such London street-names means 'steep street']
Old Ford: 'old (river-)ford' [1230 (*Eldefordmelne*), 1313 (*Oldeforde*): *eald* 'old' + *ford* 'river-ford' (+ *meln, myln* 'mill' ‹ Latin)]
Old Jewry: 'former Jewish quarter' [1327–28 (*la Oldeiuwerie*), 1336 (*la Elde Jurie*): (French *la* 'the' +) *eald* 'old' + Middle English *giwerie, juerie* 'Jews' territory, Jews' district' (‹ Anglo-French ‹ Old French); formerly *Colechurch Lane*]
Old Oak Common: 'old-grove common' [1380 (*Eldeholt*), c.1415 (*Oldeholte*), 1650 (*Common called Old Oake*): *eald* 'old' + *oak* (by folk etymology ‹ *holt* 'holt, grove, copse') + English *common* 'common land' (‹ Latin *commūnia*)]
Old Street: 'old road' [c.1200 (*Ealdestrate*): *eald* 'old' + *strǣt* '(paved) road, street' (‹ Latin)]
Orpington: 'Orped's folk's estate' [1042 (*Orpedingtun*), 1086 (*Orpinton*), 1207 (*Orpington'*): *Orped* (name) + *-ing* '-follower of' + *tūn* 'estate, home farm']
Osterley Park ‹ Osterley: 'sheep-fold lea/grove' [1274 (*Osterle*): *eowestre* 'sheep-fold' (‹ *eowu* 'ewe') + *lēah* 'grove; meadow, lea']
Oxford Street [1720; previously called *Tyburn Road, road to Worcester, Road to Oxford*, etc.]
Oystergate [1259 (*Oystregate*); a former water*gate* where *oysters* may have been sold]

P

Paddington: 'Pad(d)a's folk's estate' [c.1045 (*Padington*): *Pad(da)* (name) + *-ing* '-follower of' + *tūn* 'estate, home farm']
Pall Mall: 'mall or alley used for playing pall-mall' [1650 (*Pall Mall Walk*): *pall-mall* 'alley for pall-mall, a game of getting a ball through a raised ring by hitting it with a mallet' (‹ Middle French ‹ Italian)]
Pancras ‹ **St. Pancras**
Paternoster Row: 'rosary-makers' row' [1307 (*Paternosterstrete*), 1320–21 (*Paternoster Lane*), 1344 (*Paternosterowe*), 1374 (*Paternostererowe*): *paternostrere* 'pater-nosterer, rosary-maker (‹ Latin) + *rǣw* 'row' (of trees or houses)]
Peckham: 'peak village' [1086 (*Pecheham*), 1241 (*Peckham*): ?*pēac* 'peak, hill' + *hām* 'settlement, village']
Penge: 'head wood, chief wood' [1067 (*Penceat*), 1206 (*Penge*), 1472 (*Pengewode*): ?Celtic *pen* 'head, top; chief' (as in *Pen(zance)*) + ?Celtic *cēt* 'wood']
Pentecost Lane [1280 (*Pentecostelane*), 1290 (*Pentecostes lane*): Middle English *Pentecoste* (Christian festival or man's Christian name) (‹ *pentecosten* ‹ Late Latin ‹ Greek) + *lane* 'lane']
Petersham Road ‹ Petersham: 'Peohtric's river-bend land' [675 (*Piterichesham*): *Peotric* (name) + *hamm* 'river-bend' land']
Petty Wales: 'little Wales' [1298–99 (*petit Walles*), 1349 (*Pety Wales*): French *petit* 'little' + *Wal(l)es* 'Wales'; perhaps from Welsh people resident here]
Philpot Lane [1480–81 (*Philpot Lane*): after Sir John *Philpot*, Lord Mayor 1378–79; formerly probably **Hubbard Lane**] *see* **Hubbard Lane**
Piccadilly [?after *Pickadilly* (Hall) (a 17th-C. tailor's house nearby) ‹ *piccadil* 'border with a cut-out pattern, ornamenting especially the edge of a collar or ruff' (‹ French ?‹ Spanish)]
Pimlico [1630 (*Pimplico*), c.1743 (*Pimlico*): ?after *Pimlico* (Walk) in **Hoxton**, named after Ben *Pimlico*, 16th-C. innkeeper there]
Pinkwell [1754 (*Pinkwell*)]
Pinner: 'pin(-shaped) (river-)bank; Pinn(a's) river-bank' [1232 (*Pinnora*), 1332 (*Pinnere*): *pinn* 'pin, peg' or *Pinn* (name) + *ōra* 'bank, edge; slope' (‹ Latin)]
Pinner Green ‹ **Pinner**
Plaistow: 'playing/sporting ground' [1278 (*Pleystowe*): *pleg* 'play'+ *stōw* 'place']
Plaistow Levels: '?Plaistow level ground' ‹ **Plaistow**
Plumstead: 'plum(-tree) place' [c.965 (*Plumstede*): *plume* 'plum; plum-tree' + *stede* 'place, stead']
Ponders End [1593 (*Ponders ende*): *Ponder* (surname of local family) + *ende* 'end, edge; district'; on the **Enfield/Edmonton** border]
Pool River ‹ Pool: 'Pool of London' [1258 (*La Pole*): *pōl* 'pool']
Poor Jewry [1366 (*la Porejewerie*)] *see* **Jewry Street**
Poplar: 'poplar(-tree)' [1327 (*Popler*): Middle English *poplere* 'poplar' (‹ Middle French)]
Potter's Bar: 'Potter's Gate (to Enfield Chase)' [1509 (*Potterys Barre*), 1548 (*Potters Barre*): *(le) Pottere* (attested surname) + Middle English *barre* 'rod, bar; gate, barrier' (‹ Old French)]
Poultry: 'poultry-market' [1301 (*Poletria*), 1422 (*Pulyterye*): Middle English *pultrie* 'poultry; poultry-market' (‹ Old French)]
Primrose Hill [1586 (*Prymrose Hill*); allegedly from the former profusion of *primrose(s)* there]
Pudding Lane (near Billingsgate): 'guts lane' [1360 (*Puddynglane*): Middle English *pudding* 'guts, entrails' + *lane* 'lane'; perhaps whence "the Butchers of Eastcheape" got rid of such parts of their animals]
Purley: 'pear-tree lea/grove' [1200 (*Pirlee*), 1220 (*Purle*): *pirige* 'pear-tree' (‹ *peru, pere* 'pear' ‹ Latin) + *lēah* 'grove; meadow, lea']
Putney: 'Put(t)a's landing' [1086 (*Putelei*), 1279 (*Puttenhuthe*): *Putten* (from name) + *hȳð* 'landing-place, harbour']
Putney Heath ‹ **Putney**
Pyl Brook ‹ Pylford Bridge [1548 (*Pillefordebrudge*)]
Pymme's Brook [after the family of Reginald *Pymme* of Edelmetone (**Edmonton**), attested locally since the 14th C.; formerly *Medeseye* (c.1200)]

Q

Quaggy River: 'quagmire river; boggy river' [from its sluggish flow]
Queen Street [after Catherine of Braganza (1638–1705), *Queen* as wife of King Charles II; includes the former **Soper Lane**] *see* **Soper Lane**

Queen Victoria Street [opened 1871]
Queenhithe: 'Queen('s) dock' [898 (*Æðeredes hyd*). *Æðered* '?Ethelred, Alderman of Mercia' + *hȳð* 'landing-place, harbour'; now *Queenhithe Dock* perhaps because formerly owned by Isabella of Angoulême]

R

Radlett: 'cross-roads' [1453 (*Radelett*): ?*rād-(ge)lǣt(e)* 'road-junction' (‹ *rād* 'riding; road' + *-(ge)lǣt(e)* 'junction of roads, cross-roads')]
Rainham (Essex): 'top-people's settlement' [1086 (*Renaham, Raineham*): ?*roeginga-ham* (as attested for *Rainham* in Kent) ‹ *roegingas* 'dominant folk' + *hām* 'settlement, village']
Red Cross Street [1275 (*Redecrochestrete*), 1341 (*Redecrouchestrete*), 1502 (*Redcrosse strete*): *rēad* 'red' + Middle English *crouche* 'cross' (‹ Latin) or *cros* 'cross' (‹ Old Irish ‹ Latin) + *strǣt* '(paved) road, street' (‹ Latin); perhaps after a local house or a boundary *cross*]
Redbridge [after a *red bridge* across the **River Roding** between **Wanstead** and **Ilford**]
Regent's Park [1817 (*The Regents Park*): after the Prince *Regent*, later George IV]
Richmond [1502 (*Richemont*): after Henry VII, Earl of *Richmond* in Yorkshire; formerly (*West*) *Sheen*]
Richmond Park ‹ **Richmond**
Richmond upon Thames ‹ **Richmond, River Thames**
River Brent ‹ **Brent**
River Ching [1562 (*the Boorne*), 1585 (*the Brook*): *burna* 'stream, brook'; *Ching* is a later back-formation from **Chingford**] *see* **Chingford**
River Colne ‹ **Colne**: 'water stream' [1301 (*Collee*), 1351 (*Colne*): ?Celtic *colūn* 'water' + *ēa* 'stream'; found elsewhere too as a river-name]
River Crane [1825 (*Cran Brook*); formerly *Fishbourne*] ‹ **Cranford**
River Effra ‹ **Effra**: 'river-bank' [?*efre* 'bank' (of river); cognate with German *Ufer* 'bank, shore']
River Fleet ‹ **Fleet**: 'stream' [c.1012 (*Fleta*): *fleot* 'inlet, stream']
River Gade ‹ **Gade**: 'Gǣte's stream' [1242 (*Gatesee*), 1349–96 (*Gateseye*), 1728 (*river Gade*): ?*Gǣtesēa* 'Gǣte's stream' (‹ *Gǣte* (name or nickname ‹ *gat* 'goat') + *ēa* 'stream')]
River Graveney 'river by Tooting Graveney' [1272 (*Thoting Gravenel*): after (Richard de) *Gravenel*, lord of the manor of Lower/South **Tooting** in 1215 (whose family were perhaps from *Graveney* in Kent)]
River Lea ‹ **Lea**: 'bright' [895 (*Lygan*); perhaps related to *lēah* 'lea, meadow as light-filled place' (‹ Indo-European base ?*leuk, louk* 'light, brightness')]
River Mole [1214 (*aqua de Mulesia*), 1595 (*Moulsey River*)] ‹ **Molesey**
River Pinn [from **Pinner**] *see* **Pinner**
River Ravensbourne ‹ **Ravensbourne**: 'raven's stream' [1575 (*Ravensburn*): *hrǣfn* 'raven' + *burna* 'stream, brook']
River Roding [1576 (*Rodon*), 1622 (*Roding*); formerly *Hyle*] ‹ **Roding** (Essex): 'Rod(da)'s folk' [c.1050 (*Rodinges*): *Rod(da)* (name) + *-ingas, -inges* '-followers of']
River Thames ‹ **Thames**: 'dark water' [?‹ Celtic base cognate with Sanskrit *tamasa-* 'dark']
River Wandle [from the *Wa(e)nd(e)l* of **Wandsworth**] *see* **Wandsworth**
River Wey ‹ **Wey**: 'flowing' [675 (*Waie*): ?‹ Indo-European *wegh* -(referring to motion, as in *wǣg* 'wave')]
Romford: 'ample ford' [1177 (*Romfort*), 1199 (*Rumford*): *rūm* 'roomy, spacious' + *ford* '(river-)ford']
Roper Lane: 'rope-maker's lane; Roper's lane' [1313 (*Ropereslane*): Middle English *roper* 'rope-maker' or *Roper(e)* (attested local surname) + *lane* 'lane'; now *Love Lane*]
The Ropery, Roper Street [1271 (*Roperestrete*), 1307 (*la Roperie*); after the *rope*-makers there; now **Thames Street**]
Rotherhithe: 'cattle landing-place' [c.1105 (*Rederheia*), 1301 (*Rotherhethe*): *hrīðer* 'horned beast, ox; cattle' + *hȳð* 'landing-place, harbour']
Royal Botanic Gardens *see* **Kew Gardens**
Ruislip: 'rush(y) leap' [1806 (*Rislepe*), 1341 (*Ruysshlep*): *rysc* 'rush(-plant)' + ?*hlype* 'leap'; ?from a nearby crossing place of the **River Pinn**]

S

St. Botolph's Lane [1348–49 (*Seyntbotulfeslane*), 1432 (*Botulpheslane*), 1544 (*Botulphe Lane*); after the church of *St. Botulph Billingsgate*; now *Botolph Lane*]
St. Bride Street [?after *St. Bride*'s churchyard nearby]
St. Clement's Lane [1348 (*Seint Clementeslane*); by the church of *St. Clement Eastcheap*; now *Clement's Lane*]
St. Dunstans Lane [1329 (*Donstoneslane*), 1363 (*Seint Dunstoneslone*); by the church of *St. Dunstan in the East*; now *St. Dunstan's Hill*]
St. James ‹ **St. James's Palace**
St. James's Palace [built on the site of a leprosy hospital dedicated to *St. James* the Less]
St. James's Park ‹ **St. James's Palace**
St. Katharine's Dock [1422 (*Katerines Dokke*): *St. Katherine's* (from the name of a former local hospital founded 1148) + Middle English *dok* 'dock; wharf' (?‹ Middle Dutch ‹ Latin)]
St. Laurence Lane [1320 (*Seint Laurencelane*), c.1600 (*Poultney lane*); after the church of *St. Laurence Pountney*; now *Laurence Pountney Lane*]
St. Margaret Patten's Lane [1577 (*Rood Lane*): Middle English *rood* 'cross' (‹ *rōd*) + *lane* 'lane'; from a *rood* put before 1538 in the churchyard of *St. Margaret Pattens*, from which church comes the previous name of this lane now called *Rood Lane*]
St. Mary Axe: 'St. Mary at/of the Axe' [1275 (*strata Sancte Marie atte Ax*); after the church of *St. Mary Axe* (demolished 1561), housing the *axe* with which St. Ursula was said to have been martyred]
St. Mary (Axe) Street [now **St. Mary Axe**] *see* **St. Mary Axe**
St. Mary Cray: 'St. Mary('s church by the River) Cray' [1257 (*Creye Sancte Marie*)] *see* **Crayford**
St. Mary at Hill Lane [1275 (*venella Sancte Marie de la Hulle*), 1520–21 (*seint mary hill lane*); after the church of *St. Mary at Hill*]
St. Marylebone ‹ **Marylebone**
St. Martin Orgar Lane [1236–37 (*venella Sancti Martini*), c.1600 (*Saint Martins Orgar Lane*); after the church of *St. Martin Orgar*; now *Martin Lane*]
St. Martin's Le Grand: 'St. Martin the Great's' [1265 (*St. Martin le Grand*); after the former local church of *St. Martin le Grand*]
St. Michael's Lane [1303 (*Seint Micheleslane*); by the church of *St. Michael Crooked Lane*; later *Miles's Lane* (*Miles* ‹ *Michael*)]
St. Nicholas Lane [1381 (*Seint Nicholaslane*); by the church of *St. Nicholas Acon*; now *Nicholas Lane*]
St. Pancras [1086 (*Sanctum Pancratiū*), 1588 (*Pankeridge al. St Pancras*); after *St. Pancras*, martyred under Diocletian (Roman emperor 284–305)]
St. Paul's Cathedral [built 1675–1710; replacing old *St. Paul's* (burnt 1666)]
St. Paul's Churchyard [after **St. Paul's Cathedral** or old *St. Paul's*]
St. Peter's Hill [1263 (*Venella sancti Petri*), 1378 (*Seint Petrelane*), 1564 (*Peter Lane*) c.1600 (*Saint Peters Hill, Peter hill lane*); *hill* in such London street-names means 'steep street'; by the church of *St. Peter (the little) Paul's Wharf*; formerly *Peter Lane*]
Salmon's Brook [1754]: after (the family of John) *Salmon* (attested 1274 at **Edmonton**)]
Sanderstead: 'sandy place' [c.880 (*Sandenstede*), 1086 (*Sandestede*), 1221 (*Sanderstede*): ?sanden 'sandy' + *stede* 'place, stead']
Seacoal Lane: 'coal lane' [1253 (*sacolelane*), c.1600 (*Seacole lane*): *sǣcol* 'coal, not charcoal' (delivered by *sea* or mined by the *sea*) + *lane* 'lane'; *coal* may have been delivered here from the **River Fleet**]
Sewardstone: 'Sigeweard's estate' [1176–90 (*Sidwardeston'*): *Sigeweard* (name) + *tūn* 'estate, home farm']
Shambles, Butchery: 'meat-market; slaughterhouse' [1349 (*Bocherie*), 1425–26 (*Shameles*), 1530 (*le Fleshambles*): (*flǣsc* 'flesh, meat' +) Middle English *shambles* 'meat-market; slaughterhouse' (‹ Middle English *shamble* 'meat-seller's table' ‹ *sceamel* 'stool' ‹ Late Latin) or Middle English *butchery* 'slaughterhouse' (‹ Old French); now *Newgate Street*]
Shepherds Bush [1635 (*Sheppards Bush Green*), 1675 (*Shepperds Bush*)]
Shepperton: 'shepherd farm' [959 (*Scepertune*): ?*sceaphir(de), sceaphier(de)* 'shepherd' + *tūn* 'estate, home farm']
Shepperton Green [1754] ‹ **Shepperton**
Shitbourn Lane: 'shithouse lane' [1272–73 (*Shitteboruelane*), 1321 (*Shiteburghlane*), 1313 (*Shitebournelane*), 1467 (*Shirbouruelane alias Shetbouruelane*), 1540 (*Shirborne lane*), c.1600 (*Sherborne lane*): Middle English *Shitebourne* 'shit stream' (by scribal error ‹ Middle English ?*shiteburgh* 'shithouse, privy' ‹ *scite* 'shit' + *burh, burg* 'stronghold, fortified manor') + *lane* 'lane'; now *Sherborne Lane* (by euphemism)]
Shoe Lane: 'shoe(-shaped) land; shelter-land' [1187–1216 (*Solande*), 1272 (*Sholand*), 1279 (*Sholane*): *scoh* 'shoe' or ?*scēo* 'shelter' + *land* 'land']
Shooters Hill: 'archer's slope' [1292 (*Shetereshelde*): Middle English *sheter* 'shooter, archer' (‹ ?*scēotere*) + *helde* 'slope']
Shoreditch: 'slope-ditch' [c.1148 (*Soredich*): ?*scora* 'shore, bank; slope' + *dīc* 'ditch, trench; dyke'; the name's referent is obscure]
Sidcup: 'flat-top; camp-site top' [1254 (*Cetecopp'*), 1332 (*Sedecoppe*); ?*set* 'seat-shaped, flattened; camp' + *copp* 'hill-top']
Silk Stream: 'gully stream' [957 (*Sulh, Sulue, Sulc*), 13th C. (*Solke, Selke*): ?*sulh* 'plough; ?furrow' (?with *h* changed to *c* or *k* before *stream*)]
Sipson: 'Sibwine's estate' [13th C. (*Sibwineston*), 1391 (*Sibston*), 1638 (*Sipson*): *Sibwine* (name) + *tūn* 'estate, home farm']
Smallbury: 'narrow mound' [1436 (*Smalborow*), 1680 (*Smallbury Green*): *smæl* 'thin, narrow; small' + *beorg* 'hill, mound; barrow']
Smithfield: 'level field' [*smēðe* 'smooth, level' + *feld* 'field']
Soper Lane, Soper's Lane: 'soaper's lane' [c.1246 (*Sopereslane*), 1282 (*Soperlane*), 1600 (*Sopers lane*): Middle English *sopere* 'soaper: soap-maker; soap-seller' (‹ *sāpe* + *-ere*) + *lane* 'lane'; now part of **Queen Street**] *see* **Queen Street**
South Mimms [1086 (*Mimes*), 1211 (*Mimmes*), 1253 (*Suthmimes*); "*South* in contrast to North Mimms in Hertfordshire....The name must remain an unsolved problem." – *The Place-Names of Middlesex*, p.76]
Southend [*sūð* 'south' + *ende* 'end, edge; district']
Southgate [1370 (*Suthgate, Southgate*): *sūð* 'south' + *geat* 'gap; gate'; by the *south gate* to **Enfield** Chase]
Southall: 'south corner' [1198 (*Suhaull*), 1204 (*Sudhale*), 1261 (*Suthall(e)*): *sūð* 'south' + *halh* 'corner/nook of land'; contrasted with **Northolt**]
Southwark: 'south fortress' [1086 (*Sudwearca*): *sūð* 'south' + (ge)*weorc* 'construction, fortification']
Spittlefields: 'hospital fields' [1561 (*Spyttlefeildes*): Middle English *spitel* 'hospital' (here, of St. Mary Spital, ‹ Medieval Latin) + *feld* 'field'; now *Spitalfields*]
Staines: 'stone(s)' [969 (*Stána*), 1086 (*Stanes*): *stān(as)* 'stone(s)'; probably after a nearby Roman mile*stone*]
Stamford Brook: 'stony ford brook' [1650 (*Stamford Brooke*) ‹ **Stamford**: 'stony ford' [1274 (*Staunford*): Middle English *stoon, ston, stan* ‹ *stān* 'stone' + *ford* '(river-)ford']
Stamford Hill: 'sand-ford hill' [1225 (*Sanford*), 1924 (*Saundfordhull*), 1675 (*Stamford Hill*)]
Stanmore [793 (*Stanmere*)] *see* **Great Stanmore**
Stanwell: 'stony spring' [1086 (*Stanwelle*): *stān* 'stone' + *well(a)* 'well; spring']
Stepney: 'Stybba's landing' [c.1000 (*Stybbanhyþe*), 1542 (*Stebenheth al. Stepney*): *Stybban* (from name) + *hȳð* 'landing-place, harbour']
Stinking Lane [1228 (*Styngkynglane*); presumably from the *stink* of the nearby **Shambles**; now **King Edward Street**] *see* **King Edward Street**
Stockwell: 'tree-stump well' [1197 (*Stokewell*): *stocc* 'tree-trunk, stump, log' + *well(a)* 'well; spring']
Stoke Newington: 'log new estate' [1086 (*Neutone*), 1255 (*Newinthon*), 1274 (*Neweton Stoken, Stokeneweton*): *stocc* 'tree-trunk, stump, log' + *nīwe* 'new' + *-ing-* (perhaps as in **Newington** in Surrey) + *tūn* 'estate, home farm'] *see* **Newington** (Surrey)
The Strand: 'the bank (of the Thames)' [1185 (*Stronde*): *strand* 'shore, bank'; the Thames used to be wider]
Stratford: '(Roman-)road ford' [1066 (*Stratforde*): *strǣt* '(paved) road, street' (‹ Latin) + *ford* '(river-)ford'; where the old London-Colchester road crossed the **River Lea**]
Stratford-le-Bow: '(Roman-)road ford (at) the arched bridge' [1177 (*Stratford*), 1279 (*Stratford atte Bowe*), c.1560 (*Stratford le Bow(e)*): *strǣt* '(paved) road, street' (‹ Latin) + *ford* '(river-)ford' (across the **River Lea**) + French *le* 'the' + *boga* '(archery) bow; arch, arched bridge'; now *Bow*]
Streatham: '(Roman-)road village' [1086 (*Estreham*), 1175 (*Stratham*): *strǣt* '(paved) road, street' (‹ Latin) + *hām* 'settlement, village']
Sudbury: 'south stronghold' [1292 (*Suthbery*): *sūð* 'south' + *burh* 'stronghold, fortified manor']
Sunbury: 'Sunna's stronghold' [9592 (*Sunnabyri*): *Sunn(a)* (name) + *burh* 'stronghold, fortified manor']
Surbiton: 'south grain-farm, south grange' [1179 (*Suberton*): *sūð* 'south' + *bertūn* 'grain-farm; lord's grange' (‹ *bere* 'barley' + *tūn* 'estate, home farm')]

Sutton: 'south estate' [1181 (*Suthtona*): *sūð* 'south' + *tūn* 'estate, home farm']

Swithin Lane [1269–70 (*vicus Sancti Swithuni*), 1410–11 (*Seint Swithoneslane*), 1532 (*St. Swithens Lane*); after the church of *St. Swithin* in **Cannon Street**; now *St. Swithin's Lane*]

Sydenham: 'Chippa's village' [1206 (*Chipenham*), 1315 (*Shippenham*), 1690 (*Sidenham*): *Syden* (from name ‹ *Shippen* ‹ *Chipen*) + *hām* 'settlement, village'; similar to *Chippenham* (Camb, Wilts), *Cippenham* (Bucks)]

Syvethe Lane, Syvthe Lane: 'chaff lane' [1259–59 (*Syvidlane*), 1322 (*Syvthelane*), 1533 (*Sedyng Lane*): *sifeða* 'siftings, chaff' + *lane* 'lane'; perhaps from threshing done nearby; now *Seething Lane*]

T

Teddington: 'Tuda's folk's estate' [969 (*Tudinton*), 1274 (*Tedinton*): *Tud(a)* (name) + *-ing* '-follower of' + *tūn* 'estate, home farm']

Thames Ditton: 'Thames ditch estate' [1005 (*Dictun*), 1235 (*Temes Ditton*): (**River**) **Thames** + *dīc* 'ditch; dyke' + *tūn* 'estate, home farm']

Thames Street [1222 (*vicus super Ripam Tamis*), 13th C. (*la rue de Thamise*), 1275 (*Tamisestrete*), 1308 (*Temestret*)] ‹ **River Thames**

Threadneedle Street: 'three-needle street; street where *threadneedle* is played' [1598 (*Three needle street*), 1616 (*Thred-needle-street*); ?from a local signboard or coat of arms displaying *three needles*, or from the children's game *threadneedle*]

Tilbury: 'Til(la)'s stronghold' [c.735 (*Tilaburg*), 1066–87 (*Tillabyri*), 1218 (*Tylleber, Tyllebery*): *Til(la)* (name) + *burh* 'stronghold, fortified manor']

Tooting: 'Tota's folk' [675 (*Totinge*): *Tot-* (from name) + *-ing* '-follower of']

Tooting Common ‹ **Tooting**

Tottenham: 'Tota's village' [1086 (*Toteham*), 1189 (*Totenham*), 1254 (*Tottenham*): *Tote(n)* (from name) + *hām* 'settlement, village']

Tottenham Court: 'Totta's-corner manor' [c.1000 (*Þottanheale*), 1083 (*Totenhala*), 1487 (*Totenhalecourt*), 1593 (*Totten Court*), 1741–45 (*Tottenham Court*): *Totten* (from name) + *halh, healh* 'corner/nook of land' (to *ham* influenced by **Tottenham**) + Middle English *court* 'manor' (‹ Old French)] *compare* **Tottenham**

Tottenham Court Road [1708 (*Tottenham Court Row*)] ‹ **Tottenham Court**

Tower Hamlets: 'hamlets near the Tower (of London)'

Tower Hill [after the adjacent *Tower* of London]

Turnagain Lane: 'blind alley' [1415 (*Turneageyne lane*): Middle English *turne-agayne lane* 'blind alley, cul-de-sac'; formerly *Wendageyneslane* (from 1293)]

Turnbaston Lane [1328 (*Tornebastonlane, Tornebastoneslane*), 1436 (*Turnebastlane*), 1568 (*Turnebaslane, Turnesbaslane*): Middle English *?turnebaston* '?tollgate' (‹ Middle French) + *lane* 'lane'; now part of **Cannon Street**]

Turnham Green: 'round-village green; river-bend-land green' [c.1235 (*Turneham*), 1396 (*Turnhamgrene*): *?trun, turn* 'circular, round' + *hām* 'settlement, village' or *hamm* 'river-bend land' + *grēne* '(village) green'; near a big bend in the Thames]

Twickenham: 'Tuic(c)a's river-bend land' [704 (*Tuican hom, Tuiccanham*): *Tuic(c)an* (from name) + *hamm* 'river-bend land']

Twickenham Common ‹ **Twickenham**

Tyburn Street ‹ Tyburn: 'boundary brook' [959 (*Teobernan*), 1222 (*Tyburn*): *?tēo* 'boundary' + *burna* 'stream, brook'; formerly marking the boundary of **Westminster** Abbey lands; sometimes also called *Marybourn*] *see also* **Marylebone**

U

Upminster: '(high-)up monastery' [1062 (*Upmynstre*): *upp* 'up' + *mynster* 'monastery, church']

Upper Clapton ‹ **Clapton**

Upper Norwood ‹ **Norwood**

Upper Sydenham ‹ **Sydenham**

Upper Tooting ‹ **Tooting**

Uxbridge: 'the Wixans' bridge' [c.1145 (*Oxebruge, Wixebrug'*): *Wixan* (from tribal name) + *brycg* 'bridge' (over the **River Colne**)]

V

Vedast Lane *see* **Foster Lane**

Victoria [after Queen *Victoria* (1819–1901), reigned 1837–1901]

W

Walbrook: '(Celtic) Britons' brook' [1104 (*Walebroch*): *wal(h)* '(Celtic) stranger' + *brōc* 'brook']

Walham Green: 'de Wenden's Green' [1386 (*Wendenegrene*), 1615 (*Wandon's Green*), 1710 (*Wallam Green*), 1819 (*Walham Green*): *de Wenden(e), de Wanden(e)* (name of local family, perhaps originally from *Wendens* in Essex) + *grēne* '(village) green']

Waltham Abbey ‹ Waltham: 'wood-land village; wood-land river-bend land' [1062 (*Waltham*): *wald, weald* 'wood-land, forest' + *hām* 'settlement, village' or *hamm* 'river-bend land']

Waltham Cross [**Waltham** + *cros* 'cross' (‹ Old Irish ‹ Latin); from the (Eleanor) *Cross* put here in 1291 by Edward I to mark the penultimate stage in the funeral procession of Eleanor of Castile] *see* **Waltham Abbey**; *compare* **Charing Cross**

Waltham Forest [London borough comprising **Walthamstow, Chingford** and **Leyton**]

Walthamstow: 'welcome place; Celts' place' [c.1076 (*Wilcumestowe*), 1446 (*Walthamstowe*): *wilcume* 'welcome' or *walh* '(Celtic) stranger' + *stōw* 'place']

Walthamstow Mead: 'Walthamstow meadow' [**Walthamstow** + *mǣd* 'meadow'] ‹ **Walthamstow**

Walworth: 'Celts' ward' [1006 (*Wealawyrð*), 1086 (*Waleorde*), 1196 (*Wallewurd*), 1354 (*Walworth*): *wealh, walh* '(Celtic) stranger' + *worð* 'ward, enclosure']

Wanstead: '(wen-like) mound site' [c.1050 (*Wænstede*): *wænn* 'wen' + *stede* 'place, stead']

Wapping Dock ‹ Wapping: 'Wæppa's folk' [c.1220 (*Wapping'*), 1231 (*Wappinges*): *Wæpp(a)* (name) + *-ingas* '-followers of']

Warwick Lane [1474–75 (*Werwyk Lane*); after the Earls of *Warwick*, who held property locally; formerly **Old Dean's Lane**]

Waterloo [after *Waterloo* in Belgium, site of the famous defeat of Napoleon in 1815]

Watford: 'hunters' ford' [944–46 (*Watford*), c.1180 (*Wathford, Wathforda*): *wað* 'chase, hunting' + *ford* '(river-)ford']

Watling Street: 'prince's street' [c. 1213 (*Aphelingestrate*), 1289 (*Athelingstrate*), 1307 (*Watlingstrate*): *æðeling* 'prince; nobleman' [becoming *Watling* perhaps by folk etymology through similarity of sound to the Roman road *Watling* Street) + *strǣt* '(paved) road, street' (‹ Latin)]

Wealdstone Brook [1453 (*le Weldebroke*), 1548 (*Weyldbrooke*); also *Kenton Brook*; formerly *Lyddying (Water)*] ‹ **Wealdstone**: 'woodland (boundary-)stone' ‹ **Harrow Weald**: 'Harrow woodland' [1282 (*Weldewode*), 1388 (*Harewewelde*), 1603 (*Harrow weale*): **Harrow** + *weald* 'woodland, forest'] *see* **Harrow**

Weir Hall [1086 (*Wirehel(l)e*), 1198 (*Wylehale*), 1207–8 (*Wirhale, Wilehal'*), 1593 (*Wirehall, Wyerhall*): *Wylehale, Wyrhale* (attested surname)]

Welling [1362 (*Wellyngs*): *Welling* (surname of 14th-C. local landowners)]

Wembley: 'Wemba's lea/grove' [825 (*Wemba Lea*): *Wemba* (name) + *lēah* 'grove; meadow, lea']

West Bedfont [1086 (*Westbedefund*)] ‹ **Bedfont**

West Cheap: 'west market' [1304 (*Chepe*), 1249 (*Westchepe*): *west* 'west' (by contrast with **Eastcheap**) + *cēap* 'market; trade'; also *Cheap*; now **Cheapside**] *see* **Cheapside, Eastcheap**

West Drayton: 'west portage farm' [939 (*Drægton*), 1086 (*Draitone*), 1465 (*Westdrayton*): *west* 'west' (added perhaps to contrast with Ealing's *Drayton* (Green) + *dræg* 'drag; portage, slipway' (perhaps in reference to the adjacent **River Colne**) + *tūn* 'estate, home farm']

West End (Middlesex, near Northolt) [1274 (*(atte) Westende*), 1660 (*West End*)]

West End (Middlesex, near Pinner) [1448 (*le Westhend*)]

West Ham: 'west river-bend land' [958 (*Hamme*), 1186 (*Westhamma*): *west* 'west' + *hamm* 'river-bend land']

West Molesey [1200 (*Westmoleseie*)] ‹ **Molesey**

West Smithfield [*west* 'west' + **Smithfield**] ‹ **Smithfield**

West Thurrock [1219 (*West Turroc*, etc.): *west* 'west' + **Thurrock**] ‹ **Thurrock**: 'bilge; muck-heap' [1086 (*Turoc*): Þurruc 'bilge; ship's bottom; muck-heap']

West Wickham: 'west farm village; west Romano-British-site village' [973 (*Wichamm*), 1086 (*Wicheham*), 1284 (*Westwycham*): *west* 'west' + *wīc-hām* 'farm village; village on Romano-British site']

West Wood Common [c.1350 (*Westwode*)]

Westbourne [formerly *Knightsbridge Brook, Bayswater Rivulet*; flows into the Serpentine in Hyde Park] ‹ **Westbourne Green**: 'west-stream green; green west of the stream' [1222 (*Westeburne*), 1294 (*Westbourne*), 1548 (*Westborne Grene*): *west* 'west' + Middle English *bourne, burne* ‹ *burna* 'stream, brook' + *grēne* '(village) green']

Westminster: 'west monastery' [c.975 (*Westmynster*): *west* 'west' + *mynster* 'monastery, church'; previously *Thorney* (969)]

Whetstone [1417 (*Wheston*), 1437 (*Whetestonesstret*), 1492 (*Whetstone*): *hwetstān* 'whetstone']

White Chapel [1282 (*St Mary de Mattefelon*), 1340 (*Whitechapele by Algate*); *hwīt* 'white' + Middle English *chapel* 'chapel' (‹ Old French ‹ Late Latin); now *Whitechapel*]

White Cross Street [1226 (*Whitecruchestrete*), 1309–10 (*Whitecrouchestrate*), 1502 (*Whitecrosse Strete*): *hwīt* 'white' + Middle English *crouche* 'cross' (‹ Latin) or *cros* 'cross' (‹ Old Irish ‹ Latin) + *strǣt* '(paved) road, street' (‹ Latin); after a local *white cross*]

Whitehall ‹ Whitehall Palace [1530 (*Whytehale*); from the name of the Lords' chamber in the old Parliament; previously called *York Place* when the London residence of the Archbishops of York]

Willesden: 'spring's hill' [939 (*Wellesdune, Willesdone*), 1290 (*Willesden*): *well(a), wiell(a)* 'well; spring' + *dūn* 'hill']

Wimbledon: 'Wynman('s) hill; Winebeald('s) hill' [c.950 (*Wunemannedune*), 1202 (*Wimeldon*), 13th C. (*Wymendon*), 1211 (*Wimbeldon, Wimbeldona*): *Wunemanne* (name) or *Winebeald* (name) + *dūn* 'hill']

Wimbledon Common ‹ Wimbledon

Winchmore Hill: 'Wynsige('s) boundary hill' [1319 (*Wynsemerhull*), 1543 (*Wynsmore hill*), 1586 (*Winchmore Hill*): *Winsige* (name) + (*ge*)*mǣre* 'boundary, border' + *hyll* 'hill'; near the southern boundary of **Edmonton** parish]

Wood End [1531 (*Wodehende*): *wudu* 'wood' + *ende* 'end, edge; district']

Wood Green [1502 (*Wodegrene*): *wudu* 'wood' + *grēne* '(village) green']

Wood Hall [1271 (*Wodehalle*), 1349 (*Wodhall*): *wudu* 'wood' + *hall* 'hall, manor']

Wood Street: 'street where wood was sold' [1156–57 (*Wodestrata*): *wudu* 'wood' + Latin *strāta* (source of *street*)]

Woodford: 'wood(-side) ford' [1062 (*Wodeforda*), 1225 (*Wudeforde*): *wudu* 'wood' + *ford* '(river-)ford']

Woodford Bridge [1238 ((Thomas de) *ponte de Wodeford*), 1429 (*Woodfordbrigge*): **Woodford** + *brycg* 'bridge'; name of **Woodford** east of the **River Roding**] ‹ **Woodford**

Woodford Wells [1285 ((William de) *fonte de Wodeford*)] ‹ **Woodford**

Woodruff Lane, Woodroffe Lane [1260 (*Woderouelane*), c.1600 (*Woodroffe lane*): Middle English *woderove* 'woodruff (plant)' (‹ *wudurōfe*) + *lane* 'lane'; now probably *Cooper's Row*]

Woodside [1686 (*Woodside*): *wudu* 'wood' + *sīde* 'side']

Woodwich: 'wool harbour' [918 (*Uuluuich*): *wull* 'wool' + *wīc* 'farm or harbour of the stated kind']

Y

Yeading Brook ‹ Yedding

Yedding, Yeading: 'Geddi's folk' [757 (*Geddinges*), 1325 (*Yedding(g)s*), 1331 (*Yeddyng*): *Gedd(i)* (name) + *-(i)ngas* '-followers of']

TOPIC INDEX

MAP REFERENCES

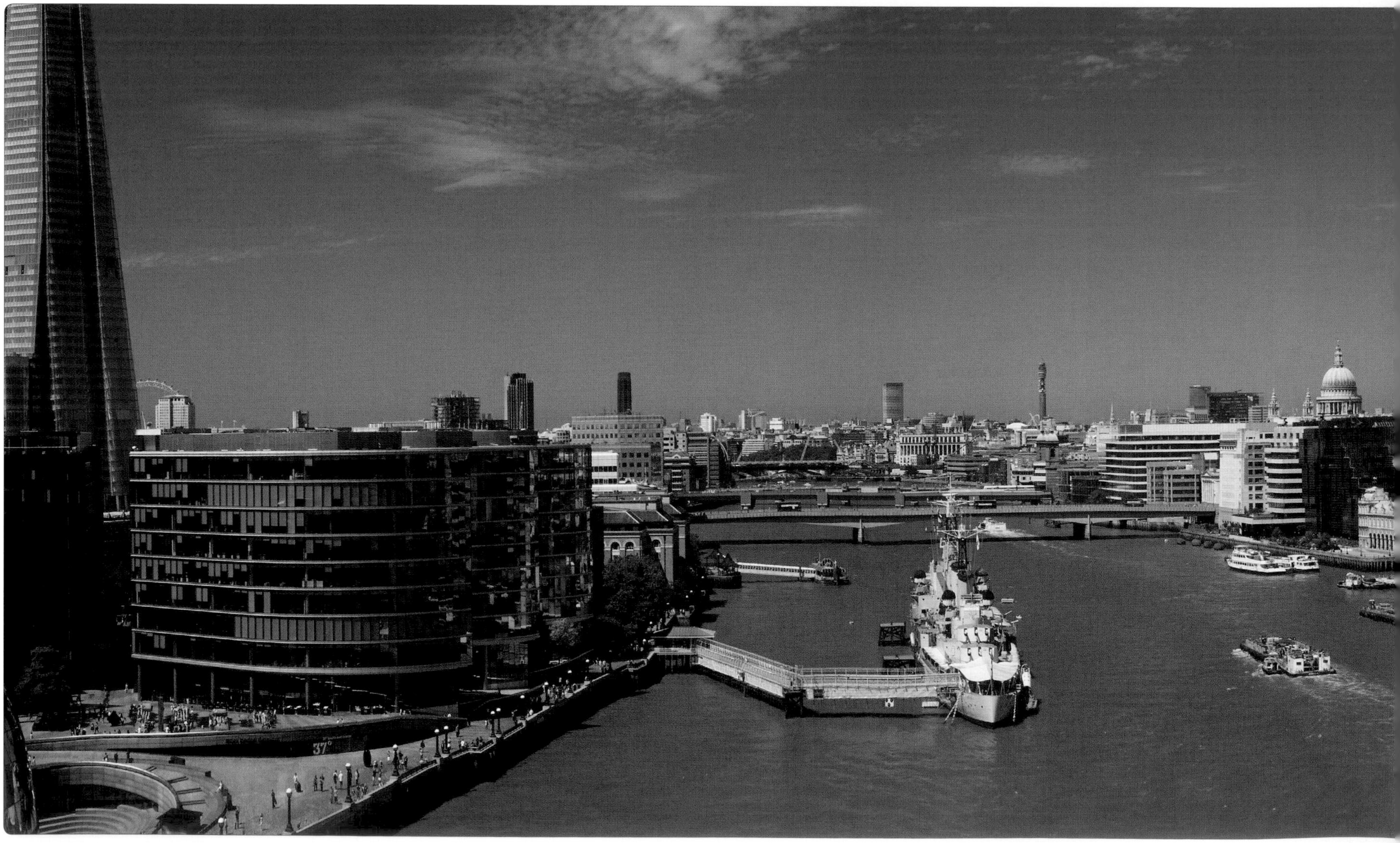

The River Thames as viewed from the top of Tower Bridge. From the left: the Shard with the London Eye behind, HMS *Belfast*, London Bridge, with the BT Tower, St Paul's Cathedral and the Monument in the distance, and to the right the City of London and the Traitors' Gate of the Tower of London.

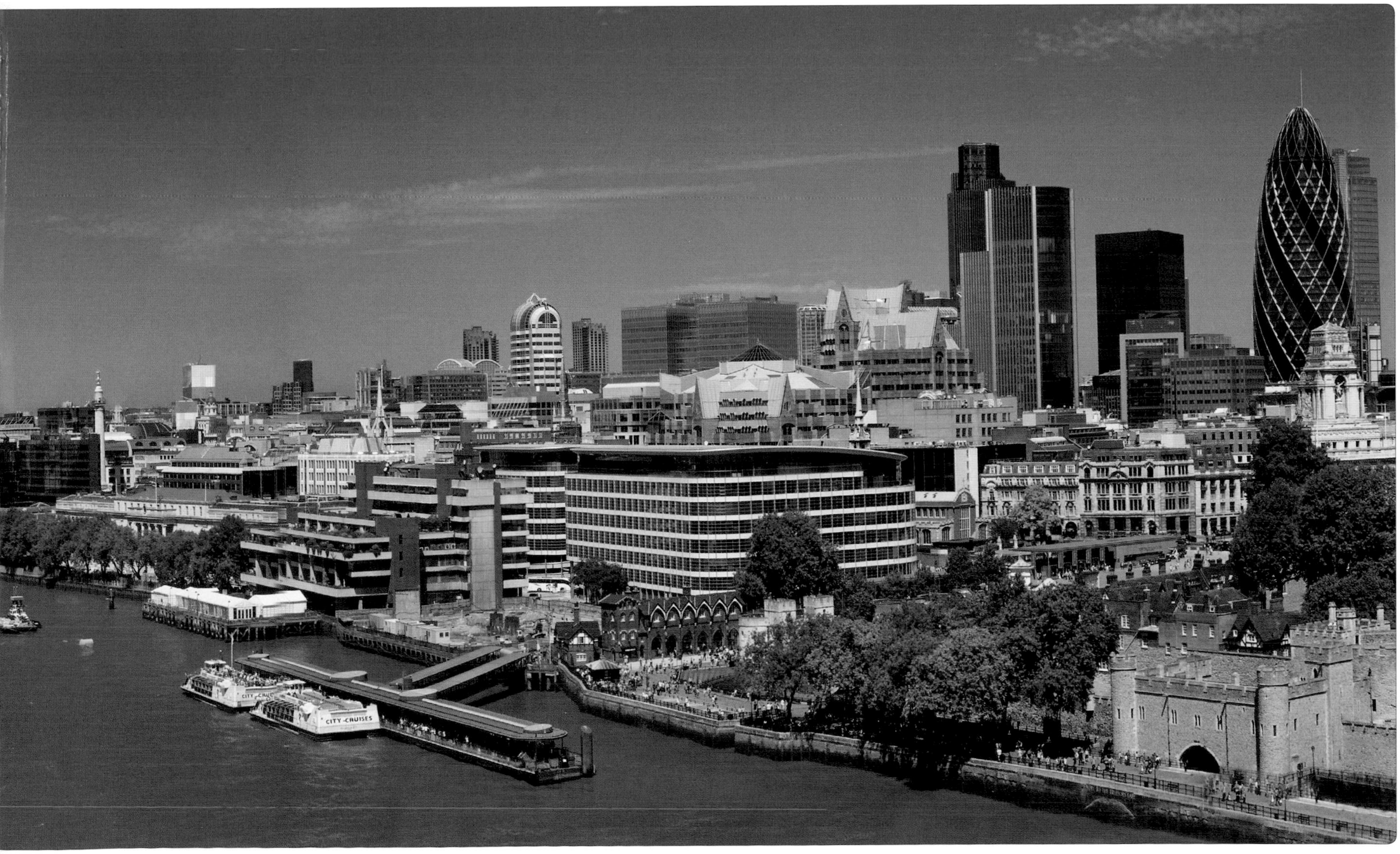

ACKNOWLEDGEMENTS

While every effort has been made to trace the owners of copyright material reproduced herein and secure permissions, the publishers would like to apologize for any omissions and will be pleased to incorporate missing acknowledgements in any future edition of this book.

Author: Christopher Riches

MAPS AND ILLUSTRATIONS

We are grateful to the following companies and organizations for supplying the historical maps and illustrations included on these pages. All other mapping © Collins Bartholomew

National Library of Scotland (www.nls.uk): pages **14, 19** (from *Collins County Atlas of England and Wales*, 1877), **24–25, 61, 62–69** (by Thomas Allom), **70–71** (This extract was published by Edward Stanford in 1859), **94** (from the *Pocket Atlas and Guide To London* by J.G.Bartholomew for John Walker & Co 1908), **110–111, 135** (top), **147** (top), **152, 162–163, 181** (the original of this held by NLS is printed in one colour), **205, 245** (John Rocque's map of the Environs of London 1744–6), **252–253** and **270–271**.
Reproduced by permission of the Trustees of the National Library of Scotland.

The Bridgeman Art Library: pages **9, 11 and 13**. © Museum of London, UK/ The Bridgeman Art Library (www.bridgemanart.com).

British Museum (www.britishmuseum.org): page **8** ©The Trustees of the British Museum. All rights reserved.

Mapseeker (www.mapseeker.co.uk): pages **58–59, 92–93** (*The Thames* by Cpt. G. Collins 1693) and **215**. ©Mapseeker Archive Publishing Ltd 2010

Wikimedia Creative Commons (commons.wikimedia.org): pages **10, 12, 54–55, 56–57, 134, 135** (bottom) and **259**.

Other historical maps and images: **15** © TfL from the London Transport Museum collection; **17** John Davies (www.Sovietmaps.com); **170** © Transport for London; ; **244** Wanstead House, original print, published 1787, Harrison & Co., Paternoster Row, London

We are grateful to the borough councils of London for giving us permission to use their historical coat of arms throughout this book and to Robert Young (www.civicheraldry.co.uk) for providing the illustrations.

TEXT AND DIAGRAMS

In compiling this work a wide range of sources have been consulted, and the most important of these are listed below.

Books

Peter Ackroyd (2000), *London: the Biography*, Chatto and Windus, London.
Diane Burstein (2009), *London Then and Now*, Batsford, London.
Hugh Clout (ed.) (1999), *The Times History of London*, Times Books, London (first published as *The Times Atlas of London History*, 1991). As a successor to this title, *The Times Atlas of London* has reused some material from this book, in particular the Chronology (which has been updated), **72–77**, London Names and Their Meanings, **292–297**, and selected texts and illustrations on the geology and history of London, **22, 128, 133** (Livery Companies), **134, 165.** All material © Times Books.
Philip Davies (2009), *Lost London*, Transatlantic Press, Croxley Green.
Ed Glinert (2004), *The London Compendium*, Penguin Books, London
A. D. Mills (2001), *A Dictionary of London Place Names*, Oxford University Press, Oxford.
Oxford Dictionary of National Biography (online edition www.oxforddnb.com), Oxford University Press.
Cathy Ross and John Clark (2008), *London: the Illustrated History*, Allen lane, London.
Richard Tames (2006), *London: a Literary and Cultural History*, Signal Books, Oxford.
Ben Weinreb, Christopher Hibbert, Julia Keay and John Key (2008), *The London Encyclopaedia*, Third Edition, Macmillan, London.
Peter Whitfield (2006), *London: a Life in Maps*, British Library, London.
Russ Willey (2010), *Brewer's Dictionary of London Phrase and Fable*, Chambers Harrap, Edinburgh.
Thomas Wright (ed.) (2004), *A Traveller's Companion to London*, Robinson, London.

Statistics

An invaluable resource is the London Datastore (www.data.london.gov.uk) established by the Greater London Authority to bring together a mass of data about London from a wide range of sources. For employment data by borough, the Labour Market Profile at www.nomisweb.co.uk provides a wide range of information. For historic population figures A Vision of Britain Through Time (www.visionofBritain.org.uk) has retrospectively calculated London borough populations on the basis of today's boundaries from Census data from 1801 onwards. On population, also consult *Focus on London 2010: Population and Migration* (Greater London Authority).

The sources of the data given at the start of each borough's entry are as follows:
Population: Office for National Statistics 2009 Mid-Year Estimates.
Area and *Area of Green Space*: Figures rounded from the 2005 Generalised Land Use Database, accessed through the London Datastore (http://data.london.gov.uk/datastore/package/population-density-2009-borough).
Jobs in borough: This is the total jobs figure for 2009 given by Nomis (www.nomisweb.co.uk) in its Job Density section for each borough's Labour Market Profile and is based on ONS jobs density. The total jobs includes employees, self-employed, government-supported trainees and H.M. Forces.
House prices: This is the mean annual housing price in the borough for 2009, based on Land Registry data, compiled by the Department for Communities and Local Government and accessed through the London Datastore (http://data.london.gov.uk/datastore/package/average-house-prices-borough).

Data for charts, diagrams and tables were sourced as below:
27: Data for Greenwich 1971 to 2000, compiled by the Meteorological Office.
28: Gross value added per head data from the Office for National Statistics (ONS) *Regional Trends* released June 2011; data for Main Economic Sectors chart from the Greater London Authority Economics' Medium Term Forecast and available through the London Datastore (http://data.london.gov.uk/datastore/package/londons-economic-outlook-forecast); data for London as the Economic Centre of Britain diagram from ONS *Regional Trends* released June 2011.
30: All data from Nomis Labour Market Profile for boroughs and regions (www.nomisweb.co.uk)
31: Data for employment pie charts from Nomis Labour Market Profile for boroughs (www.nomisweb.co.uk); data for Business Turnover and Employment diagram from Inter-Departmental Business Register (IDBR) maintained by the ONS and sourced through the London Datastore (http://data.london.gov.uk/datastore/package/enterprises-and-local-units-counts-employment-and-turnover).
32: Data for graph of population growth 1801–2001 from A Vision of Britain Through Time (www.visionofBritain.org.uk); borough populations by racial origin from estimates by the Greater London Authority and sourced through London Datastore (http://data.london.gov.uk/datastore/package/egp-2010rnd-shlaa-borough).
33: Population figures for diagram from ONS 2009 Mid-Year Estimates; population growth from Greater London Authority, 2010, and sourced through the London Datastore (http://data.london.gov.uk/datastore/package/popproj-2010rnd-shlaa-borough-sya).
34: Population of major UK conurbations and cities from ONS 2009 Mid-Year Estimates; data for house prices from the Land Registry of England and Wales, Registers of Scotland Executive Agency and the University of Ulster in partnership with the Bank of Ireland; data for the percentage of children receiving free school meals from the Department for Education; the Scottish Government; the Welsh Assembly Government; and the Northern Ireland Executive.
35 City population figures reproduced with permission from the City Mayors Foundation (www.citymayors.com); data on the most expensive cities and the cost of daily items from the Mercer *2010 Global Cost of Living Information Services* (www.mercer.com/costoflivingservices), and reproduced by permission; data from *Cities of Opportunity* 2011 edition (www.pwc.com/us/en/cities-of-opportunity), reproduced by permission of PricewaterhouseCoopers LLP.
82: Table adapted from Annual Business Inquiry Workplace Analysis by Industry, ONS, sourced through London Datastore (http://data.london.gov.uk/datastore/package/enterprises-and-local-units-counts-employment-and-turnover); chart sourced from Nomis Official Labour Market Statistics (www.nomisweb.co.uk).
106: Data for pie charts from the 2005 Generalised Land Use Database created by the Department for Communities and Local Government in 2007, accessed through the London Datastore (http://data.london.gov.uk/datastore/package/population-density-2009-borough).
112: Chart of museum visitor numbers adapted from 2010 visitor numbers published by the Association of Leading Visitor Attractions (ALVA) (http://www.alva.org.uk/visitor_statistics/).
138: Transport for London projections of 2011–12 from Transport for London *Business Plan 2009–10 to 2017–18*, Appendix B.
142–3: Student number figures for 2009–10 from the Higher Education Statistics Agency (www.hesa.ac.uk).
146: Licensed vehicle numbers 2009 (http://data.london.gov.uk/search/node/licensed%20 vehicle) and licensed vehicles per borough 2009 (http://data.london.gov.uk/datastore/package/licensed-vehicles-type-0) prepared by the Department for Transport and sourced through the London Datastore.
186: Data for map of household recycling for2009/10 from Department for Environment, Food and Rural Affairs, Local Authority collected waste for England annual statistics 2009/10 (www.defra.gov.uk/statistics/environment/waste/wrfg23-wrmsannual/).
213: Data for chart from Office of Rail Regulation *National Rail Trends Yearbook 2010–11*, Regional Usage Profiles 2009–10.
230: Figures on household tenure from Annual Population Survey (ONS) sourced through the London Datastore (http://data.london.gov.uk/datastore/package/housing-tenure-households-borough).
253: Art gallery visitor numbers sourced from the *Art Newspaper* 2010 survey (www.theartnewspaper.com/articles/Japanese-old-master-tops-the-attendance-tree/23408).

London websites

There are many websites providing information about London. Official websites include the Greater London Authority (www.london.gov.uk), each of the London boroughs (particularly useful for current information and for the history of the borough) and their lobbying and policy organization, London Councils (www.londoncouncils.gov.uk), the London Development Agency (www.lda.gov.uk) and Transport for London (www.tfl.gov.uk). Among the many other websites, particularly recommended are the Museum of London (www.museumoflondon.org.uk), the London Transport Museum (www.ltmuseum.co.uk) and Hidden London (www.hidden-london.com), and, of course, the websites for the museums, art galleries and other visitor attractions in the London along with those for the many organizations and businesses who have interests in particular aspects of London life.

PHOTO CREDITS

Images from www.alamy.com, AY
Images from www.shutterstock.co.uk, SS
Images from www.flickr.com, FL

Cover image (top), ©Getty Images (www.gettyimages.com, from *Views of London*, published by Laurie and Whittle, 1794)
Cover image (bottom): ©Mark Steward (www.marksteward.co.uk)
22 View from Parliament Hill ©John Farnham AY; **22** River Fleet joining Thames ©Timewatch Images AY; **26** The Great Freeze ©Mary Evans Picture Library AY; **26** Office workers enjoy the sunshine ©CalamityJane AY; **27** Dense smog ©Trinity Mirror / Mirrorpix AY; **27** October 1987 storm ©Imagestate Media Partners Limited - Impact Photos AY; **28** Inside Lloyd's building ©Arcaid Images AY; **29** Tallest buildings in the City ©QQ7 SS; **30** Worker's wives demonstrate ©The Art Archive AY; **30** Marcing against cuts ©Bjanka Kadic AY; **32** Multi-ethnic crowd ©Jon Arnold Images Ltd AY; **34** View from the Shard ©glychuk FL; **79** City Hall ©LOOK Die Bildagentur der Fotografen GmbH AY; **80** Eastbury Manor House ©David Burrows SS; **81** Barking Flood Barrier ©David Ramkalawon AY; **82** Fullers Beer Sign ©Andrew Holt AY; **83** Silvertown and Royal Victoria Dock ©Andrew Holt AY; **83** Tate & Lyle sugar refinery ©June Jones AY; **84** Lawrence Campe Almshouses ©David Bleeker Photography.com AY; **84** Hendon RAF Museum ©elsie FL; **86** Parade ©Trinity Mirror / Mirrorpix AY; **86** East End entertainer ©The Print Collector AY; **86** Jewish community ©Lebrecht Music and Arts Photo Library AY; **87** Pearly Kings and Queens ©Jim Holden AY; **87** Chelsea pensioners ©Chris Harvey SS; **88** Festival of Vaisakhi ©Photofusion Picture Library AY; **88** Young girl at Notting Hill Carnival ©Adina Tovy AY; **88** Polish community ©piotr adamski SS; **89** British Bangladeshis ©LondonPhotos AY; **89** Chinatown ©David Berrecloth AY; **89** Common surnames maps ©James Cheshire; **90** The Red House ©The National Trust Photolibrary AY; **90** Crossness Pumping Station ©Eric Nathan AY; **91** Five Arch Bridge ©zoonabar FL; **95** Tower Bridge and the Thames, 1931 ©The Print Collector AY; **95** Tower Bridge and the Thames today ©Mike Hughes AY; **96** Millennium Bridge ©cristapper SS; **97** Thames Flood Barrier ©Marc Pinter SS; **97** Blackfriars Bridge ©Patrick Wang SS; **98** BAPS Shri Swaminarayan Mandir ©Jon Arnold Images Ltd AY; **99** Former Gaumont State cinema ©Roberto Herret AY; **99** Wembley Stadium ©Chunni4691 SS; **100** Boleyn Ground Stadium (Upton Park) ©Neil Tingle AY; **100** Loftus Road Stadium ©Neil Tingle AY; **101** Stamford Bridge Stadium ©London Aerial Photo Library AY; **101** White Hart Lane Stadium ©David Goddard AY; **101** The Emirates Stadium ©David Wootton AY; **102** Wembley 1923 ©The Print Collector AY; **102** Wembley 1999 ©London Aerial Photo Library AY; **103** New Wembley u/c ©chris gorman AY; **103** New Wembley completed ©chris gorman AY; **104** Grave of Charles Darwin's wife ©Tony Watson AY; **106** Goldfinch in Rainham Marshes ©Garry Bowden AY; **107** London Wetland Centre ©Meridian Images AY; **107** Information Centre at Rainham Marshes ©Chris Mattison AY; **108** Keats House, Hampstead ©Greg Balfour Evans AY; **108** Sir John Soane's mausoleum ©grahamc99 FL; **109** Regent's Canal at Camden Lock ©Londonstills.com AY; **110** St Pancras u/c ©National Railway Museum FL; **112** British Museum & Senate House of the University of London ©Robert Harding Picture Library Ltd AY; **113** Statue of Charles Darwin ©Mark Steward SS; **113** Victoria and Albert Museum ©Ant Clausen SS; **113** Battleship gun barrels, Imperial War Museum ©godrick SS; **113** Darwin Centre building ©Mark Steward; **120** Karl Marx's tomb in Highgate Cemetery ©Kamira SS; **121** Grave of the writer and journalist Daniel Defoe ©psd FL; **121** Headstones, Highgate Cemetery ©Don Cline SS; **122** The Gherkin and St Andrew Undershaft ©Elena Elisseeva SS; **122** The Monument ©N/A SS; **123** Staple Inn on High Holborn ©Jim Linwood FL; **123** Lloyd's Building ©tonyz20 SS; **124** Looking west from the Dome of St Paul's, 1846 ©courtesy National Library of ScotlandNLS; **124** Looking west from the Dome of St Paul's today ©r.nagy SS; **125** An aerial view of St Paul's Cathedral today ©Mike Hughes AY; **125** An aerial view of St Paul's Cathedral in 1932, AFL03/AEROFILMS/37976 ©English Heritage. NMR. Aerofilms Collection; **126** The Mansion House around 1926 ©The Print Collector AY; **126** The Bank of England and the Royal Exchange, mid 1920s ©The Print Collector AY; **127** Cheapside, around 1900 ©Niday Picture Library AY; **128** An artist's impression of Londinium ©Times Atlas of London HistoryTimes History Atlas; **129** A bastion of the City Wall at the Barbican ©Londonstills.com AY; **129** A section of the Roman Wall at Tower Hill ©Elena Elisseeva SS; **132** Lord Mayor and Lord Mayor's Coach, 2010 ©Malcolm Park London events AY; **133** Plaque at the Church of St Michael Paternoster Royal ©Michael K Berman-Wald AY; **133** The Lord Mayor's procession ©Paul Gapper AY; **135** Sir Christopher Wren's 1666 vision for the rebuilding of London ©Mary Evans Picture Library AY; **136** Croydon Aerodrome, from the cover of Airways, 1925 ©World History Archive AY; **137** Shirley Windmill ©Marijus Seskauskas SS; **138** Westminster Bridge traffic in the 1920s ©INTERFOTO AY; **138** Mock-up of the New Bus for London ©Jeffrey Blackler AY; **139** Boarding a bus, from the late 1920s ©The Print Collector AY; **139** The last tram to run to New Cross, 1952 ©Trinity Mirror / Mirrorpix AY; **139** The iconic Routemaster ©Chris Jenner SS; **140** Pitzhanger Manor House ©Gregory Wrona AY; **140** The Art Deco Hoover building ©kyz FL; **141** Ealing Studios ©Maurice Savage AY; **142** Motto outside King's College, London ©Roberto Herrett AY; **144** Forty Hall ©Imagestate Media Partners Limited - Impact Photos AY; **144** Enfield Market ©Greg Balfour Evans AY; **145** Former Royal Small Arms Factory, Enfield Lock ©Shangara Singh AY; **147** Queen Elizabeth II Bridge ©Derek Croucher AY; **148** O2 Arena and Ravensbourne College ©Colin Palmer Photography AY; **148** Cutty Sark ©Péter Gudella SS; **149** The Royal Observatory ©Andrew Holt AY; **150** Dick Turpin ©Mary Evans Picture Library AY; **150** The Spaniards Inn, Hampstead ©WinePix AY; **151** 50 Berkeley Square ©Trinity Mirror / Mirrorpix AY; **151** Memorial plaque to William Terriss ©Eric Nathan AY; **153** Greenwich today ©Sergio Azenha AY; **153** Greenwich 1930s, AFL03/AEROFILMS/C14715 ©English Heritage. NMR. Aerofilms Collection; **158** The Tower of London ©Kamira SS; **159** Greenwich from the Thames ©Carolyn Clarke AY; **159** Temperate House, Kew Gardens ©Maria Gioberti SS; **160** Hackney Peace Carnival Mural ©Hemis AY; **161** Hackney Empire Theatre ©Robert Morris AY; **161** Hackney City Farm ©Julio Etchart AY; **164** German aircraft Heinkel HE III over the Isle of Dogs ©The Art Archive AY; **164** The Blitz from the roof of St Paul's Cathedral ©Trinity Mirror / Mirrorpix AY; **165** Bomb damage near St Pancras station, 1946 ©courtesy National Library of Scotland; **166** Bombing over Beckton and the Royal Docks ©Nigel J Clarke AY; **167** Service being held at St Mary-le-Bow church in London ©Trinity Mirror / Mirrorpix AY; **168** Inner courtyard of Fulham Palace ©Tony Watson AY; **168** Polo at the Hurlingham Club ©Julie Edwards AY; **169** BBC Television Centre ©Peter E Noyce AY; **170** Docklands Light Railway ©tim gartside london AY; **171** Inspecting the newly built Jubilee line extension in 1997 ©qaphotos.com AY; **171** Poster promoting Underground travel in 1910 ©Antiques & Collectables AY; **178** Bruce Castle Museum, Tottenham ©Shangara Singh AY; **178** Tottenham Hotspur v Roma in 2008 ©Tony Peters FL; **178** Alexandra Palace plaque ©Matt Brown FL; **178** Alexandra Palace and the BBC transmitter mast ©Gary Blakeley SS; **179** Muswell Hill ©john norman AY; **180** Globe Theatre ©PCL AY; **180** 1855 music sheet showing the Crystal Palace ©Lordprice Collection AY; **181** Royal Opera House, Covent Garden ©Greg Balfour Evans AY; **181** The Royal Albert Hall ©Karen McGaul SS; **182** Parish church of St Lawrence, Little Stanmore ©Simon White FL; **182** Memorial stained glass window, RAF Bentley Priory ©greentool2002 FL; **183** Former RAF Bentley Priory ©N/A FL; **183** Harrow School © jennyt SS; **184** A 1910 advertisement for Romford Garden Suburb ©mikeyashworth FL; **184** Romford Market ©Justin Kase z08z AY; **186** Crossness Sludge Incinerator ©Mick Sinclair AY; **187** Mayor Boris Johnson and Arnold Schwarzenegger try the Barclay's cycle hire scheme ©OnTheRoad AY; **187** Charging point for electric cars ©Justin Kase zsixz AY; **187** Barclays cycle hire scheme ©Neil Lang SS; **188** Terminal 5 at Heathrow Airport ©Peter Lane AY; **188** Regeneration of Harmondsworth Moor ©Clive Collie AY; **189** The great medieval barn at Harmondsworth ©eogin21 FL; **190** Terminal 5B ©david pearson AY; **191** An aeroplane coming in to land at City Airport ©frank'n'focus AY; **191** A poster for Hendon Aerodrome from 1910 ©Antiques & Collectables AY; **192** Waterside housing development at Brentford Dock ©Peter Lane AY; **192** The Gillette Building ©Maxwell Hamilton FL; **192** Osterley Park ©Stephen Mulligan SS; **194** 15th-century Great Hall at Eltham Palace ©Arcaid Images AY; **194** Charlton House ©Erikas SS; **195** Spencer House ©alessandro0770 SS; **195** Chiswick House ©Anthony Shaw Photography SS; **196** The Ante Room at Syon House ©Angelo Hornak AY; **196** Kenwood House ©tonyz20 SS; **197** Waterloo Gallery, Apsley House ©V&A Images AY; **197** 2 Willow Road, Hampstead ©The National Trust Photolibrary AY; **197** Leighton House, Holland Park ©LondonPhotos - Homer Sykes AY; **197** The restored Gallery at Strawberry Hill ©Strawberry Hill Trust; **198** Emirates Stadium ©Mayday AY; **199** Wesley's Chapel ©Jeremy Hoare AY; **199** Sadler's Wells Theatre, Clerkenwell ©Eric Nathan AY; **200** The Bibendum Restaurant ©Roberto Herrett AY; **200** Riverside eating and drinking in Richmond ©Gregory Wrona AY; **201** Food stalls in the Stables Market, Camden ©Gregory Wrona AY; **201** Trafalgar Tavern ©tim gartside london AY; **201** A traditional English 'chop house' ©Kevin George AY; **202** Central Hall of the Natural History Museum ©Francisco Javier Ballester Calonge SS; **203** Portobello Road Market, Notting Hill ©Michael Kemp AY; **203** L'Occitane Garden, Chelsea Flower Show 2010 ©Ros Drinkwater AY; **203** Grand Victorian terraces ©r.nagy SS; **203** Kensington Palace ©Irina Korshunova SS; **204** The Victoria and Albert Museum at South Kensington ©Robert Harding Picture Library Ltd AY; **206** Last Night of the Proms, Royal Albert Hall ©LondonPhotos AY; **206** Notting Hill Carnival costume ©jeff gynane SS; **207** Trooping the Colour on Horse Guards Parade ©Travelshots.com AY; **208** Buckingham Palace ©Kevin Allen AY; **209** The wedding of the Duke and Duchess of Cambridge, 2011 ©Trinity Mirror / Mirrorpix AY; **209** Hampton Court Palace ©St. Nick SS; **210** The circular auditorium of the Rose Theatre ©Chris Pearsall AY; **210** Houseboat at Kingston Bridge ©Anthony Worsdell SS; **211** Coronation Stone outside the Guildhall, Kingston upon Thames ©Gregory Wrona AY; **212** Poster advertising train travel, 1910 ©The Art Archive AY; **212** St Pancras International station ©Mike Hughes AY; **213** Charing Cross Station ©Debbie O'Hare SS; **213** Eurostar ©Baloncici SS; **214** Paddington station in the 1920s ©The Print Collector AY; **214** Paddington station, 2009 ©david pearson AY; **215** King's Cross station, around 1930 ©Trinity Mirror / Mirrorpix AY; **216** London Eye ©ricardomiguel.pt SS; **216** Secret Intelligence Service headquarters ©ffolas SS; **217** Brixton Academy ©Greg Balfour Evans AY; **217** The Oval in August 2009 ©Kevin Allen AY; **218** South Bank 1951 ©Trinity Mirror / Mirrorpix AY; **218** South Bank today ©Kevin Allen AY; **226** Covent Garden in the 1920s ©The Print Collector AY; **226** Whitechapel Market, Tower Hamlets ©Oliver Knight AY; **226** Harrods ©sonewfangled FL; **227** Porters outside Billingsgate fish market mid 1920s ©The Print Collector AY; **227** Covent Garden today ©Michael Jones AY; **228** The Laban dance centre at Creekside ©VIEW Pictures Ltd AY; **229** Mosaic artwork, Horniman Museum entrance ©Pres Panayotov SS; **229** All Saints' Church, Blackheath ©David Burrows SS; **229** The clock tower of the Horniman Museum, Forest Hill ©Pres Panayotov SS; **230** Belgrave Square ©Bildarchiv Monheim GmbH AY; **230** Metro-Land magazine ©Mary Evans Picture Library AY; **230** Terraced housing on the Becontree Estate ©Justin Kase z11z AY; **231** Ronan Point tower block in Newham, 1968 ©Trinity Mirror / Mirrorpix AY; **231** Residential building in the Docklands ©Chris Harvey SS; **231** New apartment buildings, part of the Canary Wharf development ©r.nagy SS; **232** Wimbledon Tennis Championships, 2010 ©Neil Tingle AY; **232** Snuff Mill and the River Wandle, Morden Hall Park ©Jim Linwood FL; **233** Wimbledon Windmill ©flash bang wallop AY; **233** The Nelson Arms, Merton High Street ©sarflondondunc FL; **234** England against Scotland at Twickenham in the 1920s ©The Print Collector AY; **234** England against Scotland at Twickenham, 2011 ©Neil Balderson SS; **235** Centre Court, Wimbledon ©Nimbus AY; **235** The Media Centre at Lord's Cricket Ground ©markhillary FL; **236** 1875 depiction of the Oxford and Cambridge Boat Race course ©Lordprice Collection AY; **237** London Marathon course map ©London Marathon; **237** Runners in the London Marathon in 2007 ©Chris Mole SS; **238** Stratford International ©Justin Kase z08z AY; **238** Waves of hedges, Thames Barrier Park ©DavidYoung SS; **239** Halls of residence, University of East London Docklands Campus ©andrew parker AY; **239** London City Airport ©UggBoy&UggGirl FL; **240** The finish of the marathon in the White City Stadium, 1908 Olympic Games ©The Print Collector AY; **240** 2012 Olympic Stadium ©branchlake AY; **241** Programme from the 1948 Olympic Games ©Mary Evans Picture Library AY; **242** The Hospital Chapel of St Mary the Virgin and St Thomas of Canterbury, Ilford ©Mike Booth AY; **242** Snaresbrook Crown Court ©Matt Brown FL; **243** Charlie Brown's roundabout ©Andrew Holt AY; **244** Temple at Wanstead House ©E.J.Westmacott AY; **244** St Mary's Church, Wanstead ©Mike Booth AY; **244** Wanstead House ©N/A; **245** Rocque Wanstead map ©courtesy National Library of ScotlandNLS; **246** The Temple to Shakespeare by the Thames at Hampton ©Colin Hutchings AY; **246** Ham House ©Patrick Wang SS; **246** White Lodge, Richmond Park ©Anthony Shaw Photography SS; **247** Richmond Lock ©Anthony Worsdell SS; **248** The Serpentine, Hyde Park ©Londonstills.com AY; **248** Richmond Park in winter ©piotr adamski SS; **249** Formal planting in The Regent's Park ©Kevin Allen AY; **250** The tower of Southwark Cathedral, now dwarfed by the Shard ©Julio Etchart AY; **250** HMS Belfast and Tower Bridge ©shanneong SS; **251** Robert Morris's interactive installation ©Chris Harvey SS; **254** Saatchi Gallery ©Robert Clayton AY; **254** Tate Modern ©Mike Hughes AY; **255** National Gallery, Trafalgar Square ©Alex Segre AY; **256** BedZED ©telex4 FL; **257** Nonsuch Palace ©The Art Gallery Collection AY; **257** Carshalton Lavender ©Charlotte Gilhooly FL; **258** St John's Chapel in the White Tower ©JOHN KELLERMAN AY; **258** Yeoman Warder ©Thomas Owen Jenkins SS; **259** Tower of London, 2010 ©Robert Harding Picture Library Ltd AY; **259** Tower of London plan 1597 ©wikimedia creative commons; **260** Columbia Road Flower Market ©Greg Balfour Evans AY; **260** Brick Lane ©Alex Segre AY; **260** Brushfield Street, Spitalfields ©Edward Herdwick AY; **261** Canary Wharf, 2009 ©Kevin Allen AY; **262** Isle of Dogs 1934, AFL03/AEROFILMS/C18403 ©English Heritage. NMR. Aerofilms Collection; **263** Isle of Dogs today ©Mike Hughes AY; **268** An aerial view of the Royal Docks in the 1950s, AFL03/AEROFILMS/A46498 ©English Heritage. NMR. Aerofilms Collection; **269** London City Airport ©Victor Abbott AY; **272** Walthamstow Market ©Peter Forsberg AY; **273** Epping Forest ©Carolyn Clarke AY; **273** The Ancient House, Walthamstow ©Kevin White AY; **274** Battersea Power Station in 1949 ©Trinity Mirror / Mirrorpix AY; **274** Refurbished Battersea Dogs and Cats Home, 2011 ©Maurice Savage AY; **275** Charity Santa Run in Battersea Park ©Londonstills.com AY; **275** Railway lines close to Clapham Junction ©Elsie esq. FL; **276** The Chancel Screen, Westminster Abbey ©Ricardo Rafael Alvarez AY; **277** West London Synagogue ©Art Directors & TRIP AY; **277** Wat Buddhapadipa ©Guy Somerset. AY; **277** London Central Mosque ©godrick SS; **278** Broadcasting House ©Michael Kemp AY; **278** The Royal Arcade ©Greg Balfour Evans AY; **278** Allies, the statue of Franklin D. Roosevelt and Winston Churchill in New Bond Street ©Ktylerconk FL; **279** Piccadilly Circus ©Matt Brown FL; **280** Regent Street, 1920 ©Mary Evans Picture Library AY; **280** Regent Street, Christmas 2008 ©Londonstills.com AY; **281** Westminster Abbey and the Houses of Parliament, 1931 ©The Print Collector AY; **281** Westminster Abbey and the Houses of Parliament, 2011 ©Mike Hughes AY; **282** Fountains in Trafalgar Square, around 1865 ©V&A Images AY; **282** Fountains in Trafalgar Square, 2009 ©Jon Arnold Images Ltd AY; **283** Trafalgar Square and the Admiralty Arch, 1937 ©Trinity Mirror / Mirrorpix AY; **283** Trafalgar Square and the Admiralty Arch, 2010 ©Mike Hughes AY; **284** HM Treasury, the Foreign and Commonwealth Office etc. ©Mike Hughes AY; **285** Home Office, Marsham Street ©Arcaid Images AY; **285** House of Lords Chamber ©Lisa Ryder AY; **290** Docklands skyline ©N/A FL; **290** Pinacle ©The Pinacle/Savills, www.londonpinnacle.com; **290–291** Canary Wharf Station ©Crossrail Ltd.; **291** Personal Rapid Transport pod ©Maurice Savage AY; **291** Cable car ©Transport For London

Flickr images are licensed under the Creative Commons 2.0 Attribution License. To view a copy of this license, visit *http://creativecommons.org/licenses/by/2.0/*